STUDEN SOLUTIONS MANUAL

RANDY GALLAHER ▪ KEVIN BODDEN
KATHY KOPELOUSOS ▪ MIKE ZIEGLER

Lewis & Clark Community College

INTRODUCTORY ALGEBRA

for collegstudents

URTH EDITION

Blitzer

PEARSON
Prentice Hall

Upper Saddle River, NJ 07458

Editor-in-Chief: Chris Hoag
Executive Editor: Paul Murphy
Supplements Editor: Christina Simoneau
Executive Managing Editor: Kathleen Schiaparelli
Assistant Managing Editor: Becca Richter
Production Editor: Allyson Kloss
Supplement Cover Manager: Paul Gourhan
Supplement Cover Designer: Joanne Alexandris
Manufaturing Buyer: Ilene Kahn

Pearson Prentice Hall
Pearson Education, Inc.
Upper Saddle River, NJ 07458

Printed in the United ates of America

10 9 8 7 6 5 3 2

ISBN 0-13-92185-1 Standalone
0-13-15799-1 Student Study Pack Component

Pearson Education Ltd. *ondon*
Pearson Education Austlia Pty. Ltd., *Sydney*
Pearson Education Singa ore, Pte. Ltd.
Pearson Education North sia Ltd., *Hong Kong*
Pearson Education Canad Inc., *Toronto*
Pearson Educación de Me co, S.A. de C.V.
Pearson Education—Japan *Tokyo*
Pearson Education Malaysi Pte. Ltd.

Table of Contents

Chapter 1
The Real Number System

1.1 Exercise Set

1. $2\frac{3}{8} = \frac{2\cdot 8+3}{8} = \frac{16+3}{8} = \frac{19}{8}$

3. $7\frac{3}{5} = \frac{7\cdot 5+3}{5} = \frac{35+3}{5} = \frac{38}{5}$

5. $8\frac{7}{16} = \frac{8\cdot 16+7}{16} = \frac{128+7}{16} = \frac{135}{16}$

7. 23 divided by 5 is 4 with a remainder of 3, so $\frac{23}{5} = 4\frac{3}{5}$.

9. 76 divided by 9 is 8 with a remainder of 4, so $\frac{76}{9} = 8\frac{4}{9}$.

11. 711 divided by 20 is 35 with a remainder of 11, so $\frac{711}{20} = 35\frac{11}{20}$.

13. $22 = 2\cdot 11$

15. $20 = 4\cdot 5 = 2\cdot 2\cdot 5$

17. 37 has no factors other than 1 and 37, so 37 is prime.

19. $36 = 4\cdot 9 = 2\cdot 2\cdot 3\cdot 3$

21. $140 = 10\cdot 14 = 2\cdot 5\cdot 2\cdot 7$
$= 2\cdot 2\cdot 5\cdot 7$

23. 79 has no factors other than 1 and 79, so 79 is prime.

25. $81 = 9\cdot 9 = 3\cdot 3\cdot 3\cdot 3$

27. $240 = 10\cdot 24$
$= 2\cdot 5\cdot 2\cdot 12$
$= 2\cdot 5\cdot 2\cdot 3\cdot 4$
$= 2\cdot 5\cdot 2\cdot 3\cdot 2\cdot 2$
$= 2\cdot 2\cdot 2\cdot 3\cdot 5$

29. $\frac{10}{16} = \frac{\not{2}\cdot 5}{\not{2}\cdot 8} = \frac{5}{8}$

31. $\frac{15}{18} = \frac{\not{3}\cdot 5}{\not{3}\cdot 6} = \frac{5}{6}$

33. $\frac{35}{50} = \frac{\not{5}\cdot 7}{\not{5}\cdot 10} = \frac{7}{10}$

35. $\frac{32}{80} = \frac{\not{16}\cdot 2}{\not{16}\cdot 5} = \frac{2}{5}$

37. $\frac{44}{50} = \frac{\not{2}\cdot 22}{\not{2}\cdot 25} = \frac{22}{25}$

39. $\frac{120}{86} = \frac{\not{2}\cdot 60}{\not{2}\cdot 43} = \frac{60}{43}$

41. $\frac{2}{5}\cdot\frac{1}{3} = \frac{2\cdot 1}{5\cdot 3} = \frac{2}{15}$

43. $\frac{3}{8}\cdot\frac{7}{11} = \frac{3\cdot 7}{8\cdot 11} = \frac{21}{88}$

45. $9\cdot\frac{4}{7} = \frac{9}{1}\cdot\frac{4}{7} = \frac{9\cdot 4}{1\cdot 7} = \frac{36}{7}$ or $5\frac{1}{7}$

47. $\frac{1}{10}\cdot\frac{5}{6} = \frac{1\cdot 5}{10\cdot 6} = \frac{5}{60} = \frac{5\cdot 1}{5\cdot 12} = \frac{1}{12}$

49. $\frac{5}{4}\cdot\frac{6}{7} = \frac{5\cdot 6}{4\cdot 7} = \frac{30}{28} = \frac{2\cdot 15}{2\cdot 14} = \frac{15}{14}$ or $1\frac{1}{14}$

51. $\left(3\frac{3}{4}\right)\left(1\frac{3}{5}\right)=\frac{15}{4}\cdot\frac{8}{5}=\frac{120}{20}=\frac{\cancel{20}\cdot 6}{\cancel{20}\cdot 1}=6$

53. $\frac{5}{4}\div\frac{4}{3}=\frac{5}{4}\cdot\frac{3}{4}=\frac{5\cdot 3}{4\cdot 4}=\frac{15}{16}$

55. $\frac{18}{5}\div 2=\frac{18}{5}\cdot\frac{1}{2}$

$=\frac{18\cdot 1}{5\cdot 2}=\frac{18}{10}=\frac{\cancel{2}\cdot 9}{\cancel{2}\cdot 5}=\frac{9}{5}$ or $1\frac{4}{5}$

57. $2\div\frac{18}{5}=\frac{2}{1}\cdot\frac{5}{18}=\frac{10}{18}=\frac{\cancel{2}\cdot 5}{\cancel{2}\cdot 9}=\frac{5}{9}$

59. $\frac{3}{4}\div\frac{1}{4}=\frac{3}{4}\cdot\frac{4}{1}=\frac{3\cdot 4}{4\cdot 1}=\frac{12}{4}=3$

61. $\frac{7}{6}\div\frac{5}{3}=\frac{7}{6}\cdot\frac{3}{5}=\frac{7\cdot 3}{6\cdot 5}=\frac{21}{30}=\frac{\cancel{3}\cdot 7}{\cancel{3}\cdot 10}=\frac{7}{10}$

63. $\frac{1}{14}\div\frac{1}{7}=\frac{1}{14}\cdot\frac{7}{1}=\frac{7}{14}=\frac{\cancel{7}\cdot 1}{\cancel{7}\cdot 2}=\frac{1}{2}$

65. $6\frac{3}{5}\div 1\frac{1}{10}=\frac{33}{5}\div\frac{11}{10}$

$=\frac{33}{5}\cdot\frac{10}{11}=\frac{33}{55}=\frac{\cancel{11}\cdot 3}{\cancel{11}\cdot 5}=\frac{3}{5}$

67. $\frac{2}{11}+\frac{4}{11}=\frac{2+4}{11}=\frac{6}{11}$

69. $\frac{7}{12}+\frac{1}{12}=\frac{8}{12}=\frac{\cancel{4}\cdot 2}{\cancel{4}\cdot 3}=\frac{2}{3}$

71. $\frac{5}{8}+\frac{5}{8}=\frac{10}{8}=\frac{\cancel{2}\cdot 5}{\cancel{2}\cdot 4}=\frac{5}{4}$ or $1\frac{1}{4}$

73. $\frac{7}{12}-\frac{5}{12}=\frac{2}{12}=\frac{\cancel{2}\cdot 1}{\cancel{2}\cdot 6}=\frac{1}{6}$

75. $\frac{16}{7}-\frac{2}{7}=\frac{14}{7}=\frac{\cancel{7}\cdot 2}{\cancel{7}\cdot 1}=2$

77. $\frac{1}{2}+\frac{1}{5}=\frac{1}{2}\cdot\frac{5}{5}+\frac{1}{5}\cdot\frac{2}{2}$

$=\frac{5}{10}+\frac{2}{10}=\frac{5+2}{10}=\frac{7}{10}$

79. $\frac{3}{4}+\frac{3}{20}=\frac{3}{4}\cdot\frac{5}{5}+\frac{3}{20}$

$=\frac{15}{20}+\frac{3}{20}$

$=\frac{18}{20}=\frac{\cancel{2}\cdot 9}{\cancel{2}\cdot 10}=\frac{9}{10}$

81. $\frac{3}{8}+\frac{5}{12}=\frac{3}{8}\cdot\frac{3}{3}+\frac{5}{12}\cdot\frac{2}{2}$

$=\frac{9}{24}+\frac{10}{24}=\frac{19}{24}$

83. $\frac{11}{18}-\frac{2}{9}=\frac{11}{18}-\frac{2}{9}\cdot\frac{2}{2}=\frac{11}{18}-\frac{4}{18}=\frac{7}{18}$

85. $\frac{4}{3}-\frac{3}{4}=\frac{4}{3}\cdot\frac{4}{4}-\frac{3}{4}\cdot\frac{3}{3}$

$=\frac{16}{12}-\frac{9}{12}=\frac{7}{12}$

87. $\frac{7}{10}-\frac{3}{16}=\frac{7}{10}\cdot\frac{8}{8}-\frac{3}{16}\cdot\frac{5}{5}$

$=\frac{56}{80}-\frac{15}{80}=\frac{41}{80}$

89. $3\frac{3}{4}-2\frac{1}{3}=\frac{15}{4}-\frac{7}{3}$

$=\frac{15}{4}\cdot\frac{3}{3}-\frac{7}{3}\cdot\frac{4}{4}$

$=\frac{45}{12}-\frac{28}{12}=\frac{17}{12}$ or $1\frac{5}{12}$

91. $\frac{3}{4}\cdot\frac{a}{5}=\frac{3\cdot a}{4\cdot 5}=\frac{3a}{20}$

92. $\frac{2}{3}\div\frac{a}{7}=\frac{2}{3}\cdot\frac{7}{a}=\frac{2\cdot 7}{3\cdot a}=\frac{14}{3a}$

93. $\frac{11}{x}+\frac{9}{x}=\frac{11+9}{x}=\frac{20}{x}$

94. $\frac{10}{y}-\frac{6}{y}=\frac{10-6}{y}=\frac{4}{y}$

95. $$\left(\frac{1}{2}-\frac{1}{3}\right)\div\frac{5}{8}=\left(\frac{3}{6}-\frac{2}{6}\right)\div\frac{5}{8}$$
$$=\frac{1}{6}\div\frac{5}{8}$$
$$=\frac{1}{6}\cdot\frac{8}{5}=\frac{8}{30}=\frac{\not{2}\cdot 4}{\not{2}\cdot 15}=\frac{4}{15}$$

96. $$\left(\frac{1}{2}+\frac{1}{4}\right)\div\left(\frac{1}{2}+\frac{1}{3}\right)=\left(\frac{2}{4}+\frac{1}{4}\right)\div\left(\frac{3}{6}+\frac{2}{6}\right)$$
$$=\frac{3}{4}\div\frac{5}{6}$$
$$=\frac{3}{4}\cdot\frac{6}{5}$$
$$=\frac{18}{20}=\frac{\not{2}\cdot 9}{\not{2}\cdot 10}=\frac{9}{10}$$

97. **a.** The number of adults that do not find television the most believable news source is

$$\frac{1}{4}+\frac{3}{25}+\frac{2}{25}$$
$$=\frac{25}{100}+\frac{12}{100}+\frac{8}{100}=\frac{45}{100}$$

The number of adults that do find television the most believable news source is

$$1-\frac{45}{100}=\frac{100}{100}-\frac{45}{100}=\frac{55}{100}=\frac{11}{20}.$$

b. $$2000\cdot\frac{3}{25}=\frac{2000}{1}\cdot\frac{3}{25}=240$$

240 people found radio the most believable news source.

99. $\frac{\text{Hispanic}}{\text{female}}=\frac{16}{40}=\frac{2}{5}$

The ratio of Hispanic judges to female judges appointed by Carter was $\frac{2}{5}$.

101. $\frac{\text{desired}}{\text{recipe}}\times\text{amount in recipe}$

$$=\frac{8}{5}\times\frac{3}{4}=\frac{24}{20}=\frac{6}{5}=1\frac{1}{5}\text{cups}$$

103. Total distance covered is

$\frac{3}{4}+\frac{2}{5}=\frac{15}{20}+\frac{8}{20}=\frac{23}{20}=1\frac{3}{20}$ miles.

Subtract to find out how much further you walked.

$\frac{3}{4}-\frac{2}{5}=\frac{15}{20}-\frac{8}{20}=\frac{7}{20}$ miles farther.

105. $2\frac{3}{8}\cdot 16=\frac{19}{8}\cdot\frac{16}{1}=\frac{304}{8}=38$ miles

107. – 115. Answers will vary.

117. Statements a, b, and c are false. The methods illustrated are incorrect. The only true statement is d.

1.2 Exercise Set

1. –20

3. 8

5. –3000

7. −4 billion

9. 2

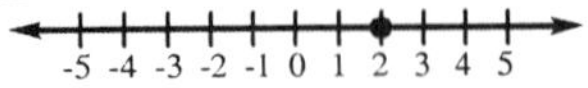

11. −5

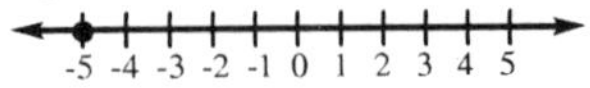

13. $3\frac{1}{2}$

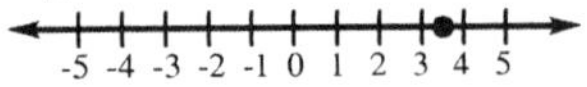

15. $\frac{11}{3}$

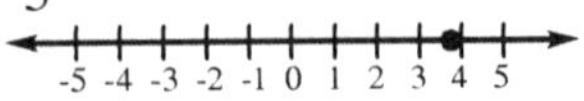

17. −1.8

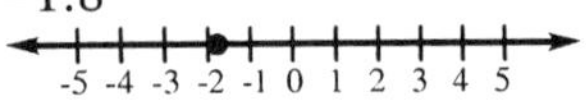

19. $-\frac{16}{5}$

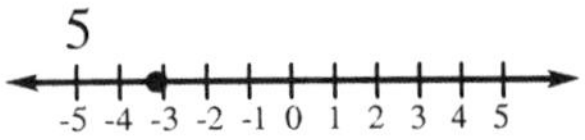

21.
$$\begin{array}{r} 0.75 \\ 4\overline{)3.00} \\ \underline{28} \\ 20 \\ \underline{20} \\ 0 \end{array}$$
$\frac{3}{4} = 0.75$

23.
$$\begin{array}{r} 0.35 \\ 20\overline{)7.00} \\ \underline{60} \\ 100 \\ \underline{100} \\ 0 \end{array}$$
$\frac{7}{20} = 0.35$

25.
$$\begin{array}{r} 0.875 \\ 8\overline{)7.000} \\ \underline{64} \\ 60 \\ \underline{56} \\ 40 \\ \underline{40} \\ 0 \end{array}$$
$\frac{7}{8} = 0.875$

27.
$$\begin{array}{r} 0.818... \\ 11\overline{)9.000...} \\ \underline{88} \\ 20 \\ \underline{11} \\ 90 \\ \underline{88} \\ 20 \end{array}$$
$\frac{9}{11} = 0.\overline{81}$

29.
$$\begin{array}{r} 0.5 \\ 2\overline{)1.0} \\ \underline{1.0} \\ 0 \end{array}$$
$-\frac{1}{2} = -0.5$

31.
$$\begin{array}{r} 0.833... \\ 6\overline{)5.000...} \\ \underline{48} \\ 20 \\ \underline{18} \\ 20 \\ \underline{18} \\ 20 \end{array}$$
$\frac{5}{6} = 0.8\overline{3}$

33. **a.** $\sqrt{100}$ (=10)

b. 0, $\sqrt{100}$

c. −9, 0, $\sqrt{100}$

d. $-9, -\frac{4}{5}$, 0, 0.25, 9.2, $\sqrt{100}$

e. $\sqrt{3}$

f. $-9, -\frac{4}{5}$, 0, 0.25, $\sqrt{3}$, 9.2, $\sqrt{100}$

35. **a.** $\sqrt{64}$ (= 8)

b. 0, $\sqrt{64}$

c. −11, 0, $\sqrt{64}$

d. $-11, -\frac{5}{6}$, 0, 0.75, $\sqrt{64}$

e. $\sqrt{5}$, π

f. $-11, -\frac{5}{6}$, 0, 0.75, $\sqrt{5}$, π, $\sqrt{64}$

37. The only whole number that is not a natural number is 0.

39. Answers will vary. As an example, one rational number that is not an integer is $\frac{1}{2}$.

41. Answers will vary. As an example, 6 is a number that is an integer, a whole number, and a natural number.

43. Answers will vary. As an example, one number that is an irrational number and a real number is π.

45. $\frac{1}{2} < 2$ since $\frac{1}{2}$ is to the left of 2 on the number line.

47. $3 > -\frac{5}{2}$ since 3 is to the right of $-\frac{5}{2} = -2\frac{1}{2}$.

49. −4 > −6 since −4 is to the right of −6

51. −2.5 < 1.5 since −2.5 is to the left of 1.5

53. $-\frac{3}{4} > -\frac{5}{4}$ since $-\frac{3}{4}$ is to the right of $-\frac{5}{4}$

55. −4.5 < 3 since −4.5 is to the left of 3

57. $\sqrt{2} < 1.5$ since $\sqrt{2} \approx 1.414$ is to the left of 1.5.

59. $0.\bar{3} > 0.3$ since $0.\bar{3} = 0.333...$ is to the right of 0.3

61. $-\pi > -3.5$ since $-\pi \approx -3.14$ is to the right of −3.5

63. $-5 \geq -13$ is true because $-5 > -13$ is true.

65. $-9 \geq -9$ is true because −9 = −9 is true.

67. $0 \geq -6$ is true because 0 > −6 is true.

69. $-17 \geq 6$ is false because neither −17 > 6 nor −17 = 6 is true.

71. $|6| = 6$ because the distance between 6 and 0 on the number line is 6 units.

73. $|-7| = 7$ because the distance between −7 and 0 on the number line is 7 units.

75. $\left|\frac{5}{6}\right| = \frac{5}{6}$ because the distance between $\frac{5}{6}$ and 0 on the number line is $\frac{5}{6}$ units.

77. $\left|-\sqrt{11}\right| = \sqrt{11}$ because the distance between $-\sqrt{11}$ and 0 on the number line is $\sqrt{11}$ units.

79. $|-6| \,\square\, |-3|$

$6 \,\square\, 3$

$6 > 3$

Since $6 > 3$, $|-6| > |-3|$.

80. $|-20| \,\square\, |-50|$

$20 \,\square\, 50$

$20 < 50$

Since $20 < 50$, $|-20| < |-50|$.

81. $\left|\frac{3}{5}\right| \,\square\, |-0.6|$

$|0.6| \,\square\, |-0.6|$

$0.6 \,\square\, 0.6$

$0.6 = 0.6$

Since $0.6 = 0.6$, $\left|\frac{3}{5}\right| = |-0.6|$.

82. $\left|\frac{5}{2}\right| \,\square\, |-2.5|$

$|2.5| \,\square\, |-2.5|$

$2.5 \,\square\, 2.5$

$2.5 = 2.5$

Since $2.5 = 2.5$, $\left|\frac{5}{2}\right| = |-2.5|$.

83. $\frac{30}{40} - \frac{3}{4} \,\square\, \frac{14}{15} \cdot \frac{15}{14}$

$\frac{30}{40} - \frac{30}{40} \,\square\, \frac{\cancel{14}}{\cancel{15}} \cdot \frac{\cancel{15}}{\cancel{14}}$

$0 \,\square\, 1$

$0 < 1$

Since $0 < 1$, $\frac{30}{40} - \frac{3}{4} < \frac{14}{15} \cdot \frac{15}{14}$.

84. $\frac{17}{18} \cdot \frac{18}{17} \,\square\, \frac{50}{60} - \frac{5}{6}$

$\frac{\cancel{17}}{\cancel{18}} \cdot \frac{\cancel{18}}{\cancel{17}} \,\square\, \frac{50}{60} - \frac{50}{60}$

$1 \,\square\, 0$

$1 > 0$

Since $1 > 0$, $\frac{17}{18} \cdot \frac{18}{17} > \frac{50}{60} - \frac{5}{6}$.

85. $\frac{8}{13} \div \frac{8}{13} \,\square\, |-1|$

$\frac{8}{13} \cdot \frac{13}{8} \,\square\, 1$

$1 \,\square\, 1$

$1 = 1$

Since $1 = 1$, $\frac{8}{13} \div \frac{8}{13} = |-1|$.

86. $|-2| \,\square\, \frac{4}{17} \div \frac{4}{17}$

$2 \,\square\, \frac{4}{17} \cdot \frac{17}{4}$

$2 \,\square\, 1$

$2 > 1$

Since $2 > 1$, $|-2| > \frac{4}{17} \div \frac{4}{17}$.

87. -2

89. The years for which money collected < money spent are 1997 and 2002. There was a budget deficit in these years.

91. – 101. Answers will vary

103. Statement *c* is true since there are an infinite number of rational numbers that are not positive. -5 is one example.

105. Since $\sqrt{36} = 6$ and $\sqrt{49} = 7$, $-\sqrt{47}$ is between -7 and -6.

107. $\sqrt{3} \approx 1.732$ and should be graphed between 1 and 2.

109. $1-\sqrt{2} \approx -0.414$ and should be graphed between -1 and 0.

1.3 Exercise Set

1. Quadrant I

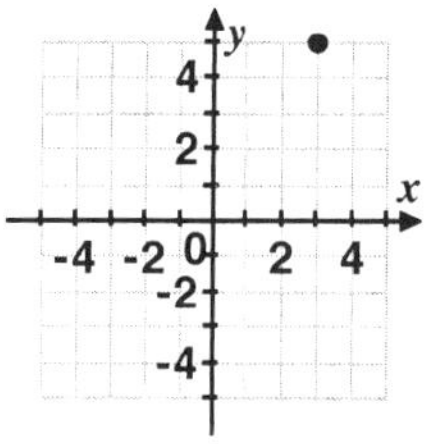

3. Quadrant II

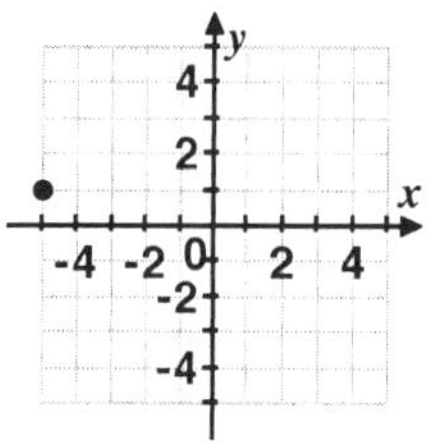

5. Quadrant III

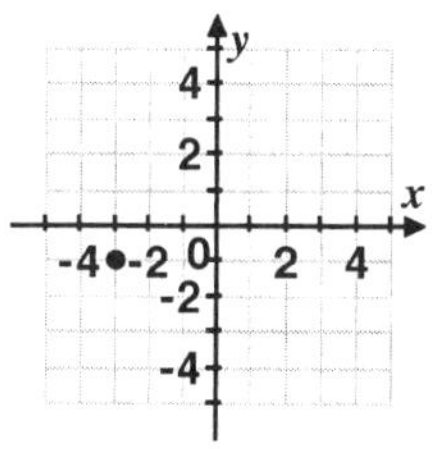

7. Quadrant IV

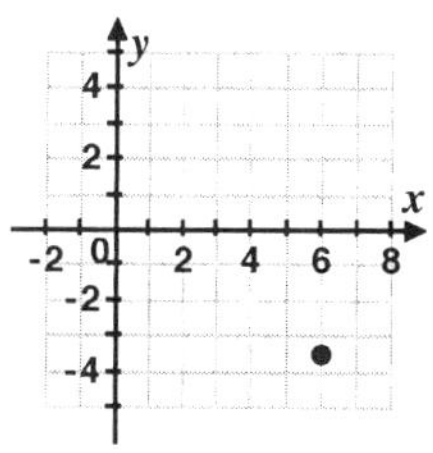

9-23. All points for Exercises 9 through 23 are graphed on the same set of axes and labeled accordingly.

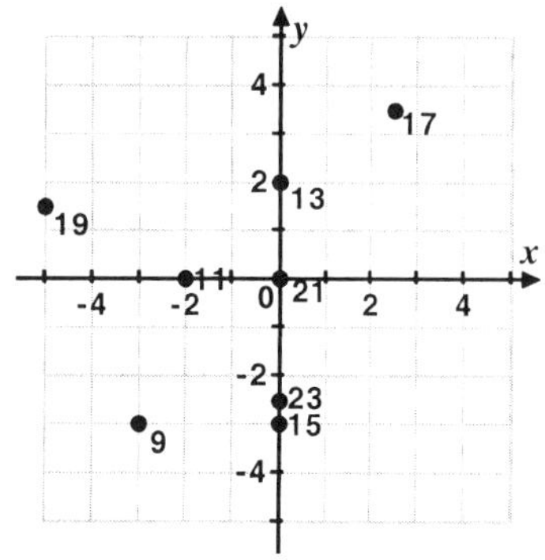

25. A (5,2)

27. C (−6,5)

29. E(−2,−3)

31. G(5,−3)

33. The y-coordinates are positive in Quadrants I and II.

35. The x- and y-coordinates have the same sign in Quadrants I and III.

37. Answers will vary. Some examples are (−2, 2) and (2, 2), and (−1, 1) and (1, 1).

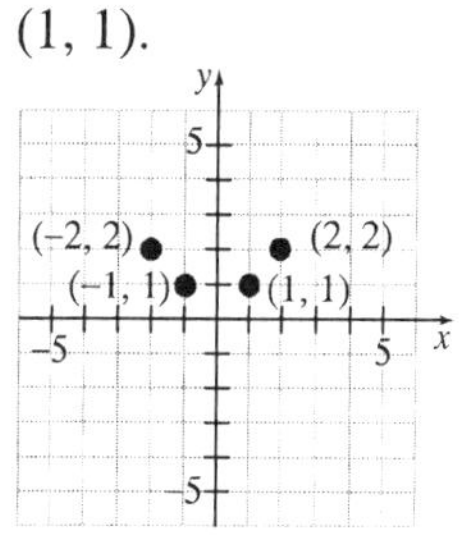

38. Answers will vary. Some examples are (2, −2) and (2, 2), and (1, −1) and (1, 1).

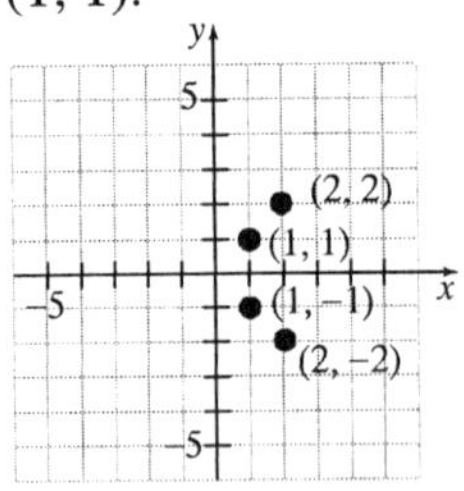

39.

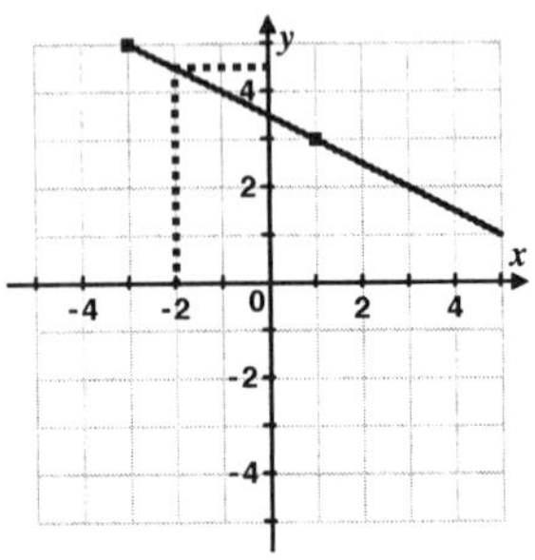

It appears that the point $\left(-2, 4\frac{1}{2}\right)$ is on the line, so y is approximately $4\frac{1}{2}$ or $\frac{9}{2}$.

41. The coordinates of point A are (2,7). When the football is 2 yards from the quarterback, its height is 7 feet.

43. The coordinates of point C are approximately (3, 9.25).

45. The football's maximum height is 12 feet. It reaches this height when it is 15 yards from the quarterback.

47. Point A is (91, 125). This means that in 1991, 125,000 acres were used to cultivate opium crops.

49. Opium cultivation was at a minimum in 2001 when approximately 25,000 acres were used.

51. Opium cultivation did not change between 1991 and 1992.

53. In 1985, oil consumption was approximately 7.1 million barrels per day.

55. In 1990, oil consumption and domestic production were the same. During that year approximately 7.2 million barrels were produced and consumed per day.

57. Domestic oil production was at an all time high in 1970 when about 9.8 million barrels per day were produced.

59. The difference between production and consumption is 1980 was about $8.7-7=1.7$ million barrels per day.

61. *The Bodyguard* grossed about $120 million.

63. *No Way Out, The Postman,* and *Dragonfly* have a box-office gross of less than $50 million.

65. Life expectancy for men born in 1900 was approximately 48 years.

67. Women born in 1996 can expect to live approximately (80 – 65 = 15) more years than men born in 1950.

69. The median income for African-American men is $22 thousand.

71. The difference in median income between Hispanic men and women is 20 – 13 = $7 thousand.

73. The average number of days before the convention that candidates declared in 1992 was approximately 270. Clinton's declaration exceeded this by 284 – 270 = 14 days.

75. The United States obtained more than $\frac{1}{2}=\frac{5}{10}$ of its oil from other countries in 2002.

77. The fraction of imported oil exceeded $\frac{1}{5}=\frac{2}{10}$ but was at most $\frac{1}{2}=\frac{5}{10}$ in 1972, 1982, and 1992.

79. In 2002, $\frac{5}{10}$ of oil was imported from other countries. Of this, $\frac{1}{10}$ was imported from Saudi Arabia. This means that $\frac{5}{10}\cdot\frac{1}{10}=\frac{1}{2}\cdot\frac{1}{10}=\frac{1}{20}$ of oil used in the U.S. in 2002 was from Saudi Arabia.

81. – 87. Answers will vary.

89. **a.** A

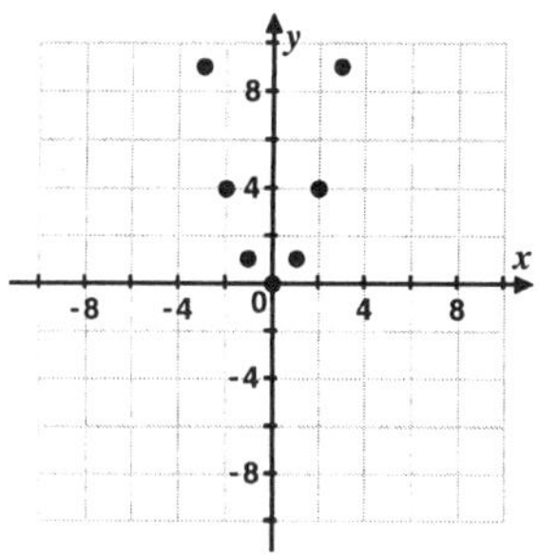

B

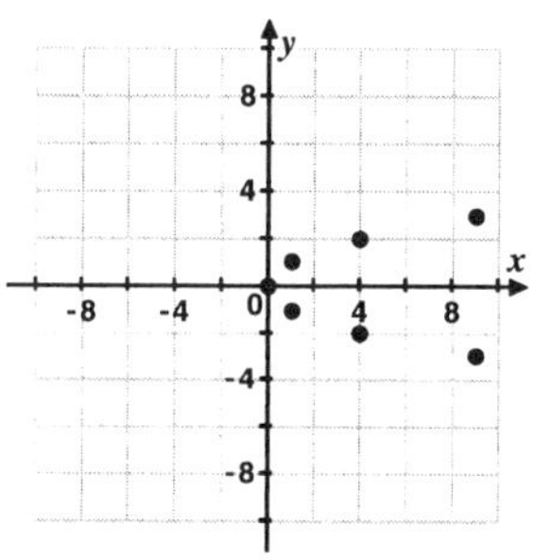

b. In set *A*, each *x*-coordinate with exactly one *y*-coordinate. In set *B*, *x*-coordinates are associated with more than one *y*-coordinate. Points line up vertically when *x*-coordinates are associated with more than one point.

91. $\frac{3}{4}+\frac{2}{5}=\frac{3}{4}\cdot\frac{5}{5}+\frac{2}{5}\cdot\frac{4}{4}=\frac{15}{20}+\frac{8}{20}=\frac{23}{20}$

92. $-\frac{1}{4}<0$ since $-\frac{1}{4}$ is to the left of 0 on the number line.

93. $|-5.83|=5.83$ because the distance between −5.83 and 0 on the number line is 5.83 units.

1.4 Exercise Set

1. When $x = 4$, $x+11=4+11=15$.

3. When $x = 10$, $8x=8\cdot 10=80$.

5. When $x = 8$,
$5x+6=5\cdot 8+6=40+6=46$.

7. When $x = 2$,
$7(x+3)=7(2+3)=7(5)=35$.

9. When $F=77$,
$\frac{5}{9}(F-32)=\frac{5}{9}(77-32)=\frac{5}{9}(45)=25$

11. $3x + 5$

a. 2 terms

b. 3

c. 5

d. No like terms

13. $x + 2 + 5x$

a. 3 terms

b. 1

c. 2

d. x and $5x$ are like terms.

15. $4y + 1 + 3$
   a. 3 terms
   b. 4
   c. 1
   d. No like terms

17. $y+4=4+y$

19. $5+3x=3x+5$

21. $4x+5y=5y+4x$

23. $5(x+3)=5(3+x)$

25. $9x=x\cdot 9$ or $x9$

27. $x+y6=x+6y$

29. $7x+23=x7+23$

31. $5(x+3)=(x+3)5$

33. $7+(5+x)=(7+5)+x=12+x$

35. $7(4x)=(7\cdot 4)x=28x$

37. $3(x+5)=3(x)+3(5)=3x+15$

39. $8(2x+3)=8(2x)+8(3)=16x+24$

41. $\frac{1}{3}(12+6r)=\frac{1}{3}(12)+\frac{1}{3}(12)+\frac{1}{3}(6r)$
$=4+2r$

43. $5(x+y)=5x+5y$

45. $3(x-2)=3(x)-3(2)=3x-6$

47. $2(4x-5)=2(4x)-2(5)=8x-10$

49. $\frac{1}{2}(5x-12)=\frac{1}{2}(5x)+\frac{1}{2}(-12)$
$=\frac{5}{2}x-6$

51. $(2x+7)4=2x(4)+7(4)=8x+28$

53. $6(x+3+2y)=6(x)+6(3)+6(2y)$
$=6x+18+12y$

55. $5(3x-2+4y)=5(3x)-5(2)+5(4y)$
$=15x-10+20y$

57. $7x+10x=(7+10)x=17x$

59. $11a-3a=(11-3)a=8a$

61. $3+(x+11)=(3+11)+x=14+x$

63. $5y-3+6y=(5y+6y)-3=11y-3$

65. $2x+5+7x-4=(2x+7x)+(5-4)$
$=9x+1$

67. $11a+12-3a-2=(11a-3a)+(12-2)$
$=8a+10$

69. $5(3x+2)-4=15x+10-4=15x+6$

71. $12+5(3x-2)=12+15x-10$
$=15x+12-10=15x+2$

73. $7(3a+2b)+5(4a+2b)$
$=21a+14b+20a+10b$
$=21a+20a+14b+10b$
$=41a+24b$

75. Commutative Property of Addition

76. Commutative Property of Addition

77. Associative Property of Addition

78. Commutative Property of Multiplication

79. False

80. True

81. True

82. False

83. When $x = 20$, $15x = 15(20) = 300$.
This means that you can stay in the sun for 300 minutes (or 5 hours) without burning with a number 15 lotion.

85. When $x = 8$,
$$405x + 5565 = 405(8) + 5565$$
$$= 3240 + 5565 = 8805$$
According to the graph in the year 1994 + 8 = 2002, credit card debt per U.S. household was \$8940. The model fits the data fairly well.

87. **a.** $2(0.18x + 0.01) + 0.02x$
$$= 0.36x + 0.03 + 0.02x$$
$$= 0.38x + 0.03$$

b. 2002 – 1997 = 5, so evaluate the expression for $x = 5$.
$$0.38x + 0.03 = 0.38(5) + 0.03$$
$$= 1.9 + 0.03 = 1.93$$
According to the graph, the number of testosterone prescriptions in 2002 was approximately 1.9 million. The model is fairly accurate.

89. – 99. Answers will vary.

101. The only correct statement is *c*, which is an example of the distributive property.

103. **a.** When $x = 100$,
$$\frac{0.5x + 5000}{x} = \frac{0.5(100) + 5000}{100}$$
$$= \frac{50 + 5000}{100}$$
$$= \frac{5050}{100} = 50.5$$
The average cost per clock for 100 clocks is \$50.50.

When $x = 1000$,
$$\frac{0.5x + 5000}{x} = \frac{0.5(1000) + 5000}{1000}$$
$$= \frac{500 + 5000}{1000}$$
$$= \frac{5500}{1000} = 5.5$$
The average cost per clock for 1000 clocks is \$5.50.

When $x = 10{,}000$,
$$\frac{0.5x + 5000}{x} = \frac{0.5(10{,}000) + 5000}{10{,}000}$$
$$= \frac{5000 + 5000}{10{,}000}$$
$$= \frac{10{,}000}{10{,}000} = 1$$
The average cost per clock for 10,000 clocks is \$1.

b. When $x = 2000$,
$$\frac{0.5x + 5000}{x} = \frac{0.5(2000) + 5000}{2000}$$
$$= \frac{1000 + 5000}{2000}$$
$$= \frac{6000}{2000} = 3$$

The average cost per clock to manufacture 2000 clocks is \$3.

Since the clocks cannot be sold for more than \$1.50, the business cannot make a profit so it doesn't have a promising future.

104. $$\begin{array}{r} 0.44\ldots \\ 9\overline{)4.00\ldots} \\ \underline{36} \\ 40 \\ \underline{36} \\ 40 \\ \vdots \end{array}$$

$$\frac{4}{9}=0.\overline{4}$$

105.

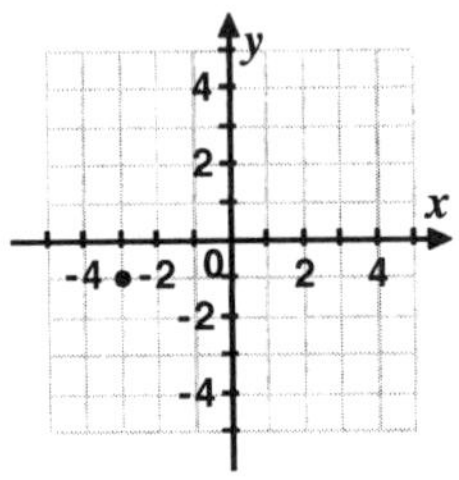

106. $\frac{3}{7}\div\frac{15}{7}=\frac{3}{7}\cdot\frac{7}{15}=\frac{21}{105}=\frac{1\cdot 21}{5\cdot 21}=\frac{1}{5}$

Mid-Chapter Check Point – Chapter 1

1. $15a+14+9a-13=15a+9a+14-13$
$=24a+1$

2. The LCD for 10 and 15 is 30.

$$\frac{7}{10}-\frac{8}{15}=\frac{7}{10}\cdot\frac{3}{3}-\frac{8}{15}\cdot\frac{2}{2}$$
$$=\frac{21}{30}-\frac{16}{30}=\frac{5}{30}=\frac{1}{6}$$

3. $\frac{2}{3}\cdot\frac{3}{4}=\frac{2}{3}\cdot\frac{3}{4}=\frac{2}{4}=\frac{1}{2}$

4. $$7(9x+3)+\frac{1}{3}(6x-15)$$
$$7(9x)+7(3)+\frac{1}{3}(6x)-\frac{1}{3}(15)$$
$$=63x+21+2x-5$$
$$=63x+2x+21-5=65x+16$$

5. $\frac{5}{22}+\frac{5}{33}=\frac{5}{22}\cdot\frac{3}{3}+\frac{5}{33}\cdot\frac{2}{2}=\frac{15}{66}+\frac{10}{66}=\frac{25}{66}$

6. $\frac{3}{5}\div\frac{9}{10}=\frac{3}{5}\cdot\frac{10}{9}=\frac{3}{5}\cdot\frac{2\cdot 5}{3\cdot 3}=\frac{3}{5}\cdot\frac{2\cdot 5}{3\cdot 3}=\frac{2}{3}$

7. $\frac{23}{105}-\frac{2}{105}=\frac{21}{105}=\frac{3\cdot 7}{3\cdot 5\cdot 7}=\frac{1}{5}$

8. $2\frac{7}{9}\div 3=\frac{25}{9}\div\frac{3}{1}=\frac{25}{9}\cdot\frac{1}{3}=\frac{25}{27}$

9. $$5\frac{2}{9}-3\frac{1}{6}=\frac{47}{9}-\frac{19}{6}$$
$$=\frac{47}{9}\cdot\frac{2}{2}-\frac{19}{6}\cdot\frac{3}{3}$$
$$=\frac{94}{18}-\frac{57}{18}=\frac{37}{18}\text{ or }2\frac{1}{18}$$

10.

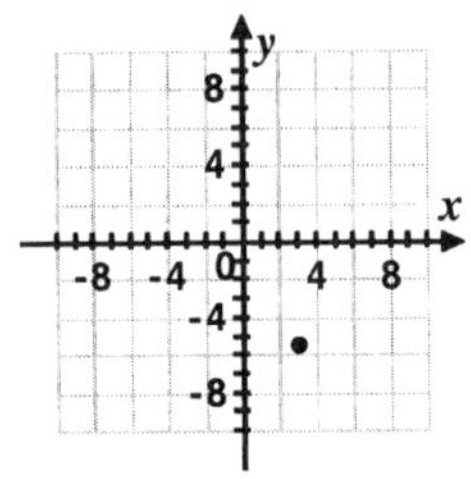

The point lies in Quadrant IV.

11. $5(x+3)=(x+3)5$

12. $5(x+3)=5(3+x)$

13. $5(x+3)=5\cdot x+5\cdot 3=5x+15$

14. 13% – 6% = 7%
There was about a 7% increase in the number of people listening to internet radio between 2001 and 2004.

15. The percentage exceeded 7% in 2002, 2003, and 2004.

16. $-8000 < -8\frac{1}{4}$

17. $-11,\ -\frac{3}{7},\ 0,\ 0.45,$ and $\sqrt{25}$ are rational numbers.

18. When $x = \frac{3}{5}$,

$$10x + 7 = 10\left(\frac{3}{5}\right) + 7 = 6 + 7 = 13.$$

19. When $x = \frac{5}{2}$,

$$8(x-2) = 8\left(\frac{5}{2} - 2\right) = 8\left(\frac{5}{2} - \frac{4}{2}\right) = 8\left(\frac{1}{2}\right) = 4$$

20. (67, 20); In 1967, 20% of grades earned by undergraduates were A's.

21. The percentage of grades of C or below reached a maximum in 1970. Approximately 23% of grades were C or below.

22. The difference between the percentage of A's and the percentage of C's or below in 2003 was about $45 - 5 = 40\%$.

23. $|-19.3| = 19.3$

24. $\frac{1}{11} = 0.\overline{09}$

25. $8(7x - 10 + 3y) = 8 \cdot 7x - 8 \cdot 10 + 8 \cdot 3y = 56x - 80 + 24y$

1.5 Exercise Set

1. $7 + (-3) = 4$

3. $-2 + (-5) = -7$

5. $-6 + 2 = -4$

7. $3 + (-3) = 0$

9. $-7 + 0 = -7$

11. $30 + (-30) = 0$

13. $-30 + (-30) = -60$

15. $-8 + (-10) = -18$

17. $-0.4 + (-0.9) = -1.3$

19. $-\frac{7}{10} + \left(-\frac{3}{10}\right) = -\frac{10}{10} = -1$

21. $-9 + 4 = -5$

23. $12 + (-8) = 4$

25. $6 + (-9) = -3$

27. $-3.6 + 2.1 = -1.5$

29. $-3.6 + (-2.1) = -5.7$

31. $\frac{9}{10} + \left(-\frac{3}{5}\right) = \frac{9}{10} + \left(-\frac{6}{10}\right) = \frac{3}{10}$

33. $-\frac{5}{8} + \frac{3}{4} = -\frac{5}{8} + \frac{6}{8} = \frac{1}{8}$

35. $-\frac{3}{7} + \left(-\frac{4}{5}\right) = -\frac{15}{35} + \left(-\frac{28}{35}\right) = -\frac{43}{35}$

37. $4+(-7)+(-5)=[4+(-7)]+(-5)$
$=-3+(-5)$
$=-8$

39. $85+(-15)+(-20)+12$
$=[85+(-15)]+(-20)+12$
$=70+(-20)+12$
$=[70+(-20)]+12$
$=50+12$
$=62$

41. $17+(-4)+2+3+(-10)$
$=13+2+3+(-10)$
$=15+3+(-10)$
$=18+(-10)$
$=8$

43. $-45+\left(-\frac{3}{7}\right)+25+\left(-\frac{4}{7}\right)$
$=(-45+25)+\left[-\frac{3}{7}+\left(-\frac{4}{7}\right)\right]$
$=-20+\left(-\frac{7}{7}\right)$
$=-20+(-1)$
$=-21$

45. $3.5+(-45)+(-8.4)+72$
$=[3.5+(-8.4)]+(-45+72)$
$=-4.9+27$
$=22.1$

47. $-10x+2x=(-10+2)x=-8x$

49. $25y+(-12y)=[25+(-12)]y=13y$

51. $-8a+(-15a)=[-8+(-15)]a$
$=-23a$

53. $-4+7x+5+(-13x)$
$=-4+5+7x+(-13x)$
$=(-4+5)+[7+(-13)]x$
$=1-6x$

55. $7b+2+(-b)+(-6)$
$=7b+(-b)+2+(-6)$
$=[7+(-1)]b+[2+(-6)]$
$=6b-4$ or $-4+6b$

57. $7x+(-5y)+(-9x)+2y$
$=7x+(-9x)+(-5y)+2y$
$=[7+(-9)]x+(-5+2)y$
$=-2x-3y$

59. $4(5x-3)+6=4\cdot 5x+4(-3)+6$
$=20x-12+6$
$=20x-6$

61. $8(3-4y)+35y=8\cdot 3+8(-4y)+35y$
$=24-32y+35y$
$=24+(-32+35)y$
$=24+3y$

63. $6(2-9a)+7(3a+5)$
$=6\cdot 2+6(-9a)+7\cdot 3a+7\cdot 5$
$=12-54a+21a+35$
$=(12+35)+(-54+21a)$
$=47-33a$

65. $|-3+(-5)|+|2+(-6)|=|-8|+|-4|$
$=8+4$
$=12$

66. $|4+(-11)|+|-3+(-4)| = |-7|+|-7|$
$= 7+7$
$= 14$

67. $-20+\left[-|15+(-25)|\right]$
$= -20+\left[-|-10|\right]$
$= -20+[-10]$
$= -30$

68. $-25+\left[-|18+(-26)|\right]$
$= -25+\left[-|-8|\right]$
$= -25+[-8]$
$= -33$

69. $6+[2+(-13)]\square-3+[4+(-8)]$
$6+[-11]\square-3+[-4]$
$-5\square-7$
$-5>-7$

70. $[(-8)+(-6)]+10 \;\square\; -8+[9+(-2)]$
$-14+10 \;\square\; -8+7$
$-4 \;\square\; -1$
$-4<-1$

71. $-56+100=44$
The high temperature was 44°F.

73. $-1312+712=-600$
The elevation of the person is 600 feet below sea level.

75. $-7+15-5=3$
The temperature at 4:00 P.M. was 3°F.

77. $27+4-2+8-12$
$=(27+4+8)+(-2-12)$
$=34-14$
$=25$
The location of the football at the end of the fourth play is at the 25-yard line.

79. $126+110-109-233-349$
$=(126+110)+(-109-233-349)$
$=236+(-691)$
$=-455$
There was a \$455 billion deficit in 2003.

81. – 87. Answers will vary.

89. Statement *d* is true. (Statement *a* is sometimes true, but not considered true because it is not always true.)

91. $\_\_+11x+(-3y)+3x=7(2x-3y)$
$11x+3x+\_\_+(-3y)=7\cdot 2x-7\cdot 3y$
$14x+\_\_+(-3y)+=14x-21y$
Since the x terms are the same, the y terms must match. This means that $\_\_+(-3y)+=-21y$ and the missing term must be $-18y$.

93. Answers will vary according to the exercises chosen. For example, $3\sqrt{5}-2\sqrt{7}-\sqrt{11}+4\sqrt{3}\approx 5.0283$.

94. $-19\ge -18$ is true because $-19>-18$ is true.

95.
a. $\sqrt{4}\,(=2)$
b. $0, \sqrt{4}$
c. $-6, 0, \sqrt{4}$
d. $-6, 0, 0.\overline{7}, \sqrt{4}$
e. $-\pi, \sqrt{3}$
f. $-6, -\pi, 0, 0.\overline{7}, \sqrt{3}, \sqrt{4}$

96. Quadrant IV

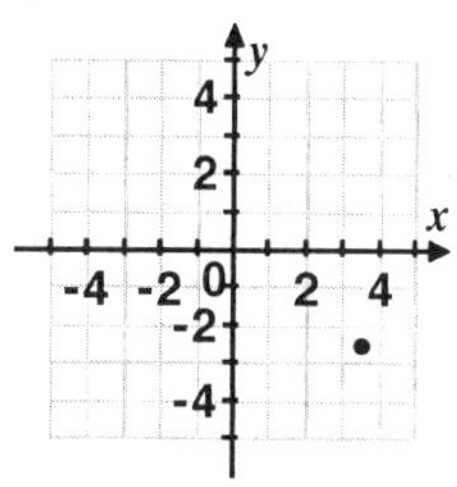

Exercise Set 1.6

1. **a.** -12
b. $5-12=5+(-12)$

3. **a.** 7
b. $5-(-7)=5+7$

5. $14-8=14+(-8)=6$

7. $8-14=8+(-14)=-6$

9. $3-(-20)=3+20=23$

11. $-7-(-18)=-7+18=11$

13. $-13-(-2)=-13+2=-11$

15. $-21-17=-21+(-17)=-38$

17. $-45-(-45)=-45+45=0$

19. $23-23=23+(-23)=0$

21. $13-(-13)=13+13=26$

23. $0-13=0+(-13)=-13$

25. $0-(-13)=0+13=13$

27. $\frac{3}{7}-\frac{5}{7}=\frac{3}{7}+\left(-\frac{5}{7}\right)=-\frac{2}{7}$

29. $\frac{1}{5}-\left(-\frac{3}{5}\right)=\frac{1}{5}+\frac{3}{5}=\frac{4}{5}$

31. $-\frac{4}{5}-\frac{1}{5}=-\frac{4}{5}+\left(-\frac{1}{5}\right)=-\frac{5}{5}=-1$

33. $-\frac{4}{5}-\left(-\frac{1}{5}\right)=-\frac{4}{5}+\frac{1}{5}=-\frac{3}{5}$

35. $\frac{1}{2}-\left(-\frac{1}{4}\right)=\frac{1}{2}+\frac{1}{4}=\frac{2}{4}+\frac{1}{4}=\frac{3}{4}$

37. $\frac{1}{2}-\frac{1}{4}=\frac{1}{2}+\left(-\frac{1}{4}\right)=\frac{2}{4}+\left(-\frac{1}{4}\right)=\frac{1}{4}$

39. $9.8-2.2=9.8+(-2.2)=7.6$

41. $-3.1-(-1.1)=-3.1+1.1=-2$

43. $1.3-(-1.3)=1.3+1.3=2.6$

45. $-2.06-(-2.06)=-2.06+2.06=0$

47. $5\pi-2\pi=5\pi+(-2\pi)=3\pi$

49. $3\pi-(-10\pi)=3\pi+10\pi=13\pi$

51.
$$\begin{aligned}13-2-(-8)&=13+(-2)+8\\&=(13+8)+(-2)\\&=21+(-2)\\&=19\end{aligned}$$

53.
$$\begin{aligned}9-8+3-7&=9+(-8)+3+(-7)\\&=(9+3)+[(-8)+(-7)]\\&=12+(-15)\\&=-3\end{aligned}$$

55.
$$\begin{aligned}&-6-2+3-10\\&=-6+(-2)+3+(-10)\\&=[(-6)+(-2)+(-10)]+3\\&=-18+3\\&=-15\end{aligned}$$

57.
$$\begin{aligned}&-10-(-5)+7-2\\&=-10+5+7+(-2)\\&=[(-10)+(-2)]+(5+7)\\&=-12+12\\&=0\end{aligned}$$

59. $-23-11-(-7)+(-25)$
$=(-23)+(-11)+7+(-25)$
$=[(-23)+(-11)+(-25)]+7$
$=-59+7$
$=-52$

61. $-823-146-50-(-832)$
$=-823+(-146)+(-50)+832$
$=[(-823)+(-146)+(-50)]+832$
$=-1019+832$
$=-187$

63. $1-\frac{2}{3}-\left(-\frac{5}{6}\right)=1+\left(-\frac{2}{3}\right)+\frac{5}{6}$
$=\left(1+\frac{5}{6}\right)+\left(-\frac{2}{3}\right)$
$=\left(\frac{6}{6}+\frac{5}{6}\right)+\left(-\frac{2}{3}\right)$
$=\frac{11}{6}+\left(-\frac{2}{3}\cdot\frac{2}{2}\right)$
$=\frac{11}{6}+\left(-\frac{4}{6}\right)$
$=\frac{7}{6}$ or $1\frac{1}{6}$

65. $-0.16-5.2-(-0.87)$
$=-0.16+(-5.2)+0.87$
$=[(-0.16)+(-5.2)]+0.87$
$=-5.36+0.87$
$=-4.49$

67. $-\frac{3}{4}-\frac{1}{4}-\left(-\frac{5}{8}\right)=-\frac{3}{4}+\left(-\frac{1}{4}\right)+\frac{5}{8}$
$=-\frac{4}{4}+\frac{5}{8}$
$=-\frac{8}{8}+\frac{5}{8}=-\frac{3}{8}$

69. $-3x-8y=-3x+(-8y)$
The terms are $-3x$ and $-8y$.

71. $12x-5xy-4=12x+(-5xy)+(-4)$
The terms are $12x$, $-5xy$, and -4.

73. $3x-9x=3x+(-9x)$
$=[3+(-9)]x=-6x$

75. $4+7y-17y=4+7y+(-17y)$
$=4+[7+(-17)]y$
$=4-10y$

77. $2a+5-9a=2a+5+(-9a)$
$=2a+(-9a)+5$
$=[2+(-9)]a+5$
$=-7a+5a$ or $5-7a$

79. $4-6b-8-3b$
$=4+(-6b)+(-8)+(-3b)$
$=4+(-8)+(-6b)+(-3b)$
$=4+(-8)+[-6+(-3)]b$
$=-4-9b$

81. $13-(-7x)+4x-(-11)$
$=13+7x+4x+11$
$=13+11+7x+4x$
$=24+11x$

83. $-5x-10y-3x+13y$
$=-5x+(-10y)+(-3x)+13y$
$=-5x+(-3x)+(-10y)+13y$
$=[-5+(-3)]x+(-10+13)y$
$=-8x+3y$ or $3y-8x$

85. $-|-9-(-6)|-(-12)=-|-9+6|+12$
$=-|-3|+12$
$=-3+12$
$=9$

86. $-|-8-(-2)|-(-6) = -|-8+2|+6$
$= -|-6|+6$
$= -6+6$
$= 0$

87. $\frac{5}{8}-\left(\frac{1}{2}-\frac{3}{4}\right) = \frac{5}{8}-\left(\frac{1}{2}\cdot\frac{2}{2}-\frac{3}{4}\right)$
$= \frac{5}{8}-\left(\frac{2}{4}+\left(-\frac{3}{4}\right)\right)$
$= \frac{5}{8}-\left(-\frac{1}{4}\right)$
$= \frac{5}{8}+\frac{1}{4}$
$= \frac{5}{8}+\frac{1}{4}\cdot\frac{2}{2}$
$= \frac{5}{8}+\frac{2}{8}$
$= \frac{7}{8}$

88. $\frac{9}{10}-\left(\frac{1}{4}-\frac{7}{10}\right) = \frac{9}{10}-\left(\frac{1}{4}\cdot\frac{5}{5}-\frac{7}{10}\cdot\frac{2}{2}\right)$
$= \frac{9}{10}-\left(\frac{5}{20}-\frac{14}{20}\right)$
$= \frac{9}{10}-\left[\frac{5}{20}+\left(-\frac{14}{20}\right)\right]$
$= \frac{9}{10}-\left(-\frac{9}{20}\right)$
$= \frac{9}{10}\cdot\frac{2}{2}+\frac{9}{20}$
$= \frac{18}{20}+\frac{9}{20}$
$= \frac{27}{20}$ or $1\frac{7}{20}$

89. $|-9-(-3+7)|-|-17-(-2)|$
$= |-9-4|-|-17+2|$
$= |-9+(-4)|-|-17+2|$
$= |-13|-|-15|$
$= 13+(-15)$
$= -2$

90. $|24-(-16)|-|-51-(-31+2)|$
$= |24+16|-|-51-(-29)|$
$= |24+16|-|-51+29|$
$= |40|-|-22|$
$= 40-22$
$= 18$

91. Elevation of Mount Kilimanjaro – elevation of Qattara Depression
$= 19,321-(-436) = 19,757$
The difference in elevation between the two geographic locations is 19,757 feet.

93. Increase teachers – decrease farmers
$= 711-(-328) = 711+328 = 1039$
The difference is 1039 thousand jobs.

95. phone – farmers $= -60-(-328)$
$= -60+328$
$= 268$
The decline for phone workers exceeds the decline for farmers by 268 thousand jobs.

97. $2-(-19) = 2+19 = 21$
The difference between the average daily low temperature for March and February is 21°F.

99. $-19-(-22) = -19+22 = 3$
February's average low temperature is 3°F warmer than January's.

101. The maximum point on the graph is (3, 0.05). This means that the drug's maximum concentration is 0.05 milligrams per 100 milliliters and this occurs 3 hours after the injection.

103. $0.045-0.03=0.045+(-0.03)=0.015$
The difference in concentrations between 4 hours and 1 hour after injection is about 0.015 milligrams.

105. The drug's concentration is increasing between 0 and 3 hours after the injection (from the time of the injection to three hours later).

107. – 111. Answers will vary.

113. Consider dates B.C. as negative numbers and dates A.D. as positive numbers:
$500-(-212)=500+212=712$.
Because there was no year 0, the number of elapsed time is 712 – 1 = 711 years.

115. Student answers will vary according to the exercises chosen.

117. 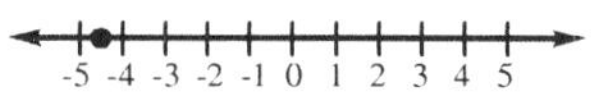

118. $10(a+4)=10(4+a)$

119. Examples will vary. One integer that is not a natural number is –7.

1.7 Exercises Set

1. $5(-9)=-(5\cdot 9)=-45$

3. $(-8)(-3)=+(8\cdot 3)=24$

5. $(-3)(7)=-21$

7. $(-19)(-1)=19$

9. $0(-19)=0$

11. $\frac{1}{2}(-24)=-12$

13. $\left(-\frac{3}{4}\right)(-12)=\frac{3\cdot 12}{4\cdot 1}=9$

15. $-\frac{3}{5}\cdot\left(-\frac{4}{7}\right)=\frac{3\cdot 4}{5\cdot 7}=\frac{12}{35}$

17. $-\frac{7}{9}\cdot\frac{2}{3}=-\frac{7\cdot 2}{9\cdot 3}=-\frac{14}{27}$

19. $3(-1.2)=-3.6$

21. $-0.2(-0.6)=0.12$

23. $(-5)(-2)(3)=30$

25. $(-4)(-3)(-1)(6)=-72$

27. $-2(-3)(-4)(-1)=24$

29. $(-3)(-3)(-3)=9(-3)=-27$

31. $5(-3)(-1)(2)(3)=90$

33. $(-8)(-4)(0)(-17)(-6)=0$

35. The multiplicative inverse of 4 is $\frac{1}{4}$.

37. The multiplicative inverse of $\frac{1}{5}$ is 5.

39. The multiplicative inverse of −10 is $-\frac{1}{10}$.

41. The multiplicative inverse of $-\frac{2}{5}$ is $-\frac{5}{2}$.

43. **a.** $-32 \div 4 = -32 \cdot \frac{1}{4}$

b. $-32 \cdot \frac{1}{4} = -8$

45. **a.** $\frac{-60}{-5} = -60 \cdot \left(-\frac{1}{5}\right)$

b. $-60 \cdot \left(-\frac{1}{5}\right) = 12$

47. $\frac{12}{-4} = 12 \cdot \left(-\frac{1}{4}\right) = -3$

49. $\frac{-21}{3} = -21 \cdot \frac{1}{3} = -7$

51. $\frac{-90}{-3} = -90 \cdot \left(-\frac{1}{3}\right) = 30$

53. $\frac{0}{-7} = 0$

55. $\frac{-7}{0}$ is undefined.

57. $-15 \div 3 = -15 \cdot \frac{1}{3} = -5$

59. $12 \div (-10) = 120 \cdot \left(-\frac{1}{10}\right) = -12$

61. $(-180) \div (-30) = -180 \cdot \left(-\frac{1}{30}\right) = 6$

63. $0 \div (-4) = 0$

65. $-4 \div 0$ is undefined.

67. $\frac{-12.9}{3} = -12.9 \cdot \frac{1}{3} = -4.3$

69. $-\frac{1}{2} \div \left(-\frac{3}{5}\right) = -\frac{1}{2} \cdot \left(-\frac{5}{3}\right) = \frac{5}{6}$

71.
$$-\frac{14}{9} \div \frac{7}{8} = -\frac{14}{9} \cdot \frac{8}{7} = -\frac{112}{63} = \frac{\cancel{7} \cdot 16}{\cancel{7} \cdot 9} = -\frac{16}{9}$$

73. $\frac{1}{3} \div \left(-\frac{1}{3}\right) = \frac{1}{3} \cdot (-3) = -1$

75. $6 \div \left(-\frac{2}{5}\right) = 6 \cdot \left(-\frac{5}{2}\right) = -\frac{30}{2} = -15$

77. $-5(2x) = (-5 \cdot 2)x = -10x$

79. $-4\left(-\frac{3}{4}y\right) = \left[-4 \cdot \left(-\frac{3}{4}\right)\right]y = 3y$

81. $8x + x = 8x + 1x = (8+1)x = 9x$

83. $-5x + x = -5x + 1x = (-5+1)x = -4x$

85. $6b - 7b = (6-7)b = -1b = -b$

87. $-y + 4y = -1y + 4y = (-1+4)y = 3y$

89. $-4(2x-3) = -4(2x) - 4(-3) = -8x + 12$

91. $-3(-2x+4) = -3(-2x) - 3(4) = 6x - 12$

93. $-(2y-5) = -2y + 5$

95.
$$\begin{aligned} &4(2y-3) - (7y+2) \\ &= 4(2y) + 4(-3) - 7y - 2 \\ &= 8y - 12 + 7y - 2 \\ &= 8y - 7y - 12 - 2 \\ &= y - 14 \end{aligned}$$

97. $4(-10) + 8 = -40 + 8 = -32$

98. $3(-15) + 14 = -45 + 14 = -31$

99. $(-9)(-3) - (-2) = 27 + 2 = 29$

100. $(-6)(-4)-(-5)=24+5=29$

101. $\frac{-18}{-15+12}=\frac{-18}{-3}=6$

102. $\frac{-25}{-21+16}=\frac{-25}{-5}=5$

103. $-6-\left(\frac{12}{-4}\right)=-6-(-3)=-6+3=-3$

104. $-11-\left(\frac{20}{-5}\right)=-11-(-4)$
$=-11+4=-7$

105. Since 2000 − 1994 = 6, let t = 6:
$-1.4t+14.7=-1.4(6)+14.7$
$=-8.4+14.7=6.3$
The model predicts that there were 6.3 million welfare recipients in 2000. The graph shows approximately 6 million so the model gives a slight overestimation.

107. **a.** From the graph, a reasonable estimate is 11 words.

b. $\frac{5x+30}{x};x=5$
$\frac{5x+30}{x}=\frac{5(5)+30}{5}$
$=\frac{25+30}{5}=\frac{55}{5}=11$
According to the model, 11 Latin words will be remembered after 5 days. This is the same as the estimate from part (a).

109. **a.** $\frac{200x}{100-x};x=50$
$\frac{200x}{100-x}=\frac{200(50)}{100-50}$
$=\frac{10,000}{50}=200$
The cost for removing 50% of the containments is 200($10,000) = $2,000,000.

b. $\frac{200x}{100-x};x=80$
$\frac{200x}{100-x}=\frac{200(80)}{100-80}$
$=\frac{16,000}{20}=800$
The cost for removing 80% of the containments is 80($10,000) = $8,000,000.

c. As the percentage of contaminant removed increases, the cost of the cleanup rises very rapidly.

111. – 117. Answers will vary.

119. Statement b is true.

121. $5x$

123. $\frac{x}{12}$

125. Student solutions will vary according to the exercises chosen.

127. $0.3(4.7x-5.9)-0.07(3.8x-61)$
$=0.3(4.7x)+0.3(-5.9)-(0.07)(3.8x)$
$\quad-(0.07)(-61)$
$=1.41x-1.77-0.266x+4.27$
$=[1.41x+(-0.266x)]+(-1.77+4.27)$
$=1.144x+2.5$

129. $-6+(-3)=-9$

130. $-6-(-3)=-6+3=-3$

131. $-6\div(-3)=-6\left(-\frac{1}{3}\right)=2$

1.8 Exercise Set

1. $9^2=9\cdot9=81$

3. $4^3=4\cdot4\cdot4=64$

5. $(-4)^2=(-4)(-4)=16$

7. $(-4)^3=(-4)(-4)(-4)=-64$

9. $(-5)^4=(-5)(-5)(-5)(-5)=625$

11. $5^4=-5\cdot5\cdot5\cdot5=-625$

13. $-10^2=-10\cdot10=-100$

15. $7x^2+12x^2=(7+12)x^2=19x^2$

17. $10x^3+5x^3=(10+5)x^3=15x^3$

19. $8x^4+x^4=8x^4+1x^4=(8+1)x^4=9x^4$

21.
$$\begin{aligned}26x^2-27x^2&=26x^2+(-27x^2)\\&=[26+(-27)]x^2\\&=-1x^2=-x^2\end{aligned}$$

23.
$$\begin{aligned}27x^3-26x^3&=27x^3+(-26x^2)\\&=1x^3=x^3\end{aligned}$$

25. $5x^2+5x^3$ cannot be simplified. The terms $5x^2$ and $5x^3$ are not like terms because they have different variable factors, namely, x^2 and x^3.

27.
$$\begin{aligned}16x^2-16x^2&=16x^2+(-16x^2)\\&=[16+(-16)]x^2\\&=0x^2=0\end{aligned}$$

29. $7+6\cdot3=7+18=25$

31. $45\div5\cdot3=9+18=27$

33. $6\cdot8\div4=48\div4=12$

35. $14-2\cdot6+3=14-12+3=2+3=5$

37.
$$\begin{aligned}8^2-16\div2^2\cdot4-3&=64-16\div4\cdot4-3\\&=64-4\cdot4-3\\&=64-16-3\\&=48-3\\&=45\end{aligned}$$

39.
$$\begin{aligned}3(-2)^2-4(-3)^2&=3\cdot4-4\cdot9\\&=12\quad36\\&=12+(-36)\\&=-24\end{aligned}$$

41.
$$\begin{aligned}(4\cdot5)^2-4\cdot5^2&=20^2-4\cdot25\\&=400-100\\&=300\end{aligned}$$

43.
$$\begin{aligned}(2-6)^2-(3-7)^2&=(-4)^2-(-4)^2\\&=16-16\\&=0\end{aligned}$$

45.
$$\begin{aligned}&6(3-5)^3-2(1-3)^3\\&=6(-2)^3-2(-2)^3\\&=6(-8)-2(-8)\\&=-48+16\\&=-32\end{aligned}$$

47. $[2(6-2)]^2=(2\cdot4)^2=8^2=64$

49. $2[5+2(9-4)]=2[5+2(5)]$
$=2(5+10)$
$=2\cdot 15=30$

51. $[7+3(2^3-1)]+21$
$=[7+3(8-1)]\div 21$
$=(7+3\cdot 7)\div 21$
$=(7+21)\div 21$
$=28\div 21=\frac{28}{21}=\frac{\cancel{7}\cdot 4}{\cancel{7}\cdot 3}=\frac{4}{3}$

53. $\frac{10+8}{5^2-4^2}=\frac{18}{25-16}=\frac{18}{9}=2$

55. $\frac{37+15\div(-3)}{2^4}=\frac{37+(-5)}{16}=\frac{32}{16}=2$

57. $\frac{(-11)(-4)+2(-7)}{7-(-3)}=\frac{44+(-14)}{7+3}$
$=\frac{30}{10}=3$

59. $4|10-(8-20)|=4|10-(-12)|$
$=4|10+12|$
$=4|22|=4\cdot 22=88$

61. $8(-10)+|4(-5)|=-80+|-20|$
$=-80+20=-60$

63. $-2^2+4[16+(3-5)]$
$=-4+4[16+(-2)]$
$=-4+4(-8)=-4-32=-36$

65. $24\div\frac{3^2}{8-5}-(-6)=24\div\frac{9}{3}-(-6)$
$=24\div 3-(-6)$
$=8+6=14$

67. $\frac{\frac{1}{4}-\frac{1}{2}}{\frac{1}{3}}=\frac{\frac{1}{4}-\frac{2}{4}}{\frac{1}{3}}=\frac{-\frac{1}{4}}{\frac{1}{3}}=-\frac{1}{4}\cdot\frac{3}{1}=-\frac{3}{4}$

69. $-\frac{9}{4}\left(\frac{1}{2}\right)+\frac{3}{4}\div\frac{5}{6}=-\frac{9}{4}\left(\frac{1}{2}\right)+\frac{3}{4}\cdot\frac{6}{5}$
$=-\frac{9}{8}+\frac{18}{20}$
$=-\frac{45}{40}+\frac{36}{40}=-\frac{9}{40}$

71. $\frac{\frac{7}{9}-3}{\frac{5}{6}}\div\frac{3}{2}+\frac{3}{4}=\frac{\frac{7}{9}-\frac{27}{9}}{\frac{5}{6}}\cdot\frac{3}{2}+\frac{3}{4}$
$=\frac{-\frac{20}{9}}{\frac{5}{6}}\cdot\frac{3}{2}+\frac{3}{4}$
$=-\frac{20}{9}\cdot\frac{6}{5}\cdot\frac{2}{3}+\frac{3}{4}$
$=-\frac{240}{135}+\frac{3}{4}$
$=-\frac{15\cdot 16}{15\cdot 9}+\frac{3}{4}$
$=-\frac{16}{9}+\frac{3}{4}$
$=-\frac{64}{36}+\frac{27}{36}$
$=-\frac{37}{36}$ or $-1\frac{1}{36}$

73. $x^2+5x;\ x=3$
$x^2+5x=3^2+5\cdot 3$
$=9+5\cdot 3=9+15=24$

75. $3x^2 - 8x;\ x = -2$

$$3x^2 - 8x = 3(-2)^2 - 9(-2)$$
$$= 3 \cdot 4 - 8(-2) = 12 + 16 = 28$$

77. $-x^2 - 10x;\ x = -1$

$$-x^2 - 10x = -(-1)^2 - 10(-1)$$
$$= -1 + 10 = 9$$

79. $\dfrac{6y - 4y^2}{y^2 - 15};\ y = 5$

$$\frac{6y - 4y^2}{y^2 - 15} = \frac{6(5) - 4(5^2)}{5^2 - 15}$$
$$= \frac{6(5) - 4(25)}{25 - 15}$$
$$= \frac{30 - 100}{25 - 15} = \frac{-70}{10} = -7$$

81. $3[5(x-2)+1] = 3(5x - 10 + 1)$
$$= 3(5x - 9)$$
$$= 15x - 27$$

83. $3[6 - (y+1)] = 3(6 - y - 1)$
$$= 3(5 - y)$$
$$= 15 - 3y$$

85. $7 - 4[3 - (4y - 5)]$
$$= 7 - 4(3 - 4y + 5)$$
$$= 7 - 12 + 16y - 20$$
$$= -25 + 16y \text{ or } 16y - 25$$

87. $2(3x^2 - 5) - [4(2x^2 - 1) + 3]$
$$= 6x^2 - 10 - (8x^2 - 4 + 3)$$
$$= 6x^2 - 10 - (8x^2 - 1)$$
$$= 6x^2 - 10 - 8x^2 - 1$$
$$= -2x^2 - 9$$

89. $-10 - (-2)^3 = -10 - (-8) = -10 + 8 = -2$

90. $-100 - (-5)^3 = -100 - (-125)$
$$= -100 + 125$$
$$= 25$$

91. $[2(7-10)]^2 = [2(-3)]^2 = [-6]^2 = 36$

92. $[2(9-11)]^4 = [2(-2)]^4 = [-4]^4 = 256$

93. $x - (5x + 8) = x - 5x - 8 = -4x - 8$

94. $x - (3x + 9) = x - 3x - 9 = -2x - 9$

95. $5(x^3 - 4) = 5x^3 - 20$

96. $4(x^3 - 6) = 4x^3 - 24$

97. $R = 165 - 0.75A;\ A = 40$

$$R - 165 - 0.75A = 165 - 0.75(40)$$
$$= 165 - 30 = 135$$

The desirable heart rate during exercise for a 40-year old man is 135 beats per minute. This corresponds to the point (40, 135) on the graph.

99. Since 2000 – 1995 = 5, the year 2005 corresponds to $x = 5$.

$N = 1.2x^2 + 15.2x + 181.4;\ \ x = 5$

$$N = 1.2x^2 + 15.2x + 181.4$$
$$= 1.2(5^2) + 152.5(5) + 181.4$$
$$= 1.2(25) + 15.2(5) + 181.4$$
$$= 30 + 76 + 181.4$$
$$= 287.4$$

According to the formula, the cost of Medicare in 2000 was $287.4 billion. This is a very good estimate for the cost shown by the bar graph.

101. Since 2002 – 1992 = 10, let x = 10

$$N = 0.12x^3 - x^2 + 3x + 15$$
$$= 0.12(10)^3 - 10^2 + 3(10) + 15$$
$$= 0.12(1000) - 100 + 3(10) + 15$$
$$= 120 - 100 + 30 + 15 = 65$$

According to the formula, approximately 65 thousand bariatric surgeries were performs in 2002. The graph shows approximately 63 thousand so this is a slight overestimation.

103. $C = \frac{5}{9}(F - 32);\ \ F = 68$

$$C = \frac{5}{9}(F - 32)$$
$$= \frac{5}{9}(68 - 32)$$
$$= \frac{5}{9}(36) = \frac{5}{9} \cdot \frac{36}{1} = \frac{180}{9} = 20$$

Thus, 68°F = 20°V.

105. $C = \frac{5}{9}(F - 32);\ \ F = -22$

$$C = \frac{5}{9}(F - 32)$$
$$= \frac{5}{9}(-22 - 32)$$
$$= \frac{5}{9}(-54) = \frac{5}{9} \cdot \frac{54}{1} = -\frac{270}{9} = -30$$

Thus, –22°F = –30°C.

107. – 111. Answers will vary.

113. $\frac{1}{4} - 6(2+8) \div \left(-\frac{1}{3}\right)\left(-\frac{1}{9}\right)$

$$= \frac{1}{4} - 6(10) \div \left(-\frac{1}{3}\right)\left(-\frac{1}{9}\right)$$
$$= \frac{1}{4} - 60 \div \left(-\frac{1}{3}\right)\left(-\frac{1}{9}\right)$$
$$= \frac{1}{4} - 60 \div (-3)\left(-\frac{1}{9}\right)$$
$$= \frac{1}{4} + 180\left(-\frac{1}{9}\right)$$
$$= \frac{1}{4} - 20 = \frac{1}{4} - \frac{80}{4} = \frac{79}{4}$$

115. $\left(2 \cdot 5 - \frac{1}{2} \cdot 10\right) \cdot 9 = (10 - 5) \cdot 9$

$$= 5 \cdot 9 = 45$$

117. Answers will vary.

119. $-8 - 2 - (-5) + 11$

$$= -8 + (-2) + 5 + 11$$
$$= [(-8) + (-2)] + (5 + 11)$$
$$= -10 + 16 = 6$$

120. $-4(-1)(-3)(2) = -24$

121. Any rational number is a real number that is not an irrational number. One example is $-\frac{3}{4}$.

Chapter 1 Review Exercises

1. $3\frac{2}{7} = \frac{3 \cdot 7 + 2}{7} = \frac{21 + 2}{7} = \frac{23}{7}$

2. $5\frac{9}{11} = \frac{5 \cdot 11 + 9}{11} = \frac{55 + 9}{11} = \frac{64}{11}$

3. 17 divided by 9 is 1 with a remainder of 8, so $\frac{17}{9} = 1\frac{8}{9}$.

4. 27 divided by 5 is 5 with a remainder of 2, so $\frac{27}{5} = 5\frac{2}{5}$.

5. Composite
$60 = 6 \cdot 10 = 2 \cdot 3 \cdot 2 \cdot 5 = 2 \cdot 2 \cdot 3 \cdot 5$

6. Composite
$63 = 7 \cdot 9 = 7 \cdot 3 \cdot 3 = 3 \cdot 3 \cdot 7$

7. 67 is a prime number.

8. $\frac{15}{33} = \frac{\not{3} \cdot 5}{\not{3} \cdot 11} = \frac{5}{11}$

9. $\frac{40}{75} = \frac{\not{5} \cdot 8}{\not{5} \cdot 15} = \frac{8}{15}$

10. $\frac{3}{5} \cdot \frac{7}{10} = \frac{3 \cdot 7}{5 \cdot 10} = \frac{21}{50}$

11. $\frac{4}{5} \div \frac{3}{10} = \frac{4}{5} \cdot \frac{10}{3} = \frac{40}{15} = \frac{\not{5} \cdot 8}{\not{5} \cdot 3} = \frac{8}{3}$

12. $1\frac{2}{3} \div 6\frac{2}{3} = \frac{5}{3} \div \frac{20}{3}$

$= \frac{5}{\not{3}} \cdot \frac{\not{3}}{20} = \frac{5}{20} = \frac{1 \cdot \not{5}}{4 \cdot \not{5}} = \frac{1}{4}$

13. $\frac{2}{9} + \frac{4}{9} = \frac{2+4}{9} = \frac{6}{9} = \frac{2 \cdot \not{3}}{3 \cdot \not{3}} = \frac{2}{3}$

14. $\frac{5}{6} + \frac{7}{9} = \frac{5}{6} \cdot \frac{3}{3} + \frac{7}{9} \cdot \frac{2}{2}$

$= \frac{15}{18} + \frac{14}{18} = \frac{29}{18}$ or $1\frac{11}{18}$

15. $\frac{3}{4} - \frac{2}{15} = \frac{3}{4} \cdot \frac{15}{15} - \frac{2}{15} \cdot \frac{4}{4} = \frac{45}{60} - \frac{8}{60} = \frac{37}{60}$

16. $1 - \frac{1}{4} - \frac{1}{3} = \frac{12}{12} - \frac{3}{12} - \frac{4}{12} = \frac{5}{12}$

At the end of the second day, $\frac{5}{12}$ of the tank is filled.

17. -2.5

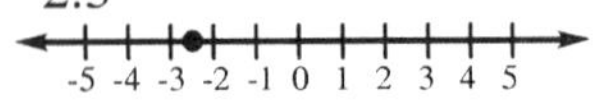

18. $4\frac{3}{4}$

19.

$$\begin{array}{r} 0.625 \\ 8\overline{)5.000} \\ \underline{48} \\ 20 \\ \underline{16} \\ 40 \\ \underline{40} \\ 0 \end{array}$$

$\frac{5}{8} = 0.625$

20.

$$\begin{array}{r} 0.2727\ldots \\ 11\overline{)3.0000\ldots} \\ \underline{22} \\ 80 \\ \underline{77} \\ 30 \\ \underline{27} \\ 30 \\ \underline{22} \\ 8 \\ \vdots \end{array}$$

$\frac{3}{11} = 0.\overline{27}$

21. **a.** $\sqrt{81}\ (=9)$

b. $0, \sqrt{81}$

c. $-17, 0, \sqrt{81}$

d. $-17, -\frac{9}{13}, 0, 0.75, \sqrt{81}$

e. $\sqrt{2}, \pi$

f. $-17, -\frac{9}{13}, 0, 0.75, \sqrt{2}, \pi, \sqrt{81}$

22. Answers will vary. One example of an integer that is not a natural number is −7.

23. Answers will vary. One example of a rational number that is not an integer is $\frac{3}{4}$.

24. Answers will vary. One example of a real number that is not a rational number is π.

25. $-93 < 17$; -93 is to the left of 17, so $-93 < 17$.

26. $-2 > -200$; -2 is to the right of -200, so $-2 > -200$.

27. $0 > -\frac{1}{3}$; 0 is to the right of $-\frac{1}{3}$, so $0 > -\frac{1}{3}$.

28. $-\frac{1}{4} < -\frac{1}{5}$; $-\frac{1}{4} = -0.25$ is to the left of $-\frac{1}{5} = -0.2$, so $-\frac{1}{4} < -\frac{1}{5}$.

29. $-13 \geq -11$ is false because neither $-13 > -11$ nor $-13 = -11$ is true.

30. $-126 \leq -126$ is true because $-126 = -126$.

31. $|-58| = 58$ because the distance between −58 and 0 on the number line is 58.

32. $|2.75| = 2.75$ because the distance between 2.75 and 0 on the number line is 2.75.

33.

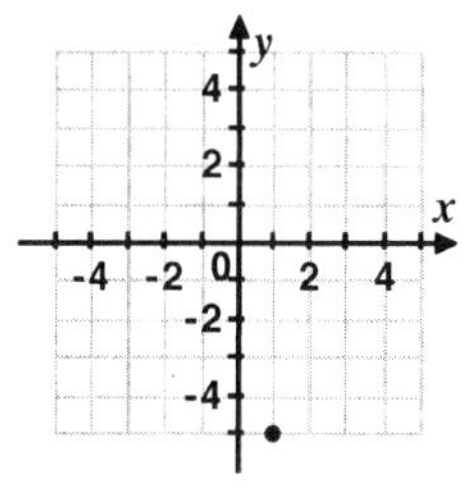

Quadrant IV

34.

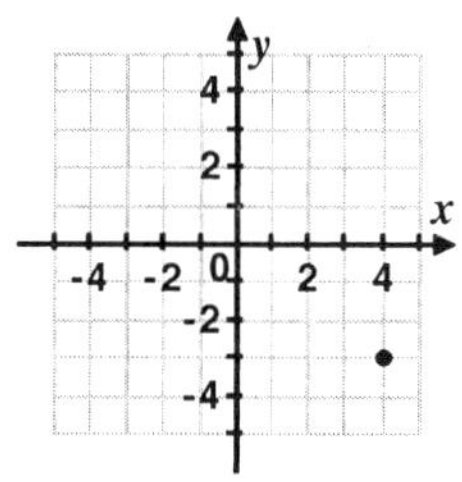

Quadrant IV

35.

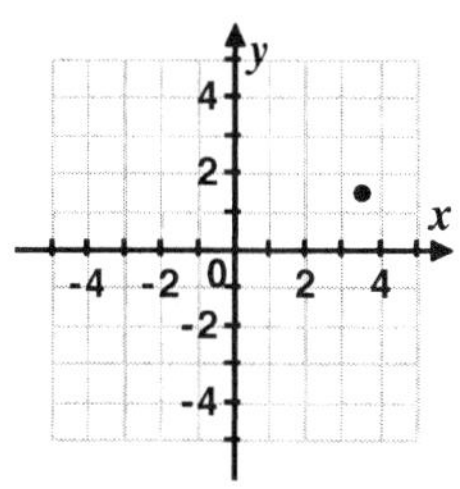

Quadrant I

36.

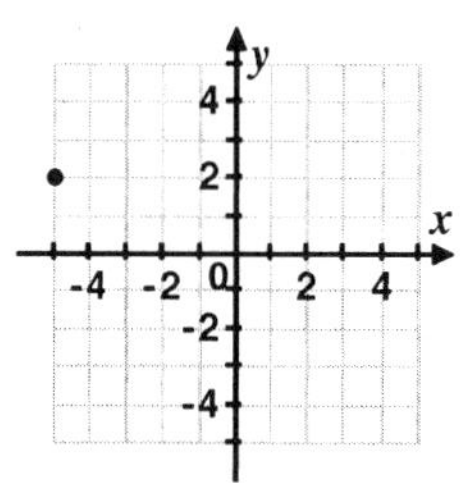

Quadrant II

37. $A(5,6)$, $B(-3,0)$, $C(-5,2)$, $D(-4,-2)$, $E(0,-5)$, $F(3,-1)$

38. There were approximately 65 democracies in 1989.

39. There were 120 – 40 = 80 more democracies in 2002 than in 1973.

40. The number of democracies increased at the greatest rate between 1989 and 1993.

41. The number of democracies increased at the slowest rate between 1981 and 1985.

42. There were 49 democracies in 1977.

43. There are approximately 85 televisions per 100 people in the U.S.

44. Finland, Germany, and Austria have more than 50 but fewer than 70 televisions per 100 people.

45. $7x+3;\ x=10$

$$7x+3=7(10)+3=70+3=73$$

46. $5(x-4);\ x=12$

$$5(x-4)=5(12-4)=5\cdot 8=40$$

47. $7+13y=13y+7$

48. $9(x+7)=(x+7)9$

49. $6+(4+y)=(6+4)+y=10+y$

50. $7(10x)=(7\cdot 10)x=70x$

51. $6(4x-2+5y)=6(4x)+6(-2)+6(5y)$

$$=24x-12+30y$$

52. $4a+9+3a-7=4a+3a+9-7$

$$=(4+3)a+(9-7)$$
$$=7a+2$$

53. $6(3x+4)+5(2x-1)$

$$=6(3x)+6(4)+5(2x)+5(-1)$$
$$=18x+24+10x-5$$
$$=18x+10x+24-5$$
$$=(18+10)x+[24+(-5)]$$
$$=28x+19$$

54. $x-0.25x;\ x=2400$

$$x-0.25x=2400-0.25(2400)$$
$$=2400-600$$
$$=1800$$

This means that a computer with a regular price of \$2400 will have a sale price of \$1800.

55. Start at –6. Move 8 units to the right because 8 is positive. Finish at 2.

56. $8+(-11)=-3$

57. $-\frac{3}{4}+\frac{1}{5}=-\frac{3}{4}\cdot\frac{5}{5}+\frac{1}{5}\cdot\frac{4}{4}$

$$=-\frac{15}{20}+\frac{4}{20}=-\frac{11}{20}$$

58. $7+(-5)+(-13)+4$

$$=[7+(-5)]+(-13)+4$$
$$=2+(-13)+4$$
$$=[2+(-13)]+4=-11+4=-7$$

59. $8x+(-6y)+(-12x)+11y$

$$=8x+(-12x)+(-6y)+11y$$
$$=[8+(-12)]x+(-6+11)y$$
$$=-4x+5y \text{ or } 5y-4x$$

60. $10(4-3y)+28y$
$=10(4)+10(-3y)+28y$
$=40-30y+28y$
$=40+(-30+28)y$
$=40-2y$

61. $-1312+512=-800$
The person's elevation is 800 feet below sea level.

62. $25-3+2+1-4+2$
$=25+(-3)+2+1+(-4)+2$
$=23$
The reservoir's water level at the end of five months is 23 feet.

63. $9-13=9+(-13)$

64. $-9-(-13)=-9+13=4$

65. $-\frac{7}{10}-\frac{1}{2}=-\frac{7}{10}-\frac{1}{2}\cdot\frac{5}{5}$
$=-\frac{7}{10}-\frac{5}{10}=-\frac{12}{10}=-\frac{6}{5}$

66. $-3.6-(-2.1)=-3.6+2.1=-1.5$

67. $-7-(-5)+11-16$
$=-7+5+11+(-16)$
$=[(-7)+(-16)]+(5+11)$
$=-23+16$
$=-7$

68. $-25-4-(-10)+16$
$=-25+(-4)+10+16$
$=[(-25)+(-4)]+(10+16)$
$=-29+26$
$=-3$

69. $3-6a-8-2a=3-8-6a-2a$
$=[3+(-8)]+[-6a-2a]$
$=-5+(-6-2)a$
$=-5-8a$

70. $26,000-(-650)=26,500+650$
$=27,150$
The difference in elevation is 27,150 feet.

71. $(-7)(-12)=84$

72. $\frac{3}{5}\left(-\frac{5}{11}\right)=-\frac{3\cdot\cancel{5}}{\cancel{5}\cdot 11}=-\frac{3}{11}$

73. $5(-3)(-2)(-4)=-120$

74. $\frac{45}{-5}=45\left(-\frac{1}{5}\right)=-9$

75. $-17\div 0$ is undefined.

76. $-\frac{4}{5}\div\left(-\frac{2}{5}\right)=-\frac{4}{5}\left(-\frac{5}{2}\right)=\frac{20}{10}=2$

77. $-4\left(-\frac{3}{4}x\right)=\left[-4\left(-\frac{3}{4}\right)\right]x=3x$

78. $-3(2x-1)-(4-5x)$
$=-3(2x)+(-3)(-1)-4+5x$
$=-6x+3-4+5x$
$=-6x+5x+3-4$
$=(-6+5)x+[3+(-4)]$
$=-1x-1=-x-1$

79. $(-6)^2=(-6)(-6)=36$

80. $-6^2=-6\cdot 6=-36$

81. $(-2)^5=(-2)(-2)(-2)(-2)(-2)=-32$

82. $4x^3+2x^3=(4+2)x^3=6x^3$

83. $4x^3+4x^2$ cannot be simplified. The terms $4x^3$ and $4x^2$ are not like terms because they have different variable factors, x^3 and x^2.

84. $-40\div 5\cdot 2=-8\cdot 2=-16$

85. $-6+(-2)\cdot 5=-6+(-10)=-16$

86. $6-5(-3+2)=6-4(-1)=6+4=10$

87.
$$\begin{aligned}28\div(2-4^2)&=28\div(2-16)\\&=28\div[2+(-16)]\\&=28\div(-14)\\&=-2\end{aligned}$$

88.
$$\begin{aligned}36-24\div 4\cdot 3-1&=36-6\cdot 3-1\\&=36-18-1\\&=18-1\\&=17\end{aligned}$$

89.
$$\begin{aligned}-8[-4-5(-3)]&=-8(-4+15)\\&=-8(11)=-88\end{aligned}$$

90.
$$\begin{aligned}\frac{6(-10+3)}{2(-15)-9(-3)}&=\frac{6(-7)}{-30+27}\\&=\frac{-42}{-3}=14\end{aligned}$$

91.
$$\begin{aligned}&\left(\frac{1}{2}+\frac{1}{3}\right)\div\left(\frac{1}{4}-\frac{3}{8}\right)\\&=\left(\frac{3}{6}+\frac{2}{6}\right)\div\left(\frac{2}{8}-\frac{3}{8}\right)\\&=\frac{5}{6}\div\left(-\frac{1}{8}\right)=\frac{5}{6}\cdot\left(-\frac{8}{1}\right)=-\frac{40}{6}=-\frac{20}{3}\end{aligned}$$

92.
$$\begin{aligned}&\frac{1}{2}-\frac{2}{3}\div\frac{5}{9}+\frac{3}{10}\\&=\frac{1}{2}-\frac{2}{\cancel{3}_1}\cdot\frac{\cancel{9}^3}{5}+\frac{3}{10}\\&=\frac{1}{2}-\frac{6}{5}+\frac{3}{10}\\&=\frac{5}{10}-\frac{12}{10}+\frac{3}{10}=-\frac{4}{10}=-\frac{2}{5}\end{aligned}$$

93. $x^2-2x+3;\ x=-1$
$$\begin{aligned}x^2-2x+3&=(-1)^2-2(-1)+3\\&=1+2+3\\&=6\end{aligned}$$

94. $-x^2-7x;\ x=-2$
$$\begin{aligned}-x^2-7x&=-(-2)^2-7(-2)\\&=-4+14\\&=10\end{aligned}$$

95.
$$\begin{aligned}4[7(a-1)+2]&=4(7a-7+2)\\&=4(7a-5)\\&=4(7a)+4(-5)\\&=28a-20\end{aligned}$$

96.
$$\begin{aligned}-6[4-(y+2)]&=-6(4-y-2)\\&=-6(2-y)\\&=-6(2)+(-6)(-y)\\&=-12+6y\text{ or }6y-12\end{aligned}$$

97. $W=1.5x+7=1.5(4)+7=6+7=13$

After 4 months, she weighs 13 pounds. This is shown on the graph as the point (4, 13).

98. $W=1.5x+7=1.5(6)+7=9+7=16$

After 6 months, she weighs 16 pounds. This is shown on the graph as the point (6, 16).

99. Since 2002 − 1997 = 5, let $x = 5$.

$$N = -26x^2 + 143x + 740$$
$$= -26(5)^2 + 143(5) + 740$$
$$= -26(25) + 143(5) + 740$$
$$= -650 + 715 + 740$$
$$= 805$$

805 million CDs were sold in 2002. According to the model, CD sales were 800 million. The model fits the data fairly well, but there is a slight overestimation.

100. Sales increase from 1998 to 2000, and decrease from 2000 to 2002.

Chapter 1 Test

1. $1.4 - (-2.6) = 1.4 + 2.6 = 4$

2.
$$-9 + 3 + (-11) + 6$$
$$= [-9 + (-11)] + (3 + 6)$$
$$= -20 + 9 = -11$$

3. $3(-17) = -51$

4.
$$\left(-\frac{3}{7}\right) \div \left(-\frac{15}{7}\right) = \left(-\frac{3}{7}\right)\left(-\frac{7}{15}\right)$$
$$= \frac{21}{105} = \frac{\cancel{21} \cdot 1}{\cancel{21} \cdot 5} = \frac{1}{5}$$

5.
$$\left(3\frac{1}{3}\right)\left(-1\frac{3}{4}\right) = \left(\frac{10}{3}\right)\left(-\frac{7}{4}\right)$$
$$= -\frac{10 \cdot 7}{3 \cdot 4} = -\frac{70}{12}$$
$$= -\frac{\cancel{2} \cdot 35}{\cancel{2} \cdot 6}$$
$$= -\frac{35}{6} \text{ or } -5\frac{5}{6}$$

6.
$$-50 \div 10 = -50\left(\frac{1}{10}\right) = -5$$

7. $-6 - (5 - 12) = -6 - (-7) = -6 + 7 = 1$

8.
$$(-3)(-4) \div (7 - 10)$$
$$= (-3)(-4) \div [7 + (-10)]$$
$$= (-3)(-4) \div (-3)$$
$$= 12 \div (-3)$$
$$= -4$$

9.
$$(6-8)^2(5-7)^3 = (-2)^2(-2)^3$$
$$= 4(-8) = -32$$

10.
$$\frac{3(-2) - 2(2)}{-2(8-3)} = \frac{-6-4}{-2(5)}$$
$$= \frac{-6 + (-4)}{-2(5)} = \frac{-10}{-10} = 1$$

11.
$$11x - (7x - 4) = 11x - 7x + 4$$
$$= 11x + (-7x) + 4$$
$$= [11 + (-7)]x + 4$$
$$= 4x + 4$$

12.
$$5(3x - 4y) - (2x - y)$$
$$= 5(3x) - 5(4y) - 2x + y$$
$$= 15x - 20y - 2x + y$$
$$= 15x - 2x - 20y + y$$
$$= 13x - 19y$$

13.
$$6 - 2[3(x+1) - 5] = 6 - 2[3x + 3 - 5]$$
$$= 6 - 2(3x - 2)$$
$$= 6 - 6x + 4$$
$$= 10 - 6x$$

14. Rational numbers can be written as the quotient of two integers.

$-7 = -\frac{7}{1}, -\frac{4}{5} = \frac{-4}{5}, 0 = \frac{0}{1}, 0.25 = \frac{1}{4},$

$\sqrt{4} = 2 = \frac{2}{1}$, and $\frac{22}{7} = \frac{22}{7}$.

Thus, -7, $-\frac{4}{5}$, 0, 0.25, $\sqrt{4}$, and $\frac{22}{7}$ are the rational numbers of the set.

15. $-1 > -100$; -1 is to the right of -100 on the number line, so -1 is greater than -100.

16. $|-12.8| = 12.8$ because the distance between 12.8 and 0 on the number line is 12.8

17. Quadrant II

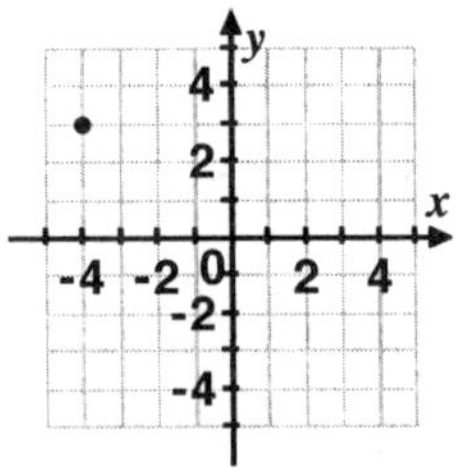

18. The coordinates of point *A* are $(-5, -2)$.

19. $5(x-7);\ x = 4$

$5(x-7) = 5(4-7) = 5(-3) = -15$

20. $x^2 - 5x;\ x = -10$

$x^2 - 5x = (-10)^2 - 5(-10)$

$= 100 + 50 = 150$

21. $2(x+3) = 2(3+x)$

22. $-6(4x) = (-6 \cdot 4)x = -24x$

23. $7(5x - 1 + 2y) = 7(5x) - 7(1) + 7(2y)$

$= 35x - 7 + 14y$

24. The coordinates of point *A* are (30, 200). This means that 30 years after the elk were introduced into the habitat, the elk population was 200.

25. The point (0, 50) indicates that 50 elk were introduced into the habitat.

26. According to the bar graph, about 725 million DVD's were sold in 2002.

27. $T = 3(A-20)^2 \div 50 + 10;\ A = 30$

$T = 3(A-20)^2 \div 50 + 10$

$= 3(30-20)^2 \div 50 + 10$

$= 3(10^2) \div 50 + 10$

$= 300 \div 50 + 10$

$= 6 + 10 = 16$

According to the formula, it takes a 30-year-old runner 16 seconds to run the 100-yard dash.

28. $16{,}200 - (-830) = 17{,}030$

The difference in elevations is 17,030 feet.

29. According to the graph, the average price of an existing single family home in 1999 was about $135,000.

30. Since *x* is years after 1989, find *N* when $x = 1999 - 1989 = 10$

$N = 0.3(10)^2 + 1.2(10) + 92.7$

$= 0.3(100) + 12 + 92.7$

$= 30 + 12 + 92.7$

$= 134.7$

Thus, the price in 1999 was $134,700.

Chapter 2
Linear Equations and Inequalities in One Variable

2.1 Exercise Set

1.
$$x-4=19$$
$$x-4+4=19+4$$
$$x+0=23$$
$$x=23$$
Check:
$$x-4=19$$
$$23-4=19$$
$$19=19$$
The solution is 23.

3.
$$z+8=-12$$
$$z+8-8=-12-8$$
$$z+0=-20$$
$$z=-20$$
Check:
$$z+8=-12$$
$$-20+8=-12$$
$$-12=-12$$
The solution is -20.

5.
$$-2=x+14$$
$$-2-14=x+14-14$$
$$-16=x$$
Check:
$$-2=-16+14$$
$$-2=-2$$
The solution is -16.

7.
$$-17=y-5$$
$$-17+5=y-5+5$$
$$-12=y$$
Check:
$$-17=-12-5$$
$$-17=-17$$
The solution is -12.

9.
$$7+z=11$$
$$z=11-7$$
$$z=4$$
Check:
$$7+4=11$$
$$11=11$$
The solution is 4.

11.
$$-6+y=-17$$
$$y=-17+6$$
$$y=-11$$
Check:
$$-6-11=-17$$
$$-17=-17$$
The solution is -11.

13.
$$x+\frac{1}{3}=\frac{7}{3}$$
$$x=\frac{7}{3}-\frac{1}{3}$$
$$x=2$$
Check:
$$2+\frac{1}{3}=\frac{7}{3}$$
$$\frac{6}{3}+\frac{1}{3}=\frac{7}{3}$$
$$\frac{7}{3}=\frac{7}{3}$$
The solution is 2.

15. $t+\frac{5}{6}=-\frac{7}{12}$

$t=-\frac{7}{12}-\frac{5}{6}$

$t=-\frac{7}{12}-\frac{10}{12}=-\frac{17}{12}$

Check:

$-\frac{17}{15}+\frac{5}{6}=-\frac{7}{12}$

$-\frac{17}{12}+\frac{10}{12}=-\frac{7}{12}$

$-\frac{7}{12}=-\frac{7}{12}$

The solution is $-\frac{17}{12}$.

17. $x-\frac{3}{4}=\frac{9}{2}$

$x-\frac{3}{4}+\frac{3}{4}=\frac{9}{2}+\frac{3}{4}$

$x=\frac{21}{4}$

Check:

$\frac{21}{4}-\frac{3}{4}=\frac{9}{2}$

$\frac{18}{4}=\frac{9}{2}$

$\frac{9}{2}=\frac{9}{2}$

The solution is $\frac{21}{4}$.

19. $-\frac{1}{5}+y=-\frac{3}{4}$

$y=-\frac{3}{4}+\frac{1}{5}$

$y=-\frac{15}{20}+\frac{4}{20}=-\frac{11}{20}$

Check:

$-\frac{1}{5}+\left(-\frac{11}{20}\right)=-\frac{3}{4}$

$-\frac{4}{20}-\frac{11}{20}=-\frac{3}{4}$

$-\frac{15}{20}=-\frac{3}{4}$

$-\frac{3}{4}=-\frac{3}{4}$ true

The solution is $-\frac{11}{20}$.

21. $3.2+x=7.5$

$3.2+x-3.2=7.5-3.2$

$x=4.3$

Check:

$3.2+4.3=7.5$

$7.5=7.5$

The solution is 4.3

23. $x+\frac{3}{4}=-\frac{9}{2}$

$x+\frac{3}{4}-\frac{3}{4}=-\frac{9}{2}-\frac{3}{4}$

$x=-\frac{21}{4}$

Check:

$-\frac{21}{4}+\frac{3}{4}=-\frac{9}{2}$

$-\frac{18}{4}=-\frac{9}{2}$

$-\frac{9}{2}=-\frac{9}{2}$

The solution is $-\frac{21}{4}$.

25. $5 = -13 + y$
$5 + 13 = y$
$18 = y$
Check:
$5 = -13 + 18$
$5 = 5$
The solution is 18.

27. $-\frac{3}{5} = -\frac{3}{2} + s$
$-\frac{3}{5} + \frac{3}{2} = s$
$-\frac{6}{10} + \frac{15}{10} = s$
$\frac{9}{10} = s$
Check:
$-\frac{3}{5} = -\frac{3}{2} + \frac{9}{10}$
$-\frac{6}{10} = -\frac{15}{10} + \frac{9}{10}$
$-\frac{6}{10} = -\frac{6}{10}$
The solution is $\frac{9}{10}$.

29. $830 + y = 520$
$y = 520 - 830$
$y = -310$
Check:
$830 - 310 = 520$
$520 = 520$
The solution is -310.

31. $r + 3.7 = 8$
$r = 8 - 3.7$
$r = 4.3$
Check:
$4.3 + 3.7 = 8$
$8 = 8$
The solution is 4.3

33. $-3.7 + m = -3.7$
$m = -3.7 + 3.7$
$m = 0$
Check:
$-3.7 + 0 = -3.7$
$-3.7 = -3.7$
The solution is 0.

35. $6y + 3 - 5y = 14$
$y + 3 = 14$
$y = 14 - 3$
$y = 11$
Check:
$6(11) + 3 - 5(11) = 14$
$66 + 3 - 55 = 14$
$14 = 14$
The solution is 11.

37. $7 - 5x + 8 + 2x + 4x - 3 = 2 + 3 \cdot 5$
$x + 12 = 2 + 15$
$x = 17 - 12$
$x = 5$
Check:
$7 - 5(5) + 8 + 2(5) + 4(5) - 3 = 2 + 3 \cdot 5$
$7 - 25 + 8 + 10 + 20 - 3 = 2 + 15$
$45 - 28 = 17$
$17 = 17$
The solution is 5.

39. $7y+4=6y-9$

$7y-6y+4=-9$

$y=-9-4$

$y=-13$

Check:

$7(-13)+4=6(-13)-9$

$-91+4=-78-9$

$-87=-87$

The solution is -13.

41. $12-6x=18-7x$

$12+x=18$

$x=6$

Check:

$12-6(6)=18-7(6)$

$12-36=18-42$

$-24=-24$

The solution is 6.

43. $4x+2=3(x-6)+8$

$4x+2=3x-18+8$

$4x+2=3x-10$

$4x-3x+2=-10$

$x+2=-10$

$x=-10-2$

$x=-12$

Check:

$4(-12)+2=3(-12-6)+8$

$-48+2=3(-18)+8$

$-46=-54+8$

$-46=-46$

The solution is -12.

45. $x-\square=\triangle$

$x-\square+\square=\triangle+\square$

$x=\triangle+\square$

46. $x+\square=\triangle$

$x+\square-\square=\triangle-\square$

$x=\triangle-\square$

47. $2x+\triangle=3x+\square$

$\triangle=3x-2x+\square$

$\triangle=x+\square$

$\triangle-\square=x+\square-\square$

$\triangle-\square=x$

48. $6x-\triangle=7x-\square$

$6x-\triangle-6x=7x-\square-6x$

$-\triangle=x-\square$

$-\triangle+\square=x-\square+\square$

$\square-\triangle=x$

49. $x-12=-2$

$x=-2+12$

$x=10$

The number is 10.

50. $x-23=-8$

$x-23+23=-8+23$

$x=15$

The number is 15.

51. $\frac{2}{5}x-8=\frac{7}{5}x$

$-8=\frac{7}{5}x-\frac{2}{5}x$

$-8=\frac{5}{5}x$

$-8=x$

The number is -8.

52.
$$3-\frac{2}{7}x=\frac{5}{7}x$$
$$3-\frac{2}{7}x+\frac{2}{7}x=\frac{5}{7}x+\frac{2}{7}x$$
$$3=\frac{7}{7}x$$
$$3=x$$
The number is 3.

53. $C+M=S;\ S=1850,\ M=150$
$$C+M=S$$
$$C+150=1850$$
$$C=1850-150$$
$$C=1700$$
The cost of the computer is $1700.

55. $d+525{,}000=5000c;\ c=210$
$$d+525{,}000=5000c$$
$$d+525{,}000=1{,}050{,}000$$
$$d=1{,}050{,}000-525{,}000$$
$$d=525{,}000$$

According to the formula, 525,000 deaths per year from heart disease can be expected at this cholesterol level.

57.
$$S-1.6x=5.8$$
$$S-1.6(7)=5.8$$
$$S-11.2=5.8$$
$$S=5.8+11.2$$
$$S=17$$
According to the model, Americans will spend $17 billion of statins in 2005.

For Exercises 59-63, answers will vary.

65. Answers will vary. Any equation with $x-100$ on one side and a number ≥ -101 on the other side.

One example is as follows.
$x-100=-101$

67.
$$6.9825=4.2296+y$$
$$6.9825-4.2296=y$$
$$2.7529=y$$
The solution is 2.7529.

68.

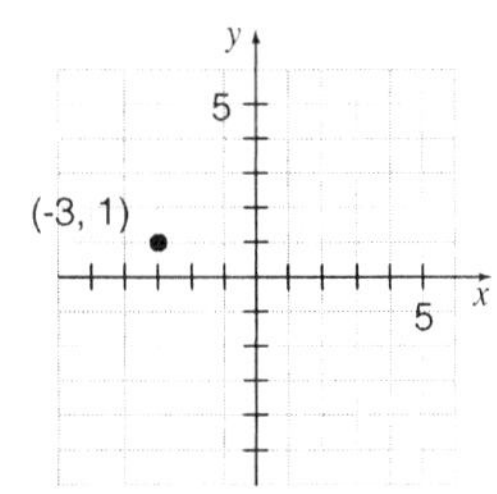

Quadrant II

69.
$$-16-8\div 4\cdot(-2)$$
$$=-16-2(-2)$$
$$=-16+4$$
$$=-12$$

70.
$$3[7x-2(5x-1)]$$
$$=3(7x-10x+2)$$
$$=3(-3x+2)$$
$$=-9x+6 \text{ or } 6-9x$$

2.2 Exercise Set

1.
$$\frac{x}{6}=5$$
$$6\cdot\frac{x}{6}=6\cdot 5$$
$$1x=30$$
$$x=30$$
Check:
$$\frac{30}{6}=5$$
$$5=5$$
The solution is 30.

3.
$$\frac{x}{-3}=11$$
$$-3\cdot\frac{x}{-3}=-3(11)$$
$$1x=-33$$
$$x=-33$$
Check:
$$\frac{-33}{-3}=11$$
$$11=11$$
The solution is −33.

5.
$$5y=35$$
$$\frac{5y}{5}=\frac{35}{5}$$
$$y=7$$
Check:
$$5(7)=35$$
$$35=35$$
The solution is 7.

7.
$$-7y=63$$
$$\frac{-7y}{-7}=\frac{63}{-7}$$
$$y=-9$$
Check:
$$-7(-9)=63$$
$$63=63$$
The solution is −9.

9.
$$-28=8z$$
$$\frac{-28}{8}=\frac{8z}{8}$$
$$-\frac{7}{2}=z$$
Check:
$$-28=8\left(-\frac{7}{2}\right)$$
$$-28=-\frac{56}{2}$$
$$-28=-28$$
The solution is $-\frac{7}{2}$ or $-3\frac{1}{2}$.

11.
$$-18=-3z$$
$$\frac{-18}{-3}=\frac{-3z}{-3}$$
$$6=z$$
Check:
$$-18=-3(6)$$
$$-18=-18$$
The solution is 6.

13.
$$-8x=6$$
$$\frac{-8x}{-8}=\frac{6}{-8}$$
$$x=-\frac{6}{8}=-\frac{3}{4}$$

Check:

$$-8\left(-\frac{3}{4}\right)=6$$
$$\frac{24}{4}=6$$
$$6=6$$

The solution is $-\frac{3}{4}$.

15. $17y=0$

$$\frac{17y}{17}=\frac{0}{17}$$
$$y=0$$

Check:

$$17(0)=0$$
$$0=0$$

The solution is 0.

17. $\frac{2}{3}y=12$

$$\frac{3}{2}\left(\frac{2}{3}y\right)=\frac{3}{2}(12)$$
$$1y=\frac{3}{2}\cdot\frac{12}{1}=\frac{36}{2}$$
$$y=18$$

Check:

$$\frac{2}{3}(18)=12$$
$$\frac{2}{3}\cdot\frac{18}{1}=12$$
$$\frac{36}{3}=12$$
$$12=12$$

The solution is 18.

19. $28=-\frac{7}{2}x$

$$-\frac{2}{7}(28)=-\frac{2}{7}\left(-\frac{7}{2}x\right)$$
$$-\frac{56}{7}=1x$$
$$-8=x$$

Check:

$$28=-\frac{7}{2}(-8)$$
$$28=\frac{56}{2}$$
$$28=28$$

The solution is −8.

21. $-x=17$

$$-1x=17$$
$$-1(-1x)=-1(17)$$
$$x=-17$$

Check:

$$-(-17)=17$$
$$17=17$$

The solution is −17.

23. $-47=-y$

$$47=y$$

Check:

$$-47=-47$$

The solution is 47.

25. $-\frac{x}{5}=-9$

$$5\left(-\frac{x}{5}\right)=5(-9)$$
$$-x=-45$$
$$x=45$$

Check:

$$-\frac{45}{5}=-9$$
$$-9=-9$$

The solution is 45.

27.
$$2x-12x=50$$
$$(2-12)x=50$$
$$-10x=50$$
$$\frac{-10x}{-10}=\frac{50}{-10}$$
$$x=-5$$
Check:
$$2(-5)-12(-5)=50$$
$$-10+60=50$$
$$50=50$$
The solution is -5.

29.
$$2x+1=11$$
$$2x+1-1=11-1$$
$$2x=10$$
$$\frac{2x}{2}=\frac{10}{2}$$
$$x=5$$
Check:
$$2(5)+1=11$$
$$10+1=11$$
$$11=11$$
The solution is 5.

31.
$$2x-3=9$$
$$2x-3+3=9+3$$
$$2x=12$$
$$\frac{2x}{2}=\frac{12}{2}$$
$$x=6$$
Check:
$$2(6)-3=9$$
$$12-3=9$$
$$9=9$$
The solution is 6.

33.
$$-2y+5=7$$
$$-2y+5-5=7-5$$
$$-2y=2$$
$$\frac{-2y}{2}=\frac{2}{-2}$$
$$y=-1$$
Check:
$$-2(-1)+5=7$$
$$2+5=7$$
$$7=7$$
The solution is -1.

35.
$$-3y-7=-1$$
$$-3y-7+7=-1+7$$
$$-3y=6$$
$$\frac{-3y}{-3}=\frac{6}{-3}$$
$$y=-2$$
Check:
$$-3(-2)-7=-1$$
$$6-7=-1$$
$$-1=-1$$
The solution is -2.

37.
$$12=4z+3$$
$$12-3=4z+3-3$$
$$9=4z$$
$$\frac{9}{4}=\frac{4z}{4}$$
$$\frac{9}{4}=z$$
Check:
$$12=4\left(\frac{9}{4}\right)+3$$
$$12=9+3$$
$$12=12$$
The solution is $\frac{9}{4}$.

39.

$$-x-3=3$$
$$-x-3+3=3+3$$
$$-x=6$$
$$x=-6$$

Check:

$$-(-6)-3=3$$
$$6-3=3$$
$$3=3$$

The solution is –6.

41.

$$6y=2y-12$$
$$6y+12=2y-12+12$$
$$6y+12=2y$$
$$6y+12-6y=2y-6y$$
$$12=-4y$$
$$\frac{12}{-4}=\frac{-4y}{-4}$$
$$-3=y$$

Check:

$$6(-3)=2(-3)-12$$
$$-18=-6-12$$
$$-18=-18$$

The solution is –3.

43.

$$3z=-2z-15$$
$$3z+2z=-2z-15+2z$$
$$5z=-15$$
$$\frac{5z}{5}=\frac{-15}{3}$$
$$z=-3$$

Check:

$$3(-3)=-2(-3)-15$$
$$-9=6-15$$
$$-9=-9$$

The solution is –3.

45.

$$-5x=-2x-12$$
$$-5x+2x=-2x-12+2x$$
$$-3x=-12$$
$$\frac{-3x}{3}=\frac{-12}{-3}$$
$$x=4$$

Check:

$$-5(4)=2(4)-12$$
$$-20=-8-12$$
$$-20=-20$$

The solution is 4.

47.

$$8y+4=2y-5$$
$$8y+4-2y=2y-5-2y$$
$$6y+4=-5$$
$$6y+4-4=-5-4$$
$$6y=-9$$
$$\frac{6y}{6}=\frac{-9}{6}$$
$$y=-\frac{3}{2}$$

Check:

$$8\left(-\frac{3}{2}\right)+4=2\left(-\frac{3}{2}\right)-5$$
$$-12+4=-3-5$$
$$-8=-8$$

The solution is $-\frac{3}{2}$.

49.

$$6z-5=z+5$$
$$6z-5-z=z+5-z$$
$$5z-5=5$$
$$5z-5+5=5+5$$
$$5z=10$$
$$\frac{5z}{5}=\frac{10}{5}$$
$$z=2$$

Check:

$$6(2)-5=2+5$$
$$12-5=2+5$$
$$7=7$$

The solution is 2.

51.
$$6x+14=2x-2$$
$$6x-2x+14=-2$$
$$4x=-2-14$$
$$4x=-16$$
$$x=-4$$

Check:

$$6(-4)+14=2(-4)-2$$
$$-24+14=-8-2$$
$$-10=-10$$

The solution is −4.

53.
$$-3y-1=5-2y$$
$$-3y+2y-1=5$$
$$-y=5+1$$
$$-y=6$$
$$y=-6$$

Check:

$$-3(-6)-1=5-2(-6)$$
$$18-1=5+12$$
$$17=17$$

The solution is −6.

55.
$$\frac{x}{\square}=\triangle$$
$$\square\cdot\frac{x}{\square}=\triangle\cdot\square$$
$$x=\triangle\square$$

56.
$$\triangle=\square x$$
$$\frac{\triangle}{\square}=\frac{\square x}{\square}$$
$$\frac{\triangle}{\square}=x$$

57.
$$\triangle=-x$$
$$\triangle(-1)=-x(-1)$$
$$-\triangle=x$$

58.
$$\frac{-x}{\square}=\triangle$$
$$-\square\cdot\frac{-x}{\square}=-\square\cdot\triangle$$
$$x=-\square\cdot\triangle$$

59.
$$6x=10$$
$$\frac{6x}{6}=\frac{10}{6}$$
$$x=\frac{10}{6}=\frac{5}{3}$$

The number is $\frac{5}{3}$.

60.
$$-6x=20$$
$$\frac{-6x}{6}=\frac{20}{-6}$$
$$x=\frac{20}{-6}=-\frac{10}{3}$$

The number is $-\frac{10}{3}$.

61.
$$\frac{x}{-9}=5$$
$$\frac{x}{-9}(-9)=5(-9)$$
$$x=-45$$

The number is -45.

62.
$$\frac{x}{-7}=8$$
$$-7\cdot\frac{x}{-7}=-7\cdot 8$$
$$x=-56$$

The number is -56.

63. $M = \frac{n}{5}; M = 2$

$$M = \frac{n}{5}$$
$$2 = \frac{n}{5}$$
$$5(2) = 5\left(\frac{n}{5}\right)$$
$$10 = n$$

If you are 2 miles away from the lightening flash, it will take 10 seconds for the sound of thunder to reach you.

65. $M = \frac{A}{740}; M = 2.03$

$$M = \frac{A}{740}$$
$$2.03 = \frac{A}{740}$$
$$740(2.03) = 740\left(\frac{A}{740}\right)$$
$$1502.2 = A$$

The speed is 1502.2 miles per hour.

67. $P = -0.5d + 100; P = 70$

$$P = -0.5d + 100$$
$$70 = -0.5d + 100$$
$$70 - 100 = -0.5d + 100 - 100$$
$$-30 = -0.5d$$
$$\frac{-30}{-0.5} = \frac{-0.5d}{-0.5}$$
$$60 = d$$

The parallel distance of separation is 60 yards.

For Exercises 69-71, answers will vary.

73. Statement d is true since the solution to $6x = 0$ is 0, which is not a natural number.

75. Answers will vary. As an example, start with an integer solution, such as 10, and set it equal to x. That is, we have $x = 10$. The solution was obtained by multiplying both sides by $\frac{4}{5}$. To undo this, we multiply both sides of our equation by the reciprocal, $\frac{5}{4}$. This give,

$$\frac{5}{4}x = \frac{5}{4}(10)$$
$$\frac{5}{4}x = \frac{25}{2}$$

Therefore, an example equation would be $\frac{5}{4}x = \frac{25}{2}$.

77.

$$-72.8y - 14.6 = -455.43 - 4.98y$$
$$-72.8y - 14.6 + 4.98y = -455.43 - 4.98y + 4.98y$$
$$-67.82y - 14.6 = -455.43$$
$$-67.82y - 14.6 + 14.6 = -455.43 + 14.6$$
$$-67.82y = -440.83$$
$$\frac{-67.82y}{-67.82} = \frac{-440.83}{-67.82}$$
$$y = 6.5$$

The solution is 6.5.

78. $(-10)^2 = (-10)(-10) = 100$

79. $-10^2 = -10 \cdot 10 = -100$

80. $x^3 - 4x; x = -1$

$$x^3 - 4x = (-1)^3 - 4(-1) = -1 + 4 = 3$$

2.3 Exercise Set

For exercises 1-45, students should check the proposed solutions. The checks will not be shown here.

1.
$$\begin{aligned} 5x+3x-4x &= 10+2 \\ 8x-4x &= 12 \\ 4x &= 12 \\ \frac{4x}{4} &= \frac{12}{4} \\ x &= 3 \end{aligned}$$
The solution is 3.

3.
$$\begin{aligned} 4x-9x+22 &= 3x+30 \\ -5x+22 &= 3x+30 \\ -5x-3x+22 &= 30 \\ -8x+22 &= 30 \\ -8x &= 30-22 \\ -8x &= 8 \\ \frac{-8x}{-8} &= \frac{8}{-8} \\ x &= -1 \end{aligned}$$
The solution is −1.

5.
$$\begin{aligned} 3x+6-x &= 8+3x-6 \\ 2x+6 &= 2+3x \\ 2x+6-2 &= 2+3x-2 \\ 2x+4 &= 3x \\ 2x+4-2x &= 3x-2x \\ 4 &= x \end{aligned}$$
The solution is 4.

7.
$$\begin{aligned} 4(x+1) &= 20 \\ 4x+4 &= 20 \\ 4x &= 20-4 \\ 4x &= 16 \\ \frac{4x}{4} &= \frac{16}{4} \\ x &= 4 \end{aligned}$$
The solution is 4.

9.
$$\begin{aligned} 7(2x-1) &= 42 \\ 14x-7 &= 42 \\ 14x-7+7 &= 42+7 \\ 14x &= 49 \\ \frac{14x}{14} &= \frac{49}{14} \\ x &= \frac{7}{2} \end{aligned}$$
The solution is $\frac{7}{2}$.

11.
$$\begin{aligned} 38 &= 30-2(x-1) \\ 38 &= 30-2x+2 \\ 38 &= 32-2x \\ 38-32 &= -2x \\ 6 &= -2x \\ \frac{6}{-2} &= \frac{-2x}{-2} \\ -3 &= x \end{aligned}$$
The solution is −3.

13.
$$\begin{aligned} 2(4z+3)-8 &= 46 \\ 8z+6-8 &= 46 \\ 8z-2 &= 46 \\ 8z-2+2 &= 46+2 \\ 8z &= 48 \\ \frac{8z}{3} &= \frac{48}{8} \\ z &= 6 \end{aligned}$$
The solution is 6.

15.
$$\begin{aligned} 6x-(3x+10) &= 14 \\ 6x-3x-10 &= 14 \\ 3x-10 &= 14 \\ 3x-10+10 &= 14+10 \\ 3x &= 24 \\ \frac{3x}{3} &= \frac{24}{3} \\ x &= 8 \end{aligned}$$
The solution is 8.

17.
$$\begin{aligned} 5(2x+1) &= 12x-3 \\ 10x+5 &= 12x-3 \\ 10x-10x+5 &= 12x-10x-3 \\ 5 &= 2x-3 \\ 5+3 &= 2x-3+3 \\ 8 &= 2x \\ \frac{8}{2} &= \frac{2x}{2} \\ x &= 4 \end{aligned}$$

The solution is 4

19.
$$\begin{aligned} 3(5-x) &= 4(2x+1) \\ 15-3x &= 8x+4 \\ 15-3x-8x &= 8x+4-8x \\ 15-11x &= 4 \\ 15-11x-15 &= 4-15 \\ -11x &= -11 \\ \frac{-11x}{-11} &= \frac{-11}{-11} \\ x &= 1 \end{aligned}$$

The solution is 1.

21.
$$\begin{aligned} 8(y+2) &= 2(3y+4) \\ 8y+16 &= 6y+8 \\ 8y+16-16 &= 6y+8-16 \\ 8y &= 6y-8 \\ 8y-6y &= 6y-8-6y \\ 2y &= -8 \\ y &= -4 \end{aligned}$$

The solution is −4.

23.
$$\begin{aligned} 3(x+1) &= 7(x-2)-3 \\ 3x+3 &= 7x-14-3 \\ 3x+3 &= 7x-17 \\ 3x+3-3 &= 7x-17-3 \\ 3x &= 7x-20 \\ 3x-7x &= 7x-20-7x \\ -4x &= -20 \\ \frac{-4x}{-4} &= \frac{-20}{-4} \\ x &= 5 \end{aligned}$$

The solution is 5.

25.
$$\begin{aligned} 5(2x-8)-2 &= 5(x-3)+3 \\ 10x-40-2 &= 5x-15+3 \\ 10x-42 &= 5x-12 \\ 10x-42+42 &= 5x-12+42 \\ 10x &= 5x+30 \\ 10x &= 5x+30-5x \\ 5x &= 30 \\ \frac{5x}{5} &= \frac{30}{5} \\ x &= 6 \end{aligned}$$

The solution is 6.

27.
$$\begin{aligned} 6 &= -4(1-x)+3(x+1) \\ 6 &= -4+4x+3x+3 \\ 6 &= -1+7x \\ 6+1 &= -1+7x+1 \\ 7 &= 7x \\ \frac{7}{7} &= \frac{7x}{7} \\ 1 &= x \end{aligned}$$

The solution is 1.

29. $10(z+4)-4(z-2)=3(z-1)+2(z-3)$

$$10z+40-4z+8=3z-3+2z-6$$
$$6z+48=5z-9$$
$$6z+48-48=5z-9-48$$
$$6z-5z=5z-57-5z$$
$$z=-57$$

The solution is −57.

31. $\frac{x}{5}-4=-6$

To clear the equation of fractions, multiply both sides by the least common denominator (LCD), which is 5.

$$5\left(\frac{x}{5}-4\right)=5(-6)$$
$$5\cdot\frac{x}{5}-5\cdot 4=-30$$
$$x-20=-30$$
$$x-20+20=-30+20$$
$$x=-10$$

The solution is −10.

33. $\frac{2x}{3}-5=7$

LCD = 3

$$3\left(\tfrac{2}{3}x-5\right)=3(7)$$
$$3\cdot\tfrac{2}{3}x-3\cdot 5=21$$
$$2x-15=21$$
$$2x-15+15=21+15$$
$$2x=36$$
$$\frac{2x}{2}=\frac{36}{2}$$
$$x=18$$

The solution is 18.

35. $\frac{2y}{3}-\frac{3}{4}=\frac{5}{12}$

LCD = 12

$$12\left(\frac{2y}{3}-\frac{3}{4}\right)=12\left(\frac{5}{12}\right)$$
$$12\left(\frac{2y}{3}\right)-12\left(\frac{3}{4}\right)=5$$
$$8y-9=5$$
$$8y-9+9=5+9$$
$$8y=14$$
$$\frac{8y}{8}=\frac{14}{8}$$
$$y=\tfrac{14}{8}=\tfrac{7}{4}$$

The solution is $\frac{7}{4}$.

37. $\frac{x}{3}+\frac{x}{2}=\frac{5}{6}$, LCD = 6

$$6\left(\frac{x}{3}+\frac{x}{2}\right)=6\left(\frac{5}{6}\right)$$
$$2x+3x=5$$
$$5x=5$$
$$\frac{5x}{5}=\frac{5}{5}$$
$$x=1$$

The solution is 1.

39. $20-\frac{z}{3}=\frac{z}{2}$, LCD = 6

$$6\left(20-\frac{z}{3}\right)=6\left(\frac{z}{2}\right)$$
$$120-2z=3z$$
$$120-2z+2z=3z+2z$$
$$120=5z$$
$$\frac{120}{5}=\frac{5z}{5}$$
$$24=z$$

The solution is 24.

41. $\frac{y}{3}+\frac{2}{5}=\frac{y}{5}-\frac{2}{5}$

LCD = 15

$$15\left(\frac{y}{3}+\frac{2}{5}\right)=15\left(\frac{y}{5}+\frac{2}{5}\right)$$
$$15\left(\frac{y}{3}\right)+15\left(\frac{2}{5}\right)=15\left(\frac{y}{5}\right)+15\left(-\frac{2}{5}\right)$$
$$5y+6=3y-6$$
$$5y+6-3y=3y-6-3y$$
$$2y+6=-6$$
$$2y+6-6=-6-6$$
$$2y=-12$$
$$\frac{2y}{2}=\frac{-12}{2}$$
$$y=-6$$

The solution is –6.

43. $\frac{3x}{4}-3=\frac{x}{2}+2$

LCD = 8

$$8\left(\frac{3x}{4}-3\right)=8\left(\frac{x}{2}+2\right)$$
$$8\left(\frac{3x}{4}\right)-8\cdot 3=8\left(\frac{x}{2}\right)+8\cdot 2$$
$$6x-24=4x+16$$
$$6x-24-4x=4x+16-4x$$
$$2x-24=16$$
$$2x-24+24=16+24$$
$$2x=40$$
$$\frac{2x}{2}=\frac{40}{2}$$
$$x=20$$

The solution is 20.

45. $\frac{x-3}{5}-1=\frac{x-5}{4}$

LCD = $4\cdot 5=20$

$$(20)\left(\frac{x-3}{5}-1\right)=20\left(\frac{x-5}{4}\right)$$
$$4(x-3)-20=5(x-5)$$
$$4x-12-20=5x-25$$
$$4x-5x-32=5x-5x-25$$
$$-x-32=-25$$
$$-x-32+32=-25+32$$
$$-x=7$$
$$-1(-x)=-1(7)$$
$$x=-7$$

The solution is -7.

47.
$$3x-7=3(x+1)$$
$$3x-7=3x+3$$
$$3x-7-3x=3x+3-3x$$
$$-7=3$$

The original equation is equivalent to the false statement –7 = 3, so the equation is inconsistent and has no solution.

49.
$$2(x+4)=4x+5-2x+3$$
$$2x+8=2x+8$$
$$2x-8-2x=2x+8-2x$$
$$8=8$$

The original equation is equivalent to the true statement 8 = 8, so the equation is an identity and all real numbers are solutions.

51. $7+2(3x-5)=8-3(2x+1)$

$$7+6x-10=8-6x-3$$
$$6x-3=5-6x$$
$$6x+6x-3=5-6x+6x$$
$$12x-3=5$$
$$12x-3+3=5+3$$
$$12x=8$$
$$\frac{12x}{12}=\frac{8}{12}$$
$$x=\frac{2}{3}$$

The solution is $\frac{2}{3}$.

53. $4x+1-5x=5-(x+4)$

$$-x+1=5-x-4$$
$$-x+1=1-x$$
$$-x+1+x=1-x+x$$
$$1=1$$

Since 1 = 1 is a true statement, the original equation is an identity and all real numbers are solutions.

55. $4(x+2)+1=7x-3(x-2)$

$$4x+8+1=7x-3x+6$$
$$4x+9=4x+6$$
$$4x-4x+9=4x-4x+6$$
$$9=6$$

Since 9 = 6 is a false statement, the original equation is inconsistent and has no solution.

57. $3-x=2x+3$

$$3-x+x=2x+x+3$$
$$3=3x+3$$
$$3-3=3x+3-3$$
$$0=3x$$
$$\frac{0}{3}=\frac{3x}{3}$$
$$0=x$$

The solution is $x = 0$.

59. $\frac{x}{3}+2=\frac{x}{3}$

Multiply by the LCD, which is 6.

$$6\left(\frac{x}{3}+2\right)=6\left(\frac{x}{3}\right)$$
$$2x+12=2x$$
$$2x+12-2x=2x-2x$$
$$12=0$$

Since 12 = 0 is a false statement, the original equation has no solution.

61. $\frac{x}{2}-\frac{x}{4}+4=x+4$

LCD = 4

$$4\left(\frac{x}{2}-\frac{x}{4}+4\right)=4(x+4)$$
$$4\left(\frac{x}{2}\right)-4\left(\frac{x}{4}\right)+16=4x+16$$
$$2x-x+16=4x+16$$
$$x+16=4x+16$$
$$x-x+16=4x-x+16$$
$$16=3x+16$$
$$16-16=3x+16-16$$
$$0=3x$$
$$\frac{0}{3}=\frac{3x}{3}$$
$$0=x$$

The solution is 0.

63.
$$\frac{2}{3}x = 2 - \frac{5}{6}x$$
LCD = 6
$$6\left(\frac{2}{3}x\right) = 6(2) - 6\left(\frac{5}{6}x\right)$$
$$2(2x) = 12 - 5x$$
$$4x = 12 - 5x$$
$$4x + 5x = 12 - 5x + 5x$$
$$9x = 12$$
$$\frac{9x}{9} = \frac{12}{9}$$
$$x = \frac{12}{9} = \frac{4}{3}$$
The solution is $\frac{4}{3}$.

65.
$$\frac{x}{\square} + \triangle = \$$$
$$\frac{x}{\square} + \triangle - \triangle = \$ - \triangle$$
$$\frac{x}{\square} = \$ - \triangle$$
$$\square\left(\frac{x}{\square}\right) = \square(\$ - \triangle)$$
$$x = \square\$ - \square\triangle$$

66.
$$\frac{x}{\square} - \triangle = -\$$$
$$\frac{x}{\square} - \triangle + \triangle = -\$ + \triangle$$
$$\frac{x}{\square} = -\$ + \triangle$$
$$\square \cdot \frac{x}{\square} = \square(-\$ + \triangle)$$
$$x = -\square\$ + \square\triangle$$

67.
$$\frac{x}{5} - 2 = \frac{x}{3}$$
$$\frac{x}{5} - \frac{x}{5} - 2 = \frac{x}{3} - \frac{x}{5}$$
$$-2 = \frac{5x}{15} - \frac{3x}{15}$$
$$-2 = \frac{2x}{15}$$
$$15(-2) = 15\left(\frac{2x}{15}\right)$$
$$-30 = 2x$$
$$\frac{-30}{2} = \frac{2x}{2}$$
$$-15 = x$$
If $x = -15$, evaluate $x^2 - x$.
$$(-15)^2 - (-15) = 225 + 15 = 240$$

68.
$$\frac{3x}{2} + \frac{3x}{4} = \frac{x}{4} - 4$$
LCD = 4
$$4\left(\frac{3x}{2} + \frac{3x}{4}\right) = 4\left(\frac{x}{4} - 4\right)$$
$$6x + 3x = x - 16$$
$$9x = x - 16$$
$$9x - x = x - 16 - x$$
$$8x = -16$$
$$\frac{8x}{8} = \frac{-16}{8}$$
$$x = -2$$
If $x = -2$, evaluate $x^2 - x$.
$$(-2)^2 - (-2) = 4 + 4 = 8$$

69.
$$\frac{1}{3}x+\frac{1}{5}x=16$$
$$\text{LCD} = 15$$
$$15\left(\frac{1}{3}x\right)+15\left(\frac{1}{5}x\right)=15(16)$$
$$5x+3x=240$$
$$8x=240$$
$$\frac{8x}{8}=\frac{240}{8}$$
$$x=30$$
The number is 30.

70.
$$\frac{2}{5}x+\frac{1}{4}x=13$$
$$\text{LCD} = 20$$
$$20\left(\frac{2}{5}x+\frac{1}{4}x\right)=20(13)$$
$$8x+5x=260$$
$$13x=260$$
$$\frac{13x}{13}=\frac{260}{13}$$
$$x=20$$
The number is 20.

71.
$$\frac{3}{4}x-3=\frac{1}{2}x$$
$$\text{LCD} = 4$$
$$4\left(\frac{3}{4}x\right)-4(3)=4\left(\frac{1}{2}x\right)$$
$$3x-12=2x$$
$$3x-2x-12=2x-2x$$
$$x-12=0$$
$$x-12+12=0+12$$
$$x=12$$
The number is 12.

72.
$$\frac{7}{8}x-30=\frac{1}{2}x,\quad \text{LCD} = 8$$
$$8\left(\frac{7}{8}x-30\right)=8\left(\frac{1}{2}x\right)$$
$$7x-240=4x$$
$$7x-240-7x=4x-7x$$
$$-240=-3x$$
$$\frac{-240}{-3}=\frac{-3x}{-3}$$
$$80=x$$
The number is 80.

73.
$$F=10(x-65)+50;\; F=250$$
$$F=10(x-65)+50$$
$$250=10(x-65)+50$$
$$250-50=10(x-65)+50-50$$
$$200=10x-650$$
$$200+650=10x-650+650$$
$$850=10x$$
$$\frac{850}{10}=\frac{10x}{10}$$
$$85=x$$
A person receiving a \$250 fine was driving 85 miles per hour.

75. Substitute 10 for D in the low humor formula. The LCD is 9.
$$10=\frac{10}{9}N+\frac{53}{9}$$
$$9(10)=9\left(\frac{10}{9}N\right)+9\left(\frac{53}{9}\right)$$
$$90=10N+53$$
$$90-53=10N+53-53$$
$$37=10N$$
$$\frac{37}{10}=\frac{10N}{10}$$
$$3.7=N$$
The intensity of the event was 3.7. This is shown as the point (3.7, 10) on the graph.

77. $p = 15 + \frac{5d}{11};\ p = 201$

$$201 = 15 + \frac{5d}{11}$$
$$201 - 15 = 15 + \frac{5d}{11} - 15$$
$$186 = \frac{5d}{11}$$
$$11(186) = 11\left(\frac{5d}{11}\right)$$
$$2046 = 5d$$
$$\frac{2046}{5} = d \text{ or } 409.2 = d$$

He descended to a depth of 409.2 feet below the surface.

For Exercises 79-81, answers will vary.

83. Statement c is true. The solution to the linear equation is −3. When −3 is substituted into $y^2 + 2y - 3$, the result is 0.

85. $\frac{2x-3}{9} + \frac{x-3}{2} = \frac{x+5}{6} - 1$

LCD = 18

$$18\left(\frac{2x-3}{9} + \frac{x-3}{2}\right) = 18\left(\frac{x+5}{6} - 1\right)$$
$$18\left(\frac{2x-3}{9}\right) + 18\left(\frac{x-3}{2}\right) = 18\left(\frac{x+5}{6}\right) - 18 \cdot 1$$
$$2(2x-3) + 9(x-3) = 3(x+5) - 18$$
$$4x - 6 + 9x - 27 = 3x + 15 - 18$$
$$13x - 33 = 3x - 3$$
$$13x - 33 - 3x = 3x - 3 - 3x$$
$$10x - 33 = -3$$
$$10x - 33 + 33 = -3 + 33$$
$$10x = 30$$
$$\frac{10x}{10} = \frac{30}{10}$$
$$x = 3$$

Check:

$$\frac{2(3)-3}{9} + \frac{3-3}{2} = \frac{3+5}{6} - 1$$
$$\frac{6-4}{9} + \frac{0}{2} = \frac{8}{6} - 1$$
$$\frac{3}{9} + 0 = \frac{4}{3} - 1$$
$$\frac{1}{3} = \frac{1}{3}$$

The solution is 3.

87.

$$2.24y - 9.28 = 5.74y + 5.42$$
$$2.24y - 9.28 - 5.74y = 5.74y + 5.42 - 5.74y$$
$$-3.5y - 9.25 = 5.42$$
$$-3.5y - 9.28 + 9.28 = 5.42 + 9.28$$
$$-3.5y = 14.7$$
$$\frac{-3.5y}{-3.5} = \frac{14.7}{-3.5}$$
$$y = -4.2$$

The solution is −4.2

89. $-24 < -20$; −24 is to the left of −20 on the number line, so −24 is less than −20.

90. $-\frac{1}{3} < -\frac{1}{5}$; $-\frac{1}{3}$ is to the left of $-\frac{1}{5}$ on the number line, so $-\frac{1}{3}$ is less than $-\frac{1}{5}$.

To compare these numbers, write them with a common denominator:

$-\frac{1}{3} = -\frac{5}{15}, -\frac{1}{5} = -\frac{3}{15}.$

91. $-9-11+7-(-3)$
$=(-9)+(-11)+7+3$
$=(7+3)+[(-9)+(-11)]$
$=10+(-20)$
$=-10$

2.4 Exercise Set

1. $d = rt$ for r

$\frac{d}{t} = \frac{rt}{t}$

$\frac{d}{t} = r$ or $r = \frac{d}{t}$

This is the distance traveled formula: distance = rate · time.

3. $I = Prt$ for P

$\frac{I}{rt} = \frac{Prt}{rt}$

$\frac{I}{rt} = P$ or $P = \frac{I}{rt}$

This is the formula for simple interest:
interest = principal · rate · time.

5. $C = 2\pi r$ for r

$\frac{C}{2\pi} = \frac{2\pi r}{2\pi}$

$\frac{C}{2\pi} = r$ or $r = \frac{C}{2\pi}$

This is the formula for finding the circumference of a circle if you know its radius.

7. $E = mc^2$

$\frac{E}{c^2} = \frac{mc^2}{c^2}$

$\frac{E}{c^2} = m$ or $m = \frac{E}{c^2}$

This is Einstein's formula relating energy, mass, and the speed of light.

9. $y = mx + b$ for m

$y - b = mx$

$\frac{y-b}{x} = \frac{mx}{x}$

$\frac{y-b}{x} = m$ or $m = \frac{y-b}{x}$

This is the slope-intercept formula for the equation of a line. (This formula will be discussed later in the textbook.)

11. $T = D + pm$ for p

$T - D = D + pm - D$

$T - D = pm$

$\frac{T-D}{m} = \frac{pm}{m}$

$\frac{T-D}{m} = p$ or $p = \frac{T-D}{m}$

13. $A = \frac{1}{2}bh$ for b

$2A = 2\left(\frac{1}{2}bh\right)$

$2A = bh$

$\frac{2A}{h} = \frac{bh}{h}$

$\frac{2A}{h} = b$ or $b = \frac{2A}{h}$

This is the formula for the area of a triangle: area = $\frac{1}{2}$ · base · height.

15. $M = \frac{n}{5}$ for n

$5M = 5\left(\frac{n}{5}\right)$

$5M = n$ or $n = 5M$

17. $\frac{c}{2}+80=2F$ for c

$$\frac{c}{2}+80-80=2F-80$$
$$\frac{c}{2}=2F-80$$
$$2\left(\frac{c}{2}\right)=2(2F-80)$$
$$c=4F-160$$

19. $A=\frac{1}{2}(a+b)$ for a

$$2A=2\left[\frac{1}{2}(a+b)\right]$$
$$2A=a+b$$
$$2A-b=a+b-b$$
$$2A-b=a \text{ or } a=2A-b$$

This is the formula for finding the average of two numbers.

21. $S=P+Prt$ for r

$$S-P=P+Prt\ -P$$
$$S-P=Prt$$
$$\frac{S-P}{Pt}=\frac{Prt}{Pt}$$
$$\frac{S-P}{Pt}=r \text{ or } r=\frac{S-P}{Pt}$$

This is the formula for finding the total amount owed (or earned) using simple interest.
Total = Principle + Interest

23. $A=\frac{1}{2}h(a+b)$ for b

$$2A=2\left[\frac{1}{2}h(a+b)\right]$$
$$2A=h(a+b)$$
$$2A=ha+hb$$
$$2A-ha=ha+hb-ha$$
$$2A-ha=hb$$
$$\frac{2A-ha}{h}=\frac{hb}{h}$$
$$\frac{2A-ha}{h}=b \quad \text{or} \quad b=\frac{2A}{h}-a$$

This is the formula for the area of a trapezoid.

25. $Ax+By=C$ for x

$$Ax+By-By=C-By$$
$$Ax=C-By$$
$$\frac{Ax}{A}=\frac{C-By}{A}$$
$$x=\frac{C-By}{A}$$

This is the standard form of the equation of a line.

27. To change a decimal number to a percent, move the decimal point two places to the right and add a percent sign. 0.89 = 89%

29. 0.002 = 0.2%

31. 4.78 = 478%

33. 100 = 10,000%

35. To change a percent to a decimal number, move the decimal point two places to the left and remove the percent sign. 27% = 0.27

37. 63.4% = 0.634

39. 170% = 1.7

41. $3\% = 0.03$

43. $\frac{1}{2}\% = 0.5\% = 0.005$

45. $A = PB$; $P = 3\% = 0.03, B = 200$

$A = PB$

$A = 0.03 \cdot 200$

$A = 6$

3% of 200 is 6.

47. $A = PB$; $P = 18\% = 0.18,\ B = 40$

$A = PB$

$A = 0.18 \cdot 40$

$A = 7.2$

18% of 40 is 7.2.

49. $A = PB$; $A = 3, P = 60\% = 0.6$

$A = PB$

$3 = 0.6 \cdot B$

$\frac{3}{0.6} = \frac{0.6B}{0.6}$

$5 = B$

3 is 60% of 5.

51. $A = PB$; $A = 40.8, P = 24\% = 0.24$

$A = PB$

$40.8 = 0.24 \cdot B$

$\frac{40.8}{0.24} = \frac{0.24B}{0.24}$

$170 = B$

24% of 170 is 40.8.

53. $A = PB$; $A = 3,\ B = 15$

$A = PB$

$3 = P \cdot 15$

$\frac{3}{15} = \frac{P \cdot 15}{15}$

$0.2 = P$

$0.2 = 20\%$

3 is 20% of 15.

55. $A = PB$; $A = 0.3,\ B = 2.5$

$A = PB$

$0.3 = P \cdot 2.5$

$\frac{0.3}{2.5} = \frac{P - 2.5}{2.5}$

$0.12 = P$

$0.12 = 12\%$

0.3 is 12% of 2.5

57. Use the formula,
increase = percent · original.
The increase is 8 – 5 = 3.

$3 = P \cdot 5$

$\frac{3}{5} = \frac{P \cdot 5}{5}$

$0.60 = P$

This is a 60% increase.

59. Use the formula, decrease = percent · original. The decrease is 4 – 1 = 3.

$3 = P \cdot 4$

$\frac{3}{4} = \frac{P \cdot 4}{4}$

$0.75 = P$

This is a 75% decrease.

61.

$$y = (a+b)x$$

$$\frac{y}{(a+b)} = \frac{(a+b)x}{(a+b)}$$

$$\frac{y}{a+b} = x \text{ or } x = \frac{y}{a+b}$$

62.

$$y = (a-b)x$$

$$\frac{y}{(a-b)} = \frac{(a-b)x}{(a-b)}$$

$$\frac{y}{a-b} = x \text{ or } x = \frac{y}{a-b}$$

63.
$$y=(a-b)x+5$$
$$y-5=(a-b)x+5-5$$
$$y-5=(a-b)x$$
$$\frac{y-5}{a-b}=\frac{(a-b)x}{a-b}$$
$$\frac{y-5}{a-b}=x \quad \text{or} \quad x=\frac{y-5}{a-b}$$

64.
$$y=(a+b)x-8$$
$$y+8=(a+b)x-8+8$$
$$y+8=(a+b)x$$
$$\frac{y+8}{(a+b)}=\frac{(a+b)x}{(a+b)}$$
$$\frac{y+8}{a+b}=x \quad \text{or} \quad x=\frac{y+8}{a+b}$$

65.
$$y=cx+dx$$
$$y=(c+d)x$$
$$\frac{y}{c+d}=\frac{(c+d)x}{c+d}$$
$$\frac{y}{c+d}=x \quad \text{or} \quad x=\frac{y}{c+d}$$

66.
$$y=cx-dx$$
$$y=(c-d)x$$
$$\frac{y}{(c-d)}=\frac{(c-d)x}{(c-d)}$$
$$\frac{y}{c-d}=x \quad \text{or} \quad x=\frac{y}{c-d}$$

67.
$$y=Ax-Bx-C$$
$$y=(A-B)x-C$$
$$y+C=(A-B)x-C+C$$
$$y+C=(A-B)x$$
$$\frac{y+C}{A-B}=\frac{(A-B)x}{A-B}$$
$$\frac{y+C}{A-B}=x \quad \text{or} \quad x=\frac{y+C}{A-B}$$

68.
$$y=Ax+Bx+C$$
$$y-C=Ax+Bx+C-C$$
$$y-C=Ax+Bx$$
$$y-C=(A+B)x$$
$$\frac{y-C}{(A+B)}=\frac{(A+B)x}{(A+B)}$$
$$\frac{y-C}{A+B}=x \quad \text{or} \quad x=\frac{y-C}{A+B}$$

69. **a.** $A=\frac{x+y+z}{3}$ for z
$$3A=3\left(\frac{x+y+z}{3}\right)$$
$$3A=x+y+z$$
$$3A-x-y=x+y+z-x-y$$
$$3A-x-y=z$$

b. $A=90, x=86, y=88$
$$z=3A-x-y$$
$$z=3(90)-86-88=96$$
You need to get 96% on the third exam to have an average of 90%

71. **a.** $d=rt$ for t
$$\frac{d}{r}=\frac{rt}{r}$$
$$\frac{d}{r}=t$$

b. $t = \frac{d}{r};\ d = 100, r = 40$

$t = \frac{100}{40} = 2.5$

You would travel for 2.5 $\left(\text{or } 2\frac{1}{2}\right)$ hours.

73. $0.34 \cdot 1200 = 408$
408 single women would marry someone other than the perfect mate.

75.
$$A = P \cdot B$$
$$710{,}760 = 0.30B$$
$$\frac{710{,}760}{0.30} = \frac{0.30B}{0.30}$$
$$2{,}369{,}200 = B$$
The total number of deaths in 2002 was 2,369,200.

77.
$$A - P \cdot B$$
$$7080 = P \cdot 12{,}000$$
$$\frac{7080}{12{,}000} = \frac{P \cdot 12{,}000}{12{,}000}$$
$$0.59 = P$$
0.59 = 59% of hate crimes were motivated by race.

79. $A = PB;\ A = 7500, B = 60{,}000$
$$A = PB$$
$$7500 = P \cdot 60{,}000$$
$$\frac{7500}{60{,}000} = \frac{P \cdot 60{,}000}{60{,}000}$$
$$0.125 = P$$
The charity has raised 0.125 = 12.5% of its goal.

81. $A = PB;\ p = 15\% = 0.15, B = 60$
$$A = PB$$
$$A = 0.15 \cdot 60 = 09$$
The tip was $9.

83. **a.** The sales tax is 6% of $16,800.
$$0.06(16{,}800) = 1008$$
The sales tax due on the car is $1008.

b. The total cost is the sum of the price of the car and the sales tax.
$$\$16{,}800 + \$1008 = \$17{,}808$$
The car's total cost is $17,808.

85. **a.** The discount is 12% of $860.
$$0.12(860) = 103.20$$
The discount amount is $103.20.

b. The sale price is the regular price minus the discount amount: $\$860 - \$103.20 = \$756.80$.

87. Use the formula, decrease = percent · original. The decrease is $840 – $714 = $126.
$$126 = P \cdot 840$$
$$\frac{126}{840} = \frac{P \cdot 840}{840}$$
$$0.15 = P$$
This is a 0.15 = 15% decrease.

89. Investment dollars decreased in year 1 are $0.30 \cdot \$10{,}000 = \$3000$. This means that $10,000 – $3000 = $7000 remains. Investment dollars increased in year 2 are $0.40 \cdot \$7000 = \$2800$. This means that $7000 + $2800 = $9800 of the original investment remains. This is an overall loss of $200 over the two years.
decrease = percent · original
$$200 = P \cdot 10{,}000$$
$$\frac{200}{10{,}000} = \frac{P \cdot 10{,}000}{10{,}000}$$
$$0.02 = P$$
The financial advisor is not using percentages properly. Instead of a 10% increase, this is a 0.02 = 2% decrease.

For Exercises 91-95, answers will vary.

97. Statement d is true.

99. $v = -32t + 64;\ v = 16$

$$16 = -32t + 64$$
$$-48 = -32t$$
$$\frac{-48}{-32} = \frac{-32t}{-32}$$
$$1.5 = t$$
$$h = -16t^2 + 64t;\ t = 1.5$$
$$h = -16(1.5^2) + 64(1.5) = 60$$

When the velocity is 16 feet per second, the time is 1.5 seconds and the height is 60 feet.

100.
$$5x + 20 = 8x - 16$$
$$5x + 20 - 8x = 8x - 16 - 8x$$
$$-3x + 20 = -16$$
$$-3x + 20 - 20 = -16 - 20$$
$$-3x = -36$$
$$\frac{-3x}{-3} = \frac{-36}{-3}$$
$$x = 12$$

Check:
$$5(12) + 20 = 9(12) - 16$$
$$60 + 20 = 96 - 16$$
$$80 = 80$$

The solution is 12.

101.
$$5(2y - 3) - 1 = 4(6 + 2y)$$
$$10y - 15 - 1 = 24 + 8y$$
$$10y - 16 = 24 + 8y$$
$$10y - 16 - 8y = 24 + 8y - 8y$$
$$2y - 16 = 24y$$
$$2y - 16 + 16 = 24 + 16$$
$$2y = 40$$
$$\frac{2y}{2} = \frac{40}{2}$$
$$y = 20$$

Check:
$$5(2 \cdot 20 - 3) - 1 = 4(6 + 2 \cdot 20)$$
$$5(40 - 3) - 1 = 4(6 + 40)$$
$$5(37) - 1 = 4(46)$$
$$185 - 1 = 184$$
$$184 = 184$$

The solution is 20.

102. $x - 0.3x = 1x - 0.3x = (1 - 0.3)x = 0.7x$

Chapter 2 Mid-Chapter Check Points

1. $\frac{x}{2} = 12 - \frac{x}{4}$

The LCD is 4, so multiply both sides by 4.

$$\frac{x}{2} = 12 - \frac{x}{4}$$
$$4\left(\frac{x}{2}\right) = 4(12) - 4\left(\frac{x}{4}\right)$$
$$2x = 48 - x$$
$$2x + x = 48 - x + x$$
$$3x = 48$$
$$\frac{3x}{3} = \frac{48}{3}$$
$$x = 16$$

The solution is 16.

2.
$$
\begin{aligned}
5x-42&=-57\\
5x-42+42&=-57+42\\
5x&=-15\\
\frac{5x}{5}&=\frac{-15}{5}\\
x&=-3
\end{aligned}
$$
The solution is −3.

3.
$$
\begin{aligned}
H&=\frac{EC}{825}\\
H\cdot 825&=\frac{EC}{825}\cdot 825\\
825H&=EC\\
\frac{825H}{E}&=\frac{EC}{E}\\
\frac{825H}{E}&=C
\end{aligned}
$$

4.
$$
\begin{aligned}
A&=P\cdot B\\
A&=0.06\cdot 140\\
A&=8.4
\end{aligned}
$$
8.4 is 6% of 140.

5.
$$
\begin{aligned}
\frac{-x}{10}&=-3\\
10\left(\frac{-x}{10}\right)&=10(-3)\\
-x&=-30\\
-1(-x)&=-1(-30)\\
x&=30
\end{aligned}
$$

6.
$$
\begin{aligned}
1-3(y-5)&=4(2-3y)\\
1-3y+15&=8-12y\\
-3y+16&=8-12y\\
-3y+12y+16&=8-12y+12y\\
9y+16&=8\\
9y+16-16&=8-16\\
9y&=-8\\
\frac{9y}{9}&=\frac{-8}{9}\\
y&=-\frac{8}{9}
\end{aligned}
$$

7.
$$
\begin{aligned}
S&=2\pi rh\\
\frac{S}{2\pi h}&=\frac{2\pi rh}{2\pi h}\\
\frac{S}{2\pi h}&=r
\end{aligned}
$$

8.
$$
\begin{aligned}
A&=P\cdot B\\
12&=0.30\cdot B\\
\frac{12}{0.30}&=\frac{0.30\cdot B}{0.30}\\
40&=B
\end{aligned}
$$
12 is 30% of 40.

9.
$$\frac{3y}{5}+\frac{y}{2}=\frac{5y}{4}-3$$
To clear fractions, multiply both sides by the LCD, 20.
$$
\begin{aligned}
20\left(\frac{3y}{5}\right)+20\left(\frac{y}{2}\right)&=20\left(\frac{5y}{4}\right)-20(3)\\
4(3y)+10y&=5(5y)-60\\
12y+10y&=25y-60\\
22y&=25y-60\\
22y-25y&=25y-25y-60\\
-3y&=-60\\
\frac{-3y}{-3}&=\frac{-60}{-3}\\
y&=20
\end{aligned}
$$
The solution is 20.

10.
$$5z+7=6(z-2)-4(2z-3)$$
$$5z+7=6z-12-8z+12$$
$$5z+7=-2z$$
$$5z-5z+7=-2z-5z$$
$$7=-7z$$
$$\frac{7}{-7}=\frac{-7z}{-7}$$
$$-1=z$$
The solution is −1.

11.
$$Ax-By=C$$
$$Ax-By+By=C+By$$
$$Ax=C+By$$
$$\frac{Ax}{A}=\frac{C+By}{A}$$
$$x=\frac{C+By}{A} \text{ or } \frac{By+C}{A}$$

12.
$$6y+7+3y=3(3y-1)$$
$$9y+7=9y-3$$
$$9y-9y+7=9y-9y-3$$
$$7=-3$$
Since this is a false statement, there is no solution.

13.
$$D=0.12x+5.44$$
$$6.4=0.12x+5.44$$
$$6.4-5.44=0.12x+5.44-5.44$$
$$0.96=0.12x$$
$$\frac{0.96}{0.12}=\frac{0.12x}{0.12}$$
$$8=x$$
In the year 2000 + 8 = 2008, there will be 6.4 million children with disabilities.

14.
$$10\left(\frac{1}{2}x+3\right)=10\left(\frac{3}{5}x-1\right)$$
$$10\left(\frac{1}{2}x\right)+10(3)=10\left(\frac{3}{5}x\right)-10(1)$$
$$5x+30=6x-10$$
$$5x-5x+30=6x-5x-10$$
$$30=x-10$$
$$30+10=x-10+10$$
$$40=x$$
The solution is 40.

15.
$$A=P\cdot B$$
$$50=P\cdot 400$$
$$\frac{50}{400}=\frac{P\cdot 400}{400}$$
$$0.125=P$$
50 is 0.125 = 12.5% of 400.

16.
$$\frac{3(m+2)}{4}=2m+3$$
$$4\cdot\frac{3(m+2)}{4}=4(2m+3)$$
$$3(m+2)=4(2m+3)$$
$$3m+6=8m+12$$
$$3m-3m+6=8m-3m+12$$
$$6=5m+12$$
$$6-12=5m+12-12$$
$$-6=5m$$
$$\frac{-6}{5}=\frac{5m}{5}$$
$$-\frac{6}{5}=m$$

17. Use the formula, increase = percent · original. The increase is 50 − 40 = 10.
$$10=P\cdot 40$$
$$\frac{10}{40}=\frac{P\cdot 40}{40}$$
$$0.25=P$$
This is a 0.25 = 25% increase.

18.
$$12w-4+8w-4=4(5w-2)$$
$$20w-8=20w-8$$
$$20w-20w-8=20w-20w-8$$
$$-8=-8$$
Since $-8 = -8$ is a true statement, the solution is all real numbers.

2.5 Exercise Set

1. $x + 7$

3. $25 - x$

5. $9 - 4x$

7. $\frac{83}{x}$

9. $2x + 40$

11. $9x - 93$

13. $8(x + 14)$

15.
$$x+60=410$$
$$x+60-60=410-60$$
$$x=350$$
The number is 350.

17.
$$x-23=214$$
$$x-23+23=214+23$$
$$x=237$$
The number is 237.

19.
$$7x=126$$
$$\frac{7x}{7}=\frac{126}{7}$$
$$x=18$$
The number is 18.

21.
$$\frac{x}{19}=5$$
$$19\left(\frac{x}{19}\right)=19(5)$$
$$x=95$$
The number is 95.

23.
$$4+2x=56$$
$$4-4+2x=56-4$$
$$2x=52$$
$$\frac{2x}{2}=\frac{52}{2}$$
$$x=26$$
The number is 26.

25.
$$5x-7=178$$
$$5x-7+7=178+7$$
$$5x=185$$
$$\frac{5x}{5}=\frac{185}{5}$$
$$x=37$$
The number is 37.

27.
$$x+5=2x$$
$$x+5-x=2x-x$$
$$5=x$$
The number is 5.

29.
$$2(x+4)=36$$
$$2x+8=36$$
$$2x=28$$
$$x=14$$
The number is 14.

31.
$$9x=30+3x$$
$$6x=30$$
$$x=5$$
The number is 5.

33. $\frac{3x}{5}+4=34$

$\frac{3x}{5}=30$

$3x=150$

$x=50$

The number is 50.

35. *Step 1* Let x = the cost to make *Waterworld* (in millions of dollars).
Step 2 $x + 25$ = the cost to make *Titanic.*
Step 3 The combined cost was \$375 million, so the equation is
$x+(x+25)=375$
Step 4
$x+x+25=375$
$2x+25=375$
$2x=350$
$x=175$
It would cost \$175 million to make *Waterworld* and \$175 million + \$25 million = \$200 million to make *Titanic.*

37. Let x = the percentage of Conservatives.
Then $2x + 4.4$ = the percentage of Liberals.
$x+(2x+4.4)=57.2$
$x+2x+4.4=57.2$
$3x+4.4=57.2$
$3x+4.4-4.4=57.2-4.4$
$3x=52.8$
$\frac{3x}{3}=\frac{52.8}{3}$
$x=17.6$
The percentage of Conservatives is 17.6% and the percentage of Liberals is $2x+4.4=2(17.6)+4.4=39.6\%$.

39. Let x = the number of the left-hand page.
Let $x + 1$ = the number of the right-hand page.
$x+(x+1)=629$
$x+x+1=629$
$2x+1=629$
$2x+1-1=629-1$
$2x=628$
$\frac{2x}{2}=\frac{628}{2}$
$x=314$
The pages are 314 and 315.

41. Let x = the amount grossed by Springsteen.
Let $x + 1$ = the amount grossed by the Stones.
$x+(x+1)=241$
$x+x+1=241$
$2x+1=241$
$2x+1-1=241-1$
$2x=240$
$\frac{2x}{2}=\frac{240}{2}$
$x=120$
Springsteen grossed \$120 million and the Rolling Stones grossed 120 + 1 = \$121 million.

43. Let x = the smaller integer.
Then $x + 2$ = the larger integer.
$x+(x+2)=66$
$2x+2=66$
$2x=34$
$x=32$
The smaller integer is 32. The larger integer is 32 + 2 = 34. Their sum is 32 + 34 = 66.

45. Let x = the number of miles you can travel in one week for \$320.

$$200+0.15x=320$$
$$200+0.15x-200=320-200$$
$$0.15x=120$$
$$\frac{0.15x}{0.15}=\frac{120}{0.15}$$
$$x=800$$

You can travel 800 miles in one week for \$320. This checks because \$200 + 0.15(\$800) = \$320.

47. Let x = the number of months it will take for a baby girl to weigh 16 pounds.

$$7+1.5x=16$$
$$7+1.5x-4=16-7$$
$$1.5x=9$$
$$\frac{1.5x}{1.5}=\frac{9}{1.5}$$
$$x=6$$

The average baby girl weighs 16 pounds after 6 months.

49. Let w = the width of the field (in yards).
Let $4w$ = the length.
The perimeter of a rectangle is twice the width plus twice the length, so
$2w+2(4w)=500.$
Solve this equation.

$$2w+8w=500$$
$$10w=500$$
$$w=50$$

The width is 50 yards and the length is 4(50) = 200 yards. This checks because 2(50) + 2(200) = 500.

51. Let w = the width of a football field (in feet).
Let w + 200 = the length.

$$2w+2(w+200)=1040$$
$$2w+2w+400=1040$$
$$4w+400=1040$$
$$4w=640$$
$$w=160$$

The width 160 feet and the length is 160 + 200 = 360 feet. This checks because 2(160) + 2(200) = 720.

53. As shown in the diagram, let x = the height and $3x$ = the length. To construct the bookcase, 3 heights and 4 lengths are needed. Since 60 feet of lumber is available,
$3x+4(3x)=60.$
Solve this equation.

$$3x+12x=60$$
$$15x=60$$
$$x=4$$

If $x=4,\ 3x=3\cdot4=12.$
The bookcase is 12 feet long and 4 feet high.

55. Let x = the price before the reduction.

$$x-0.20x=320$$
$$1x-0.20x=320$$
$$0.80x=320$$
$$\frac{0.80x}{0.80}=\frac{320}{0.80}$$
$$x=400$$

The price before the reduction was \$400.

57. Let x = the average salary in 2001

$$x + 0.30x = 87{,}100$$
$$1.30x = 87{,}100$$
$$\frac{1.30x}{1.30} = \frac{87{,}100}{1.30}$$
$$x = 67{,}000$$

The average salary in 2001 was $67,000.

59. Let x = the price of the car without tax.

$$x + 0.06x = 15{,}370$$
$$1x + 0.06x = 15{,}370$$
$$1.06x = 15{,}370$$
$$\frac{1.06x}{1.06} = \frac{15{,}370}{1.06}$$
$$x = 14{,}500$$

The price of the car without sales tax was $14,500.

61. Let x = the number of hours of labor.

$$63 + 35x = 448$$
$$63 + 35x - 63 = 448 - 63$$
$$35x = 385$$
$$\frac{35x}{35} = \frac{385}{35}$$
$$x = 11$$

It took 11 hours of labor to repair the car.

For Exercises 63-65, answers will vary.

67. Statement **a.** should be translated as $x - 10 = 160$ and statement **b.** should be translated as $5x + 4 = 6x - 1$. Statement **c.** should be translated as $7 = x + 3$. Since none of these statements was translated correctly, the correct response is **d.**

69. Let x = the number of inches over 5 feet

$$W = 100 + 5x$$
$$135 = 100 + 5x$$
$$135 - 100 = 100 - 100 + 5x$$
$$35 = 5x$$
$$\frac{35}{5} = \frac{5x}{5}$$
$$7 = x$$

The height 5' 7" corresponds to 135 pounds.

71. Let x = the woman's age.
Let $3x$ = the "uncle's" age.

$$3x + 20 = 2(x + 20)$$
$$3x + 20 = 2x + 40$$
$$3x - 2x + 20 = 2x - 2x + 40$$
$$x + 20 = 40$$
$$x + 20 - 20 = 40 - 20$$
$$x = 20$$

The woman is 20 years old and the "uncle" is $3x = 3(20) = 60$ years old.

73.

$$\frac{4}{5}x = -16$$
$$\frac{5}{4}\left(\frac{4}{5}x\right) = \frac{5}{4}(-16)$$
$$x = -20$$

Check:

$$\frac{4}{5}(-20) = -16$$
$$\frac{4}{5} \cdot \frac{-20}{1} = -16$$
$$\frac{-80}{5} = -16$$
$$-16 = -16$$

The solution is −20.

74.
$$6(y-1)+7=9y-y+1$$
$$6y-6+7=9y-y+1$$
$$6y+1=8y+1$$
$$6y+1-1=8y+1-1$$
$$6y=8y$$
$$6y-8y=8y-8y$$
$$-2y=0$$
$$\frac{-2y}{-2}=\frac{0}{-2}$$
$$y=0$$

Check:
$$6(0-1)+7=9(0)-0+1$$
$$6-10+7=0-0+1$$
$$-6+7=1$$
$$1=1$$

The solution is 0.

75. $V=\frac{1}{3}lwh$ for w
$$V=\frac{1}{3}lwh$$
$$3V=3\left(\frac{1}{3}lwh\right)$$
$$3v=lwh$$
$$\frac{3V}{lh}=\frac{lwh}{lh}$$
$$\frac{3V}{lh}=w \quad \text{or} \quad w=\frac{3V}{lh}$$

2.6 Exercise Set

1. $x>5$

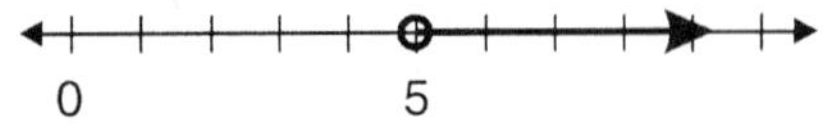

3. $x<-2$

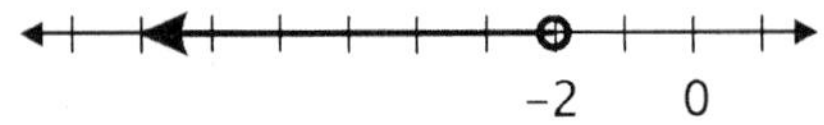

5. $x\geq -4$

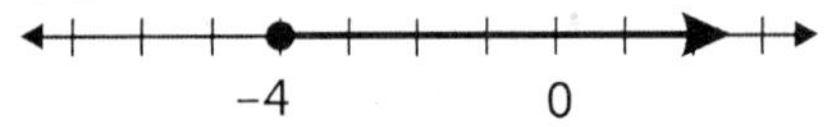

7. $x\leq 4.5$

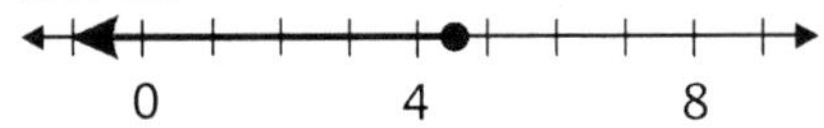

9. $-2<x\leq 6$

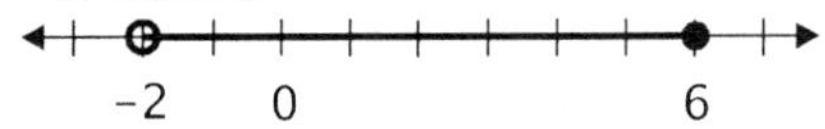

11. $-1<x<3$

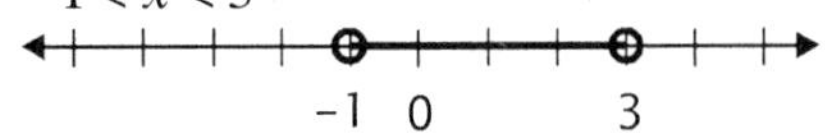

13. $\{x|x>-2\}$

15. $\{x|x\geq 4\}$

17. $\{x|x\geq 3\}$

19.
$$x-3>4$$
$$x-3+3>4+3$$
$$x>7$$
$$\{x|x>7\}$$

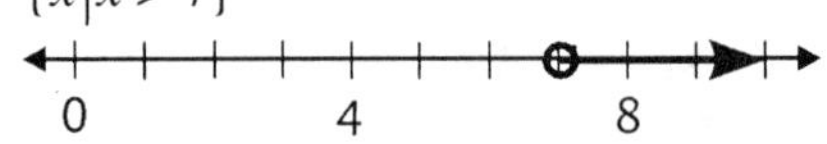

21.
$$x+4\leq 10$$
$$x+4-4\leq 10-4$$
$$x\leq 6$$
$$\{x|x\leq 6\}$$

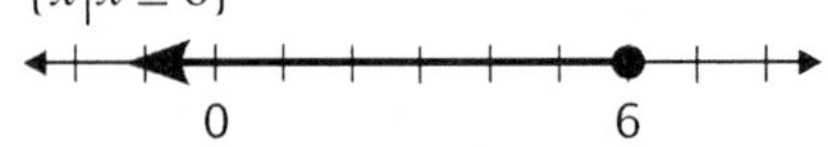

23.
$$y-2<0$$
$$y-2+2<0+2$$
$$y<2$$
$$\{y|y<2\}$$

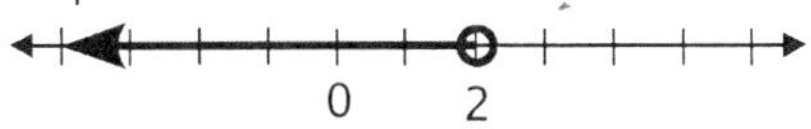

25.
$$3x+4\le 2x+7$$
$$3x-2x\le 7-4$$
$$x\le 3$$
$$\{x|x\le 3\}$$

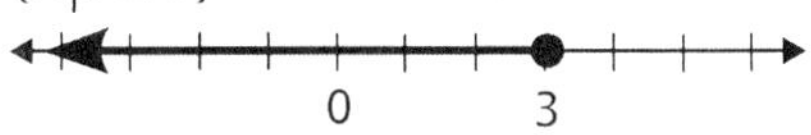

27.
$$5x-9<4x+7$$
$$5x-4x<7+9$$
$$x<16$$
$$\{x|x<16\}$$

29.
$$7x-7>6x-3$$
$$7x-6x>-3+7$$
$$x>4$$
$$\{x|x>4\}$$

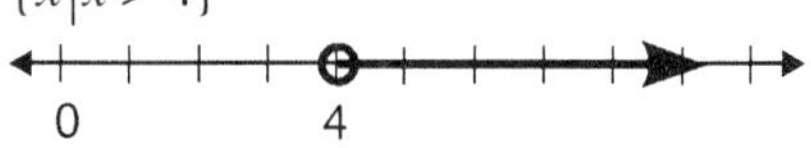

31.
$$x-\frac{2}{3}>\frac{1}{2}$$
$$x-\frac{2}{3}+\frac{2}{3}>\frac{1}{2}+\frac{2}{3}$$
$$x>\frac{3}{6}+\frac{4}{6}$$
$$x>\frac{7}{6}$$
$$\left\{x\,|\,x>\frac{7}{6}\right\}$$

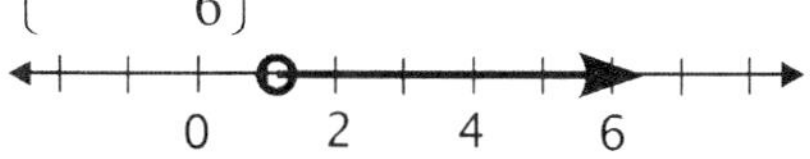

33.
$$y+\frac{7}{8}\le\frac{1}{2}$$
$$y+\frac{7}{8}-\frac{7}{8}\le\frac{1}{2}-\frac{7}{8}$$
$$y\le\frac{4}{8}-\frac{7}{8}$$
$$y\le-\frac{3}{8}$$
$$\left\{y\middle|y\le-\frac{3}{8}\right\}$$

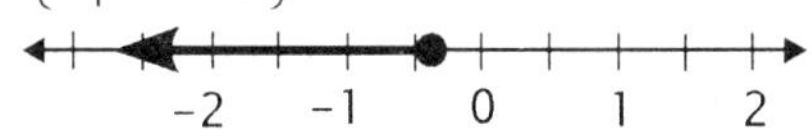

35.
$$-15y+13>13-16y$$
$$-15y+13+16y>13-16y+16y$$
$$y+13>13$$
$$y+13-13>13-13$$
$$y>0$$
$$\{y|y>0\}$$

37.
$$\frac{1}{2}x<4$$
$$2\left(\frac{1}{2}x\right)<2(4)$$
$$1x<8$$
$$x<8$$
$$\{x|x<8\}$$

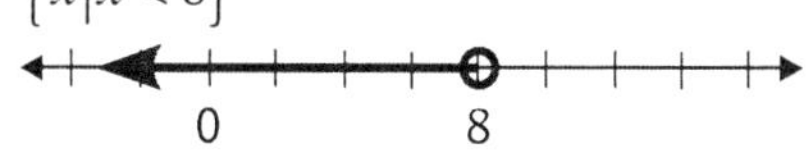

39.
$$\frac{x}{3}>-2$$
$$3\left(\frac{x}{3}\right)>3(-2)$$
$$x>-6$$
$$\{x|x>-6\}$$

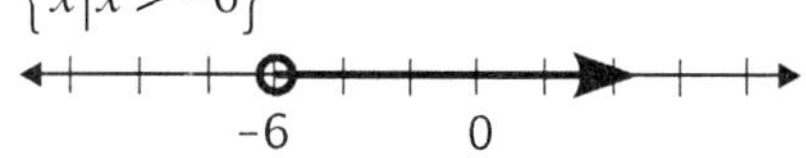

41.

$$4x < 20$$
$$\frac{4x}{4} < 20$$
$$x < 5$$
$$\{x|x < 5\}$$

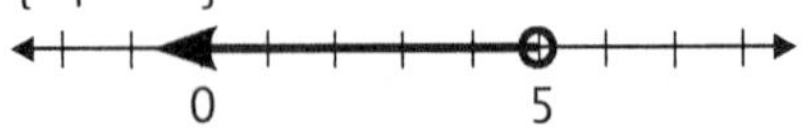

43.

$$3x \geq -21$$
$$\frac{3x}{3} \geq \frac{-21}{3}$$
$$x \geq -7$$
$$\{x|x \geq -7\}$$

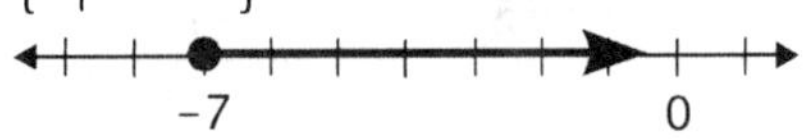

45.

$$-3x < 15$$
$$\frac{-3x}{-3} > \frac{15}{-3}$$

Notice that the direction of the inequality symbol was reversed when both sides were divided by a negative number.

$$x > -5$$
$$\{x|x > -5\}$$

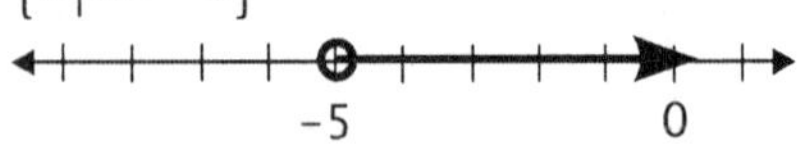

47.

$$-3x \geq 15$$
$$\frac{-3x}{-3} \leq \frac{15}{-3}$$
$$x \leq -5$$
$$\{x|x \leq -5\}$$

49.

$$-16x > -48$$
$$\frac{-16x}{-16} < \frac{-48}{-16}$$
$$x < 3$$
$$\{x|x < 3\}$$

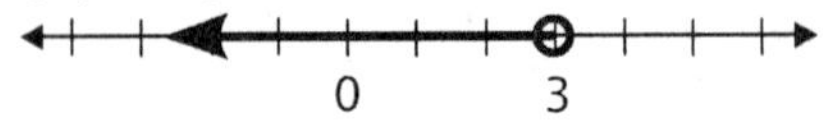

51.

$$-4y \leq \frac{1}{2}$$
$$2(-4y) \leq 2\left(\frac{1}{2}\right)$$
$$-8y \leq 1$$
$$\frac{-8y}{-8} \geq \frac{1}{-8}$$
$$y \geq -\frac{1}{8}$$
$$\left\{y \middle| y \geq -\frac{1}{8}\right\}$$

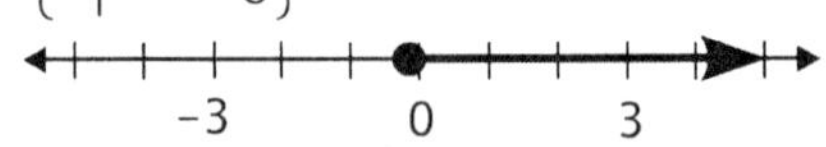

53.

$$-x < 4$$
$$-1(-x) > -1(4)$$
$$x > -4$$
$$\{x|x > -4\}$$

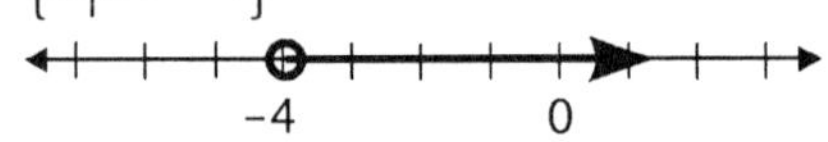

55.

$$2x - 3 > 7$$
$$2x - 3 + 3 > 7 + 3$$
$$2x > 10$$
$$\frac{2x}{2} > \frac{10}{2}$$
$$x > 5$$
$$\{x|x > 5\}$$

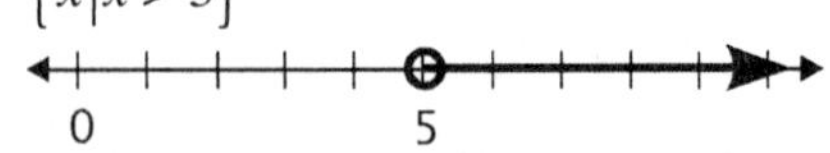

57.
$$\begin{aligned} 3x+3&<18 \\ 3x+3-3&<18-3 \\ 3x&<15 \\ \frac{3x}{3}&<\frac{15}{3} \\ x&<5 \end{aligned}$$
$\{x|x<5\}$

59.
$$\begin{aligned} 3-7x&\le 17 \\ 3-7x-3&\le 17-3 \\ -7x&\le 14 \\ \frac{-7x}{-7}&\ge\frac{14}{-7} \\ x&\ge -2 \end{aligned}$$
$\{x|x\ge -2\}$

61.
$$\begin{aligned} -2x-3&<3 \\ -2x-3+3&<3+3 \\ -2x&<6 \\ \frac{-2x}{-2}&>\frac{6}{-2} \\ x&>-3 \end{aligned}$$
$\{x|x>-3\}$

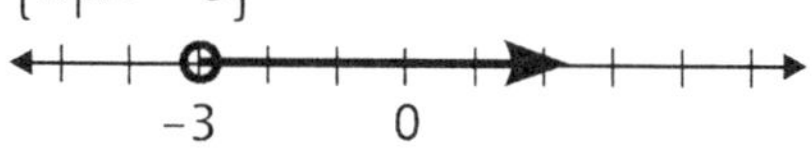

63.
$$\begin{aligned} 5-x&\le 1 \\ 5-x-5&\le 1-5 \\ -x&\le -4 \\ -1(-x)&\ge -1(-4) \\ x&\ge 4 \end{aligned}$$
$\{x|x\ge 4\}$

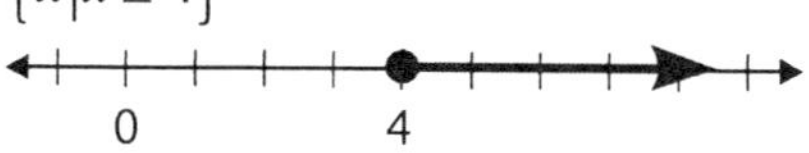

65.
$$\begin{aligned} 2x-5&>-x+6 \\ 2x-5+x&>-x+6+x \\ 3x-5&>6 \\ 3x-5+5&>6+5 \\ 3x&>11 \\ \frac{3x}{3}&>\frac{11}{3} \\ x&>\frac{11}{3} \end{aligned}$$
$\left\{x\middle|x>\frac{11}{3}\right\}$

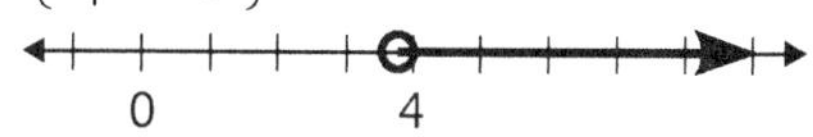

67.
$$\begin{aligned} 2y-5&<5y-11 \\ 2y-5-5y&<5y-11-5y \\ -3y-5&<-11 \\ -3y-5+5&<-11+5 \\ -3y&<-6 \\ \frac{-3y}{-3}&>\frac{-6}{-3} \\ y&>2 \end{aligned}$$
$\{y|y>2\}$

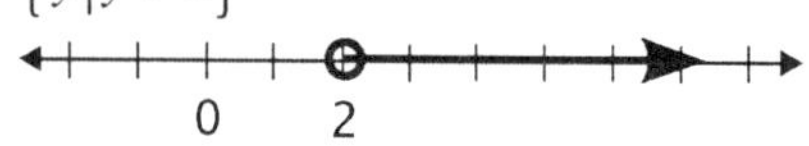

69.
$$\begin{aligned} 3(2y-1)&<9 \\ 6y-3&<9 \\ 6y-3+3&<9+3 \\ 6y&<12 \\ \frac{6y}{6}&<\frac{12}{6} \\ y&<2 \end{aligned}$$

$\{y|y<2\}$

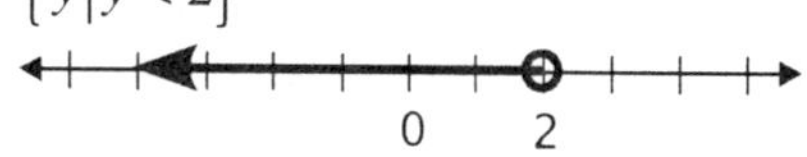

71.

$$3(x+1)-5<2x+1$$
$$3x+3-5<2x+1$$
$$3x-2<2x+1$$
$$3x-2-2x<2x+1-2x$$
$$x-2<1$$
$$x-2+2<1+2$$
$$x<3$$
$$\{x|x<3\}$$

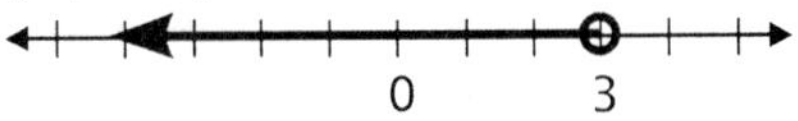

73.

$$8x+3>3(2x+1)-x+5$$
$$8x+3>6x+3-x+5$$
$$8x+3>5x+8$$
$$8x+3-5x>5x+8-5x$$
$$3x+3>8$$
$$3x+3-3>8-3$$
$$3x>5$$
$$x>\frac{5}{3}$$
$$\left\{x\middle|x>\frac{5}{3}\right\}$$

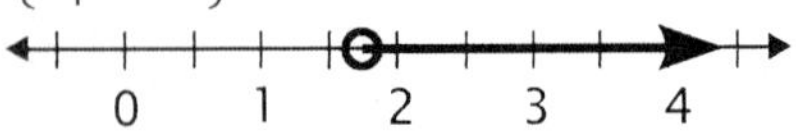

75.

$$\frac{x}{3}-2\geq 1$$
$$\frac{x}{3}-2+2\geq 1+2$$
$$\frac{x}{3}\geq 3$$
$$3\left(\frac{x}{3}\right)\geq 3(3)$$
$$x\geq 9$$
$$\{x|x\geq 9\}$$

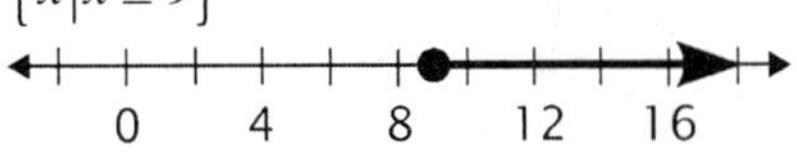

77.

$$1-\frac{x}{2}>4$$
$$1-\frac{x}{2}-1>4-1$$
$$-\frac{x}{2}>3$$
$$2\left(-\frac{x}{2}\right)>2(3)$$
$$-x>6$$
$$-1(-x)<-1(6)$$
$$x<-6$$
$$\{x|x<-6\}$$

79.

$$4x-4<4(x-5)$$
$$4x-4<4x-20$$
$$4x-4+4<4x-20+4$$
$$4x<4x-16$$
$$4x-4x<4x-16-4x$$
$$0<-16$$

The original inequality is equivalent to the false statement $0<-16$, so the inequality has no solution. The solution set is Ø (the empty set).

81.

$$x+3<x+7$$
$$x+3-x<x+7-x$$
$$3<7$$

The original inequality is equivalent to the true statement $3<7$, so the solution is the set of all real numbers, written $\{x|x \text{ is a real number}\}$.

83. $7x \le 7(x-2)$

$7x \le 7x - 14$

$7x - 7x \le 7x - 14 - 7x$

$0 \le -14$

Since $0 \le -14$ is a false statement, the original inequality has no solution. The solution set is Ø.

85. $2(x+3) > 2x+1$

$2x + 6 > 2x + 1$

$2x + 6 - 2x > 2x + 1 - 2x$

$6 > 1$

Since 6 > 1 is a true statement, the original inequality is true for all real numbers the solution set is $\{x | x \text{ is a real number}\}$.

87. $5x - 4 \le 4(x-1)$

$5x - 4 \le 4x - 4$

$5x - 4 + 4 \le 4x - 4 + 4$

$5x \le 4x$

$5x - 4x \le 4x - 4x$

$x \le 0$

$\{x | x \le 0\}$

89. $3x + a > b$

$3x > b - a$

$\frac{3x}{3} > \frac{b-a}{3}$

$x > \frac{b-a}{3}$

91. $y \le mx + b$

$y - b \le mx$

Reverse the inequality since $m < 0$.

$\frac{y-b}{m} \ge \frac{mx}{m}$

$\frac{y-b}{m} \ge x$

93. x is between −2 and 2, so $|x| < 2$.

95. x is less than −2 and greater than 2, so $|x| > 2$

97. Denmark, Netherlands, and Norway

99. Japan and Mexico

101. Netherlands, Norway, Canada, and U.S.

103. $N = 550 - 9x$; $N < 370$

$550 - 9x < 370$

$550 - 9x - 550 < 370 - 550$

$-9x < -180$

$\frac{-9x}{-9} > \frac{-180}{-9}$

$x > 20$

According to the model, there will be 370 billion cigarettes consumed in 1988 + 20 = 2008 and less than 370 billion after 2008 (from 2009 onward).

105. **a.** Let x = your grade on the final exam.

$\frac{86 + 88 + x}{3} \ge 90$

$3\left(\frac{86 + 88 + x}{3}\right) \ge 3(90)$

$86 + 88 + x \ge 270$

$174 + x \ge 270$

$174 + x - 174 \ge 270 - 174$

$x \ge 96$

You must get at least a 96% on the final exam to earn an A in the course.

b.

$$\frac{86+88+x}{3}<80$$
$$3\left(\frac{86+88+x}{3}\right)<3(80)$$
$$86+88+x<240$$
$$174+x<240$$
$$174+x-174<240-174$$
$$x<66$$

If you get less than a 66 on the final exam, your grade will be below a B.

107. Let x = number of miles driven.

$$80+0.25x\le 400$$
$$80+0.25x-80\le 400-80$$
$$0.25x\le 320$$
$$\frac{0.25x}{0.25}\le\frac{320}{0.25}$$
$$x\le 1280$$

You can drive up to 1280 miles.

109. Let x = number of cement bags.

$$245+95x\le 3000$$
$$245+95x-245\le 3000-245$$
$$95x\le 2755$$
$$\frac{95x}{95}\le\frac{2755}{95}$$
$$x\le 29$$

Up to 29 bags of cement can safely be listed on the elevator in one trip.

For Exercises 111.-115., answers will vary.

117. Let x = number of miles driven.
Weekly cost for Basic Rental: \$260.
Weekly cost for Continental: \$80 + $0.25x$
The cost for Basic Rental is a better deal if $80+0.25x>260$.
Solve this inequality.

$$80+0.25x-80>260-80$$
$$0.25x>180$$
$$\frac{0.25x}{0.25}>\frac{180}{0.25}$$
$$x>720$$

Basic Car Rental is a better deal if you drive more than 720 miles in a week.

119.

$$1.45-7.23x>-1.442$$
$$1.45-7.23x-1.45>-1.442-1.45$$
$$-7.23x>-2.892$$
$$\frac{-7.23x}{-7.23}<\frac{-2.892}{-7.23}$$
$$x<0.4$$

$\{x|x<0.4\}$

121. $A = PB$, $A = 8$, $P = 40\% = 0.4$

$$A=PB$$
$$8=0.4B$$
$$\frac{8}{0.4}=\frac{0.4B}{0.4}$$
$$20=B$$

8 is 40% of 20.

122. Let w = the width of the rectangle.
Let $w + 5$ = the length.
The perimeter is 34 inches.
$2(\text{width}) + 2(\text{length}) = \text{perimeter}$

$$\begin{aligned} 2w + 2(w+5) &= 34 \\ 2w + 2w + 10 &= 34 \\ 4w + 10 &= 34 \\ 4w &= 24 \\ w &= 6 \end{aligned}$$

The width is 6 inches and the length is 6 + 5 = 11 inches.

123.

$$\begin{aligned} 5x+16 &= 3(x+8) \\ 5x+16 &= 3x+24 \\ 5x+16-3x &= 3x+24-3x \\ 2x+16 &= 24 \\ 2x+16-16 &= 24-16 \\ 2x &= 8 \\ \frac{2x}{2} &= \frac{8}{2} \\ x &= 4 \end{aligned}$$

Check: $5(4)+16 \stackrel{?}{=} 3(4+8)$

$$20+16 \stackrel{?}{=} 3(12)$$

$$36 = 36 \quad \text{true}$$

The solution is 4.

Chapter 2 Review Exercises

For Exercises 1-18 and 20-28, students should check all proposed solutions by substituting in the original equations. Checks will not be shown here.

1.

$$\begin{aligned} x-10 &= 22 \\ x-10+10 &= 22+10 \\ x &= 32 \end{aligned}$$

The solution is 32.

2.

$$\begin{aligned} -14 &= y+8 \\ -14-8 &= y+8-8 \\ -22 &= y \end{aligned}$$

The solution is −22

3.

$$\begin{aligned} 7z-3 &= 6z+9 \\ 7z-3-6z &= 6z+9-6z \\ z-3 &= 9 \\ z-3+3 &= 9+3 \\ z &= 12 \end{aligned}$$

The solution is 12.

4.

$$\begin{aligned} 4(x+3) &= 3x-10 \\ 4x+12 &= 3x-10 \\ 4x+2-3x &= 3x-10-3x \\ x+12 &= -10 \\ x+12-12 &= -10-12 \\ x &= -22 \end{aligned}$$

The solution is −22.

5.

$$\begin{aligned} 6x-3x-9+1 &= -5x+7x-3 \\ 3x-8 &= 2x-3 \\ 3x-8-2x &= 2x-3-2x \\ x-8 &= -3 \\ x-8+8 &= -3+8 \\ x &= 5 \end{aligned}$$

The solution is 5.

6.

$$\begin{aligned} \frac{x}{8} &= 10 \\ 8\left(\frac{x}{8}\right) &= 8(10) \\ x &= 80 \end{aligned}$$

The solution is 80.

7.
$$\frac{y}{-8}=7$$
$$-8\left(\frac{y}{-8}\right)=-8(7)$$
$$y=-56$$
The solution is −56.

8.
$$7z=77$$
$$\frac{7z}{7}=\frac{77}{7}$$
$$z=11$$
The solution is 11.

9.
$$-36=-9y$$
$$\frac{-36}{-9}=\frac{-9y}{-9}$$
$$4=y$$
The solution is 4.

10.
$$\frac{3}{5}x=-9$$
$$\frac{5}{3}\left(\frac{3}{5}x\right)=\frac{5}{3}(-9)$$
$$1x=-15$$
$$x=-15$$
The solution is −15.

11.
$$30=-\frac{5}{2}y$$
$$-\frac{2}{5}(30)=-\frac{2}{5}\left(-\frac{5}{2}y\right)$$
$$-12=y$$
The solution is −12.

12.
$$-x=25$$
$$-1(-x)=-1(25)$$
$$x=-25$$
The solution is −25.

13.
$$\frac{-x}{10}=-1$$
$$10\left(\frac{-x}{10}\right)=10(-1)$$
$$-x=-10$$
$$-1(-x)=-1(-10)$$
$$x=10$$
The solution is 10.

14.
$$4x+9=33$$
$$4x+9-9=33-9$$
$$4x=24$$
$$\frac{4x}{4}=\frac{24}{4}$$
$$x=6$$
The solution is 6.

15.
$$-3y-2=13$$
$$-3y-2+2=13+2$$
$$-3y=15$$
$$\frac{-3y}{-3}=\frac{15}{-3}$$
$$y=-5$$
The solution is −5.

16.
$$5z+20=3z$$
$$5z+20-3z=3z-3z$$
$$2z+20=0$$
$$2z+20-20=0-20$$
$$2z=-20$$
$$\frac{2z}{2}=\frac{-20}{2}$$
$$z=-10$$
The solution is −10.

17.
$$\begin{aligned} 5x-3&=x+5\\ 5x-3-x&=x+5-x\\ 4x-3&=5\\ 4x-3+3&=5+3\\ 4x&=8\\ \frac{4x}{4}&=\frac{8}{4}\\ x&=2 \end{aligned}$$
The solution is 2.

18.
$$\begin{aligned} 3-2x&=9-8x\\ 3-2x+8x&=9-8x+8x\\ 3+6x&=9\\ 3+6x-3&=9-3\\ 6x&=6\\ \frac{6x}{6}&=\frac{6}{6}\\ x&=1 \end{aligned}$$
The solution is 1.

19.
$$\begin{aligned} F&=1.2x+21.6\\ 40.8&=1.2x+21.6\\ 40.8-21.6&=1.2x+21.6-21.6\\ 19.2&=1.2x\\ \frac{19.2}{1.2}&=\frac{1.2x}{1.2}\\ 16&=x \end{aligned}$$
In the year, 1990 + 16 = 2006, the average income for a Puerto Rican family will be $40,800.

20.
$$\begin{aligned} 5x+9-7x+6&=x+18\\ -2x+15&=x+18\\ -2x+15-x&=x+18-x\\ -3x+15&=18\\ -3x+15-15&=18-15\\ -3x&=3\\ \frac{-3x}{-3}&=\frac{3}{-3}\\ x&=-1 \end{aligned}$$
The solution is −1.

21.
$$\begin{aligned} 3(x+4)&=5x-12\\ 3x+12&=5x-12\\ 3x+12-5x&=5x-12-5x\\ -2x+12&=-12\\ -2x+12-12&=-12-12\\ -2x&=-24\\ \frac{-2x}{-2}&=\frac{-24}{-2}\\ x&=12 \end{aligned}$$
The solution is 12.

22.
$$\begin{aligned} 1-2(6-y)&=3y+2\\ 1-12+2y&=3y+2\\ 2y-11&=3y+2\\ 2y-11-3y&=3y+2-3y\\ -y-11&=2\\ -y-11+11&=2+11\\ -y&=13\\ -1(-y)&=-1(13)\\ y&=-13 \end{aligned}$$
The solution is −13.

23. $$\begin{aligned} 2(x-4)+3(x+5) &= 2x-2 \\ 2x-8+3x+15 &= 2x-2 \\ 5x+7 &= 2x-2 \\ 5x+7-2x &= 2x-2-2x \\ 3x+7 &= -2 \\ 3x+7-7 &= -2-7 \\ 3x &= -9 \\ \frac{3x}{3} &= \frac{-9}{3} \\ x &= -3 \end{aligned}$$

The solution is −3.

24. $$\begin{aligned} -2(y-4)-(3y-2) &= -2-(6y-2) \\ -2y+8-3y+2 &= -2-6y-2 \\ -5y+10 &= -6y \\ -5y+10+6y &= -6y+6y \\ 10+y &= 0 \\ 10+y-10 &= 0-10 \\ y &= -10 \end{aligned}$$

The solution is −10.

25. $\frac{2x}{3} = \frac{x}{6}+1$

To clear fractions, multiply both sides by the LCD, which is 6.

$$\begin{aligned} 6\left(\frac{2x}{3}\right) &= 6\left(\frac{x}{6}+1\right) \\ 6\left(\frac{2x}{3}\right) &= 6\left(\frac{x}{6}\right)+6(1) \\ 4x &= x+6 \\ 4x-x &= x+6-x \\ 3x &= 6 \\ \frac{3x}{3} &= \frac{6}{3} \\ x &= 2 \end{aligned}$$

The solution is 2.

26. $\frac{x}{2}-\frac{1}{10} = \frac{x}{5}+\frac{1}{2}$

Multiply both sides by the LCD, which is 10.

$$\begin{aligned} 10\left(\frac{x}{2}-\frac{1}{10}\right) &= 10\left(\frac{x}{5}+\frac{1}{2}\right) \\ 10\left(\frac{x}{2}\right)-10\left(\frac{1}{10}\right) &= 10\left(\frac{x}{5}\right)+10\left(\frac{1}{2}\right) \\ 5x-1 &= 2x+5 \\ 5x-1-2x &= 2x+5-2x \\ 3x-1 &= 5 \\ 3x-1+1 &= 5+1 \\ 3x &= 6 \\ \frac{3x}{3} &= \frac{6}{3} \\ x &= 2 \end{aligned}$$

The solution is 2.

27. $$\begin{aligned} 3(8x-1) &= 6(5+4x) \\ 24x-3 &= 30+24x \\ 24x-3-24x &= 30+24x-24x \\ -3 &= 30 \end{aligned}$$

Since −3 = 30 is a false statement, the original equation is inconsistent and has no solution.

28. $$\begin{aligned} 4(2x-3)+4 &= 8x-8 \\ 8x-12+4 &= 8x-8 \\ 8x-8 &= 8x-8 \\ 8x-8-8x &= 8x-8-8x \\ -8 &= -8 \end{aligned}$$

Since −8 = −8 is a true statement, the original equation is an identity and all real numbers are solutions.

29. $r = 0.06(220 - a);\ \ r = 120$

$$r = 0.6(220 - a)$$
$$120 = 0.6(220 - a)$$
$$120 = 132 - 0.6a$$
$$120 - 132 = -.06a$$
$$-12 = -0.6a$$
$$\frac{-12}{-0.6} = \frac{-0.6a}{-0.6}$$
$$20 = a$$

If the optimal heart rate is 120 beats per minute, the person is 20 years old.

30. $I = Pr$ for r

$$\frac{I}{P} = \frac{Pr}{P}$$
$$\frac{I}{P} = r \text{ or } r = \frac{I}{P}$$

31. $V = \frac{1}{3}Bh$ for h

$$3V = 3\left(\frac{1}{3}Bh\right)$$
$$3V = Bh$$
$$\frac{3V}{B} = \frac{Bh}{B}$$
$$\frac{3V}{B} = h \text{ or } h = \frac{3V}{B}$$

32. $P = 2l + 2w$ for w

$$P - 2l = 2l + 2w - 2l$$
$$P - 2l = 2w$$
$$\frac{P - 2l}{2} = \frac{2w}{2}$$
$$\frac{P - 2l}{2} = w \text{ or } w = \frac{P - 2l}{2}$$

33. $A = \frac{B + C}{2}$ for B

$$2A = 2\left(\frac{B + C}{2}\right)$$
$$2A = B + C$$
$$2A - C = B + C - C$$
$$2A - c = b \text{ or } B = 2A - C$$

34. $T = D + pm$ for m

$$T - D = D + pm - D$$
$$T - D = pm$$
$$\frac{T - D}{p} = \frac{pm}{p}$$
$$\frac{T - D}{p} = m \text{ or } m = \frac{T - D}{p}$$

35. $0.72 = 72\%$

36. $0.0035 = 0.35\%$

37. $65\% = 0.65$

38. $150\% = 1.50$

39. $3\% = 0.03$

40. $A = PB;\ P = 8\% = 0.08,\ B = 120$

$$A = PB$$
$$A = 0.08 \cdot 120$$
$$A = 9.6$$

8% of 120 is 9.6

41. $A = PB;\ A = 90,\ P = 45\% = 0.45$

$$A = PB$$
$$90 = 0.45B$$
$$\frac{90}{0.45} = \frac{0.45B}{0.45}$$
$$200 = B$$

90 is 45% of 200.

42. $A = PB;\ A = 36,\ B = 75$

$$A = PB$$
$$36 = P \cdot 75$$
$$\frac{36}{75} = \frac{P \cdot 75}{75}$$
$$0.48 = P$$

36 is 48% of 75.

43. Increase = Percent · Original
First, find the increase: 12 − 6 = 6

$$6 = P \cdot 6$$
$$\frac{6}{6} = \frac{P \cdot 6}{6}$$
$$1 = P$$

The percent increase is 1 = 100%.

44. Decrease = Percent · Original
First, find the decrease: 5 − 3 = 2

$$2 = P \cdot 5$$
$$\frac{2}{5} = \frac{P \cdot 5}{5}$$
$$0.4 = P$$

The percent decrease is 0.4 = 40%.

45. Increase = Percent · Original
First, find the increase: 45 − 40 = 5

$$5 = P \cdot 40$$
$$\frac{5}{40} = \frac{P \cdot 40}{40}$$
$$0.125 = P$$

The percent increase is 0.125 = 12.5%.

46. Investment dollars lost last year were $0.10 \cdot \$10{,}000 = \$1000$. This means that \$10,000 − \$1000 = \$9000 remains. Investment dollars gained this year are $0.10 \cdot \$9000 = \$900$. This means that \$9000 + \$900 = \$9900 of the original investment remains. This is an overall loss of \$100.
decrease = percent · original

$$100 = P \cdot 10{,}000$$
$$\frac{100}{10{,}000} = \frac{P \cdot 10{,}000}{10{,}000}$$
$$0.01 = P$$

The statement is not true. Instead of recouping losses, there is an overall 1% decrease in the portfolio.

47. a.

$$r = \frac{h}{7}$$
$$7r = 7\left(\frac{h}{7}\right)$$
$$7r = h \text{ or } h = 7r$$

b. $h = 7r;\ r = 9$

$$h = 7(9) = 63$$

The woman's height is 63 inches or 5 feet, 3 inches.

48.

$$A = P \cdot B$$
$$91 = 0.26 \cdot B$$
$$\frac{91}{0.26} = \frac{0.26 \cdot B}{0.26}$$
$$350 = B$$

The average U.S. household uses 350 gallons of water per day.

49. Let x = the unknown number.

$$6x - 20 = 4x$$
$$6x - 20 - 4x = 4x - 4x$$
$$2x - 20 = 0$$
$$2x - 20 + 20 = 0 + 20$$
$$2x = 20$$
$$x = 10$$

The number is 10.

50. Let x = the number of unhealthy air days in New York.
Then $3x + 48$ = the number of unhealthy air days in Los Angeles.

$$x+(3x+48)=268$$
$$4x+48=268$$
$$4x=200$$
$$x=55$$

New York has 55 unhealthy air days and Los Angeles has $3(55) + 48 =$ 213 unhealthy air days.

51. Let x = the smaller page number.
Then $x + 1$ = the larger page number.

$$x+(x+1)=93$$
$$2x+1=93$$
$$2x=92$$
$$x=46$$

The page numbers are 46 and 47. This solution checks because 46 + 47 = 93.

52. Let x = the number of Madonna's platinum records.
Then $x + 2$ = the number of Barbra Streisand's platinum records.

$$x+(x+2)=96$$
$$2x+2=96$$
$$2x=94$$
$$x=47$$

Madonna has 47 platinum records and Barbra Streisand has 47 + 2 =49 platinum records. This solution checks because 47 + 49 = 96.

53. Let x = number of years after 2003.

$$612+15x=747$$
$$612+15x-612=747-612$$
$$15x=135$$
$$\frac{15x}{15}=\frac{135}{15}$$
$$x=9$$

According to this model, the average weekly salary will reach $747 in 9 years after 2003 (in 2012).

54. Let x = the number of checks written.

$$6+0.05x=6.90$$
$$6+0.05x-6=6.90-6$$
$$0.05x=0.90$$
$$\frac{0.05x}{0.05}=\frac{0.90}{0.05}$$
$$x=18$$

You wrote 18 checks that month.

55. Let w = the width of the field.
Then $3w$ = the length.
The perimeter of a rectangle is twice the length plus twice the width, so the perimeter equation is

$$2(3w)+2w=400.$$

Solve the equation.

$$6w+2w=400$$
$$8w=400$$
$$w=50$$

The width is 50 yards and the length is 3(50) = 150 yards.

56. Let x = the original price of the table.

$$x-0.25x=180$$
$$0.75x=180$$
$$\frac{0.75x}{0.75}=\frac{180}{0.75}$$
$$x=240$$

The table's price before the reduction was $240.

57. $x < -1$

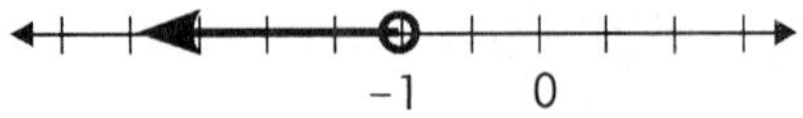

58. $-2 < x \le 4$

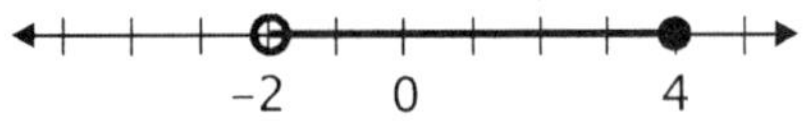

59. $\{x | x > 4\}$

60. $\{x | x \le -3\}$

61.
$$\begin{aligned} 2x - 5 &< 3 \\ 2x - 5 + 5 &< 3 + 5 \\ 2x &< 8 \\ \frac{2x}{2} &< \frac{8}{2} \\ x &< 4 \end{aligned}$$
$\{x | x < 4\}$

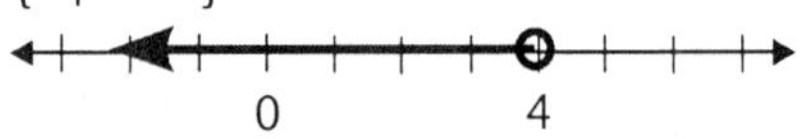

62.
$$\begin{aligned} \frac{x}{2} &> -4 \\ 2\left(\frac{x}{2}\right) &> 2(-4) \\ x &> -8 \end{aligned}$$
$\{x | x > -8\}$

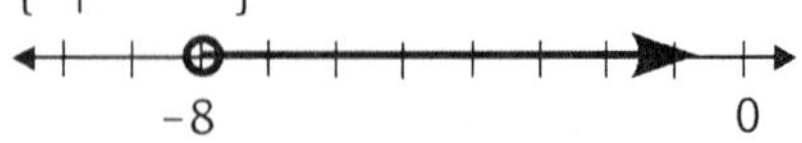

63.
$$\begin{aligned} 3 - 5x &\le 18 \\ 3 - 5x - 3 &\le 18 - 3 \\ -5x &\le 15 \\ \frac{-5x}{-5} &\ge \frac{15}{-5} \\ x &\ge -3 \end{aligned}$$
$\{x | x \ge -3\}$

64.
$$\begin{aligned} 4x + 6 &< 5x \\ 4x + 6 - 5x &< 5x - 5x \\ -x + 6 &< 0 \\ -x + 6 - 6 &< 0 - 6 \\ -x &< -6 \\ -1(-x) &> -1(-6) \\ x &> 6 \end{aligned}$$
$\{x | x > 6\}$

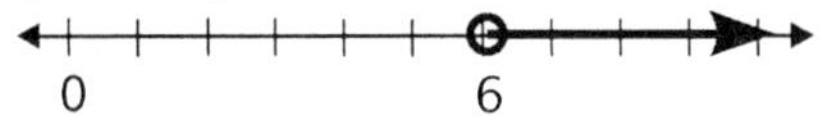

65.
$$\begin{aligned} 6x - 10 &\ge 2(x + 3) \\ 6x - 10 &\ge 2x + 6 \\ 6x - 10 - 2x &\ge 2x + 6 - 2x \\ 4x - 10 &\ge 6 \\ 4x - 10 + 10 &\ge 6 + 10 \\ 4x &\ge 16 \\ \frac{4x}{4} &\ge \frac{16}{4} \\ x &\ge 4 \end{aligned}$$
$\{x | x \ge 4\}$

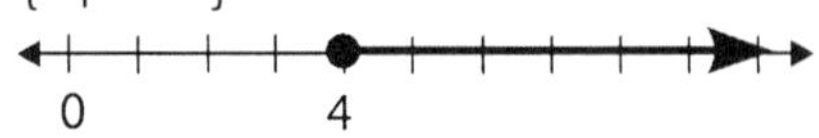

66.
$$\begin{aligned} 4x + 3(2x - 7) &\le x - 3 \\ 4x + 6x - 21 &\le x - 3 \\ 10x - 21 &\le x - 3 \\ 10x - 21 - x &\le x - 3 - x \\ 9x - 21 &\le -3 \\ 9x - 21 + 21 &\le -3 + 21 \\ 9x &\le 18 \\ \frac{9x}{9} &\le \frac{18}{9} \\ x &\le 2 \end{aligned}$$
$\{x | x \le 2\}$

67. $$2(2x+4)>4(x+2)-6$$
$$4x+8>4x+8-6$$
$$4x+8>4x+2$$
$$4x+8-4x>4x+2-4x$$
$$8>2$$

Since $8>2$ is a true statement, the original inequality is true for all real numbers, and the solution set is $\{x|x \text{ is a real number}\}$.

68. $$-2(x-4)\le 3x+1-5x$$
$$-2x+8\le -2x+1$$
$$-2x+8+2x\le 2x+1+2x$$
$$8\le 1$$

Since $8\le 1$ is a false statement, the original inequality has no solution. The solution set is Ø.

69. Let x = the student's score on the third test.
$$\frac{42+74+x}{3}\ge 60$$
$$3\left(\frac{42+74+x}{3}\right)\ge 3(60)$$
$$42+74+x\ge 180$$
$$116+x\ge 180$$
$$116+x-116\ge 180-116$$
$$x\ge 64$$

The student must score at least 64 on the third test to pass the course.

70. $$C=10+5(x-1);\ C\le 500$$
$$10+5(x-1)\le 500$$
$$10+5x-5\le 500$$
$$5x+5\le 500$$
$$5x+5-5\le 500-5$$
$$5x\le 495$$
$$\frac{5x}{5}\le\frac{495}{5}$$
$$x\le 99$$

You can talk no more than 99 minutes.

Chapter 2 Test

1. $$4x-5=13$$
$$4x+5+5=13+5$$
$$4x=18$$
$$\frac{4x}{4}=\frac{18}{4}=\frac{9}{2}$$
$$x=\frac{9}{2}$$

The solution is $\frac{9}{2}$.

2. $$12x+4=7x-21$$
$$12x+4-7x=7x-21-7x$$
$$5x+4=-21$$
$$5x+4-4=-21-4$$
$$5x=-25$$
$$\frac{5x}{5}=\frac{-25}{5}$$
$$x=-5$$

The solution is –5.

3. $$8-5(x-2)=x+26$$
$$8-5x+10=x+26$$
$$18-5x=x+26$$
$$18-5x-x=x+26-x$$
$$18-6x=26$$
$$18-6x-18=26-18$$
$$-6x=8$$
$$\frac{-6x}{-6}=\frac{8}{-6}$$
$$x=-\frac{8}{6}=-\frac{4}{3}$$

The solution is $-\frac{4}{3}$.

4.
$$3(2y-4)=9-3(y+1)$$
$$6y-12=9-3y-3$$
$$6y-12=6-3y$$
$$6y-12+3y=6-3y+3y$$
$$9y-12=6$$
$$9y-12+12=6+12$$
$$9y=18$$
$$\frac{9y}{9}=\frac{18}{9}$$
$$y=2$$
The solution is 2.

5.
$$\frac{3}{4}x=-15$$
$$\frac{4}{3}\left(\frac{3}{4}x\right)=\frac{4}{3}(-15)$$
$$x=-20$$
The solution is –20.

6.
$$\frac{x}{10}+\frac{1}{3}=\frac{x}{5}+\frac{1}{2}$$
Multiply both sides by the LCD, 30.
$$30\left(\frac{x}{10}+\frac{1}{3}\right)=30\left(\frac{x}{5}+\frac{1}{2}\right)$$
$$30\left(\frac{x}{10}\right)+30\left(\frac{1}{3}\right)=30\left(\frac{x}{5}\right)+30\left(\frac{1}{2}\right)$$
$$3x+10=6x+15$$
$$3x+10-6x=6x+15-6x$$
$$-3x+10=15$$
$$-3x+10-10=15-10$$
$$-3x=5$$
$$\frac{-3x}{-3}=\frac{5}{-3}$$
$$x=-\frac{5}{3}$$
The solution is $-\frac{5}{3}$.

7.
$$N=2.4x+180;\ N=324$$
$$2.4x+180=324$$
$$2.4x+180-180=324-180$$
$$2.4=144$$
$$\frac{2.4x}{2.4}=\frac{144}{2.4}$$
$$x=60$$
The US population is expected to reach 324 million 60 years after 1960, in the year 2020.

8.
$$V=\pi r^2h \text{ for } h$$
$$\frac{V}{\pi r^2}=\frac{\pi r^2h}{\pi r^2}$$
$$\frac{V}{\pi r^2}=h \text{ or } h=\frac{V}{\pi r^2}$$

9.
$$l=\frac{P-2w}{2} \text{ for } w$$
$$2l=2\left(\frac{P-2w}{2}\right)$$
$$2l=P-2w$$
$$2l-P=P-2w-P$$
$$2l-P=-2w$$
$$\frac{2l-P}{-2}=\frac{-2w}{-2}$$
$$\frac{2l-P}{-2}=w \quad\text{or}\quad w=\frac{P-2l}{2}$$

10.
$$A=PB;\ P=6\%=0.06,\ B=140$$
$$A=PB$$
$$A=0.06(140)$$
$$A=8.4$$
6% of 140 is 8.4

11. $A = PB$; A=120, $P = 80\% = 0.80$

$$A = PB$$
$$120 = 0.80B$$
$$\frac{120}{0.80} = \frac{0.80B}{0.80}$$
$$150 = B$$

120 is 80% of 150.

12. $A = PB$; $A = 12$, $B = 240$

$$A = PB$$
$$12 = P \cdot 240$$
$$\frac{12}{240} = \frac{P \cdot 240}{240}$$
$$0.05 = P$$

12 is 5% of 240.

13. Let x = the unknown number.

$$5x - 9 = 306$$
$$5x - 9 + 9 = 306 + 9$$
$$5x = 315$$
$$\frac{5x}{5} = \frac{315}{5}$$
$$x = 63$$

The number is 63.

14. Let x = the amount earned by a preschool teacher
Let x + 22,870 = the amount earned by a fitness instructor

$$x + (x + 22{,}870) = 79{,}030$$
$$x + x + 22{,}870 = 79{,}030$$
$$2x + 22{,}870 = 79{,}030$$
$$2x + 22{,}870 - 22{,}870 = 79{,}030 - 22{,}870$$
$$2x = 79{,}030 - 22{,}870$$
$$2x = 56{,}160$$
$$\frac{2x}{2} = \frac{56{,}160}{2}$$
$$x = 28{,}080$$

A preschool teacher makes \$28,080 and a fitness trainer makes \$28,080 + \$22,870 = \$50,950

15. Let x = number of minutes of long distance calls.

$$15 + 0.05x = 45$$
$$0.05x = 30$$
$$x = \frac{30}{0.05}$$
$$x = 600$$

You can talk long distance for 600 minutes.

16. Let w = width of field (in yards).
Then $2w$ = length of field.

$$2(2w) + 2w = 450$$
$$4w + 2w = 450$$
$$6w = 450$$
$$w = 75$$

The width is 75 yards and the length is 2(75) = 150 yards.

17. Let x = the book's original price.

$$x - 0.20x = 28$$
$$0.80x = 28$$
$$x = \frac{28}{0.80}$$
$$x = 35$$

The price of the book before the reduction was \$35.

18. $x > -2$

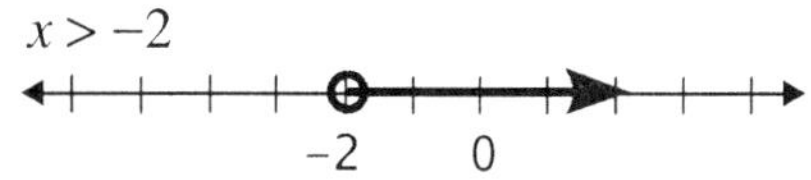

19. $-4 \le x < 1$

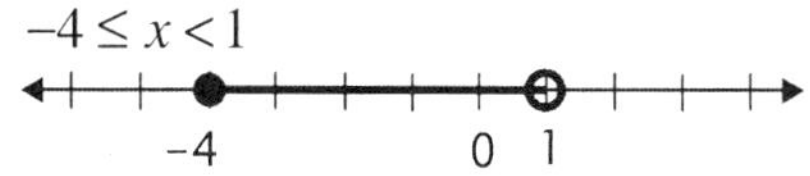

20. $\{x \mid x \le -1\}$

21.

$$\frac{x}{2} < -3$$
$$2\left(\frac{x}{2}\right) < 2(-3)$$
$$x < -6$$
$$\{x \mid x < -6\}$$

22.

$$6 - 9x \geq 33$$
$$6 - 9x - 6 \geq 33 - 6$$
$$-9x \geq 27$$
$$\frac{-9x}{-9} \leq \frac{27}{-9}$$
$$x \leq -3$$
$$\{x \mid x \leq -3\}$$

23.

$$4x - 2 > 2(x + 6)$$
$$4x - 2 > 2x + 12$$
$$4x - 2 - 2x > 2x + 12 - 2x$$
$$2x - 2 > 12$$
$$2x > 14$$
$$x > 7$$
$$\{x \mid x > 7\}$$

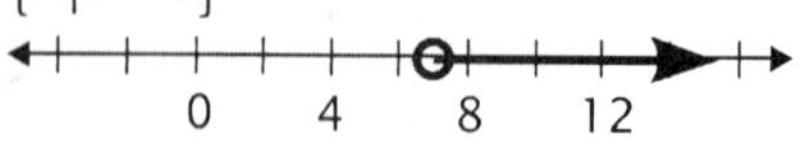

24. Let x = the student's score on the fourth exam.

$$\frac{76 + 80 + 72 + x}{4} \geq 80$$
$$4\left(\frac{76 + 80 + 72 + x}{4}\right) \geq 4(80)$$
$$76 + 80 + 72 + x \geq 320$$
$$228 + x \geq 320$$
$$x \geq 92$$

The student must score at least 92 on the fourth exam to have an average of at least 80.

25. Let w = the width of rectangle.

$$2(20) + 2w > 56$$
$$40 + 2w > 56$$
$$2w > 16$$
$$w > 8$$

The width must be greater than 8 inches.

Cumulative Review Exercises (Chapters 1-2)

1. $-8 - (12 - 16) = -8 - (-4) = -8 + 4 = -4$

2. $(-3)(-2) + (-2)(4) = 6 + (-8) = -2$

3.

$$(8 - 10)^3 (7 - 11)^2 = (-2)^3 (-4)^2$$
$$= -8(16) = -128$$

4.

$$2 - 5[x + 3(x + 7)]$$
$$= 2 - 5(x + 3x + 21)$$
$$= 2 - 5(4x + 21)$$
$$= 2 - 20x - 105$$
$$= -103 - 20x$$

5. The rational numbers are $-4, -\frac{1}{3}, 0, \sqrt{4}\,(= 2)$, and 1063.

6.

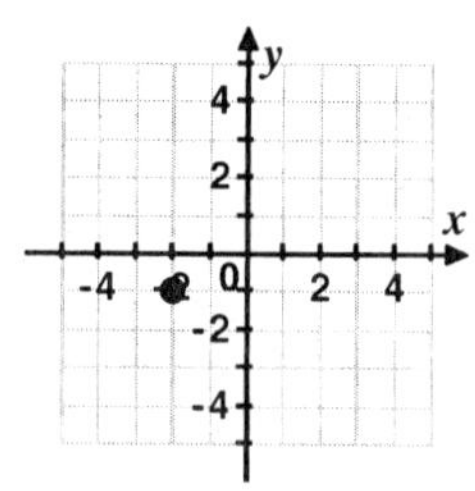

Quadrant III

7. $-10{,}000 < -2$ since $-10{,}000$ is to the left of -2 on the number line.

8. $6(4x-1-5y)=6(4x)-6(1)-6(5y)$
$=24x-6-30y$

9. Unemployment was a minimum of 2000, with about 4% unemployed.

10. The unemployment rate reached a maximum during 1992 of about 7.8%.

11.
$$5-6(x+2)=x-14$$
$$5-6x-12=x-14$$
$$-7-6x=x-14$$
$$-7-6x-x=x-14-x$$
$$-7-7x=-14$$
$$-7-7x+7=-14+7$$
$$-7x=-7$$
$$\frac{-7x}{-7}=\frac{-7}{-7}$$
$$x=1$$
The solution is 1.

12. $\frac{x}{5}-2=\frac{x}{3}$
Multiply both sides by the LCD, 15.
$$15\left(\frac{x}{5}-2\right)=15\left(\frac{x}{3}\right)$$
$$15\left(\frac{x}{5}\right)-15(2)=15\left(\frac{x}{3}\right)$$
$$3x-30=5x$$
$$3x-30-3x=5x-3x$$
$$-30=2x$$
$$\frac{-30}{2}=\frac{2x}{2}$$
$$-15=x$$
The solution is −15.

13. $V=\frac{1}{3}Ah$ for A
$$V=\frac{1}{3}Ah$$
$$3V=3\left(\frac{1}{3}Ah\right)$$
$$3V=Ah$$
$$\frac{3V}{h}=\frac{Ah}{h}$$
$$\frac{3V}{h}=A \text{ or } A=\frac{3V}{h}$$

14. $A = PB;\ A = 48,\ P = 30\% = 0.30$
$$A=PB$$
$$48=0.30B$$
$$\frac{48}{0.30}=\frac{0.30B}{0.30}$$
$$160=B$$
48 is 30% of 160.

15. Let w = width of parking lot (in yards).
Let $2w - 10$ = length of parking lot.
$$2(2w-10)+2w=400$$
$$4w-20+2w=400$$
$$6w-20=400$$
$$6w=420$$
$$w=70$$
The width is 70 yards and the length is 2(70) − 10 = 130 yards.

16. Let x = number of gallons of gasoline.
$$0.40x=30{,}000$$
$$\frac{0.40x}{0.40}=\frac{30{,}000}{0.40}$$
$$x=75{,}000$$
75,000 gallons of gasoline must be sold.

17. $-2 < x \leq 3$

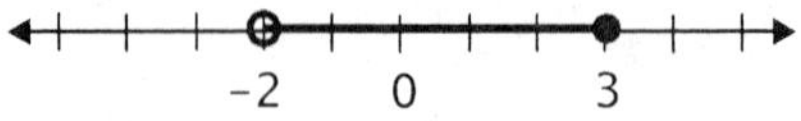

18.

$$3-3x > 12$$
$$3-3x-3 > 12-3$$
$$-3x > 9$$
$$\frac{-3x}{-3} < \frac{9}{-3}$$
$$x < -3$$

$\{x|x < -3\}$

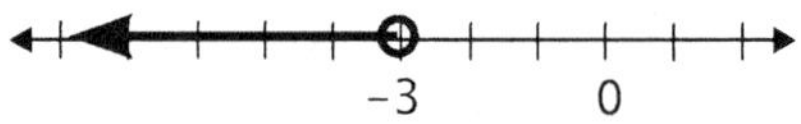

19.

$$5-2(3-x) \leq 2(2x+5)+1$$
$$5-6+2x \leq 4x+10+1$$
$$2x-1 \leq 4x+11$$
$$2x-1-4x \leq 4x+11-4x$$
$$-2x-1 \leq 11$$
$$-2x-1+1 \leq 11+1$$
$$-2x \leq 12$$
$$\frac{-2x}{-2} \geq \frac{12}{-2}$$
$$x \geq -6$$

$\{x|x \geq -6\}$

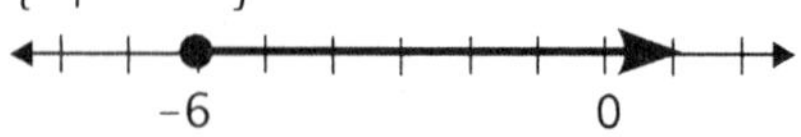

20. Let x = value of medical supplies sold.

$$600+0.04x > 2500$$
$$600+0.04x-600 > 2500-600$$
$$0.04x > 1900$$
$$\frac{0.04x}{0.04} > \frac{1900}{0.04}$$
$$x > 47{,}500$$

You must sell more than \$47,500 worth of medical supplies.

Chapter 3
Problem Solving

3.1 Exercise Set

1. $I = Prt; P = 4000, r = 4\% = 0.04, t = 1$
$I = Prt = (4000)(0.04)(1) = 160$
The interest at the end of one year is \$160.

3.

	Principal	·	Rate	=	Interest
7% Investment	x		0.07		$0.07x$
8% Investment	$20,000 - x$		0.08		$0.08(20,000 - x)$

The interest for the two investments combined must be \$1520, so the equation is
$0.07x + 0.08(20,000 - x) = 1520.$
Solve for x.

$$\begin{aligned} 0.07x + 1600 - 0.08x &= 1520 \\ -0.01x + 1600 &= 1520 \\ -0.10x + 1600 - 1600 &= 1520 - 1600 \\ -0.01x &= -80 \\ \frac{-0.01x}{-0.01} &= \frac{80}{-0.01} \\ x &= 8000 \end{aligned}$$

\$8000 should be invested at 7% and \$20,000 – \$8000 = \$12,000 should be invested at 8%.

5.

	Principal	·	Rate	=	Interest
8% Loan	x		0.08		$0.08x$
18% Loan	$120,000 - x$		0.18		$0.18(120,000 - x)$

$$\begin{aligned} 0.08x + 0.18(120,000 - x) &= 10,000 \\ 0.08x + 21,600 - 0.18x &= 10,000 \\ -0.10x + 21,600 &= 10,000 \\ -0.10x + 21,600 - 21,600 &= 10,000 - 21,600 \\ -0.10x &= -11,600 \\ \frac{-0.10x}{-0.10} &= \frac{-11,600}{-0.10} \\ x &= 116,000 \end{aligned}$$

\$116,000 was loaned at 8% and \$120,000 – \$116,000 = \$4000 was loaned at 18%.

7. Let x = amount invested at 6%.
Let 6000 – x = amount invested at 9%.
The accounts earned the same amount of interest, so the equation is $0.06x = 0.09(600 - x)$.
Solve for x.

$$0.06x = 540 - 0.09x$$
$$0.06x + 0.09x = 540$$
$$0.15x = 540$$
$$\frac{0.15x}{0.15} = \frac{540}{0.15}$$
$$x = 3600$$

\$3600 was invested at 6% and \$6000 – \$3600 = \$2400 was invested at 9%.

9. Let x = amount invested at 15%.
Let 50,000 – x = amount invested at 7%.

$$0.15x + 0.07(50{,}000 - x) = 6000$$
$$0.15x + 3500 - 0.07x = 6000$$
$$0.08x = 2500$$
$$\frac{0.08x}{0.08} = \frac{2500}{0.08}$$
$$x = 31{,}250$$

\$31,250 should be invested at 15% and \$50,000 – \$31,250 = \$18,750 should be invested at 7%.

11. Let x = the amount of acid that is in the solution.
$x = 0.30(20) = 6$
There are 6 milliliters of acid in the solution.

13.

	Numbers of Liters	·	Percent Fungicide	=	Amount of Fungicide
5% Fungicide Solution	x		0.05		$0.05x$
10% Fungicide Solution	$50 - x$		0.01		$0.1(50 - x)$
8% Fungicide Solution	50		0.08		0.08(50)

$$0.05x + 0.1(50 - x) = 0.08(50)$$
$$0.05x + 5 - 0.1x = 4$$
$$-0.05x + 5 = 4$$
$$-0.05x = -1$$
$$\frac{-0.05x}{-0.05} = \frac{-1}{-1.05}$$
$$x = 20$$

20 liters of 5% fungicide solution and 50 – 20 = 30 liters of 10% fungicide solution should be used.

15.

	Number Ounces ·	Percent Alcohol =	Amount of Alcohol
15% Alcohol	x	0.15	$0.15x$
20% Alcohol	4	0.2	4(0.2)
17% Alcohol	$x+4$	0.17	$0.17(x+4)$

$$0.15x+4(0.2)=0.17(x+4)$$
$$0.15x+0.8=0.17x+0.68$$
$$0.15x+0.8-0.17x=0.17x+0.68-0.17x$$
$$-0.02x+0.8=0.68$$
$$-0.02x+0.8-0.8=0.68-0.8$$
$$-0.02x=-0.12$$
$$-0.02x=-0.12$$
$$\frac{-0.02x}{-0.02}=\frac{-0.12}{-0.02}$$
$$x=6$$

To make a 17% alcohol solution, 6 ounces of 15% alcohol should be mixed with the 4 ounces of 20% alcohol solution.

17. Let x = number of students at north campus before merger.
Let $1000-x$ = number of students at south campus before merger.

$$0.1x+0.9(1000-x)=0.42(1000)$$
$$0.1x+900-0.9x=420$$
$$-0.8x+900=420$$
$$-0.8x=-480$$
$$\frac{-0.8x}{-0.8}=\frac{-420}{-0.8}$$
$$x=600$$

There were 600 students at the north campus and 1000 – 600 = 400 students at the south campus.

19.

	Rate ·	Time =	Distance
Slower Cyclist	10	x	$10x$
Faster Cyclist	12	x	$12x$

After x hours, the cyclists are 66 miles apart, so the equation is $10x+12x=66$.
Solve for x.

$$22x=66$$
$$x=3$$

They will be 66 miles apart after 3 hours.

21.

	Rate ·	Time =	Distance
Faster Truck	$x+5$	5	$5(x+5)$
Slower Truck	x	5	$5x$

$$5(x+5)+5x=600$$
$$5x+25+5x=600$$
$$10x+25=600$$
$$10x=575$$
$$x=57.5$$

The rate of the slower truck is 57.5 miles per hour and the rate of the faster truck is 57.5 + 5 = 62.5 miles per hour.

23.

	Rate ·	Time =	Distance
Car	55	x	$55x$
Bus	45	x	$45x$

The cars traveled a total of 240 miles, so the equation is $55x+45x=240$. Solve for x.

$$55x+45x=240$$
$$100x=240$$
$$x=2.4$$

The car and bus meet after 2.4 hours (2 hours and 24 minutes).

25.

	Rate ·	Time =	Distance
First Part of Trip	50	x	$50x$
Second Part of Trip	40	$5-x$	$40(5-x)$

$$50x+40(5-x)=220$$
$$50x+200-40x=220$$
$$10x+200=220$$
$$10x=20$$
$$x=2$$

The bus traveled for 2 hours at 50 miles per hour and for 3 hours at 40 miles per hour.

27.

	Pounds ·	Cost Per Pound =	Cost
A-Grade Coffee	x	\$9.50	$9.50x$
B- Grade Coffee	$20-x$	\$7.00	$7.00(20-x)$
Mixture	20	\$8.50	20(8.50)

$$9.50x + 7.00(20 - x) = 20(8.50)$$
$$9.50x + 140 - 7.00x = 170$$
$$2.50x + 140 = 170$$
$$2.50x = 30$$
$$x = 12$$

The mixture should contain 12 pounds of the A-grade coffee and 20 – 12 = 8 pounds of the B-grade coffee.

28.

	Pounds ·	Cost Per Pound	= Cost
More expensive tea	x	\$5.00	$5.00x$
Less expensive tea	$100 - x$	\$3.00	$3.00(100 - x)$
Blend	100	\$4.50	100(4.50)

$$5.00x + 3.00(100 - x) = 100(4.50)$$
$$5.00x + 300 - 3.00x = 450$$
$$2.00x + 300 = 450$$
$$2.00x = 150$$
$$x = 75$$

The blend should contain 75 pounds of the more expensive tea and 100 – 75 = 25 pounds of the less expensive tea.

29.

	Pounds ·	Cost Per Pound	= Cost
Cashews	x	\$7.40	$7.40x$
Peanuts	6	\$2.60	6(2.60)
Mixture	$x + 6$	\$5.80	$5.80(x + 6)$

$$7.40x + 6(2.60) = 5.80(x + 6)$$
$$7.40x + 15.60 = 5.80x + 34.80$$
$$1.60x + 15.60 = 34.80$$
$$1.60x = 19.20$$
$$x = 12$$

The mixture should contain 12 pounds of cashews.

30.

	Pounds ·	Cost Per Pound	= Cost
Cashews	x	\$8.96	$8.96x$
Chocolates	12	\$4.48	12(4.48)
Mixture	$x + 12$	\$7.28	$7.28(x + 12)$

$$8.96x + 12(4.48) = 7.28(x + 12)$$
$$8.96x + 53.76 = 7.28x + 87.36$$
$$1.68x + 53.76 = 87.36$$
$$1.68x = 33.60$$
$$x = 20$$

The mixture should contain 20 pounds of cashews.

31.

	Coins ·	Denomination =	Total Value
Dimes	x	0.10	$0.10x$
Quarters	$32-x$	0.25	$0.25(32-x)$

$$\begin{aligned} 0.10x+0.25(32-x)&=5.00 \\ 0.10x+8-0.25x&=5.00 \\ 8.00-0.15x&=5.00 \\ -0.15x&=-3.00 \\ x&=20 \end{aligned}$$

There are 20 dimes and 32 – 20 = 12 quarters.

33.

	Bills ·	Denomination =	Total Value
\$5 bills	$x+25$	5	$5(x+25)$
\$10 bills	x	10	$10x$

$$\begin{aligned} 5(x+25)+10x&=200 \\ 5x+125+10x&=200 \\ 15x+125&=200 \\ 15x&=75 \\ x&=5 \end{aligned}$$

There are 5 \$10 bills and 5 + 25 = 30 \$5 bills.

35.

	Number of Tickets ·	Cost =	Total Cost
Adult Tickets	x	\$25	$25x$
Children's Tickets	$305-x$	\$5	$5(305-x)$

$$\begin{aligned} 25x+5(305-x)&=6025 \\ 25x+1525-5x&=6025 \\ 20x+1525&=6025 \\ 20x&=4500 \\ x&=225 \end{aligned}$$

225 adult tickets and 305 – 225 = 80 children's tickets were sold.

37. – 43. Answers will vary.

45.

	Milliliters ·	Percent Minoxidil =	Amount of Minoxidil
15% Minoxidil	50	0.15	0.15(50)
Water	x	0	$0(x)$
10% Minoxidil	$50 + x$	0.10	$0.10(50 + x)$

$$0.15(50)+0(x)=0.10(x+50)$$
$$7.50=0.10x+5$$
$$2.50=0.10x$$
$$x=25$$

25 milliliters of water should be mixed with 50 milliliters of 15% minoxidil to make a 10% solution.

47. $3^2-5[4-3(2-6)]$

$=3^2-5[4-3(-4)]$

$=3^2-5(4+12)$

$=3^2-5(16)$

$=9-80$

$=-71$

48. The integers are -100, 0, and $\sqrt{16}=4$.

49.
$$3(x+3)=5(2x+6)$$
$$3x+9=10x+30$$
$$3x+9-10x=10x+30-10x$$
$$-7x+9-9=30-9$$
$$-7x=21$$
$$\frac{-7x}{-7}=\frac{21}{-7}$$
$$x=-3$$

The solution is -3.

3.2 Exercise Set

1. 24 to 48

$$\frac{24}{48}=\frac{24\cdot 1}{24\cdot 2}=\frac{1}{2}$$

3. 48 to 20

$$\frac{48}{20}=\frac{4\cdot 12}{4\cdot 5}=\frac{12}{5}$$

5. 27:36

$$\frac{27}{36}=\frac{9\cdot 3}{9\cdot 4}=\frac{3}{4}$$

7. 20 men to 10 women

$\frac{20}{10}=\frac{2}{1}$ or $2:1$

9. 10 women to 30 students

$\frac{10}{30}=\frac{1}{3}$ or $1:3$

11.
$$\frac{20}{x}=\frac{5}{3}$$
$$5x=20\cdot 3$$
$$5x=60$$
$$x=12$$

13. $\frac{x}{3}=\frac{5}{2}$
$2x=3\cdot 5$
$2x=15$
$x=\frac{15}{2}=7.5$

15. $\frac{x}{12}=-\frac{3}{4}$
$4x=12(-3)$
$4x=-36$
$x=-9$

17. $\frac{x-2}{12}=\frac{8}{3}$
$3(x-2)=12(8)$
$3x-6=96$
$3x=102$
$x=34$

19. $\frac{x}{7}=\frac{x+14}{5}$
$5x=7(x+14)$
$5x=7x+98$
$-2x=98$
$x=-49$

21. $\frac{x+9}{5}=\frac{x-10}{11}$
$5(x-10)=11(x+9)$
$5x-50=11x+99$
$-50=6x+99$
$-149=6x$
$-\frac{149}{6}=x$

23. $\frac{\text{price of 3 boxes}}{\text{3 boxes}}=\frac{\text{price of 8 boxes}}{\text{8 boxes}}$

$\frac{\text{3 boxes}}{\text{8 boxes}}=\frac{\text{price of 3 boxes}}{\text{price of 8 boxes}}$

$\frac{\text{8 boxes}}{\text{3 boxes}}=\frac{\text{price of 8 boxes}}{\text{price of 3 boxes}}$

24. $\frac{b}{a}=\frac{d}{c};\ \frac{a}{c}=\frac{b}{d};\ \frac{c}{a}=\frac{d}{b}$

25. $\frac{x}{a}=\frac{b}{c}$
$xc=ab$
$x=\frac{ab}{c}$

26. $\frac{a}{x}=\frac{b}{c}$
$xb=ac$
$x=\frac{ac}{b}$

27. $\frac{a+b}{c}=\frac{x}{d}$
$xc=d(a+b)$
$x=\frac{d(a+b)}{c}$ or $\frac{ad+bd}{c}$

28. $\frac{a-b}{c}=\frac{x}{d}$
$xc=d(a-b)$
$x=\frac{d(a-b)}{c}$ or $\frac{ad-bd}{c}$

29. $$\frac{x+a}{a}=\frac{b+c}{c}$$
$$a(b+c)=c(x+a)$$
$$ab+ac=cx+ca$$
$$ab+ac-ca=cx$$
$$ab=cx$$
$$\frac{ab}{c}=x$$

30. $$\frac{ax-b}{b}=\frac{c-d}{d}$$
$$d(ax-b)=b(c-d)$$
$$dax-db=bc-bd$$
$$dax=bc-bd+db$$
$$dax=bc$$
$$x=\frac{bc}{ad}$$

31. The ratio of the number of extinct languages in Brazil to that in the United States is $\frac{30}{22}=\frac{15}{11}$ or $15:11$.

33. Answers may vary.

35. Let x = the tax on a property with an assessed value of \$162,500.

$$\frac{\text{Tax on \$62,000 house}}{\text{Assessed value (\$62,000)}}=\frac{\text{Tax on \$162,500 house}}{\text{Assessed value \$162,500}}$$
$$\frac{\$720}{\$65,000}=\frac{\$x}{\$162,500}$$
$$\frac{720}{65,000}=\frac{x}{\$162,500}$$
$$65,000x=(720)(162,500)$$
$$65,000x=117,000,000$$
$$\frac{65,000x}{65,000}=\frac{117,000,000}{65,000}$$
$$x=1800$$

The tax on a property assessed at \$162,500 is \$1800.

37. Let x = the total number of fur seal pups in the rookery.

$$\frac{\text{Original number tagged fur seal pups}}{\text{Total number fur seal pups}}=\frac{\text{Number tagged fur seal pups in sample}}{\text{Number fur seal pups in sample}}$$
$$\frac{4963}{x}=\frac{218}{900}$$
$$218x=(4963)(900)$$
$$218x=4,466,700$$
$$\frac{218x}{218}=\frac{4,466,700}{218}$$
$$x\approx 20,490$$

There were approximately 20,490 fur seal pups in the rookery.

39. Let x = the monthly amount of child support for a father earning \$38,000 annually.

$$\frac{x}{\$38,000}=\frac{1}{40}$$
$$40x=38,000$$
$$x=950$$

A father earning \$38,000 annually has to pay \$950 in monthly child support.

41. Let x = the height of the critter.

$$\frac{\text{foot length person}}{\text{height of person}}=\frac{\text{foot length critter}}{\text{height of critter}}$$
$$\frac{10\text{ inches}}{67\text{ inches}}=\frac{23\text{ inches}}{x}$$
$$\frac{10}{67}=\frac{23}{x}$$
$$10x=(67)(23)$$
$$10x=1541$$
$$x=154.1$$

The height of the critter is 154.1 in.

43. 5 years after installation:

$$\frac{C_{\text{gas}}}{C_{\text{solar}}} = \frac{12{,}000+700x}{30{,}000+150x}$$
$$= \frac{12{,}000+700(5)}{30{,}000+150(5)}$$
$$= \frac{15{,}500}{30{,}750} = \frac{62}{123} \text{ or } 62:123$$

40 years after installation:

$$\frac{C_{\text{gas}}}{C_{\text{solar}}} = \frac{12{,}000+700(40)}{30{,}000+150(40)}$$
$$= \frac{40{,}000}{36{,}000} = \frac{10}{9} \text{ or } 10:9$$

The ratio of the total cost of gas to solar heating increases over time. Over a short period of time, gas heating is more economical, but over many years, solar heating becomes more economical.

45. – 49. Answers will vary.

51. Statement *b* is true.

53.
$$\frac{10+x}{20+x} = \frac{0.60}{1}$$
$$10+x = 0.60(20+x)$$
$$10+x = 12+0.60x$$
$$10+0.40x = 12$$
$$0.40x = 2$$
$$x = 5$$

5 consecutive pitches must be hit to raise the batting average to 0.600.

55. Let x = actual distance represented by 9.85 inches on a map.

$$\frac{2 \text{ inches}}{13.47 \text{ miles}} = \frac{9.85 \text{ inches}}{x \text{ miles}}$$
$$\frac{2}{13.47} = \frac{9.85}{x}$$
$$2x = (13.47)(9.85)$$
$$2x = 132.6795$$
$$x \approx 66.34$$

The person plans to travel 66.34 miles.

56.
$$-6x+2 \le 2(5-x)$$
$$-6x+2 \le 10-2x$$
$$-6x+2+2x \le 10-2x+2x$$
$$-4x+2 \le 10$$
$$-4x+2-2 \le 10-2$$
$$-4x \le 8$$
$$\frac{-4x}{-4} \ge \frac{8}{-4}$$
$$x \ge -2$$

The solution set is $\{x \mid x \ge -2\}$.

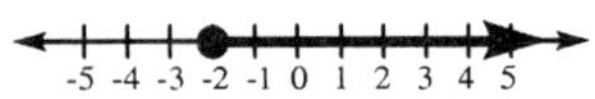

57. $A = PB$; $A = 112$, $P = 40\% = 0.40$
$$A = PB$$
$$112 = 0.40 \cdot B$$
$$\frac{112}{0.40} = \frac{0.40B}{0.40}$$
$$280 = B$$

112 is 40% of 280.

58.
$$9-2\left[4(x-3)+7\right]$$
$$= 9-2(4x-12+7)$$
$$= 9-2(4x-5)$$
$$= 9-8x+10$$
$$= 19-8x$$

Mid-Chapter Check Point – Chapter 3

1. Let x = the number of days it will take to type the manuscript.

$$\frac{600}{21} = \frac{230}{x}$$
$$600x = 21 \cdot 230$$
$$600x = 4830$$
$$x = 8.05$$

It will take 8.05 days to type the manuscript.

2.

	Number of Liters ·	Percent Alcohol =	Amount Of Alcohol
30% Alcohol Solution	x	0.30	$0.30x$
70% Alcohol Solution	$12 - x$	0.70	$0.70(12 - x)$
60% Alcohol Solution	12	0.60	0.60(12)

$$0.30x + 0.70(12 - x) = 0.60(12)$$
$$0.30x + 8.4 - 0.70x = 7.2$$
$$8.4 - 0.40x = 7.2$$
$$-0.40x = -1.2$$
$$x = 3$$

3 liters of 30% alcohol solution must be mixed with the 70% alcohol solution.

3.
$$\frac{4x}{9} = \frac{5}{-15}$$
$$-60x = 45$$
$$x = -\frac{45}{60} = -\frac{3}{4}$$

4.

	Principal ·	Rate =	Interest
8% Investment	x	0.08	$0.08x$
9% Investment	$25{,}000 - x$	0.09	$0.09(25{,}000 - x)$

$$0.08x + 0.09(25{,}000 - x) = 2135$$
$$0.08x + 2250 - 0.09x = 2135$$
$$2250 - 0.01x = 2135$$
$$-0.01x = -115$$
$$x = 11{,}500$$

She invested \$11,500 at 8% and \$25,000 - \$11,500 = \$13,500 at 9%.

5. $\dfrac{\text{number of men}}{\text{number of students}} = \dfrac{25}{60} = \dfrac{5}{12}$ or 5:12 or 5 to 12

6.

	Rate ·	Time =	Distance
Slower Plane	x	5	$5x$
Faster Plane	$x + 100$	5	$5(x + 100)$

$$5x + 5(x + 100) = 4250$$
$$5x + 5x + 500 = 4250$$
$$10x + 500 = 4250$$
$$10x = 3750$$
$$x = 375$$

The slow plane is traveling at 375 miles per hour and the fast plane is traveling at 375 + 100 = 475 miles per hour.

7. Let x = the total number of elk at the refuge.

$$\frac{\text{Original number of tagged elk}}{\text{Total number of elk}} = \frac{\text{Number of tagged elk in sample}}{\text{Total number of elk in sample}}$$

$$\frac{40}{x} = \frac{4}{80}$$
$$4x = 40 \cdot 80$$
$$4x = 3200$$
$$x = 800$$

There are approximately 800 elk at the refuge.

8.

	Quarts ·	Percent Milk Fat =	Amount Of Fat
1/2% Milk Fat	x	0.005	$0.005x$
2% Milk Fat	4	0.02	0.02(4)
1% Milk Fat	$x+4$	0.01	$0.01(x+4)$

$$0.005x + 0.02(4) = 0.01(x+4)$$
$$0.005x + 0.08 = 0.01x + 0.04$$
$$0.08 = 0.005x + 0.04$$
$$0.04 = 0.005x$$
$$8 = x$$

8 quarts of the $\frac{1}{2}$% milk fat should be added.

9.

$$\frac{2}{x+1} = \frac{3}{2x+3}$$
$$2(2x+3) = 3(x+1)$$
$$4x + 6 = 3x + 3$$
$$x + 6 = 3$$
$$x = -3$$

10.

	Principal ·	Rate =	Interest
4% Gain	x	0.04	$0.04x$
3% Loss	$4000 - x$	-0.03	$-0.03(4000 - x)$

$$0.04x - 0.03(4000 - x) = 55$$
$$0.04x - 120 + 0.03x = 55$$
$$0.07x - 120 = 55$$
$$0.07x = 175$$
$$x = 2500$$

She earned 4% on \$2500 and lost 3% on \$4000 – \$2500 = \$1500.

11.

	Rate	·	Time	=	Distance
Plane	450		t		$450t$
Car	50		$t-2$		$50(t-2)$

$$\begin{aligned} 450t+50(t-2)&=1900 \\ 450t+50t-100&=1900 \\ 500t-100&=1900 \\ 500t&=2000 \\ t&=4 \end{aligned}$$

You travel 4 hours by plane and 4 – 2 = 2 hours by car.

12. Let x = the distance that the spring stretches with an 80 pound weight.

$$\frac{\text{weight}_{(60)}}{\text{distance}_{(60)}}=\frac{\text{weight}_{(80)}}{\text{distance}_{(80)}}$$

$$\begin{aligned} \frac{60}{4}&=\frac{80}{x} \\ 60x&=4\cdot 80 \\ 60x&=320 \\ x&=\frac{16}{3}=5\frac{1}{3} \end{aligned}$$

An 80-pound weight will stretch the spring $5\frac{1}{3}$ inches.

3.3 Exercise Set

1. Use the formulas for the perimeter and area of a rectangle. The length is 6 m and the width is 3 m.

$P=2l+2w$

$\quad=2(6)+2(3)=12+6=18$

$A=lw=6\cdot 3=18$

The perimeter is 18 meters, and the area is 18 square meters.

3. Use the formula for the area of a triangle. The base is 14 in and the height is 8 in. The lengths of the other two sides are not used in calculating the area:

$A=\frac{1}{2}bh=\frac{1}{2}(14)(8)=56$

The area is 56 square inches.

5. Use the formula for the area of a trapezoid. The bases are 16 m and 10 m and the height is 7 m. The lengths of the other two sides of the trapezoid are not used in calculating the area.

$A=\frac{1}{2}h(a+b)$

$\quad=\frac{1}{2}(7)(16+10)=\frac{1}{2}\cdot 7\cdot 26=91$

The area is 91 square meters.

7. $A=lw;\ A=1250,\ w=25$

$A=lw$

$1250=l\cdot 25$

$50=l$

The length of the swimming pool is 50 feet.

9. $A = \frac{1}{2}bh; A = 20, b = 5$

$$A = \frac{1}{2}bh$$
$$20 = \frac{1}{2} \cdot 5 \cdot h$$
$$20 = \frac{5}{2}h$$
$$\frac{2}{5}(20) = \frac{2}{5}\left(\frac{5}{2}h\right)$$
$$8 = h$$

The height of the triangle is 8 feet.

11. $P = 2l + 2w;\ P = 188,\ w = 44$

$$188 = 2l + 2(44)$$
$$188 = 2l + 88$$
$$100 = 2l$$
$$50 = l$$

The length of the rectangle is 50 cm.

13. Use the formulas for the area and circumference of a circle. The radius is 4 cm.

$A = \pi r^2 = \pi(4)^2 = 16\pi \approx 50$

$C = 2\pi r = 2\pi(4) = 8\pi \approx 25$

The area is 16π cm^2 or approximately 50 cm^2, and the circumference is 8π cm or approximately 25 cm.

15. Since the diameter is 12 yd, the radius is $\frac{12}{2} = 6$ yd.

$A = \pi r^2 = \pi(6)^2 = 36\pi \approx 113$

$C = 2\pi r = 2\pi \cdot 6 = 12\pi \approx 38$

The area is 36π yd^2 or approximately 113 yd^2, and the circumference is 12π yd or approximately 38 yd.

17. $C = 2\pi r;\ C = 14\pi$

$$C = 2\pi r$$
$$14\pi = 2\pi r$$
$$\frac{14\pi}{2\pi} = \frac{2\pi r}{2\pi}$$
$$7 = r$$

The radius is 7 in and the diameter is 2(7 in) = 14 in.

19. Use the formula for the volume of a rectangular solid. The length and width are each 3 inches and the height is 4 inches.

$V = lwh = 3 \cdot 3 \cdot 4 = 36$

The volume is 36 in^3.

21. Use the formula for the volume of a cylinder. The radius is 5 cm and the height is 6 cm.

$$V = \pi r^2 h$$
$$= \pi(5)^2 6 = \pi(25)6 = 150\pi \approx 471$$

The volume of the cylinder is 150π cm^3 or approximately 471 cm^3.

23. Use the formula for the volume of a sphere. The diameter is 18 cm, so the radius is 9 cm.

$$V = \frac{4}{3}\pi r^3 = \frac{4}{3}\pi(9)^3 = 972\pi \approx 3052$$

The volume is 972π cm^3 or approximately 3052 cm^3.

25. Use the formula for the volume of a cone. The radius is 4 m and the height is 9 m.

$$V = \frac{1}{3}\pi r^2 h = \frac{1}{3}\pi(4)^2 \cdot 9 = 48\pi \approx 151$$

The volume is 48π m^3 or approximately 151 m^3.

27. Solve $V = \pi r^2 h$ for h

$$\frac{V}{\pi r^2} = \frac{\pi r^2 h}{\pi r^2}$$

$$\frac{V}{\pi r^2} = h$$

29. Smaller cylinder: $r = 3$ in, $h = 4$ in.

$V = \pi r^2 h = \pi(3)^2 \cdot 4 = 36\pi$

The volume of the smaller cylinder is $36\pi\, in^3$.

Larger cylinder: r = 3(3 in) = 9 in, h = 4 in.

$V = \pi r^2 h = \pi(9)^2 \cdot 4 = 324\pi$

The volume of the larger cylinder is 324π. The ratio of the volumes of the two cylinders is

$$\frac{V_{\text{larger}}}{V_{\text{smaller}}} = \frac{324\pi}{36\pi} = \frac{9}{1}.$$

So, the volume of the larger cylinder is 9 times the volume of the smaller cylinder.

31. The sum of the measures of the three angles of any triangle is $180°$, so $x + x + (x + 30) = 180$.

Solve for x.

$$3x + 30 = 180$$
$$3x = 150$$
$$x = 50$$

If $x = 50$, $x + 30 = 80$, so the three angle measures are $50°, 50°, \text{and}\, 80°$.

This solution checks because $50° + 50° + 80° = 180°$.

33. $4x + (3x + 4) + (2x + 5) = 180$

$$9x + 9 = 180$$
$$9x = 171$$
$$x = 19$$

If $x = 19$, then $4x = 76$, $3x + 4 = 61$, and $2x + 5 = 43$. Therefore, the angle measures are $76°$, $61°$, and $43°$.

This solution checks because $76° + 61° + 43° = 180°$.

35. Let x = the measure of the smallest angle.

Let $2x$ = the measure of the second angle.

Let $x + 20$ = the measure of the third angle.

$$x + 2x + (x + 20) = 180$$
$$4x + 20 = 180$$
$$4x = 160$$
$$x = 40$$

Measure of smallest angle is $40°$.

Measure of second angle is $2x = 80°$.

Measure of third angle is $x + 20 = 60°$.

37. If the measure of an angle is $58°$, the measure of its complement is $90° - 58° = 32°$.

39. If the measure of an angle is $88°$, the measure of its complement is $2°$.

41. If the measure of an angle is $132°$, the measure of its supplement is $180° - 132° = 48°$.

43. If the measure of an angle is $90°$, the measure of its supplement is $180° - 90° = 90°$.

45. Let x = the measure of the angle.
Let $90 - x$ = the measure of its complement.
The angle's measure is $60°$ more than that of its complement, so the equation is $x = (90 - x) + 60$.
Solve for x.

$$x = 90 - x + 60$$
$$x = 150 - x$$
$$2x = 150$$
$$x = 75$$

The measure of the angle is $75°$.
The complement of the angle is $90° - 75° = 15°$, and $75°$ is $60°$ more than $15°$.

47. Let x = the measure of the angle.
Let $180 - x$ = the measure of its supplement.

$$x = 3(180 - x)$$
$$x = 540 - 3x$$
$$4x = 540$$
$$x = 135$$

The measure of the angle is $135°$.
The measure of its supplement is $180° - 135° = 45°$, and $135° = 3(45°)$, so the proposed solution checks.

49. Let x = the measure of the angle.
Let $180 - x$ = the measure of its supplement, and, $90 - x$ = the measure of its complement.

$$180 - x = 3(90 - x) + 10$$
$$180 - x = 270 - 3x + 10$$
$$180 - x = 280 - 3x$$
$$2x = 100$$
$$x = 50$$

The measure of the angle is $50°$.
The measure of its supplement is $130°$ and the measure of its complement is $40°$. Since $130° = 3(40°) + 10°$, the proposed solution checks.

51.

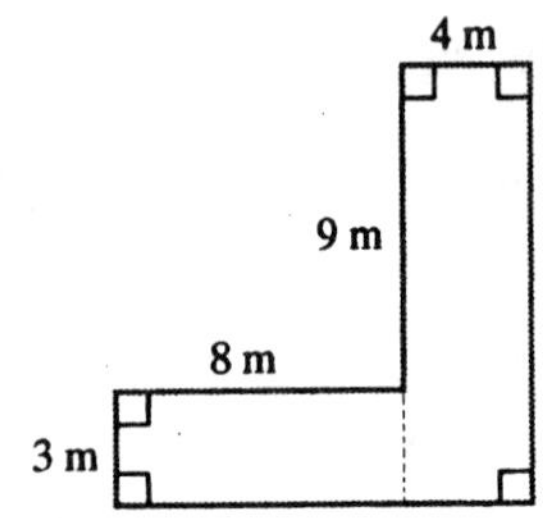

Divide the shape into two rectangles.

$$A_{\text{entire figure}} = A_{\text{bottom rectangle}} + A_{\text{side rectangle}}$$
$$A_{\text{entire figure}} = 3 \cdot 8 + 4(9 + 3)$$
$$= 24 + 4(12)$$
$$= 24 + 48$$
$$= 72$$

The area of the figure is 72 square meters.

52.

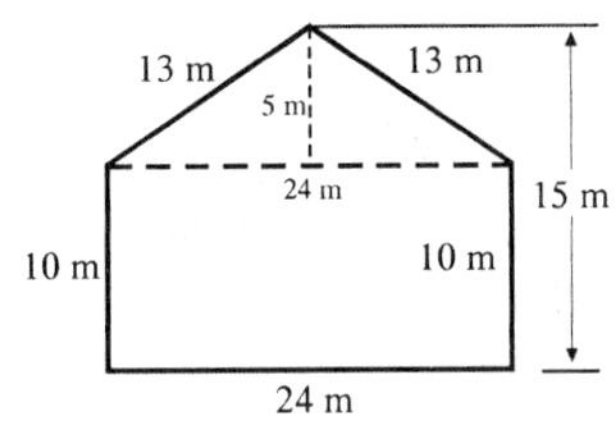

Divide the shape into a triangle and a rectangle.

$$A_{\text{entire figure}} = A_{\text{rectangle}} + A_{\text{triangle}}$$
$$A_{\text{entire figure}} = lw + \frac{1}{2}bh$$
$$= 10(24) + \frac{1}{2}(24)(15 - 10)$$
$$= 240 + \frac{1}{2}(24)(5)$$
$$= 240 + 60 = 300$$

The area of the figure is 300 m^2.

53.

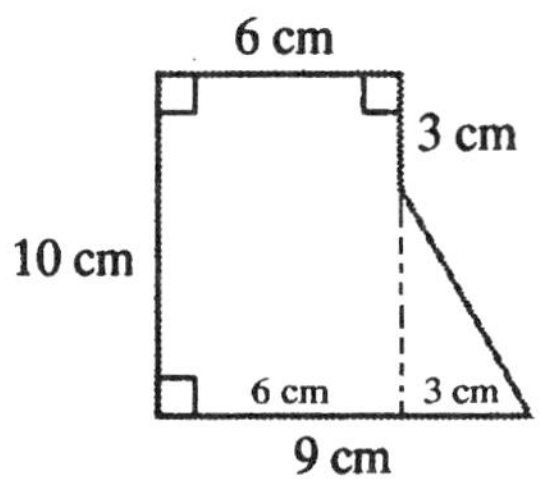

Divide the shape into a rectangle and a triangle.

$$A_{\text{entire figure}} = A_{\text{rectangle}} + A_{\text{triangle}}$$

$$\begin{aligned} A_{\text{entire figure}} &= lw + \frac{1}{2}bh \\ &= 10(6) + \frac{1}{2}(3)(10-3) \\ &= 60 + \frac{1}{2}(3)(7) \\ &= 60 + 10.5 = 70.5 \end{aligned}$$

The area of the figure is $70.5\ \text{cm}^2$.

54.

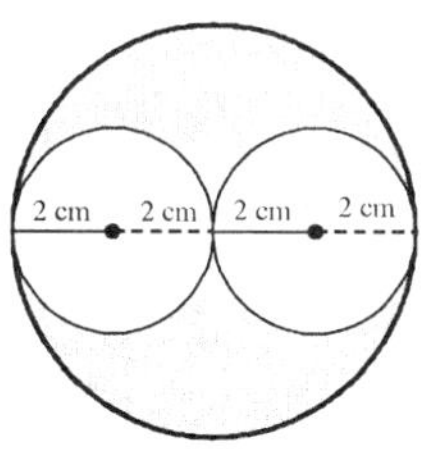

Subtract the area of the two smaller circles from the area of the larger circle. Note that the two smaller circles are the same size.

$$\begin{aligned} A_{\text{shaded}} &= A_{\text{larger circle}} - 2 \cdot A_{\text{smaller circle}} \\ &= \pi R^2 - 2 \cdot \pi r^2 \\ &= \pi(2+2)^2 - 2 \cdot \pi(2)^2 \\ &= \pi(4)^2 - 2 \cdot \pi(4) \\ &= 16\pi - 8\pi \\ &= 8\pi \end{aligned}$$

The shaded area is $8\pi\ \text{cm}^2$.

55. Subtract the volume of the pyramid from the volume of the rectangular solid.

$$\begin{aligned} V_{\text{shaded}} &= V_{\text{rectangular solid}} - V_{\text{pyramid}} \\ &= lwh - \frac{1}{3}lwh \\ &= (6)(6)(7) - \frac{1}{3}(6)(6)(7) \\ &= 252 - 84 \\ &= 168 \end{aligned}$$

The volume of the shaded region is 168 cubic centimeters.

56. Subtract the volume of the smaller cylinder from the volume of the larger cylinder.

$$\begin{aligned} V_{\text{shaded}} &= V_{\text{larger cylinder}} - V_{\text{smaller cylinder}} \\ &= \pi R^2 h - \pi r^2 h \\ &= \pi\left(\frac{6}{2}\right)^2 \cdot 10 - \pi\left(\frac{2}{2}\right)^2 \cdot 10 \\ &= \pi(3)^2 \cdot 10 - \pi(1)^2 \cdot 10 \\ &= 90\pi - 10\pi \\ &= 80\pi \end{aligned}$$

The volume of the shaded region is 80π cubic inches.

57. The area of the office is $(20\text{ ft})(16\text{ ft}) = 320\text{ ft}^2$. Use a proportion to determine how much of the yearly electric bill is deductible.

Let x = the amount of the electric bill that is deductible.

$$\begin{aligned} \frac{320}{2200} &= \frac{x}{4800} \\ 2200x &= (320)(4800) \\ 2200x &= 1{,}536{,}000 \\ \frac{2200x}{2200} &= \frac{1{,}546{,}000}{2200} \\ x &\approx 698.18 \end{aligned}$$

\$698.18 of the yearly electric bill is deductible.

59. The radius of the large pizza is $\frac{1}{2}\cdot 14$ $= 7$ inches, and the radius of the medium pizza is $\frac{1}{2}\cdot 7 \text{ inches} = 3.5 \text{ inches}$.

large pizza:
$A = \pi r^2 = \pi(7\,in.)^2$
$= 49\pi \text{ in}^2 \approx 154 \text{ in}^2$
medium pizza:
$A = \pi r^2 = \pi(3.5 \text{ in})^2$
$= 12.25 \text{ in}^2 \approx 38.465 \text{ in}^2$

For each pizza, find the price per inch by dividing the price by the area. Price per square inch for the large pizza $= \frac{\$12.00}{154 \text{ in}^2} \approx \frac{\$0.08}{\text{in}^2}$ and the price per square inch for the medium pizza $= \frac{\$5.00}{28.465 \text{ in}^2} \approx \frac{\$0.13}{\text{in}^2}$.
The large pizza is the better buy.

61. The area of the larger circle is $A = \pi r^2 = \pi \cdot 50^2 = 2500\pi \text{ ft}^2$.
The area of the smaller circle is $A = \pi r^2 = \pi \cdot 40^2 = 1600\pi \text{ ft}^2$.
The area of the circular road is the difference between the area of the larger circle and the area of the smaller circle.
$A = 2500\pi \text{ ft}^2 - 1600\pi \text{ ft}^2 = 900\pi \text{ ft}^2$
The cost to pave the circular road is $\$0.80(900\pi) \approx \$2262$.

63. To find the perimeter of the entire window, first find the perimeter of the lower rectangular portion. This is the bottom and two sides of the window, which is 3 ft + 6 ft + 6 ft = 15 ft. Next, find the perimeter or circumference of the semicircular portion of the window. The radius of the semicircle is $\frac{1}{2}\cdot 3\text{ft} = 1.5\text{ft}$, so the circumference is $\frac{1}{2}\cdot 2\pi r \approx 3.14(1.5) = 4.7\text{ft}$. So, approximately 15 ft + 4.7 ft = 19.7 ft of stripping would be needed to frame the window.

65. First, find the volume of water when the reservoir was full.
$V = lwh = 50 \cdot 0 \cdot 20 = 30{,}000$
The volume was 30,000 yd^3. Next, find the volume when the height of the water was 6 yards.
$V = 50 \cdot 30 \cdot 6 = 9000$
The volume was 9000 yd^3. The amount of water used in the three-month period was 30,000 yd^3 – 9000 yd^3 = 21,000 yd^3.

67. For the first can, the diameter is 6 in so the radius is 3 in and $V = \pi r^2 h = \pi(3)^2 \cdot 5 = 45\pi \approx 141.3$.
The volume of the first can is 141.3 in^3. For the second can, the diameter is 5 in, so the radius is 2.5 in and $V = \pi r^2 h = \pi(2.5)^2 \cdot 6 = 37.5\pi \approx 117.75$.
The volume of the second can is 117.75 in^2. Since the cans are the same price, the can with the greater volume is the better buy. Choose the can with the diameter of 3 inches and height of 5 inches.

69. Find the volume of a cylinder with radius 3 feet and height 2 feet 4 inches.

$2 \text{ ft } 4 \text{ in} = 2\frac{1}{3} \text{ feet} = \frac{7}{3} \text{ feet}$

$$V = \pi r^2 h$$
$$= \pi(3)^2\left(\frac{7}{3}\right) = \pi \cdot 9 \cdot \frac{7}{3} = 21\pi \approx 65.94$$

The volume of the tank is approximately 65.94 ft^3. This is a little over 1 ft^3 smaller than 67 ft^3 so it is too small to hold 500 gallons of water. Yes, you should be able to win your case.

71. – 79. Answers will vary

81. Area of smaller deck = (8 ft)(10 ft) = 80 ft^2
Area of larger deck = (12 ft)(15 ft) = 180 ft^2
Find the ratio of the areas.

$$\frac{A_{\text{larger}}}{A_{\text{smaller}}} = \frac{180\, ft^2}{80\, ft^2} = \frac{2.25}{1} \text{ or } 2.25:1$$

The cost will increase 2.25 times.

83. Let x = the radius of the original sphere.
Let $2x$ = the radius of the larger sphere.
Find the ratio of the volumes of the two spheres.

$$\frac{A_{\text{larger}}}{A_{\text{original}}} = \frac{\frac{4}{3}\pi(2x)^3}{\frac{4}{3}\pi x^3} = \frac{8x^3}{x^3} = \frac{8}{1} \text{ or } 8:1$$

If the radius of a sphere is doubled, the volume increases 8 times.

85. The angles marked $(2x)°$ and $(2x+40)°$ in the figure are supplementary, so their sum is 180°.

$$2x + (2x+40) = 180.$$
$$2x + 2x + 40 = 180$$
$$4x + 40 = 180$$
$$4x = 10$$
$$x = 35$$

The angle of inclination is 35°.

86.
$$P = 2s + b \text{ for } s$$
$$P - b = 2s$$
$$\frac{P-b}{2} = \frac{2s}{2}$$
$$\frac{P-b}{2} = s \text{ or } s = \frac{P-b}{2}$$

87.
$$\frac{x}{2} + 7 = 13 - \frac{x}{4}$$

Multiply both sides by the LCD, 4.

$$4\left(\frac{x}{2}+7\right) = 4\left(13 - \frac{x}{4}\right)$$
$$2x + 28 = 52 - x$$
$$2x + 28 + x = 52 - x + x$$
$$3x + 28 = 52$$
$$3x + 28 - 28 = 52 - 28$$
$$3x = 24$$
$$\frac{3x}{3} = \frac{24}{3}$$
$$x = 8$$

88.
$$\left[3\left(12 \div 2^2 - 3\right)^2\right]^2$$
$$= \left[3\left(12 \div 4 - 3\right)^2\right]^2$$
$$= \left[3\left(3-3\right)^2\right]^2 = \left(3 \cdot 0^2\right)^2 = 0^2 = 0$$

Chapter 3 Review Exercises

1.

	Principal ·	Rate =	Interest
8% Investment	x	0.08	$0.08x$
10% Investment	$10{,}000 - x$	0.10	$0.10(10{,}000 - x)$

The interest for the two investments combined must be \$940, so the equation is $0.08x + 0.10(10,000 - x) = 940$.

Solve for x.

$$0.08x + 1000 - 0.10x = 940$$
$$-0.02x + 1000 = 940$$
$$-0.02x + 1000 - 1000 = 940 - 1000$$
$$-0.02x = -60$$
$$\frac{-0.02x}{-0.02} = \frac{-60}{-0.02}$$
$$x = 3000$$

\$3000 was invested at 8% and \$10,000 – \$3000 = \$7000 was invested at 10%.

2. Let x = amount invested at 10%.
Let $x + 6000$ = amount invested at 12%.

$$0.10x + 0.12(x + 6000) = 2480$$
$$0.10x + 0.12x + 720 = 2480$$
$$0.22x + 720 = 2480$$
$$0.22x + 720 - 720 = 2480 - 720$$
$$0.22x = 1760$$
$$\frac{0.22x}{0.22} = \frac{1760}{0.22}$$
$$x = 8000$$

\$8000 was invested at 10% and \$8000 + \$6000 = \$14,000 was invested at 12%.

3.

	Gallons ·	Percent Salt =	Amount of Salt
75% Saltwater Solution	x	0.75	0.75
50% Saltwater Solution	$10 - x$	0.50	$0.50(10 - x)$
60% Saltwater Solution	10	0.60	0.60(10)

$$0.75x + 0.50(10 - x) = 0.60(10)$$
$$0.75x + 5 - 0.50x = 6$$
$$0.25x + 5 = 6$$
$$0.25x = 1$$
$$\frac{0.25x}{0.25} = \frac{1}{0.25}$$
$$x = 4$$

To obtain 10 gallons of a 60% saltwater solution, 4 gallons of a 75% saltwater solution and 10 – 4 = 6 gallons of a 50% saltwater solution must be used.

4. In a mixture of two alloys, the percentage of copper will fall between the percentages of the two alloys being combined. Since 70% is greater than both 30% and 50%, it is not possible to obtain an alloy that is 70% copper.

5. Let x = number of students at north campus before merger.
Let $150 - x$ = number of students at south campus before merger.

$$0.05x + 0.80(150 - x) = 0.05(150)$$
$$0.95x + 120 - 0.80x = 75$$
$$-0.75x + 120 = 75$$
$$-0.75x = -45$$
$$\frac{-0.75x}{-0.75} = \frac{-45}{-0.75}$$
$$x = 60$$

Before the merger, there were 60 students in the department at the north campus and 150 – 60 = 90 students at south campus.

6.

	Rate ·	Time =	Distance
Slower Train	60	x	$60x$
Faster Train	80	x	$80x$

$$60x + 80x = 420$$
$$140x = 420$$
$$\frac{40x}{140} = \frac{420}{140}$$
$$x = 3$$

They will be 400 miles apart after 3 hours.

7.

	Rate ·	Time =	Distance
Slower Bus	x	3	$3x$
Faster Bus	$x + 10$	3	$3(x + 10)$

$$3x + 3(x + 10) = 210$$
$$3x + 3x + 30 = 210$$
$$6x + 30 = 210$$
$$6x = 180$$
$$x = 30$$

The rate of the slower bus is 30 miles per hour and the rate of the faster bus is 30 + 10 = 40 miles per hour.

8.

	Bills	· Denomination	= Total Value
\$5 Bills	x	5	$5x$
\$10 Bills	$15 - x$	10	$10(15 - x)$

$$5x + 10(15 - x) = 120$$
$$5x + 150 - 10x = 120$$
$$150 - 5x = 120$$
$$-5x = -30$$
$$x = 6$$

There were 6 \$10 bills and 15 – 6 = 9 \$10 bills.

9. There is exactly enough information to solve the problem.

10. There is not enough information to solve the problem. Either the total quantity of the 15% solution, or the relationship between the quantities of the 12% and 20% solutions is needed.

11. There is exactly enough information to solve the problem.

12. There are 10 women and a total of 25 students in the class. The ratio of the number of women to the number of students in the class is $\frac{10}{25} = \frac{2}{5}$ or $2:5$.

13. The percentage of Americans who sleep 7 hours a night is 30% and the percentage who sleep 8 hours a night is 28%, so the ratio is $\frac{30\%}{28\%} = \frac{0.30}{0.28} = \frac{30}{28} = \frac{15}{14}$ or $15:14$.

14. The percentage of Americans who sleep less than 6 hours a night is 12% and the percentage who sleep more than 8 hours a night is 3%, so the ratio is $\frac{12\%}{3\%} = \frac{4}{1}$ or $4:1$.

15.

$$\frac{3}{x} = \frac{15}{25}$$
$$15x = 3 \cdot 25$$
$$15x = 75$$
$$\frac{15x}{15} = \frac{75}{15}$$
$$x = 5$$

16.

$$\frac{-7}{5} = \frac{91}{x}$$
$$-7x = 5 \cdot 9$$
$$-7x = 455$$
$$\frac{-7x}{-7} = \frac{455}{-7}$$
$$x = -65$$

17.

$$\frac{x+2}{2} = \frac{4}{5}$$
$$5(x+2) = 3 \cdot 4$$
$$5x + 10 = 12$$
$$5x = 2$$
$$x = \frac{2}{5}$$

18. $$\frac{5}{x+7}=\frac{3}{x+3}$$
$$5(x+3)=3(x+7)$$
$$5x+15=3x+21$$
$$5x+15-3x=3x+21-3x$$
$$2x+15=21$$
$$2x+15-15=21-15$$
$$2x=6$$
$$x=3$$

19. Let x = number of teachers needed for 5400 students.
$$\frac{3}{50}=\frac{x}{5400}$$
$$50x=3\cdot 5400$$
$$50x=16,200$$
$$\frac{50x}{50}=\frac{16,200}{50}$$
$$x=324$$
For an enrollment of 5400 students, 324 teachers are needed.

20. Let x = number of trout in the lake.
$$\frac{\text{Original Number Tagged Deer}}{\text{Total Number of Deer}}=\frac{\text{Number Tagged Deer in Sample}}{\text{Total Number Deer in Sample}}$$
$$\frac{112}{x}=\frac{32}{82}$$
$$32x=112\cdot 82$$
$$32x=9184$$
$$\frac{32x}{32}=\frac{9184}{32}$$
$$x=287$$
There are 287 trout in the lake.

21. Let x = monthly sales if \$96,000 is spent on advertising.
$$\frac{12,000\text{ skates}}{\$60,000}=\frac{x\text{ skates}}{\$96,000}$$
$$\frac{12,000}{60,000}=\frac{x}{96,000}$$
$$\frac{1}{5}=\frac{x}{96,000}$$
$$5x=96,000$$
$$x=19,200$$
If \$96,00 is spent on advertising, they will sell 19,200 pairs of skates.

22. Find the area of a rectangle with length 6.5 ft and width 5 ft.
$A=lw=(6.5)(5)=32.5$
The area is 32.5 ft^2.

23. Find the area of a triangle with base 20 cm and height 5 cm.
$$A=\frac{1}{2}bh=\frac{1}{2}(20)(5)=50$$
The area is 50 cm^2.

24. Find the area of a trapezoid with bases 22 yd and 5 yd and height 10 yd.
$$A=\frac{1}{2}h(a+b)$$
$$=\frac{1}{2}(10)(22+5)$$
$$=\frac{1}{2}\cdot 10\cdot 27=135$$
The area is 135 yd^2.

25. Since the diameter is 20 m, the radius is $\frac{20}{2}=10$ m.
$$C=2\pi=2\pi(10)=20\pi\approx 63$$
$$A=\pi r^2=\pi(10)^2=100\approx 314$$
The circumference is 20π m or approximately 63 m; the area is 100π m^2 or approximately 314 m^2.

26. $A = \frac{1}{2}bh; A = 42, b = 14$

$A = \frac{1}{2}bh$

$42 = \frac{1}{2} \cdot 14 \cdot h$

$42 = 7h$

$6 = h$

The height of the sail is 6 ft.

27. Area of floor:

$A = bh = (12\,\text{ft})(15\,\text{ft}) = 180\,\text{ft}^2$

Area of base of stove:

$A = bh = (3\,\text{ft})(4\,\text{ft}) = 12\,\text{ft}^2$

Area of bottom of refrigerator:

$A = bh = (3\,\text{ft})(14\,\text{ft}) = 12\,\text{ft}^2$

The area to be covered with floor tile is $180\,\text{ft}^2 - 12\,\text{ft}^2 - 12\,\text{ft}^2 = 156\,\text{ft}^2$.

28. First, find the area of a trapezoid with bases 80 ft and 100 ft and height 60 ft.

$A = \frac{1}{2}h(a+b)$

$= \frac{1}{2}(60)(80+100) = 5400$

The area of the yard is 5400 ft^2. The cost is \$0.35(5400) = \$1890.

29. The radius of the medium pizza is $\frac{1}{2} \cdot 14 \text{ inches} = 7 \text{ inches}$, and the radius of each small pizza is $\frac{1}{2} \cdot 8 \text{ inches} = 4 \text{ inches}$.

Medium pizza:

$A = \pi r^2 = \pi(7\text{ in.})^2$

$= 49\pi\,\text{in}^2 \approx 154\,\text{in}^2$

Small pizza:

$A = \pi r^2 = \pi(4\,\text{in.})^2$

$= 16\pi\,\text{in}^2 \approx 50.24\,\text{in}^2$

The area of one medium pizza is approximately 154 in^2 and the area of two small pizzas is approximately 2(50.24) = 100.48 in^2. Since the price of one medium pizza is the same as the price of two small pizzas and the medium pizza has the greater area, the medium pizza is the better buy. (Because the prices are the same, it is not necessary to find price per square inch in this case.)

30. Find the volume of a rectangular solid with length 5 cm, width 3 cm, and height 4 cm.

$A = lwh = 5 \cdot 3 \cdot 4 = 60$

The volume is 60 cm^3.

31. Find the volume of a cylinder with radius 4 yd and height 8 yd.

$V = \pi r^2 h$

$= \pi(4)^2 \cdot 8 = 128\pi \approx 402$

The volume is 138π $\text{yd}^3 \approx 402$ yd^3.

32. Find the volume of a sphere with radius 6 m.

$V = \frac{4}{3}\pi r^3$

$= \frac{4}{3}\pi(6)^3 = \frac{4}{3} \cdot \pi \cdot 216$

$= 288\pi \approx 904$

The volume is 288π $\text{m}^3 \approx 904$ m^3.

33. Find the volume of each box.

$V = lwh = (8\text{m})(4\text{m})(3\text{m}) = 96\text{m}^3$

The space required for 50 containers is $50(96\text{ m}^3) = 4800\text{ m}^3$.

34. Since the diameter of the fish tank 6 ft, the radius is 3 ft.
$V = \pi r^2 h = \pi(3)^2 \cdot 3 = 27\pi \approx 84.78$
The volume of the tank is approximately 85 ft^3. Divide by 5 to determine how many fish can be put in the tank.
$\frac{84.78}{5} \approx 16.96$
There is enough water in the tank for 16 fish. Round down to 16, since 0.96 of a fish cannot be purchased.

35. The sum of the measures of the angles of any triangle is $180°$, so $x + 3x + 2x = 180$.
Solve the equation for x.
$6x = 180$
$x = 30$
If $x = 30$, then $3x = 90$ and $2x = 60$, so the angles measure $30°$, $60°$, and $90°$.

36. Let x = the measure of the second angle.
Let $2x + 15$ = the measure of the first angle.
Let $x + 25$ = the measure of the third angle.
$$x + (2x + 15) + (x + 25) = 180$$
$$4x + 40 = 180$$
$$4x = 140$$
$$x = 35$$
If $x = 35$, then $2x + 15 = 2(35) + 15 = 85$ and $x + 25 = 35 + 25 = 60$. The angles measure $35°$, $85°$, and $60°$.

37. If the measure of an angle is $57°$, the measure of its complement is $90° - 57° = 33°$

38. If the measure of an angle is $75°$, the measure of its supplement is $180° - 75° = 105°$.

39. Let x = the measure of the angle.
Let $90 - x$ = the measure of its complement.
angle = 25 more than complement
angle = complement + 25
$$x = (90 - x) + 25$$
$$x = 115 - x$$
$$2x = 115$$
$$x = 57.5$$
The measure of the angle is $57.5°$.

40. Let x = the measure of the angle.
Let $180 - x$ = the measure of its supplement.
supplement = 45 less than 4 times angle
supplement = 4 times angle − 45
$$180 - x = 4x - 45$$
$$180 - 5x = -45$$
$$-5x = -225$$
$$x = 45$$
If $x = 45$, then $180 - x = 135$. The measure of the angle is $45°$ and the measure of its supplement is $135°$.

Chapter 3 Test

1. Let x = amount invested at 9%.
Let $6000 - x$ = amount invested at 6%.

$$0.09x + 0.06(6000 - x) = 480$$
$$0.09x + 360 - 0.06x = 480$$
$$0.03x + 360 = 480$$
$$0.03x = 120$$
$$\frac{0.03x}{0.03} = \frac{120}{0.03}$$
$$x = 4000$$

\$4000 was invested at 9% at \$6000 – \$4000 = \$2000 was invested at 6%.

2. Let x = number of milliliters of 50% acid solution.
Let $100 - x$ = number of milliliters of 80% acid solution.

$$0.50x + 0.80(100 - x) = 0.68(100)$$
$$0.50x + 80 - 0.80x = 68$$
$$-0.03x = -12$$
$$\frac{-0.30x}{-0.30} = \frac{-12}{-0.30}$$
$$x = 40$$

40 milliliters of 50% acid solution and 100 – 40 = 60 milliliters of 80% acid solution must be used.

3.

	R	· T	= D
Fast Car	45	x	$45x$
Slow Car	35	x	$35x$

$$45x + 35x = 400$$
$$80x = 400$$
$$x = 5$$

The two cars will meet after 5 hours.

4. $\frac{\text{men}}{\text{students}} = \frac{20}{20+15} = \frac{20}{35} = \frac{4}{7}$ or 4 : 7

5.
$$\frac{-5}{8} = \frac{x}{12}$$
$$8x = -60$$
$$x = \frac{60}{8} = -\frac{15}{2}$$

6. Let x = number of tule elk in the park.

$$\frac{200}{x} = \frac{5}{150}$$
$$5x = 30{,}000$$
$$x = 6000$$

There are 6000 tule elk in the park.

7. Let x = pressure on object 330 feet below the surface.

$$\frac{\frac{25\text{ pounds per}}{\text{square inch}}}{60\text{ feet}} = \frac{\frac{x\text{ pounds per}}{\text{square inch}}}{330\text{ feet}}$$
$$\frac{25}{60} = \frac{x}{330}$$
$$60x = 25 \cdot 330$$
$$60x = 8250$$
$$x = 137.5$$

The pressure 330 feet below the surface is 137.5 pounds per square inch.

8. Find the area of a triangle with base 47 m and height 22 m.

$$A = \frac{1}{2}bh = \frac{1}{2}(47)(22) = 517$$

The area of the triangle is 517 m^2.

9. Find the area of a trapezoid with height 15 in, lower base 40 in and upper base 30 in.

$$A = \frac{1}{2}h(a+b)$$
$$= \frac{1}{2}(15)(40+30)$$
$$= \frac{1}{2}\cdot 15\cdot 70 = 525$$

The area is 525 in^2.

10. Find the volume of a rectangular solid with length 3 in, width 2 in, and height 3 in.

$V = lwh = 3\cdot 2\cdot 3 = 18$

The volume is 18 in^3.

11. Find the volume of a cylinder with radius 5 cm and height 7 cm.

$$V = \pi r^2 h$$
$$= \pi(5)^2\cdot 7 = \pi\cdot 25\cdot 7$$
$$= 175\pi \approx 550$$

The volume is 175π cm^3 or approximately 550 cm^3.

12. The area of the floor is

$A = (40\,\text{ft})(50\,\text{ft}) = 2000\,\text{ft}^2$.

The area of each tile is

$A = (2\,\text{ft})(2\,\text{ft}) = 4\,\text{ft}^2$.

The number of tiles needed is

$\frac{2000\,\text{ft}^2}{4\,\text{ft}^2} = 500.$

Since there are 10 tiles in a package, the number of packages needed is

$\frac{500}{10} = 50.$

Since each package costs \$13, the cost for enough tiles to cover the floor is $50(\$13) = \$650$.

13. $A = \frac{1}{2}bh; A = 56, b = 8$

$$A = \frac{1}{2}bh$$
$$56 = \frac{1}{2}\cdot 8\cdot h$$
$$56 = 4h$$
$$14 = h$$

The height of the sail is 14 feet.

14. Let x = the measure of the second angle.
Let $3x$ = the measure of the first angle.
Let $x - 30$ = the measure of the third angle.

$$x + 3x + (x-30) = 180$$
$$5x - 30 = 180$$
$$5x = 210$$
$$x = 42$$

The measure of the first angle = $3x$ = $3(42°) = 126°$.
The measure of the second angle = x = $42°$.
The measure of the third angle = x $-30 = 42° - 30° = 12°$.

15. Let x = the measure of the angle.
Let $90 - x$ = the measure of its complement.

$$x = (90-x)+16$$
$$x = 106 - x$$
$$2x = 106$$
$$x = 53$$

The measure of the angle is $53°$.

Cumulative Review Exercises (Chapters 1-3)

1. $\frac{-9(3-6)}{(-12)(3)+(-3-5)(8-4)}$
$= \frac{-9(-3)}{-36+(-8)(4)}$
$= \frac{27}{-36-32} = \frac{27}{-68} = -\frac{27}{68}$

2. $8-3[2(x-1)+5]$
$= 8-3(2x-2+5)$
$= 8-3(2x+3)$
$= 8-6x-9$
$= -1-6x$

3. The integers are $-3, 0,$ and $\sqrt{9}=3$.

4.

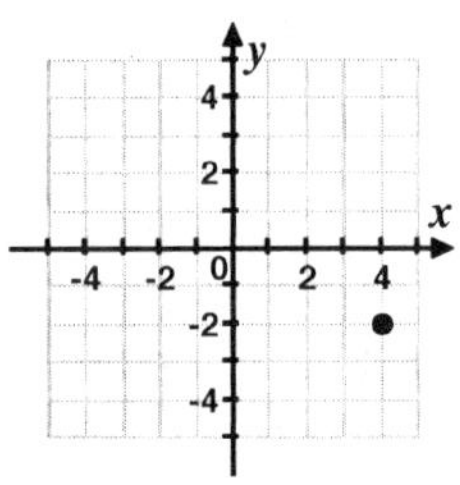

Quadrant IV

5. $-x^2-10x; x=-3$
$-x^2-10x = (-3)^2-10(-3)$
$= 9+30 = 39$

6. -2000 is to be left of -3 on the number line, so $-2000 < -3$.

7. $-4+(-11)+21 = -15+21 = 6$
The temperature at noon was $6\,°\text{F}$.

8. $10(2x-1) = 8(2x+1)+14$
$20x-10 = 16x+8+14$
$20x-10 = 16x+22$
$4x-10 = 22$
$4x = 32$
$x = 8$
The solution is 8.

9. $\frac{x}{5}+\frac{2x}{3} = x+\frac{1}{15}$
$15\left(\frac{x}{5}+\frac{2x}{3}\right) = 15\left(x+\frac{1}{15}\right)$
$3x+10x = 15x+1$
$13x = 15x+1$
$-2x = 1$
$\frac{-2x}{-2} = \frac{1}{-2}$
$x = -\frac{1}{2}$
The solution is $-\frac{1}{2}$.

10. $A = \frac{m+n}{2}$
$2A = 2\left(\frac{m+n}{2}\right)$
$2A = m+n$
$2A-n = m$ or $m = 2A-n$

11. $D = 4x+30; D = 150$
$150 = 4x+30$
$120 = 4x$
$30 = x$
According to the formula, the average debt for graduating doctors will be \$150,000 in 1985 + 30 = 2015.

12. $A = PB; A = 144, P = 60\% = 0.6$

$$A = PB$$
$$144 = 0.06 \cdot B$$
$$\frac{144}{0.60} = \frac{0.60 \cdot B}{B}$$
$$240 = B$$

144 is 60% of 240.

13. Let w = the width of the field.
Let $2w + 14$ = the length of the field.

$$2w + 2(2w + 14) = 346$$
$$2w + 4w + 80 = 346$$
$$6w + 28 = 318$$
$$w = 53$$

If $w = 53$, then $2w + 14 = 2(53) + 14 = 106 + 14 = 120$. The width is 53 meters and the length is 120 meters.

14. Let x = the person's weight before the weight loss.

$$x - 0.10x = 180$$
$$0.90 = 180$$
$$\frac{0.90x}{0.90} = \frac{180}{0.90}$$
$$x = 200$$

The person's weight was 200 pounds.

15.

$$5x - 5 \le -5$$
$$5x + 5 + 5 \le -5 + 5$$
$$5x \le 0$$
$$\frac{5x}{5} \le \frac{0}{5}$$
$$x \le 0$$

$\{x | x \le 0\}$

16.

$$-5x + 9 > -2x + 6$$
$$-5x + 9 + 2x > -2x + 6 + 2x$$
$$-3x + 9 > 6$$
$$-3x + 9 - 9 > 6 - 9$$
$$-3x > -3$$
$$\frac{-3x}{-3} < \frac{-3}{-3}$$
$$x < 1$$

$\{x | x < 1\}$

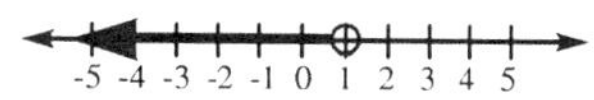

17.

	R · T = D		
Slow Runner	6	x	$6x$
Fast Runner	8	x	$8x$

$$6x + 8x = 21$$
$$14x = 21$$
$$x = \frac{21}{14} = \frac{3}{2} \text{ or } 1\frac{1}{2}$$

They will be 21 miles apart in $1\frac{1}{2}$ hours.

18.

$$\frac{-5}{20} = \frac{x}{21}$$
$$20x = (-5)(21)$$
$$20x = -105$$
$$\frac{20x}{20} = \frac{-105}{20}$$
$$x = -\frac{21}{4}$$

19. Let x = Buchanan's age.
Let $x + 4$ = Reagan's age.

$$x+(x+4)=134$$
$$2x+4=134$$
$$2x=130$$
$$x=65$$

Buchanan was 65 years old and Reagan was $x + 4 = 65 + 4 = 69$ years old.

20. Use the formula increase = percent · original. The increase is $13 - 4 = 9$.

$$9 = P\cdot 4$$
$$\frac{9}{4}=\frac{P\cdot 4}{4}$$
$$2.25 = P$$

9 is 2.25 = 225% of 4. This means that the PBS audience increased by 225%. John Tesh did not report the percent increase correctly.

Chapter 4
Linear Equations and Inequalities in Two Variables

4.1 Exercise Set

1. $y = 3x$

(2,3):
$3 = 3(2)$
$3 = 6$ false
(2,3) is not a solution.

(3,2):
$2 = 3(3)$
$2 = 9$ false
(3,2) is not a solution.

(−4,−12):
$-12 = 3(-4)$
$-12 = -12$ true
(−4,−12) is a solution.

3. $y = -4x$

$(-5,-20)$:
$-20 = -4(-5)$
$-20 = 20$ false
$(-5,-20)$ is not a solution.

(0,0):
$0 = -4(0)$
$0 = 0$ true
$(0,0)$ is a solution.

$(9,-36)$:
$-36 = -4(9)$
$-36 = -36$ true
$(9,-36)$ is a solution.

5. $y = 2x + 6$

$(0,6)$:
$6 = 2(0) + 6$
$6 = 6$ true
$(0,6)$ is a solution.

$(-3,0)$:
$0 = 2(-3) + 6$
$0 = 0$ true
$(-3,0)$ is a solution.

$(2,-2)$:
$-2 = 2(2) + 6$
$-2 = 10$ false
$(2,-2)$ is not a solution.

7. $3x + 5y = 15$

$(-5,6)$:
$3(-5) + 5(6) = 15$
$-15 + 30 = 15$
$15 = 15$ true
$(-5,6)$ is a solution.

$(0,5)$:
$3(0) + 5(5) = 15$
$0 + 25 = 15$
$25 = 15$ false
$(0,5)$ is not a solution.

$(10,-3)$:
$3(10) + 5(-3) = 15$
$30 - 15 = 15$
$15 = 15$ true
$(10,-3)$ is a solution.

9. $x+3y=0$

$(0,0)$:

$0+3(0)=0$

$0=0$ true

$(0,0)$ is a solution.

$\left(1,\frac{1}{3}\right)$:

$1+3\left(\frac{1}{3}\right)=0$

$1+1=0$

$2=0$ false

$\left(1,\frac{1}{3}\right)$ is not a solution.

$\left(2,-\frac{2}{3}\right)$:

$2+3\left(-\frac{2}{3}\right)=0$

$2-2=0$

$0=0$ true

$\left(2,-\frac{2}{3}\right)$ is a solution.

11. $x-4=0$

$(4,7)$:

$4-4=0$

$0=0$ true

$(4,7)$ is a solution.

$(3,4)$:

$3-4=0$

$-1=0$ false

$(3,4)$ is not a solution.

$(0,-4)$:

$0-4=0$

$-4=0$ false

$(0,-4)$ is not a solution.

13.

x	$y=12x$	(x,y)
-2	$y=12(-2)=-24$	$(-2,-24)$
-1	$y=12(-1)=-12$	$(-1,-12)$
0	$y=12(0)=0$	$(0,0)$
1	$y=12(1)=12$	$(1,12)$
2	$y=12(2)=24$	$(2,24)$

15.

x	$y=-10x$	(x,y)
-2	$y=-10(-2)=20$	$(-2,20)$
-1	$y=-10(-1)=10$	$(-1,10)$
0	$y=-10(0)=0$	$(0,0)$
1	$y=-10(1)=-10$	$(1,-10)$
2	$y=-10(2)=-20$	$(2,-20)$

17.

x	$y=8x-5$	(x,y)
-2	$y=8(-2)-5=-21$	$(-2,-21)$
-1	$y=8(-1)-5=-13$	$(-1,-13)$
0	$y=8(0)-5=-5$	$(0,-5)$
1	$y=8(1)-5=3$	$(1,3)$
2	$y=8(2)-5=11$	$(2,11)$

19.

x	$y=-3x+7$	(x,y)
-2	$y=-3(-2)+7=13$	$(-2,13)$
-1	$y=-3(-1)+7=10$	$(-1,10)$
0	$y=-3(0)+7=7$	$(0,7)$
1	$y=-3(1)+7=4$	$(1,4)$
2	$y=-3(2)+7=1$	$(2,1)$

21.

x	$y=x$	(x,y)
-2	$y=-2$	$(-2,-2)$
-1	$y=-1$	$(-1,-1)$
0	$y=0$	$(0,0)$
1	$y=1$	$(1,1)$
2	$y=2$	$(2,2)$

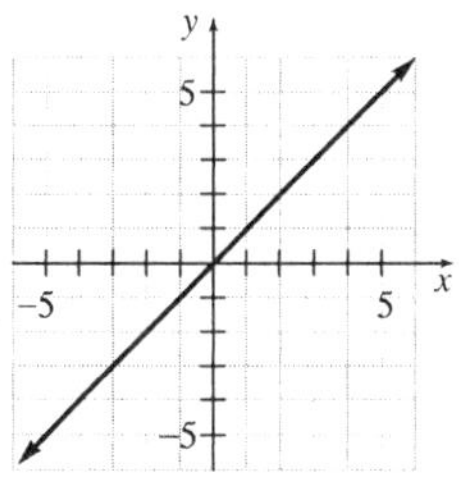

23.

x	$y=x-1$	(x,y)
-2	$y=-2-1=-3$	$(-2,-3)$
-1	$y=-1-1=-2$	$(-1,-2)$
0	$y=0-1=-1$	$(0,-1)$
1	$y=1-1=0$	$(1,0)$
2	$y=2-1=1$	$(2,1)$

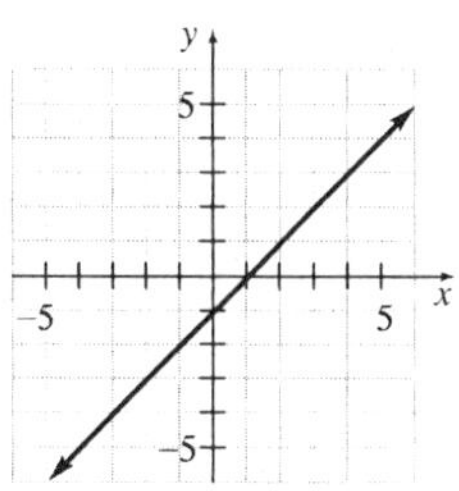

25.

x	$y=2x+1$	(x,y)
-2	$y=2(-2)+1=-3$	$(-2,-3)$
-1	$y=2(-1)+1=-1$	$(-1,-1)$
0	$y=2(0)+1=1$	$(0,1)$
1	$y=2(1)+1=3$	$(1,3)$
2	$y=2(2)+1=5$	$(2,5)$

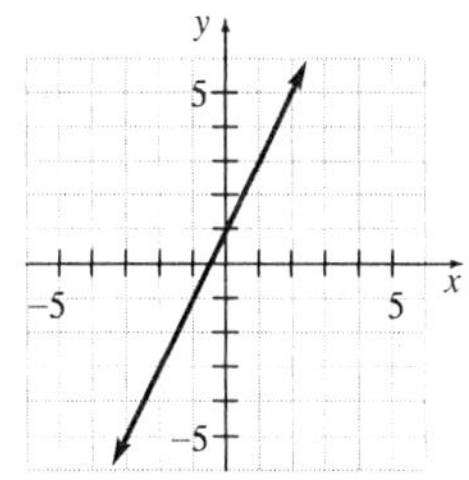

27.

x	$y=-x+2$	(x,y)
-2	$y=-(-2)+2=4$	$(-2,4)$
-1	$y=-(-1)+2=3$	$(-1,3)$
0	$y=-0+2=2$	$(0,2)$
1	$y=-1+2=1$	$(1,1)$
2	$y=-2+2=0$	$(2,0)$

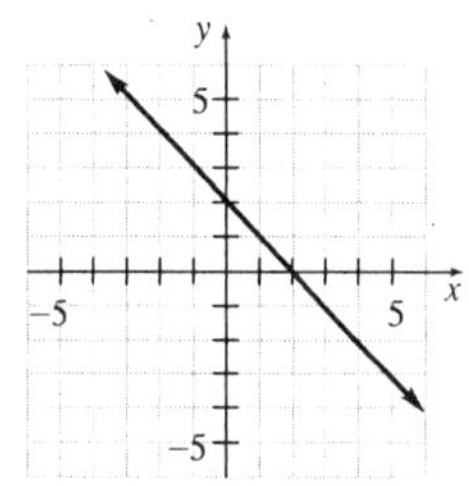

29.

x	$y=-3x-1$	(x,y)
-2	$y=-3(-2)-1=5$	$(-2,5)$
-1	$y=-3(-1)-1=2$	$(-1,2)$
0	$y=-3(0)-1=-1$	$(0,-1)$
1	$y=-3(1)-1=-4$	$(1,-4)$
2	$y=-3(2)-1=-7$	$(2,-7)$

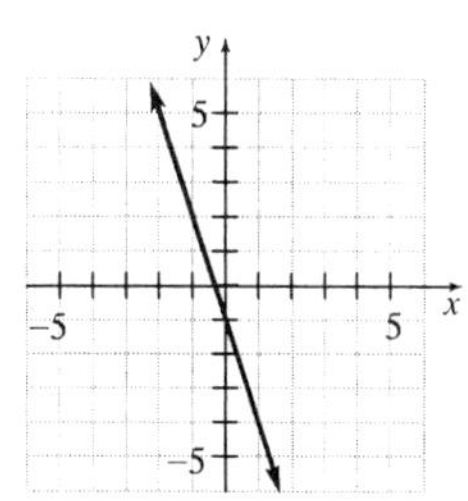

31.

x	$y=\frac{1}{2}x$	(x, y)
-4	$y=\frac{1}{2}(-4)=-2$	$(-4,-2)$
-2	$y=\frac{1}{2}(-2)=-1$	$(-2,-1)$
0	$y=\frac{1}{2}(0)=0$	$(0,0)$
2	$y=\frac{1}{2}(2)=1$	$(2,1)$
4	$y=\frac{1}{2}(4)=2$	$(4,2)$

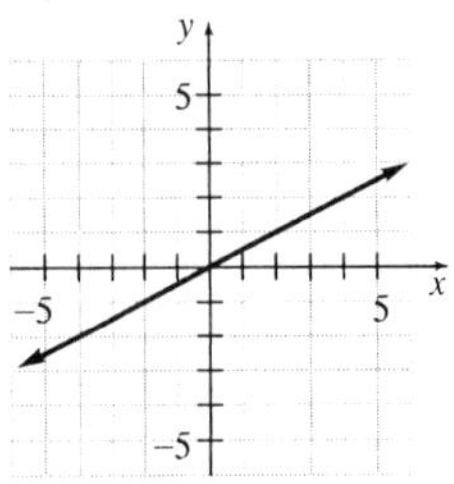

35.

x	$y=\frac{1}{3}x+1$	(x, y)
-6	$y=\frac{1}{3}(-6)+1=-1$	$(-6,-1)$
-3	$y=\frac{1}{3}(-3)+1=0$	$(-3,0)$
0	$y=\frac{1}{3}(0)+1=1$	$(0,-1)$
3	$y=\frac{1}{3}(3)+1=2$	$(3,2)$
6	$y=\frac{1}{3}(6)+1=3$	$(6,3)$

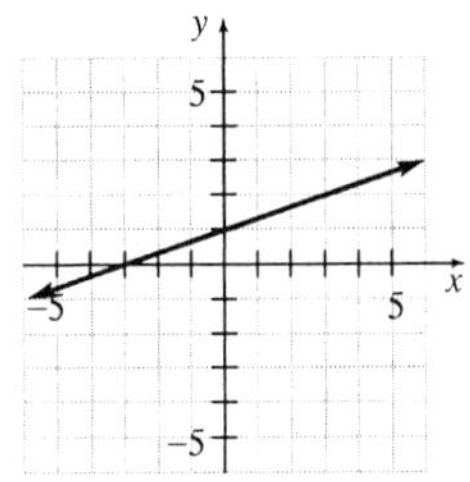

33.

x	$y=-\frac{1}{4}x$	(x, y)
-8	$y=-\frac{1}{4}(-8)=2$	$(-8,2)$
-4	$y=-\frac{1}{4}(-4)=1$	$(-4,1)$
-0	$y=-\frac{1}{4}(0)=0$	$(0,0)$
4	$y=-\frac{1}{4}(4)=-1$	$(4,-1)$
8	$y=-\frac{1}{4}(8)=-2$	$(8,-2)$

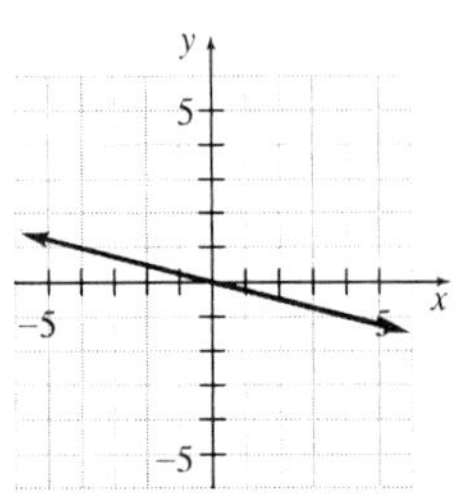

37.

x	$y=-\frac{3}{2}x+1$	(x, y)
-4	$y=-\frac{3}{2}(-4)+1=7$	$(-4,7)$
-2	$y=-\frac{3}{2}(-2)+1=4$	$(-2,4)$
0	$y=-\frac{3}{2}(0)+1=1$	$(0,1)$
2	$y=-\frac{3}{2}(2)+1=-2$	$(2,-2)$
4	$y=-\frac{3}{2}(4)+1=-5$	$(4,-5)$

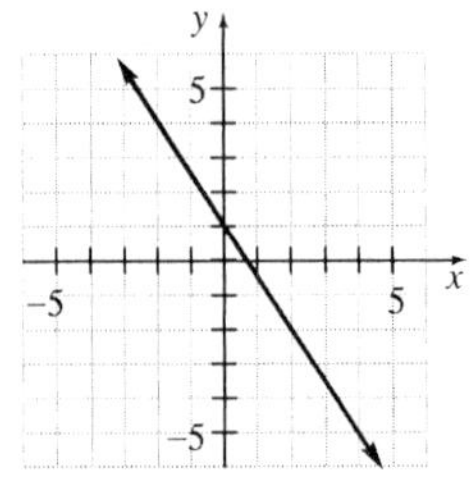

39.

x	$y=-\frac{5}{2}x-1$	(x, y)
-4	$y=-\frac{5}{2}(-4)-1=9$	$(-4,9)$
-2	$y=-\frac{5}{2}(-2)-1=4$	$(-2,4)$
0	$y=-\frac{5}{2}(0)-1=-1$	$(0,-1)$
2	$y=-\frac{5}{2}(2)-1=-6$	$(2,-6)$
4	$y=-\frac{5}{2}(4)-1=-11$	$(4,-11)$

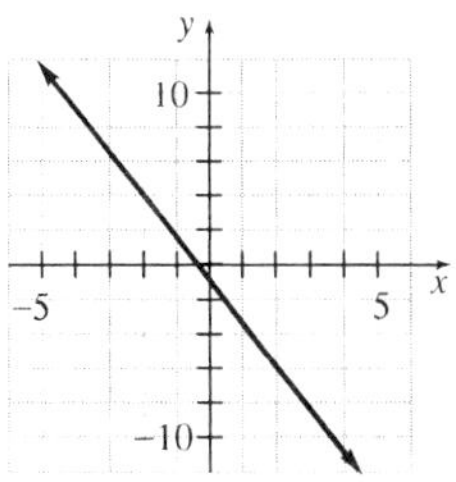

41.

x	$y=x+\frac{1}{2}$	(x, y)
-4	$y=-4+\frac{1}{2}=-3.5$	$(-4,-3.5)$
-2	$y=-2+\frac{1}{2}=-1.5$	$(-2,-1.5)$
0	$y=0+\frac{1}{2}=0.5$	$(0,0.5)$
2	$y=2+\frac{1}{2}=2.5$	$(2,2.5)$
4	$y=4+\frac{1}{2}=4.5$	$(4,4.5)$

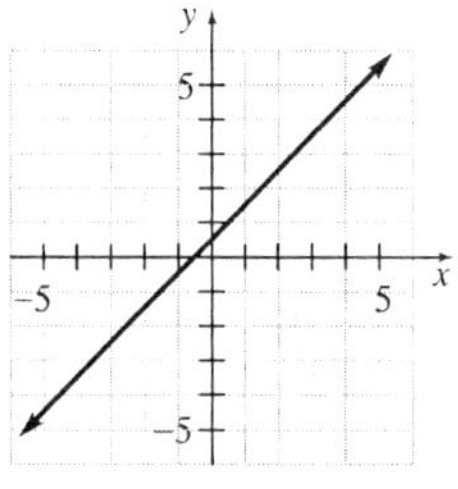

43.

x	$y=0x+4$	(x, y)
-6	$y=0(-6)+4=4$	$(-6,4)$
-3	$y=0(-3)+4=4$	$(-3,4)$
0	$y=0(0)+4=4$	$(0,4)$
3	$y=0(3)+4=4$	$(3,4)$
6	$y=0(6)+4=4$	$(6,4)$

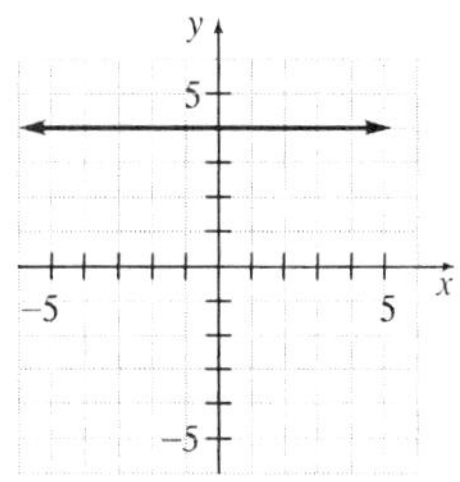

45.

x	$y=x^2$	(x, y)
-3	$y=(-3)^2=9$	$(-3,9)$
-2	$y=(-2)^2=4$	$(-2,4)$
-1	$y=(-1)^2=1$	$(-1,1)$
0	$y=0^2=0$	$(0,0)$
1	$y=1^2=1$	$(1,1)$
2	$y=2^2=4$	$(2,4)$
3	$y=3^2=9$	$(3,9)$

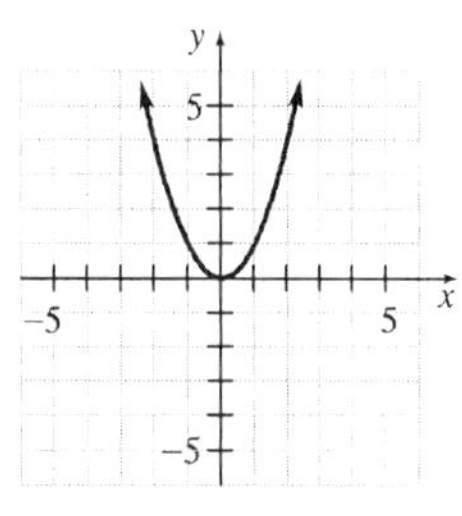

47.

x	$y = x^2 + 1$	(x, y)
-3	$y=(-3)^2+1=10$	$(-3,10)$
-2	$y=(-2)^2+1=5$	$(-2,5)$
-1	$y=(-1)^2+1=2$	$(-1,2)$
0	$y=0^2+1=1$	$(0,1)$
1	$y=1^2+1=2$	$(1,2)$
2	$y=2^2+1=5$	$(2,5)$
3	$y=3^2+1=10$	$(3,10)$

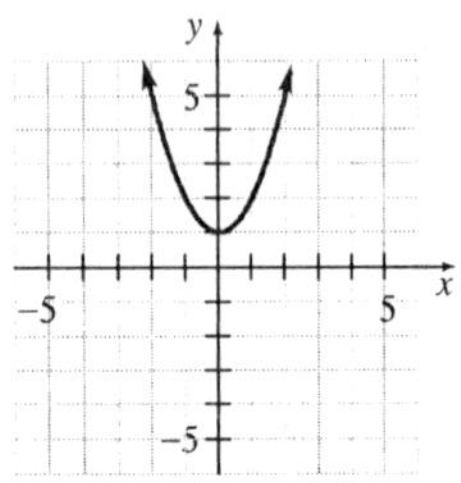

49.

x	$y = 4 - x^2$	(x, y)
-3	$y=4-(-3)^2=-5$	$(-3,-5)$
-2	$y=4-(-2)^2=0$	$(-2,0)$
-1	$y=4-(-1)^2=3$	$(-1,3)$
0	$y=4-0^2=4$	$(0,4)$
1	$y=4-1^2=3$	$(1,3)$
2	$y=4-2^2=0$	$(2,0)$
3	$y=4-3^2=-5$	$(3,-5)$

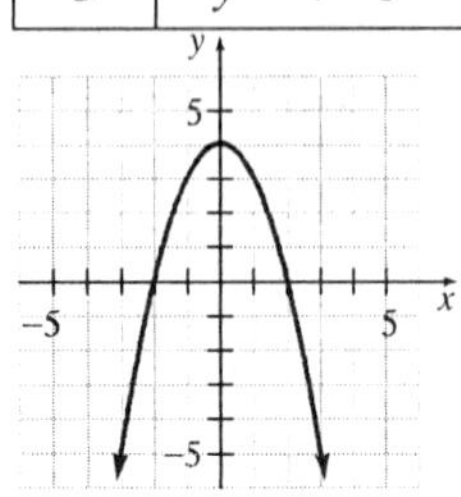

51. $y = x + 3$

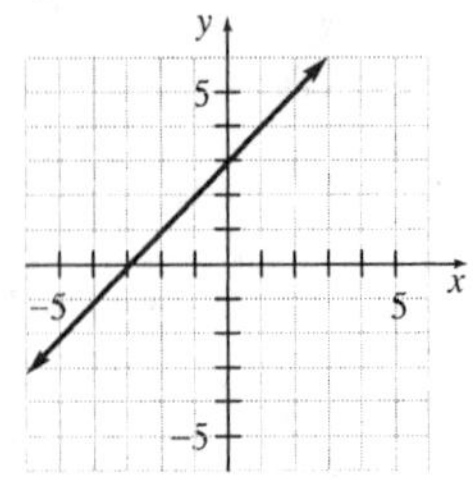

52. $y = x + 4$

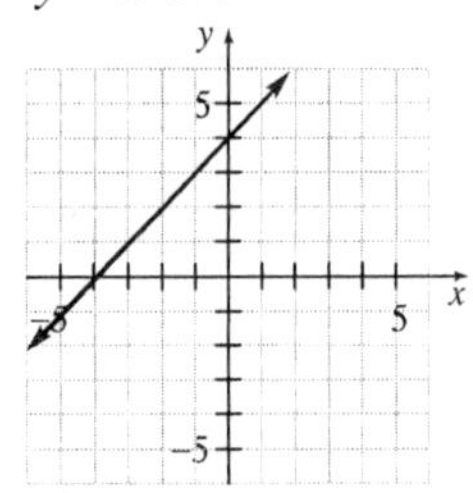

53. $y = 2x + 5$

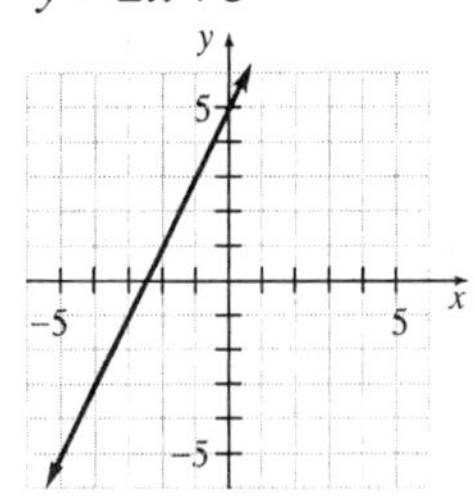

54. $y = 3x - 2$

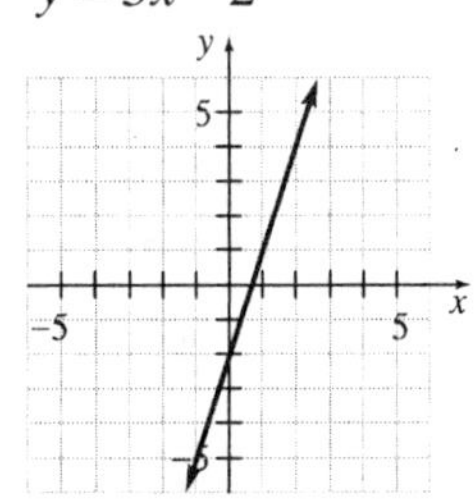

55. **a.** $8x + 6y = 14.50$

b.

$$8x + 6(0.75) = 14.50$$
$$8x + 4.50 = 14.50$$
$$8x = 10.00$$
$$x = 1.25$$

Pens cost $1.25.

56. **a.** $3x + 4y = 22.00$

b. $3x + 4(2.50) = 22.00$

$3x + 10.00 = 22.00$

$3x = 12.00$

$x = 4.00$

Orange trees cost $4.00.

57. **a.**

x	$y = 0.24x + 5.2$	(x, y)
0	$y = 0.24(0) + 5.2 = 5.2$	(0, 5.2)
10	$y = 0.24(10) + 5.2 = 7.6$	(10, 7.6)
20	$y = 0.24(20) + 5.2 = 10$	(20, 10)
30	$y = 0.24(30) + 5.2 = 12.4$	(30,12.4)

The model does not fit the data very well. Some years are underestimated while others are overestimated.

b.

x	$y = 0.22x + 3.4$	(x, y)
0	$y = 0.22(0) + 3.4 = 3.4$	(0, 3.4)
10	$y = 0.22(10) + 3.4 = 5.6$	(10, 5.6)
20	$y = 0.22(20) + 3.4 = 7.8$	(20,7.8)
30	$y = 0.22(30) + 3.4 = 9.0$	(30,9.0)

The model fits the data moderately well.

c.

x	$y = 0.13x + 4.2$	(x, y)
0	$y = 0.13(0) + 4.2 = 4.2$	(0, 4.2)
10	$y = 0.13(10) + 4.2 = 5.5$	(10, 5.5)
20	$y = 0.13(20) + 4.2 = 6.8$	(20,6.8)
30	$y = 0.13(30) + 4.2 = 8.1$	(30,8.1)

The model fits the data fairly well.

58. **a.**

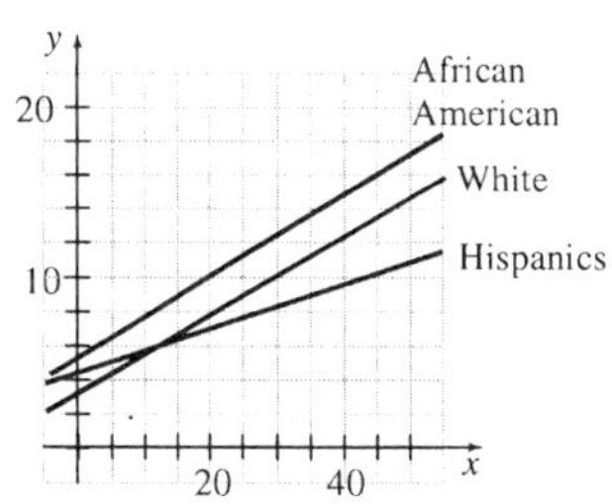

b. From the graph we obtain the following predictions for percent divorced in 2010:
African American: 14.8%
Whites: 10%
Hispanics: 9.4%

59. **a.** The x-coordinate of the intersection point is 40. This means that if you drive the moving truck 40 miles, the rental charge will be the same with both companies.

b. A reasonable estimate of the y-coordinate of the intersection point is 55.

c. $y = 40 + 35;\ x = 40$

$y = 40 + 0.35(40)$

$y = 40 + 14 = 54$

$y = 36 + 0.45x;\ x = 40$

$y = 36 + 0.45(40)$

$y = 36 + 18 = 54$

This value indicates that if you drive the moving truck 40 miles, the rental charge with either company will be $54. This is almost the same as the estimate in part (b).]

60. a.

x	$y=166x+1781$	(x,y)
0	$y=166(0)+1781$ $=1781$	$(0,1781)$
5	$y=166(5)+1781$ $=2611$	$(0,2611)$
10	$y=166(10)+1781$ $=3441$	$(10,3441)$
15	$y=166(15)+1781$ $=4271$	$(15,4271)$
20	$y=166(20)+1781$ $=5101$	$(20,5101)$

b.

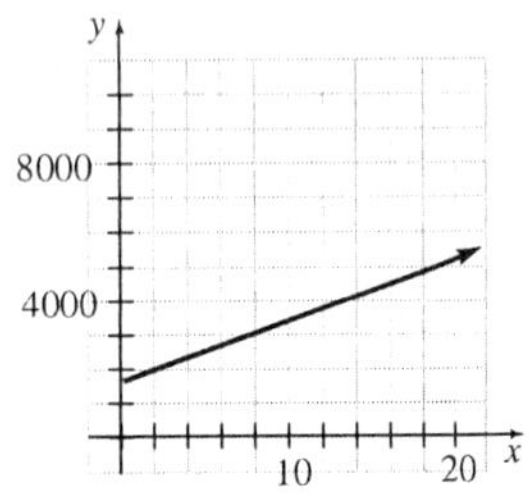

The cost of a four-year college has been increasing and will continue to increase at the same rate.

61. a.

x	$y=50x+30{,}000$	(x,y)
0	$y=30{,}000$	$(0,30{,}000)$
10	$y=30{,}500$	$(10,30{,}500)$
20	$y=31{,}000$	$(20,31{,}000)$
30	$y=31{,}500$	$(30,31{,}500)$
40	$y=32{,}000$	$(40,32{,}000)$

b.

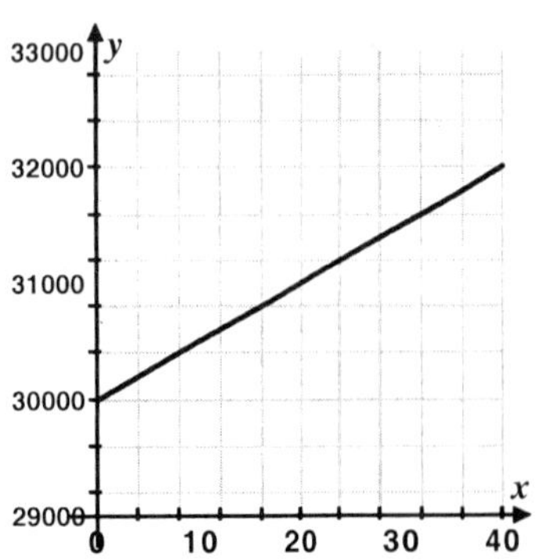

For Exercises 63-65, answers will vary.

67.

x	$y=\lvert x\rvert$	(x,y)
-3	$y=\lvert -3\rvert=3$	$(-3,3)$
-2	$y=\lvert -2\rvert=2$	$(-2,2)$
-1	$y=\lvert -1\rvert=1$	$(-1,1)$
0	$y=\lvert 0\rvert=0$	$(0,0)$
1	$y=\lvert 1\rvert=1$	$(1,1)$
2	$y=\lvert 2\rvert=2$	$(2,2)$
3	$y=\lvert 3\rvert=3$	$(3,3)$

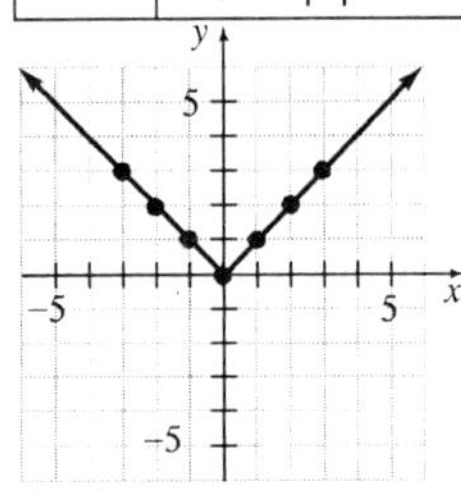

69. a. Set $x = 0$, and simplify.

$$y=0.1x^2-0.4x+0.6$$
$$=0.1(0)^2-0.4(0)+0.6$$
$$=0.6$$

This solution is the pair, (0, 0.6).
Set $x = 1$, and simplify.

$$y=0.1x^2-0.4x+0.6$$
$$=0.1(1)^2-0.4(1)+0.6$$
$$=0.1(1)-0.4+0.6$$
$$=0.1-0.4+0.6$$
$$=0.3$$

This solution is the pair, (1, 0.3). Using similar calculations, we have (2, 0.2), (3, 0.3), (4, 0.6), and (5, 1.1).

b. Runners should run between 10:00 A.M. and noon in order to avoid unsafe air.

71. Answers will vary depending upon the points chosen. One example is shown here.

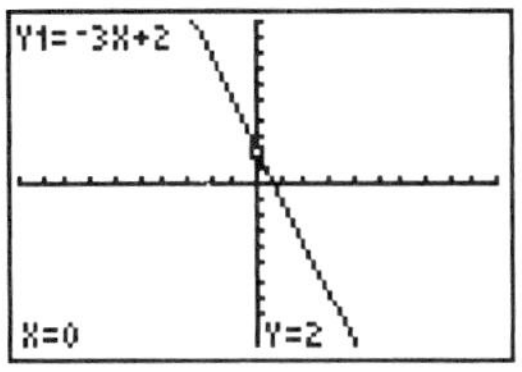

73. Answers will vary depending upon the points chosen. One example is shown here.

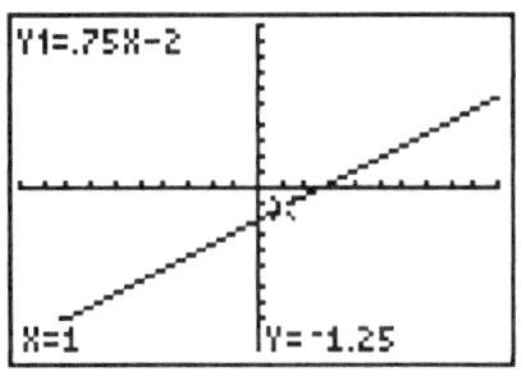

75.

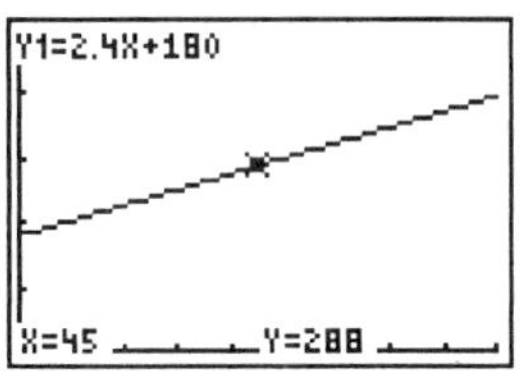

U.S. population is increasing over time.

76.

$$\begin{aligned} 3x+5 &= 4(2x-3)+7 \\ 3x+5 &= 8x-12+7 \\ 3x+5 &= 8x-5 \\ 3x+5-8x &= 8x-5-8x \\ -5x+5 &= -5 \\ -5x+5-5 &= -5-5 \\ -5x &= -10 \\ \frac{-5x}{-5} &= \frac{-10}{-5} \\ x &= 2 \end{aligned}$$

The solution is 2.

77. $3(1-2\cdot 5)-(-28) = 3(1-10)+28$
$= 3(-9)+28$
$= -27+28 = 1$

78. $V = \frac{1}{3}Ah$ for h

$$\begin{aligned} V &= \frac{1}{3}Ah \\ 3V &= 3\left(\frac{1}{3}Ah\right) \\ 3V &= Ah \\ \frac{3V}{A} &= \frac{Ah}{A} \\ \frac{3V}{A} &= h \text{ or } h = \frac{3V}{A} \end{aligned}$$

4.2 Exercise Set

1. **a.** The graph crosses the x-axis at (3,0). Thus, the x-intercept is 3.

b. The graph crosses the y-axis at (0,4). Thus, the y-intercept is 4.

3. **a.** The graph crosses the x-axis at (–4,0). Thus, the x-intercept is –4.

b. The graph crosses the y-axis at (0,–2). Thus, the y-intercept is –2.

5. **a.** The graph crosses the x-axis at (0,0) (the origin). Thus, the x-intercept is 0.

b. The graph also crosses the y-axis at (0,0).Thus, the y-intercept is 0.

7. **a.** The graph does not cross the x-axis. Thus, there is no x-intercept.

b. The graph crosses the y-axis at (0,–2). Thus the y-intercept is –2.

9. To find the x-intercept, let $y = 0$ and solve for x.

$$2x+5y=20$$
$$2x+5(0)=20$$
$$2x=20$$
$$x=10$$

The x-intercept is 10.

To find the y-intercept, let $x = 0$ and solve for y.

$$2x+5y=20$$
$$2(0)+5y=20$$
$$5y=20$$
$$y=4$$

The y-intercept is 4.

11. To find the x-intercept, let $y = 0$ and solve for x.

$$2x-3y=15$$
$$2x-3(0)=15$$
$$2x=15$$
$$x=\frac{15}{2}$$

The x-intercept is $\frac{15}{2}$.

To find the y-intercept, let $x = 0$ and solve for y.

$$2x-3y=15$$
$$2(0)-3y=15$$
$$-3y=15$$
$$y=-5$$

The y-intercept is –5.

13. x-intercept:

$$-x+3(0)=-8$$
$$-x=-8$$
$$x=8$$

y-intercept:

$$-0+3y=-8$$
$$3y=-8$$
$$y=-\frac{8}{3}$$

x-intercept: 8; y-intercept: $-\frac{8}{3}$.

15. x-intercept:

$$7x-9(0)=0$$
$$7x=0$$
$$x=0$$

y-intercept:

$$7(0)-9y=0$$
$$-9y=0$$
$$y=0$$

x-intercept: 0; y-intercept: 0

17. x-intercept:

$$2x=3(0)-11$$
$$2x=-11$$
$$x=-\frac{11}{2}$$

y-intercept:

$$2(0)=3y-11$$
$$0=3y-11$$
$$11=3y$$
$$\frac{11}{3}=y$$

x-intercept: $-\frac{11}{2}$; y-intercept: $\frac{11}{3}$

19. $x+y=5$

x-intercept: 5
y-intercept: 5
checkpoint: (2,3)
Draw a line through (5,0), (0,5), and (2,3).

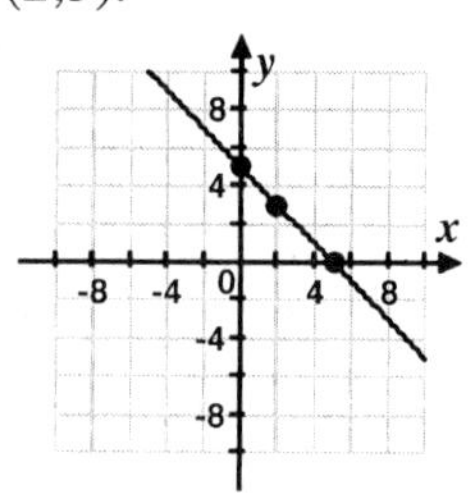

21. $x+3y=6$
x-intercept: 6
y-intercept: 2
checkpoint: (3,1)
Draw a line through (6,0), (0,2), and (3,1).

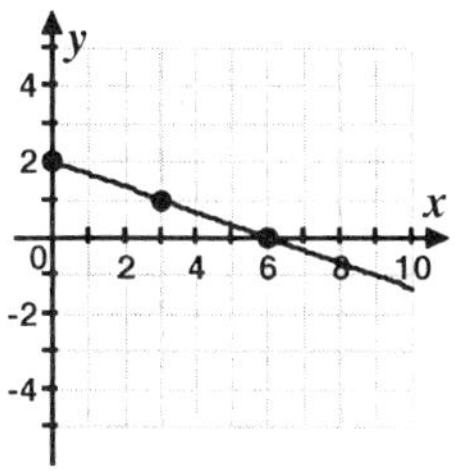

23. $6x-9y=18$
x-intercept: 3
y-intercept: -2
checkpoint: $\left(1,-\frac{4}{3}\right)$

Draw a line through (3,0), (0,–2), and $\left(1,-\frac{4}{3}\right)$.

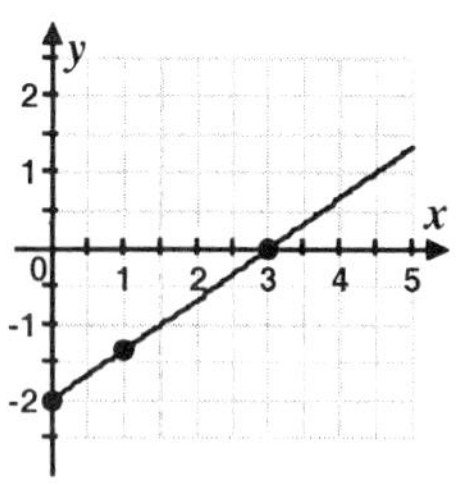

25. $-x+4y=6$
x-intercept: -6
y-intercept: $\frac{3}{2}$
checkpoint: (2,2)

Draw a line through (–6,0), $\left(0,\frac{3}{2}\right)$, and (2,2).

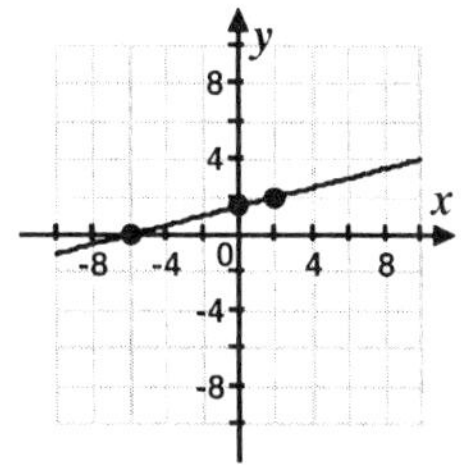

27. $2x-y=7$

x-intercept: $\frac{7}{2}$

y-intercept: -7
checkpoint: (1,–5)

Draw a line through $\left(\frac{7}{2},0\right)$, (0,7), and (1,–5).

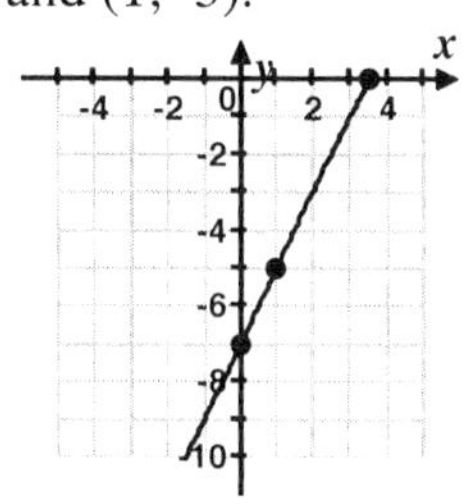

29. $3x=5y-15$
x-intercept: -5
y-intercept: 3
checkpoint: $\left(-\frac{10}{3},1\right)$

Draw a line through (–5,0), (0,3), and $\left(-\frac{10}{3},1\right)$.

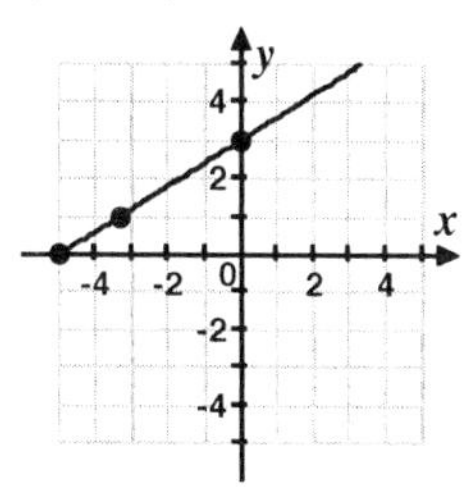

31. $25y = 100 - 50x$
x-intercept: 2
y-intercept: 4
checkpoint: (1, 2)
Draw a line through (2,0), (0,4), and (1, 2).

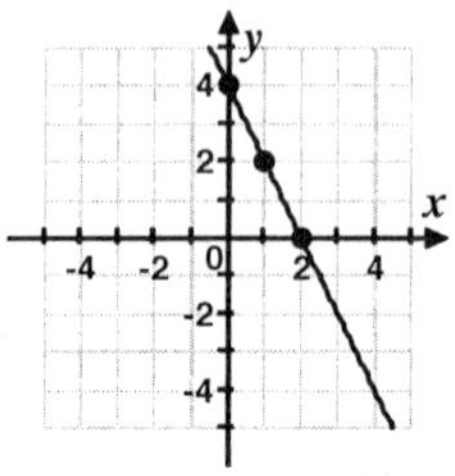

33. $2x - 8y = 12$
x-intercept: 6
y-intercept: $-\frac{3}{2}$
checkpoint: (2, −1)
Draw a line through (6,0), $\left(0, -\frac{3}{2}\right)$,
and (2, −1).

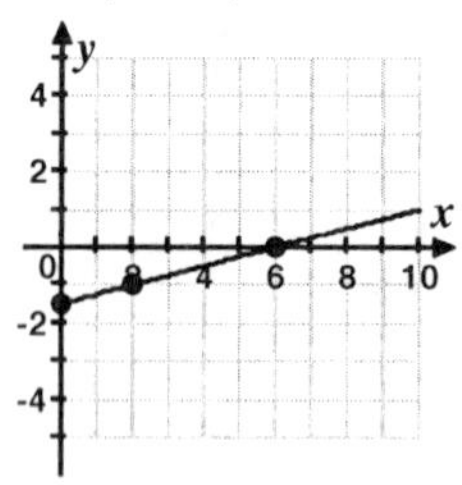

35. $x + 2y = 0$
x-intercept: 0
y-intercept: 0
Since the line goes through the origin, find two additional points.
checkpoint: (2, −1)
checkpoint: (4, −2)
Draw a line through (0,0), (2, −1), and (4, −2).

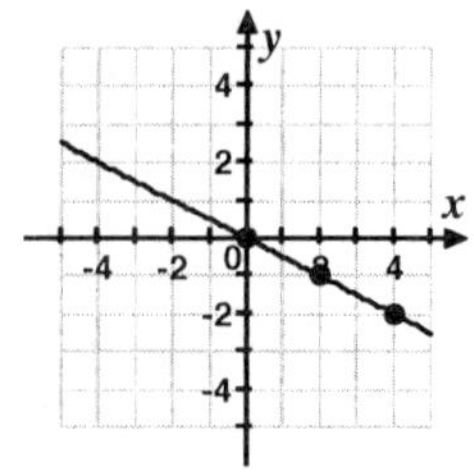

37. $y - 3x = 0$
x-intercept: 0
y-intercept: 0
Since the line goes through the origin, find two additional points.
checkpoint: (1, 3)
checkpoint: (2, 6)
Draw a line through (0,0), (1, 3), and (2, 6).

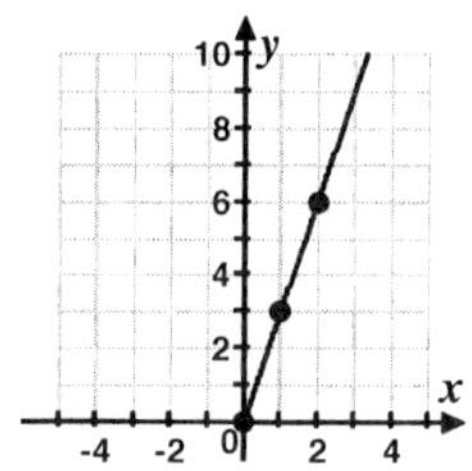

39. $2x - 3y = -11$
x-intercept: $-\frac{11}{2}$
y-intercept: $\frac{11}{3}$
checkpoint: (−1, 3)
Draw a line through $\left(-\frac{11}{2}, 0\right)$, $\left(0, \frac{11}{3}\right)$
and (−1, 3).

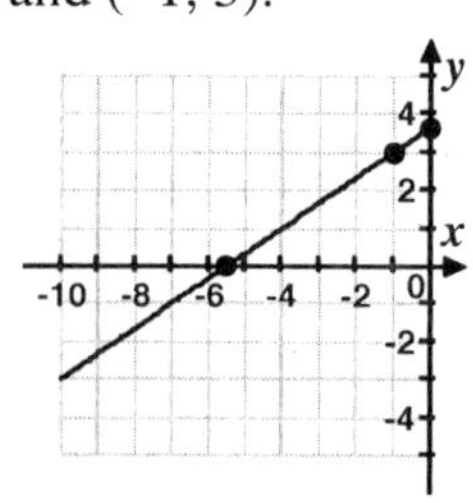

41. The equation for this horizontal line is $y = 3$.

43. The equation for this vertical line is $x = -3$.

45. The equation for this horizontal line, which is the x-axis is $y = 0$.

47. $y = 4$

All ordered pairs that are solutions will have a value of y that is 4. Any value can be used for x. Three ordered pairs that are solutions are $(-2,4)$, $(0,4)$, and $(3,4)$.
Plot these points and draw the line through them. The graph is a horizontal line.

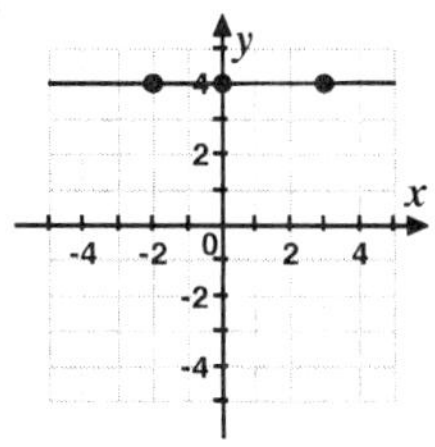

49. $y = -2$

Three ordered pairs are $(-3,-2)$, $(0,-2)$, and $(4,-2)$. The graph is a horizontal line.

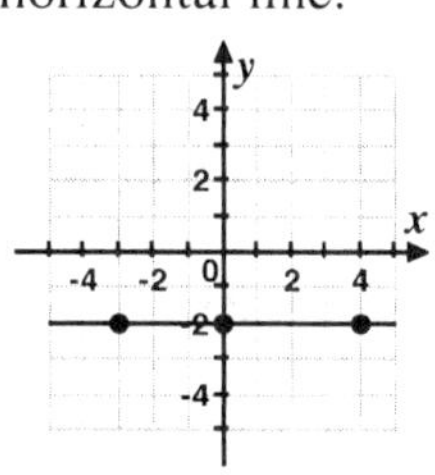

51. $x = 2$

All ordered pairs that are solutions will have a value of x that is 2. Any value can be used for y. Three ordered pairs that are solutions are $(2, -3)$, $(2,0)$, and $(2,2)$.
The graph is a vertical line.

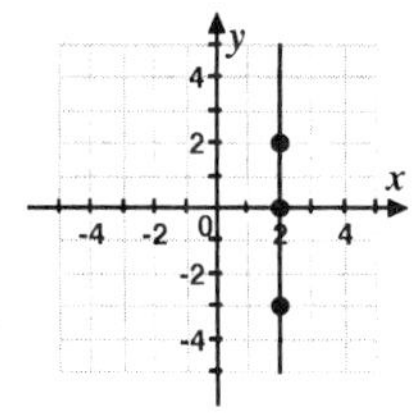

53. $x + 1 = 0$

$x = -1$

Three ordered pairs are $(-1,-3)$, $(-1,0)$, and $(-1,3)$. The graph is a vertical line.

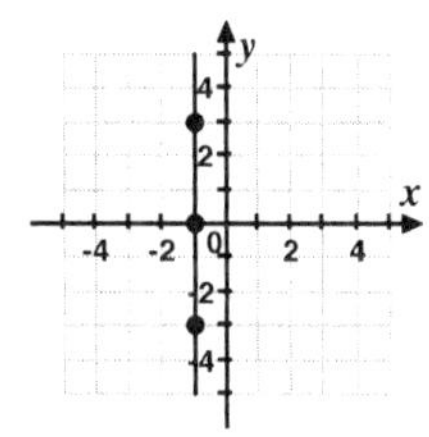

55. $y - 3.5 = 0$

$y = 3.5$

Three ordered pairs are $(-2, 3.5)$, $(0, 3.5)$, and $(3.5, 3.5)$. The graph is a horizontal line.

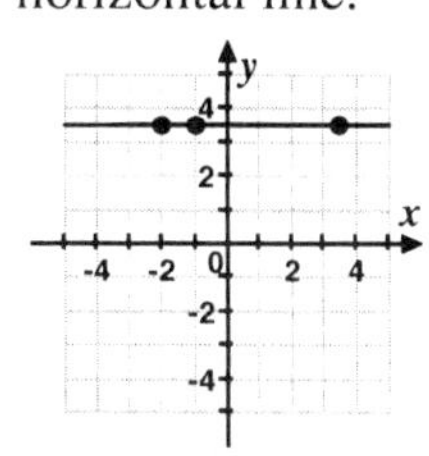

57. $x = 0$

Three ordered pairs are $(0,-2)$, $(0,0)$, and $(0,4)$. The graph is a vertical line, the y-axis.

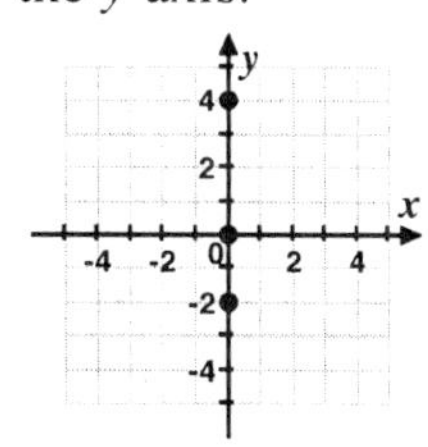

59 $3y = 9$

$y = 3$

Three ordered pairs are (–3,3), (0,3), and (3,3). The graph is a horizontal line.

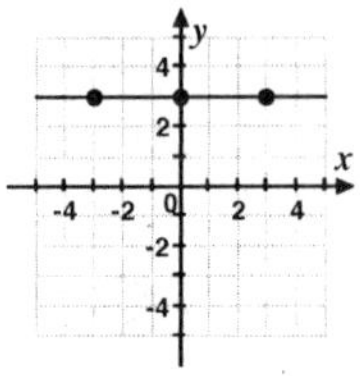

61. $12 - 3x = 0$

$-3x = -12$

$x = 4$

Three ordered pairs are (4,–2), (4,1), and (4,3). The graph is a vertical line.

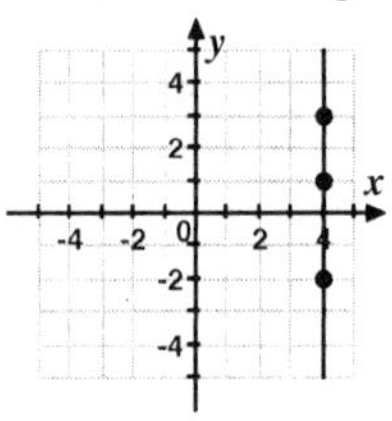

63. Using the x- and y-intercepts, we see that $3x + 2y = -6$ corresponds to Exercise 4.

64. $x + 2y = -4$

x-intercept: $x + 2(0) = -4$, $x = -4$

y-intercept: $0 + 2y = -4$, $2y = -4$, $y = -2$

Using the x- and y-intercepts, we see that $x + 2y = -4$ corresponds to Exercise 3.

65. Since $y = -2$ is a horizontal line at –2, it corresponds to Exercise 7.

66. Since $x = -3$ is a vertical line at -3, it corresponds to Exercise 8.

67. Using the x- and y-intercepts, we see that $4x + 3y = 12$ corresponds to Exercise 1.

68. $2x + 5y = 10$

x-intercept: $2x + 5(0) = 10$, $2x = 10$, $x = 5$

y-intercept: $2(0) + 5y = 10$, $5y = 10$, $y = 2$

Using the x- and y-intercepts, we see that $2x + 5y = 10$ corresponds to Exercise 2.

69. **a.** Let $x + 5 + 5 = x + 10$ = the width. Let $y + 8$ = length. Using the formula for the perimeter of a rectangle, we have

$$2(x+10) + 2(y+8) = 58$$
$$2x + 20 + 2y + 16 = 58$$
$$2x + 2y + 36 = 58$$
$$2x + 2y = 22$$
$$x + y = 11$$

b.

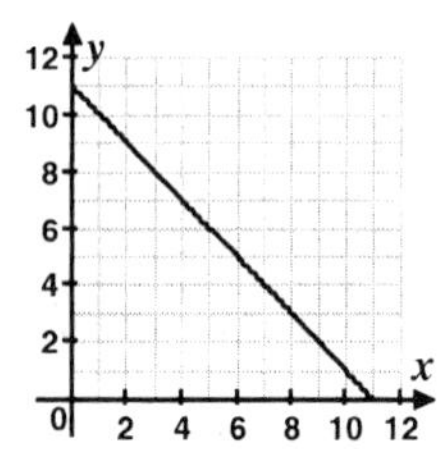

70. **a.** The base of the trapezoid has length x and the top has length $x - 2y$. The two sides each have length 25, so the perimeter equation for the trapezoid is given by:

$$x + (x - 2y) + 2(25) = 84$$
$$x + x - 2y + 50 = 84$$
$$2x - 2y = 34$$
$$x - y = 17$$

b. 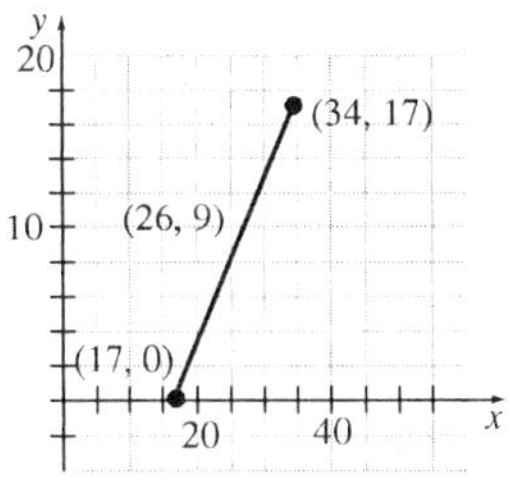

The total perimeter is 84 feet and two sides are each 25 feet. This leaves 34 feet for the remaining two sides. Thus, the largest value possible for x is 34, which is when we have an isosceles triangle.

71. The vulture's height is decreasing from 3 seconds to 12 seconds.

73. The y-intercept is 45. This means that the vulture's height was 45 meters at the beginning of the observation.

75. Five x-intercepts of the graph are 12, 13, 14, 15, and 16. During these times (12-16 minutes), the vulture was on the ground.

77. Your temperature is decreasing from 8 A.M. to 11 A.M.

79. Your temperature is increasing from 11 A.M. to 1 P.M.

81. **a.**
$$0.57x + y = 80$$
$$0.57(0) + y = 80$$
$$y = 80$$
The y-intercept is 80. This means that in 1994, carbonated beverages had 80% of the market share.

b. The model approximates the data very well for 1994.

c.
$$0.57x + y = 80$$
$$0.57x + 0 = 80$$
$$0.57x = 80$$
$$x \approx 140$$
The x-intercept is 140. This means that in 1994 + 140 = 2134, carbonated beverages will have 0% of the market share. This means that there will be no consumption of carbonated beverages. Since this is extremely unlikely, model breakdown has occurred.

For Exercises 83-91, answers will vary.

93. $y = -1$ is a horizontal line. A line parallel to a horizontal line is also horizontal. The equation of a horizontal line passing through (5,6) is $y = 6$.

95. Since the x-intercept is -2, $y = 0$ when $x = -2$.
$$\square x + \square y = 12$$
$$\square(-2) + \square(0) = 12$$
$$\square(-2) = 12$$
$$\square = -6$$
So, the coefficient of x is -6. Similarly, since the y-intercept is 4, $x = 0$ when $y = 4$.
$$\square x + \square y = 12$$
$$\square(0) + \square(4) = 12$$
$$\square(4) = 12$$
$$\square = 3$$
So, the coefficient of y is 3. The equation of the line is $-6x + 3y = 12$.

97. $2x + y = 4$

$$y = -2x + 4$$

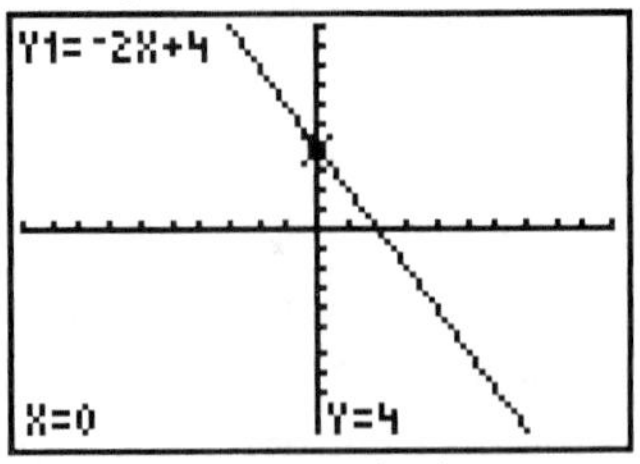

The y-intercept is 4.

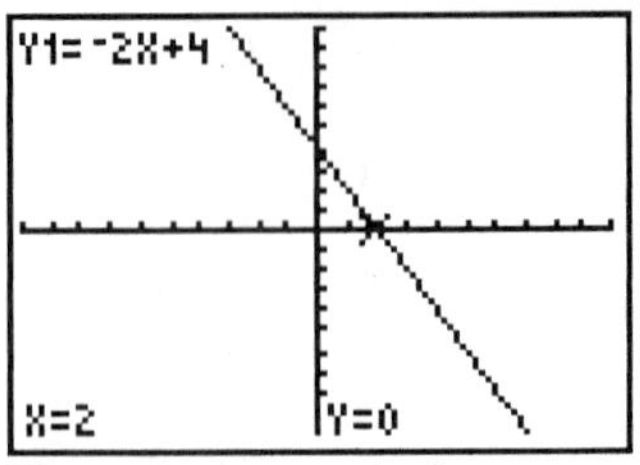

The x-intercept is 2.

99. $2x + 3y = 30$

$$3y = -2x + 30$$

$$y = -\frac{2}{3}x + \frac{30}{3}$$

$$y = -\frac{2}{3}x + 10$$

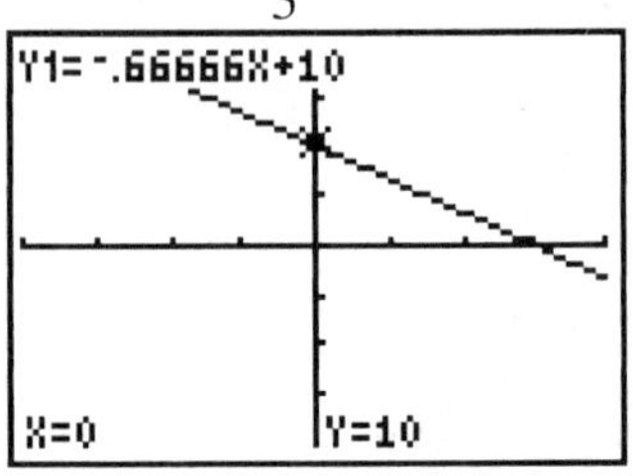

The y-intercept is 10.

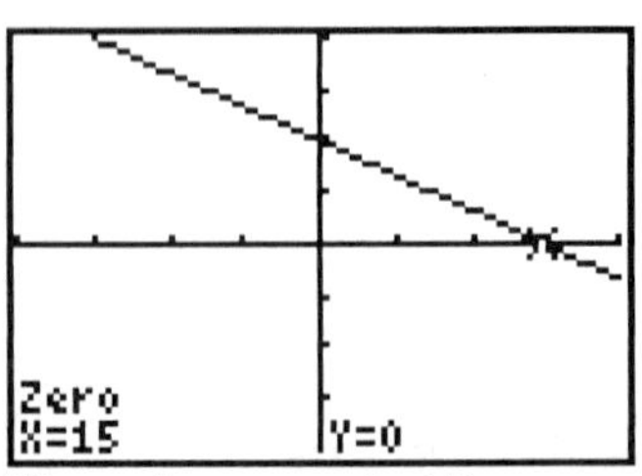

The x-intercept is 15.

101. $|-13.4| = 13.4$

102. $7x - (3x - 5) = 7x - 3x + 5 = 4x + 5$

103. $-2 \le x < 4$

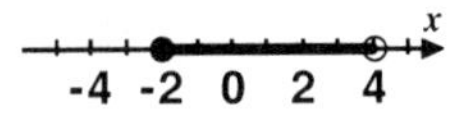

4.3 Exercise Set

1. Let $(x_1, y_1) = (4,7)$ and $(x_2, y_2) = (8,10)$.

$$m = \frac{\text{Change in } y}{\text{Change in } x} = \frac{y_2 - y_1}{x_2 - x_1}$$

$$= \frac{10-7}{8-4} = \frac{3}{4}$$

The slope is $\frac{3}{4}$. Since the slope is positive, the line rises.

3. (−2,1) and (2,2)

$$m = \frac{2-1}{2-(-2)} = \frac{1}{4}$$

Since the slope is positive, the line rises.

5. (4,−2) and (3,−2)

$$m = \frac{-2-(-2)}{3-4} = \frac{0}{-1} = 0$$

Since the slope is zero, the line is horizontal.

7. (−2,4) and (−1,−1)

$$m = \frac{-1-4}{-1-(-2)} = \frac{-5}{1} = -5$$

Since the slope is negative, the line falls.

9. (5,3) and (5,−2)

$$m = \frac{-2-3}{5-5} = \frac{-5}{0}$$

Since the slope is undefined, the line is vertical.

11. Line through (–2,2) and (2,4):

$$m=\frac{4-2}{2-(-2)}=\frac{2}{4}=\frac{1}{2}$$

13. Line through (–3,4) and (3,2):

$$m=\frac{2-4}{3-(-3)}=\frac{-2}{6}=-\frac{1}{3}$$

15. Line through (–2,1), (0,0), and (2,–1)
Use any two of these points to find the slope.

$$m=\frac{0-1}{0-(-2)}=\frac{-1}{2}=-\frac{1}{2}$$

17. Line through (0,2) and (3,0):

$$m=\frac{0-2}{3-0}=-\frac{2}{3}$$

19. Line through (–2,1) and (4,1):

$$m=\frac{1-1}{4-(-2)}=\frac{0}{6}=0$$

(Since the line is horizontal, it is not necessary to do this computation. The slope of every horizontal line is 0.)

21. Line through (–3,4) and (–3,–2):

$$m=\frac{-2-4}{-3-(-3)}=\frac{-6}{0};\text{ undefined}$$

(Since the line is vertical, it is not necessary to do this computation. The slope of every vertical line is undefined.)

23. Line through (–2,0) and (0,6):

$$m=\frac{6-0}{0-(-2)}=3$$

Line through (1,8) and (0,5):

$$m=\frac{5-8}{0-1}=\frac{-3}{-1}=3$$

Since their slopes are equal, the lines are parallel.

25. Line through (0,3) and (1,5):

$$m=\frac{5-3}{1-0}=\frac{2}{1}=2$$

Line through (–1,7) and $(1,10)$:

$$m=\frac{10-7}{1-(-1)}=\frac{3}{2}$$

Since their slopes are not equal, the lines are not parallel.

27.

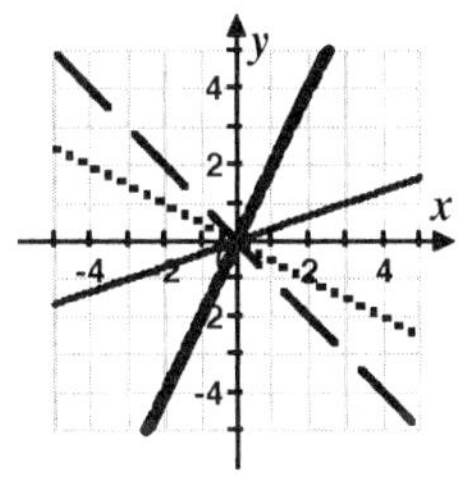

28.

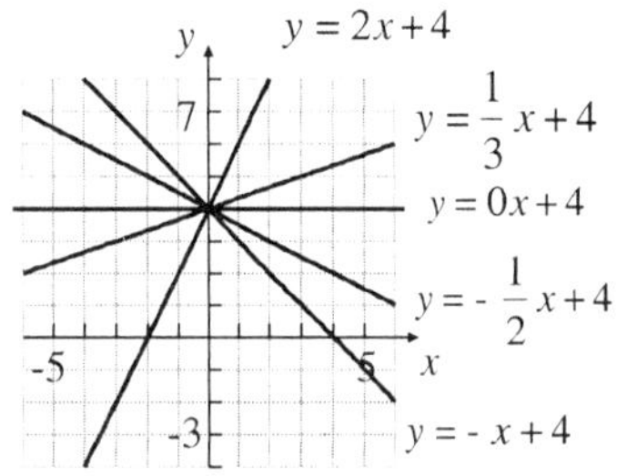

29.

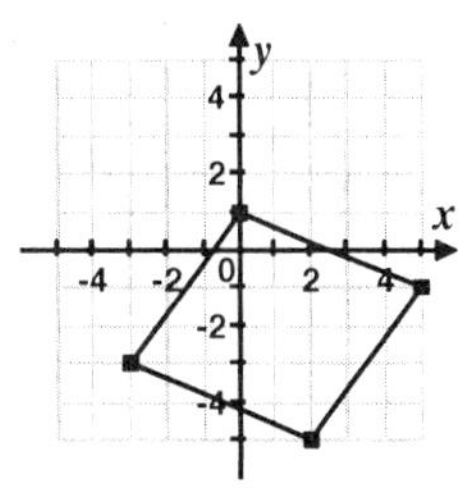

$$m=\frac{y_2-y_1}{x_2-x_1}=\frac{-3-1}{-3-0}=\frac{-4}{-3}=\frac{4}{3}$$

$$m=\frac{y_2-y_1}{x_2-x_1}=\frac{-1-1}{5-0}=\frac{-2}{5}=-\frac{2}{5}$$

$$m=\frac{y_2-y_1}{x_2-x_1}=\frac{-5-(-1)}{2-5}=\frac{-4}{-3}=\frac{4}{3}$$

$$m=\frac{y_2-y_1}{x_2-x_1}=\frac{-3-(-5)}{-3-2}=\frac{2}{-5}=-\frac{2}{5}$$

Slopes of opposite sides are equal, so the figure is a parallelogram.

30.

$$m_1 = \frac{y_2 - y_1}{x_2 - x_1} = \frac{-3-6}{2-(-3)} = -\frac{9}{5}$$

$$m_2 = \frac{y_2 - y_1}{x_2 - x_1} = \frac{2-(-3)}{11-2} = \frac{5}{9}$$

$$m_3 = \frac{y_2 - y_1}{x_2 - x_1} = \frac{11-2}{6-11} = -\frac{9}{5}$$

$$m_4 = \frac{y_2 - y_1}{x_2 - x_1} = \frac{6-11}{-3-6} = \frac{5}{9}$$

Since m_1 and m_3 are the same, the line connecting $(-3,6)$ and $(2,-3)$ is parallel to the line connecting $(11,2)$ and $(6,11)$. Since m_2 and m_4 are the same, the line connecting $(-3,6)$ and $(6,11)$ is parallel to the line connecting $(2,-3)$ and $(11,2)$.

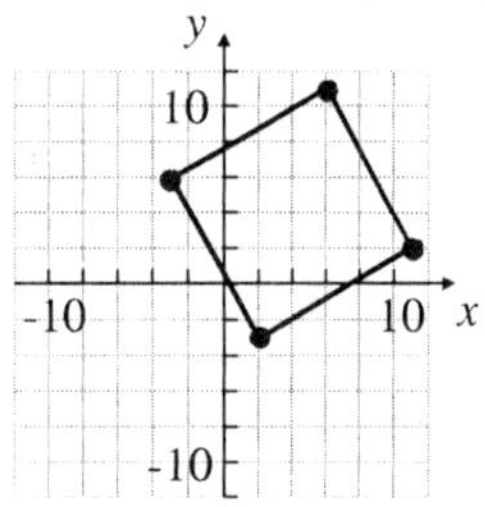

31. First find the slope of the line passing through (2, 3) and (−2, 1).

$$m = \frac{y_2 - y_1}{x_2 - x_1} = \frac{3-1}{2-(-2)} = \frac{2}{4} = \frac{1}{2}$$

Now, use the slope formula, the slope and the points (5, y) and (1, 0) to find y.

$$\frac{1}{2} = \frac{y-0}{5-1}$$

$$\frac{1}{2} = \frac{y}{4}$$

$$4\left(\frac{1}{2}\right) = 4\left(\frac{y}{4}\right)$$

$$2 = y$$

32. First find the slope of the line passing through $(-3,4)$ and $(-5,-2)$.

$$m = \frac{-2-4}{-5-(-3)} = \frac{-6}{-2} = 3$$

Now, use the slope formula, the slope and the points (1, y) and (7, 12) to find y.

$$3 = \frac{12-y}{7-1}$$

$$3 = \frac{12-y}{6}$$

$$18 = 12 - y$$

$$6 = -y$$

$$y = -6$$

33. (1, 2) and (3,12)

$$m = \frac{y_2 - y_1}{x_2 - x_1} = \frac{12-2}{3-1} = \frac{10}{2} = 5$$

(3, 12) and (6, 27)

$$m = \frac{y_2 - y_1}{x_2 - x_1} = \frac{27-12}{6-3} = \frac{15}{3} = 5$$

(6, 27) and (1, 2)

$$m = \frac{y_2 - y_1}{x_2 - x_1} = \frac{2-27}{1-6} = \frac{-25}{-5} = 5$$

The slope from $(1,2)$ to $(3,12)$ is the same as the slope from $(3,12)$ to $(6,27)$. Therefore, the three points are collinear.

34. $(1,3)$ and $(3,11)$

$$m = \frac{11-3}{3-1} = \frac{8}{2} = 4$$

$(3,11)$ and $(6,22)$

$$m = \frac{22-11}{6-3} = \frac{11}{3}$$

These two slopes are different, so the three points are not collinear.

35. Line through (1999,1000) and (2001,1500):

$$m=\frac{1500-1000}{2001-1999}=\frac{500}{2}=250$$

The amount spent online per U.S. online household was projected to increase by \$250 each year from 1999 to 2001.

37. Two points on the line segment representing men are (1972, 98) and (2002, 86).

$$m=\frac{98-86}{1972-2002}=\frac{12}{-30}=-0.4$$

The percentage of fill-time police officers who are men is decreasing at a rate of 0.4% per year.

39. Two points on the line segment representing highest-income are (2002, 161,800) and (1980, 98,000).

$$m=\frac{161{,}800-98{,}000}{2002-1980}=\frac{63{,}800}{22}=2900$$

Mean income is increasing by \$2900 per year.

41. Two points on the line are (20,000, 8000) and (40,000, 16,000).

$$m=\frac{16{,}000-8{,}000}{40{,}000-20{,}000}=\frac{8{,}000}{20{,}000}=0.4$$

The cost increases \$0.40 per mile driven.

43. $$m=\frac{\text{Change in } y}{\text{Change in } x}=\frac{6}{18}=\frac{1}{3}$$

The pitch of the roof is $\frac{1}{3}$.

45. The grade an access ramp is

$$\frac{1\text{ foot}}{12\text{ feet}}=\frac{1}{12}\approx 0.083=8.3\%.$$

For Exercises 47-51, answers will vary.

53. Statement *b* is true.

55. Use the graph to observe where each line crosses the *y*-axis. In order of decreasing size, the *y*-intercepts are b_2, b_1, b_4, b_3.

57.

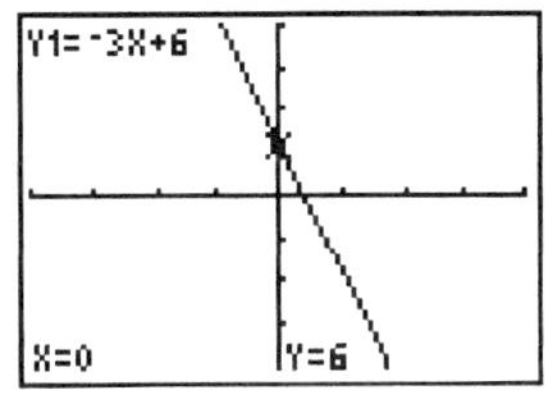

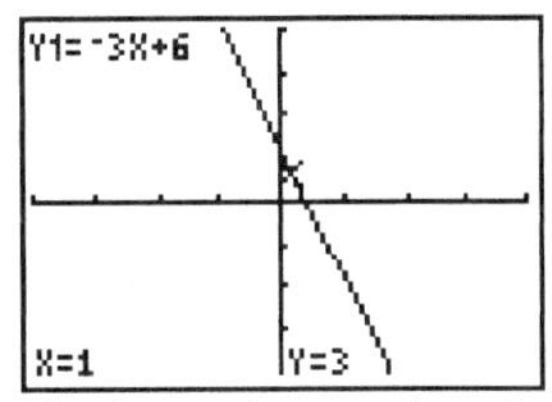

Find the slope using the points (0, 6) and (1, 3). Other points can be used, but the slope should be the same.

$$m=\frac{6-3}{0-1}=\frac{3}{-1}=-3$$

59.

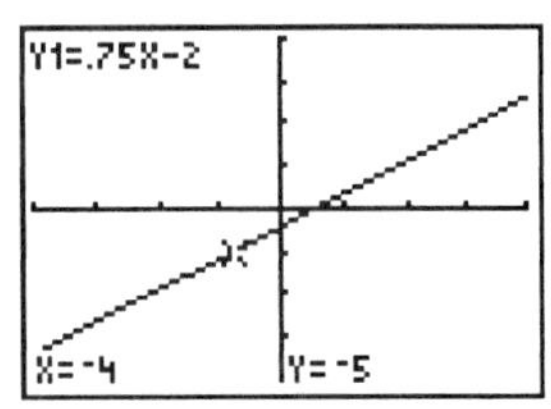

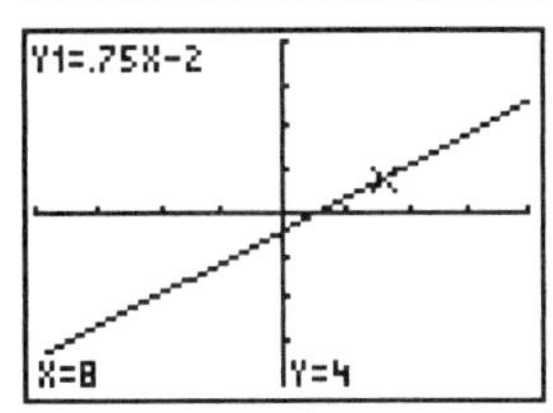

Two points on the graph are (–4,–5) and (8,4).

$$m=\frac{4-(-5)}{8-(-4)}=\frac{9}{12}=\frac{3}{4}$$

61. Let x = length of shorter piece (in inches).
Let $2x$ = length of longer piece.
$$x+2x=36$$
$$3x=36$$
$$x=12$$
The pieces are 12 inches and 24 inches.

62. $$-10+16\div2(-4)=-10+8(-4)$$
$$=-10-32$$
$$=-10+(-32)=-42$$

63. $$2x-3\le5$$
$$2x\le8$$
$$x\le4$$
$\{x|x\le4\}$

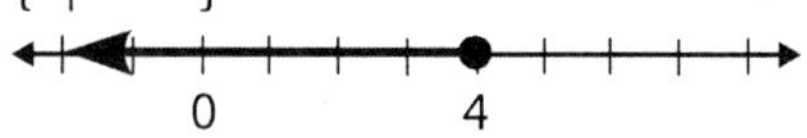

4.4 Exercise Set

1. $y=3x+2$
The slope is the x-coefficient, which is 3. The y-intercept is the constant term, which is 2.

3. $$y=3x-5$$
$$y=3x+(-5)$$
$m=3$; $y-$intercept $=-5$

5. $$y=-\frac{1}{2}x+5$$
$m=-\frac{1}{2}$; y-intercept $=5$

7. $$y=7x$$
$$y=7x+0$$
$m=7$; y-intercept $=0$

9. $$y=10$$
$$y=0x+10$$
$m=0$; y-intercept $=10$

11. $$y=4-x$$
$$y=-x+4=-1x+4$$
$m=-1$; y-intercept $=4$

13. $$-5x+y=7$$
$$-5x+y+5x=5x+7$$
$$y=5x+7$$
$m=5$; y-intercept $=7$

15. $$x+y=6$$
$$y=-x+6=-1x+6$$
$m=-1$; y-intercept $=6$

17. $$6x+y=0$$
$$y=-6x=-6x+0$$
$m=-6$; y-intercept $=0$

19. $$3y=6x$$
$$y=2x$$
$m=2$; y-intercept $=0$

21. $$2x+7y=0$$
$$7y=-2x$$
$$y=-\frac{2}{7}x$$
$m=-\frac{2}{7}$; y-intercept $=0$

23. $$3x+2y=3$$
$$2y=-3x+3$$
$$y=-\frac{3}{2}x+\frac{3}{2}$$
$m=-\frac{3}{2}$; y-intercept $=\frac{3}{2}$

25. $3x - 4y = 12$

$$-4y = -3x + 12$$

$$y = \frac{3}{4}x - 3$$

$m = \frac{3}{4}$; y-intercept $= -3$

27. $y = 2x + 4$

Step 1. Plot (0,4) on the y-axis.

Step 2. $m = \frac{2}{1} = \frac{\text{rise}}{\text{run}}$

Start at (0,4). Using the slope, move 2 units *up* (the rise) and 1 unit to the *right* (the run) to reach the point (1,6).

Step 3. Draw a line through (0,4) and (1,6).

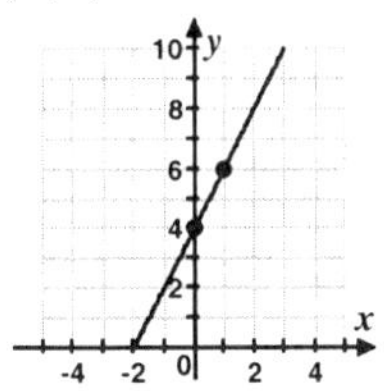

29. $y = -3x + 5$

Slope $= -3 = \frac{-3}{1}$; y-intercept = 5.

Plot (0,5) on the y-axis. From this point, move 3 units *down* (because −3 is negative) and 1 unit to the *right* to reach the point (1,2). Draw a line through (0,5) and (1,2).

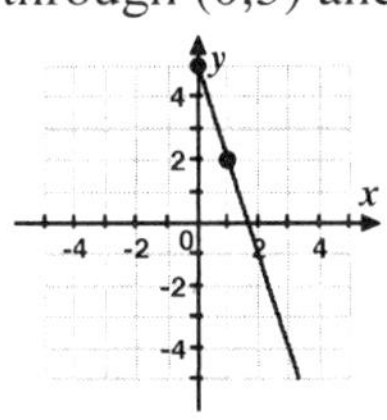

31. $y = \frac{1}{2}x + 1$

Slope $= \frac{1}{2}$; y-intercept = 1

Plot (0,1). From this point, move 1 unit *up* and 2 units to the *right* to reach the point (2,2). Draw a line through (0,1) and (2,2).

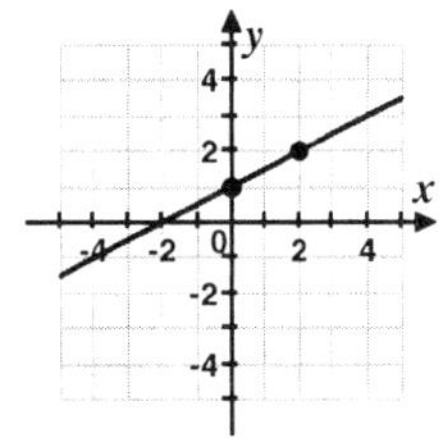

33. $y = \frac{2}{3}x - 5$

Slope $= \frac{2}{3}$; y-intercept $= -5$

Plot (0,−5). From this point move 2 units *up* and 3 units to the *right* to reach the point (3,−3). Draw a line through (0,−5) and (3,−3).

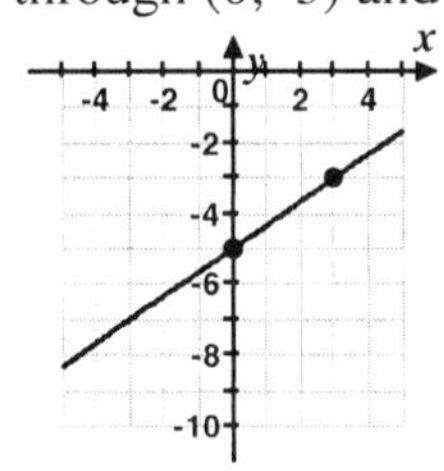

35. $y = -\frac{3}{4}x + 2$

Slope $= -\frac{3}{4} = \frac{-3}{4}$; y-intercept = 2

Plot (0,2). From this point move 3 units *down* and 4 units to the *right* to reach the point (4,−1).

Draw a line through (0,2) and (4,−1)

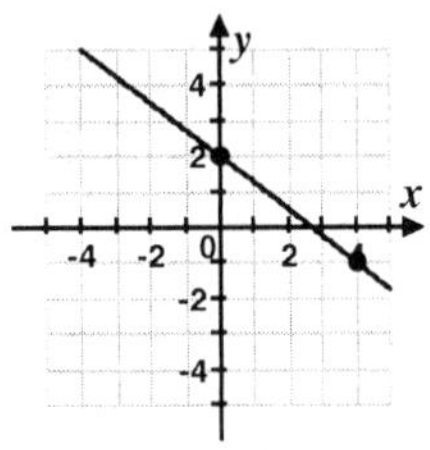

37. $y = -\frac{5}{3}x$

Slope $= -\frac{5}{3} = \frac{-5}{3}$; y-intercept $= 0$

Plot (0,0). From this point, move 5 units *down* and 3 units to the *right* to reach the point (3,–5). Draw a line through (0,0) and (3,–5).

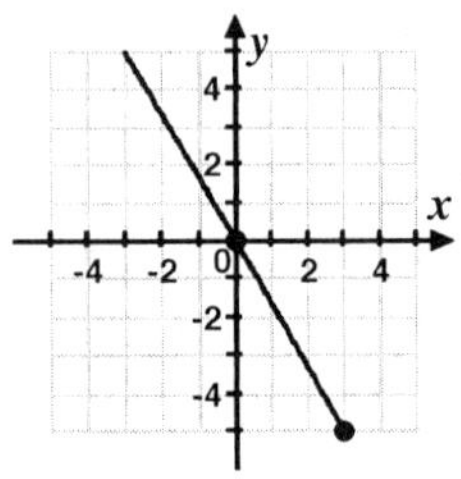

39. **a.** $3x + y = 0$

$y = -3x$

b. $m = -3$; y-intercept $= 0$

c. Plot (0,0). Since $m = -3 = -\frac{3}{1}$, move 3 units *down* and 1 units to the *right* to reach the point (1,–3). Draw a line through (0,0) and (1,–3).

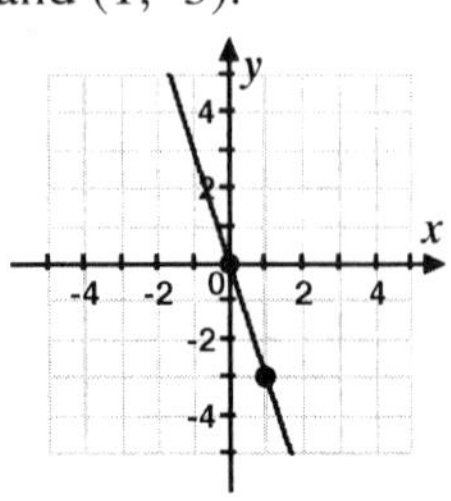

41. **a.** $3y = 4x$

$y = \frac{4}{3}x$

b. $m = \frac{4}{3}$; y-intercept $= 0$

c. Plot (0,0). Move 4 units *up* and 3 units to the *right* to reach the point (3,4).
Draw a line through (0,0) and (3,4).

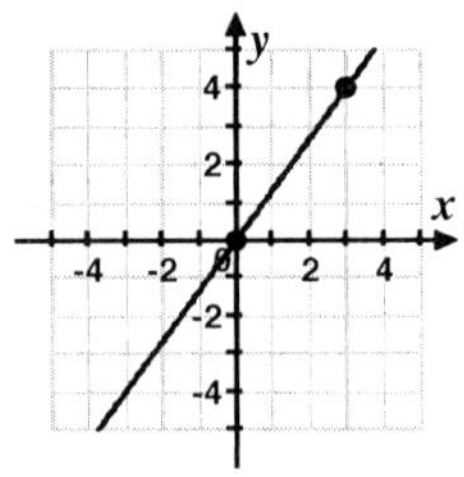

43. **a.** $2x + y = 3$

$y = -2x + 3$

b. $m = -2$; y-intercept $= 3$

c. Plot (0,3). Since $m = -2 = -\frac{2}{1}$, move 2 units *down* and 1 units to the *right* to reach the point (1,1). Draw a line through (0,3) and (1,1).

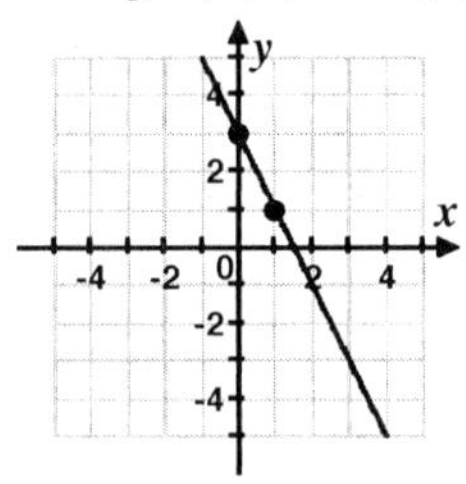

45. **a.** $7x + 2y = 14$

$$2y = -7x + 14$$

$$\frac{2y}{2} = \frac{-7x + 14}{2}$$

$$y = -\frac{7}{2}x + 7$$

b. $m=-\frac{7}{2}$; y-intercept = 7

c. Plot (0,7). Since $m=-\frac{7}{2}=-\frac{7}{2}$, move 7 units *down* and 2 units to the *right* to reach the point (2,0). Draw a line through (0,7) and (2,0).

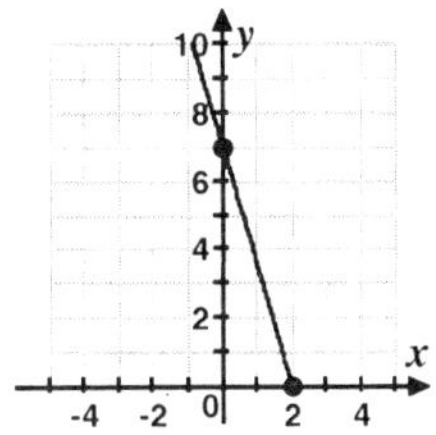

47. $y=3x+1$:

$m=3$; y-intercept $=1$

$y=3x-3$:

$m=3$; y-intercept $=-3$

The lines are parallel because their slopes are equal.

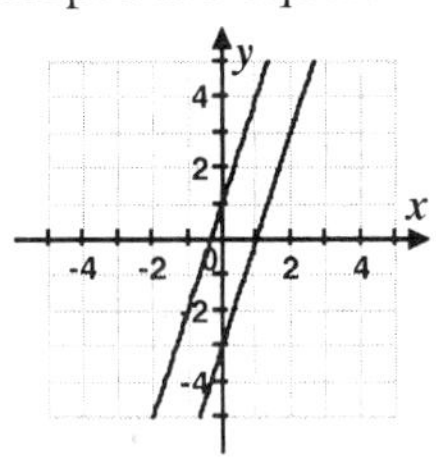

49. $y=-3x+2$:

$m=-3$; y-intercept $=2$

$y=3x+2$:

$m=3$; y-intercept $=2$

The lines are not parallel because their slopes are not equal.

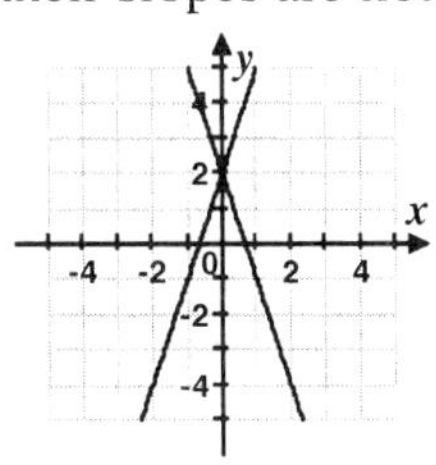

51. $x-2y=2 \rightarrow y=\frac{1}{2}x-1$

$2x-4y=3 \rightarrow y=\frac{1}{2}x-\frac{3}{4}$

The lines are parallel because their slopes are equal.

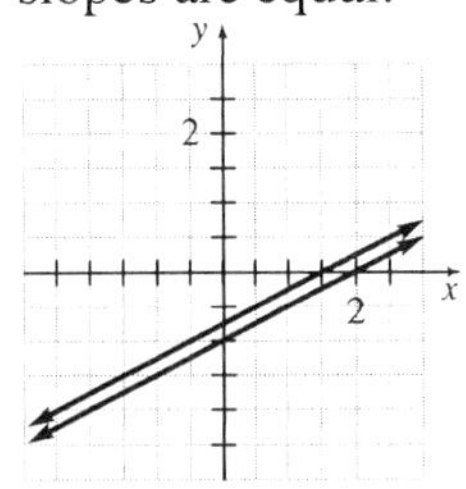

53. Find the slope of the parallel line.

$3x+y=6$

$y=-3x+6$

The slope is -3. We are given that the y-intercept is 5, so using slope-intercept form, we have $y=-3x+5$.

54. Find the slope of the parallel line.

$2x+y=8$

$y=-2x+8$

The slope is -2. We are given that the y-intercept is -4, so using the slope-intercept form, we have $y=-2x-4$.

55. Find the y-intercept of the line.

$16y=8x+32$

$\frac{16}{16}y=\frac{8}{16}x+\frac{32}{16}$

$y=\frac{1}{2}x+2$

The y-intercept is 2.

Find the slope of the parallel line.

$3x+3y=9$

$3y=-3x+9$

$y=-x+3$

The slope is -1. Using slope-intercept form, we have $y=-x+2$.

56. Find the y-intercept of the line.

$2y = 6x + 8$

$\frac{2y}{2} = \frac{6x}{2} + \frac{8}{2}$

$y = 3x + 4$

The y-intercept is 4.
Now, find the slope of the parallel line.

$4x + 4y = 20$

$4y = -4x + 20$

$\frac{4y}{4} = \frac{-4x}{4} + \frac{20}{4}$

$y = -x + 5$

The slope is -1. Using the slope-intercept form, we have $y = -x + 4$.

57. If the line rises from left to right, it has a positive slope. It passes through the origin, (0, 0) and a second point with equal x- and y-coordinates. The point (2, 2) is one example.
Use the two points to find the slope.

$m = \frac{0-2}{0-2} = \frac{-2}{-2} = 1$

The slope is 1. The y-intercept is 0. Using slope-intercept form, we have $y = 1x + 0$ or $y = x$.

58. If the line falls from left to right, the slope must be negative. It passes through the origin, $(0,0)$, and has a second point with opposite x- and y-coordinates. The point $(2,-2)$ is one example.
Use the two points to find the slope.

$m = \frac{-2-0}{2-0} = -\frac{2}{2} = -1$

The slope is -1. The y-intercept is 0. Using the slope-intercept form, we have $y = -x + 0$ or $y = -x$.

59. **a.** $y = -0.4x + 38$

1980; $x = 0$

$y = -0.4(0) + 38 = 38$

1981; $x = 1$

$y = -0.4(1) + 38 = 37.6$

1982; $x = 2$

$y = -0.4(2) + 38 = 37.2$

1983; $x = 3$

$y = -0.4(3) + 38 = 36.8$

1990; $x = 10$

$y = -0.4(10) + 38 = 34$

2000; $x = 20$

$y = -0.4(20) + 38 = 30$

According to the formula, 38% of U.S. men smoked in 1980, 37.6% in 1981, 37.2% in 1982, 36.8% in 1983, 34% in 1990, and 30% in 2000.

b. The slope of this model is –0.4. This indicates that the percentage of U.S. men smoking is decreasing by 0.4% each year.

c. The y-intercept is 38. This indicates that in 1980 (the initial year for the model), there were 38% of U.S. men smoking.

61. **a.** The y-intercept is 21. This means that 21 million people were living with AIDS in sub-Saharan Africa in 1997.

b. $m = \frac{29-21}{5-0} = \frac{8}{5} = 1.6$

The number of people living with AIDS in sub-Saharan Africa is increasing by 1.6 million each year.

c. $y = mx + b$

$y = 1.6x + 21$

d. Since 2006 – 1997 = 9, find y when x =9.

$y=1.6(9)+21=14.4+21=35.4$

35.4 million people will be living with the virus in 2006.

For Exercises 63-65, answers will vary.

67. First, find the slope using the points $(0,32)$ and $(100,212)$.

$m=\dfrac{212-32}{100-0}=\dfrac{180}{100}=\dfrac{9}{5}$

The slope is $\dfrac{9}{5}$. We also know that the y-intercept is 32. Using slope-intercept form, we have $F=\dfrac{9}{5}C+32$.

69. $\dfrac{x}{2}+7=13-\dfrac{x}{4}$

Multiply by the LCD, which is 4.

$4\left(\dfrac{x}{2}+7\right)=4\left(13-\dfrac{x}{4}\right)$

$2x+28=52-x$

$3x+28=52$

$3x=24$

$x=8$

The solution is 8.

70. $3\left(12\div 2^2-3\right)^2$

$=3(12\div 4-3)^2$

$=3(3-3)^2$

$=3\cdot 0^2=3\cdot 0=0$

71. $A=PB$; A = 14, P = 25% = 0.25

$A=PB$

$14=0.25\cdot B$

$\dfrac{14}{0.25}=\dfrac{0.25B}{0.25}$

$56=B$

14 is 25% of 56.

Chapter 4 Mid-Chapter Check Points

1. **a.** The x-intercept is 4.

b. The y-intercept is 2.

c. The points (4, 0) and (0, 2) lie on the line.

$m=\dfrac{2-0}{0-4}=\dfrac{2}{-4}=-\dfrac{1}{2}$

2. **a.** The x-intercept is –5.

b. There is no y-intercept.

c. It is a vertical line, so the slope is undefined.

3. **a.** The x-intercept is 0.

b. The y-intercept is 0.

c. The points (0, 0) and (5, 3) lie on the line.

$m=\dfrac{3-0}{5-0}=\dfrac{3}{5}$

4. $y=-2x$

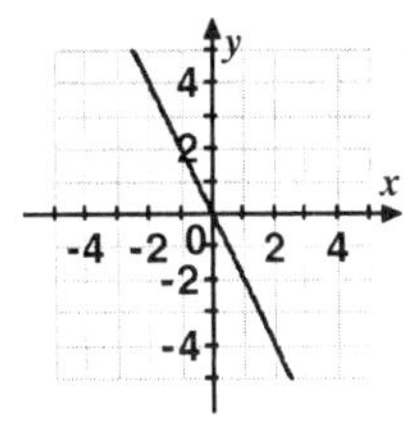

5. $y=-2$

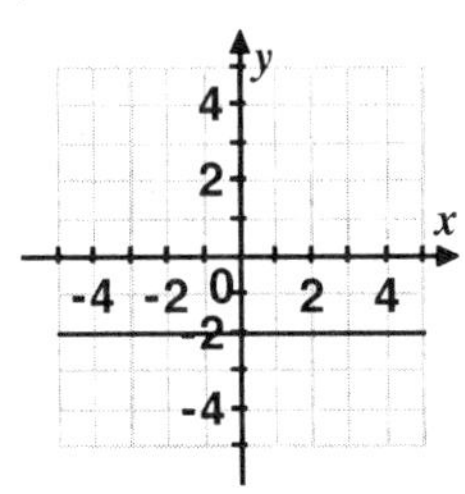

6. $x + y = -2$

$y = -x - 2$

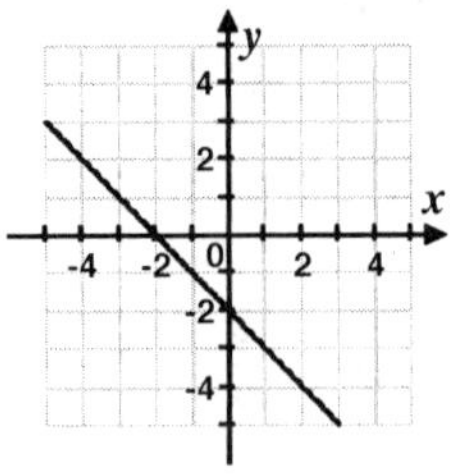

7. $y = \frac{1}{3}x - 2$

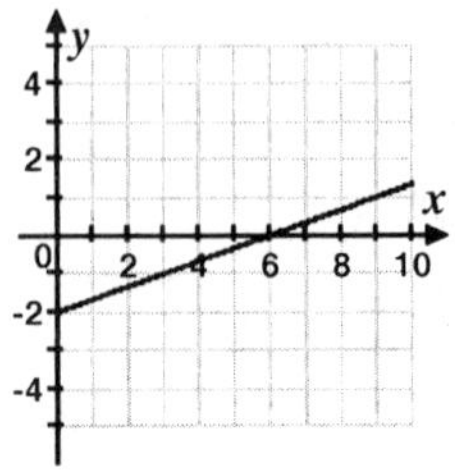

8. $x = 3.5$

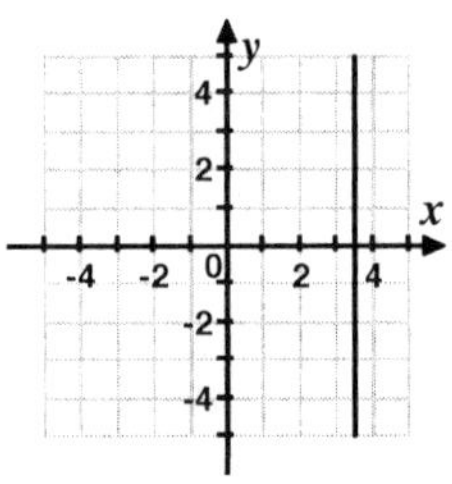

9. $4x - 2y = 8$

$-2y = -4x + 8$

$\frac{-2y}{-2} = \frac{-4x}{-2} + \frac{8}{-2}$

$y = 2x - 4$

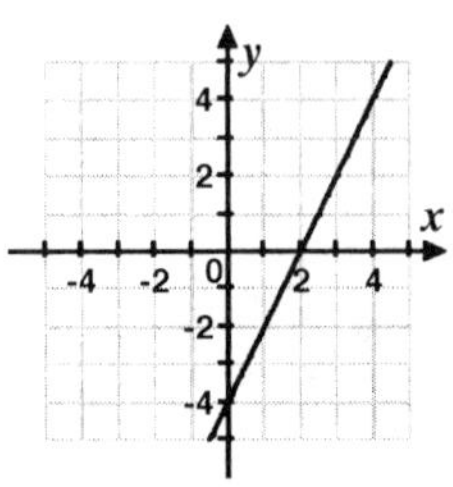

10. $y = 3x + 2$

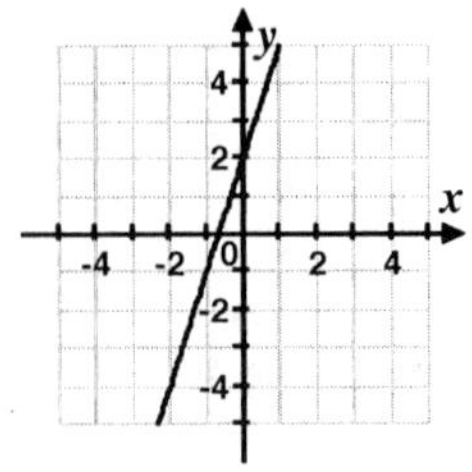

11. $3x + y = 0$

$y = -3x$

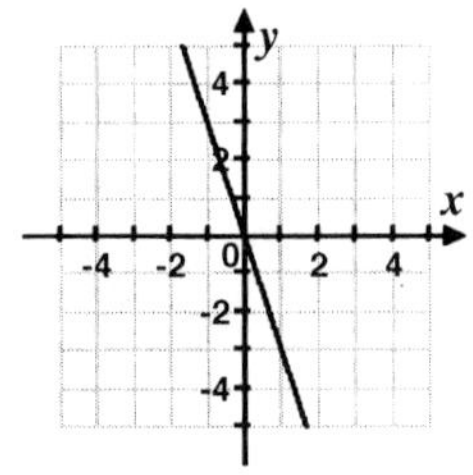

12. $y = x^2 - 4$

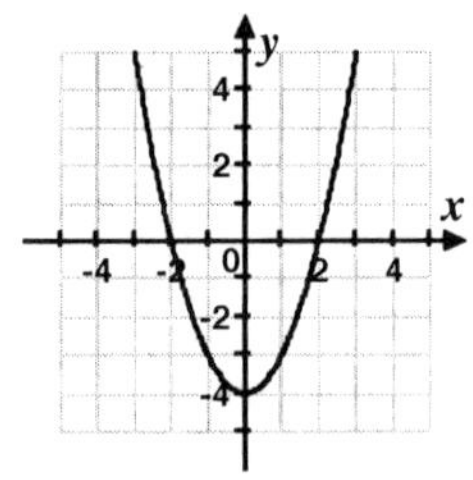

13. $y = x - 4$

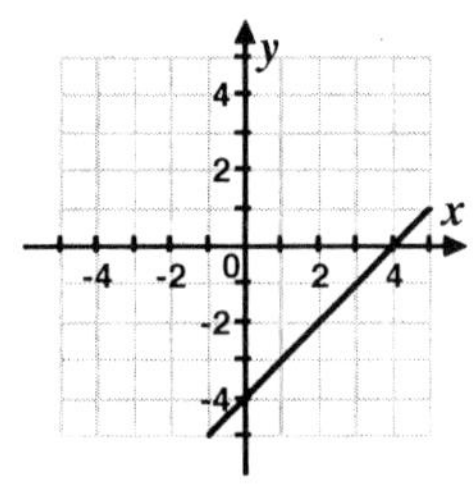

14. $5y = -3x$

$y = -\frac{3}{5}x$

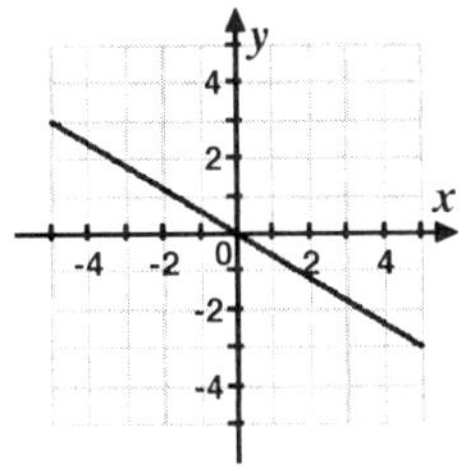

15. $5y = 20$

$y = 4$

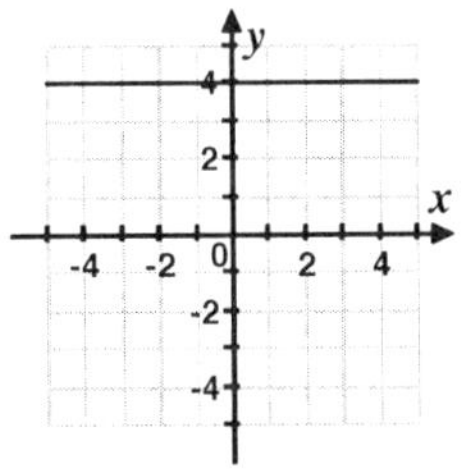

16. $5x - 2y = 10$

$-2y = -5x + 10$

$y = \frac{5}{2}x - 5$

The slope is $\frac{5}{2}$ and the y-intercept is -5.

17. $(2,-4)$ and $(7,0)$: $m = \frac{0-(-4)}{7-2} = \frac{4}{5}$

$(-4,2)$ and $(1,6)$: $m = \frac{6-2}{1-(-4)} = \frac{4}{5}$

Since the slopes are the same, the lines are parallel.

18. **a.** The line is in slope-intercept form, so the y-intercept is 33.

b. In 1995, 33% of U.S. colleges offered distance learning by computer.

c. The line is in slope intercept form, so the coefficient of the x-term, 7.8, is the slope.

d. For the years 1993 through 2002, the percentage of colleges that offered distance learning by computer increased by 7.8% each year.

4.5 Exercise Set

1. Line with a slope 3 that passes through the point (2,5).
Begin with the point-slope equation of a line with $m = 3$, $x_1 = 2$, and $y_1 = 5$.

$y - y_1 = m(x - x_1)$

$y - 5 = 3(x - 2)$

Now solve this equation for y and write an equivalent equation in slope-intercept form.

$y - 5 = 3x - 6$

$y = 3x - 1$

3. Line with a slope 5 that passes through the point (−2, 6).
Begin with the point-slope equation of a line with $m = 5$, $x_1 = -2$, and $y_1 = 6$.

$y - y_1 = m(x - x_1)$

$y - 6 = 5(x - (-2))$

$y - 6 = 5(x + 2)$

Now solve this equation for y and write an equivalent equation in slope-intercept form.

$y - 6 = 5(x + 2)$

$y - 6 = 5x + 10$

$y = 5x + 16$

5. Line with a slope −8 that passes through the point (−3, −2).
Begin with the point-slope equation of a line with $m=-8$, $x_1=-3$, and $y_1=-2$.

$$y-y_1=m(x-x_1)$$
$$y-(-2)=-8(x-(-3))$$
$$y+2=-8(x+3)$$

Now solve this equation for y and write an equivalent equation in slope-intercept form.

$$y+2=-8(x+3)$$
$$y+2=-8x-24$$
$$y=-8x-26$$

7. Line with a slope −12 that passes through the point (−8, 0).
Begin with the point-slope equation of a line with $m=-12$, $x_1=-8$, and $y_1=0$.

$$y-y_1=m(x-x_1)$$
$$y-0=-12(x-(-8))$$
$$y=-12(x+8)$$
$$y=-12x-96$$

Now solve this equation for y and write an equivalent equation in slope-intercept form.

$$y=-12(x+8)$$
$$y=-12x-96$$

9. Slope = −1, passing through $\left(-\frac{1}{2},-2\right)$

point-slope form:

$$y+2=-1\left(x+\frac{1}{2}\right)$$
$$y+2=-x-\frac{1}{2}$$

slope-intercept form: $y=-x-\frac{5}{2}$

11. Slope = $\frac{1}{2}$, passes through the origin: (0,0)

point-slope form: $y-0=\frac{1}{2}(x-0)$

slope-intercept form: $y=\frac{1}{2}x$

13. Slope = $-\frac{2}{3}$, passing through (6, −2)

point-slope form:

$$y+2=-\frac{2}{3}(x-6)$$
$$y+2=-\frac{2}{3}x+4$$

slope-intercept form: $y=-\frac{2}{3}x+2$

15. Passing through (1,2) and (5,10)

slope = $\frac{10-2}{5-1}=\frac{8}{4}=2$

point-slope form: $y-2=2(x-1)$
or $y-10=2(x-5)$

slope-intercept form:

$$y-2=2x-2$$
$$y=2x$$

17. Passing through (−3,0) and (0,3)

slope = $\frac{3-0}{0+3}=\frac{3}{3}=1$

point-slope form: $y-0=1(x+3)$ or $y-3=1(x-0)$

slope-intercept form: $y=x+3$

19. Passing through (−3, −1) and (2,4)

slope = $\frac{4+1}{2+3}=\frac{5}{5}=1$

point-slope form: $y+1=1(x+3)$
or $y-4=1(x-2)$

slope-intercept form: $y=x+2$

21. Passing through (−4, −1) and (3, 4)

slope = $\frac{4-(-1)}{3-(-4)} = \frac{5}{7}$

point-slope form: $y-4=\frac{5}{7}(x-3)$

or $y+1=\frac{5}{7}(x+4)$

slope-intercept form: $y=\frac{5}{7}x+\frac{13}{7}$

23. Passing through (−3, −1) and (4, −1)

slope = $\frac{-1+1}{4+3}=\frac{0}{7}=0$

point-slope form: $y+1=0(x+3)$

or $y+1=0(x-4)$

slope-intercept form: $y=-1$

25. Passing through (2,4) with x-intercept = −2

Use the points (2,4) and (−2,0) to find the slope.

slope = $\frac{0+4}{-2-2}=\frac{-4}{-4}=1$

point-slope form: $y-4=1(x-2)$

slope-intercept form: $y=x+2$

27. x-intercept = $-\frac{1}{2}$ and y-intercept = 4

Use the points $\left(-\frac{1}{2},0\right)$ and (0,4).

slope = $\frac{4-0}{0+\frac{1}{2}}=\frac{4}{\frac{1}{2}}=8$

point-slope form: $y-0=8\left(x+\frac{1}{2}\right)$

or $y-4=8(x-0)$

slope-intercept form: $y=8x+4$

29. Through (−3, 2) and parallel to $y = 4x + 2$.

The slope of the line is 4 since the line is parallel to a line with a slope of 4. Use point-slope form to find the equation of the line.

$$y-2=4(x-(-3))$$
$$y-2=4(x+3)$$
$$y-2=4x+12$$
$$y=4x+14$$

30. Through $(5,-3)$ and parallel to $y=2x+1$.

The slope of the line is 2 since the line is parallel to a line with slope 2. Use the point-slope form to find the equation of the line.

$$y-(-3)=2(x-5)$$
$$y+3=2x-10$$
$$y=2x-13$$

31. Through (−1, −5) and parallel to $3x + y = 6$.

Solve the equation for y to obtain the slope.

$$3x+y=6$$
$$y=-3x+6$$

The slope is −3. Use the slope and the point to obtain the equation of the line.

$$y-(-5)=-3(x-(-1))$$
$$y+5=-3(x+1)$$
$$y+5=-3x-3$$
$$y=-3x-8$$

32. Through $(-4,-7)$ and parallel to the line $6x+y=8$.

$$6x+y=8$$
$$y=-6x+8$$

The slope of the line is -6 since the line is parallel to a line with slope -6. Use the point-slope form to find the equation of the line.

$$y-(-7)=-6(x-(-4))$$
$$y+7=-6(x+4)$$
$$y+7=-6x-24$$
$$y=-6x-31$$

33. Through (2, 4) and same y-intercept as $x-4y=8$. Solve the equation to obtain the y-intercept.

$$x-4y=8$$
$$-4y=-x+8$$
$$y=\frac{1}{4}x-2$$

Now, use the two points to find the slope.

$$m=\frac{4-(-2)}{2-0}=\frac{6}{2}=3$$

Now use the slope and one of the points to find the equation of the line.

$$y-4=3(x-2)$$
$$y-4=3x-6$$
$$y=3x-2$$

34. Through $(2,6)$ with the same y-intercept as the graph of $x-3y=18$.

Find the y-intercept:

$$0-3y=18$$
$$-3y=18$$
$$\frac{-3y}{-3}=\frac{18}{-3}$$
$$y=-6$$

The y-intercept is -6 so the point $(0,-6)$ is on the graph. Use the two points to obtain the slope of the line.

$$m=\frac{-6-6}{0-2}=\frac{-12}{-2}=6$$

Using the slope-intercept form, the equation of the line is $y=6x-6$.

35. x-intercept at -4 and parallel to the line containing (3, 1) and (2, 6)

First, find the slope of the line going through the points (3, 1) and (2, 6).

$$m=\frac{6-1}{2-3}=\frac{5}{-1}=-5$$

The slope of the line is -5. Since this line is parallel to the line we are writing the equation for, its slope is also -5. Since the x-intercept is -4, the line goes through the point $(-4, 0)$. Use the point and the slope to find the equation of the line.

$$y-0=-5(x-(-4))$$
$$y=-5(x+4)$$
$$y=-5x-20$$

36. x-intercept at -6 and parallel to the line containing $(4,-3)$ and $(2,2)$.

Find the slope of the line.

$$m=\frac{2-(-3)}{2-4}=\frac{5}{-2}=-\frac{5}{2}$$

The slope of the line is $-\frac{5}{2}$. Since this line is parallel to the new line, the slope of our line is also $-\frac{5}{2}$. Since the x-intercept is -6, the line goes through the point $(-6,0)$. Use the point and the slope to find the equation of the new loan.

$$y-0=-\frac{5}{2}(x-(-6))$$
$$y=-\frac{5}{2}x-15$$

37. **a.** Line through (2,162) and (8,168)

$m = \frac{168-162}{8-2} = \frac{6}{6} = 1$

Using the point (2,162) as (x_1, y_1), the point-slope equation is $y - 162 = 1(x-2)$.

b. $y - 162 = x - 2$

$y = x + 160$

c. The year 2010 corresponds to $x = 20$.

$y = 20 + 160 = 180$

According to the equation, the average American adult will weigh 180 pounds in 2010.

39. Two points on the line are (12,3) and (15,1).

$m = \frac{1-3}{15-12} = \frac{-2}{3} = -\frac{2}{3}$

point-slope form using (12,3):

$y - 3 = -\frac{2}{3}(x-12)$

Use this equation to find the point-slope equation.

$y - 3 = -\frac{2}{3}x + 8$

$y = -\frac{2}{3}x + 11$

If $x = 7$, $y = -\frac{2}{3}(7) + 11 = -\frac{14}{3} + 11 \approx 6.3$.

The model predicts that a person with 7 years of education will score about 6.3 on the prejudice test.

41. **a.** Answers will vary.

b. Two points on the line are (50,6) and (80,5).

The slope is $m = \frac{5-6}{80-50} = -\frac{1}{30}$.

Using the point (50,6), the point-slope form is $y - 6 = -\frac{1}{30}(x-50)$.

Use this equation to find the slope-intercept equation.

$y - 6 = -\frac{1}{30}x + \frac{5}{3}$

$y = -\frac{1}{30}x + \frac{23}{3}$

$y \approx -0.03x + 7.67$

c. If $x = 130$, $y = -0.03(130) + 7.67$ $= 3.77$. This model predicts that a person exercising 130 minutes per week will have 3.77 or about 4 headaches per week.

d. As minutes per week spent exercising increases, the number of headaches per month decreases.

43. Answers will vary.

45. Statement *c* is true.

The line through (2, −5) and (2,6) is vertical, so its slope is undefined.

47. Answers will vary.

49. **a.**

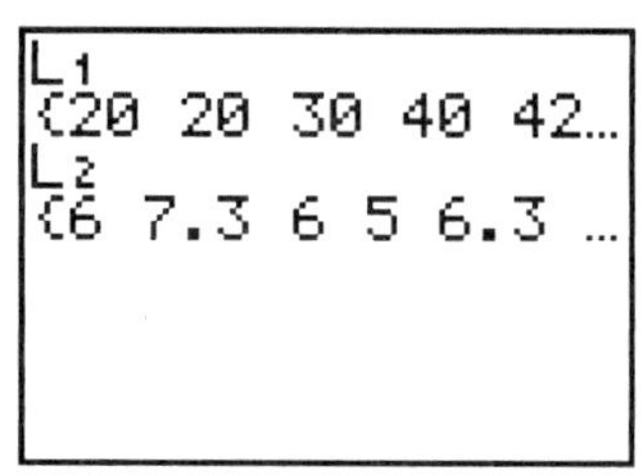

b.

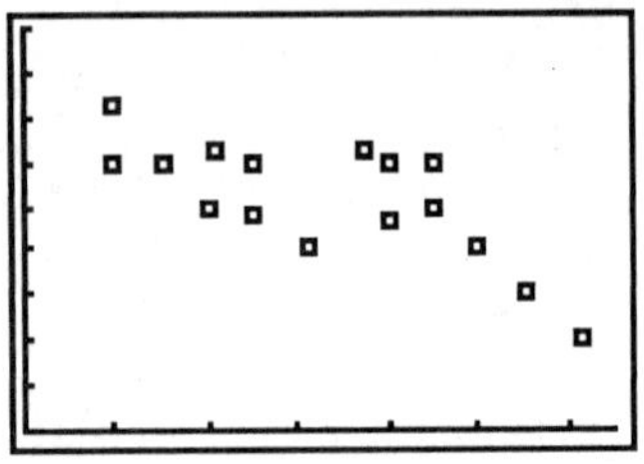

c.

```
LinReg
 y=ax+b
 a=-.0311817572
 b=7.219689132
```

d.

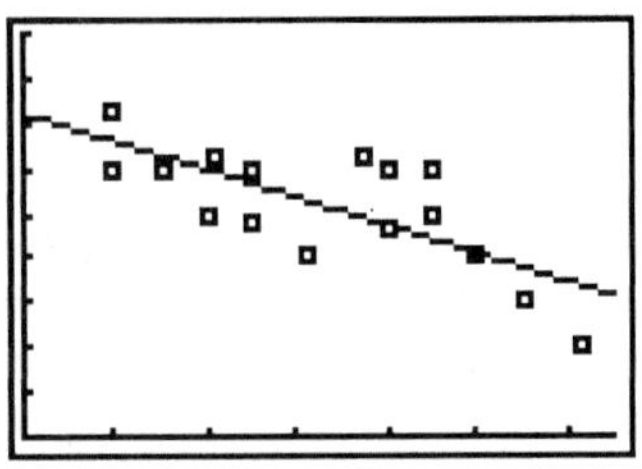

50. Let x = the number of sheets of paper.

$$4+2x \le 29$$
$$2x \le 25$$
$$x \le \frac{25}{2} \text{ or } 12\frac{1}{2}$$

Since the number of sheets of paper must be a whole number, at most 12 sheets of paper can be put in the envelope.

51. The only natural numbers in the given set are 1 and $\sqrt{4}(=2)$

52. $3x-5y=15$

x-intercept:
$$3x-5(0)=15$$
$$3x=15$$
$$x=5$$

y-intercept:
$$3(0)-5y=15$$
$$-5y=15$$
$$y=-3$$

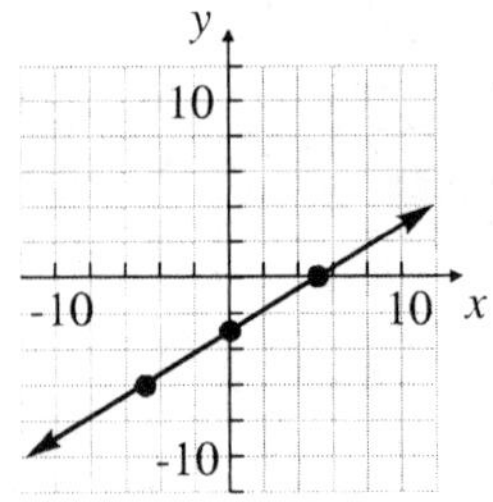

4.6 Exercise Set

1. $x+y>4$

$(2,2)$: $2+2>4$; $4>4$ false

$(2,2)$ is not a solution.

$(3,2)$: $3+2>4$; $5>4$ true

$(3,2)$ is a solution.

$(-3,8)$: $-3+8>4$; $5>4$ true

$(-3,8)$ is a solution.

3. $2x+y\ge 5$

$(4,0)$: $8+0\ge 5$; true

$(4,0)$ is a solution.

$(1,3)$: $2+3\ge 5$ true

$(1,3)$ is a solution.

$(0,0)$: $0+0\ge 5$ false

$(0,0)$ is not a solution.

5. $y\ge -2x+4$

$(4,0)$: $0\ge -8+4$ true

$(4,0)$ is a solution.

$(1,3)$: $3\ge -2+4=2$ true

$(1,3)$ is a solution.

$(-2,-4)$: $-4\ge 4+4=8$ false

$(-2,-4)$ is not a solution.

7. $y > -2x+1$

$(2,3)$: $3 > -4+1 = -3$ true

(2,3) is a solution.

$(0,0)$: $0 > 0+1 = 1$ false

$(0,0)$ is not a solution.

$(0,5)$: $5 > 0+1 = 1$ true

$(0,5)$ is a solution.

9. $x+y \geq 3$

Step 1. Replace $\geq$ with = and graph the linear equation $x+y=3$. The x-intercept is 4 and the y-intercept is 3, so the line passes through (3,0) and (0,3). Draw a solid line because the inequality contains a $\geq$symbol.

Step 2. Use (0,0) as a test point.

$x+y \geq 3$

$0+0 \geq 3$

$0 \geq 3$ false

Step 3. The test point (0,0) is part of the solution set, so shade the half-plane *not* containing (0,0).

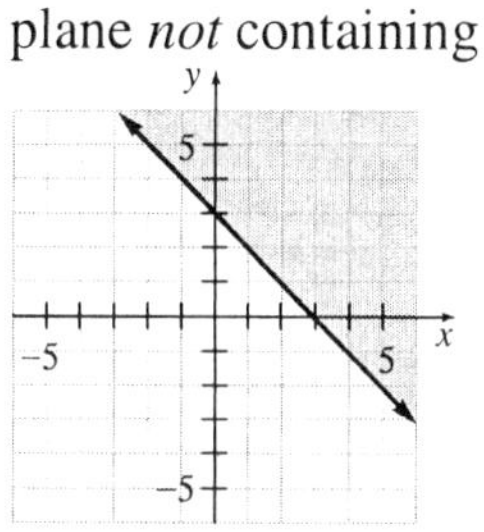

11. $x-y<5$

Graph the equation $x-y=5$, which passes through the points (3,0) and (0, −5). Draw a dashed line because the inequality contains a < symbol. Use (0,0) as a test point. Since $0-0<5$ is a true statement, shade the half-plane containing (0,0).

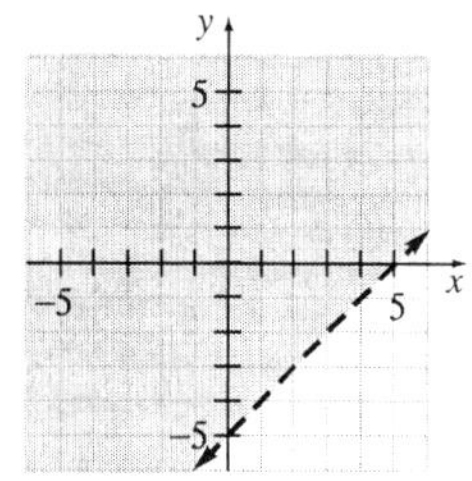

13. $x+2y>4$

Graph the equation $x+2y=4$ as a dashed line through (4,0) and (0,2). Use (0,0) as a test point. Since $0+2(0)>4$ is false, shade the half-plane *not* containing (0,0).

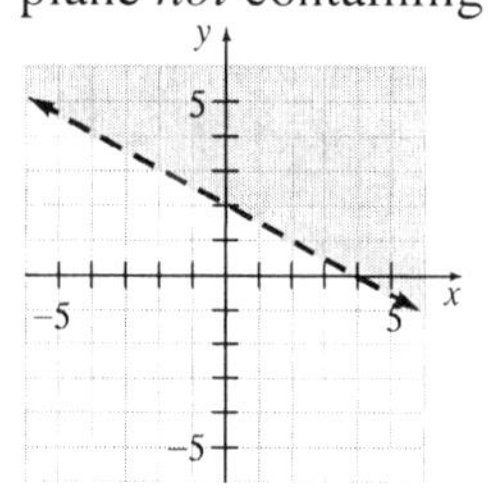

15. $3x-y \leq 6$

Graph the equation $3x-y=6$ as a solid line through (2,0) and (0, −6). Use (0,0) as a test point. Since $3(0)- \leq 6$ is true, shade the half-plane containing (0,0).

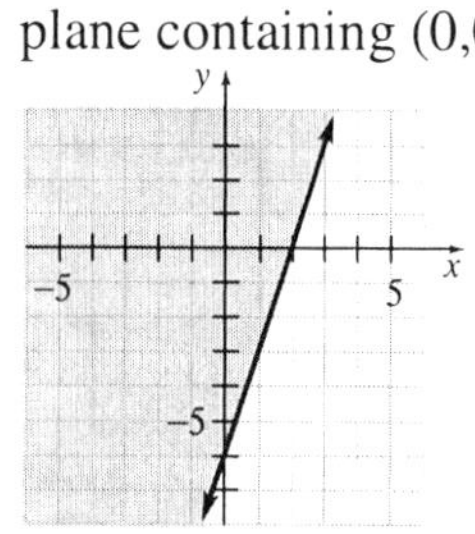

17. $3x-2y \leq 8$

Graph the equation $3x-2y=8$ as a solid line through $\left(\frac{8}{3},0\right)$ and (0, −4). Use (0,0) as a test point. Since $3(0)-2(0) \leq 8$ is true, shade the half-plane containing (0,0).

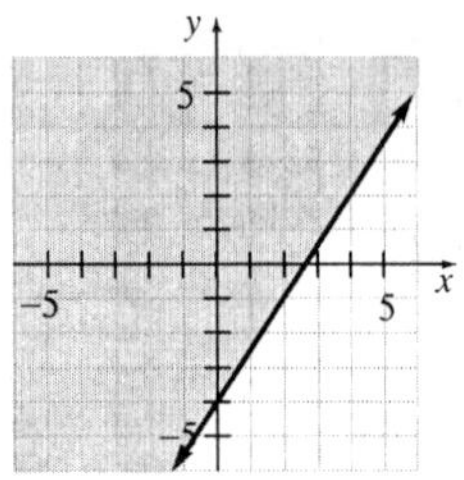

19. $4x+3y>15$

Graph $4x+3y=15$ as a dashed line through $\left(\frac{15}{4},0\right)$ and (0,5).

Use (0,0) as a test point. Since $4(0)+3(0)>15$ is false, shade the half-plane not containing (0,0).

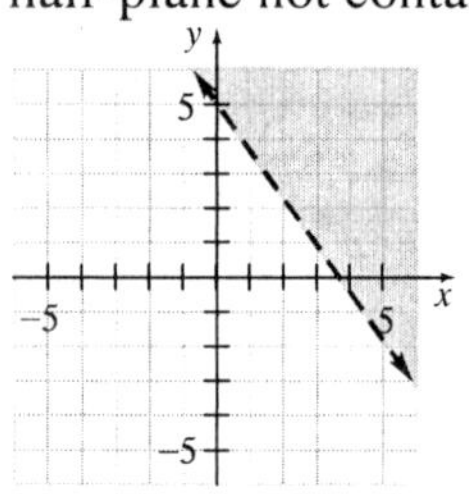

21. $5x-y<-7$

Graph the equation $5x-y=-7$ as a dashed line through $\left(-\frac{7}{5},0\right)$ and (0,7). Use (0,0) as a test point. Since $5(0)-0<-7$ is false, shade the half-plane *not* containing (0,0).

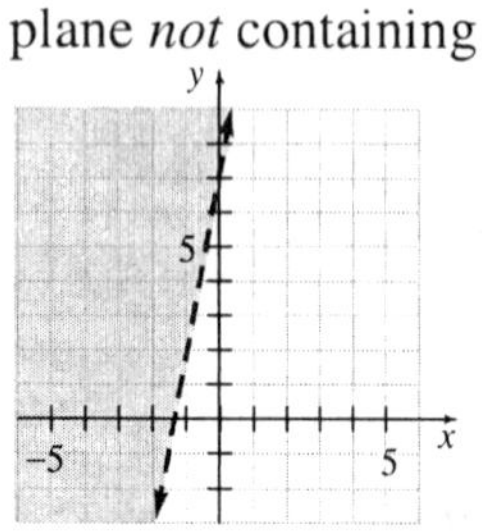

23. $y\le\frac{1}{3}x$

Graph the equation $y=\frac{1}{3}x$ as a solid line through (0,0) and (3,1). Because (0,0) lies on the line, it cannot be used as a test point. Instead use a point not on the line, such as (0,6). Since $6\le\frac{1}{2}(0)$ is false, shade the half-plane *not* containing (0,6).

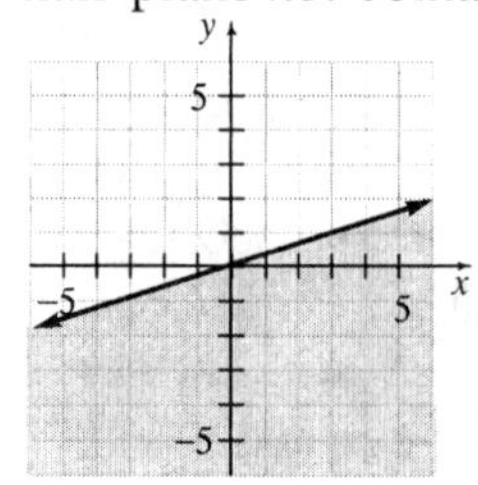

25. $y>2x$

Graph the equation $y=2x$ as a dashed line through the origin with slope 2. Use (3,3) as a test point. Since $3>2(3)$ is false, shade the half-plane *not* containing (3,3).

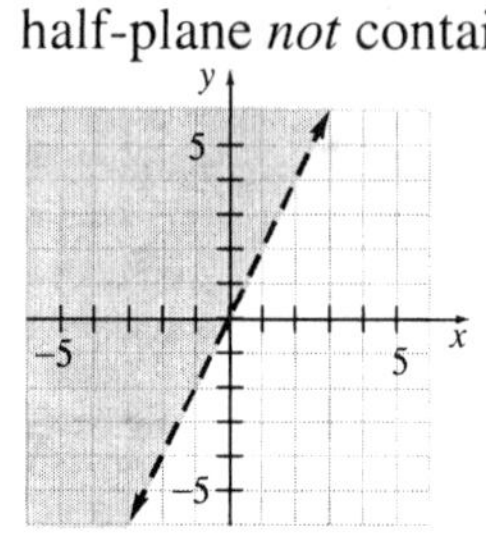

27. $y > 3x + 2$

Graph $y = 3x + 2$ as a dashed line using the slope and *y*-intercept. Use (0,0) as a test point. Since $0 > 3(0) + 2$ is false, shade the half-plane *not* containing (0,0).

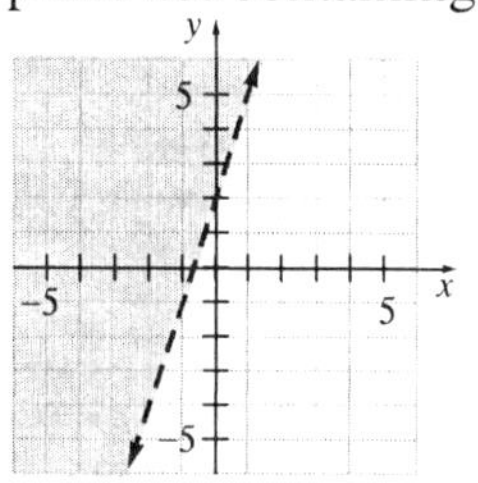

29. $y < \frac{3}{4}x - 3$

Graph $y = \frac{3}{4}x - 3$ as a dashed line using the slope and *y*-intercept. (Plot (0, −3) and move 3 units up and 4 units to the right to the point (4,0).) Use (0,0) as a test point. Since $0 < \frac{3}{4}(0) - 3$ is false, shade the half-plane *not* containing (0,0).

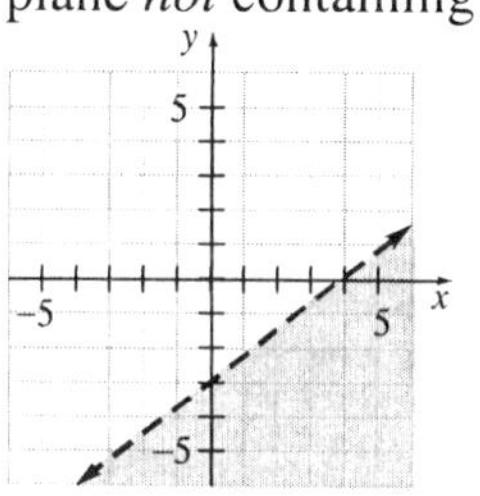

31. $x \le 1$

Graph the vertical line $x = 1$ as a solid line. Use (0,0) as a test point. Since $0 \le 1$ is true, shade the half-plane containing (0,0), which is the half-plane to the *left* of the line.

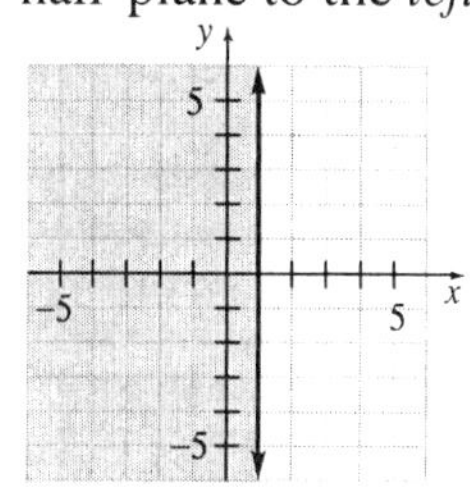

33. $y > 1$

Graph the horizontal line $y = 1$ as a dashed line. Use (0,0) as a test point. Since $0 > 1$ is false, shade the half-plane *not* containing (0,0), which is the half-plane *above* the line.

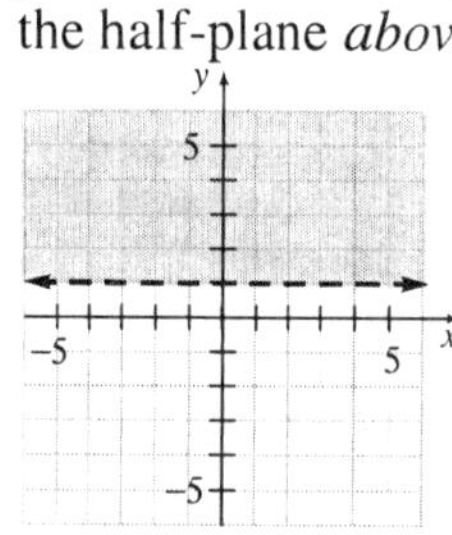

35. $x \ge 0$

Graph the vertical line $x = 0$ (the *y*-axis) as a solid line. Since (0,0) is on the line, choose a different test point, such as (3,3). Since $3 > 0$ is true, shade the half-plane containing (3,3), which is the half-plane to the *right* of the *y*-axis.

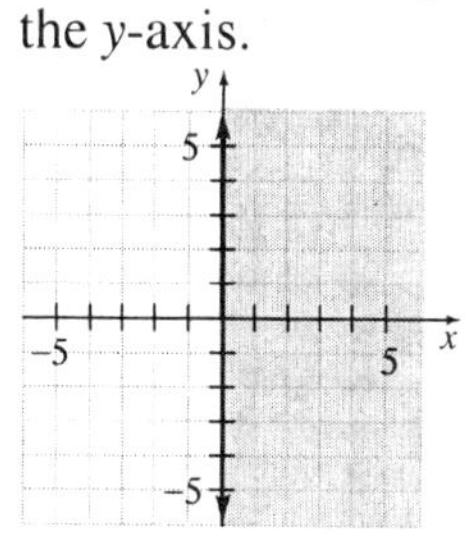

37. $x + y \geq 2$

Rewrite: $y \geq -x + 2$

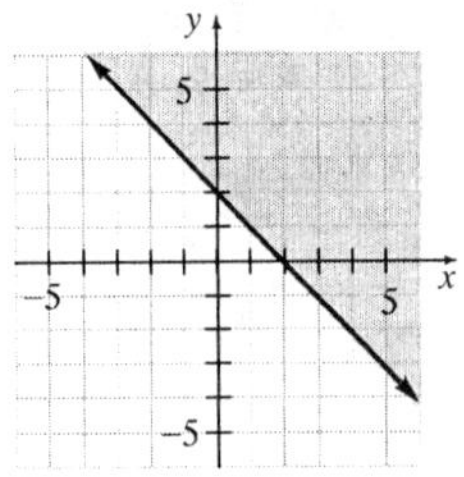

38. $x - y \geq 3$

Rewrite: $y \leq x - 3$

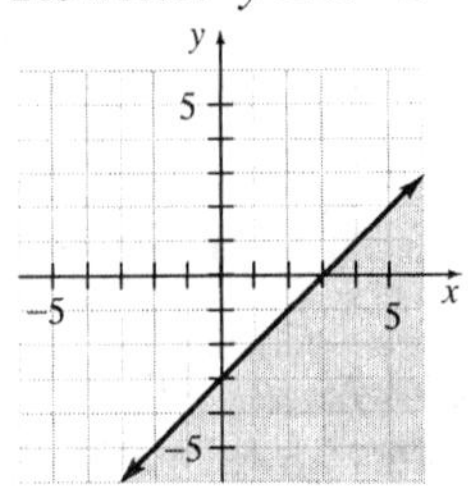

39. $5x - 2y \leq 10$

Rewrite: $y \geq \frac{5}{2}x - 5$

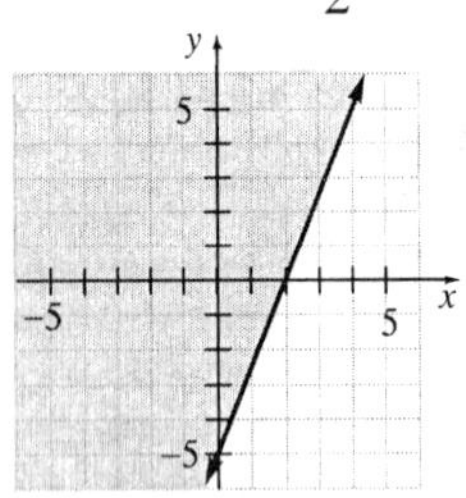

40. $4x + 2y \leq 8$

Rewrite: $y \leq -2x + 4$

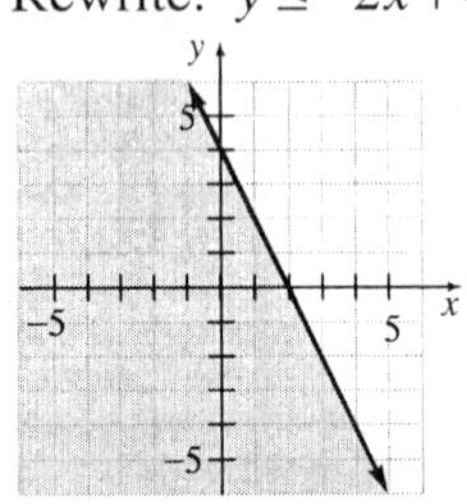

41. $y \geq \frac{1}{2}x$

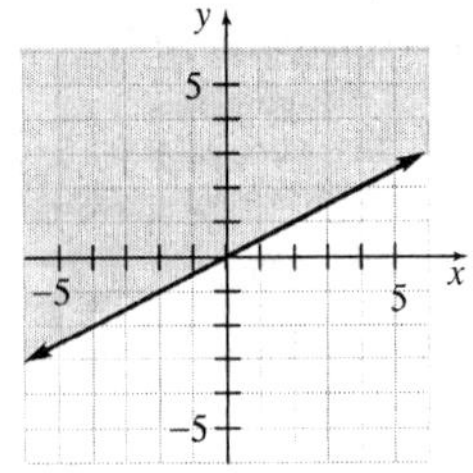

42. $y \geq \frac{1}{4}x$

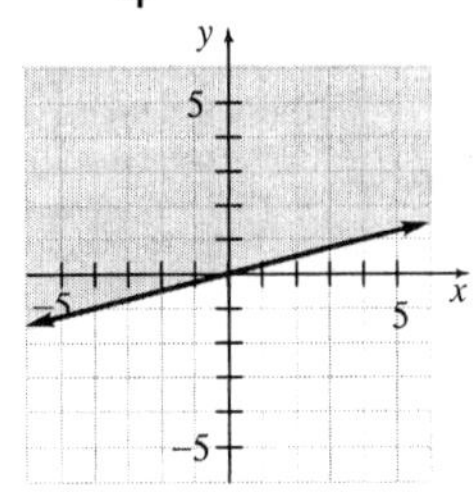

43. $y \leq -1$

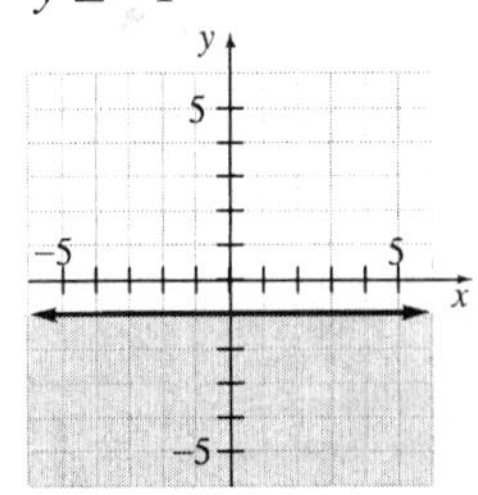

44. $y \leq -2$

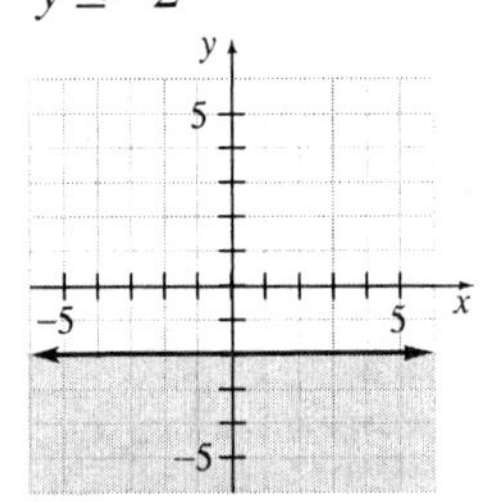

45. a. $20x + 10y \le 80{,}000$
Graph the line $20x + 10y = 80{,}000$ as a solid line, using the x-intercept 4000 and the y-intercept 8000. Use (1000,1000) as a test point. Since $20(1000) + 10(1000)$ $= 30{,}000 \le 80{,}000$ is true, shade the half-plane containing (1000,1000). Draw the graph in quadrant I only.

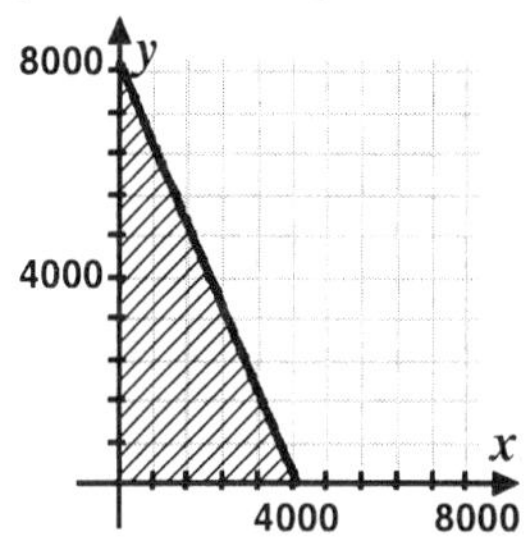

b. Answers will vary. One example is (1000, 2000) since $20(1000) + 10(2000)$
$= 20{,}000 + 20{,}000$
$= 40{,}000 < 80{,}000.$
This indicates that the plane can carry 1000 bottles of water and 2000 medical kits.

47. a. $50x + 150y > 2000$

b. Graph $50x + 150y = 2000$ as a dashed line, using the x-intercept 40 and y-intercept $\dfrac{2000}{150} \approx 13.3$. Use (10,20) as a test point. Since $50(10) + 150(20) = 3500 > 2000$ is true, shade the half-plane containing (10,20). Draw the graph in quadrant I only.

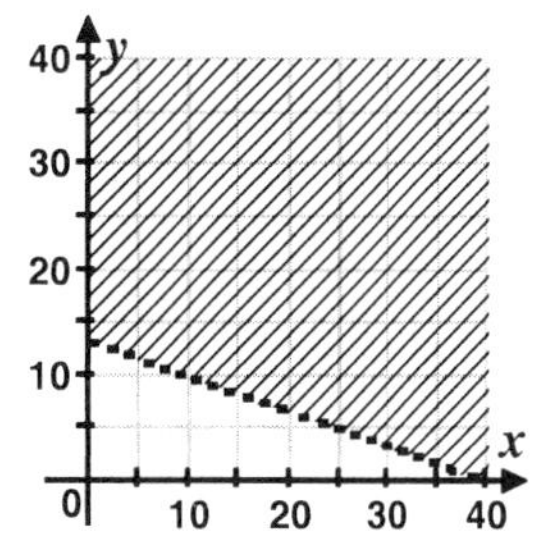

c. Answers will vary. One example is (20,15) since $50(20) + 150(150)$ $= 3200 > 2000$. This indicates that the elevator cannot carry 20 children and 15 adults.

49. a. $BMI = \dfrac{703W}{H^2}; W = 200, H = 72$

$$BMI = \frac{703(200)}{72^2}$$
$$= \frac{140{,}600}{5184} \approx 27.1$$

b. Locate the point (20,27.1) on the graph for males. The point falls in the "Borderline" region, so the man is borderline overweight.

For Exercises 51-57, answers may vary.

59. The x-and y-intercepts of the line are both 3, so the equation of the line is $x + y = 3$ or $y = -x + 3$. The line is solid, so the inequality symbol must be either $\ge$ or $\le$. Choose a test point in the shaded region, for example (4,4). Since $4 + 4 > 3$, the inequality symbol must be $\ge$. Therefore, the inequality is $x + y \ge 3$ or $y \ge -x + 3$.

61. $y \le 4x + 4$

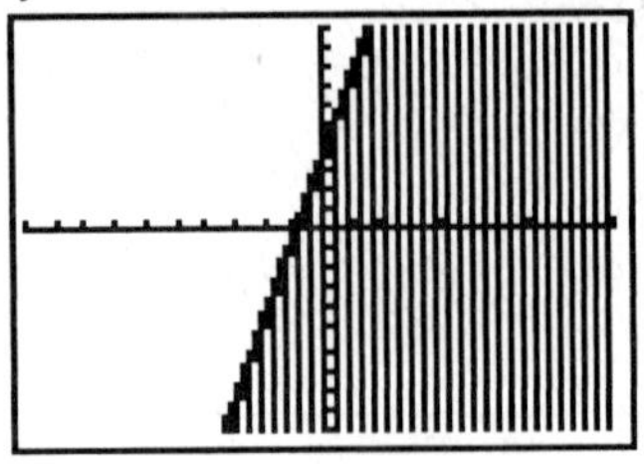

63. $y \ge \frac{1}{2}x + 4$

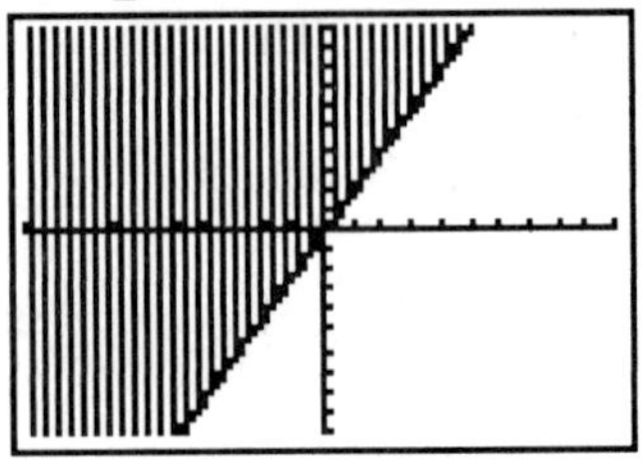

65. $V = lwh$ for h

$$V = lwh$$
$$\frac{V}{lw} = \frac{lwh}{lw}$$
$$\frac{V}{lw} = h \text{ or } h = \frac{V}{lw}$$

66. $\frac{2}{3} \div \left(-\frac{5}{4}\right)$

$$= \frac{2}{3} \cdot \left(-\frac{4}{5}\right)$$
$$= -\frac{8}{15}$$

67. $x^2 - 4;\ x = -3$

$$x^2 - 4 = (-3)^2 - 4 = 9 - 4 = 5$$

Chapter 4 Review Exercises

1. $(-3,3)$:

$$3 = 3(-3) + 6$$
$$3 = -6 + 9$$
$$3 = -3 \text{ false}$$

$(-3,3)$ is not a solution.

$(0,6)$:

$$6 = 3(0) + 6$$
$$6 = 6 \text{ true}$$

$(0,6)$ is a solution.

$(1,9)$:

$$9 = 3(1) + 6$$
$$9 = 9 \text{ true}$$

$(1,9)$ is a solution.

2. $(0,4)$:

$$3(0) - 4 = 12$$
$$-4 = 12 \text{ false}$$

$(0,4)$ is not a solution.

$(4,0)$:

$$3(4) - 0 = 12$$
$$12 = 12 \text{ true}$$

$(4,0)$ is a solution.

$(-1,15)$:

$$3(-1) - 15 = 12$$
$$-3 - 15 = 12$$
$$-18 = 12 \text{ false}$$

$(-1,15)$ is not a solution.

3. a.

x	$y=2x-3$	(x,y)
-2	$y=2(-2)-3=-7$	$(-2,-7)$
-1	$y=2(-1)-3=-5$	$(-1,-5)$
0	$y=2(0)-3=-5$	$(0,-3)$
1	$y=2(1)-3=-1$	$(1,-1)$
2	$y=2(2)-3=1$	$(2,1)$

b.

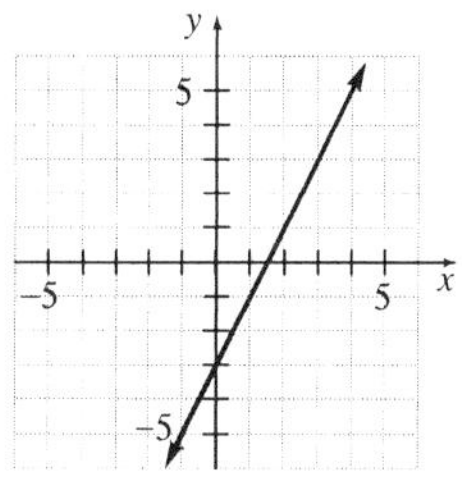

4. a.

x	$y=\frac{1}{2}x+1$	(x,y)
-4	$y=\frac{1}{2}(-4)+1=-1$	$(-4,-1)$
-2	$y=\frac{1}{2}(-2)+1=0$	$(-2,0)$
0	$y=\frac{1}{2}(0)+1=1$	$(0,1)$
2	$y=\frac{1}{2}(2)+1=2$	$(2,2)$
4	$y=\frac{1}{2}(4)+1=3$	$(4,3)$

b.

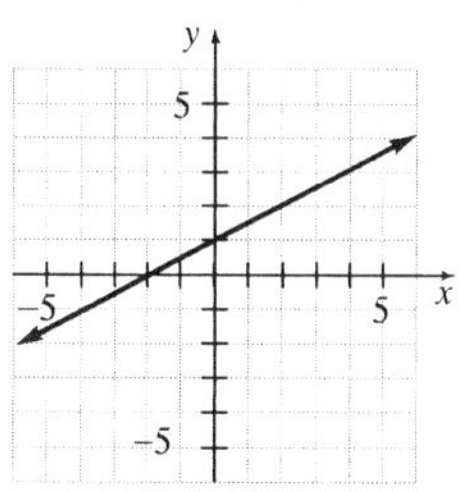

5.

x	$y=x^2-3$	(x,y)
-3	$y=(-3)^2-3=6$	$(-3,6)$
-2	$y=(-2)^2-3=1$	$(-2,1)$
-1	$y=(-1)^2-3=-2$	$(-1,-2)$
0	$y=0^2-3=-3$	$(0,-3)$
1	$y=1^2-3=-2$	$(1,-2)$
2	$y=2^2-3=1$	$(2,1)$
3	$y=3^2-1=6$	$(3,6)$

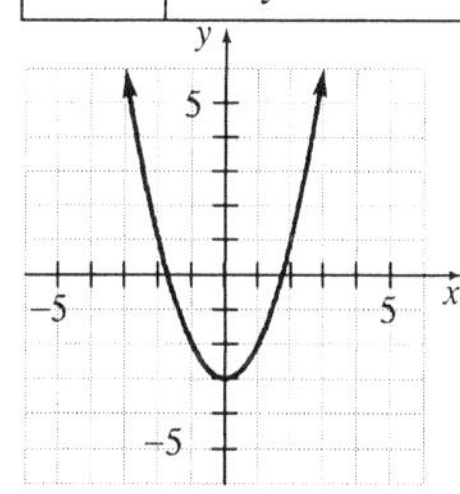

6. a.

x	$y=5x-41$	(x,y)
10	$y=5(10)-41=9$	$(10,9)$
12	$y=5(12)-41=19$	$(12,19)$
14	$y=5(14)-41=29$	$(14,29)$
16	$y=5(16)-41=39$	$(16,39)$

b. Answers will vary.

7. a. The graph crosses the x-axis at $(-2,0)$, so the x-intercept is -2.

b. The graph crosses the y-axis at $(0, -4)$, so the y-intercept is-4.

8. a. The graph does not cross the x-axis, so there is no x-intercept.

b. The graph crosses the y-axis at $(0,2)$, so the y-intercept is 2.

9. a. The graph crosses the x-axis at $(0,0)$ (the origin), so the x-intercept is 0.

b. The graph also crosses the y-axis at (0,0), so the y-intercept is 0.

10. $2x + y = 4$

x-intercept:
$$2x + 0 = 4$$
$$2x = 4$$
$$x = 2$$

y-intercept:
$$2(0) + y = 4$$
$$y = 4$$

x-intercept: (2,0); y-intercept: (0,4)
Find one other point as a checkpoint.
For example, substitute 1 for x.
$$2(1) + y = 4$$
$$2 + y = 4$$
$$y = 2$$
checkpoint: (1,2)
Draw a line through (2,0), (0,4), and (1,2).

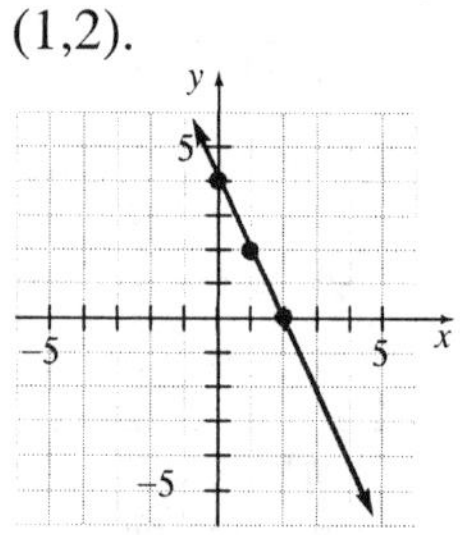

11. $3x - 2y = 12$
x-intercept: (4,0)
y-intercept: (0, −6)
checkpoint: (2, −3)
Draw a line through (4,0), (0, −6) and (2, −3)

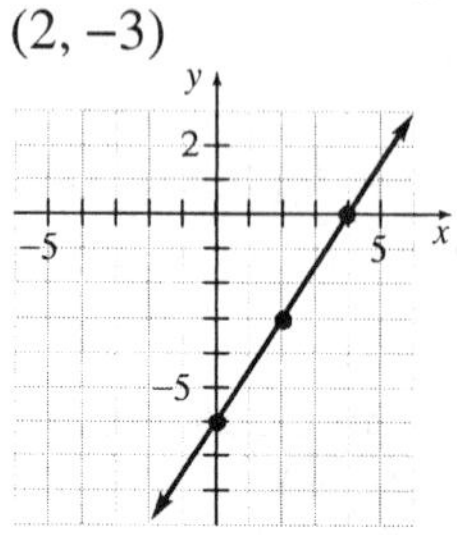

12. $3x = 6 - 2y$
x-intercept: (2,0)
y-intercept: (0,3)
checkpoint: (4, −3)
Draw a line through (2,0), (0,3) and (4, −3)

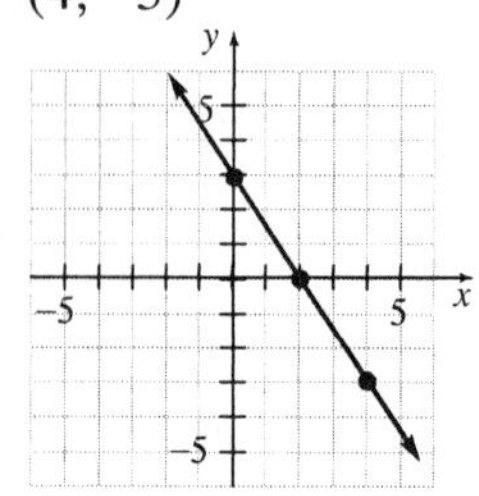

13. $3x - y = 0$
x-intercept: 0
y-intercept: 0
second point: (1,3)
checkpoint: (−1, −3)
Draw a line through (0,0), (1,3) and (−1, −3)

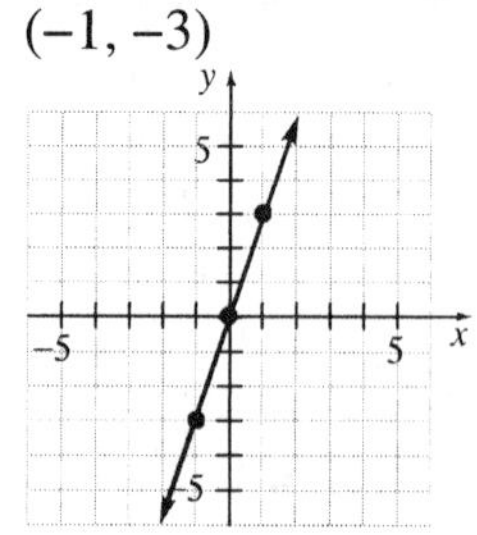

14. $x = 3$
Three ordered pairs are (3, −2), (3,0), and (3,2). The graph is a vertical line.

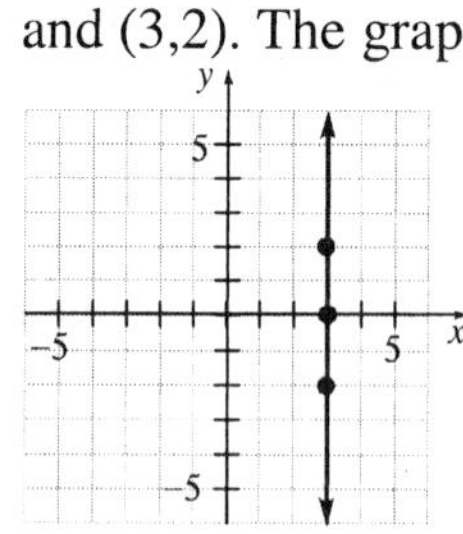

15. $y = -5$
Three ordered pairs are (−2, −5), (0, −5), and (2, −5). The graph is a horizontal line.

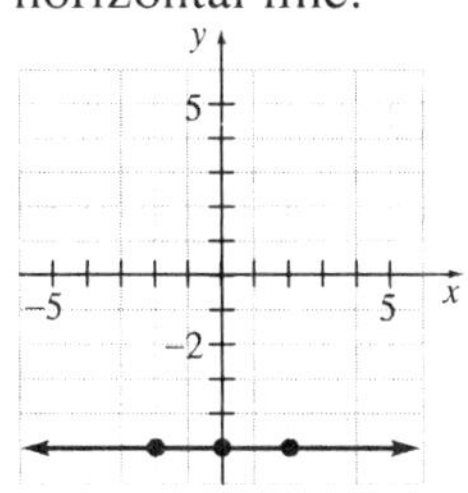

16. $y + 3 = 5$
$y = 2$
Three ordered pairs are (−2,2), (0,2), and (2,2). The graph is a horizontal line.

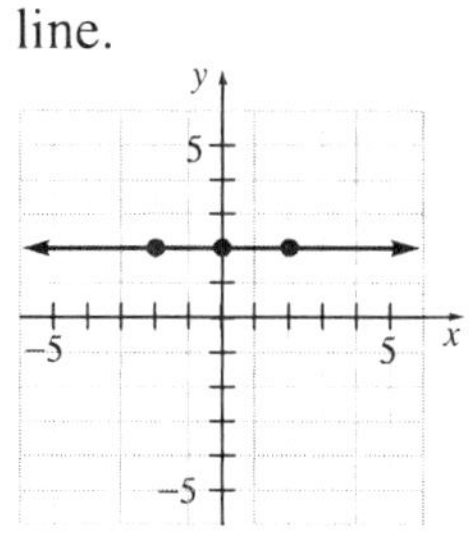

17. $2x = -8$
$x = -4$
Three ordered pairs (−4, −2), (−4,0), and (−4,2). The graph is a vertical line.

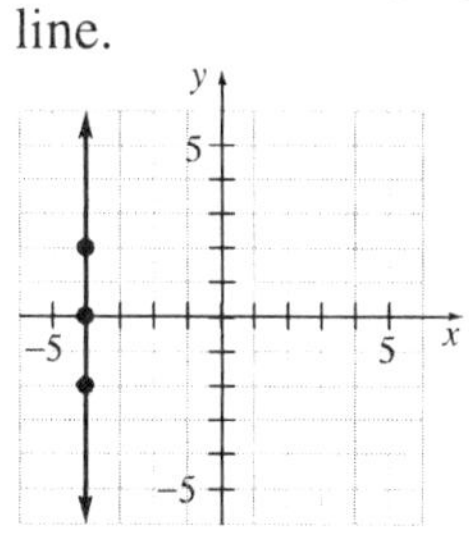

18. **a.** The minimum temperature occurred at 5 P.M. and was −4°F.

b. The maximum temperature occurred at 8 P.M. and was at 16°F.

c. The x-intercepts are 4 and 6. This indicates that 4 P.M. and 6 P.M., the temperature was 0°F.

d. The y-intercept is 12. This indicates that at noon the temperature was 12°F.

e. This indicates that the temperature stayed the same, at 12°F, from 9 P.M. until midnight.

19. Let $(x_1, y_1) = (3,2)$ and $(x_2, y_2) = (5,1)$.
$$m = \frac{y_2 - y_1}{x_2 - x_1} = \frac{1-2}{5-3} = -\frac{1}{2}$$
The slope is $-\frac{1}{2}$. Since the slope is negative, the line falls.

20. (−1,2) and (−3, −4)
$$m = \frac{-4-2}{-3-(-1)} = \frac{-6}{-2} = 3$$
Since the slope is positive, the line rises.

21. (−3,4) and (6,4)
$$m = \frac{4-4}{6-(-3)} = \frac{0}{9} = 0$$
Since the slope is 0, the line is horizontal.

22. (5,3) and (5, −3)
$$m = \frac{-3-3}{5-5} = \frac{-6}{0}\text{; undefined}$$
Since the slope is undefined, the line is vertical.

23. Line through (−3, −2) and (2,1):
$$m = \frac{1-(-2)}{2-(-3)} = \frac{3}{5}$$

24. Line through (–2,3) and (–2, –3): The line is vertical, so its slope is undefined.

25. Line through (–4, –1) and (2, –3):
$$m = \frac{-3-(-1)}{2-(-4)} = \frac{-2}{6} = -\frac{1}{3}$$

26. Line through (–2,2) and (3,2): The line is horizontal, so its slope is 0.

27. Line through (–1, –3) and (2, –8):
$$m = \frac{-8-(-3)}{2-(-1)} = \frac{-5}{3} = -\frac{5}{3}$$
Line through (8, –7) and (9,10):
$$m = \frac{10-(-7)}{9-8} = \frac{17}{1} = 17$$
Since their slopes are not equal, the lines are not parallel.

28. Line through (5,4) and (9,7):
$$m = \frac{7-4}{9-5} = \frac{3}{4}$$
Line through (–6,0) and (–2,3):
$$m = \frac{3-0}{-2-(-6)} = \frac{3}{4}$$
Since their slopes are equal, the lines are parallel.

29. **a.** $(1999,41315)$ and $(2001,41227)$
$$m = \frac{41227-41315}{2001-1999} = \frac{-88}{2} = -44$$
The number of new AIDS diagnoses decreased at a rate of 44 each year from 1999 to 2001.

b. $(2001,41227)$ and $(2003,43045)$
$$m = \frac{43045-41227}{2003-2001} = \frac{1818}{2} = 909$$
The number of new AIDS diagnoses increased at a rate of 909 each year from 2001 to 2003.

c. $(1999,41315)$ and $(2003,43045)$
$$m = \frac{43045-41315}{2003-1999} = \frac{1730}{4} = 432.5$$
$$\frac{-44+909}{2} = \frac{865}{2} = 432.5$$
Yes, the slope equals the average of the two values. Explanations will vary.

30. $y = 5x - 7$

$y = 5x + (-7)$

The slope is the x-coefficient, which is 5. The y-intercept is the constant term, which is –7.

31. $y = 6 - 4x$

$y = -4x + 6$

$m = -4$; y-intercept = 6

32. $y = 3$

$m = 0$; y-intercept = 3

33.
$$2x + 3y = 6$$
$$3y = -2x + 6$$
$$y = \frac{-2x+6}{3}$$
$$y = -\frac{2}{3}x + 2$$
$m = -\frac{2}{3}$; y-intercept = 2

34. $y = 2x - 4$

slope = $2 = \frac{2}{1}$; y-intercept = –4

Plot (0, –4) on the y-axis. From this point, move 2 units *up* (because 2 is positive) and 1 unit to the *right* to reach the point (1, –2). Draw a line through (0, –4) and (1, –2).

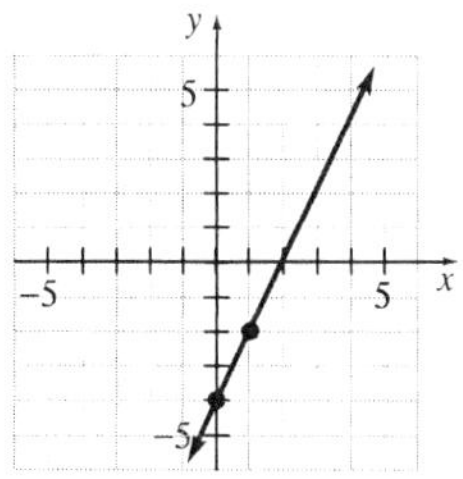

35. $y = \frac{1}{2}x - 1$

slope $= \frac{1}{2}$; y-intercept $= -1$

Plot (0, −1). From the point, move 1 unit *up* and 2 units to the *right* to reach the point (2,0). Draw a line through (0, −1) and (2,0).

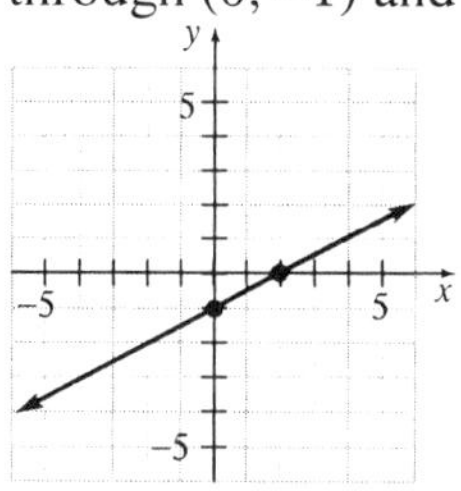

36. $y = -\frac{2}{3}x + 5$

slope $= -\frac{2}{3} = \frac{-2}{3}$; y-intercept $= 5$

Plot (0,5). Move 2 units *down* (because −2 is negative) and 3 units to the *right* to reach the point (3,3). Draw a line through (0,5) and (3,3).

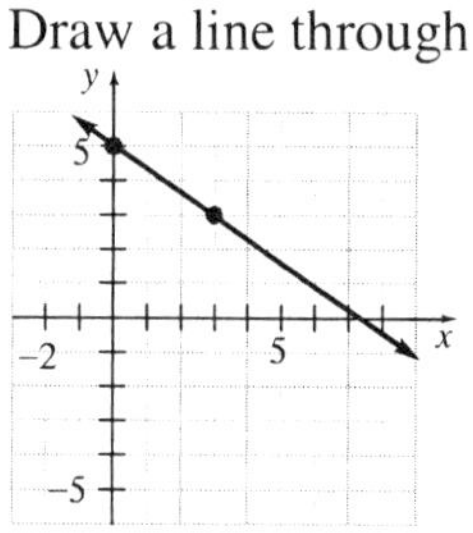

37. $y - 2x = 0$

$y = 2x$

slope $= 2 = \frac{2}{1}$; y-intercept $= 0$

Plot (0,0) (the origin). Move 2 units *up* and 1 unit to the *right* to reach the point (1,2). Draw a line through (0,0) and (1,2).

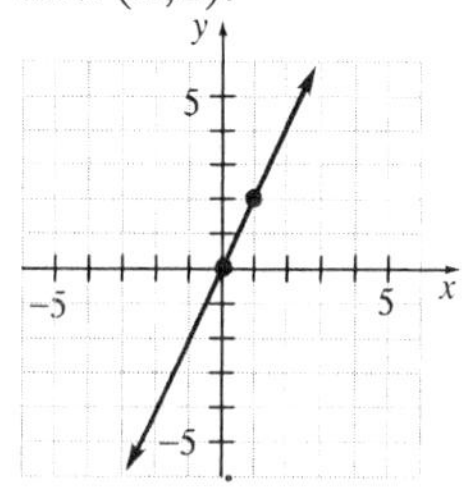

38. $\frac{1}{3}x + y = 2$

$y = -\frac{1}{3}x + 2$

slope $= -\frac{1}{3} = \frac{-1}{3}$; y-intercept $= 2$

Plot (0,2). Move 1 unit *down* and 3 units to the *right* to reach the point (3,1). Draw line through (0,2) and (3,1).

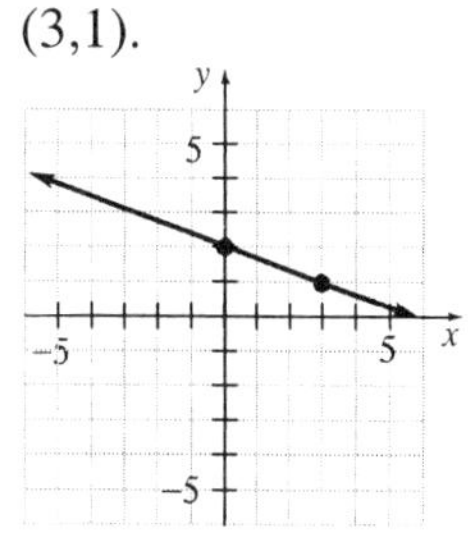

39. $y = -\frac{1}{2}x + 4$ $\qquad$ $y = -\frac{1}{2}x - 1$

slope $= -\frac{1}{2} = \frac{-1}{2}$ $\qquad$ slope $= -\frac{1}{2} = \frac{-1}{2}$

y-intercept $= 4$ $\qquad$ y-intercept $= -1$

Graph each line using its slope and y-intercept.

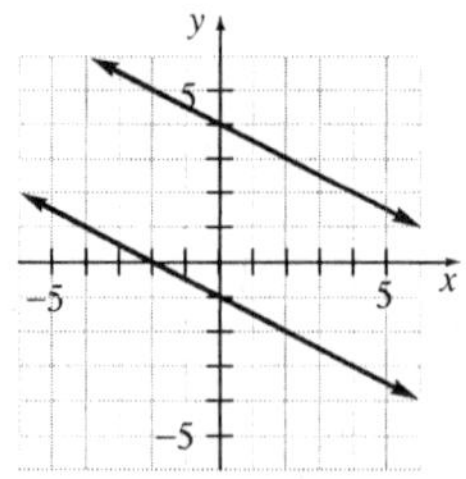

Yes, they are parallel since both lines have a slope of $-\frac{1}{2}$ and different y-intercepts

40. **a.** The smallest *y*-intercept is 25. This indicates that in 1990 the average age of U.S. Hispanics was 25.

b. Line through (0,35) and (10,38):
$$m = \frac{38-35}{10-0} = \frac{3}{10} = 0.3$$
This means that the average age for U.S. whites increased at a rate of about 0.3 each year from 1990 to 2000.

c. $y = 0.3x + 35$

d. The year 2010 corresponds to $x = 20$. If $x = 20$,
$y = 0.3(20) + 35 = 41$.
According to the model, the average age for U.S. whites in 2010 will be 41 years old.

41. Slope = 6, passing through (–4,7)
point-slope form:
$$y - 7 = 6[x - (-4)]$$
$$y - 7 = 6(x + 4)$$
slope-intercept form:
$$y - 7 = 6x + 24$$
$$y = 6x + 31$$

42. Passing through (3,4) and (2,1)
First, find the slope.
$$m = \frac{1-4}{2-3} = \frac{-3}{-1} = 3$$
Next, use the slope and one of the points to write the equation of the line in point-slope form.
$$y - y_1 = m(x - x_1)$$
$$y - 4 = 3(x - 3)$$
Solve for *y* to obtain slope-intercept form.
$$y - 4 = 3x - 9$$
$$y = 3x - 5$$

43. **a.** First, find the slope. $(1, 1.5)$ and $(3, 3.4)$.
$$m = \frac{3.4-1.5}{3-1} = \frac{1.9}{2} = 0.95$$
Next, use the slope and one of the points to write the point-slope equation of the line.
$y - 1.5 = 0.95(x - 1)$ or
$y - 3.4 = 0.95(x - 3)$

b.
$$y - 1.5 = 0.95(x - 1)$$
$$y - 1.5 = 0.95x - 0.95$$
$$y = 0.95x + .55$$

c. Since 2009 is 2009-1999 = 10, let *x* = 10.
$$y = 0.95(10) + .55$$
$$= 9.5 + .55 = 10.05$$
$10.05 billion in revenue was earned from online gambling in 2009.

44. $3x-4y>7$

$(0,0)$: $0-0>7$

$0>7$ false

$(0,0)$ is not a solution.

$(3,-6)$: $9+24>7$

$33>7$ true

$(3,-6)$ is a solution.

$(-2,-5)$: $-6+20>7$

$14>7$ true

$(-2,-5)$ is a solution

$(-3,4)$: $-9-12>7$

$-21>7$ false

$(-3,4)$ is not a solution.

45. $x-2y>6$

Graph the equation $x-2y=6$ as a dashed line through (6,0) and (0, –3). Use (0,0) as a test point. Since $0-2(0)>6$ is false, shade the half-plane *not* containing (0,0).

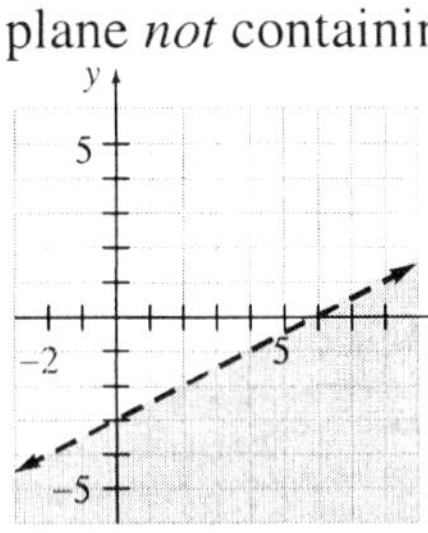

46. $4x-6y\le 12$

Graph the equation $4x-6y=12$ as a solid line through (3,0) and (0, –2). Use (0,0) as a test point. Since $4(0)-6(0)\le 12$ is true, shade the half-plane containing (0,0).

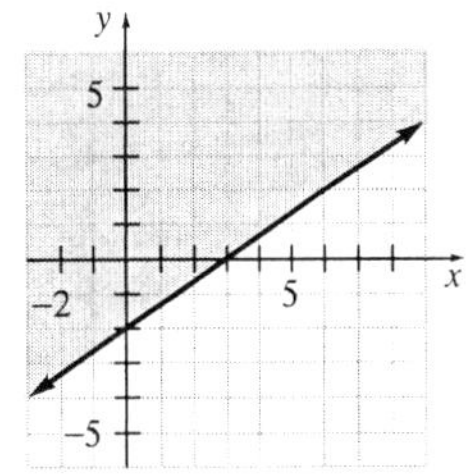

47. $y>3x+2$

Graph $y=3x+2$ as a dashed line using the slope and y-intercept. Use (0,0) as a test point. Since $0>3(0)+2$ is false, shade the half-plane *not* containing (0,0).

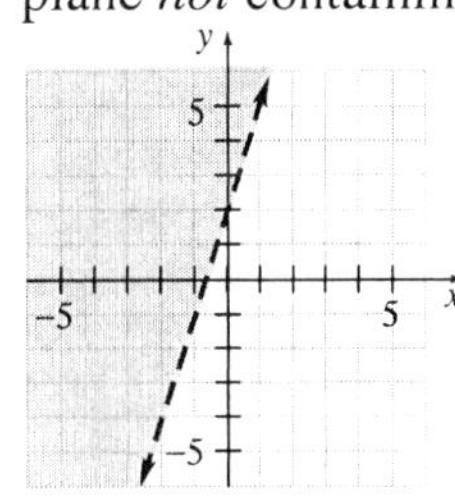

48. $y\le \frac{1}{3}x-1$

Graph $y=\frac{1}{3}x-1$ as a solid line using slope and y-intercept. Use (0,0) as a test point. Since $0\le \frac{1}{3}(0)-1$ is false, shade the half-plane *not* containing (0,0).

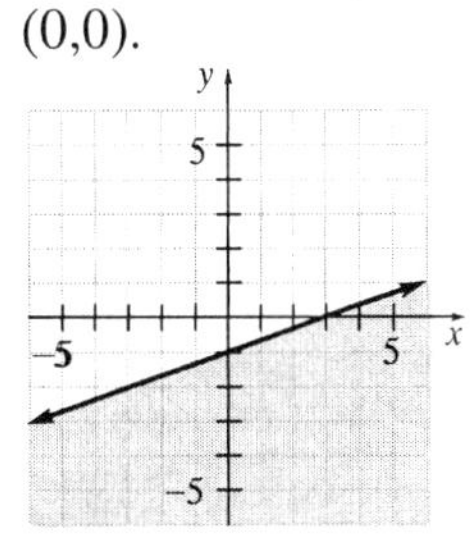

49. $y < -\frac{1}{2}x$

Graph $y = -\frac{1}{2}x$ as a solid line using the slope and y-intercept. Since the line passes through the origin, a point other than (0,0) must be chosen as the test point, for example (4,4). Since $4 \le -\frac{1}{2}(4)$ is false, shade the half-plane not containing (4,4).

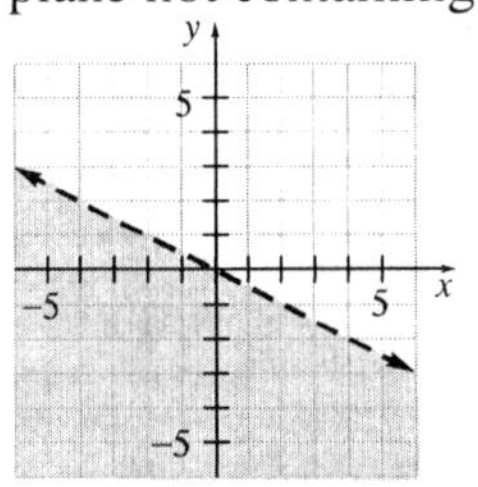

50. $x < 4$

Graph the vertical line $x = 4$ as a dashed line. Use (0,0) as a test point. Since $0 < 4$ is true, shade the half-plane containing (0,0), which is the half-plane to the *left* of the line.

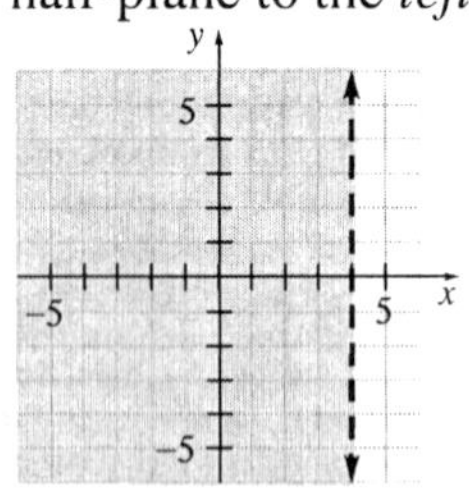

51. $y \ge -2$

Graph the horizontal line $y = -2$ as a solid line. Use (0,0) as a test point. Since $0 \ge -2$ is true, shade the half-plane containing (0,0), which is the half-plane *above* the line.

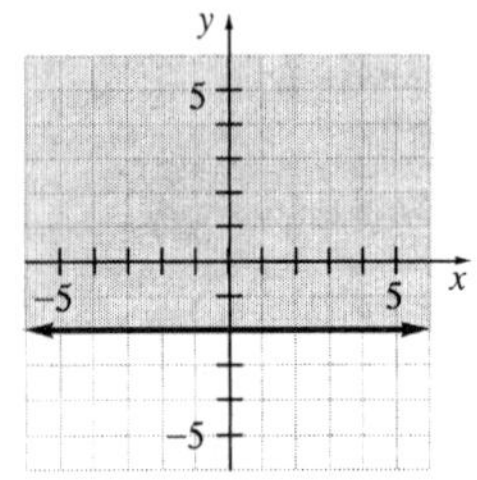

52. $x + 2y \le 0$

Graph $x + 2y = 0$ as a solid line through (0,0) and (2, −1). Since the line goes through the origin, choose another point as the test point, for example (1,1).

Since $1 + 2(1) \le 0$ is false, shade the half-plane *not* containing (1,1).

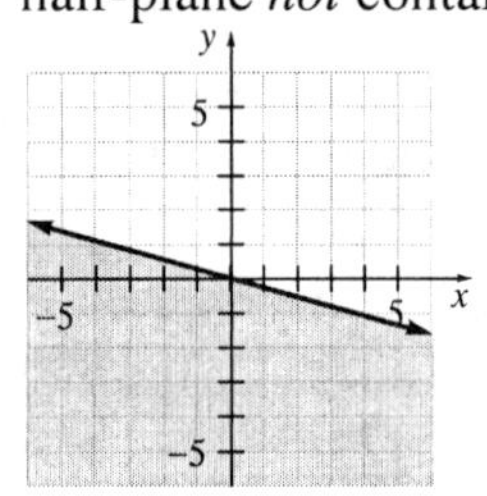

Chapter 4 Test

1. $4x - 2y = 10$

$(0, -5)$:

$4(0) - 2(-5) = 10$

$0 + 10 = 10$

$10 = 10$ true

$(0, -5)$ is a solution

$(-2, 1)$:

$4(-2) - 2(1) = 10$

$-8 - 2 = 10$

$-10 = 10$ false

$(-2,1)$ is not a solution.

$(4, 3)$:

$4(4) - 2(3) = 10$

$16 - 6 = 10$

$10 = 10$ true

$(4, 3)$ is a solution.

2. $y = 3x + 1$

x	$y = 3x+1$	(x, y)
-2	$y=3(-2)+1=-5$	$(-2,-5)$
-1	$y=3(-1)+1=-2$	$(-1,-2)$
0	$y=3(0)+1=1$	$(0,1)$
1	$y=3(1)+1=4$	$(1,4)$
2	$y=3(2)+1=7$	$(2,7)$

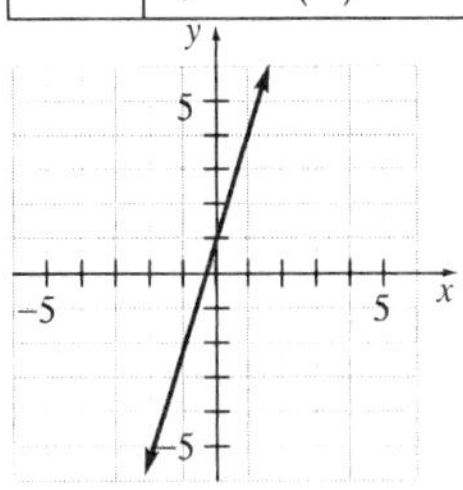

3. $y = x^2 - 1$

x	$y = x^2 - 1$	(x, y)
-3	$y=(-3)^2-1=8$	$(-3,8)$
-2	$y=(-2)^2-1=3$	$(-2,3)$
-1	$y=(-1)^2-1=0$	$(-1,0)$
0	$y=0^2-1=-1$	$(0,-1)$
1	$y=1^2-1=0$	$(1,0)$
2	$y=2^2-1=3$	$(2,3)$
3	$y=3^2-1=8$	$(3,8)$

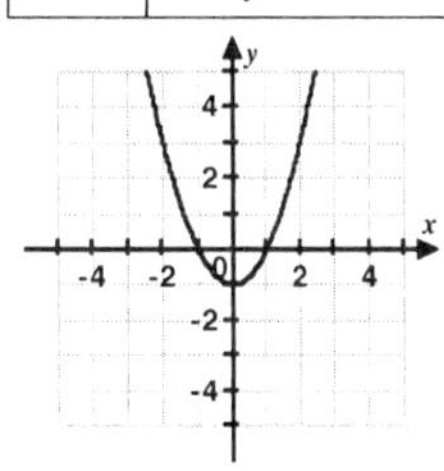

4. **a.** The graph crosses the x-axis at (2,0), so the x-intercept is 2.

b. The graph crosses the y-axis at (0, −3), so the y-intercept is −3.

5. $4x - 2y = -8$

x-intercept:
$$4x - 2(0) = -8$$
$$4x = -8$$
$$x = -2$$

y-intercept:
$$4(0) - 2y = -8$$
$$-2y = -8$$
$$y = 4$$

Find one other point as a checkpoint. For example, substitute −4 for x.
$$4(-4) - 2y = -8$$
$$-16 - 2y = -8$$
$$-2y = -8$$
$$y = -4$$

checkpoint: (−4, −4)

Draw a line through (−2,0), (0,4) and (−4, −4).

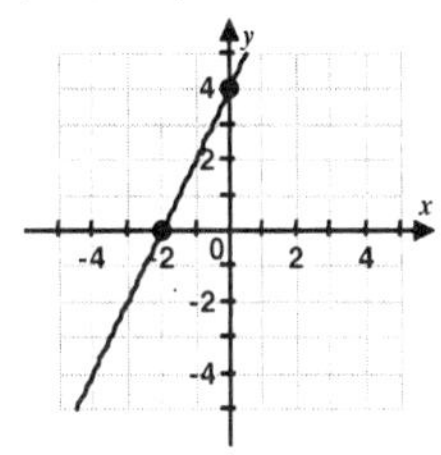

6. $y = 4$

Three ordered pairs are (−2,4), (0,4), and (2,4). The graph is a horizontal line.

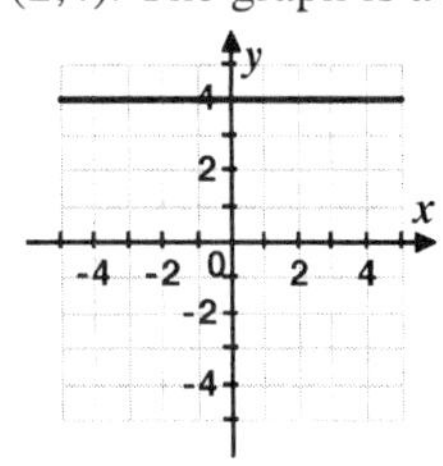

7. (−3,4) and (−5, −2)
$$m = \frac{-2-4}{-5(-3)} = \frac{-6}{-2} = 3$$
The slope is 3. Since the slope is positive, the line rises.

8. (6, −1) and (6,3)
$$m = \frac{3-(-1)}{6-6} = \frac{4}{0}; \text{ undefined}$$
Since the slope is undefined, the line is vertical.

9. Line through (−1, −2) and (1,1):

$$m = \frac{1-(-2)}{1-(-1)} = \frac{3}{2}$$

10. Line through (2,4) and (6,1):

$$m = \frac{1-4}{6-2} = \frac{-3}{4} = -\frac{3}{4}$$

Line through (−3,1) and (1, −2):

$$m = \frac{-2-1}{1-(-3)} = \frac{-3}{4} = -\frac{3}{4}$$

Since the slopes are equal, the lines are parallel.

11. $y = -x + 10$

$y = -1x + 10$

The slope is the coefficient of x, which is −1. The y-intercept is the constant term, which is 10.

12. $2x + y = 6$

$y = -2x + 6$

$m = -2$; y-intercept = 6

13. $y = \frac{2}{3}x - 1$

slope = $\frac{2}{3}$; y-intercept = −1

Plot (0, −1). From this point, move 2 units *up* and 3 units to the *right* to reach the point (3,1). Draw a line through (0, −1) and (3,1).

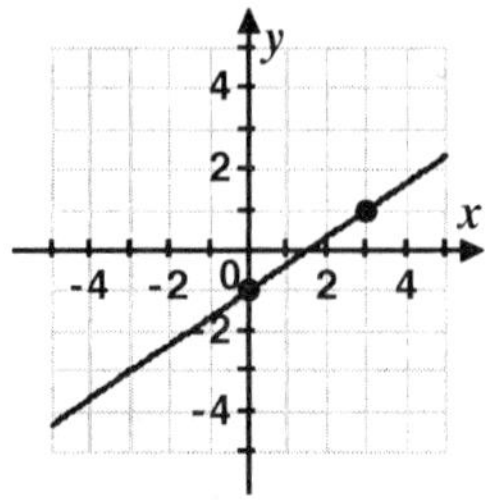

14. $y = -2x + 3$

slope = $-2 = \frac{-2}{1}$; y-intercept = 3

Plot (0,3). Move 2 units *down* and 1 unit to the right to reach the point (1,1). Draw a line through (0,3) and (1,1).

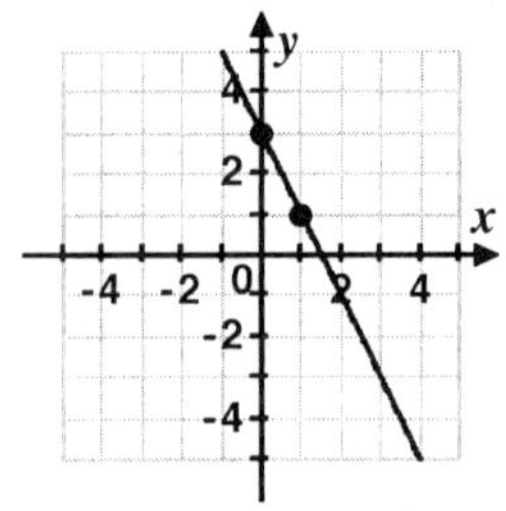

15. Slope = −2; passing through (−1,4)

point-slope form:

$y - 4 = -2[x - (-1)]$

$y - 4 = -2(x + 1)$

slope-intercept form:

$y - 4 = -2x - 2$

$y = -2x + 2$

16. Passing through (2,1) and (−1, −8)

$$m = \frac{-8-1}{-1-2} = \frac{-9}{-3} = 3$$

Using the point (2,1), the point-slope equation is

$y - 1 = 3(x - 2)$.

Rewrite this equation in slope-intercept form

$y - 1 = 3x - 6$

$y = 3x - 5$

17. $3x - 2y < 6$

Graph the line $3x - 2y = 6$ as a dashed line through (2,0) and (0, −3). Use (0,0) as a test point. Since $3(0) - 2(0) < 6$ is true, shade the half-plane containing (0,0).

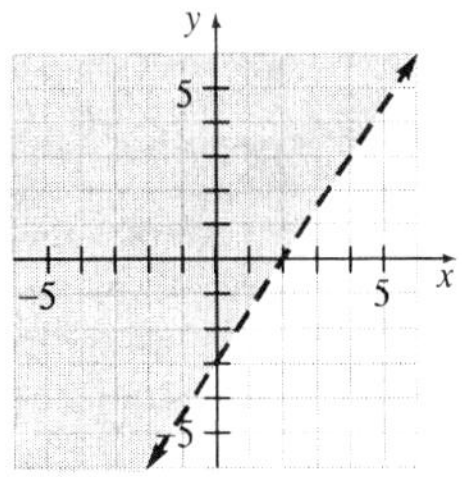

18. $y \geq 2x - 2$
Graph the line $y = 2x - 2$ as a solid line using the slope and y-intercept. Use (0,0) as a test point. Since $0 \geq 2(0) - 2$ is true, shade the half-plane containing (0,0).

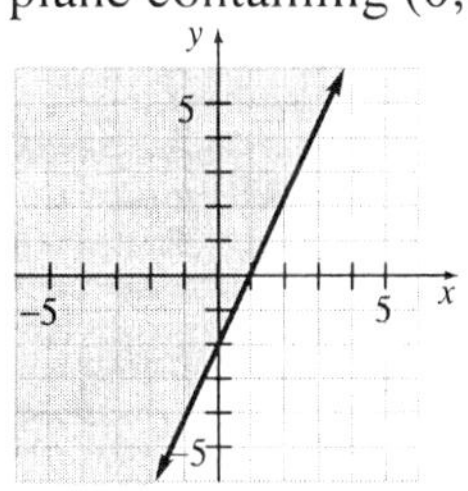

19. $x > -1$
Graph the vertical line $x = -1$ as a dashed line. Use (0,0) as a test point. Since $0 > -1$ is true, shade the half-plane containing (0,0), which is the half-plane to the *right* of the line.

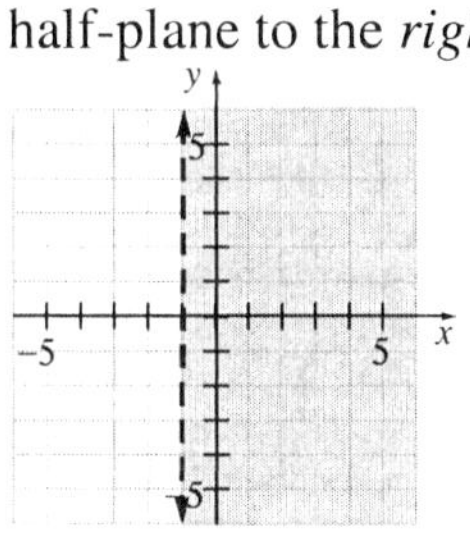

20. Line through (1970,2100) and (2000,5280):
$$m = \frac{5280 - 2100}{2000 - 1970} = \frac{3180}{30} = 106$$
This slope indicates that per-pupil spending increases by about \$106 each year.

Cumulative Review Exercises (Chapters 1-4)

1. $$\frac{10 - (-6)}{3^2 - (4 - 3)} = \frac{10 + 6}{9 - 1} = \frac{16}{8} = 2$$

2. $$\begin{aligned} &6 - 2[3(x-1) + 4] \\ &= 6 - 2(3x - 3 + 4) = 6 - 2(3x + 1) \\ &= 6 - 6x - 2 = 4 - 6x \end{aligned}$$

3. The only irrational number in the given set is $\sqrt{5}$.

4. $$\begin{aligned} 6(2x - 1) - 6 &= 11x + 7 \\ 12x - 6 - 6 &= 11x + 7 \\ 12x - 12 &= 11x + 7 \\ x - 12 &= 7 \\ x &= 19 \end{aligned}$$
The solution is 19.

5. $$\begin{aligned} x - \frac{3}{4} &= \frac{1}{2} \\ x - \frac{3}{4} + \frac{3}{4} &= \frac{1}{2} + \frac{3}{4} \\ x &= \frac{2}{4} + \frac{3}{4} = \frac{5}{4} \end{aligned}$$
The solution is $\frac{5}{4}$.

6. $y = mx + b$ for x.
$$\begin{aligned} y &= mx + b \\ y - b &= mx + b - b \\ y - b &= mx \\ \frac{y - b}{m} &= \frac{mx}{m} \\ \frac{y - b}{m} &= x \text{ or } x = \frac{y - b}{m} \end{aligned}$$

7. $A = PB;\ A = 120;\ P = 15\% = 0.15$

$$A = PB$$
$$120 = 0.15 \cdot B$$
$$\frac{120}{0.15} = \frac{0.15B}{0.15}$$
$$800 = B$$

120 is 15% of 800.

8. $y = 4.5x - 46.7;\ y = 133.3$

$$133.3 = 4.5x - 46.7$$
$$133.3 + 46.7 = 4.5x - 46.7 + 46.7$$
$$180 = 4.5x$$
$$\frac{180}{4.5} = \frac{4.5x}{4.5}$$
$$40 = x$$

The car is traveling 40 miles per hour.

9.

$$2 - 6x \ge 2(5 - x)$$
$$2 - 5x \ge 10 - 2x$$
$$2 - 6x + 2x \ge 10 - 2x + 2x$$
$$2 - 4x \ge 10$$
$$2 - 4x - 2 \ge 10 - 2$$
$$-4x \ge 8$$
$$\frac{-4x}{4} \le \frac{8}{-4}$$
$$x \le -2$$

$\{x | x \le -2\}$

10.

$$6(2 - x) > 12$$
$$12 - 6x > 12$$
$$12 - 6x - 12 > 12 - 12$$
$$-6x > 0$$
$$\frac{-6x}{-6} < \frac{0}{-6}$$
$$x < 0$$

$\{x | x < 0\}$

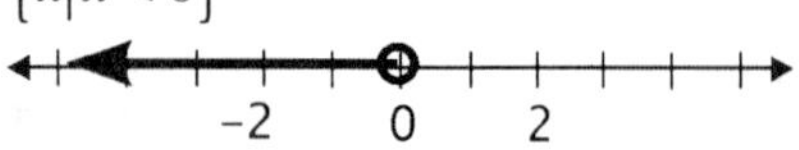

11. Let x = the number of hours the plumber worked.

$$18 + 35x = 228$$
$$35x = 210$$
$$x = 6$$

The plumber worked 6 hours.

12.

	Number Liters	%	Amount Of Acid
40%	x	0.40	$0.40x$
70%	$12 - x$	0.70	$0.70(12 - x)$
50%	12	0.50	$0.50(12)$

$$0.40x + 0.70(12 - x) = 0.50(12)$$
$$0.40x + 8.4 - 0.70x = 6$$
$$-0.30x + 8.4 = 6$$
$$-0.30x + 8.4 - 8.4 = 6 - 8.4$$
$$-0.30x = -2.4$$
$$x = 8$$

To obtain 12 liters of a 50% acid solution, 8 liters of a 40% solution and $12 - 8 = 4$ liters of a 70% solution should be used.

13.

	R	· T	= D
Slow Car	40	x	$40x$
Fast Car	60	x	$60x$

$$40x + 60x = 350$$
$$100x = 350$$
$$x = 3.5$$

The cars will be 350 miles apart after 3.5 hours.

14. Let x = the measure of the first angle.
Let $x + 20$ = the measure of the second angle.
Let $2x$ = the measure of third angle.

$$x + (x + 20) + 2x = 180$$
$$4x + 20 = 180$$
$$4x = 160$$
$$x = 40$$

The angles measure $x = 40°$, $x + 20 = 60°$, and $2x = 80°$.

15. $\dfrac{45}{2} = \dfrac{360}{x}$

$45x = 2 \cdot 360$

$45x = 720$

$\dfrac{45x}{45} = \dfrac{720}{45}$

$x = 16$

16. $2x - y = 4$

x-intercept: 2 and y-intercept : -4

checkpoint: (4,4)

Draw a line through (2,0), (0, −4), and (4,4)

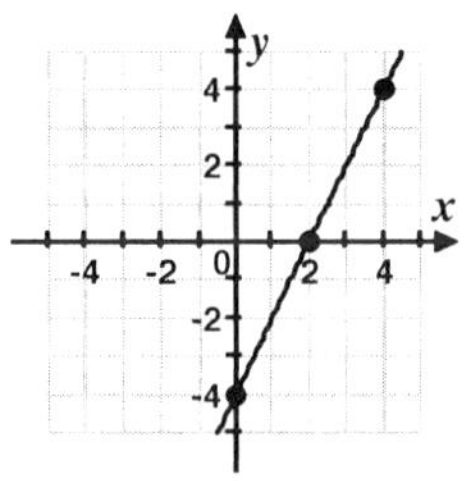

17.

x	$y = x^2 - 5$	(x, y)
-3	$y=(-3)^2-5=4$	$(-3,4)$
-2	$y=(-2)^2-5=-1$	$(-2,-1)$
-1	$y=(-1)^2-5=-4$	$(-1,-4)$
0	$y=0^2-5=-5$	$(0,-5)$
1	$y=1^2-5=-4$	$(1,-4)$
2	$y=2^2-5=-1$	$(2,-1)$
3	$y=3^2-5=4$	$(3,4)$

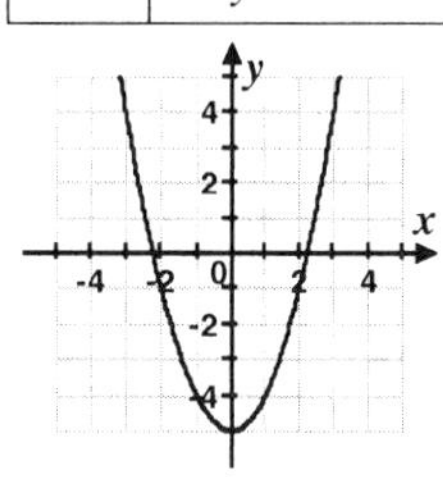

18. $y = -4x + 3$

slope = $-4 = \dfrac{-4}{1}$; y-intercept = 3

Plot (0,3). Move 4 units *down* and 1 unit to the *right* to reach the point (1, −1). Draw a line through (0,3) and (1, −1).

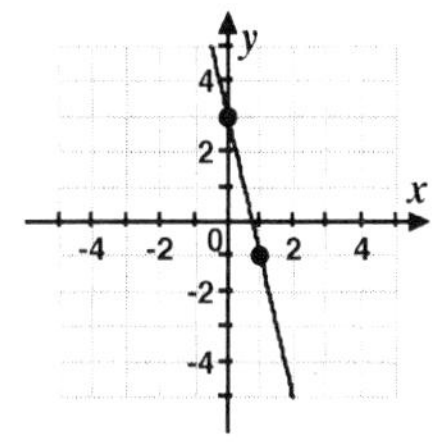

19. $3x - 2y < -6$

Graph the equation $3x - 2y = -6$ as a dashed line through (−2,0) and (0,3). Use (0,0) as a test point. Since $3(0) - 2(0) < -6$ is false, shade the half-plane not containing (0,0).

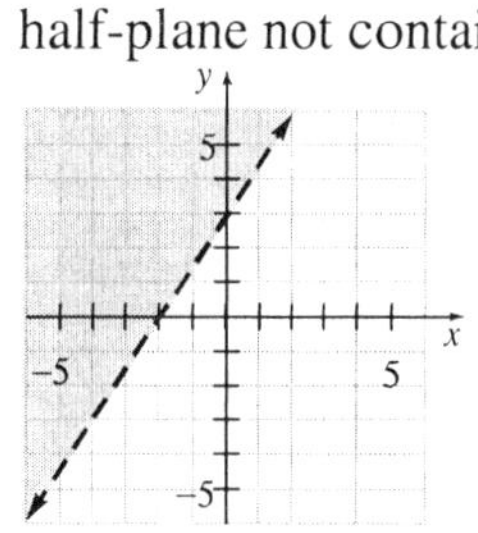

20. $y \geq -1$

Graph the horizontal line $y = -1$ as a solid line. Use (0,0) as a test point. Since $0 \geq -1$ is true, shade the half-plane containing (0,0).

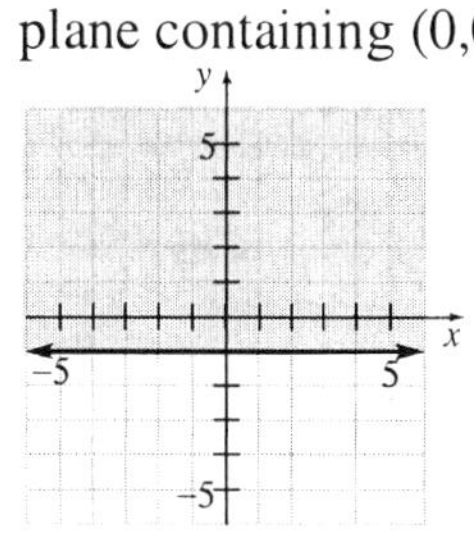

Chapter 5
Systems of Linear Equations and Inequalities

5.1 Exercise Set

1. (2, −3)

To determine if (2, −3) is a solution to the system, replace x with 2 and y with −3 in both equations.

$$2x+3y=-5$$
$$2(2)+3(-3)=-5$$
$$4+(-9)=-5$$
$$-5=-5 \quad \text{true}$$

$$7x-3y=23$$
$$7(2)-3(-3)=23$$
$$14+9=23$$
$$23=23 \text{ true}$$

The ordered pair does satisfy both equations, so it is a solution to the system.

3. $\left(\frac{2}{3},\frac{1}{9}\right)$

$$x+3y=1$$
$$\frac{2}{3}+3\left(\frac{1}{9}\right)=1$$
$$\frac{2}{3}+\frac{1}{3}=1$$
$$1=1 \quad \text{true}$$

$$4x+3y=3$$
$$4\left(\frac{2}{3}\right)+3\left(\frac{1}{9}\right)=3$$
$$\frac{8}{3}+\frac{1}{3}=3$$
$$\frac{9}{3}=3$$
$$3=3 \text{ true}$$

Since the ordered pair satisfies both equations, the pair is a solution to the system.

5. (−5, 9)

$$5x+3y=2$$
$$5(-5)+3(9)=2$$
$$-25+27=2$$
$$2=2 \quad \text{true}$$

$$x+4y=14$$
$$-5+4(9)=14$$
$$-5+36=14$$
$$31=14 \text{ false}$$

The ordered pair does not satisfy both equations, so it is not a solution to the system.

7. (1400,450)

$$x-2y=500$$
$$1400-2(450)=500$$
$$1400-900=500$$
$$500=500 \quad \text{true}$$

$$0.03x+0.02y=51$$
$$0.03(1400)+0.02(450)=51$$
$$42+9=51$$
$$51=51 \quad \text{true}$$

The ordered pair satisfies both equations, so the ordered pair is a solution to the system.

9. (8,5)

$$5x-4y=20$$
$$5(8)-4(5)=20$$
$$40-20=20$$
$$20=20 \quad \text{true}$$

$$3y = 2x + 1$$
$$3(5) = 2(8) + 1$$
$$15 = 16 + 1$$
$$15 = 17 \quad \text{false}$$

The ordered pair does not satisfy both equations, so it is not a solution to the system.

11. Graph both equations on the same axes.
$x + y = 6$:
x-intercept = 6; y-intercept = 6
$x - y = 2$:
x-intercept = 2; y-intercept = −2

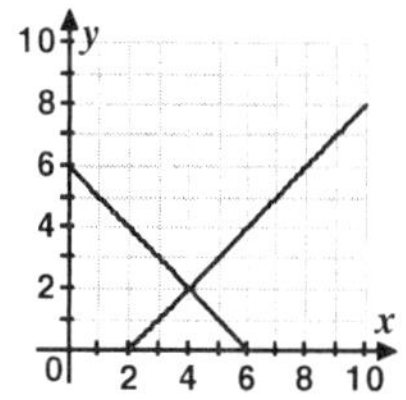

The lines intersect at (4, 2), so it is the solution to the system.

13. Graph both equations on the same axes.
$x + y = 1$:
x-intercept = 1; y-intercept = 1
$y - x = 3$
x-intercept = −3; y-intercept = 3

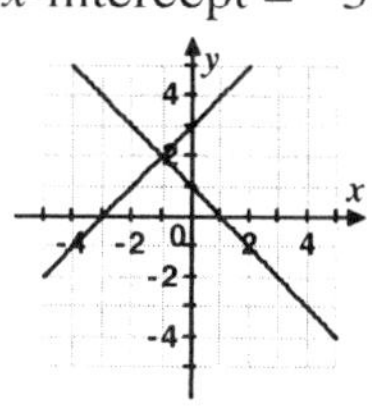

The lines intersect at (−1, 2), so it is the solution to the system.

15. Graph both equations.
$2x - 3y = 6$:
x-intercept = 3: y-intercept = −2
$4x + 3y = 12$:
x-intercept = 3: y-intercept = 4

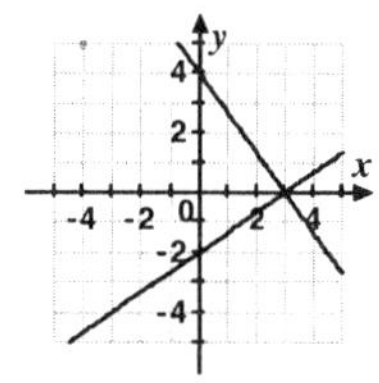

Solution: (3, 0)

17. Graph both equations.
$4x + y = 4$:
x-intercept = 1: y-intercept = 4
$3x - y = 3$:
x-intercept = 1: y-intercept = −3

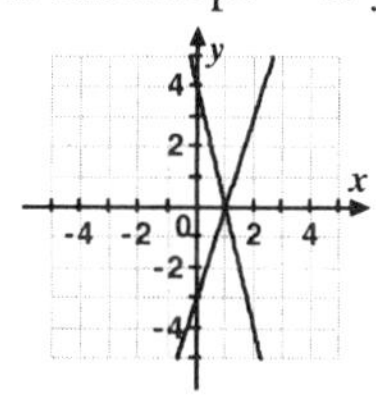

Solution: (1, 0)

19. Graph both equations.
$y = x + 5$:
Slope = 1; y-intercept = 5
$y = -x + 3$:
Slope = −1; y-intercept = 3

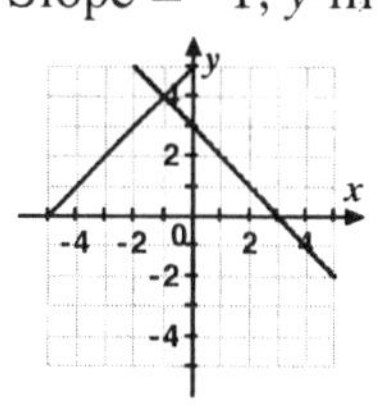

Solution: (−1, 4)

21. Graph both equations.
$y = 2x$:
slope =2; y-intercept = 0
$y = -x + 6$:
slope = −1; y-intercept = 6

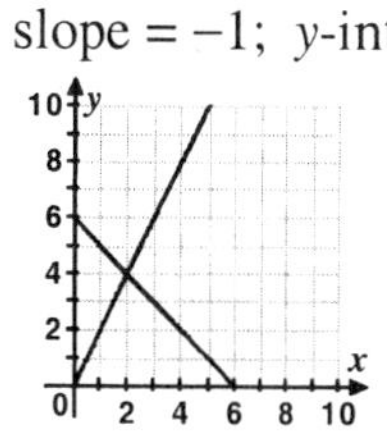

Solution: (2, 4)

23. Graph both equations.
$y = -2x + 3$:
slope = −2; y-intercept = 3
$y = -x + 1$:
slope = −1; y-intercept = 1

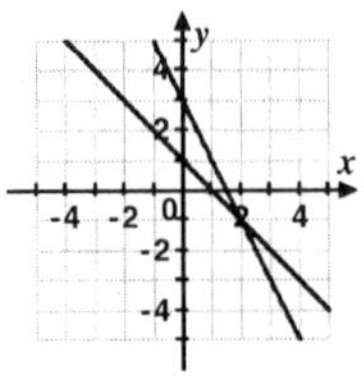

Solution: (2, −1)

25. Graph both equations.
$y = 2x - 1$:
Slope = 2; y-intercept = −1
$y = 2x + 1$:
Slope = 2; y-intercept = 1

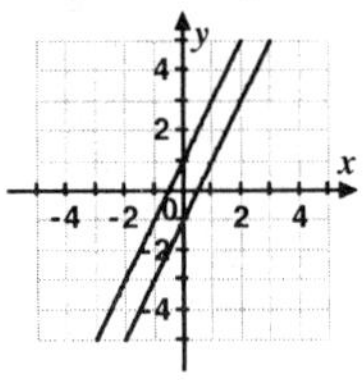

The two lines are parallel. (Note that the lines have the same slope, but different y-intercepts.) The system has no solution.

27. Graph each equation.
$x + y = 4$:
x-intercept = 4; y-intercept = 4
$x = -2$:
vertical line with x-intercept −2

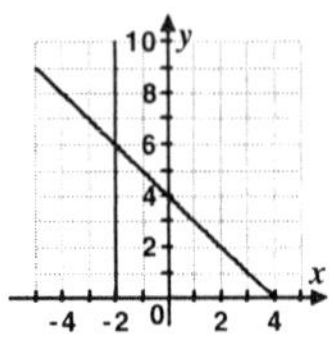

Solution: (−2, 6)

29. Graph each equation.
$x - 2y = 4$:
x-intercept = 4; y-intercept = −2
$2x - 4y = 8$:
x-intercept = 4; y-intercept = −2

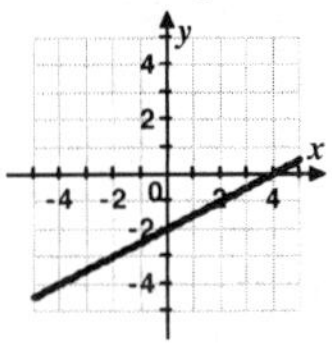

Since the lines have the same slope and y-intercept, the two equations are the same line. The lines coincide, and the system has infinitely many solutions.

31. Graph both lines.
$y = 2x - 1$:
slope = 2; y-intercept = −1
$x - 2y = -4$:
x-intercept = −4; y-intercept = 2

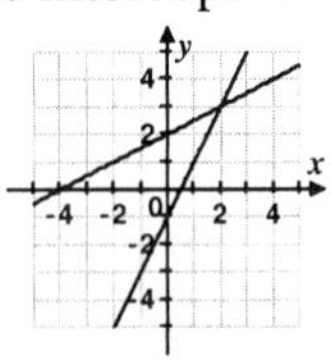

Solution: (2, 3)

33. Graph both lines.
$x + y = 5$:
x-intercept = 5; y-intercept = 5
$2x + 2y = 12$:
x-intercept = 6; y-intercept = 6

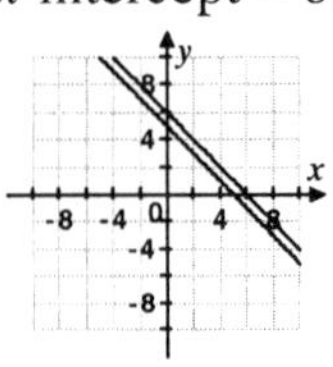

The lines are parallel, so the system has no solution.

35. $x - y = 0$
$y = x$

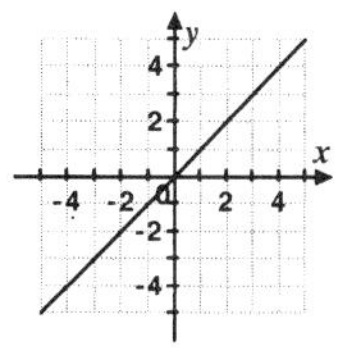

Because the lines coincide, the system has an infinite number of solutions.

37. $x = 2$
$y = 4$

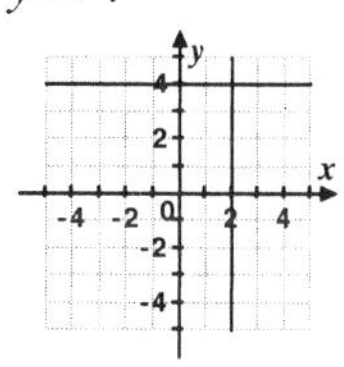

The vertical and horizontal line intersect at (2, 4), so the solution is (2, 4).

39. $x = 2$
$x = -1$

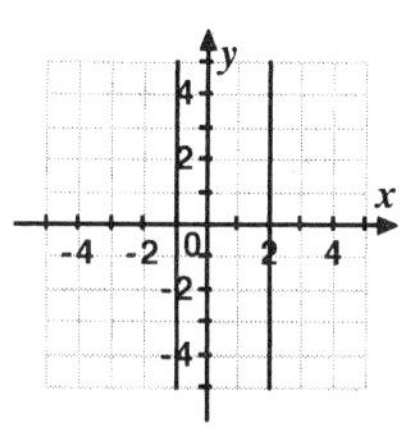

The two vertical lines are parallel, so the system has no solution.

41. $y = 0$
$y = 4$

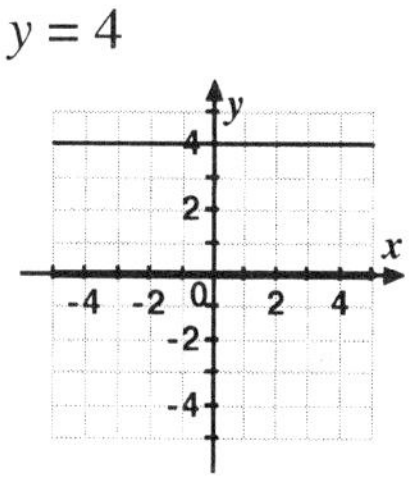

The two horizontal lines are parallel, so the system has no solution.

43. $y = \frac{1}{2}x + 3$:

slope = $\frac{1}{2}$, y-intercept = 3

$y = \frac{1}{2}x - 5$:

slope = $\frac{1}{2}$, y-intercept = −5

Since the slopes are the same, but the y-intercepts are different, the lines are parallel and there is no solution.

44. $y = \frac{3}{4}x - 2$:

slope = $\frac{3}{4}$, y-intercept = −2

$y = \frac{3}{4}x + 1$:

slope = $\frac{3}{4}$, y-intercept = 1

Since the slopes are the same, but the y-intercepts are different, the lines are parallel and there is no solution.

45. $y = -\frac{1}{2}x + 4$

slope = $-\frac{1}{2}$, y-intercept = 4

$3x - y = -4$
$-y = -3x - 4$
$y = 3x + 4$

slope = 3, y-intercept = 4

Since the lines have different slopes, there will be one solution.

46. $y = -\frac{1}{4}x + 3$

slope = $-1/4$, y-intercept = 3

$4x - y = -3$
$-y = -4x - 3$
$y = 4x + 3$

slope = 4, y-intercept = 3
Since the lines have different slopes, there will be one solution.

47. $3x - y = 6$

$$-y = -3x + 6$$
$$y = 3x - 6$$

slope = 3, y-intercept = –6

$$x = \frac{y}{3} + 2$$
$$3x = y + 6$$
$$3x - 6 = y$$
$$y = 3x - 6$$

slope = 3, y-intercept = –6
Since the lines have the same slopes and y-intercepts, the graphs will coincide and there are an infinite number of solutions.

48. $2x - y = 4$

$$-y = -2x + 4$$
$$y = 2x - 4$$

slope = 2, y-intercept = –4

$$x = \frac{y}{2} + 2$$
$$2x = y + 4$$
$$2x - 4 = y$$
$$y = 2x - 4$$

slope = 2, y-intercept = –4
Since the lines have the same slopes and y-intercepts, the graphs will coincide and there are an infinite number of solutions.

49. $3x + y = 0$

$$y = -3x$$

slope = –3, y-intercept = 0
$y = -3x + 1$
slope = –3, y-intercept = 1
Since the slopes are the same, but the y-intercepts are different, the lines are parallel and there is no solution.

50. $2x + y = 0$

$$y = -2x$$

slope = –2, y-intercept = 0
$y = -2x + 1$
slope = –2, y-intercept = 1

Since the slopes are the same, but the y-intercepts are different, the lines are parallel and there is no solution.

51. **a.** The intersection point is approximately (1996, 41). This means that mothers 30 years old and older in Massachusetts had about 41 thousand (41,000) births in 1996.

b. Since 1996, there have been more births in Massachusetts to mothers 30 years old and older than to those under 30 years old.

53.-59. Answers will vary.

61. Statement c is true.
If two lines have two points in common, they must coincide (be on the same line), so they will have equal slopes and equal y-intercepts.

63. Answers will vary.

65. Answers will vary depending on exercises chosen.

67. $y = -x + 5$
$y = x - 7$

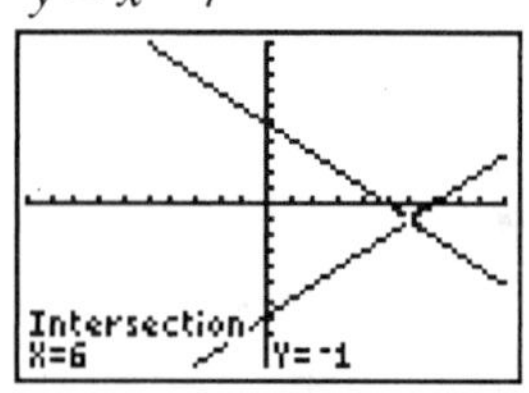

Solution: (6, –1)

69. $2x - 3y = 6$

$$-3y = -2x + 6$$
$$y = \frac{2}{3}x - 2$$

$4x + 3y = 12$

$$3y = -4x + 12$$
$$y = -\frac{4}{3}x + 4$$

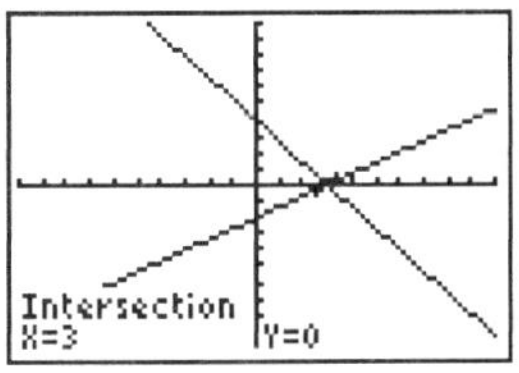

Solution: (3, 0)

71. $2x - 3y = 7$

$$-3y = -2x + 7$$
$$y = \frac{2}{3}x - \frac{7}{3}$$

$3x + 5y = 1$

$$5y = -3x + 1$$
$$y = -\frac{3}{5}x + \frac{1}{5}$$

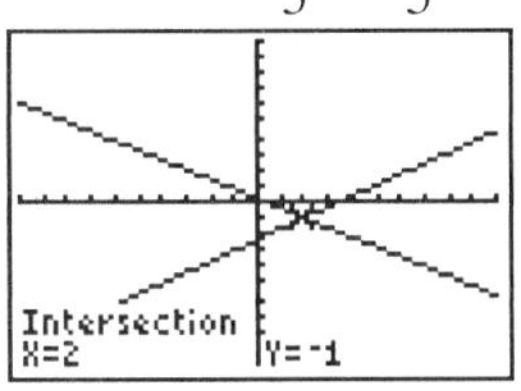

Solution: (2, −1)

73. $y = -\frac{1}{2}x + 2$

$y = \frac{3}{4}x + 7$

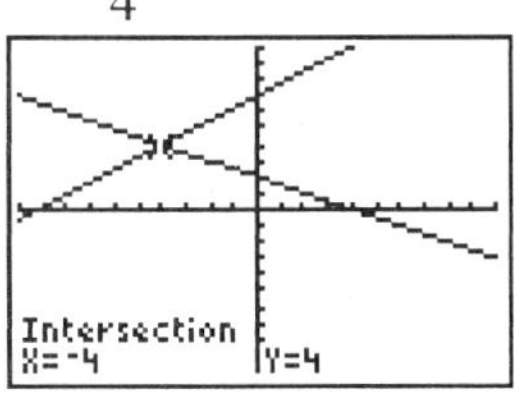

Solution: (−4, 4)

74. $-3 + (-9) = -3 - 9 = -12$

75. $-3 - (-9) = -3 + 9 = 6$

76. $-3(-9) = 27$

5.2 Exercise Set

1. $x + y = 4$

$y = 3x$

Substitute $3x$ for y in the first equation.

$$x + y = 4$$
$$x + (3x) = 4$$

Solve this equation for x.

$$4x = 4$$
$$x = 1$$

Back substitute 1 for x into the second equation.

$$y = 3x$$
$$y = 3(1) = 3$$

The solution is (1, 3).

3. $x + 3y = 8$

$y = 2x - 9$

Substitute $2x - 9$ for y in the first equation and solve for x.

$$x + 3y = 8$$
$$x + 3(2x - 9) = 8$$
$$x + 6x - 27 = 8$$
$$7x - 27 = 8$$
$$7x = 35$$
$$x = 5$$

Back-substitute 5 for x into the second equation and solve for y.

$$y = 2x - 9$$
$$y = 2(5) - 9 = 1$$

Solution: (5, 1)

5. $x+3y=5$

$4x+5y=13$

Solve the first equation for x.

$x+3y=5$

$x=5-3y$

Substitute $5-3y$ for x in the second equation and solve for y.

$$4x+5y=13$$
$$4(5-3y)+5y=13$$
$$20-12y+5y=13$$
$$20-7y=13$$
$$-7y=-7$$
$$y=1$$

Back-substitute 1 for y in the equation $x=5-3y$ and solve for x.

$x=5-3y$

$x=5-3(1)=2$

Solution: (2, 1)

7. $2x-y=-5$

$x+5y=14$

Solve the second equation for x.

$x+5y=14$

$x=14-5y$

Substitute $14-5y$ for x in the first equation.

$$2(14-5y)-y=-5$$
$$28-10y-y=-5$$
$$28-11y=-5$$
$$-11y=-33$$
$$y=3$$

Back-substitute.

$x=14-5y$

$x=14-5(3)=14-15=-1$

Solution: (−1, 3)

9. $2x-y=3$

$5x-2y=10$

Solve the first equation for y.

$2x-y=3$

$-y=-2x+3$

$y=2x-3$

Substitute $2x-3$ for y in the second equation.

$$5x-2(2x-3)=10$$
$$5x-4x+6=10$$
$$x+6=10$$
$$x=4$$

Back-substitute.

$y=2x-3$

$y=2(4)-3=8-3=5$

Solution: (4, 5)

11. $-3x+y=-1$

$x-2y=4$

Solve the second equation for x.

$x-2y=4$

$x=2y+4$

Substitute $2y+4$ for x in the first equation.

$$-3x+y=-1$$
$$-3(2y+4)+y=-1$$
$$-6y-12+y=-1$$
$$-5y-12=-1$$
$$-5y=11$$
$$y=-\frac{11}{5}$$

Back-substitute

$x = 2y + 4$

$x = 2\left(-\frac{11}{5}\right) + 4$

$x = -\frac{22}{5} + 4$

$x = -\frac{22}{5} + \frac{20}{5}$

$x = -\frac{2}{5}$

Solution: $\left(-\frac{2}{5}, -\frac{11}{5}\right)$

13. $x = 9 - 2y$

$x + 2y = 13$

The first equation is already solved for x.

Substitute $9 - 2y$ for x in the second equation.

$x + 2y = 13$

$(9 - 2y) + 2y = 13$

$9 = 13$ false

The false statement 9=13 indicates that the system is inconsistent and has no solution.

15. $y = 3x - 5$

$21x - 35 = 7y$

Substitute $3x–5$ for y in the second equation.

$21x - 35 = 7y$

$21x - 35 = 7(3x - 5)$

$21x - 35 = 21x - 35$

$-35 = -35$ true

The true statement $-35 = -35$ indicates that the system contains dependent equations and has infinitely many solutions.

17. $5x + 2y = 0$

$x - 3y = 0$

Solve the second equation for x.

$x - 3y = 0$

$x = 3y$

Substitute $3y$ for x in the first equation.

$5x + 2y = 0$

$5(3y) + 2y = 0$

$15y + 2y = 0$

$17y = 0$

$y = 0$

Back-substitute.

$x = 3y$

$x = 3(0) = 0$

Solution: (0,0)

19. $2x - y = 6$

$3x + 2y = 5$

Solve the first equation for y.

$2x - y = 6$

$-y = -2x + 6$

$y = 2x - 6$

Substitute $2x - 6$ for y in the second equation.

$3x + 2y = 5$

$3x + 2(2x - 6) = 5$

$3x + 4x - 12 = 5$

$7x - 12 = 5$

$7x = 17$

$x = \frac{17}{7}$

Back-substitute.

$y = 2x - 6 = 2\left(\frac{17}{7}\right) - 6$

$= \frac{34}{7} - 6 = \frac{34}{7} - \frac{42}{7} = -\frac{8}{7}$

Solution: $\left(\frac{17}{7}, -\frac{8}{7}\right)$

21. $2(x-1)-y=-3$

$y=2x+3$

Substitute $2x+3$ for y in the first equation.

$$2(x-1)-(2x+3)=-3$$
$$2x-2-2x-3=-3$$
$$-5=-3 \text{ false}$$

The false statement $-5 = -5$ indicates that the system has no solution.

23. $x=2y+9$

$x=7y+10$

Substitute $7y + 10$ for x in the first equation.

$$x=2y+9$$
$$7y+10=2y+9$$
$$5y+10=9$$
$$5y=-1$$
$$y=-\frac{1}{5}$$

Back-substitute.

$$x=2y+9=2\left(-\frac{1}{5}\right)+9$$
$$=-\frac{2}{5}+9=-\frac{2}{5}+\frac{45}{5}=\frac{43}{5}$$

Solution: $\left(\frac{43}{5},-\frac{1}{5}\right)$

25. $4x-y=100$

$0.05x-0.06y=-32$

Solve the first equation for y.

$$4x-y=100$$
$$-y=-4x+100$$
$$y=4x-100$$

Substitute $4x-100$ for y in the second equation.

$$0.05x-0.06y=-32$$
$$0.05x-0.06(4x-100)=-32$$
$$0.05x-0.24x+6=-32$$
$$-0.19x+6=-32$$
$$-0.19x=-38$$
$$x=200$$

Back-substitute.

$$y=4x-100$$
$$=4(200)-100$$
$$=800-100=700$$

Solution: $(200,700)$

27. $y=\frac{1}{3}x+\frac{2}{3}$

$y=\frac{5}{7}x-2$

First, clear both equations of fractions. Multiply the first equation by the LCD, 3.

$$3y=3\left(\frac{1}{3}x+\frac{2}{3}\right)$$
$$3y=3x+2$$

Multiply the second equation by the LCD, 7.

$$7y=7\left(\frac{5}{7}x-2\right)$$
$$7y=5x-14$$

Now solve the new system

$3y=x+2$

$7y=5x-14$

Solve the first of these equations for x.

$$3y=x+2$$
$$3y-2=x$$

Substitute $3y-2$ for x in the second equation of the new system.

$$7y = 5x - 14$$
$$7y = 5(3y - 2) - 14$$
$$7y = 15y - 10 - 14$$
$$7y = 15y - 24$$
$$-8y = -24$$
$$y = 3$$

Back-substitute.

$x = 3y - 2$

$x = 3(3) - 2 = 9 - 2 = 7$

Solution: (7, 3)

29. $\frac{x}{6} - \frac{y}{2} = \frac{1}{3}$

$x + 2y = -3$

Clear the first equation of fractions by multiplying 6.

$$6\left(\frac{x}{6} - \frac{y}{2}\right) = 6\left(\frac{1}{3}\right)$$
$$x - 3y = 2$$

Solve this equation for x.

$x = 3y + 2$

Substitute $3y + 2$ for x in the second equation of the system.

$$(3y + 2) + 2y = -3$$
$$5y + 2 = -3$$
$$5y = -5$$
$$y = -1$$

Back-substitute.

$x = 3y + 2 = 3(-1) + 2 = -1$

Solution: (−1, −1)

31. $2x - 3y = 8 - 2x$

$3x + 4y = x + 3y + 14$

Simplify the first equation.

$$2x - 3y = 8 - 2x$$
$$2x - 3y + 2x = 8 - 2x + 2x$$
$$4x - 3y = 8$$

Simplify the second equation.

$$3x + 4y = x + 3y + 14$$
$$3x + 4y - x - 3y = x + 3y + 14 - x - 3y$$
$$2x + y = 14$$

Solve the last equation for y.

$y = 14 - 2x$

Substitute $14 - 2x$ for y in the equation $4x - 3y = 8$.

$$4x - 3y = 8$$
$$4x - 3(14 - 2x) = 8$$
$$4x - 42 + 6x = 8$$
$$10x - 42 = 8$$
$$10x = 50$$
$$x = 5$$

$y = 14 - 2x = 14 - 2(5) = 14 - 10 = 4$

Solution: (5, 4)

33. $x + y = 81$

$x = y + 41$

Substitute $y + 41$ for x in the first equation.

$$x + y = 81$$
$$(y + 41) + y = 81$$
$$2y + 41 = 81$$
$$2y = 40$$
$$y = 20$$

Back-substitute.

$x = y + 41 = 20 + 41 = 61$

The numbers are 20 and 61.

34. $x + y = 62$

$x = y + 12$

Substitute $y + 12$ for x in the first equation.

$$x + y = 62$$
$$(y + 12) + y = 62$$
$$y + 12 + y = 62$$
$$2y + 12 = 62$$
$$2y = 50$$
$$y = 25$$

Back-substitute.

$x = y + 12 = 25 + 12 = 37$

The numbers are 25 and 37.

35. $x - y = 5$
$4x = 6y$
Solve the first equation for x.
$x - y = 5$
$x = y + 5$
Substitute $y + 5$ for x in the second equation.
$4x = 6y$
$4(y+5) = 6y$
$4y + 20 = 6y$
$20 = 2y$
$10 = y$
Back-substitute.
$x = y + 5 = 10 + 5 = 15$
The numbers are 10 and 15.

36. $x - y = 25$
$2x = 12y$
Solve the first equation for x.
$x - y = 25$
$x = y + 25$
Substitute $y + 25$ for x in the second equation.
$2x = 12y$
$2(y+25) = 12y$
$2y + 50 = 12y$
$50 = 10y$
$5 = y$
Back-substitute.
$x = y + 25 = 5 + 25 = 30$
The numbers are 5 and 30.

37. $x - y = 1$
$x + 2y = 7$
Solve the first equation for x.
$x - y = 1$
$x = y + 1$
Substitute $y + 1$ for x in the second equation.
$x + 2y = 7$
$(y+1) + 2y = 7$
$y + 1 + 2y = 7$
$3y + 1 = 7$
$3y = 6$
$y = 2$
Back-substitute.
$x = y + 1 = 2 + 1 = 3$
The numbers are 2 and 3.

38. $x - y = 5$
$x + 2y = 14$
Solve the first equation for x.
$x - y = 5$
$x = y + 5$
Substitute $y + 5$ for x in the second equation.
$x + 2y = 14$
$(y+5) + 2y = 14$
$y + 5 + 2y = 14$
$3y + 5 = 14$
$3y = 9$
$y = 3$
Back-substitute.
$x = y + 5 = 3 + 5 = 8$
The numbers are 3 and 8.

39. $0.7x - 0.1y = 0.6$
$0.8x - 0.3y = -0.8$
Multiply both sides of both equations by 10.
$7x - y = 6$
$8x - 3y = -8$
Solve the first equation for y.
$7x - y = 6$
$7x = 6 + y$
$7x - 6 = y$
Substitute $7x - 6$ for y in the second equation.
$8x - 3y = -8$
$8x - 3(7x - 6) = -8$
$8x - 21x + 18 = -8$
$-13x + 18 = -8$
$-13x = -26$
$x = 2$
Back-substitute.
$y = 7x - 6 = 7(2) - 6 = 14 - 6 = 8$
Solution: (2, 8)

40. $1.25x - 0.01y = 4.5$
$0.5x - 0.02y = 1$
Multiply both sides of both equations by 100.
$125x - 1y = 450$
$50x - 2y = 100$
Solve the first equation for y.
$125x - 1y = 450$
$125x - y = 450$
$125x = y + 450$
$125x - 450 = y$
Substitute $125x - 450$ for y in the second equation.
$50x - 2y = 100$
$50x - 2(125x - 450) = 100$
$50x - 250x + 900 = 100$
$-200x + 900 = 100$
$-200x = -800$
$x = 4$
Back-substitute.
$y = 125x - 450 = 125(4) - 450$
$= 500 - 450 = 50$
Solution: (4, 50)

41. Demand model: $N = -25p + 7500$
Supply model: $N = 5p + 6000$

a. Substitute 40 for p in both models.
$N = -25(40) + 7500 = 6500$
$N = 5(40) + 6000 = 6200$
At \$40 per ticket, 6500 tickets can be sold, but only 6200 tickets will be supplied.

b. To find the price at which supply and demand are equal, solve the demand-supply linear system. Substitute $-25p + 7500$ for N in the supply equation.
$N = 5p + 6000$
$-25p + 7500 = 5p + 6000$
$-30p = -1500$
$p = 50$
If $p = 50$,
$N = 5(50) + 6000 = 6250.$
Supply and demand are equal when the ticket price is \$50. At this price, 6250 tickets are supplied and sold.

43. Weekly costs: $y = 1.2x + 1080$
Weekly revenue: $y = 1.6x$
The station will break even when costs = revenue. Solve the cost-revenue linear system. Substitute $1.6x$ for y in the cost equation.
$y = 1.2x + 1080$
$1.6x = 1.2x + 1080$
$0.4x = 1080$
$\frac{0.4x}{0.4} = \frac{1080}{0.4}$
$x = 2700$
The station will break even if 2700 gallons of gasoline are sold weekly.

45. Blacks: $M = -0.41x + 22$
Whites: $M = -0.18x + 10$
To find out when infant mortality will be the same for blacks and whites, solve this system. Substitute $-0.41x + 22$ for M in the second equation.
$M = -0.18x + 10$
$-0.41x + 22 = -0.18x + 10$
$-0.23x + 22 = 10$
$-0.23x = -12$
$x \approx 52$
x = 52 corresponds to the year 1980 + 52 = 2032. Substitute 52 for x in either equation of the system.
$M = -0.18(52) + 10 = 0.6$
The model projects that the infant mortality for both groups will be about 0.6 deaths per 1000 live births in the year 2032.

47. – 51. Answers will vary.

53. $x = 3 - y - z$
$2x + y - z = -6$
$3x - y + z = 11$
This is a system of three linear equations with three variables. It can be solved by the substitution method. First substitute $3 - y - z$ for x in the second equation.

$$2x + y - z = -6$$
$$2(3 - y - z) + y - z = -6$$
$$6 - 2y - 2z + y - z = -6$$
$$6 - y - 3z = -6$$
$$6 - y - 3z - 6 = -6 - 6$$
$$-y - 3z = -12$$

Solve this equation for y.

$$-y = -12 + 3z$$
$$y = 12 - 3z$$

Now substitute $3 - y - z$ in the third equation of the given system.

$$3x - y + z = 11$$
$$3(3 - y - z) - y + z = 11$$
$$9 - 3y - 3z - y + z = 11$$
$$9 - 4y - 2z = 11$$

Substitute $12 - 3z$ in the last equation.

$$9 - 4y - 2z = 11$$
$$9 - 4(12 - 3z) - 2z = 11$$
$$9 - 48 + 12z - 2z = 11$$
$$-39 + 10z = 11$$
$$10z = 50$$
$$z = 5$$

Now back-substitute the equation $y = 12 - 3z$ to find the value of y.

$$y = 12 - 3z = 12 - 3(5) = -3$$

Finally, back-substitute in the equation $x = 3 - y - z$ to find the value of x.

$$x = 3 - y - z = 3 - (-3) - 5 = 1$$

Thus, $x = 1$, $y = -3$, and $z = 5$.

55. $4x + 6y = 12$
x-intercept: 3
y-intercept: 2
Checkpoint: (–3,4)
Draw a line through (3,0), (0, 2), and (–3, 4).

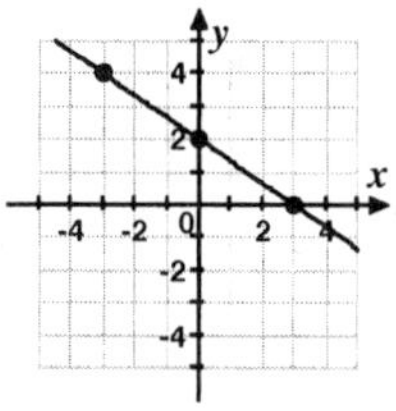

56. $4(x + 1) = 25 + 3(x - 3)$

$$4x + 4 = 25 + 3x - 9$$
$$x + 4 = 16$$
$$x = 12$$

The solution is 12.

57. The integers in the given set are –73, 0, and $\frac{3}{1} = 3$.

5.3 Exercise Set

1. $x + y = -3$
$x - y = 11$
Add the equations to eliminate the y-terms.
$x + y = -3$
$x - y = 11$
$2x \quad = 8$
Now solve for x.

$2x = 8$

$x = 4$

Back-substitute into either of the original equations to solve for y.

$x + y = -3$

$4 + y = -3$

$y = -7$

The proposed solution, (4, −7), satisfies both equations of the system since 4 + (−7) = -3 and 4 – (−7) = 11.
Solution: (4, −7)

3. $2x + 3y = 6$

$\underline{2x - 3y = 6}$

$4x = 12$

$x = 3$

$2(3) + 3y = 6$

$3y = 0$

$y = 0$

Solution: (3,0)

5. $x + 2y = 7$

$\underline{-x + 3y = 18}$

$5y = 25$

$y = 5$

$x + 2(5) = 7$

$x + 10 = 7$

$x = -3$

Solution: (−3, 5)

7. $5x - y = 14$

$\underline{-5x + 2y = -13}$

$y = 1$

$5x - (1) = 14$

$5x = 15$

$x = 3$

Solution: (3, 1)

9. $3x + y = 7$

$2x - 5y = -1$

Multiply each term of the first equation by 5 and add the equations to eliminate y.

$15x + 5y = 35$

$\underline{2x - 5y = -1}$

$17x = 34$

$x = 2$

Substitute 2 for x in one of the original equations and solve for y.

$3x + y = 7$

$3(2) + y = 7$

$6 + y = 7$

$y = 1$

Solution: (2, 1)

11. $x + 3y = 4$

$4x + 5y = 2$

Multiply each term of the first equation by −4 and add the equations to eliminate x.

$-4x - 12y = -16$

$\underline{4x + 5y = 2}$

$-7y = -14$

$y = 2$

Substitute 2 for y in one of the original equations and solve for x.

$x + 3y = 4$

$x + 3(2) = 4$

$x + 6 = 4$

$x = -2$

Solution: (−2, 2)

13. $-3x+7y = 14$
$2x - y = -13$
Multiply each term of the second equation by 7 and add the equations to eliminate y.

$$\begin{aligned} -3x+7y &= 14 \\ 14x-7y &= -91 \\ \hline 11x \quad &= -77 \\ x \quad &= -7 \end{aligned}$$

Substitute -7 for x in one of the original equations and solve for y.

$$\begin{aligned} 2x - y &= -13 \\ 2(-7) - y &= -13 \\ -14 - y &= -13 \\ -y &= 1 \\ y &= -1 \end{aligned}$$

Solution: $(-7, -1)$

15. $3x-14y = 6$
$5x+7y = 10$
Multiply each term of the second equation by 2 and add the equations to eliminate y.

$$\begin{aligned} 3x-14y &= 6 \\ 10x+14y &= 20 \\ \hline 13x \quad &= 26 \\ x \quad &= 2 \end{aligned}$$

Substitute 2 for x in one of the original equations and solve for y.

$$\begin{aligned} 5x+7y &= 10 \\ 5(2)+7y &= 10 \\ 10+7y &= 10 \\ 7y &= 0 \\ y &= 0 \end{aligned}$$

Solution: $(2, 0)$

17. $3x-4y = 11$
$2x+3y = -4$
Multiply the first equation by 3, and the second equation by 4.

$$\begin{aligned} 9x-12y &= 33 \\ 8x+12y &= -16 \\ \hline 17x \quad &= 17 \\ x \quad &= 1 \end{aligned}$$

Substitute 1 for x in one of the original equations and solve for y.

$$\begin{aligned} 2(1)+3y &= -4 \\ 3y &= -6 \\ y &= -2 \end{aligned}$$

Solution: $(1, -2)$

19. $3x+2y = -1$
$-2x+7y = 9$
Multiply the first equation by 2 and the second equation by 3.

$$\begin{aligned} 6x+4y &= -2 \\ -6x+21y &= 27 \\ \hline 25y &= 25 \\ y &= 1 \end{aligned}$$

Substitute 1 for y in one of the original equations and solve for x.

$$\begin{aligned} 3x+2(1) &= -1 \\ 3x &= -3 \\ x &= -1 \end{aligned}$$

Solution: $(-1, 1)$

21. $3x = 2y + 7$
$5x = 2y + 13$
Rewrite:
$3x - 2y = 7$
$5x - 2y = 13$
Multiply equation 1 by −1 and add the equations to eliminate y.

$$\begin{array}{r} -3x + 2y = -7 \\ \underline{5x - 2y = 13} \\ 2x = 6 \\ x = 3 \end{array}$$

Substitute 3 for x in one of the original equations and solve for y.

$$\begin{aligned} 3(3) &= 2y + 7 \\ 2 &= 2y \\ 1 &= y \end{aligned}$$

Solution: (3, 1)

23. $2x = 3y - 4$
$-6x + 12y = 6$
Rewrite the first equation.
$2x - 3y = -4$
Multiply the first equation by 3 and add to eliminate x.

$$\begin{array}{r} 6x - 9y = -12 \\ \underline{-6x + 12y = \quad 6} \\ 3y = -6 \\ y = -2 \end{array}$$

Substitute −2 for y in one of the original equations and solve for x.

$$\begin{aligned} 2x &= 3(-2) - 4 \\ 2x &= -6 - 4 \\ 2x &= -10 \\ x &= -5 \end{aligned}$$

Solution: (−5, −2)

25. $2x - y = 3$
$4x + 4y = -1$
Multiply the first equation by 4 and add to eliminate y.

$$\begin{array}{r} 8x - 4y = 12 \\ \underline{4x + 4y = -1} \\ 12x = 11 \\ x = \frac{11}{12} \end{array}$$

Instead of back-substituting $\frac{11}{12}$ and working with fractions, go back to the original system. Multiply the first equation by −2 and add the equations to eliminate x.

$$\begin{array}{r} -4x + 2y = -6 \\ \underline{4x + 4y = -1} \\ 6y = -7 \\ y = -\frac{7}{6} \end{array}$$

Solution: $\left(\frac{11}{12}, -\frac{7}{6}\right)$

27. $4x = 5 + 2y$

$2x + 3y = 4$

Rewrite the first equation, and multiply the second equation by −2.

$$\begin{array}{r} 4x - 2y = \ \ 5 \\ \underline{-4x - 6y = -8} \\ -8y = -3 \\ y = \frac{3}{8} \end{array}$$

Instead of back-substituting $\frac{3}{8}$ and working with fractions, go back to the original system. Use the rewritten form of the first equation, and multiply by −3. Solve by addition.

$$\begin{array}{r} -12x + 6y = -15 \\ \underline{-4x - 6y = -8} \\ -16x = -23 \\ x = \frac{23}{16} \end{array}$$

Solution: $\left(\frac{23}{16}, \frac{3}{8}\right)$

29. $3x - y = 1$

$\underline{3x - y = 2}$

Multiply equation 1 by −1.

$$\begin{array}{r} -3x + y = -1 \\ \underline{3x - y = 2} \\ 0 = 1 \quad \text{false} \end{array}$$

The false statement 0 = 1 indicates that the system is inconsistent and has no solution.

31. $x + 3y = 2$

$\underline{3x + 9y = 6}$

Multiply equation 1 by −3.

$$\begin{array}{r} -3x - 9y = -6 \\ \underline{3x + 9y = 6} \\ 0 = 0 \quad \text{true} \end{array}$$

The true statement 0 = 0 indicates that the system has infinitely many solutions.

33. $7x - 3y = 4$

$-14x + 6y = -7$

Multiply equation 1 by 2.

$$\begin{array}{r} 14x - 6y = 8 \\ \underline{-14x + 6y = -7} \\ 0 = 1 \end{array}$$

The false statement 0 = 1 indicates that the system has no solution.

35. $5x + y = 2$

$3x + y = 1$

Multiply equation 2 by −1.

$$\begin{array}{r} 5x + y = 2 \\ \underline{-3x - y = -1} \\ 2x = 1 \\ x = \frac{1}{2} \end{array}$$

Back-substitute $\frac{1}{2}$ for x and solve for y.

$$3\left(\frac{1}{2}\right) + y = 1$$

$$y = -\frac{1}{2}$$

Solution: $\left(\frac{1}{2}, -\frac{1}{2}\right)$

37. $x = 5 - 3y$
$2x + 6y = 10$
Rewrite equation 1.
$x + 3y = 5$
Multiply this equation by −2.
$-2x - 6y = -10$
$2x + 6y = 10$
$0 = 0$
The true statement 0 = 0 indicates that the system has infinitely many solutions.

39. $4(3x - y) = 0$
$3(x + 3) = 10y$
Rewrite both equations.
$12x - 4y = 0$
$3x - 10y = -9$
Multiply the second equation by −4 and add the equations to eliminate x.
$12x - 4y = 0$
$\underline{-12x + 40y = 36}$
$36y = 36$
$y = 1$
Back-substitute 1 for y in one of the original equations and solve for x.
$12x - 4y = 0$
$12x - 4(1) = 0$
$12x = 4$
$x = \frac{1}{3}$
Solution: $\left(\frac{1}{3}, 1\right)$

41. $x + y = 11$
$\frac{x}{5} + \frac{y}{7} = 1$
Multiply the second equation by the LCD, 35, to clear fractions.
$35\left(\frac{x}{5} + \frac{y}{7}\right) = 35(1)$
$7x + 5y = 35$
Now solve the system.
$x + y = 11$
$7x + 5y = 35$
Multiply the first equation by −5 and add the result to the second equation.
$-5x - 5y = -55$
$\underline{7x + 5y = 35}$
$2x = -20$
$x = -10$

$-10 + y = 11$
$y = 21$
Solution: (−10, 21)

43. $\frac{4}{5}x - y = -1$
$\frac{2}{5}x + y = 1$
Multiply both equations by 5 to clear fractions.
$4x - 5y = -5$
$\underline{2x + 5y = 5}$
$6x = 0$
$x = 0$

Back-substitute 0 for x and solve for y.
$\frac{2}{5}(0) + y = 1$
$y = 1$
Solution: (0, 1)

45. $3x-2y=8$

$x=-2y$

The substitution method is a good choice because the second equation is already solved for *x*. Substitute $-2y$ for *x* in the first equation

$$3x-2y=8$$
$$3(-2y)-2y=8$$
$$-6y-2y=8$$
$$-8y=8$$
$$y=-1$$

Back-substitute -1 for *y* in the second equation.

$x=-2y=-2(-1)=2$

Solution: $(2, -1)$

47. $3x+2y=-3$

$2x-5y=17$

The addition method is a good choice because both equations are written in the form $Ax+By=C$.

Multiply the first equation by 2 and the second equation by -3.

$$6x+4y=-6$$
$$-6x+15y=-51$$
$$19y=-57$$
$$y=-3$$

Back-substitute -3 for *y* and solve for *x*.

$$3x+2(-3)=-3$$
$$3x-6=-3$$
$$3x=3$$
$$x=1$$

Solution: $(1, -3)$

49. $3x-2y=6$

$y=3$

The substitution method is a good choice because the second equation is already solved for *y*. Substitute 3 for *y* in the first equation.

$$3x-2y=6$$
$$3x-2(3)=6$$
$$3x-6=6$$
$$3x=12$$
$$x=4$$

It is not necessary to back-substitute to find the value of *y* because $y = 3$ is one of the equations of the given system. The solution is (4, 3).

51. $y=2x+1$

$y=2x-3$

The substitution method is a good choice, because both equations are already solved for *y*. Substitute $2x+1$ for *y* in the second equation.

$$y=2x-3$$
$$2x+1=2x-3$$
$$2x+1-2x=2x-3-2x$$
$$1=-3 \text{ false}$$

The false statement $1=-3$ indicates that the system has no solution.

53. $2(x+2y)=6$

$3(x+2y-3)=0$

The addition method is a good choice since the left-hand sides of the equations can easily be simplified to give equations of the form $Ax+By=C$.

$2x+4y=6$ $\qquad$ $3x+6y-9=0$

$\qquad\qquad\qquad\qquad 3x+6y=9$

So, solve the system.

$2x+4y=6$

$3x+6y=9$

Multiply the first equation by -3 and the second by 2 and solve by addition.

$$\begin{aligned} -6x-12y &= -18 \\ \underline{6x+12y} &\underline{= 18} \\ 0 &= 0 \text{ true} \end{aligned}$$

The true statement $0 = 0$ indicates that the original system has infinitely many solutions.

55. $3y = 2x$

$2x+9y=24$

The substitution method is a good choice because the first equation can easily be solved for one of the variables. Solve this equation for y.

$3y = 2x$

$y = \frac{2}{3}x$

Substitute $\frac{2}{3}x$ for y in the second equation.

$$\begin{aligned} 2x+9y &= 24 \\ 2x+9\left(\frac{2}{3}x\right) &= 24 \\ 2x+6x &= 24 \\ 8x &= 24 \\ x &= 3 \end{aligned}$$

Back-substitute 3 for x in the equation, $y = \frac{2}{3}x$.

$y = \frac{2}{3}x = \frac{2}{3}(3) = 2$

Solution: $(3, 2)$

57. $\frac{3x}{5}+\frac{4y}{5}=1$

$\frac{x}{4}-\frac{3y}{8}=-1$

Multiply the first equation by 5 and the second equation by 8 to clear fractions.

$\frac{3x}{5}+\frac{4y}{5}=1 \qquad \frac{x}{4}-\frac{3y}{8}=-1$

$3x+4y=5 \qquad 2x-3y=-8$

The addition method is a good choice since both equations are of the form $Ax+By=C$.

$3x+4y=5$

$2x-3y=-8$

Multiply the first equation by 3 and the second equation by 4.

$$\begin{aligned} 9x+12y &= 15 \\ \underline{8x-12y} &\underline{= -32} \\ 17x \quad &= -17 \\ x \quad &= -1 \end{aligned}$$

Back-substitute -1 for x in the equation and solve for y.

$$\begin{aligned} 3x+4y &= 5 \\ 3(-1)+4y &= 5 \\ -3+4y &= 5 \\ 4y &= 8 \\ y &= 2 \end{aligned}$$

Solution: $(-1, 2)$

58. $\frac{x}{3}-\frac{y}{2}=\frac{2}{3}$

$\frac{2x}{3}+y=\frac{4}{3}$

Multiply the first equation by 6 and the second equation by 3 to clear fractions.

$\frac{x}{3}-\frac{y}{2}=\frac{2}{3}$ $\qquad$ $\frac{2x}{3}+y=\frac{4}{3}$

$2x-3y=4$ $\qquad$ $2x+3y=4$

The addition method is a good choice since both equations are of the form $Ax+By=C$.

$$\begin{aligned} 2x-3y&=4\\ \underline{2x+3y}&\underline{=4}\\ 4x\quad\;\; &=8\\ x\quad\;\; &=2 \end{aligned}$$

Back-substitute 2 for *x* in the equation and solve for *y*.

$$\begin{aligned} 2x-3y&=4\\ 2(2)-3y&=4\\ 4-3y&=4\\ -3y&=0\\ y&=0 \end{aligned}$$

Solution: (2, 0)

59. $5(x+1)=7(y+1)-7$

$6(x+1)+5=5(y+1)$

Simplify both equations.

$$\begin{aligned} 5(x+1)&=7(y+1)-7\\ 5x+5&=7y+7-7\\ 5x+5&=7y\\ 5x-7y+5&=0\\ 5x-7y&=-5 \end{aligned}$$

$$\begin{aligned} 6(x+1)+5&=5(y+1)\\ 6x+6+5&=5y+5\\ 6x+11&=5y+5\\ 6x-5y+11&=5\\ 6x-5y&=-6 \end{aligned}$$

The rewritten system is as follows.

$5x-7y=-5$

$6x-5y=-6$

Multiply the first equation by -6 and the second equation by 5, and solve by addition.

$$\begin{aligned} -30x+42y&=\;\;30\\ \underline{30x-25y}&\underline{=-30}\\ 17y&=\;\;0\\ y&=\;\;0 \end{aligned}$$

Back-substitute 0 for *y* to find *x*.

$$\begin{aligned} 5x-7y&=-5\\ 5x-7(0)&=-5\\ 5x-0&=-5\\ 5x&=-5\\ x&=-1 \end{aligned}$$

The solution is $(-1, 0)$.

60. $6x=5(x+y+3)-x$

$3(x-y)+4y=5(y+1)$

Simplify both equations.

$$\begin{aligned} 6x&=5(x+y+3)-x\\ 6x&=5x+5y+15-x\\ 6x&=4x+5y+15\\ 2x-5y&=15 \end{aligned}$$

$$\begin{aligned} 3(x-y)+4y&=5(y+1)\\ 3x-3y+4y&=5y+5\\ 3x+y&=5y+5\\ 3x-4y&=5 \end{aligned}$$

The rewritten system is as follows.
$2x-5y=15$
$3x-4y=5$
Multiply the first equation by -3 and the second equation by 2, and solve by addition.

$$\begin{array}{r} -6x+15y=-45 \\ \underline{6x-8y=10} \\ 7y=-35 \\ y=-5 \end{array}$$

Back-substitute -5 for y to find x.

$$\begin{aligned} 2x-5y&=15 \\ 2x-5(-5)&=15 \\ 2x+25&=15 \\ 2x&=-10 \\ x&=-5 \end{aligned}$$

The solution is $(-5, -5)$.

61. $0.4x+\quad y=2.2$
$0.5x-1.2y=0.3$
Multiply the first equation by 1.2 and solve by addition.

$$\begin{array}{l} 0.48x+1.2y=2.64 \\ \underline{0.50x-1.2y=0.30} \\ 0.98x \qquad\quad = 2.94 \\ \quad x \qquad\quad\ = 3 \end{array}$$

Back-substitute 3 for x to find y.

$$\begin{aligned} 0.4x+y&=2.2 \\ 0.4(3)+y&=2.2 \\ 1.2+y&=2.2 \\ y&=1 \end{aligned}$$

The solution is $(3, 1)$.

62. $1.25x-1.5y=2$
$3.5x-1.75y=10.5$
Multiply the first equation by -2.8 and solve by addition.

$$\begin{array}{r} -3.5x+4.2y=-5.6 \\ \underline{3.5x-1.75y=10.5} \\ 2.45y=-4.9 \\ y=2 \end{array}$$

Back-substitute 2 for y to find x.

$$\begin{aligned} 1.25x-1.5y&=2 \\ 1.25x-1.5(2)&=2 \\ 1.25x-3&=2 \\ 1.25x&=5 \\ x&=4 \end{aligned}$$

The solution is $(4, 2)$.

63. $\frac{x}{2}=\frac{y+8}{3}$
$\frac{x+2}{2}=\frac{y+11}{3}$
Simplify both equations.

$$\begin{aligned} \frac{x}{2}&=\frac{y+8}{3} \\ 3x&=2(y+8) \\ 3x&=2y+16 \\ 3x-2y&=16 \end{aligned}$$

$$\begin{aligned} \frac{x+2}{2}&=\frac{y+11}{3} \\ 3(x+2)&=2(y+11) \\ 3x+6&=2y+22 \\ 3x-2y+6&=22 \\ 3x-2y&=16 \end{aligned}$$

When simplified, the equations are the same. This means that the system is dependent and there are an infinite number of solutions.

64. $\frac{x}{2}=\frac{y+8}{4}$
$\frac{x+3}{2}=\frac{y+5}{4}$

Simplify both equations.

$$\frac{x}{2}=\frac{y+8}{4}$$
$$4\left(\frac{x}{2}\right)=y+8$$
$$2x=y+8$$
$$2x-8=y$$
$$y=2x-8$$

$$\frac{x+3}{2}=\frac{y+5}{4}$$
$$4\left(\frac{x+3}{2}\right)=y+5$$
$$2(x+3)=y+5$$
$$2x+6=y+5$$
$$2x+1=y$$
$$y=2x+1$$

When simplified, the both equations have the same slope, but different *y*-intercepts. This means that the system is inconsistent and there are no solutions.

65. $13x+12y=992$
$-x+y=16$

Solve the second equation for *y*.

$-x+y=16$
$y=x+16$

Substitute $x+16$ for *y* and solve for *x*.

$$13x+12y=992$$
$$13x+12(x+16)=992$$
$$13x+12x+192=992$$
$$25x+192=992$$
$$25x=800$$
$$x=32$$

Back-substitute 32 for *x* and solve for *y*.

$y=x+16=32+16=48$

The solution is (32, 48). This means that in the year 1988 + 32 = 2020, the percent in favor and against the death penalty are both the same at 48%.

67.-71. Answers will vary.

73. $x-y=a$
$y=2x+b$

Substitute $2x+b$ for *y* and solve for *x*.

$$x-y=a$$
$$x-(2x+b)=a$$
$$x-2x-b=a$$
$$-x-b=a$$
$$-x=a+b$$
$$x=-a-b$$

Back-substitute $-a-b$ for *x* to find *y*.

$$y=2x+b$$
$$y=2(-a-b)+b$$
$$y=-2a-2b+b$$
$$y=-2a-b$$

The solution is $x=-a-b$ and $y=-2a-b$.

75. Answers will vary according to the exercises chosen.

77. $x = 5y$

$2x - 3y = 7$

Rewriting the first equation in $Ax + By = C$ form yields $x - 5y = 0$.

The system is as follows.

$x - 5y = 0$

$2x - 3y = 7$

Use the SIMULT (simultaneous equations) function on the TI-85 or higher numbered calculator. Enter 2 for two equations in two variables, then the coefficients and constant terms for each equations, one equation at a time. After entering all the coefficients, press SOLVE and read the solutions displayed on the screen.

Solution: (5, 1)

79. Let x = the unknown number.

$5x = x + 40$

$4x = 40$

$x = 10$

The number is 10.

80. Because the x-coordinate is negative and the y-coordinate is positive, $\left(-\frac{3}{2}, 15\right)$ is located in quadrant II.

81. $29{,}700 + 150x = 5000 + 1100x$

$29{,}700 - 950x = 5000$

$-950x = -24{,}700$

$x = 26$

The solution is 26.

Mid-Chapter Check Points

1. $3x + 2y = 6$

$2x - y = 4$

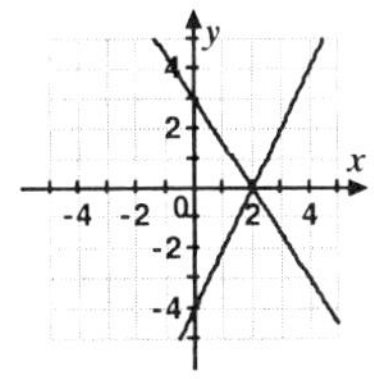

Solution: (2, 0)

2. $y = 2x - 1$

$y = 3x - 2$

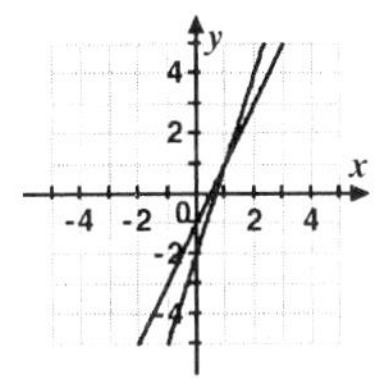

Solution: (1, 1)

3. $y = 2x - 1$

$6x - 3y = 12$

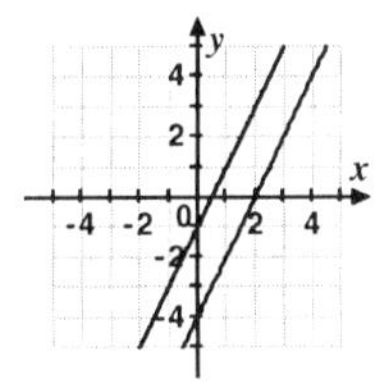

Since the lines are parallel, the system is inconsistent and there is no solution.

4. $5x-3y=1$

$y=3x-7$

Substitute $3x-7$ for y in the first equation and solve for x.

$$5x-3y=1$$
$$5x-3(3x-7)=1$$
$$5x-9x+21=1$$
$$-4x+21=1$$
$$-4x=-20$$
$$x=5$$

Back-substitute.

$$y=3x-7=3(5)-7=15-7=8$$

Solution: (5, 8)

5. $6x+5y=7$

$3x-7y=13$

Multiply the second equation by −2 and add to eliminate x.

$$6x+5y=7$$
$$-6x+14y=-26$$
$$19y=-19$$
$$y=-1$$

Back-substitute −1 for y and solve for x.

$$6x+5y=7$$
$$6x+5(-1)=7$$
$$6x-5=7$$
$$6x=12$$
$$x=2$$

Solution: $(2,-1)$

6. $x=\frac{y}{3}-1$

$6x+y=21$

Substitute $\frac{y}{3}-1$ for x in the second equation and solve for y.

$$6x+y=21$$
$$6\left(\frac{y}{3}-1\right)+y=21$$
$$2y-6+y=21$$
$$3y-6=21$$
$$3y=27$$
$$y=9$$

Back-substitute.

$$x=\frac{y}{3}-1=\frac{9}{3}-1=3-1=2$$

Solution: (2, 9)

7. $3x-4y=6$

$5x-6y=8$

Multiply the first equation by −5, the second equation by 3 and add to eliminate x.

$$-15x+20y=-30$$
$$15x-18y=24$$
$$2y=-6$$
$$y=-3$$

Back-substitute −3 for y and solve for x.

$$3x-4y=6$$
$$3x-4(-3)=6$$
$$3x+12=6$$
$$3x=-6$$
$$x=-2$$

Solution: $(-2,-3)$

8. $3x - 2y = 32$

$\frac{x}{5} + 3y = -1$

Multiply the second equation by 5 to clear the fraction.

$5\left(\frac{x}{5} + 3y\right) = 5(-1)$

$x + 15y = -5$

The system is as follows.

$3x - 2y = 32$

$x + 15y = -5$

Multiply the second equation by -3 and solve by addition.

$$\begin{array}{r} 3x - 2y = 32 \\ -3x - 45y = 15 \\ \hline -47y = 47 \\ y = -1 \end{array}$$

Back-substitute -1 for y and solve for x.

$x + 15y = -5$

$x + 15(-1) = -5$

$x - 15 = -5$

$x = 10$

Solution: $(10, -1)$

9. $x - y = 3$

$2x = 4 + 2y$

Solve the first equation for x.

$x - y = 3$

$x = y + 3$

Substitute $y + 3$ for x in the second equation and solve for y.

$2x = 4 + 2y$

$2(y + 3) = 4 + 2y$

$2y + 6 = 4 + 2y$

$6 = 4$

Notice that y has also been eliminated. The false statement $6 = 4$ indicates that the system is inconsistent and has no solution.

10. $x = 2(y - 5)$

$4x + 40 = y - 7$

Substitute $2(y - 5)$ for x in the second equation and solve for y.

$4x + 40 = y - 7$

$4(2(y - 5)) + 40 = y - 7$

$4(2y - 10) + 40 = y - 7$

$8y - 40 + 40 = y - 7$

$8y = y - 7$

$7y = -7$

$y = -1$

Back-substitute -1 for y and solve for x.

$x = 2(y - 5)$

$= 2(-1 - 5) = 2(-6) = -12$

Solution: $(-12, -1)$

11. $y = 3x - 2$

$y = 2x - 9$

Substitute $3x - 2$ for y in the second equation and solve for x.

$y = 2x - 9$

$3x - 2 = 2x - 9$

$x - 2 = -9$

$x = -7$

Back-substitute -7 for x and solve for y.

$y = 3(-7) - 2 = -21 - 2 = -23$

Solution: $(-7, -23)$

12. $2x-3y=4$

$3x+4y=0$

Multiply the first equation by 4, the second equation by 3 and add to eliminate y.

$$\begin{aligned} 8x-12y&=16\\ 9x+12y&=0\\ \hline 17x\quad&=16\\ x\quad&=\frac{16}{17} \end{aligned}$$

Back-substitute $\frac{16}{17}$ for x and solve for y.

$$\begin{aligned} 3x+4y&=0\\ 3\left(\frac{16}{17}\right)+4y&=0\\ \frac{48}{17}+4y&=0\\ 4y&=-\frac{48}{17}\\ \frac{1}{4}(4y)&=\frac{1}{4}\left(-\frac{48}{17}\right)\\ y&=-\frac{12}{17} \end{aligned}$$

Solution: $\left(\frac{16}{17},-\frac{12}{17}\right)$

13. $y-2x=7$

$4x=2y-14$

Solve the first equation for y.

$$\begin{aligned} y-2x&=7\\ y&=2x+7 \end{aligned}$$

Substitute $2x+7$ for y and solve for x.

$$\begin{aligned} 4x&=2y-14\\ 4x&=2(2x+7)-14\\ 4x&=4x+14-14\\ 0&=14-14\\ 0&=0 \end{aligned}$$

Notice that x has also been eliminated. The true statement 0 = 0 indicates that the system is dependent and has infinitely many solutions.

14. $4(x+3)=3y+7$

$2(y-5)=x+5$

First, rewrite both equations in the form $Ax+By=C$.

$$\begin{aligned} 4(x+3)&=3y+7\\ 4x+12&=3y+7\\ 4x-3y+12&=7\\ 4x-3y&=-5 \end{aligned}$$

$$\begin{aligned} 2(y-5)&=x+5\\ 2y-10&=x+5\\ -x+2y-10&=5\\ -x+2y&=15 \end{aligned}$$

The system is as follows.

$4x-3y=-5$

$-x+2y=15$

Multiply the second equation by 4 and add to eliminate x.

$$\begin{aligned} 4x-3y&=-5\\ -4x+8y&=60\\ \hline 5y&=55\\ y&=11 \end{aligned}$$

Back-substitute 11 for y and solve for x.

$$\begin{aligned} -x+2y&=15\\ -x+2(11)&=15\\ -x+22&=15\\ -x&=-7\\ x&=7 \end{aligned}$$

Solution: (7, 11)

15. $\frac{x}{2}-\frac{y}{5}=1$

$y-\frac{x}{3}=8$

Multiply the first equation by 10 and the second equation by 3 to clear fractions.

$10\left(\frac{x}{2}\right)-10\left(\frac{y}{5}\right)=10(1)$

$5x-2y=10$

$3y-3\left(\frac{x}{3}\right)=3(8)$

$3y-x=24$

$-x+3y=24$

The system is as follows.

$5x-2y=10$

$-x+3y=24$

Multiply the second equation by 5 and solve by addition.

$$\begin{aligned} 5x-\ 2y&=\ 10\\ -5x+15y&=120\\ \hline 13y&=130\\ y&=\ 10 \end{aligned}$$

Back-substitute and solve for x.

$-x+3y=24$

$-x+3(10)=24$

$-x+30=24$

$-x=-6$

$x=6$

Solution: (6, 10)

5.4 Exercise Set

1. Let x = one number.
Let y = the other number.

$$\begin{aligned} x+y&=17\\ x-y&=-3\\ \hline 2x\quad&=14\\ x\quad&=\ 7 \end{aligned}$$

Back-substitute 7 for x to find y.

$x+y=17$

$7+y=17$

$y=10$

The numbers are 7 and 10.

3. Let x = one number.
Let y = the other number.

$3x-\ y=-1$

$x+2y=23$

Solve the second equation for x.

$x+2y=23$

$x=-2y+23$

Substitute $-2y+23$ for x to find y.

$3x-y=-1$

$3(-2y+23)-y=-1$

$-6y+69-y=-1$

$-7y+69=-1$

$-7y=-70$

$y=10$

Back substitute 10 for y to find x.

$x=-2y+23=-2(10)+23$

$=-20+23=3$

The numbers are 3 and 10.

5. Let x = the number of millions of pounds of potato chips.
Let y = the number of millions of pounds of tortilla chips.

$$\begin{aligned} x+y&=10.4 \\ x-y&=1.2 \\ \hline 2x\quad&=11.6 \\ x\quad&=5.8 \end{aligned}$$

Back-substitute to find y.

$$\begin{aligned} x+y&=10.4 \\ 5.8+y&=10.4 \\ y&=4.6 \end{aligned}$$

On Super Bowl Sunday, 5.8 million pounds of potato chips and 4.6 million pounds of tortilla chips are consumed.

7. Let x = the number of calories in one pan pizza.
Let y = the number of calories in one beef burrito.

$$\begin{aligned} x+2y&=1980 \\ 2x+\quad y&=2670 \end{aligned}$$

To solve this system by the addition method, multiply the first equation by −2 and add the result to the second equation.

$$\begin{aligned} -2x-4y&=-3960 \\ 2x+\quad y&=\ 2670 \\ \hline -3y&=-1290 \\ y&=430 \end{aligned}$$

Back-substitute 430 for y and solve for x.

$$\begin{aligned} x+2y&=1980 \\ x+2(430)&=1980 \\ x+860&=1980 \\ x&=1120 \end{aligned}$$

A pan pizza has 1120 calories and a beef burrito has 430 calories.

9. Let x = number of milligrams of cholesterol in scrambled eggs.
Let y = number of milligrams of cholesterol in a Whopper.

$$\begin{aligned} x+y&=300+241 \\ 2x+3y&=1257 \end{aligned}$$

Simplify the first equation.

$$\begin{aligned} x+\quad y&=\ 541 \\ 2x+3y&=1257 \end{aligned}$$

Multiply the first equation by −2 and add to second equation.

$$\begin{aligned} -2x-2y&=-1082 \\ 2x+3y&=\ 1257 \\ \hline y&=\ 175 \end{aligned}$$

Back-substitute 175 for y and solve for x.

$$\begin{aligned} x+y&=541 \\ x+175&=541 \\ x&=366 \end{aligned}$$

The scrambled eggs have 366 mg of cholesterol, and the Double Beef Whopper has 175 mg of cholesterol.

11. Let x = the price of one sweater.
Let y = the price of one shirt.

$$\begin{aligned} x+3y&=42 \\ 3x+2y&=56 \end{aligned}$$

Multiply the first equation by −3 and add the result to the second equation.

$$\begin{aligned} -3x-9y&=-126 \\ 3x+2y&=\ 56 \\ \hline -7y&=-70 \\ y&=\ 10 \end{aligned}$$

Back-substitute 10 for y and solve for x.

$$\begin{aligned} x+3y&=42 \\ x+3(10)&=42 \\ x+30&=42 \\ x&=12 \end{aligned}$$

The price of one sweater is \$12 and the price of one shirt is \$10.

13. Let x = the length of a badminton court.
Let y = the width of a badminton court.
Use the formula for the perimeter of a rectangle to write the first equation.

$$P = 2l + 2w$$

$$128 = 2x + 2y$$

Use the other information in the problem to write the second equation.

$$6x + 9y = 444$$

The two equations form the system.

$$2x + 2y = 128$$

$$6x + 9y = 444$$

Multiply the first equation by −3 and add the result to the second equation.

$$\begin{aligned} -6x - 6y &= -384 \\ 6x + 9y &= 444 \\ \hline 3y &= 60 \\ y &= 20 \end{aligned}$$

Back-substitute 20 for y and solve for x.

$$\begin{aligned} 2x + 2y &= 128 \\ 2x + 2(20) &= 128 \\ 2x + 40 &= 128 \\ 2x &= 88 \\ x &= 44 \end{aligned}$$

The length is 44 feet and the width is 20 feet, so the dimensions of a standard badminton court are 44 feet by 20 feet.

15. Let x = the length of the lot.
Let y = the width of the lot.
Use the formula for the perimeter of a rectangle to write the first equation.

$$2x + 2y = 320$$

Use the other information in the problem to write the second equation.

$$16x + 5(2y) = 2140$$

These two equations form the system.

$$2x + 2y = 320$$

$$16x + 10y = 2140$$

Multiply the first equation by −5 and add the result to the second equation.

$$\begin{aligned} -10x - 10y &= -1600 \\ 16x + 10y &= 2140 \\ \hline 6x &= 540 \\ x &= 90 \end{aligned}$$

Back-substitute 90 for x to find y.

$$\begin{aligned} 2(90) + 2y &= 320 \\ 180 + 2y &= 320 \\ 2y &= 140 \\ y &= 70 \end{aligned}$$

The length is 90 feet and the width is 70 feet, so the dimensions of the lot are 90 feet by 70 feet.

17. **a.** Let x = the number of minutes of long distance calls.
Let y = the monthly cost of a telephone plan.
Plan A: $y = 20 + 0.05x$
Plan B: $y = 5 + 0.10x$
Solve by substitution. Substitute $5 + 0.10x$ for y in the first equation.

$$\begin{aligned} 5 + 0.10x &= 20 + 0.05x \\ 5 + 0.05x &= 20 \\ 0.05x &= 15 \\ x &= 300 \end{aligned}$$

Back-substitute 300 for x.

$$y = 20 + 0.05(300) = 35$$

The costs for the two plans will be equal for 300 minutes of long-distance calls per month. The cost for each plan will be $35.

b. $x = 10(20) = 200$

Plan A:

$y = 20 + 0.05(200) = 30$

Plan B:

$y = 5 + 0.10(200) = 25$

The monthly cost would be \$30 for Plan A and \$25 for Plan B, so Plan B should be selected to get the lower cost.

19. Let x = the number of dollars of merchandise purchased in a year.
Let y = the total cost for a year.

Plan A: $y = 100 + 0.80x$

Plan B: $y = 40 + 0.90x$

Substitute $40 = 0.90x$ for y in the first equation and solve for x.

$$40 + 0.90x = 100 + 0.80x$$
$$40 + 0.10x = 100$$
$$0.10x = 60$$
$$x = 600$$

Back-substitute 600 for x to find y.

$y = 100 + 0.80(600) = 580.$

If you purchase \$600 worth of merchandise, you will pay the \$580 under both plans.

21. Let x = the number of years after 1985.
Let y = the average high school graduate's weekly earning.
We are interested in the year in which the average college graduate earns twice as much as a high school graduate, so the average college graduate's earnings will be $2y$.
College graduates:

$2y = 508 + 25x$

High school graduates:

$y = 345x + 9x$

Substitute 345 + $9x$ for y in the first equation and solve for x

$$2(345 + 9x) = 580 + 25x$$
$$690 + 18x = 508 + 25x$$
$$690 - 7x = 508$$
$$-7x = -182$$
$$x = 26$$

Back-substitute 26 for x to find y.

$y = 345 + 9(26) = 579$

$2y = 2(579) = 1158.$

In 1985 + 26 = 2011, the average college graduate will earn \$1158 per week and the average high school graduate will earn \$579 per week.

23. Let x = the number of servings of macaroni.
Let y = the number of servings of broccoli.

$$3x + 2y = 14$$
$$16x + 4y = 48$$

Multiply the first equation by −2 and add to second equation.

$$-6x - 4y = -28$$
$$16x + 4y = 48$$
$$10x = 20$$
$$x = 2$$

Back-substitute 2 for x to find y.

$$3(2) + 2y = 14$$
$$2y = 8$$
$$y = 4$$

It would take 2 servings of macaroni and 4 servings of broccoli to get 14 grams of protein and 48 grams of carbohydrate.

25. The sum of the measures of the three angles of any triangle is 180°, so
$(x+8y-1)+(3y+4)+(7x+5)=180.$
Simplify this equation.
$$8x+11y+8=180$$
$$8x+11y=172$$
The base angles of an isosceles triangle have equal measures, so
$3y+4=7x+5$
Rewrite this equation in the form
$Ax+By=C.$
$$7x+5=3y+4$$
$$7x-3y=-1$$
Use the addition method to solve the system.
$$8x+11y=172$$
$$7x-3y=-1$$
Multiply the first equation by 3 and the second equation by 11; then add the results.
$$24x+33y=516$$
$$\underline{77x-33y=-11}$$
$$101x \quad\quad = 505$$
$$x \quad\quad = \quad 5$$
Back-substitute 5 for x to find y.
$$7(5)-3y=-1$$
$$35-3y=-1$$
$$-3y=-36$$
$$y=12$$
Use the values of x and y to find the angle measures.
Angle A:
$(x+8y-1)°=(5+8\cdot 12-1)°=100°$
Angle B:
$(3y+4)°=(3\cdot 12+4)°=40°$
Angle C:
$(7x+5)°=(7\cdot 5+5)°=40°$

27. Use the distance formula to write the equations.
Rowing with current:
$$r\cdot t=d$$
$$(x+y)\cdot 2=16$$
Rowing against current:
$$(x-y)\cdot 2=8$$
Rewrite each equation in the form
$Ax+By=C.$
$$2x+2y=16$$
$$\underline{2x-2y=\ 8}$$
$$4x \quad\quad = 24$$
$$x \quad\quad = \ 6$$
Back-substitute 6 for x to find y.
$$2(6)+2y=16$$
$$12+2y=16$$
$$2y=4$$
$$y=2$$
The rowing rate in still water is 6 miles per hour and the rate of the current is 2 miles per hour.

29.-31. Answers will vary.

33. Let x = the number of birds.
Let y = the number of lions.
Since each bird has one head and each lion has one head,
$x+y=30.$
Since each bird has two feet and each lion has four feet,
$2x+4y=100.$
Solve the first equation for y.
$y=30-x$ Substitute $30-x$ for y in the second equation.
$$2x+4(30-x)=100$$
$$2x+120-4x=100$$
$$-2x+120=100$$

$-2x = -20$

$x = 10$

Back-substitute 10 for x to find y.

$10 + y = 30$

$y = 20$

There were 10 birds and 20 lions in the zoo.

35. Let x = the number of people in the downstairs apartment.
Let y = the number of people in the upstairs apartment.
If one of the people in the upstairs apartment goes downstairs, there will be the same number of people in both apartments, so $y - 1 = x + 1$.
If one of the people in the downstairs apartment goes upstairs, there will be twice as many people upstairs as downstairs, so $y + 1 = 2(x - 1)$.
Solve the first equation for y.

$y = x + 2$

Also solve the second equation for y.

$y + 1 = 2x - 2$

$y = 2x - 3$

Substitute $x + 2$ for y in the last equation.

$x + 2 = 2x - 3$

$-x + 2 = -3$

$-x = -5$

$x = 5$

Back-substitute to find y

$y = 5 + 2 = 7$

There are 5 people downstairs and 7 people upstairs.

37. Answers will vary.

38. $2x - y < 4$
Graph $2x - y = 4$ as a dashed line with x-intercept 2 and y-intercept -4. Use (0, 0) as a test point. Since $2(0) - 0 < 4$ is true, shade the half-plane containing (0, 0).

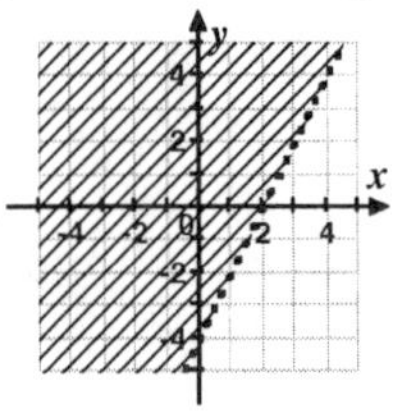

39. $y \geq x + 1$
Graph the line $y = x + 1$ using the slope of 1 and y-intercept of 1. Make the line solid because the inequality symbol is $\geq$. Use (0, 0) as a test point. Since $0 \geq 0 + 1$ is false, shade the half-plane *not* containing (0, 0).

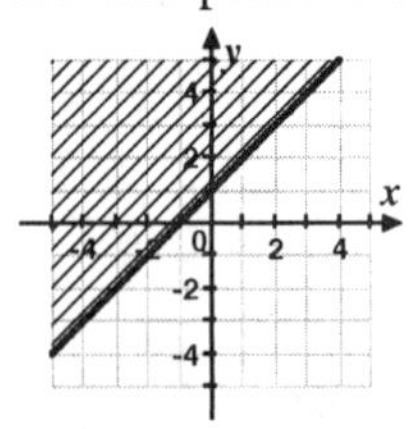

40. $x \geq 2$
Graph $x = 2$ as a solid vertical line. Use (0, 0) as a test point. Since $0 \geq 2$ is false, shade the half-plane *not* containing (0, 0). This is the region to the right of the line $x = 2$.

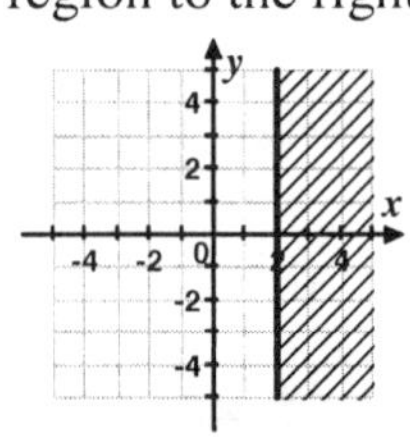

5.5 Exercise Set

1. $x+y\le 4$

$x-y\le 2$

Graph $x+y\le 4$ by graphing $x+y=4$ as a solid line using the x-intercept, 4, and the y-intercept, 4. Because (0,0) makes the inequality $x+y\le 4$ true, shade the half-plane containing (0,0).

Graph $x-y\le 2$ by graphing $x-y=2$ or $y=x-2$ as a solid line with x-intercept 2 and y-intercept –2. Because (0, 0) makes the inequality $x-y\le 2$ true, shade the half-plane containing (0,0).

The solution set of the system is the intersection of the shaded regions.

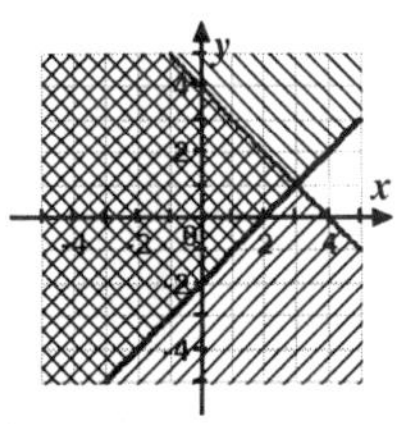

3. $2x-4y\le 8$

$x+y\ge -1$

Graph $2x-4y\le 8$ by graphing $2x-4y=8$ as a solid line using the x-intercept, 4, and the y-intercept, –2. Because $4(0)-2(0)\le 8$ is true, shade the half-plane containing (0,0).

Graph $x+y\ge -1$ by graphing $x+y=-1$ as a solid line using the x-intercept, -1, and the y-intercept, -1. Because $0+0\ge -1$ is true, shade the half-plane containing (0,0).

The solution set of the system is the intersection of the two shaded regions.

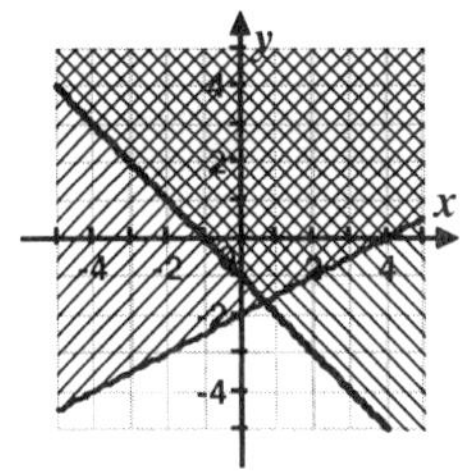

5. $x+3y\le 6$

$x-2y\le 4$

Graph $x+3y\le 6$ by graphing $x+3y=6$ as a solid line using the x-intercept, 6, and the y-intercept, 2. Because $0+3(0)\le 6$ is true, shade the half-plane containing (0,0).

Graph $x-2y\le 4$ by graphing $x-2y=4$ as a solid line using the x-intercept, 4, and the y-intercept, –2. Because $0-2(0)\le 4$ is true, shade the half-plane containing (0,0).
The solution set of the system is the intersection of the shaded regions.

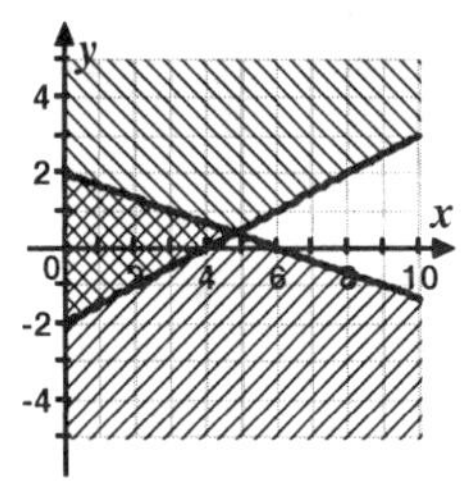

7. $x-2y>4$

$2x+y\ge 6$

Graph $x-2y>4$ by graphing $x-2y=4$ as a dashed line using the x-intercept, 4, and the y-intercept, –2. Because $0-2(0)>4$ is false, shade the half-plane *not* containing (0,0).

Graph $2x+y\ge 6$ by graphing $2x+y=6$ as a solid line using the x-

intercept, 3, and the y-intercept, 6. Because $2(0)+0 \geq 6$ is false, shade the half-plane *not* containing (0,0).

The solution set of the system is the intersection of the two shaded regions.

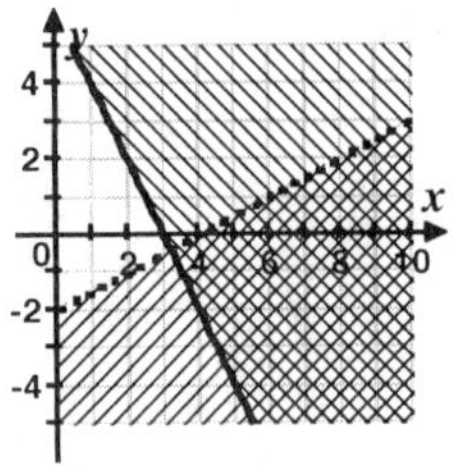

9. $x+y>1$

$x+y<4$

Graph $x+y>1$ by graphing $x+y=1$ as a dashed line using the x-intercept 1 and y-intercept 1. Because $0+0>1$ is false, *do not* shade the half-plane containing (0,0).

Graph $x+y<4$ by graphing $x+y=4$ as a dashed line using the x-intercept 4 and y-intercept 4. Because $0+0<4$ is true, shade the half-plane containing (0,0).

The solution set is the shaded region between the two dashed parallel lines.

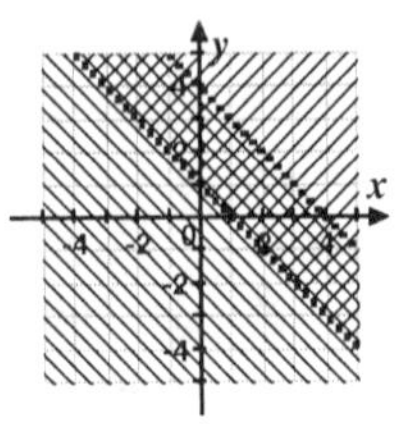

11. $y \geq 2x+1$

$y \leq 4$

Graph $y \geq 2x+1$ by graphing $y=2x+1$ as a solid line using the slope, 2, and the y-intercept, 1. Because $0 \geq 2(0)+1$ is false, shade the half-plane *not* containing (0, 0).

Graph $y \leq 4$ by graphing $y=4$ as a solid horizontal line with y-intercept 4. Because $0 \leq 4$ is true, shade the half-plane containing (0,0).

The solution set of the system is the intersection of the shaded regions.

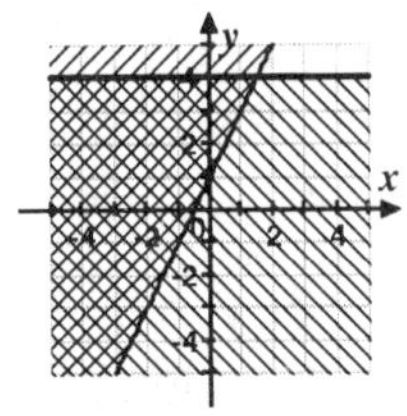

13. $y>x-1$

$x>5$

Graph $y>x-1$ by graphing $y=x-1$ as a dashed line using the slope, 1, and the y-intercept, -1. Because $0>0-1$ is true, shade the half-plane containing (0,0).

Graph $x>5$ by graphing $x=5$ as a dashed vertical line with x-intercept 5. Because $0>5$ is false, shade the half-plane not containing (0,0).

The solution set of the system is the intersection of the two shaded regions.

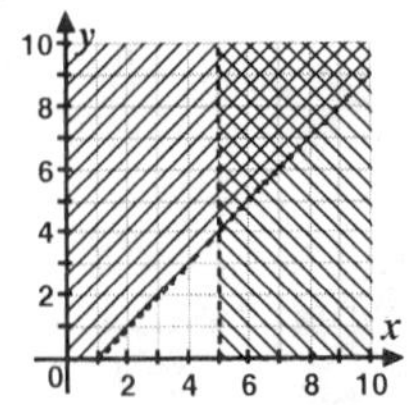

15. $y \ge 2x - 3$

$y \le 2x + 1$

Graph $y \ge 2x - 3$ by graphing $y = 2x - 3$ as a solid line using slope, 2, and y-intercept, −3. Since $0 \ge 2(0) - 3$ is true, shade the half plane containing (0,0).

Graph $y \le 2x + 1$ by graphing $y = 2x + 1$ as a solid line using its slope, 2, and y-intercept, 1. Since $0 \le 2(0) + 1$ is true, shade the half-plane containing (0,0).

The solution set of the system is the intersection of the shaded regions.

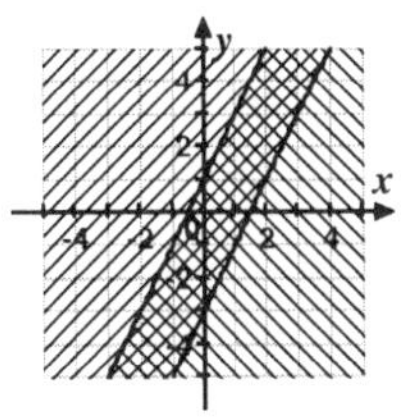

17. $y > 2x + 3$

$y \le -x + 6$

Graph $y > 2x - 3$ by graphing $y = 2x - 3$ as a dashed line using its slope, 2, and y-intercept, −3. Since $0 > 2(0) - 3$ is true, shade the half-plane containing (0,0).

Graph $y \le -x + 6$ by graphing $y = -x + 6$ as a solid line using its slope, −1, and y-intercept, 6. Since $0 \le -0 + 6$ is true, shade the half-plane containing (0,0).

The solution set of the system is the intersection of the two shaded regions.

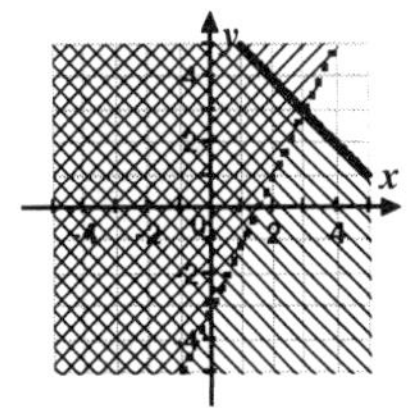

19. $x + 2y \le 4$

$y \ge x - 3$

Graph $x + 2y \le 4$ by graphing $x + 2y = 4$ as a solid line using its x-intercept, 4, and y-intercept, 2. Since $0 + 2(0) \le 4$ is true, shade the half-plane containing (0,0).

Graph $y \ge x - 3$ by graphing $y = x - 3$ as a solid line, using its slope, 1, and y-intercept, −3. Since $0 \ge 0 - 3$ is true, shade the half-plane containing (0,0).

The solution set of the system is the intersection of the two shaded regions.

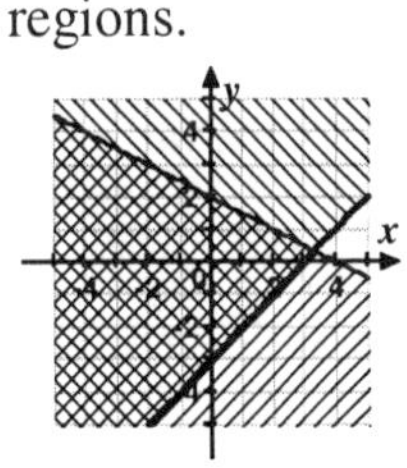

21. $x \le 3$

$y \ge -2$

Graph $x \le 3$ by graphing $x = 3$ as a solid vertical line. Since $0 \le 3$ is true, shade the half-plane containing (0,0).

Graph $y \ge -2$ by graphing $y = -2$ as a solid horizontal line. Since $0 \ge -2$ is true, shade the half-plane containing (0,0).

The solution set of the system is the intersection of the shaded regions.

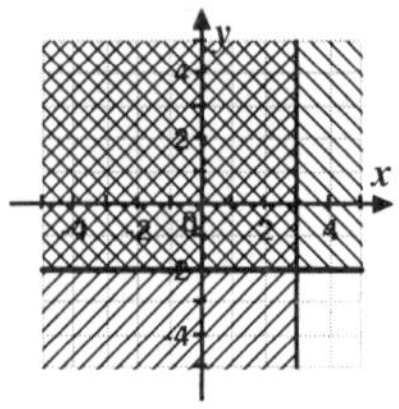

23. $x \ge 3$

$y < 2$

Graph $x \ge 3$ by graphing $x = 3$ as a solid vertical line. Since $0 \ge 3$ is false, shade the half-plane *not* containing (0,0).

Graph $y < 2$ by graphing $y = 2$ as a dashed horizontal line. Since $0 < 2$ is true, shade the half-plane containing (0,0).

The solution set of the system is the intersection of the two shaded regions.

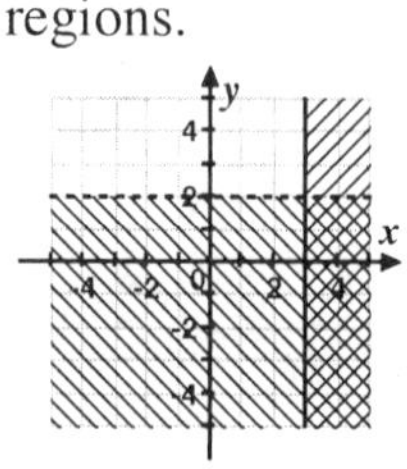

25. $x \ge 0$

$y \le 0$

Graph $x \ge 0$ by graphing $x = 0$ (the y –axis) as a solid vertical line. Shade the half-plane to the right of the axis.

Graph $y \le 0$ by graphing $y = 0$ (the x –axis) as a solid horizontal line. Shade the half-plane below the axis.

The solution set of the system is the intersection of the two shaded regions. This is all of quadrant IV, including the portions of the axes that are the boundaries of this region.

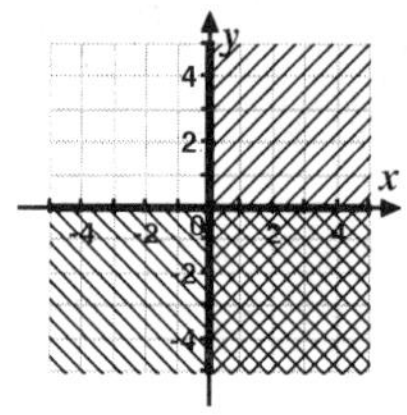

27. $x \ge 0$

$y > 0$

Graph $x \ge 0$ by graphing $x = 0$ as a solid vertical line. This is the y-axis. Shade the half-plane to the right of the y-axis.

Graph $y > 0$ by graphing $y = 0$ as a dashed solid line. This is the x-axis. Shade the half-plane above the x-axis.

The solution set of the system is the intersection of the two shaded regions. This is all of quadrant I, including the portion of the y-axis, but excluding the portion of the x-axis, that are boundaries of this region.

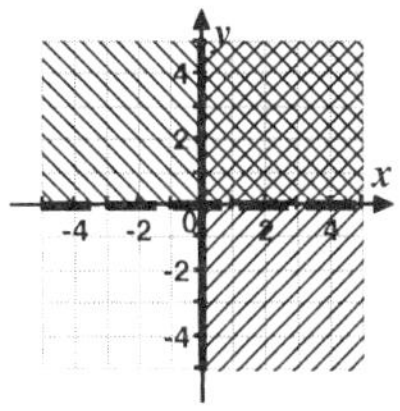

29. $x + y \le 5$

$x \ge 0$

$y \ge 0$

Graph $x + y \le 5$ by graphing $x + y = 5$ as a solid line using its *x*-intercept, 5, and *y*-intercept, 5. Since $0 + 0 \le 5$ is true, shade the half-plane containing (0,0).

Graph $x \ge 0$ by graphing $x = 0$ (the *y*-axis) as a solid line. Shade the half-plane to the right of the *y*-axis.

Graph $y \ge 0$ by graphing $y = 0$ (the *x*-axis) as a solid line. Shade the half-plane above the *x*-axis.

The solution set of the system is the intersection of the shaded regions. This is the set of points satisfying $x + y \le 5$ that lie in quadrant I, together with the portions of the axes that are boundaries of this region.

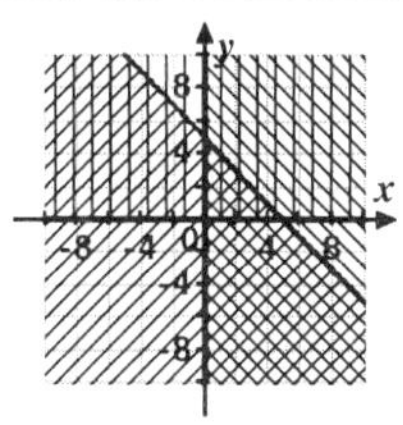

31. $4x - 3y > 12$

$x \ge 0$

$y \le 0$

Graph $4x - 3y > 12$ by graphing $4x - 3y = 12$ as a dashed line using *x*-intercept, 3, and *y*-intercept, −4. Since $4(0) - 3(0) > 12$ is false, shade the half-plane *not* including (0,0). Graph $x \ge 0$ by graphing $x = 0$ (the *y*-axis) as a solid line and shade the half-plane to the right of it.

Graph $y \le 0$ by graphing $y = 0$ (the *x*-axis) as a solid line and shade the half-plane below it.

The solution set of the system is the intersection of the three shaded regions. Notice that this is the set of points satisfying $4x - 3y > 12$ that lie in quadrant IV, together with the portions of the axes that are boundaries of these regions.

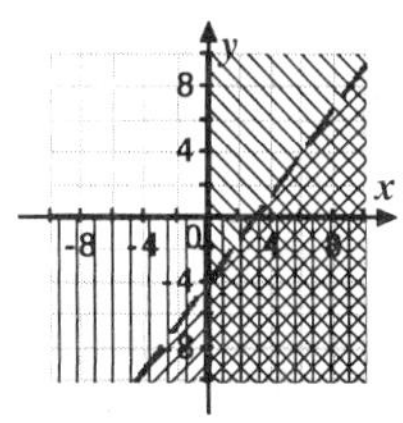

33. $0 \le x \le 3$

$0 \le y \le 3$

Graph $0 \le x \le 3$ by graphing the vertical lines $x = 0$ (the y-axis) and $x = 3$ as solid lines. Shade the region between the parallel lines.

Graph $0 \le y \le 3$ by graphing the horizontal lines $y = 0$ (the x-axis) and $y = 3$ as solid lines. Shade the region between these horizontal lines.

The solution set of the system is the intersection of the shaded regions.

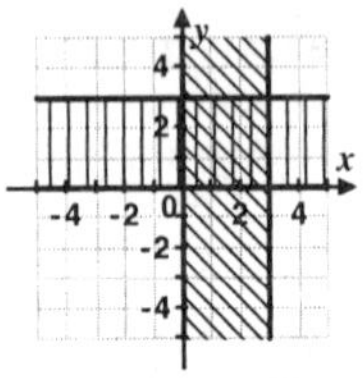

35. $x - y \le 4$

$x + 2y \le 4$

Graph $x - y \le 4$ by graphing $x - y = 4$ as a solid line using the x-intercept, 4, and the y-intercept, –4. Since $0 - 0 \le 4$ is true, shade the half-plane containing (0,0).

Graph $x + 2y \le 4$ by graphing $x + 2y = 4$ as a solid line using the x-intercept, 4, and the y-intercept, 2. Since $0 + 2(0) \le 4$ is true, shade the half-plane containing (0,0).

The solution set of the system is the intersection of the shaded regions.

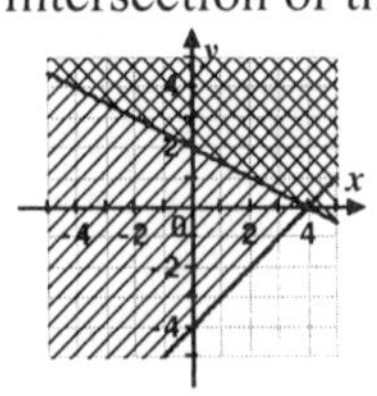

37. $x + y \ge 1$

$x - y \ge 1$

$x \ge 4$

Graph $x + y \ge 1$ by graphing $x + y = 1$ as a solid line using the x-intercept, 1, and the y-intercept, 1. Since $0 + 0 \ge 1$ is false, shade the half-plane *not* containing (0,0).

Graph $x - y \ge 1$ by graphing $x - y = 1$ as a solid line using the x-intercept, 1, and the y-intercept, -1. Since $0 - 0 \ge 1$ is false, shade the half-plane *not* containing (0,0).

Graph $x \ge 4$ by graphing $x = 4$ as a solid vertical line and shade the half-plane to the right of it.

The solution set of the system is the intersection of the shaded regions.

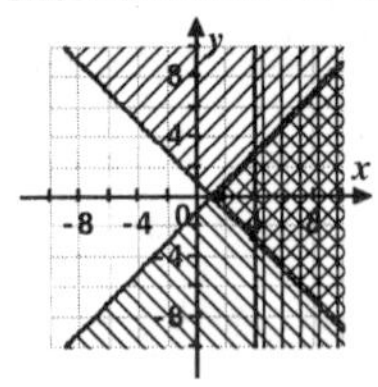

38. $x - y \le 3$

$x + y \le 3$

$x \ge -2$

Graph $x - y \le 3$ by graphing $x - y = 3$ as a solid line using the x-intercept, 3, and the y-intercept, -3. Since $0 - 0 \le 3$ is true, shade the half-plane containing (0,0).

Graph $x + y \le 3$ by graphing $x + y = 3$ as a solid line using the x-intercept, 3, and the y-intercept, 3. Since $0 + 0 \le 3$ is true, shade the half-plane containing (0,0).

Graph $x \ge -2$ by graphing $x = -2$ as a

solid vertical line and shade the half-plane to the right of it.

The solution set of the system is the intersection of the shaded regions.

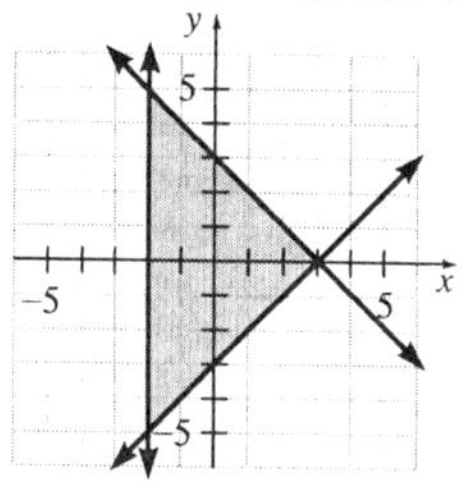

39. $x+2y<6$
$y>2x-2$
$y\geq 2$
Graph $x+2y<6$ by graphing $x+2y<6$ as a dashed line using the x-intercept, 6, and the y-intercept, 3. Since $0+2(0)<6$ is true, shade the half-plane containing (0,0).

Graph $y>2x-2$ by graphing $y=2x-2$ as a dashed line using the slope, 2, and the y-intercept, −2. Since $0>2(0)-2$ is true, shade the half-plane containing (0,0).

Graph $y\geq 2$ by graphing $y = 2$ as a solid horizontal line and shade the half-plane above it.

The solution set of the system is the intersection of the shaded regions.

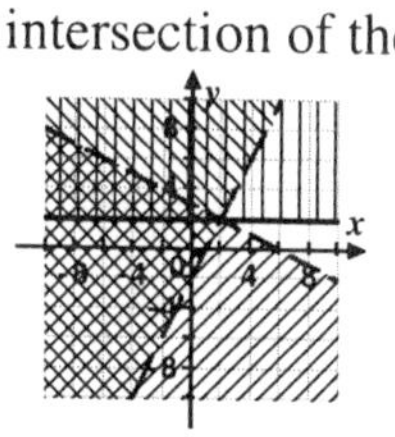

40. $2x-3y<6$
$2x-3y>-6$
$-3\leq x\leq 2$
Graph $2x-3y<6$ by graphing $2x-3y=6$ as a dashed line using the x-intercept, 3, and the y-intercept, -2. Since $2(0)-3(0)<6$ is true, shade the half-plane containing (0,0).

Graph $2x-3y>-6$ by graphing $2x-3y=-6$ as a dashed line using the x-intercept, -3, and the y-intercept, 2.
Since $2(0)-3(0)>-6$ is false, shade the half-plane *not* containing (0,0).

Graph $-3\leq x\leq 2$ by graphing the vertical lines x = -3 and x = 2 as solid lines. Shade the region between the parallel lines.

The solution set of the system is the intersection of the shaded regions.

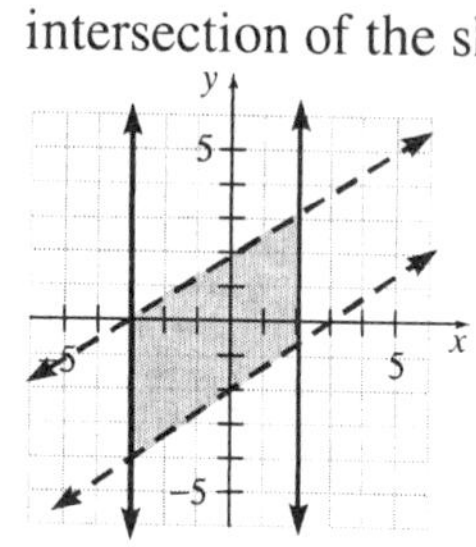

41. $y\leq -3x+3$

$y>-x-1$

$y<x+7$
Graph $y\leq -3x+3$ by graphing $y=-3x+3$ as a solid line with slope, −3, and y-intercept, 3. Since $0\leq -3(0)+3$ is true, shade the half-plane containing (0,0).

Graph $y > -x - 1$ by graphing $y = -x - 1$ as a dashed line using the slope, -1, and the y-intercept, -1. Since $0 > -0 - 1$ is true, shade the half-plane containing (0,0).

Graph $y < x + 7$ by graphing $y = x + 7$ as a dashed line with slope, 1, and y-intercept, 7. Since $0 < 0 + 7$ is true, shade the half-plane containing (0,0).

The solution set of the system is the intersection of the shaded regions.

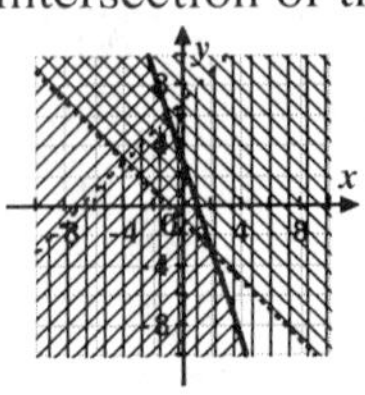

42. $y \ge -3x + 5$

$y \ge -x + 3$

$y \ge \frac{1}{2}x$

$x \ge 0$

$y \ge 0$

Graph $y \le -3x + 5$ by graphing $y = -3x + 5$ as a solid line with slope, -3, and y-intercept, 5. Since $0 \le -3(0) + 5$ is true, shade the half-plane containing (0,0).

Graph $y \ge -x + 3$ by graphing $y = -x + 3$ as a dashed line using the slope, -1, and the y-intercept, 3. Since $0 > -0 + 3$ is false, shade the half-plane *not* containing (0,0).

Graph $y \ge \frac{1}{2}x$ by graphing $y = \frac{1}{2}x$ as a solid line with slope, $\frac{1}{2}$, and y-intercept, 0. Since $0 \ge 0$ is true, shade the half-plane containing (0,0).

Graph $x \ge 0$ by graphing the vertical line $x = 0$ (the y-axis) as a solid line and shade the region to the right.

Graph $y \ge 0$ by graphing the horizontal line $y = 0$ (the x-axis) as a solid line and shade the region above it.

The solution set of the system is the intersection of the shaded regions.

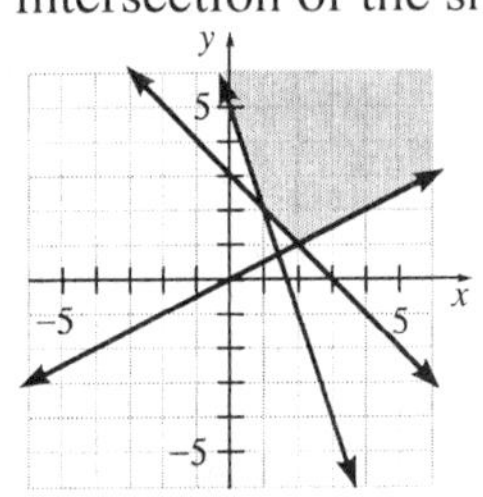

43. $y \ge 2x + 2$

$y < 2x - 3$

$x \ge 2$

Graph $y \ge 2x + 2$ by graphing $y = 2x + 2$ as a solid line with slope, 2, and y-intercept, 2. Since $0 \ge 2(0) + 2$ is false, shade the half-plane *not* containing (0,0).

Graph $y < 2x - 3$ by graphing $y = 2x - 3$ as a dashed line using the slope, 2, and the y-intercept, -3.

Since $0 < 2(0) - 3$ is false, shade the half-plane *not* containing (0,0).

Graph $x \ge 2$ by graphing $x = 2$ as a solid vertical line. Since $0 \ge 2$ is false, shade the half-plane containing (0,0).

The solution to the system is the intersection of the shaded regions. In this case, there is no region on the graph where the three shaded regions intersect, so there is no solution.

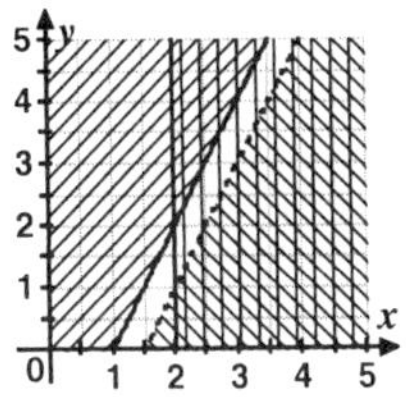

44. $y \geq -3x+2$

$y < -3x$

$x \geq 1$

Graph $y \geq -3x+2$ by graphing $y = -3x+2$ as a solid line with slope, -3, and *y*-intercept, 2. Since $0 \geq -3(0)+2$ is false, shade the half-plane *not* containing (0,0).

Graph $y < -3x$ by graphing $y == -3x$ as a dashed line using the slope, -3, and the *y*-intercept, 0. Since $0 < -3(0)$ is false, shade the half-plane *not* containing (0,0).

Graph $x \geq 1$ by graphing $x = 1$ as a solid vertical line. Since $0 \geq 1$ is false, shade the half-plane containing (0,0).

The solution to the system is the intersection of the shaded regions. In this case, there is no region on the graph where the three shaded regions intersect, so there is no solution.

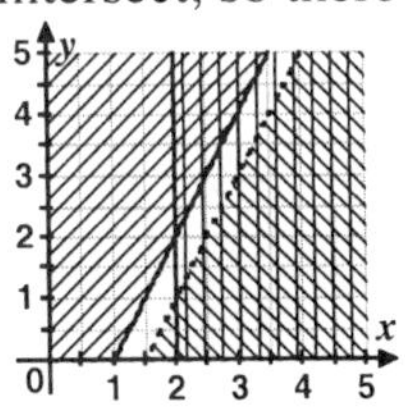

45. Answers will vary according to the student's age and the point chosen. A sample answer is given here for a student who is 25 years old.

a. A pulse rate that lies within the target zone for a 25-year-old is 150 beats per minute.

b. (25, 150)
Substitute 25 for *a* and 150 for *p* in the system of equations given in Example 3.

$$2a+3p \geq 450$$
$$2(25)+3(150) \geq 450?$$
$$50+450 \geq 450$$
$$500 \geq 450 \text{ true}$$

$$a+p \leq 190$$
$$25+150 \leq 190?$$
$$175 \leq 190 \text{ true}$$

The pair (25, 150) satisfies each inequality of the system.

47. Yes, the point (175,70) falls in the healthy weight region.

49. The recommended weight range for a person who is 6 ft (72 inches) tall is about 140 to 190 pounds.

51. Answers may vary.

53. Answers will vary. One example is as follows.

$x+y>0$

$x+y<-5$

$x + y$ cannot be both greater than 0 and less than −5 at the same time.

55. Let x = the number of \$35 tickets sold.
Let y = the number of \$50 tickets sold.
From the information given in the problem, we have the following inequalities.

$x + y \geq 25{,}000$
$35x + 50y \geq 1{,}025{,}000$

Also, the number of tickets sold and the amount of money in ticket sales cannot be negative, so we also have $x \geq 0$ and $y \geq 0$. so the system is as follows.

$x + y \geq 25{,}000$
$35x + 50y \geq 1{,}025{,}000$
$x \geq 0$
$y \geq 0$

Graph $x + y \geq 25{,}000$ by graphing $x + y = 25{,}000$ as a solid line using its x-intercept, 25,000, and y-intercept, 25,000. Since $0 + 0 \geq 25{,}000$ is false, shade the region *not* containing (0,0).
Graph $35x + 50y \geq 1{,}025{,}000$ by graphing $35x + 50y = 1{,}025{,}000$ using its x-intercept, approximately 29,286, and its y-intercept, 20,500. Since $35(0) + 50(0) \geq 1{,}025{,}000$ is false, shade the region *not* containing (0,0).

The inequalities $x \geq 0$ and $y \geq 0$ restrict the graph to quadrant I.

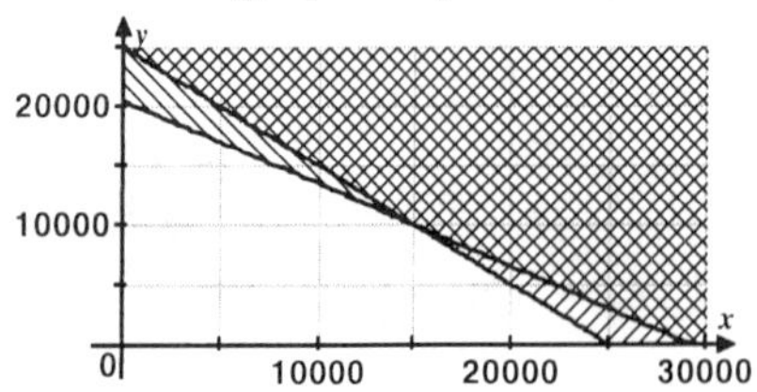

56. (−6,1) and (2, −1)

$$m = \frac{-1-1}{2-(-6)} = \frac{-2}{8} = -\frac{1}{4}$$

57. $$\frac{1}{5} + \left(-\frac{3}{4}\right) = \frac{4}{20} + \left(-\frac{15}{20}\right) = -\frac{11}{20}$$

58. $y = x^2$

Make a table of values.

x	$y = x^2$	(x,y)
−3	$y = (-3)^2 = 9$	(−3,9)
−2	$y = (-2)^2 = 4$	(−2,4)
−1	$y = (-1)^2 = 1$	(−1,1)
0	$y = 0^2 = 0$	(0,0)
1	$y = 1^2 = 1$	(1,1)
2	$y = 2^2 = 4$	(2,4)
3	$y = 3^2 = 9$	(3,9)

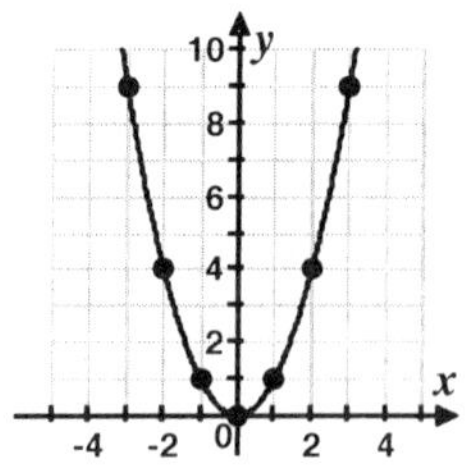

Chapter 5 Review Exercises

1.

$$\begin{aligned} 4x - y &= 9 \\ 4(1) - (-5) &= 9 \\ 4 + 5 &= 9 \\ 9 &= 9 \text{ true} \end{aligned}$$

$$\begin{aligned} 2x + 3y &= -13 \\ 2(1) + 3(-5) &= -13 \\ 2 - 15 &= -13 \\ -13 &= -13 \text{ true} \end{aligned}$$

Since the ordered pair (1, −5) satisfies both equations, it is a solution of the given system.

2. $2x+3y=-4$

$2(-5)+3(2)=-4$

$-10+6=-4$

$-4=-4$ true

$x-4y=-10$

$-5-4(-2)=-10$

$-5+8=-10$

$3=-10$ false

Since (–5,2) fails to satisfy *both* equations, it is not a solution of the given system.

3. $x+y=2$

$-1+3=2$

$2=2$ true

$2x+y=-5$

$2(-1)+3=-5$

$-2+3=-5$

$1=-5$ false

Since (–1,3) fails to satisfy *both* equations, it is not a solution of the given system. Also, the second equation in the system, which can be rewritten as $y=-2x-5$, is a line with slope –2 and y-intercept –5, while the graph shows a line with slope 2 and y-intercept 5.

4. $x+y=2$

$x-y=6$

Graph both lines on the same axes.

$x+y=2$: x-intercept = 2; y-intercept 2

$x-y=6$: x-intercept = 6, y-intercept = –6

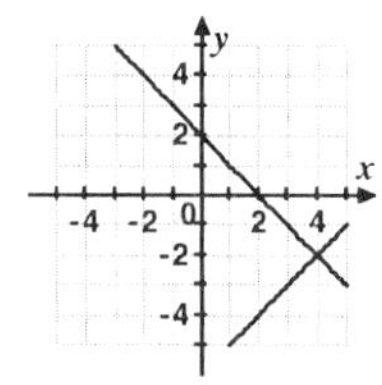

The lines appear to intersect at (4, –2). This apparent solution can be verified by substituting 4 for x and –2 for y in both equations of the original system.

5. $2x-3y=12$

$-2x+y=-8$

Graph both equations.

$2x-3y=12$: x-intercept = 6; y-intercept = –4

$-2x+y=-8$: x-intercept = 4; y-intercept = –8

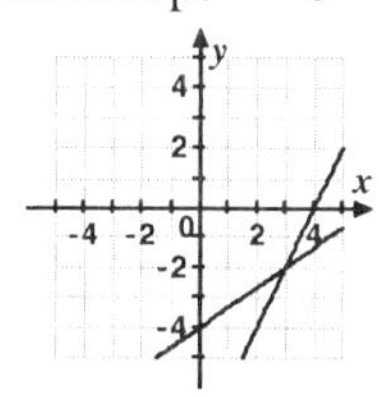

Solution: (3, –2)

6. $3x+2y=6$

$3x-2y=6$

Graph both equations.

$3x+2y=6$: x-intercept = 2; y-intercept = 3

$3x-2y=6$: x-intercept = 2; y-intercept = –3

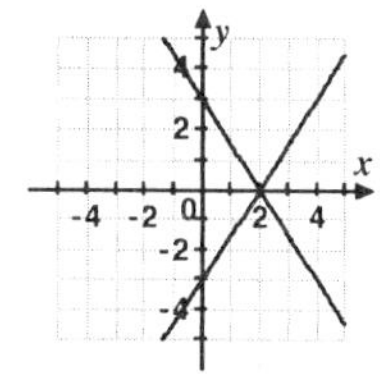

Solution: (2,0)

7. $y = \frac{1}{2}x$

$y = 2x - 3$

Graph both equations.

$y = \frac{1}{2}x$: slope = $\frac{1}{2}$; y-intercept = 0

$y = 2x - 3$: slope = 2; y-intercept = −3

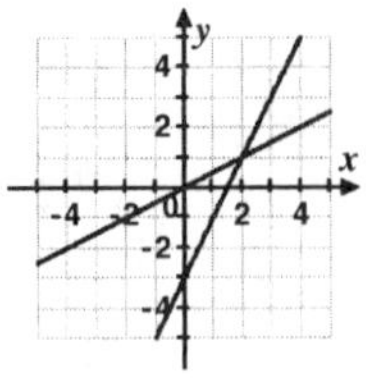

Solution: (2, 1)

8. $x + 2y = 2$

$y = x - 5$

Graph both equations.

$x + 2y = 2$: x-intercept = 2; y-intercept = 1

$y = x - 5$: slope = 1; y-intercept = −5

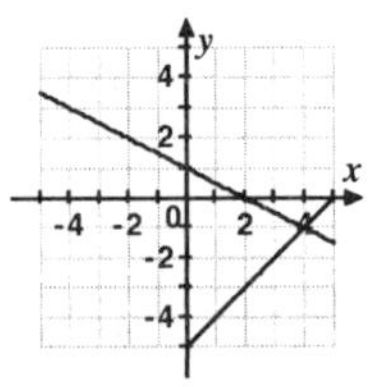

Solution: (4, −1)

9. $x + 2y = 8$

$3x + 6y = 12$

Graph both equations.

$x + 2y = 8$: x-intercept = 8; y-intercept = 4

$3x + 6y = 12$: x-intercept = 4; y-intercept = 2

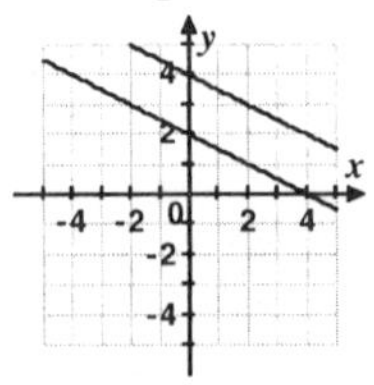

The lines are parallel. The system is inconsistent and has no solution.

10. $2x - 4y = 8$

$x - 2y = 4$

Graph both equations.

$2x - 4y = 8$: x-intercept = 4; y-intercept = −2

$x - 2y = 4$: x-intercept = 4; y-intercept = −2

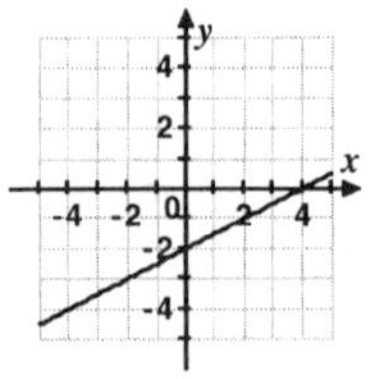

The graphs of the two equations are the same line. The system is dependent and has infinitely many solutions.

11. $y = 3x - 1$

$y = 3x + 2$

Graph both equations.

$y = 3x - 1$: slope = 3; y-intercept = −1

$y = 3x + 2$: slope = 3; y-intercept = 2

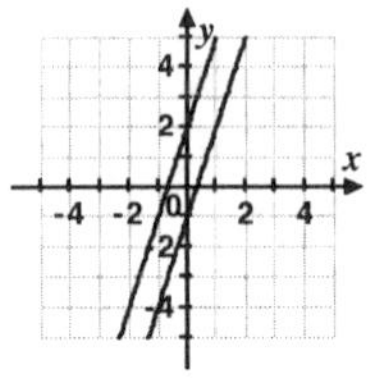

The lines are parallel, so the system is inconsistent and has no solution.

12. $x - y = 4$

$x = -2$

Graph both equations:

$x - y = 4$: x-intercept = 4; y-intercept = −4

$x = 2$: vertical line with x-intercept = −2

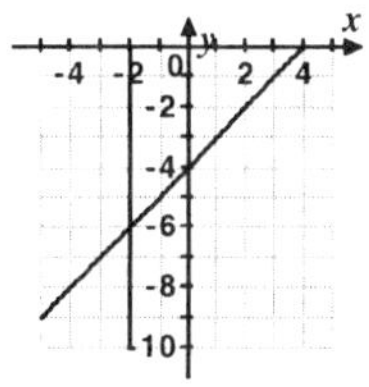

Solution: (−2, −6)

13. $x = 2$

$y = 5$

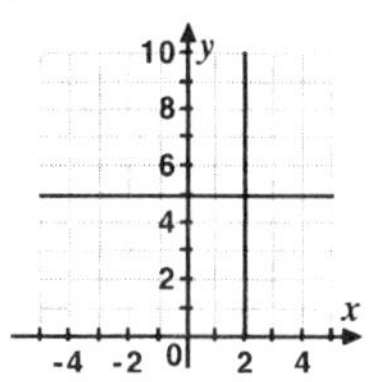

The vertical line and horizontal line intersect at (2,5).
Solution: (2,5)

14. $x = 2$

$x = 5$

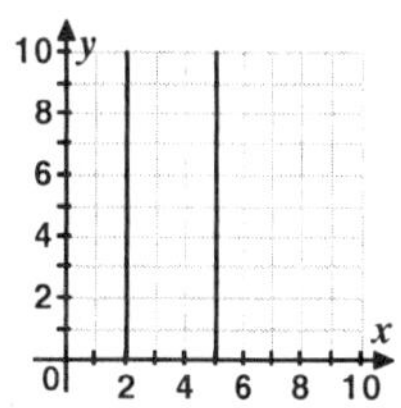

The lines are parallel, so the system inconsistent and has no solution.

15. $2x - 3y = 7$

$y = 3x - 7$

Substitute $3x - 7$ for y in the first equation.

$$2x - 3y = 7$$
$$2x - 3(3x - 7) = 7$$
$$2x - 9x + 21 = 7$$
$$-7x + 21 = 7$$
$$-7x = -14$$
$$x = 2$$

Back-substitute 7 for x into the second equation and solve for y.

$y = 3x - 7$

$y = 3(2) - 7 = -1$

Solution: (2, −1)

16. $2x - y = 6$

$x = 13 - 2y$

Substitute $13 - 2y$ for x into the first equation.

$$2x - y = 6$$
$$2(13 - 2y) - y = 6$$
$$26 - 4y - y = 6$$
$$26 - 5y = 6$$
$$-5y = -20$$
$$y = 4$$

Back-substitute 4 for y in the second equation.

$x = 13 - 2y$

$x = 13 - 2(4) = 5$

Solution: (5,4)

17. $2x - 5y = 1$

$3x + y = -7$

Solve the second equation for y.

$3x + y = -7$

$y = -3x - 7$

Substitute $-3x - 7$ in the first equation.

$$2x-5y=1$$
$$2x-5(-3x-7)=1$$
$$2x+15x+35=1$$
$$17x+35=1$$
$$17x=-34$$
$$x=-2$$

Back-substitute in the equation $y=-3x-7$.

$$y=-3x-7$$
$$y=-3(-2)-7=-1$$

Solution: (−2, −1)

18. $3x+4y=-13$

$5y-x=-21$

Solve the second equation for x.

$$5y-x=-21$$
$$-x=-5y-21$$
$$x=5y+21$$

Substitute $5y+21$ for x in the first equation.

$$3x+4y=-13$$
$$3(5y+21)+4y=-13$$
$$15y+63+4y=-13$$
$$19y+63=-13$$
$$19y=-76$$
$$y=-4$$

Back-substitute.

$$3x+4y=-13$$
$$3x+4(-4)=-13$$
$$3x-16=-13$$
$$3x=3$$
$$x=1$$

Solution: (1, −4)

19. $y=39-3x$

$y=2x-61$

Substitute $2x-61$ for y in the first equation.

$$2x-61=39-3x$$
$$5x-61=39$$
$$5x=100$$
$$x=20$$

Back-substitute.

$$y=2x-61=2(20)-61=-21$$

Solution: (20, −21)

20. $4x+y=5$

$12x+3y=15$

Solve the first equation for y.

$$4x+y=5$$
$$y=-4x+5$$

Substitute $-4x+5$ for y in the second equation.

$$12x+3y=15$$
$$12x+3(-4x+5)=15$$
$$12x-12x+15=15$$
$$15=15 \quad \text{true}$$

The true statement 15 = 15 indicates that the given system has infinitely many solutions.

21. $4x-2y=10$

$y=2x+3$

Substitute $2x+3$ for y in the first equation.

$$4x-2y=10$$
$$4x-2(2x+3)=10$$
$$4x-4x-6=10$$
$$-6=10 \text{ false}$$

The false statement −6 = 10 indicates that the system is inconsistent and has no solution.

22. $x-4=0$

$9x-2y=0$

Solve the first equation for x.

$x-4=0$

$x=4$

Substitute 4 for x in the second equation.

$9x-2y=0$

$9(4)-2y=0$

$36-2y=0$

$-2y=-36$

$y=18$

Solution: (4, 18)

23. $8y=4x$

$7x+2y=-8$

Solve the first equation for y.

$8y=4x$

$y=\frac{1}{2}x$

Substitute $\frac{1}{2}x$ for y in the second equation.

$7x+2y=-8$

$7x+2\left(\frac{1}{2}x\right)=-8$

$7x+x=-8$

$8x=-8$

$x=-1$

Back-substitute.

$y=\frac{1}{2}x=\frac{1}{2}(-1)=-\frac{1}{2}$

Solution: $\left(-1,-\frac{1}{2}\right)$

24. Demand model: $N=-60p+1000$

Supply model: $N=4p+200$

Substitute $4p+200$ for N in the demand equation.

$N=-60p+1000$

$4p+200=-60p+1000$

$64p+200=1000$

$64p=800$

$p=12.5$

Back-substitute 12.5 for p and find N.

$N=4(1.25)+200=250$

Supply and demand are equal when the price of the video is $12.50. At this price, 250 copies are supplied and sold.

25. $x+y=6$

$2x+y=8$

Multiply the first equation by -1 and add the result to the second equation to eliminate the y-terms.

$$\begin{array}{l} -x-y=-6 \\ \underline{2x+y=\ 8} \\ x\qquad = 2 \end{array}$$

Back-substitute into either of the original equations to solve for y.

$x+y=6$

$2+y=6$

$y=4$

Solution: (2, 4)

26. $3x-4y=1$

$12x-y=-11$

Multiply the first equation by –4 and add the result to the second equation.

$$\begin{array}{r} -12x+16y=-4 \\ \underline{12x-\ \ y=-11} \\ 15y=-15 \\ y=-1 \end{array}$$

Back-substitute.

$$\begin{aligned} 3x-4y&=1 \\ 3x-4(-1)&=1 \\ 3x+4&=1 \\ 3x&=-3 \\ x&=-1 \end{aligned}$$

Solution: (–1, –1)

27. $3x-7y=13$

$6x+5y=7$

Multiply the first equation by –2. Don't change the second equation.

$$\begin{array}{r} -6x+14y=-26 \\ \underline{6x+\ 5y=\ \ 7} \\ 19y=-19 \\ y=-1 \end{array}$$

Back-substitute.

$$\begin{aligned} 3x-7y&=13 \\ 3x-7(-1)&=13 \\ 3x+7&=13 \\ 3x&=6 \\ x&=2 \end{aligned}$$

Solution: (2, –1)

28. $8x-4y=16$

$4x+5y=22$

Multiply the second equation by –2. Don't change the first equation.

$$\begin{array}{r} 8x-\ 4y=\ 16 \\ \underline{-8x-10y=-44} \\ -14y=-28 \\ y=2 \end{array}$$

Back-substitute.

$$\begin{aligned} 8x-4y&=16 \\ 8x-4(2)&=16 \\ 8x-8&=16 \\ 8x&=24 \\ x&=3 \end{aligned}$$

Solution: (3, 2)

29. $5x-2y=8$

$3x-5y=1$

Multiply the first equation by 3. Multiply the second equation by –5.

$$\begin{array}{r} 15x-\ 6y=24 \\ \underline{-15x+25y=-5} \\ 19y=19 \\ y=1 \end{array}$$

Back-substitute.

$$\begin{aligned} 5x-2y&=8 \\ 5x-2(1)&=8 \\ 5x-2&=8 \\ 5x&=10 \\ x&=2 \end{aligned}$$

Solution: (2,1)

30. $2x + 7y = 0$
$7x + 2y = 0$
Multiply the first equation by 7.
Multiply the second equation by −2.
$14x + 49y = 0$
$\underline{-14x - 4y = 0}$
$45y = 0$
$y = 0$
Back-substitute.
$2x + 7y = 0$
$2x + 7(0) = 0$
$2x = 0$
$x = 0$
Solution: (0,0)

31. $x + 3y = -4$
$3x + 2y = 3$
Multiply the first equation by −3.
$-3x - 9y = 12$
$\underline{3x + 2y = 3}$
$-7y = 15$
$y = -\frac{15}{7}$

Instead of back-substituting $-\frac{15}{7}$ and working with fractions, go back to the original system. Multiply the first equation by 2 and the second equation by −3.
$2x + 6y = -8$
$\underline{-9x - 6y = -9}$
$-7x = -17$
$x = \frac{17}{7}$
Solution: $\left(\frac{17}{7}, -\frac{15}{7}\right)$

32. $2x + y = 5$
$2x + y = 7$
Multiply the first equation by −1.
Don't change the second equation.
$-2x - y = -5$
$\underline{2x + y = 7}$
$0 = 2$ false
The false statement 0 = 2 indicates that the system has no solution.

33. $3x - 4y = -1$
$-6x + 8y = 2$
Multiply the first equation by 2.
Don't change the second equation.
$6x - 8y = -2$
$\underline{-6x + 8y = 2}$
$0 = 0$ true
The true statement 0 = 0 indicates that the system is dependent and has infinitely many solutions.

34. $2x = 8y + 24$
$3x + 5y = 2$
Rewrite the first equation in the form $Ax + By = C$.
$2x - 8y = 24$
Multiply this equation by 3.
Multiply the second equation by −2.
$6x - 24y = 72$
$\underline{-6y - 10y = -4}$
$-34y = 68$
$y = -2$
Back-substitute.
$3x + 5y = 2$
$3x + 5(-2) = 2$
$3x - 10 = 2$
$3x = 12$
$x = 4$
Solution: (4, −2)

35. $5x-7y=2$

$3x=4y$

Rewrite the second equation in the form $Ax+By=C$.

$3x-4y=0$

Multiply this equation by –5.
Multiply the first equation by 3.

$$\begin{array}{r} 15x-21y=6 \\ \underline{-15x+20y=0} \\ -y=6 \end{array}$$

$y=-6$

Back-substitute.

$$\begin{aligned} 3x-4y&=0 \\ 3x-4(-6)&=0 \\ 3x+24&=0 \\ 3x&=-24 \\ x&=-8 \end{aligned}$$

Solution (–8, –6)

36. $3x+4y=-8$

$2x+3y=-5$

Multiply the first equation by 2.
Multiply the second equation by –3.

$$\begin{array}{r} 6x+8y=-16 \\ \underline{-6x-9y=\ 15} \\ -y=-1 \end{array}$$

$y=1$

Back-substitute.

$$\begin{aligned} 3x+4y&=-8 \\ 3x+4(1)&=-8 \\ 3x+4&=-8 \end{aligned}$$

$3x=-12$

$x=-4$

Solution: (–4, 1)

37. $6x+8y=39$

$y=2x-2$

Substitute $2x-2$ for y in the first equation.

$$\begin{aligned} 6x+8y&=39 \\ 6x+8(2x-2)&=39 \\ 6x+16x-16&=39 \\ 22x-16&=39 \\ 22x&=55 \\ x&=\frac{55}{22}=\frac{5}{2} \end{aligned}$$

Back-substitute $\frac{5}{2}$ for x into the second equation of the system.

$y=2x-2$

$y=2\left(\frac{5}{2}\right)-2=5-2=3$

Solution: $\left(\frac{5}{2},3\right)$

38. $x+2y=7$

$2x+y=8$

Multiply the first equation by –2.
Don't change the second equation.

$$\begin{array}{r} -2x-4y=-14 \\ \underline{2x+\ y=\ \ 8} \\ -3y=-6 \end{array}$$

$y=2$

Back-substitute.

$$\begin{aligned} x+2y&=7 \\ x+2(2)&=7 \\ x+4&=7 \\ x&=3 \end{aligned}$$

Solution: (3,2)

39. $y = 2x - 3$

$y = -2x - 1$

Substitute $-2x - 1$ for y in the first equation

$-2x - 1 = 2x - 3$

$-4x - 1 = -3$

$-4x = -2$

$x = \frac{1}{2}$

Back-substitute.

$y = 2x - 3$

$y = 2\left(\frac{1}{2}\right) - 3 = -2$

Solution: $\left(\frac{1}{2}, -2\right)$

40. $3x - 6y = 7$

$3x = 6y$

Solve the second equation for x.

$3x = 6y$

$x = 2y$

Substitute $2y$ for x in the first equation.

$3x - 6y = 7$

$3(2y) - 6y = 7$

$6y - 6y = 7$

$0 = 7$

The false statement $0 = 7$ indicates that the system has no solution.

41. $y - 7 = 0$

$7x - 3y = 0$

Solve the first equation for y.

$y - 7 = 0$

$y = 7$

Substitute 7 for y in the second equation.

$7x - 3y = 0$

$7x - 3(7) = 0$

$7x - 21 = 0$

$7x = 21$

$x = 3$

Solution: (3, 7)

42. Let x = the number of years of healthy life expectancy of people in Japan.
Let y = the number of years of healthy life expectancy of people in Switzerland.

The system to solve is

$x + y = 146.4$

$x - y = 0.8$

Add the two equations:

$$\begin{array}{r} x + y = 146.4 \\ \underline{x - y = 0.8} \\ 2x = 147.2 \end{array}$$

$x = 73.6$

Back substitute to find y:

$x + y = 146.4$

$73.6 + y = 146.4$

$y = 72.8$

The number of years of healthy life expectancy in Japan is 73.6 years and in Switzerland is 72.8 years.

43. Let x = the weight of a gorilla.
Let y = the weight of an orangutan.
$2x+3y=1465$
$x+2y=815$
Multiply the second equation by −2.
$$\begin{array}{r} 2x+3y=1465 \\ -2x-4y=-1630 \\ \hline -y=-165 \\ y=165 \end{array}$$
Back-substitute to find x.
$x+2(165)=815$
$x+330=815$
$x=485$
The weight of a gorilla is 485 pounds and the weight of an orangutan is 165 pounds.

44. Let x = the cholesterol content of one ounce of shrimp (in milligrams).
Let y = the cholesterol content in one ounce of scallops.
$3x+2y=156$
$5x+3y=300-45$
Simplify the second equation.
$5x+3y=255$
Multiply this equation by −2.
Multiply the first equation by 3.
$$\begin{array}{r} 9x+6y=468 \\ -10x-6y=-510 \\ \hline -x=-42 \\ x=42 \end{array}$$
Back-substitute.
$3x+2y=156$
$3(42)+2y=156$
$126+2y=156$
$2y=30$
$y=15$
There are 42 mg of cholesterol in an ounce of shrimp and 15 mg in an ounce of scallops.

45. Let x = the length of a tennis table top.
Let y = the width.
Use the formula for perimeter of a rectangle to write the first equation and the other information in the problem to write the second equation.
$2x+2y=28$
$4x-3y=21$
Multiply the first equation by −2.
$$\begin{array}{r} -4x+4y=-56 \\ 4x-3y=21 \\ \hline -7y=-35 \\ y=5 \end{array}$$
Back-substitute
$2x+2(5)=28$
$2x+10=28$
$2x=18$
$x=9$
The length is 9 feet and the width is 5 feet, so the dimensions of the table are 9 feet by 5 feet.

46. Let x = the length of the garden.
Let y = the width of the garden.
The perimeter of the garden is 24 yards, so $2x+2y=24$.
Since there are two lengths and two widths to be fenced, the information about the cost of fencing leads to the equation $3(2x)+2(2y)=62$.
Simplify the second equation.
$6x+4y=62$.
Multiply the first equation by −2.
$$\begin{array}{r} -4x-4y=-48 \\ 6x+4y=62 \\ \hline 2x=14 \\ x=7 \end{array}$$

Back-substitute to find y.

$2(7)+2y=24$

$14+2y=24$

$2y=10$

$y=5$

The length of the garden is 7 yards and the width is 5 yards.

47. Let x = daily cost for room.
Let y = daily cost for car.
First plan: $3x+2y=360$

Second plan: $4x+3y=500$

Multiply the first equation by 3.
Multiply the second equation by −2.

$$\begin{array}{r} 9x+6y=\ \ 1080 \\ -8x-6y=-1000 \\ \hline x\quad=\quad 80 \end{array}$$

Back-substitute to find y.

$3(80)+2y=360$

$240+2y=360$

$2y=120$

$y=60$

The cost per day is \$80 for the room and \$60 for the car.

48. Let x = the number of minutes of long-distance calls.
Let y = the monthly cost of a telephone plan.
Plan A: $y=15+0.05x$

Plan B: $y=10+0.075x$

To determine the amount of calling time that will result in the same cost for both plans, solve this system by the substitution method. Substitute $15+0.05x$ for y in the first equation.

$15+0.05x=10+0.075x$

$15-0.025x=10$

$-0.025x=-5$

$\frac{-0.025x}{-0.025}=\frac{-5}{-0.025}$

$x=200$

Back-substitute to find y.

$y=15+0.05(200)=25$

The costs for the two plans will be equal for 200 minutes of long-distance calls per month. The cost of each plan will be \$25.

49. $3x-y\le 6$

$x+y\ge 2$

Graph $3x-y\le 6$ by graphing $3x-y=6$ as a solid line using the x-intercept 2, and y-intercept −6. Because (0,0) makes the inequality true, shade the half-plane containing (0,0).

Graph $x+y\ge 2$ by graphing $x+y=2$ as a solid line using the x-intercept 2, and y-intercept 2. Because (0,0) makes the inequality false, shade the half-plane *not* containing (0,0).

The solution set of the system is the intersection (overlap) of the two shaded regions.

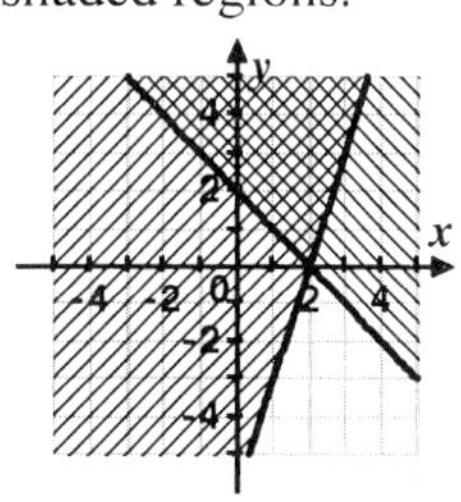

50. $x+y<4$

$x-y<4$

Graph $x+y<4$ by graphing $x+y=4$ as a dashed line using the x-intercept 4, and y-intercept 4. Because $0+0<4$ is true, shade the half-plane containing (0,0).

Graph $x-y<4$ by graphing $x-y=4$ as a dashed line using the x-intercept 4, and y-intercept −4. Because $0-0<4$ is true, shade the half-plane containing (0,0).

The solution set of the system is the intersection of the two shaded regions.

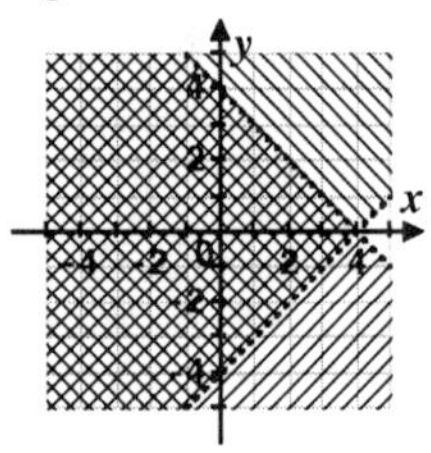

51. $y<2x-2$

$x\geq 3$

Graph $y<2x-2$ by graphing $y=2x-3$ as a dashed line using the slope 2 and y-intercept −2. Since $0<2(0)-2$ is false, shade the half-plane *not* containing (0,0).

Graph $x\geq 3$ by graphing $x=3$ as a solid vertical line with x-intercept 3. Since $0\geq 3$ is false, shade the half-plane *not* containing (0,0).

The solution set of the system is the intersection of the two shaded regions.

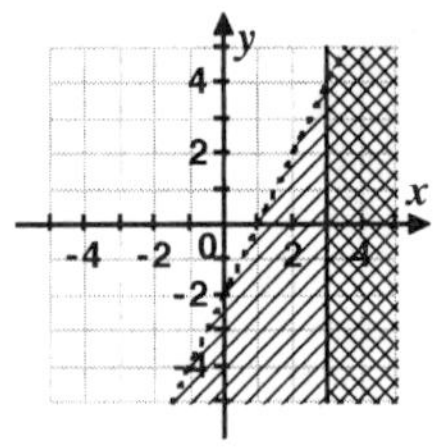

52. $4x+6y\leq 24$

$y>2$

Graph $4x+6y\leq 24$ by graphing $4x+6y=24$ as a solid line with x-intercept 6 and y-intercept 4. Since $4(0)+6(0)\leq 24$ is true, shade the half plane containing (0,0).
Graph $y>2$ by graphing the dashed horizontal line at $y=2$. Since $0>2$ is false, shade the half-plane *not* containing (0,0), the half-plane above the line.

The solution set of the system is the intersection of the two shaded regions.

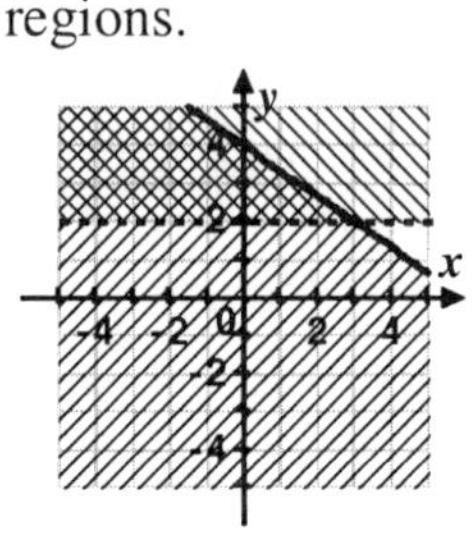

53. $x\leq 3$

$y\geq -2$

Graph $x\leq 3$ by graphing the solid vertical line at $x=3$. Since $0\leq 3$ is true, shade the half-plane containing (0,0).

Graph $y\geq -2$ by graphing $y=-2$ as a solid horizontal line. Since $0\geq -2$ is true, shade the half-plane containing (0,0).

The solution set of the system is the intersection of the two shaded regions.

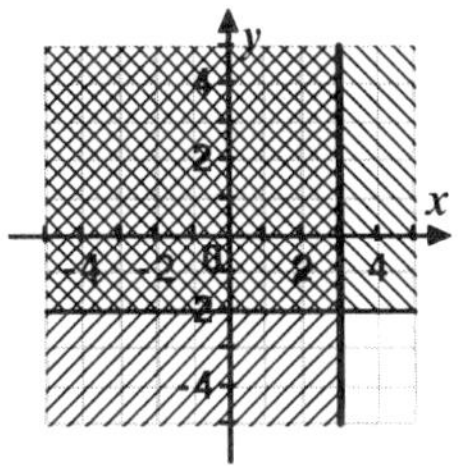

54. $y \geq \frac{1}{2}x - 2$

$y \leq \frac{1}{2}x + 1$

Graph $y \geq \frac{1}{2}x - 2$ by graphing $y = \frac{1}{2}x - 2$ as a solid line with slope $\frac{1}{2}$ and y-intercept -2. Since $0 \geq \frac{1}{2}(0) - 2$ is true, shade the half-plane containing (0,0).

Graph $y \leq \frac{1}{2}x + 1$ by graphing $y = \frac{1}{2}x + 1$ as a solid line with slope $\frac{1}{2}$ and y-intercept 1. Since $0 \leq \frac{1}{2}(0) + 1$ is true, shade the half-plane containing (0,0).

The solution set of the system is the intersection of the two shaded regions. This is the region between and including the two parallel lines.

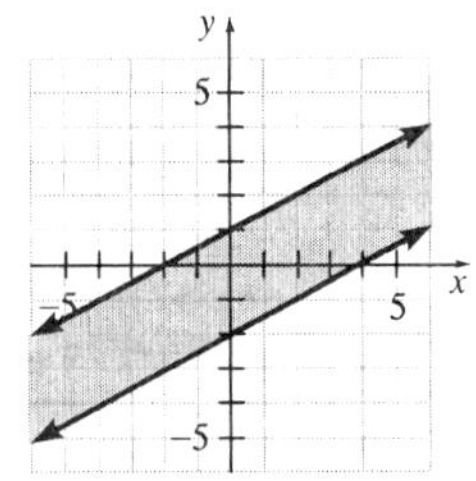

55. $x \leq 0$

$y \geq 0$

Graph $x \leq 0$ by graphing $x = 0$ (the y-axis) as a solid line. Shade the half-plane to the left of the y-axis.

Graph $y \geq 0$ by graphing $y = 0$ (the x-axis) as a solid line. Shade the half-plane above the x-axis.

The solution set of the system is the intersection of the two shaded regions. Notice that this is all of quadrant II, including the portions of the axes that are boundaries of the region.

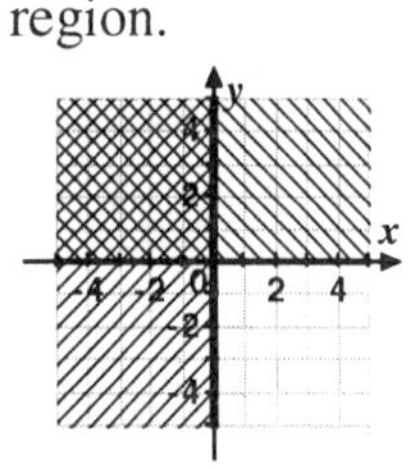

Chapter 5 Test

1. (5,–5)

$$2x + y = 5$$
$$2(5) + (-5) = 5$$
$$10 + (-5) = 5$$
$$5 = 5 \text{ true}$$

$$x + 3y = -10$$
$$5 + 3(-5) = -10$$
$$5 + (-15) = -10$$
$$-10 = -10 \text{ true}$$

Since the ordered pair (5, –5) satisfies both equations, it is a solution of the given system.

2. (–3,2)

$$x + 5y = 7$$
$$-3 + 5(2) = 7$$
$$-3 + 10 = 7$$
$$7 = 7 \text{ true}$$

$$3x - 4y = 1$$
$$3(-3) - 4(2) = 1$$
$$-9 - 8 = 1$$
$$-17 = 1 \text{ false}$$

Since the ordered pair (–3,2) fails to satisfy *both* equations, it is not a solution of the given system.

3. $x + y = 6$

$4x - y = 4$

Graph both lines on the same axes.

$x + y = 6$: x-intercept = 6; y-intercept = 6

$4x - y = 4$: x-intercept: 1; y-intercept = –4

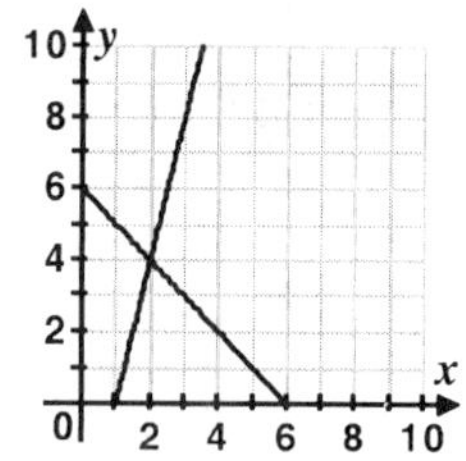

Solution: (2, 4)

4. $2x + y = 8$

$y = 3x - 2$

Graph both lines on the same axes.

$2x + y = 8$: x-intercept = 4; y-intercept = 8

$y = 3x - 2$: slope = 3; y-intercept = –2

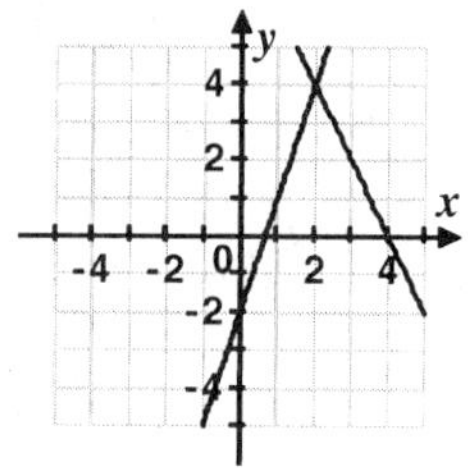

Solution: (2, 4)

5.

$$x = y + 4$$
$$3x + 7y = -18$$

Substitute $y + 4$ for x in the second equation.

$$3x + 7y = -18$$
$$3(y + 4) + 7y = -18$$
$$3y + 12 + 7y = -18$$
$$10y + 12 = -18$$
$$10y = -30$$
$$y = -3$$

Back-substitute –3 for y in the first equation.

$$x = y + 4$$
$$x = -3 + 4 = 1$$

Solution: (1, –3)

6. $2x - y = 7$
$3x + 2y = 0$
Solve the first equation for y.
$2x - y = 7$
$-y = -2x + 7$
$y = 2x - 7$
Substitute $2x - 7$ for y in the second equation.
$3x + 2y = 0$
$3x + 2(2x - 7) = 0$
$3x + 4x - 14 = 0$
$7x - 14 = 0$
$7x = 14$
$x = 2$
Back-substitute 2 for x in the equation $3x + 2y = 0$.
$3x + 2y = 0$
$3(2) + 2y = 0$
$6 + 2y = 0$
$2y = -6$
$y = -3$
Solution: (2, −3)

7. $2x - 4y = 3$
$x = 2y + 4$
Substitute $2y + 4$ for x in the first equation.

$2x - 4y = 3$
$2(2y + 4) - 4y = 3$
$4y + 8 - 4y = 3$
$8 = 3$ false
The false statement 8 = 3 indicates that the system has no solution.

8. $2x + y = 2$
$\underline{4x - y = -8}$
$6x \quad = -6$
$x = -1$
Back-substitute.
$2x + y = 2$
$2(-1) + y = 2$
$-2 + y = 2$
$y = 4$
Solution: (−1, 4)

9. $2x + 3y = 1$
$3x + 2y = -6$
Multiply the first equation by 3.
Multiply the second equation by −2.
$6x + 9y = 3$
$\underline{-6x - 4y = 12}$
$5y = 15$
$y = 3$
Back-substitute.
$2x + 3y = 1$
$2x + 3(3) = 1$
$2x + 9 = 1$
$2x = -8$
$x = -4$
Solution: (−4, 3)

10. $3x - 2y = 2$
$-9x + 6y = -6$
Multiply the first equation by 3.
Don't change the second equation.
$9x - 6y = 6$
$\underline{-9x + 6y = -6}$
$0 = 0$ true
The true statement 0 = 0 indicates that the system is dependent and the equation has infinitely many solutions.

11. Let x = the percentage of females named Mary.
Let y = the percentage of females named Patricia.

The system is
$x+y=3.7$
$x-y=1.5$
Add the two equations:
$x+y=3.7$
$x-y=1.5$
$2x \quad =5.2$
$x \quad =2.6$
Back substitute to find y:
$2.6+y=3.7$
$y=1.1$
2.6% of females are named Mary.
1.1% of females are named Patricia.

12. Let x = the length of the garden.
Let y = the width of the garden.
The perimeter of the garden is 34 yards so $2x+2y=34$.
Since there are two lengths and two widths to be fenced, the information about the cost of fencing leads to the equation $2(2x)+1(2y)=58$.
Simplify the second equation.
$4x+2y=58$
Multiply this equation by -1 and add the result to the first equation.
$2x+2y=34$
$-4x-2y=-58$
$-2x \quad =-24$
$x \quad = \quad 12$
Back-substitute.
$2(12)+2y=34$
$24+2y=34$
$2y=10$
$y=5$
The length of the garden is 12 yards and the width is 5 yards.

13. Let x = the number of minutes of long-distance calls.
Let y = the monthly cost of a telephone plan.
Plan A: $y=15+0.05x$
Plan B: $y=5+0.07x$
To determine the amount of calling time that will result in the same cost for both plans, solve this system by the substitution method. Substitute $5+0.07x$ for y in the first equation.
$5+0.07x=15+0.05x$
$5+0.02x=15$
$0.02x=10$
$\frac{0.02x}{0.02}=\frac{10}{0.02}$
$x=500$
If $x=500$, $y=15+0.05(500)=40$.
The cost of the two plans will be equal for 500 minutes per month. The cost of each plan will be $40.

14. $x-3y>6$
$2x+4y\le 8$
Graph $x-3y>6$ by graphing $x-3y=6$ as a dashed line using the x-intercept 6 and y-intercept -2. Because $0-3(0)>6$ is false, shade the half-plane *not* containing (0,0).

Graph $2x+4y\le 8$ by graphing $2x+4y=8$ as a solid line using the x-intercept 4 and y-intercept 2. Because $2(0)+4(0)\le 8$ is true, shade the half-plane containing (0,0).

The solution set of the system is the intersection (overlap) of the two shaded regions.

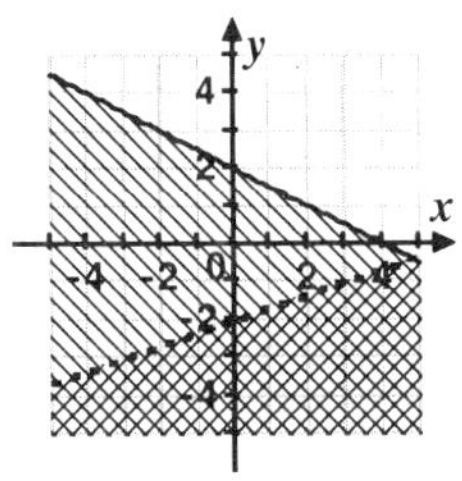

15. $y \geq 2x - 4$

$x < 2$

Graph $y \geq 2x - 4$ by graphing $y = 2x - 4$ as a solid line using the slope 2 and y-intercept −4. Since $0 \geq 2(0) - 4$ is true, shade the half-plane containing (0,0).

Graph $x < 2$ by graphing $x = 2$ as a dashed vertical line with x-intercept 2. Since $0 < 2$ is true, shade the half-plane containing (0,0).

The solution set of the system is the intersection (overlap) of the two shaded regions.

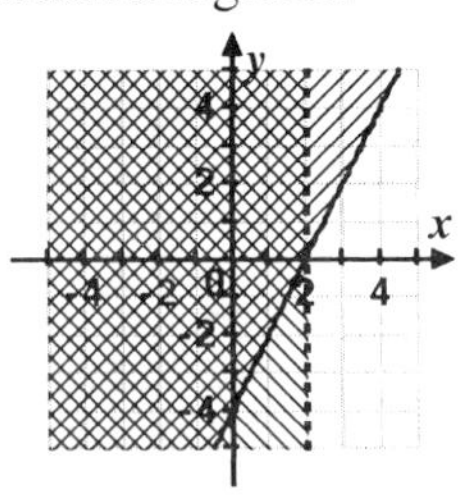

Chapter 5 Cumulative Review Exercises (Chapters 1-5)

1. $$\begin{aligned} &-14 - [18 - (6 - 10)] \\ &= -14 - [18 - (-4)] \\ &= -14 - [18 + 4] \\ &= -14 - 22 \\ &= -14 + (-22) \\ &= -36 \end{aligned}$$

2. $$\begin{aligned} 6(3x - 2) - (x - 1) &= 18x - 12 - x + 1 \\ &= 17x - 11 \end{aligned}$$

3. $$\begin{aligned} 17(x + 3) &= 13 + 4(x - 10) \\ 17x + 51 &= 13 + 4x - 40 \\ 17x + 51 &= 4x - 27 \\ 13x &= -78 \\ x &= -6 \end{aligned}$$

The solution is −6.

4. $$\frac{x}{4} - 1 = \frac{x}{5}$$

To clear fractions, multiply both sides by 20.

$$\begin{aligned} 20\left(\frac{x}{4} - 1\right) &= 20\left(\frac{x}{5}\right) \\ 5x - 20 &= 4x \\ x - 20 &= 0 \\ x &= 20 \end{aligned}$$

The solution is 20.

5. $A = P + Prt$ for t

$$\begin{aligned} A &= P + Prt \\ A - P &= Prt \\ \frac{A - P}{Pr} &= \frac{Prt}{Pr} \\ \frac{A - P}{Pr} &= t \quad \text{or} \quad t = \frac{A - P}{Pr} \end{aligned}$$

6. $$\begin{aligned} 2x - 5 &< 5x - 11 \\ -3x - 5 &< -11 \\ -3x &< -6 \\ \frac{-3x}{-3} &> \frac{-6}{-3} \\ x &> 2 \end{aligned}$$

The solution set is $\{x | x > 2\}$.

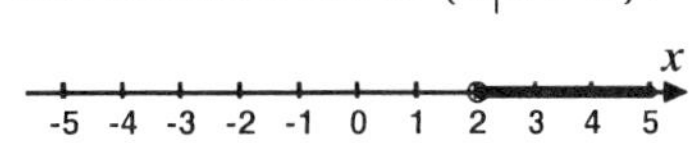

7. $x - 3y = 6$

x-intercept: 6
y-intercept: -2
Check point: $(3, -1)$

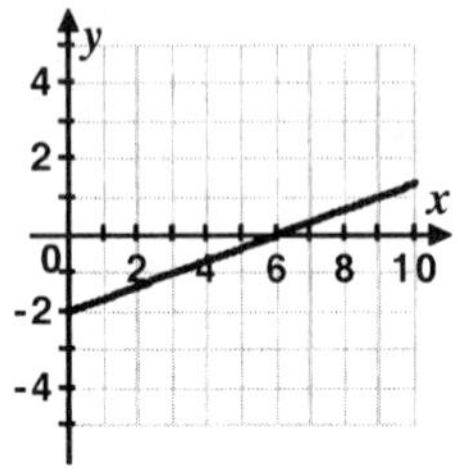

8.

x	$y = 4 - x^2$	(x,y)
-3	$y = 4 - (-3)^2 = -5$	$(-3, -5)$
-2	$y = 4 - (-2)^2 = 0$	$(-2, 0)$
-1	$y = 4 - (-1)^2 = 3$	$(-1, 3)$
0	$y = 4 - 0^2 = 4$	$(0, 4)$
1	$y = 4 - 1^2 = 3$	$(1, 3)$
2	$y = 4 - 2^2 = 0$	$(2, 0)$
3	$y = 4 - 3^2 = -5$	$(3, -5)$

Plot the ordered pairs from the table and draw a smooth curve through them..

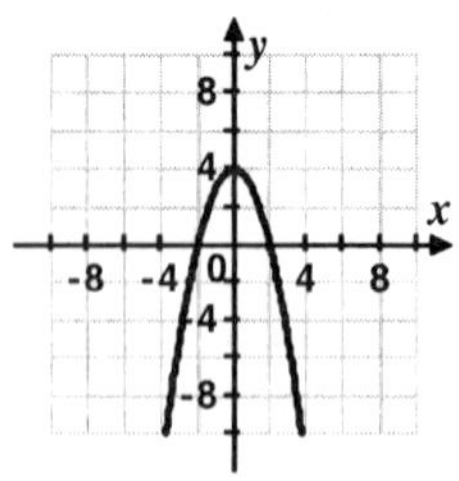

9. $y = -\frac{3}{5}x + 2$

slope $= -\frac{3}{5} = \frac{-3}{5}$; y-intercept $= 2$

Plot the point (0,2). From this point, move 3 units down (because -3 is negative) and 5 units to the right to reach the point $(5, -1)$. Draw a line through (0,2) and $(5, -1)$.

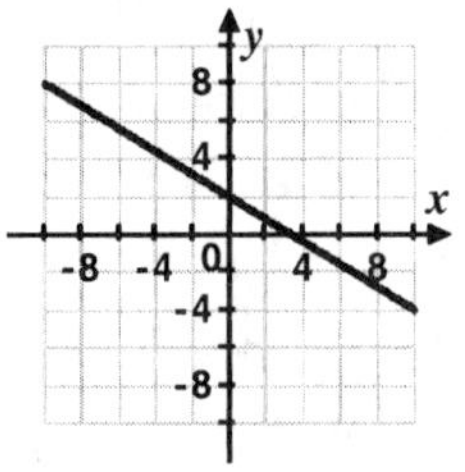

10. $3x - 4y = 8$
$4x + 5y = -10$

To solve this system by the addition method, multiply the first equation by 4 and the second equation by -3. Then add the results.

$$\begin{aligned} 12x - 16y &= 32 \\ -12x - 15y &= 30 \\ \hline -31y &= 62 \\ y &= -2 \end{aligned}$$

Back-substitute.

$$\begin{aligned} 3x - 4y &= 8 \\ 3x - 4(-2) &= 8 \\ 3x + 8 &= 8 \\ 3x &= 0 \\ x &= 0 \end{aligned}$$

Solution: $(0, -2)$

11. $2x - 3y = 9$

$y = 4x - 8$

To solve this system by the substitution method, substitute $4x - 8$ for y in the first equation.

$$2x - 3y = 9$$
$$2x - 3(4x - 8) = 9$$
$$2x - 12x + 24 = 9$$
$$-10x + 24 = 9$$
$$-10x = -15$$
$$x = \frac{15}{10} = \frac{3}{2}$$

Back-substitute $\frac{3}{2}$ for x in the second equation.

$$y = 4x - 8 = 4\left(\frac{3}{2}\right) - 8 = -2$$

Solution: $\left(\frac{3}{2}, -2\right)$

12. (5, –6) and (6, –5)

$$m = \frac{y_2 - y_1}{x_2 - x_1} = \frac{-5 - (-6)}{6 - 5} = \frac{1}{1} = 1$$

13. Passing through (–1,6) with slope = –4

point-slope form:

$$y - y_1 = m(x - x_1)$$
$$y - 6 = -4[x - (-1)]$$
$$y - 6 = -4(x + 1)$$

slope-intercept form:

$$y - 6 = -4x - 4$$
$$y = -4x + 2$$

14. Let h = the length of the altitude of the triangle.

Use the formula for the area of a triangle.

$A = \frac{1}{2}bh$; $A = 80$, $b = 16$

$$80 = \frac{1}{2} \cdot 16 \cdot h$$
$$80 = 8h$$
$$10 = h$$

The altitude is 10 feet.

15. Let x = the cost of one pen.

Let y = the cost of one pad.

$$10x + 15y = 26$$
$$5x + 10y = 16$$

Multiply the second equation by –2, and add the result to the first equation.

$$10x + 15y = 26$$
$$\underline{-10x - 20y = -32}$$
$$-5y = -6$$
$$y = \frac{6}{5} = 1.20$$

Back-substitute 1.20 for y and solve for x.

$$10x + 15(1.20) = 26$$
$$10x + 18 = 26$$
$$10x = 8$$
$$x = \frac{8}{10} = 0.8$$

One pen costs \$0.80 and one pad costs \$1.20.

16. The integers in the given set are –93, 0, $\frac{7}{1}$ (=7) and $\sqrt{100}$ (=10).

17. In 2000, 20% of U.S. households had multiple computers.

18. Both lines are rising from left to right and the line for one computer is steeper, so the graph for one computer has the greater slope. This means that the percentage of U.S. households with one computer increased at a faster rate than the percentage with multiple computers over the years 1997 – 2002.

19. Let x = the number of years after 1997.
Let y = the percentage of households having one computer.

$$y = 42 + 6x$$
$$90 = 42 + 6x$$
$$48 = 6x$$
$$8 = x$$

90% of U.S. households will have one computer 8 years after 1997, which will be in the year 2005.

20.

$$y = \frac{8}{3}x + 12$$
$$52 = \frac{8}{3}x + 12$$
$$40 = \frac{8}{3}x$$
$$\frac{3}{8}(40) = \frac{3}{8}\left(\frac{8}{3}\right)x$$
$$15 = x$$

52% of U.S. households will have multiple computers 15 years after 1997, which will be in the year 2012.

Chapter 6
Exponents and Polynomials

6.1 Exercise Set

1. $3x+7$ is a binomial of degree 1.

3. x^2-2x is a binomial of degree 3.

5. $8x^2$ is a monomial of degree 2.

7. 5 is a monomial. Because it is a nonzero constant, its degree is 0.

9. x^2-3x+4 is a trinomial of degree 2.

11. $7y^2-9y^4+5$ is a trinomial of degree 4.

13. $15x-7x^3$ is a binomial of degree 3.

15. $-9y^{23}$ is a monomial of degree 23.

17. $(9x+8)+(-17x+5)$
$9x+8+(-17)x+5$
$9x+8-17x+5$
$(9x-17x)+(8+5)$
$-8x+13$

19. $(4x^2+6x-7)+(8x^2+9x-2)$
$4x^2+6x-7+8x^2+9x-2$
$(4x^2+8x^2)+(6x+9x)+(-7-2)$
$12x^2+15x-9$

21. $(7x^2-11x)+(3x^2-x)$
$7x^2-11x+3x^2-x$
$(7x^2+3x^2)+(-11x-x)$
$10x^2-12x$

23. $(4x^2-6x+12)+(x^2+3x+1)$
$4x^2-6x+12+x^2+3x+1$
$(4x^2+x^2)+(-6x+3x)+(12+1)$
$5x^2-3x+13$

25. $(4y^3+7y-5)+(10y^2-6y+3)$
$(4y^3+7y-5)+(10y^2-6y+3)$
$4y^3+7y-5+10y^2-6y+3$
$4y^3+10y^2+(7y-6y)+(-5+3)$
$4y^3+10y^2+y-2$

27. $(2x^2-6x+7)+(3x^3-3x)$
$2x^2-6x+7+3x^3-3x$
$3x^3+2x^2+(-6x-3x)+7$
$3x^3+2x^2-9x+7$

29. $(4y^2+8y+11)+(-2y^3+5y+2)$
$4y^2+8y+11+(-2)y^3+5y+2$
$-2y^3+4y^2+(8y+5y)+(11+2)$
$-2y^3+4y^2+13y+9$

31. $(-2y^6+3y^4-y^2)+(-y^6+5y^4+2y^2)$
$-2y^6+3y^4-y^2-y^6+5y^4+2y^2$
$(-2y^6-y^6)+(3y^4+5y^4)+(-y^2+2y^2)$
$-3y^6+8y^4+y^2$

33. $$\left(9x^3 - x^2 - x - \frac{1}{3}\right) + \left(x^3 + x^2 + x + \frac{4}{3}\right)$$
$$= \left(9x^3 + x^3\right) + \left(-x^2 + x^2\right) + \left(-x + x\right)$$
$$+ \left(-\frac{1}{3} + \frac{4}{3}\right)$$
$$= 10x^3 + \frac{3}{3} = 10x^3 + 1$$

35. $$\left(\frac{1}{5}x^4 + \frac{1}{3}x^3 + \frac{3}{8}x^2 + 6\right)$$
$$+ \left(-\frac{3}{5}x^4 + \frac{2}{3}x^3 - \frac{1}{2}x^2 - 6\right)$$
$$= \left[\frac{1}{5}x^4 + \left(-\frac{3}{5}x^4\right)\right] + \left(\frac{1}{3}x^2 + \frac{2}{3}x^3\right)$$
$$+ \left[\frac{3}{8}x^2 + \left(-\frac{1}{2}x^2\right)\right] + \left[6 + (-6)\right]$$
$$= -\frac{2}{5}x^4 + x^3 - \frac{1}{8}x^2$$

37. $$\left(0.03x^5 - 0.1x^3 + x + 0.03\right)$$
$$+ \left(-0.02x^5 + x^4 - 0.7x + 0.3\right)$$
$$= \left(0.03x^5 - 0.02x^5\right) + x^4 - 0.1x^3$$
$$+ \left(x - 0.07x\right) + \left(0.03 + 0.3\right)$$
$$= 0.01x^5 + x^4 - 0.1x^3 + 0.3x + 0.33$$

39. Add:
$$\begin{array}{l} 5y^3 - 7y^2 \\ \underline{6y^3 + 4y^2} \\ 11y^3 - 3y^2 \end{array}$$

41. Add:
$$\begin{array}{l} 3x^2 - 7x + 4 \\ \underline{-5x^2 + 6x - 3} \\ -2x^2 - \ \ x + 1 \end{array}$$

43. Add:
$$\begin{array}{l} \frac{1}{4}x^4 - \frac{2}{3}x^3 - 5 \\ \underline{-\frac{1}{2}x^4 + \frac{1}{5}x^3 + 4.7} \end{array}$$

$$\begin{array}{l} \frac{1}{4}x^4 - \frac{10}{15}x^3 - 5.0 \\ \underline{-\frac{1}{2}x^2 + \frac{3}{15}x^3 + 4.7} \\ -\frac{1}{4}x^4 - \frac{7}{15}x^3 - 0.3 \end{array}$$

45. Add:
$$\begin{array}{l} y^3 + 5y^2 - 7y - 3 \\ \underline{-2y^3 + 3y^2 + 4y - 11} \\ -y^3 + 8y^2 - 3y - 14 \end{array}$$

47. Add:
$$\begin{array}{l} 4x^3 - 6x^2 + 5x - 7 \\ \underline{-9x^3 \qquad\quad - 4x + 3} \\ -5x^3 - 6x^2 + x - 4 \end{array}$$

49. Add:
$$\begin{array}{l} 7x^4 - 3x^3 + x^2 \\ \underline{\qquad\quad x^3 - x^2 + 4x - 2} \\ 7x^4 - 2x^3 \qquad\quad + 4x - 2 \end{array}$$

51. Add:
$$\begin{array}{l} 7x^2 - \ 9x + 3 \\ 4x^2 + 11x - 2 \\ \underline{-3x^2 + 5x - 6} \\ 8x^2 + 7x - 5 \end{array}$$

53.
$$\begin{array}{l} 1.2x^3 - \ \ 3x^2 + 9.1 \\ 7.8x^3 - 3.1x^2 + 8 \\ \underline{\qquad\quad 1.2x^2 - 6} \\ 9x^3 - 4.9x^2 + 11.1 \end{array}$$

55. $(x-8)-(3x+2)=(x-8)+(-3x-2)$
$=(x-3x)+(-8-2)$
$=-2x-10$

57. $(x^2-5x-3)-(6x^2-4x+9)$
$=(x^2-5x-3)+(-6x^2+4x-9)$
$=(x^2-6x^2)+(-5x-4x)+(-3-9)$
$=-5x^2-9x-12$

59. $(x^2-5x)-(6x^2-4x)$
$=(x^2-5x)+(-6x^2+4x)$
$=(x^2-6x^2)+(-5x+4x)$
$=-5x^2-x$

61. $(x^2-8x-9)-(5x^2-4x-3)$
$=(x^2-8x-9)+(-5x^2+4x+3)$
$=-4x^2-4x-6$

63. $(y-8)-(3y-2)=(y-8)+(-3y+2)$
$=-2y-6$

65. $(6y^3+2y^2-y-11)-(y^2-8y+9)$
$=(6y^3+2y^2-y-11)$
$+(-y^2+8y-9)$
$=6y^3+y^2+7y-20$

67. $(7n^3-n^7-8)-(6n^3-n^7-10)$
$=(7n^3-n^7-8)+(-6n^3+n^7+10)$
$=(7n^3-6n^3)+(-n^7+n^7)+(-8+10)$
$=n^3+2$

69. $(y^6-y^3)-(y^2-y)$
$=(y^6-y^3)+(-y^2+y)$
$=y^6-y^3-y^2+y$

71. $(7x^4+4x^2+5x)-(-19x^4-5x^2-x)$
$=(7x^4+4x^2+5x)+(19x^4+5x^2+x)$
$=26x^4+9x^2+6x$

73. $\left(\frac{3}{7}x^3-\frac{1}{5}x-\frac{1}{3}\right)-\left(-\frac{2}{7}x^3+\frac{1}{4}x-\frac{1}{3}\right)$
$=\left(\frac{3}{7}x^3-\frac{1}{5}x-\frac{1}{3}\right)+\left(\frac{2}{7}x^3-\frac{1}{4}x+\frac{1}{3}\right)$
$=\left(\frac{3}{7}x^3+\frac{2}{7}x^3\right)+\left(-\frac{1}{5}x-\frac{1}{4}x\right)$
$+\left(-\frac{1}{3}+\frac{1}{3}\right)$
$=\left(\frac{3}{7}x^3+\frac{2}{7}x^3\right)+\left(-\frac{4}{20}x-\frac{5}{20}x\right)$
$=\frac{5}{7}x^3-\frac{9}{20}x$

75. Subtract:

$$\begin{array}{r} 7x+1 \\ \underline{-(3x-5)} \end{array} \longrightarrow + \begin{array}{r} 7x+1 \\ \underline{-3x+5} \\ 4x+6 \end{array}$$

77. Subtract:

$$\begin{array}{r} 7x^2-3 \\ \underline{-(-3x^2+4)} \end{array} \longrightarrow + \begin{array}{r} 7x^2-3 \\ \underline{3x^2-4} \\ 10x^2-7 \end{array}$$

79. Subtract:

$$\begin{array}{r} 7y^2-5y+2 \\ \underline{-(11y^2+2y-3)} \end{array} \longrightarrow \begin{array}{r} 7y^2-5y+2 \\ \underline{+-11y^2-2y+3} \\ -4y^2-7y+5 \end{array}$$

81. Subtract:

$$\begin{array}{r} 7x^3+5x^2-3 \\ -(-2x^3-6x^2+5) \\ \hline \end{array} \qquad \begin{array}{r} 7x^3+5x^2-3 \\ 2x^3+6x^2-5 \\ \hline 9x^3+11x^2-8 \end{array}$$

83. Subtract:

$$\begin{array}{r} 5y^3+6y^2-3y+10 \\ -(6y^3-2y^2-4y-4) \\ \hline \end{array}$$

$$\begin{array}{r} 5y^3+6y^2-3y+10 \\ +\ -6y^3+2y^2+4y+4 \\ \hline -y^3+8y^2+\ \ y+14 \end{array}$$

85. Subtract:

$$\begin{array}{r} 7x^4-3x^3+2x^2 \\ -(\quad -x^3-x^2+x-2) \\ \hline \end{array}$$

$$\begin{array}{r} 7x^4-3x^3+2x^2 \\ +\quad x^3+\ x^2-x+2 \\ \hline 7x^4-2x^3+3x^2-x+2 \end{array}$$

87.

$$\begin{array}{r} 0.07x^3-0.01x^2+0.02x \\ -(0.02x^3-0.03x^2-\quad x) \\ \hline \end{array}$$

$$\begin{array}{r} 0.07x^3-0.01x^2+0.02x \\ +\ -0.02x^3+0.03x^2+\quad x \\ \hline 0.05x^3+0.02x^2+1.02x \end{array}$$

89. $\left[\left(4x^2+7x-5\right)-\left(2x^2-10x+3\right)\right]$

$-\left(x^2+5x-8\right)$

$=\left[2x^2+17x-8\right]-x^2-5x+8$

$=x^2+12x$

90. $\left[\left(10x^3-5x^2+4x+3\right)-\left(-3x^3-4x^2+x\right)\right]$

$-\left(7x^3-5x+4\right)$

$=\left[13x^3-x^2+3x+3\right]-7x^3+5x-4$

$=6x^3-x^2+8x-1$

91. $\left[\left(4y^2-3y+8\right)-\left(5y^2+7y-4\right)\right]$

$-\left[\left(8y^2+5y-7\right)+\left(-10y^2+4y+3\right)\right]$

$=\left[-y^2-10y+12\right]-\left[-2y^2+9y-4\right]$

$=y^2-19y+16$

92. $\left[\left(7y^2-4y+2\right)-\left(12y^2+3y-5\right)\right]$

$-\left[\left(5y^2-2y-8\right)+\left(-7y^2+10y-13\right)\right]$

$=\left[-5y^2-7y+7\right]-\left[-2y^2+8y-21\right]$

$=-3y^2-15y+28$

93. $\left[\left(4x^3+x^2\right)+\left(-x^3+7x-3\right)\right]$

$-\left(x^3-2x^2+2\right)$

$\left[3x^3+x^2+7x-3\right]+\left(-x^3+2x^2-2\right)$

$2x^3+3x^2+7x-5$

94. $\left[\left(2x^2+4x-7\right)+\left(-5x^3-2x-3\right)\right]$

$-\left(-3x^3-7x+5\right)$

$\left[-5x^3+2x^2+2x-10\right]+\left(3x^3+7x-5\right)$

$-2x^3+2x^2+9x-15$

95. $\left[\left(-5y^2+y^2+4y^3\right)-\left(-8-y+7y^3\right)\right]$

$-\left(-y^2+7y^3\right)$

$\left[-3y^3+y^2+y+3\right]+\left(y^2-7y^3\right)$

$-10y^3+2y^2+y+3$

96. $\left[\left(-6+y^2+5y^3\right)-\left(-12-y+13y^3\right)\right]$
$-\left(-2y^2+8y^3\right)$
$\left[-8y^3+y^2+y+6\right]+\left(2y^2-8y^3\right)$
$-16y^3+3y^2+y+6$

97. Let y = the number of viral particles (in billions) .
Let x = the number of days of invasion of the viral particles
$y=-0.75x^4+3x^3+5$
Substitute in $x=0$ to find the number of particles after 0 days.
$y=-0.75(0)^4+3(0)^3+5=5$
There are 5 billion particles after 0 days.
Substitute in $x=1$ to find the number of particles after 1 day.
$y=-0.75(1)^4+3(1)^3+5=7.25$
There are 7.25 billion particles after 1 day.
Substitute in $x=2$ to find the number of particles after 2 days.
$y=-0.75(2)^4+3(2)^3+5=17$
There are 17 billion particles after 2 days.
Substitute in $x=3$ to find the number of particles after 3 days.
$y=-0.75(3)^4+3(3)^3+5=25.25$
There are 25.25 billion particles after 3 days.
Substitute in $x=4$ to find the number of particles after 4 days.
$y=-0.75(4)^4+3(4)^3+5=5$
There are 5 billion particles after 4 days.
Maximum number of particles occurs after 3 days.
We should feel better after 4 days since the number of particles decreases back to the original amount.

99. Let y = cigarette consumption
Let x = the number of years after 1940.
$y=-2.3x^2+135.3x+2191$

To find cigarette consumption in the year 2000, substitute $x=60$ in the formula since 1940 + 60 = 2000.
$y=-2.3(60)^2+135.3(60)+2191=2029$

To compare the formula and the data, calculate the y-values for the years shown on the graph and compare the these values to the corresponding y-values.

Year	x	y-values from graph	y-values from formula
1940	0	2000	2191
1950	1	3500	2324
1960	2	4200	2452.4
1970	3	4000	2576.2
1980	4	3900	2695.4
1990	5	2800	2810
2000	6	2100	2920

Answers will vary.

101. Let y = median women's earnings as a percentage of median men's earnings.
Let x = the number of years after 1960.
$y=0.012x^2-0.16x+60$

(a) 73%
(b) To find median women's earnings as a percentage of median men's earnings in the year 2000, substitute $x=40$ in the formula since 1960 + 40 = 2000.
$y=0.012(40)^2-0.16(40)+60=72.8$
Women's earnings as a percentage of median men's earnings in the year 2000 was 72.8%.
(c) $\left(\dfrac{\$27,355}{\$37,339}\right)100\%=73.3\%$
Answers from parts (a) and (b) are within 0.5% of the actual percentage.

103. Let y = age in human years
Let x = age in dog years
$$y = -0.001618x^4 + 0.077326x^3 - 1.2367x^2 + 11.460x + 2.914$$

(a) A 6 year old dog is 42 human years old according to the graph.
(b)To find age in human years for a 6 year old, substitute $x = 6$ in the formula.
$$y = -0.001618(6)^4 + 0.077326(6)^3 - 1.2367(6)^2 + 11.460(6) + 2.914$$
$$= 41.8$$
To the nearest tenth, a 6 year old dog is 41.8 human years old according to the formula.

105. A 3 year old dog is 25 human years old according to the graph.

117. $5x^2 - 2x + 1 - (-3x^2 - x - 2)$
$$= (5x^2 - 2x + 1) + (3x^2 + x + 2)$$
$$= 8x^2 - x + 3$$
so the polynomial is $-3x^2 - x - 2$.

119. In a polynomial of degree 3, the highest degree term has an exponent of 3. The highest degree term of the sum will be the sum of two terms of degree 3, which will be a term of degree 3 or could be 0. It is impossible to get a term degree of 4, so it is impossible to get a polynomial of degree 4.

120. $(-10)(-7) \div (1-8) = (-10)(-7) \div (-7)$
$$= 70 \div (-7) = -10$$

121. $-4.6 - (-10.2) = -4.6 + 10.2 = 5.6$

122.
$$3(x-2) = 9(x+2)$$
$$3x - 6 = 9x + 18$$
$$3x - 6 - 9x = 9x + 18 - 9x$$
$$-6x - 6 = 18$$
$$-6x - 6 + 6 = 18 + 6$$
$$-6x = 24$$
$$\frac{-6x}{-6} = \frac{24}{-6}$$
$$x = -4$$
The solution is −4.

6.2 Exercise Set

1. $x^{15} \cdot x^3 = x^{15+3} = x^{18}$

3. $y \cdot y^{11} = y^1 \cdot y^{11} = y^{1+11} = y^{12}$

5. $x^2 \cdot x^6 \cdot x^3 = x^{2+6+3} = x^{11}$

7. $7^9 \cdot 7^{10} = 7^{9+10} = 7^{19}$

9. $(6^9)^{10} = 6^{9 \cdot 10} = 6^{90}$

11. $(x^{15})^3 = x^{15 \cdot 3} = x^{45}$

13. $\left[(-20)^3\right]^3 = (-20)^{3 \cdot 3} = (-20)^9$

15. $(2x)^3 = 2^3 \cdot x^3 = 8x^3$

17. $(-5x)^2 = (-5)^2 x^2 = 25x^2$

19. $(4x^3)^2 = 4^2 (x^3)^2 = 16x^6$

21. $(-2y^6)^4 = (-2)^4 (y^6)^4 = 16y^{24}$

23. $\left(-2x^7\right)^5 = (-2)^5\left(x^7\right)^5 = -32x^{35}$

25. $(7x)(2x) = (7\cdot 2)(x\cdot x) = 14x^2$

27. $(6x)\left(4x^2\right) = (6\cdot 4)\left(x\cdot x^2\right) = 24x^3$

29. $\left(-5y^4\right)\left(3y^3\right) = (-5\cdot 3)\left(y^4\cdot y^3\right) = -15y^7$

31. $\left(-\frac{1}{2}a^3\right)\left(-\frac{1}{4}a^2\right) = \left(-\frac{1}{2}\cdot -\frac{1}{4}\right)\left(a^3\cdot a^2\right)$
$= \frac{1}{8}a^5$

33. $\left(2x^2\right)(-3x)\left(8x^4\right)$
$= (2\cdot -3\cdot 8)\left(x^2\cdot x\cdot x^4\right) = -48x^7$

35. $4x(x+3) = 4x\cdot x + 4x\cdot 3$
$= 4x^2 + 12x$

37. $x(x-3) = x\cdot x - x\cdot 3$
$= x^2 - 3x$

39. $2x(x-6) = 2x\cdot x - 2x\cdot 6$
$= 2x^2 - 12x$

41. $-4y(3y+5) = -4y\cdot 3y - 4y\cdot 5$
$= -12y^2 - 20y$

43. $4x^2(x+2) = 4x^2\cdot x + 4x^2\cdot 2$
$= 4x^3 + 8x^2$

45. $2y^2\left(y^2+3y\right) = 2y^2\cdot y^2 + 2y^2\cdot 3y$
$= 2y^4 + 6y^3$

47. $2y^2\left(3y^2-4y+7\right)$
$= 2y^2\left(3y^2\right) + 2y^2(-4y) + 2y^2(7)$
$= 6y^4 - 8y^3 + 14y^2$

49. $\left(3x^3+4x^2\right)(2x) = 3x^3\cdot 2x + 4x^2\cdot 2x$
$= 6x^4 + 8x^3$

51. $\left(x^2+5x-3\right)(-2x)$
$= x^2(-2x) + 5x(-2x) - 3(-2x)$
$= -2x^3 - 10x^2 + 6x$

53. $-3x^2\left(-4x^2+x-5\right)$
$= -3x^2\left(-4x^2\right) - 3x^2(x) - 3x^2(-5)$
$= 12x^4 - 3x^3 + 15x^2$

55. $(x+3)(x+5)$
$= x(x+5) + 3(x+5)$
$= x\cdot x + x\cdot 5 + 3\cdot x + 3\cdot 5$
$= x^2 + 5x + 3x + 15$
$= x^2 + 8x + 15$

57. $(2x+1)(x+4)$
$= 2x(x+4) + 1(x+4)$
$= 2x^2 + 8x + x + 4$
$= 2x^2 + 9x + 4$

59. $(x+3)(x-5) = x(x-5) + 3(x-5)$
$= x^2 - 5x + 3x - 15$
$= x^2 - 2x - 15$

61. $(x-11)(x+9) = x(x+9) - 11(x+9)$
$= x^2 + 9x - 11x - 99$
$= x^2 - 2x - 99$

63. $(2x-5)(x+4)$
$= 2x(x+4)-5(x+4)$
$= 2x^2+8x-5x-20$
$= 2x^2+3x-20$

65. $\left(\frac{1}{4}x+4\right)\left(\frac{3}{4}x-1\right)$
$= \frac{1}{4}x\left(\frac{3}{4}x-1\right)+4\left(\frac{3}{4}x-1\right)$
$= \frac{1}{4}x\cdot\frac{3}{4}x+\frac{1}{4}x(-1)$
$+4\left(\frac{3}{4}x\right)+4(-1)$
$= \frac{3}{16}x^2-\frac{1}{4}x+\frac{12}{4}x-4$
$= \frac{3}{16}x^2+\frac{11}{4}x-4$

67. $(x+1)(x^2+2x+3)$
$= x(x^2+2x+3)+1(x^2+2x+3)$
$= x^3+2x^3+3x+x^2+2x+3$
$= x^3+3x^2+5x+3$

69. $(y-3)(y^2-3y+4)$
$= y(y^2-3y+4)-3(y^2-3y+4)$
$= y^3-3y^2+4y-3y^2+9y-12$
$= y^3-6y^2+13y-12$

71. $(2a-3)(a^2-3a+5)$
$= 2a(a^2-3a+5)-3(a^2-3a+5)$
$= 2a^3-6a^2+10a-3a^2+9a-15$
$= 2a^3-9a^2+19a-15$

73. $(x+1)(x^3+2x^2+3x+4)$
$= x(x^3+2x^2+3x+4)$
$+1(x^3+2x^2+3x+4)$
$= x^4+2x^3+3x^2+4x+x^3+2x^2$
$+3x+4$
$= x^4+(2x^3+x^3)+(3x^2+2x^2)$
$+(4x+3x)+4$
$= x^4+3x^3+5x^2+7x+4$

75. $\left(x-\frac{1}{2}\right)(4x^3-2x^2+5x-6)$
$= x(4x^3-2x^2+5x-6)$
$-\frac{1}{2}(4x^3-2x^2+5x-6)$
$= 4x^4-2x^3+5x^2-6x-2x^3+x^2$
$-\frac{5}{2}x+3$
$= 4x^4-4x^3+6x^2-\frac{17}{2}x+3$

77. $(x^2+2x+1)(x^2-x+2)$
$= x^2(x^2-x+2)+2x(x^2-x+2)$
$+1(x^2-x+2)$
$= x^4-x^3+2x^2+2x^3-2x^2+4x$
$+x^2-x+2$
$= x^4+x^3+x^2+3x+2$

79.
$$\begin{array}{r} x^2-5x+3 \\ \underline{x+8} \\ 8x^2-40x+24 \\ \underline{x^3-5x^2+3x} \\ x^3+3x^2-37x+24 \end{array}$$

81.
$$\begin{array}{r} x^2-3x+\ \ 9 \\ \underline{2x-\ \ 3} \\ -3x^2+9x-27 \\ \underline{2x^3-6x^2+18x\quad\quad} \\ 2x^3-9x^2+27x-27 \end{array}$$

83.
$$\begin{array}{r} 2x^3+x^2+2x+\ 3 \\ \underline{x+\ 4} \\ 8x^3+4x^2+8x+12 \\ \underline{2x^4+\ \ x^3+2x^2+3x\quad\quad} \\ 2x^4+9x^3+6x^2+11x+12 \end{array}$$

85.
$$\begin{array}{r} 4z^3-2z^2+\ \ 5z-4 \\ \underline{3z-2} \\ -8z^3+4z^2-10z+8 \\ \underline{12z^4-\ \ 5z^3+15z^2-12z\quad\quad} \\ 12z^4-14z^3+19z^2-22z+8 \end{array}$$

87.
$$\begin{array}{r} 7x^3-\ \ \ 5x^2+\ 6x \\ \underline{3x^2-\ 4x} \\ -28x^4+20x^3-24x^2 \\ \underline{21x^5-15x^4+18x^3\quad\quad\quad} \\ 21x^5-43x^4+38x^3-24x^2 \end{array}$$

89.
$$\begin{array}{r} 2y^5\qquad\quad -3y^3+\ \ y^2-2y+3 \\ \underline{2y-1} \\ -2y^5\qquad\quad +\ 3y^3-\ \ y^2+2y-3 \\ \underline{4y^6-\qquad\quad 6y^4+2y^3-4y^2+6y\quad\quad} \\ 4y^6-2y^5-6y^4+5y^3-5y^2+8y-3 \end{array}$$

91.
$$\begin{array}{r} x^2+7x-3 \\ \underline{x^2-\ \ x-1} \\ -x^2-7x+3 \\ -x^3-7x^2+3x\quad\quad \\ \underline{x^4+7x^3-3x^2\qquad\qquad} \\ x^4+6x^3-11x^2-4x+3 \end{array}$$

93. $(x+4)(x-5)-(x+3)(x-6)$
$(x^2-x-20)-(x^2-3x-18)$
$(x^2-x-20)+(-x^2+3x+18)$
$2x-2$

94. $(x+5)(x-6)-(x+2)(x-9)$
$(x^2-x-30)-(x^2-7x-18)$
$(x^2-x-30)+(-x^2+7x+18)$
$6x-12$

95. $4x^2(5x^3+3x-2)-5x^3(x^2-6)$
$(20x^5+12x^3-8x^2)+(-5x^5+30x^3)$
$15x^5+42x^3-8x^2$

96. $3x^2(6x^3+2x-3)-4x^3(x^2-5)$
$(18x^5+6x^3-9x^2)+(-4x^5+20x^3)$
$14x^5+26x^3-9x^2$

97. $(y+1)(y^2-y+1)+(y-1)(y^2+y+1)$
$= y(y^2-y+1)+1(y^2-y+1)$
$\quad + y(y^2+y+1)-1(y^2+y+1)$
$= y^3-y^2+y+y^2-y+1$
$\quad + y^3+y^2+y-y^2-y-1$
$= 2y^3$

98. $(y+1)(y^2-y+1)-(y-1)(y^2+y+1)$
$= y(y^2-y+1)+1(y^2-y+1)$
$\quad -y(y^2+y+1)+1(y^2+y+1)$
$= y^3-y^2+y+y^2-y+1$
$\quad -y^3-y^2-y+y^2+y+1$
$=2$

99. $(y+6)^2-(y-2)^2$
$(y+6)(y+6)-(y-2)(y-2)$
$(y^2+12y+36)-(y^2-4y+4)$
$16y+32$

100. $(y+5)^2-(y-4)^2$
$(y+5)(y+5)-(y-4)(y-4)$
$(y^2+10y+25)-(y^2-8y+16)$
$18y+9$

101. Use the formula for the area of a rectangle.
$A=l\cdot w$
$A=(x+5)(2x-3)$
$\quad =x(2x-3)+5(2x-3)$
$\quad =2x^2-3x+10x-15$
$\quad =2x^2+7x-15$

The area of the rug is $(2x^2+7x-15)$ square feet.

103. **a.** $(x+2)(2x+1)$

b. $x\cdot 2x+2\cdot 2x+x\cdot 1+2\cdot 1$
$=2x^2+4x+x+2$
$=2x^2+5x+2$

c. $(x+2)(2x+1)=x(2x+1)+2(2x+1)$
$=2x^2+x+4x+2$
$=2x^2+5x+2$

105. When multiplying numbers with the same base, keep the base and add the exponents.
Example: $2^3\cdot 2^5=2^{3+5}=2^8$

107. To simplify a product raised to a power, raise each factor of the product to the power, and then multiply the results.
Example: $(5\cdot x)^2=5^2\cdot x^2$

109. To multiply a monomial and a polynomial, distribute the monomial over the polynomial.
Example: $2y^2(3y^2-4y+7)$
$=2y^2(3y^2)+2y^2(-4y)+2y^2(7)$
$=6y^4-8y^3+14y^2$

111. The first is addition of two monomials of degree 2.
$2x^2+3x^2=5x^2$
The second is the multiplication of two monomials of degree 2.
$(2x^2)(3x^2)=(2\cdot 3)(x^2\cdot x^2)=6x^{2+2}=6x^4$

113. Answers will vary.

115. The area of the outer square is
$(x+4)(x+4)=x(x+4)+4(x+4)$
$=x^2+4x+4x+16$
$=x^2+8x+16$
The area of the inner square is x^2. The area of the shaded region is the difference between the areas of the two squares, which is
$$(x^2+8x+16)-x^2=8x+16$$

117. $(-8x^4)\left(-\frac{1}{4}xy^3\right)=2x^5y^3$, so the missing factor is $-8x^4$.

118.
$$\begin{aligned} 4x-7 &> 9x-2 \\ 4x-7-9x &> 9x-2-9x \\ -5x-7 &> -2 \\ -5x-7+7 &> -2+7 \\ -5x &> 5 \\ \frac{-5x}{5} &< \frac{5}{-5} \\ x &< -1 \end{aligned}$$
Solution: $\{x|x<-1\}$

119. $3x-2y=6$
x-intercept: 2
y-intercept: −3
checkpoint: (4,3)

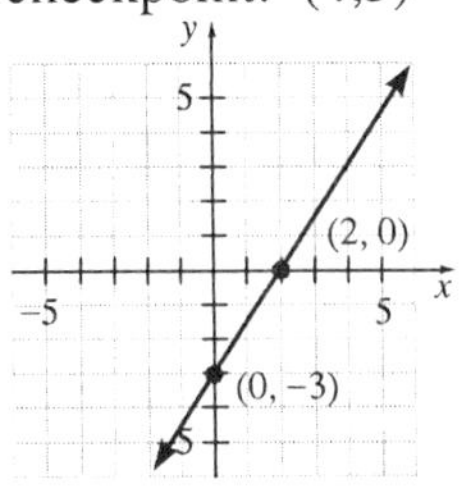

120. (−2,8) and (1,6)
$$m=\frac{y_2-y_1}{x_2-x_2} = \frac{6-8}{1-(-2)} = \frac{-2}{3} = -\frac{2}{3}$$

6.3 Exercise Set

1. $(x+4)(x+6) = x^2+6x+4x+24$
$= x^2+10x+24$

3. $(y-7)(y+3) = y^2+3y-7y-21$
$= y^2-4y-21$

5. $(2x-3)(x+5) = 2x^2+10x-3x-15$
$= 2x^2+7x-15$

7. $(4y+3)(y-1) = 4y^2-4y+3y-3$
$= 4y^2-y-3$

9. $(2x-3)(5x+3) = 10x^2+6x-15x-9$
$= 10x^2-9x-9$

11. $(3y-7)(4y-5) = 12y^2-15y-28y+35$
$= 12y^2-43y+35$

13. $(7+3x)(1-5x) = 7-35x+3x-15x^2$
$= -15x^2-32x+7$

15. $(5-3y)(6-2y) = 30-10y-18y+6y^2$
$= 30-28y+6y^2$
$= 6y^2-28y+30$

17. $(5x^2-4)(3x^2-7)$
$= (5x^2)(3x^2)+(5x^2)(-7)$
$+(-4)(3x^2)+(-4)(-7)$
$= 15x^4-35x^2-12x^2+28$
$= 15x^4-47x^2+28$

19. $(6x-5)(2-x) = 12x-6x^2-10+5x$
$= -6x^2+17x-10$

21. $(x+5)(x^2+3) = x^3+3x+5x^2+15$
$= x^3+5x^2+3x+15$

23. $(8x^3+3)(x^2+5) = 8x^5+40x^3+3x^2+15$

25. $(x+3)(x-3) = x^2-3^2 = x^2-9$

27. $(3x+2)(3x-2) = (3x)^2-2^2 = 9x^2-4$

29. $(3r-4)(3r+4) = (3r)^2-4^2$
$= 9r^2-16$

31. $(3+r)(3-r)=3^2-r^2=9-r^2$

33. $(5-7x)(5+7x)=5^2-(7x^2)=25-49x^2$

35. $\left(2x+\frac{1}{2}\right)\left(2x-\frac{1}{2}\right)=(2x)^2-\left(\frac{1}{2}\right)^2$
$=4x^2-\frac{1}{4}$

37. $(y^2+1)(y^2-1)=(y^2)^2-1^2=y^4-1$

39. $(r^3+2)(r^3-2)=(r^3)^2-2^2=r^6-4$

41. $(1-y^4)(1+y^4)=1^2-(y^4)^2=1-y^8$

43. $(x^{10}+5)(x^{10}-5)=(x^{10})^2-5^2$
$=x^{20}-25$

45. $(x+2)^2=x^2+2(2x)+2^2$
$=x^2+4x+4$

47. $(2x+5)^2=(2x)^2+2(2x)(5)+5^2$
$=4x^2+20x+25$

49. $(x-3)^2=x^2-2(3x)+3^2$
$=x^2-6x+9$

51. $(3y-4)^2=(3y)^2-2(3y)(4)+4^2$
$=9y^2-24y+16$

53. $(4x^2-1)^2=(4x^2)^2-2(4x^2)(1)+1^2$
$=16x^4-8x^2+1$

55. $(7-2x)^2=7^2-2(7)(2x)+(2x)^2$
$=49-28x+4x^2$

57. $\left(2x+\frac{1}{2}\right)^2=4x^2+2(2x)\left(\frac{1}{2}\right)+\left(\frac{1}{2}\right)^2$
$=4x^2+2x+\frac{1}{4}$

59. $\left(4y-\frac{1}{4}\right)^2=(4y)^2-2(4y)\left(\frac{1}{4}\right)+\left(\frac{1}{4}\right)^2$
$=16y^2-2y+\frac{1}{16}$

61. $(x^8+3)^2=(x^8)^2+2(x^8)(3)+3^2$
$=x^{16}+6x^8+9$

63. $(x-1)(x^2+x+1)$
$=x(x^2+x+1)-1(x^2+x+1)$
$=x^3+x^2+x-x^2-x-1$
$=x^3-1$

65. $(x-1)^2=x^2-2(x)(1)+1^2$
$=x^2-2x+1$

67. $(3y+7)(3y-7)=(3y^2)-7^2$
$=9y^2-49$

69. $3x^2(4x^2+x+9)$
$=3x^2(4x^2)+3x^2(x)+3x^2(9)$
$=12x^4+3x^3+27x^2$

71. $(7y+3)(10y-4)$
$=70y^2-28y+30y-12$
$=70y^2+2y-12$

73. $(x^2+1)^2=(x^2)^2+2(x^2)(1)+1^2$
$=x^4+2x^2+1$

75. $(x^2+1)(x^2+2)$
$= x^2 \cdot x^2 + x^2 \cdot 2 + 1 \cdot x^2 + 1 \cdot 2$
$= x^4 + 3x^2 + 2$

77. $(x^2+4)(x^2-4) = (x^2)^2 - 4^2$
$= x^4 - 16$

79. $(2-3x^5)^2 = 2^2 - 2(2)(3x^5) + (3x^5)^2$
$= 4 - 12x^5 + 9x^{10}$

81. $\left(\frac{1}{4}x^2+12\right)\left(\frac{3}{4}x^2-8\right)$
$= \frac{1}{4}x^2\left(\frac{3}{4}x^2\right) + \frac{1}{4}x^2(-8) + 12\left(\frac{3}{4}x^2\right)$
$+12(-8)$
$= \frac{3}{16}x^4 - 2x^2 + 9x^2 - 96$
$= \frac{3}{16}x^2 + 7x^2 - 96$

83. $A = (x+1)^2 = x^2 + 2x + 1$

85. $A = (2x-3)(2x+3) = (2x)^2 - 3^2$
$= 4x^2 - 9$

87. Area of outer rectangle:
$(x+9)(x+3) = x^2 + 12x + 27$
Area of inner rectangle:
$(x+5)(x+1) = x^2 + 6x + 5$
Area of shaded region:
$(x^2+12x+27) - (x^2+6x+5) = 6x + 22$

89. $[(2x+3)(2x-3)]^2$
$[4x^2-9]^2$
$16x^4 - 72x^2 + 81$

90. $[(3x+2)(3x-2)]^2$
$[9x^2-4]^2$
$81x^4 - 72x^2 + 16$

91. $(4x^2+1)[(2x+1)(2x-1)]$
$(4x^2+1)[4x^2-1]$
$16x^4 - 1$

92. $(9x^2+1)[(3x+1)(3x-1)]$
$(9x^2+1)[9x^2-1]$
$81x^4 - 1$

93. $(x+2)^3$
$(x+2)(x+2)^2$
$(x+2)(x^2+4x+4)$
$x(x^2+4x+4) + 2(x^2+4x+4)$
$x^3 + 4x^2 + 4x + 2x^2 + 8x + 8$
$x^3 + 6x^2 + 12x + 8$

94. $(x+4)^3$
$(x+4)(x+4)^2$
$(x+4)(x^2+8x+16)$
$x(x^2+8x+16) + 4(x^2+8x+16)$
$x^3 + 8x^2 + 16x + 4x^2 + 32x + 64$
$x^3 + 12x^2 + 48x + 64$

95. $[(x+3)-y][(x+3)+y]$
$(x+3)^2 - y^2$
$x^2 + 6x + 9 - y^2$

96. $[(x+5)-y][(x+5)+y]$

$(x+5)^2-y^2$

$x^2+10x+25-y^2$

97. $A=(x+1)(x+2)$ yards^2

99. If the original garden measures 6 yards on a side, substitute $x = 6$ in the formula for the larger garden:

$A=(6+1)(6+2)=(7)(8)=56$

The area of the larger garden will be 56 yards^2. The relationship corresponds to the point (6,56) on the graph.

101. The outer square (square including painting and frame) measures (x+2) inches.

$(x+2)^2=x^2+4x+4$

The area is (x^2+4x+4) square inches.

103. FOIL - First Outer Inner Last

Example:

$(4y+3)(y-1)=4y^2-4y+3y-3$

$=4y^2-y-3$

105. To square a binomial sum, square the first piece, square the last piece, multiply together and double.

Example:

$(x+5)^2=x^2+5^2+2(5)(x)$

$=x^2+25+10x$

$=x^2+10x+25$

107. The graph for exercises 97-100 is only shown in Quadrant I because the variable x represents the length and width of the original garden. Since length and width cannot be negative, we only have to graph the values of x that are greater than or equal to zero.

109. To find the correct binomial factors, try different combinations of constants in the binomials that will give a product of −20 as the last term until you find the combination that gives the correct middle term.

$(x-10)(x+2)=x^2+2x-10x-20$

$=x^2-8x-20$

so the two binomials are (x – 10) and (x + 2).

111. Divide the figure into two rectangles by drawing a vertical line.

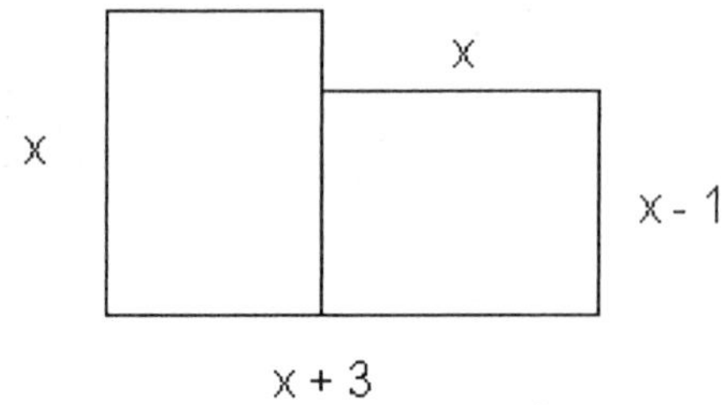

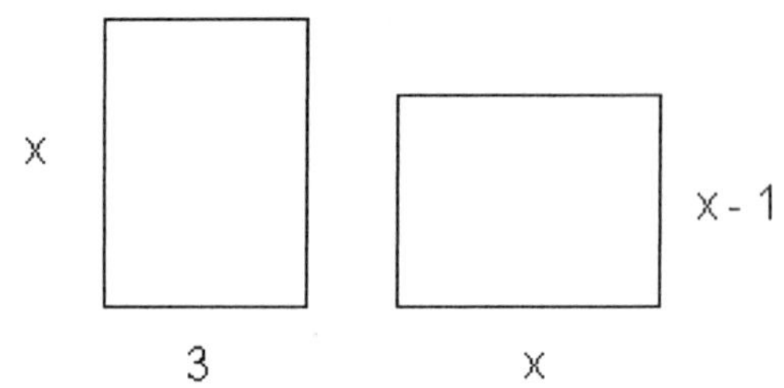

The area of the figure is the sum of the areas of the two rectangles.

$A=3\cdot x+x(x-1)$

$=3x+x^2-x$

$=x^2+2x$

113. Graph $y=(x+2)^2$ and $y=x^2+2x+4$ on the same set of axes.

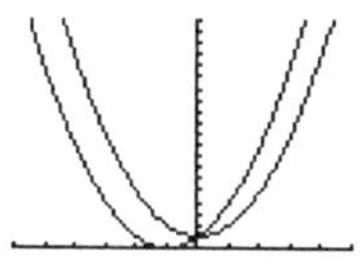

The graphs do not coincide.
$(x+2)^2=x^2+4x+4$, so x^2+2x+4 should be changed to x^2+4x+4.
Graph $y=(x+2)^2$ and $y=x^2+4x+4$ on the same set of axes.

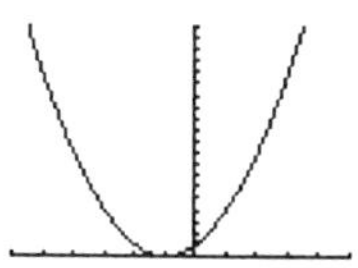

Now the graphs coincide.

115. Graph $y=(x-2)(x+2)+4$ and $y=x^2$ on the same set of axes.

The graphs coincide. We will show that both sides are equivalent.

$$(x-2)(x+2)+4=x^2$$
$$(x^2-4)+4=x^2$$
$$x^2=x^2$$

116. $2x+3y=1$
$y=3x-7$
The substitution method is a good choice because the second equation is already solved for *y*. Substitute $3x-7$ for *y* into the first equation.

$$2x+3y=1$$
$$2x+3(3x-7)=1$$
$$2x+9x-21=1$$
$$11x-21=1$$
$$11x=22$$
$$x=2$$

Back-substitute.

$$y=3x-7$$
$$y=3(2)-7=6+7=-1$$

Solution: (2, −1)

117. $3x+4y=7$
$2x+7y=9$
The addition method is a good choice because both equations are written in the form $Ax+By=C$. To eliminate *x*, multiply the first equation by 2 and the second equation by −3. Then add the results.

$$\begin{aligned} 6x+\ 8y &= \ \ 14 \\ -6x-21y &= -27 \\ \hline -13y &= -13 \\ y &= 1 \end{aligned}$$

Back-substitute 1 for *y* in either equation of the original system.

$$3x+4y=7$$
$$3x+4(1)=7$$
$$3x+4=7$$
$$3x=3$$
$$x=1$$

Solution: (1,1)

118. $y \le \frac{1}{3}x$

Graph $y = \frac{1}{3}x$ as a solid line using its slope, $\frac{1}{3}$, and y-intercept, 0. Since (0,0) is on the line, chose a different point as a test point, for example, (3,2). Since $2 \le \frac{1}{3}(3)$ is false, shade the half-plane *not* containing (3, 2).

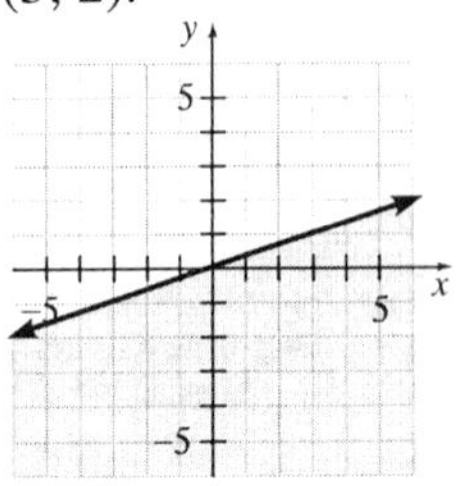

6.4 Exercise Set

1. $x^2 + 2xy + y^2;\ x = 2,\ y = -3$

$$\begin{aligned} x^2 + 2xy + y^2 &= 2^2 + 2(2)(-3) + (-3)^2 \\ &= 4 - 12 + 9 = 1 \end{aligned}$$

3.
$$\begin{aligned} xy^3 - xy + 1 &= 2(-3)^3 - 2(-3) + 1 \\ &= 2(-27) + 6 + 1 \\ &= -54 + 6 + 1 = -47 \end{aligned}$$

5.
$$\begin{aligned} &2x^2y - 5y + 3 \\ &= 2(2^2)(-3) - 5(-3) + 3 \\ &= 2(4)(-3) - 5(-3) + 3 \\ &= -24 + 15 + 3 = -6 \end{aligned}$$

7.

Term	Coefficient	Degree
x^3y^2	1	3+2=5
$-5x^2y^7$	−5	2+7=9
$6y^2$	6	2
−3	−3	0

The degree of the polynomial is the highest degree of all its terms, which is 9.

9.
$$\begin{aligned} &(5x^2y - 3xy) + (2x^2y - xy) \\ &= (5x^2y + 2x^2y) + (-3xy - xy) \\ &= 7x^2y - 4xy \end{aligned}$$

11.
$$\begin{aligned} &(4x^2y + 8xy + 11) + (-2x^2y + 5xy + 2) \\ &= (4x^2y - 2x^2y) + (8xy + 5xy) + (11 + 2) \\ &= 2x^2y + 13xy + 13 \end{aligned}$$

13.
$$\begin{aligned} &(7x^4y^2 - 5x^2y^2 + 3xy) \\ &\quad + (-18x^4y^2 - 6x^2y^2 - xy) \\ &= (7x^4y^2 - 18x^4y^2) + (-5x^2y^2 - 6x^2y^2) \\ &\quad + (3xy - xy) \\ &= -11x^4y^2 - 11x^2y^2 + 2xy \end{aligned}$$

15.
$$\begin{aligned} &(x^3 + 7xy - 5y^2) - (6x^3 - xy + 4y^2) \\ &= (x^3 + 7xy - 5y^2) + (-6x^3 + xy - 4y^2) \\ &= (x^3 - 6x^3) + (7xy + xy) + (-5y^2 - 4y^2) \\ &= -5x^3 + 8xy - 9y^2 \end{aligned}$$

17. $(3x^4y^2+5x^3y-3y)$
$-(2x^4y^2-3x^3y-4y+6x)$
$=(3x^4y^2+5x^3y-3y)$
$+(-2x^4y^2+3x^3y+4y-6x)$
$=(3x^4y^2-2x^4y^2)+(5x^3y+3x^3y)$
$+(-3y+4y)+(-6x)$
$=x^4y^2+8x^3y+y-6x$

19. $(x^3-y^3)-(-4x^3-x^2y+xy^2+3y^3)$
$=(x^3-y^3)+(4x^3+x^2y-xy^2-3y^3)$
$=(x^3+4x^3)+(-y^3-3y^3)+x^2y-xy^2$
$=5x^3-4y^3+x^2y-xy^2$
$=5x^3+x^2y-xy^2-4y^3$

21.
$$\begin{array}{r} 5x^2y^2-4xy^2+6y^2 \\ \underline{-8x^2y^2+5xy^2\ \ -y^2} \\ -3x^2y^2+\ xy^2\ \ +5y^2 \end{array}$$

23.
$$\begin{array}{r} 3a^2b^4-5ab^2+7ab \\ -(\underline{-5a^2b^4-8ab^2\ \ -ab}) \end{array}$$

$$\begin{array}{r} 3a^2b^4-5ab^2+\ 7ab \\ \underline{+5a^2b^4+8ab^2\ \ +\ ab} \\ 8a^2b^4+3ab^2\ \ +8ab \end{array}$$

25. $[(7x+13y)+(-26x+19y)]-(11x-5y)$
$[-19x+32y]+(-11x+5y)$
$-30x+37y$

27. $(5x^2y)(8xy)=(5\cdot 8)(x^2\cdot x)(y\cdot y)$
$=40x^3y^2$

29. $(-8x^3y^4)(3x^2y^5)=(-8\cdot 3)(x^3\cdot x^2)(y^4\cdot y^5)$
$=-24x^5y^9$

31. $9xy(5x+2y)$
$9xy(5x)+9xy(2y)$
$45x^2y+18xy^2$

33. $5xy^2(10x^2-3y)$
$5xy^2(10x^2)-5xy^2(3y)$
$50x^3y^2-15xy^3$

35. $4ab^2(7a^2b^3+2ab)$
$4ab^2(7a^2b^3)+4ab^2(2ab)$
$28a^3b^5+8a^2b^3$

37. $-b(a^2-ab+b^2)$
$=-b(a^2)-b(-ab)-b(b^2)$
$=-a^2b+ab^2-b^3$

39. $(x+5y)(7x+3y)$
$=x(7x)+x(3y)+5y(7x)+5y(3y)$
$=7x^2+3xy+35xy+15y^2$
$=7x^2+38xy+15y^2$

41. $(x-3y)(2x+7y)$
$=x(2x)+x(7y)-3y(2x)-3y(7y)$
$=2x^2+7xy-6xy-21y^2$
$=2x^2+xy-21y^2$

43. $(3xy-1)(5xy+2)$
$=3xy(5xy)+3xy(2)-1(5xy)-1(2)$
$=15x^2y^2+6xy-5xy-2$
$=15x^2y^2+xy-2$

45. $(2x+3y)^2 = (2x)^2 + 2(2x)(3y) + (3y)^2$
$= 4x^2 + 12xy + 9y^2$

47. $(xy-3)^2 = (xy)^2 - 2(xy)(3) + (-3)^2$
$= x^2y^2 - 6xy + 9$

49. $(x^2+y^2)^2 = (x^2)^2 + 2(x^2)(y^2) + (y^2)^2$
$= x^4 + 2x^2y^2 + y^4$

51. $(x^2-2y^2)^2$
$= (x^2) - 2(x^2)(2y^2) + (-2y^2)^2$
$= x^4 - 4x^2y^2 + 4y^4$

53. $(3x+y)(3x-y) = (3x)^2 - y^2 = 9x^2 - y^2$

55. $(ab+1)(ab-1) = (ab)^2 - 1^2 = a^2b^2 - 1$

57. $(x+y^2)(x-y^2) = x^2 - (y^2)^2 = x^2 - y^4$

59. $(3a^2b+a)(3a^2b-a) = (3a^2b)^2 - a^2$
$= 9a^4b^2 - a^2$

61. $(3xy^2-4y)(3xy^2+4y) = (3xy^2)^2 - (4y)^2$
$= 9x^2y^4 - 16y^2$

63. $(a+b)(a^2-b^2)$
$= a(a^2) + a(-b^2) + b(a^2) + b(-b^2)$
$= a^3 - ab^2 + a^2b - b^3$

65. $(x+y)(x^2+3xy+y^2)$
$= x(x^2+3xy+y^2) + y(x^2+3xy+y^2)$
$= x^3 + 3x^2y + xy^2 + x^2y + 3xy^2 + y^3$
$= x^3 + 4x^2y + 4xy^2 + y^3$

67. $(x-y)(x^2-3xy+y^2)$
$= x(x^2-3xy+y^2) - y(x^2-3xy+y^2)$
$= x^3 - 3x^2y + xy^2 - x^2y + 3xy^2 - y^3$
$= x^3 - 4x^2y + 4xy^2 - y^3$

69. $(xy+ab)(xy-ab) = (xy)^2 - (ab)^2$
$= x^2y^2 - a^2b^2$

71. $(x^2+1)(x^4y+x^2+1)$
$x^2(x^4y+x^2+1) + 1(x^4y+x^2+1)$
$= x^6y + x^4 + x^2 + x^4y + x^2 + 1$
$= x^6y + x^4y + x^4 + 2x^2 + 1$

73. $(x^2y^2-3)^2$
$= (x^2y^2)^2 - 2(x^2y^2)(3) + (-3)^2$
$= x^4y^4 - 6x^2y^2 + 9$

75. $(x+y+1)(x+y-1)$
$= x(x+y-1) + y(x+y-1)$
$+1(x+y-1)$
$= x^2 + xy - x + yx + y^2 - y + x + y - 1$
$= x^2 + 2xy + y^2 - 1$

77. $A = (3x+5y)(x+y)$
$= 3x(x) + 3x(y) + 5y(x) + 5y(y)$
$= 3x^2 + 3xy + 5xy + 5y^2$
$= 3x^2 + 8xy + 5y^2$

79. Area of a larger square $= (x+y)^2$
$= x^2 + 2xy + y^2$

Area of a smaller square $= x^2$

Area of shaded region
$= (x^2+2xy+y^2) - x^2$
$= 2xy + y^2$

81. $\left[\left(x^3y^3+1\right)\left(x^3y^3-1\right)\right]^2$

$\left[\left(x^3y^3\right)^2-(1)^2\right]^2$

$\left[x^6y^6-1\right]^2$

$\left(x^6y^6\right)^2-2\left(x^6y^6\right)(1)+(1)^2$

$x^{12}y^{12}-2x^6y^6+1$

82. $\left[\left(1-a^3b^3\right)\left(1+a^3b^3\right)\right]^2$

$\left[(1)^2-\left(a^3b^3\right)^2\right]^2$

$\left[1-a^6b^6\right]^2$

$(1)^2-2(1)\left(a^6b^6\right)+\left(a^6b^6\right)^2$

$1-2a^6b^6+a^{12}b^{12}$

83. $(xy-3)^2(xy+3)^2$

$\left[(xy-3)(xy+3)\right]^2$

$\left[(xy)^2-3^2\right]^2$

$\left[x^2y^2-9\right]^2$

$\left(x^2y^2\right)^2-2\left(x^2y^2\right)(9)+(9)^2$

$x^4y^4-18x^2y^2+81$

84. $(ab-4)^2(ab+4)^2$

$\left[(ab-4)(ab+4)\right]^2$

$\left[(ab)^2-4^2\right]^2$

$\left[a^2b^2-16\right]^2$

$\left(a^2b^2\right)^2-2\left(a^2b^2\right)(16)+(16)^2$

$a^4b^4-32a^2b^2+256$

85. $[x+y+z][x-(y+z)]$

$[x+(y+z)][x-(y+z)]$

$x^2-(y+z)^2$

$x^2-\left(y^2+2yz+z^2\right)$

$x^2-y^2-2yz-z^2$

86. $[a-b-c][a+b+c]$

$[a-(b+c)][a+(b+c)]$

$a^2-(b+c)^2$

$a^2-\left(b^2+2bc+c^2\right)$

$a^2-b^2-2bc-c^2$

87. $N=\frac{1}{4}x^2y-2xy+4y;\ x=10,\ y=16$

$$\begin{aligned}N&=\frac{1}{4}x^2y-2xy+4y\\&=\frac{1}{4}(10)^2(16)-2(10)(16)+4(16)\\&=\frac{1}{4}(100)(16)-2(10)(16)+4(16)\\&=400-320+64\\&=144\end{aligned}$$

Each tree provides 144 board feet of lumber, so 20 trees will provide 20(144) = 2880 board feet. This is not enough lumber to complete the job. Since 3000 – 2880 = 120, the contractor will need 120 more board feet.

89. $s = -16t^2 + v_0 t + s_0$; $t = 2$, $v_0 = 80$, $s_0 = 96$

$$\begin{aligned} s &= -16t^2 + v_0 t + s_0 \\ &= -16(2)^2 + 80(2) + 96 \\ &= -16(4) + 80(6) + 96 \\ &= -64 + 160 + 96 \\ &= 192 \end{aligned}$$

The ball will be 192 feet above the ground 2 seconds after being thrown.

91. $s = -16t^2 + v_0 t + s_0$; $t = 6$, $v_0 = 80$ $s_0 = 96$

$$\begin{aligned} s &= -16t^2 + v_0 t + s_0 \\ &= -16(6)^2 + 80(60) + 96 \\ &= -16(36) + 80(6) + 96 \\ &= -576 + 480 + 96 = 0 \end{aligned}$$

The ball will be 0 feet above the ground after 6 seconds. This means that the ball hits the ground 6 seconds after being thrown.

93. The ball is falling from 2.5 seconds to 6 seconds. The graph is decreasing over this interval.

95. (2,192)

97. The ball reaches its maximum height 2.5 seconds after it is thrown.

$s = -16t^2 + v_0 t + s_0$; $t = 2.5$, $v_0 = 80$ $s_0 = 96$

$$\begin{aligned} s &= -16t^2 + v_0 t + s_0 \\ &= -16(2.5)^2 + 80(2.5) + 96 \\ &= -16(6.25) + 80(2.5) + 96 \\ &= -100 + 200 + 96 \\ &= 196 \end{aligned}$$

The maximum height is 196 feet.

99. To find the degree of a polynomial in two variables, calculate the degree of each term separately by adding the powers of each variable. The degree is the maximum value of your results.

101. Statement a is false.
The term $-3x^{16}y^9$ has degree 16+9=25.
Statement b is false.
The coefficient of the term is a 1.
Statement c is true.

$$\begin{aligned} &(2x+3-5y)(2x+3+5y) \\ &= [(2x+3)-5y][(2x+3)+5y] \\ &= (2x+3)^2 - (5y)^2 \\ &= 4x^2 + 12x + 9 - 25y^2 \end{aligned}$$

Statement d is false.
The right-hand-side of the equation should be $-14xy$, not zero.

103. Area of large rectangle:
$(3x-4y)(3x+4y) = 9x^2 - 16y^2$
Area of small squares: $(x)(x) = x^2$
Area of shaded region is the area of the large rectangle minus the areas of the 4 small squares:
$9x^2 - 16y^2 - 4x = 5x^2 - 16y^2$

105. $R=\frac{L+3W}{2}$; for W

$$R=\frac{L+3W}{2}$$
$$2R=2\left(\frac{L+3W}{2}\right)$$
$$2R=L+3W$$
$$2R-L=L+3W-L$$
$$2R-L=3W$$
$$\frac{2R-L}{3}=\frac{3W}{3}$$
$$\frac{2R-L}{3}=W \text{ or } W=\frac{2R-L}{3}$$

106. $-6.4-(-10.2)=-6.4+10.2=3.8$

107. $\frac{63}{x}=\frac{3}{5}$

$$3x=63\cdot 5$$
$$3x=315$$
$$\frac{3x}{3}=\frac{315}{3}$$
$$x=105$$

The solution is 105.

Chapter 6 Mid-Chapter Check Point

1. $(11x^2y^3)(-5x^2y^3)$

$=-55x^{2+2}y^{3+3}=-55x^4y^6$

2. $11x^2y^3-5x^2y^3=6x^2y^3$

3. $(3x+5)(4x-7)$

$12x^2-21x+20x-35$

$12x^2-x-35$

4. $(3x+5)-(4x-7)$

$(3x+5)+(-4x+7)$

$-x+12$

5. $(2x-5)(x^2-3x+1)$

$2x(x^2-3x+1)-5(x^2-3x+1)$

$2x^3-6x^2+2x-5x^2+15x-5$

$2x^3-11x^2+17x-5$

6. $(2x-5)+(x^2-3x+1)$

x^2-x-4

7. $(8x-3)^2$

$(8x)^2-2(8x)(3)+3^2$

$64x^2-48x+9$

8. $(-10x^4)(-7x^5)=70x^9$

9. $(x^2+2)(x^2-2)$

$(x^2)^2-2^2$

x^4-4

10. $(x^2+2)^2$

$(x^2)^2+2(x^2)(2)+2^2$

x^4+4x^2+4

11. $(9a-10b)(2a+b)$

$18a^2+9ab-20ba-10b^2$

$18a^2+9ab-20ab-10b^2$

$18a^2-11ab-10b^2$

12. $7x^2(10x^3-2x+3)$

$70x^5-14x^3+21x^2$

13. $\left(3a^2b^3 - ab + 4b^2\right) - \left(-2a^2b^3 - 3ab + 5b^2\right)$
$\left(3a^2b^3 - ab + 4b^2\right) + \left(2a^2b^3 + 3ab - 5b^2\right)$
$5a^2b^3 + 2ab - b^2$

14. $2(3y-5)(3y+5)$
$2\left(9y^2 - 25\right)$
$18y^2 - 50$

15. $\left(-9x^3 + 5x^2 - 2x + 7\right) + \left(11x^3 - 6x^2 + 3x - 7\right)$
$2x^3 - x^2 + x$

16. $10x^2 - 8xy - 3\left(y^2 - xy\right)$
$10x^2 - 8xy - 3y^2 + 3xy$
$10x^2 - 5xy - 3y^2$

17. $\left(-2x^5 + x^4 - 3x + 10\right) - \left(2x^5 - 6x^4 + 7x - 13\right)$
$\left(-2x^5 + x^4 - 3x + 10\right) + \left(-2x^5 + 6x^4 - 7x + 13\right.$
$-4x^5 + 7x^4 - 10x + 23$

18. $(x+3y)\left(x^2 - 3xy + 9y^2\right)$
$x\left(x^2 - 3xy + 9y^2\right) + 3y\left(x^2 - 3xy + 9y^2\right)$
$x^3 - 3x^2y + 9xy^2 + 3x^2y - 9xy^2 + 27y^3$
$x^3 + 27y^3$

19. $\left(5x^4 + 4\right)\left(2x^3 - 1\right)$
$10x^7 - 5x^4 + 8x^3 - 4$

20. $(y-6z)^2$
$y^2 - 2(y)(6z) + (6z)^2$
$y^2 - 12yz + 36z^2$

21. $(2x+3)(2x-3) - (5x+4)(5x-4)$
$\left(4x^2 - 9\right) - \left(25x^2 - 16\right)$
$\left(4x^2 - 9\right) + \left(-25x^2 + 16\right)$
$-21x^2 + 7$

6.5 Exercise Set

1. $\dfrac{3^{20}}{3^5} = 3^{20-5} = 3^{15}$

3. $\dfrac{x^6}{x^2} = x^{6-2} = x^4$

5. $\dfrac{y^{13}}{y^5} = y^{13-5} = y^8$

7. $\dfrac{5^6 \cdot 2^8}{5^3 \cdot 2^4} = 5^{6-3} \cdot 2^{8-4} = 5^3 \cdot 2^4$

9. $\dfrac{x^{100}y^{50}}{x^{25}y^{10}} = x^{100-25}y^{50-10} = x^{75}y^{40}$

11. $2^0 = 1$

13. $(-2)^0 = 1$

15. $-2^0 = -\left(2^0\right) = -(1) = -1$

17. $100y^0 = 100 \cdot 1 = 100$

19. $(100y)^0 = 1$

21. $-5^0 + (-5)^0 = -1 + 1 = 0$

23. $-\pi^0 - (-\pi)^0 = -1 - 1 = -2$

25. $\left(\frac{x}{3}\right)^2=\frac{x^2}{3^2}=\frac{x^2}{9}$

27. $\left(\frac{x^2}{4}\right)^3=\frac{\left(x^2\right)^3}{4^3}=\frac{x^{2\cdot 3}}{4^3}=\frac{x^6}{64}$

29. $\left(\frac{2x^3}{5}\right)^2=\frac{2^2\left(x^3\right)^2}{5^2}=\frac{4x^6}{25}$

31. $\left(\frac{-4}{3a^3}\right)^3=\frac{(-4)^3}{3^3\left(a^3\right)^3}=\frac{-64}{27a^9}=-\frac{64}{27a^9}$

33. $\left(\frac{-2a^7}{b^4}\right)^5=\frac{\left(-2a^7\right)^5}{\left(b^4\right)^5}=\frac{(-2)^5\left(a^7\right)^5}{\left(b^4\right)^5}$

$=\frac{-32a^{35}}{b^{20}}=-\frac{32a^{35}}{b^{20}}$

35. $\left(\frac{x^2y^3}{2z}\right)^4=\frac{\left(x^2\right)^4\left(y^3\right)^4}{2^4z^4}=\frac{x^8y^{12}}{16z^4}$

37. $\frac{30x^{10}}{10x^5}=\frac{30}{10}x^{10-5}=3x^5$

39. $\frac{-8x^{22}}{4x^2}=\frac{-8}{4}x^{22-2}=-2x^{20}$

41. $\frac{-9y^8}{18y^5}=\frac{-9}{18}y^{8-5}=-\frac{1}{2}y^3$

43. $\frac{7y^{17}}{5y^5}=\frac{7}{5}y^{17-5}=\frac{7}{5}y^{12}$

45. $\frac{30x^7y^5}{5x^2y}=\frac{30}{5}x^{7-2}y^{5-1}=6x^5y^4$

47. $\frac{-18x^{14}y^2}{36x^2y^2}=\frac{-18}{36}x^{14-2}y^{2-2}$

$=-\frac{1}{2}x^{12}y^0=-\frac{1}{2}x^{12}\cdot 1$

$=-\frac{1}{2}x^{12}$

49. $\frac{9x^{20}y^{20}}{7x^{20}y^{20}}=\frac{9}{7}x^{20-20}y^{20-20}$

$=\frac{9}{7}x^0y^0=\frac{9}{7}\cdot 1\cdot 1=\frac{9}{7}$

51. $\frac{-5x^{10}y^{12}z^6}{50x^2y^3z^2}=-\frac{1}{10}x^{10-2}y^{12-3}z^{6-2}$

$=-\frac{1}{10}x^8y^9z^4$

53. $\frac{10x^4+2x^3}{2}=\frac{10x^4}{2}+\frac{2x^3}{2}=5x^4+x^3$

55. $\frac{14x^4-7x^3}{7x}=\frac{14x^4}{7x}-\frac{7x^3}{7x}$

$=2x^{4-1}-x^{3-1}=2x^3-x^2$

57. $\frac{y^7-9y^2+y}{y}=\frac{y^7}{y}-\frac{9y^2}{y}+\frac{y}{y}$

$=y^{7-1}-9y^{2-1}+y^{1-1}$

$=y^6-9y^1+y^0$

$=y^6-9y+1$

59. $\frac{24x^3-15x^2}{-3x}=\frac{24x^3}{-3x}+\frac{-15x^2}{-3x}$

$=-8x^{3-1}+5x^{2-1}=-8x^2+5x$

61. $\frac{18x^5+6x^4+9x^3}{3x^2}=\frac{18x^5}{3x^2}+\frac{6x^4}{3x^2}+\frac{9x^3}{3x^2}$

$=6x^3+2x^2+3x$

63. $\dfrac{12x^4-8x^3+40x^2}{4x}=\dfrac{12x^4}{4x}-\dfrac{8x^3}{4x}+\dfrac{40x^2}{4x}$
$=3x^3-2x^2+10x$

65. $\left(4x^2-6x\right)\div x=\dfrac{4x^2-6x}{x}=\dfrac{4x^2}{x}-\dfrac{6x}{x}$
$=4x-6$

67. $\dfrac{30z^3+10z^2}{-5z}=\dfrac{30z^3}{-5z}+\dfrac{10z^2}{-5z}=-6z^2-2z$

69. $\dfrac{8x^3+6x^2-2x}{2x}=\dfrac{8x^3}{2x}+\dfrac{6x^2}{2x}-\dfrac{2x}{2x}$
$=4x^2+3x-1$

71. $\dfrac{25x^7-15x^5-5x^4}{5x^3}=\dfrac{25x^7}{5x^3}-\dfrac{15x^5}{5x^3}-\dfrac{5x^4}{5x^3}$
$=5x^4-3x^2-x$

73. $\dfrac{18x^7-9x^6+20x^5-10x^4}{-2x^4}$
$=\dfrac{18x^7}{-2x^4}-\dfrac{9x^6}{-2x^4}+\dfrac{20x^5}{-2x^4}-\dfrac{10x^4}{-2x^4}$
$=-9x^3+\dfrac{9}{2}x^2-10x+5$

75. $\dfrac{12x^2y^2+6x^2y-15xy^2}{3xy}$
$=\dfrac{12x^2y^2}{3xy}+\dfrac{6x^2y}{3xy}-\dfrac{15xy^2}{3xy}$
$=4xy+2x-5y$

77. $\dfrac{20x^7y^4-15x^3y^2-10x^2y}{-5x^2y}$
$\dfrac{20x^7y^4}{-5x^2y}+\dfrac{-15x^3y^2}{-5x^2y}+\dfrac{-10x^2y}{-5x^2y}$
$=-4x^5y^3+3xy+2$

79. $\dfrac{2x^3(4x+2)-3x^2(2x-4)}{2x^2}$
$\dfrac{8x^4+4x^3-6x^3+12x^2}{2x^2}$
$\dfrac{8x^4-2x^3+12x^2}{2x^2}$
$\dfrac{8x^4}{2x^2}-\dfrac{2x^3}{2x^2}+\dfrac{12x^2}{2x^2}$
$4x^2-x+6$

80. $\dfrac{6x^3(3x-1)+5x^2(6x-3)}{3x^2}$
$\dfrac{18x^4-6x^3+30x^3-15x^2}{3x^2}$
$\dfrac{18x^4+24x^3-15x^2}{3x^2}$
$\dfrac{18x^4}{3x^2}+\dfrac{24x^3}{3x^2}-\dfrac{15x^2}{3x^2}$
$6x^2+8x-5$

81. $\left(\dfrac{18x^2y^4}{9xy^2}\right)-\left(\dfrac{15x^5y^6}{5x^4y^4}\right)=2xy^2-3xy^2=-xy^2$

82. $\left(\dfrac{9x^3+6x^2}{3x}\right)-\left(\dfrac{12x^2y^2-4xy^2}{2xy^2}\right)$
$\left(\dfrac{9x^3}{3x}+\dfrac{6x^2}{3x}\right)-\left(\dfrac{12x^2y^2}{2xy^2}-\dfrac{4xy^2}{2xy^2}\right)$
$3x^2+2x-(6x-2)=3x^2-4x+2$

83. $\dfrac{(y+5)^2+(y+5)(y-5)}{2y}$
$\dfrac{\left(y^2+10y+25\right)+\left(y^2-25\right)}{2y}$
$\dfrac{2y^2+10y}{2y}=\dfrac{2y^2}{2y}+\dfrac{10y}{2y}=y+5$

84. $\dfrac{(y+4)^2+(y+4)(y-4)}{2y}$

$\dfrac{(y^2+8y+16)+(y^2-16)}{2y}$

$\dfrac{2y^2+8y}{2y}=\dfrac{2y^2}{2y}+\dfrac{8y}{2y}=y+4$

85. $\dfrac{12x^{15n}-24x^{12n}+8x^{3n}}{4x^{3n}}$

$\dfrac{12x^{15n}}{4x^{3n}}-\dfrac{24x^{12n}}{4x^{3n}}+\dfrac{8x^{3n}}{4x^{3n}}$

$3x^{12n}-6x^{9n}+2$

86. $\dfrac{35x^{10n}-15x^{8n}+25x^{2n}}{5x^{2n}}$

$\dfrac{35x^{10n}}{5x^{2n}}-\dfrac{15x^{8n}}{5x^{2n}}+\dfrac{25x^{2n}}{5x^{2n}}$

$7x^{8n}-3x^{6n}+5$

87. (a)Divide the expression for the number of convictions by the expression for the number of arrests

$\dfrac{6t^4-207t^3+2128t^2-6622t+15,220}{28t^4-711t^3+5963t^2-1695t+27,424}$

(b)No. The denominator is not a monomial.

89. When dividing numbers with the same base, keep the base and subtract the exponents.

Example: $\dfrac{3^6}{3^2}=3^{6-2}=3^4$

91. $(-7)^0$ is one number -7 raised to the 0 power. So $(-7)^0=1$.

-7^0 is actually $-7^0=-1\cdot 7^0=-1\cdot 1=-1$.

93. Divide monomials by dividing coefficients and using the quotient rule on each variable expression.

95. $\dfrac{12x^2+6x}{3x}$ and $4x+2$ are not the same for $x=0$. The first expression cannot be evaluated at $x=0$ because this would make the denominator zero.

97. $\dfrac{18x^8-27x^6+36x^4}{3x^2}=6x^6-9x^4+12x^2$

so the required polynomial is

$18x^8-27x^6+36x^4$.

One way to find this polynomial is to use the relationship between division and multiplication:

$3x^2(6x^6-9x^4+12x^2)=18x^8-27x^6+36x^4$.

99. To get 2 as the coefficient of the middle term of the quotient, the coefficient in the divisor must be –3. To get the exponents shown in the three terms of the quotient, the exponent in the divisor must be 7. Since we now know that the divisor is $-3x^7$, the coefficient of the last term of the dividend must be –9.

Therefore,

$\dfrac{3x^{14}-6x^{12}-?x^7}{?x^?}=\dfrac{3x^{14}-6x^{12}-9x^7}{-3x^7}$

100. $|-20.3|=20.3$

101.

$$8\overline{)7.000}\quad \text{quotient } 0.875$$

$$\begin{array}{r} 64 \\ \hline 60 \\ 56 \\ \hline 40 \\ 40 \\ \hline 0 \end{array}$$

$$\frac{7}{8} = 0.875$$

102. $y = \frac{1}{3}x + 2$

slope = $\frac{1}{3}$; y-intercept = 2

Plot (0,2). From this point move 1 unit *up* and 3 units to the *right* to reach the point (3,3). Draw a line through (0,2) and (3,3).

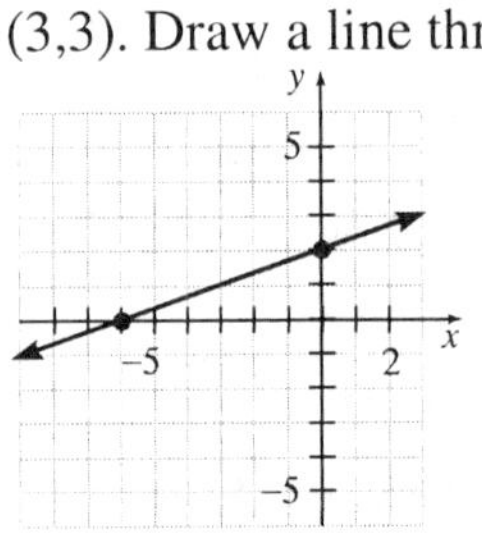

6.6 Exercise Set

1.

$$x+2\overline{)x^2+6x+8}\quad \text{quotient } x+4$$

$$\begin{array}{r} x^2+2x \\ \hline 4x+8 \\ 4x+8 \\ \hline 0 \end{array}$$

$$\frac{x^2+6x+8}{x+2} = x+4$$

3.

$$x-2\overline{)2x^2+x-10}\quad \text{quotient } 2x+5$$

$$\begin{array}{r} 2x^2-4x \\ \hline 5x-10 \\ 5x-10 \\ \hline 0 \end{array}$$

$$\frac{2x^2+x-10}{x-2} = 2x+5$$

5.

$$x-3\overline{)x^2-5x+6}\quad \text{quotient } x-2$$

$$\begin{array}{r} x^2-3x \\ \hline -2x+6 \\ -2x+6 \\ \hline 0 \end{array}$$

$$\frac{x^2-5x+6}{x-3} = x-2$$

7.

$$y+2\overline{)2y^2+5y+2}\quad \text{quotient } 2y+1$$

$$\begin{array}{r} 2y^2+4y \\ \hline y+2 \\ y+2 \\ \hline 0 \end{array}$$

$$\frac{2y^2+5y+2}{y+2} = 2y+1$$

9.

$$\begin{array}{r} x-5 \\ x+2\overline{)x^2-3x+4} \\ \underline{x^2+2x} \\ -5x+4 \\ \underline{-5x-10} \\ 14 \end{array}$$

$$\frac{x^2-3x+4}{x+2}=x-5+\frac{14}{x+2}$$

11.

$$\begin{array}{r} y+3 \\ y+2\overline{)y^2+5y+10} \\ \underline{y^2+2y} \\ 3y+10 \\ \underline{3y+6} \\ 4 \end{array}$$

$$\frac{5y+10+y^2}{y+2}=\frac{y^2+5y+10}{y+2}=y+3+\frac{4}{y+2}$$

13.

$$\begin{array}{r} x^2-5x+2 \\ x-1\overline{)x^3-6x^2+7x-2} \\ \underline{x^3-x^2} \\ -5x^2+7x \\ \underline{-5x^2+5x} \\ 2x-2 \\ \underline{2x-2} \\ 0 \end{array}$$

$$\frac{x^3-6x^2+7x-2}{x-1}=x^2-5x+2$$

15.

$$\begin{array}{r} 6y-1 \\ 2y-3\overline{)12y^2-20y+3} \\ \underline{12y^2-18y} \\ -2y+3 \\ \underline{-2y+3} \\ 0 \end{array}$$

$$\frac{12y^2-20y+3}{2y-3}=6y-1$$

17.

$$\begin{array}{r} 2a+3 \\ 2a-1\overline{)4a^2+4a-3} \\ \underline{4a^2-2a} \\ 6a-3 \\ \underline{6a-3} \\ 0 \end{array}$$

$$\frac{4a^2+4a-3}{2a-1}=2a+3$$

19.

$$\begin{array}{r} y^2-y+2 \\ 2y+1\overline{)2y^3-y^2+3y+2} \\ \underline{2y^3+y^2} \\ -2y^2+3y \\ \underline{-2y^2-y} \\ 4y+2 \\ \underline{4y+2} \\ 0 \end{array}$$

$$\frac{3y-y^2+2y^3+2}{2y+1}$$
$$=\frac{2y^3-y^2+3y+2}{2y+1}=y^2-y+2$$

21.

$$\begin{array}{r} 3x+5 \\ 2x-5\overline{)6x^2-5x-30} \\ \underline{6x^2-15x} \\ 10x-30 \\ \underline{10x-25} \\ -5 \end{array}$$

$$\frac{6x^2-5x-30}{2x-5}=3x+5-\frac{5}{2x-5}$$

23.

$$\begin{array}{r} x^2+2x+8 \\ x-2\overline{)x^3+0x^2+4x-3} \\ \underline{x^3-2x^2} \\ 2x^2+4x \\ \underline{2x^2-4x} \\ 8x-\ 3 \\ \underline{8x-16} \\ 13 \end{array}$$

$$\frac{x^2+4x-3}{x-2}=x^2+2x+8+\frac{13}{x-2}$$

25.

$$\begin{array}{r} 2y^2+y+1 \\ 2y+3\overline{)4y^3+8y^2+5y+9} \\ \underline{4y^3+6y^2} \\ 2y^2+5y \\ \underline{2y^2+3y} \\ 2y+9 \\ \underline{2y+3} \\ 6 \end{array}$$

$$\frac{4y^3+8y^2+5y+9}{2y+3}=2y^2+y+1+\frac{6}{2y+3}$$

27.

$$\begin{array}{r} 2y^2-3y+2 \\ 3y+2\overline{)6y^3-5y^2+0y+5} \\ \underline{6y^3+4y^2} \\ -9y^2+0y \\ \underline{-9y^2-6y} \\ 6y+5 \\ \underline{6y+4} \\ 1 \end{array}$$

$$\frac{6y^3-5y^2+5}{3y+2}=2y^2-3y+2+\frac{1}{3y+2}$$

29.

$$\begin{array}{r} 9x^2+3x+1 \\ 3x-1\overline{)27x^3+0x^2+0x-1} \\ \underline{27x^3-9x^2} \\ 9x^2+0x \\ \underline{9x^2-3x} \\ 3x-1 \\ \underline{3x-1} \\ 0 \end{array}$$

$$\frac{27x^3-1}{3x-1}=9x^2+3x+1$$

31.
$$\begin{array}{r} y^3-9y^2+27y-27 \\ y-3\overline{)\,y^4-12y^3+54y^2-108y+81} \\ \underline{y^4-\ 3y^3} \\ -9y^3+54y^2 \\ \underline{-9y^3+27y^2} \\ 27y^2-108y \\ \underline{27y^2-\ 81y} \\ -27y+81 \\ \underline{-27y+81} \\ 0 \end{array}$$

$$\frac{81-12y^3+54y^2+y^4-108y}{y-3}$$
$$=\frac{y^4-12y^3+54y^2-108y+81}{y-3}$$
$$=y^3-9y^2+27y-27$$

33.
$$\begin{array}{r} 2y+4 \\ 2y-1\overline{)\,4y^2+6y+0} \\ \underline{4y^2-2y} \\ 8y+0 \\ \underline{8y-4} \\ 4 \end{array}$$

$$\frac{4y^2+6y}{2y-1}=2y+4+\frac{4}{2y-1}$$

35.
$$\begin{array}{r} y^3+y^2-y-1 \\ y-1\overline{)\,y^4+0y^3-2y^2+0y+5} \\ \underline{y^4-y^3} \\ y^3-2y^2 \\ \underline{y^3-\ y^2} \\ -y^2+0y \\ \underline{-y^2+\ y} \\ -y+5 \\ \underline{-y+1} \\ 4 \end{array}$$

$$\frac{y^4-2y^2+5}{y-1}=y^3+y^2-y-1+\frac{4}{y-1}$$

37.
$$\begin{array}{r} 4x-3 \\ x^2+0x+2\overline{)\,4x^3-3x^2+x+1} \\ \underline{4x^3+0x^2+8x} \\ -3x^2-7x+1 \\ \underline{-3x^2+0x-6} \\ -7x+7 \end{array}$$

$$\frac{4x^3-3x^2+x+1}{x^2+2}=4x-3+\frac{-7x+7}{x^2+2}$$

38.
$$\begin{array}{r} 3x+4 \\ x^2+0x+1\overline{)\,3x^3+4x^2+x+7} \\ \underline{3x^3+0x^2+3x} \\ 4x^2-2x+7 \\ \underline{4x^2+0x+4} \\ -2x+3 \end{array}$$

$$\frac{3x^3+4x^2+x+7}{x^2+1}=3x+4+\frac{-2x+3}{x^2+1}$$

39.

$$
\begin{array}{r}
x^2+ax+a^2 \\
x-a\overline{)x^3+0x^2+0x-a^3} \\
\underline{x^3-ax^2} \\
ax^2+0x \\
\underline{ax^2-a^2x} \\
a^2x-a^3 \\
\underline{a^2x-a^3} \\
0
\end{array}
$$

$$\frac{x^3+0x^2+0x-a^3}{x-a}=x^2+ax+a^2$$

40.

$$
\begin{array}{r}
x^3+ax^2+a^2x+a^3 \\
x-a\overline{)x^4+0x^3+0x^2+0x-a^4} \\
\underline{x^3-ax^3} \\
ax^3+0x^2 \\
\underline{ax^3-a^2x^2} \\
a^2x^2+0x \\
\underline{a^2x^2-a^3x} \\
a^3x-a^4 \\
\underline{a^3x-a^4} \\
0
\end{array}
$$

$$\frac{x^4+0x^3+0x^2+0x-a^4}{x-a}$$

$$=x^3+ax^2+a^2x+a^3$$

41.

$$
\begin{array}{r}
2x^2-3x+2 \\
3x^2+2x-4\overline{)6x^4-5x^3-8x^2+16x-8} \\
\underline{6x^4+4x^3-8x^2} \\
-9x^3+0x^2+16x \\
\underline{-9x^3-6x^2+12x} \\
6x^2+4x-8 \\
\underline{6x^2+4x-8} \\
0
\end{array}
$$

$$\frac{6x^4-5x^3-8x^2+16x-8}{3x^2+2x-4}=2x^2-3x+2$$

42.

$$
\begin{array}{r}
2x^2+3x-2 \\
x^2+x-6\overline{)2x^4+5x^3-11x^2-20x+12} \\
\underline{2x^4+2x^3-12x^2} \\
3x^3+1x^2-20x \\
\underline{3x^3+3x^2-18x} \\
-2x^2-2x+12 \\
\underline{2x^2+2x-12} \\
0
\end{array}
$$

$$\frac{2x^4+5x^3-11x^2-20x+12}{x^2+x-6}=2x^2+3x-2$$

43. First, compute the difference:

$$\left(4x^3+x^2-2x+7\right)-\left(3x^3-2x^2-7x+4\right)$$
$$=x^3+3x^2+5x+3$$

Now, complete the division:

$$\frac{x^3+3x^2+5x+3}{x+1}$$

$$\begin{array}{r}
x^2+2x+3 \\
x+1\overline{)x^3+3x^2+5x+3} \\
\underline{x^3+x^2} \qquad\qquad \\
2x^2+5x \qquad \\
\underline{2x^2+2x} \qquad \\
3x+3 \\
\underline{3x+3} \\
0
\end{array}$$

$$\frac{x^3+3x^2+5x+3}{x+1}=x^2+2x+3$$

44. First, compute the difference:

$$\left(4x^3+2x^2-x-1\right)-\left(2x^3-x^2+2x-5\right)$$
$$=2x^3+3x^2-3x+4$$

Now, complete the division:

$$\frac{2x^3+3x^2-3x+4}{x+2}$$

$$\begin{array}{r}
2x^2-x-1 \\
x+2\overline{)2x^3+3x^2-3x+4} \\
\underline{2x^3+4x^2} \qquad\qquad \\
-x^2-3x \qquad \\
\underline{-x^2-2x} \qquad \\
-1x+4 \\
\underline{-x-2} \\
6
\end{array}$$

$$\frac{2x^3+3x^2-3x+4}{x+2}=2x^2-x-1+\frac{6}{x+2}$$

45.

$$\begin{aligned}
Area &= (length)(width) \\
x^3+3x^2+5x+3 &= (length)(x+1) \\
\frac{x^3+3x^2+5x+3}{x+1} &= length \\
length &= \frac{x^3+3x^2+5x+3}{x+1} \\
&= x^2+2x+3
\end{aligned}$$

47. **a.** Substitute $n=3$ into the formula:

$$\frac{30{,}000x^3-30{,}000}{x-1}$$

b. Factor out 30,000 from the numerator:

$$\frac{30{,}000x^3 - 30{,}000}{x-1} = 30{,}000\frac{x^3-1}{x-1}$$

Now use the formula from #39 with $a = 1$:

$$\frac{x^3 - a^3}{x-a} = x^2 + ax + a^2$$

$$\frac{x^3-1}{x-1} = \frac{x^3-1^3}{x-1}$$

$$= x^2 + 1 \cdot x + 1^2 = x^2 + x + 1$$

So

$$\frac{30{,}000x^3 - 30{,}000}{x-1} = 30{,}000\frac{x^3-1}{x-1}$$

$$= 30{,}000\left(x^2 + x + 1\right)$$

$$= 30{,}000x^2 + 30{,}000x + 30{,}000$$

c. Substitute in $x = 1.05$ into your formulas from parts (a) and (b) above:

$$\frac{30{,}000x^3 - 30{,}000}{x-1}$$

$$= \frac{30{,}000(1.05)^3 - 30{,}000}{(1.05)-1} = 94{,}575$$

$$30{,}000x^2 + 30{,}000x + 30{,}000$$

$$= 30{,}000(1.05)^2 + 30{,}000(1.05)$$

$$+ 30{,}000$$

$$= 94{,}575$$

Total salary over three years is \$94,575.

49. Answers will vary.

51. To check a division answer, the following rules must apply:

$$\frac{dividend}{divisor} = quotient + \frac{remainder}{divisor}$$

$$dividend = (quotient)(divisor) + remainder$$

53. **a.** $4x^2 + 25x - 3 = (x+6)(4x+1) - 9$

b. True. See second rule in #51 above.

c. False.

d. False.

55. Since the remainder is zero, we have

$$quotient = \frac{dividend}{divisor}$$

$$quotient = \frac{16x^2 - 2x + k}{2x-1}$$

$$\begin{array}{r} 8x+3 \\ 2x-1\overline{)16x^2-2x+k} \\ \underline{16x^2-8x} \\ 6x+k \\ \underline{6x-3} \\ 0 \end{array}$$

To make the remainder zero, we must have $k = -3$.

57. Graph $y = \dfrac{x^2-4}{x-2}$ and $y = x + 2$ on the same set of axes.

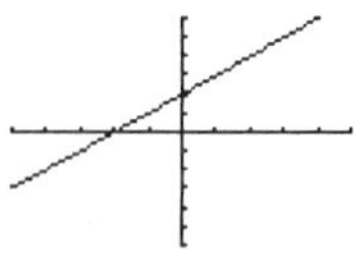

The graphs coincide because $\dfrac{x^2-4}{x-2} = x + 2$.

59. Graph $y = \dfrac{2x^2 + 13x + 15}{x-5}$ and $y = 2x + 3$ on the same set of axes.

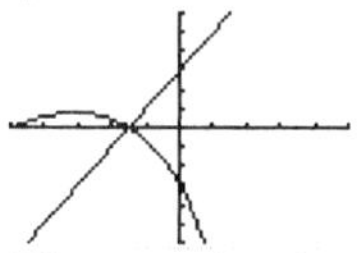

The graphs do not coincide because $\dfrac{2x^2 + 13x + 15}{x-5} = 2x + 23 + \dfrac{130}{x-5}$.

Graph $y = \dfrac{2x^2 + 13x + 15}{x-5}$ and $y = 2x + 23 + \dfrac{130}{x-5}$ on the same set of axes. The graphs coincide.

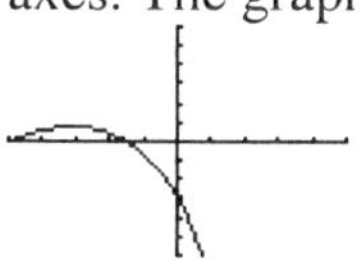

61. Graph $y = \dfrac{x^3 + 3x^2 + 5x + 3}{x+1}$ and $y = x^2 - 2x + 3$ on the same set of axes.

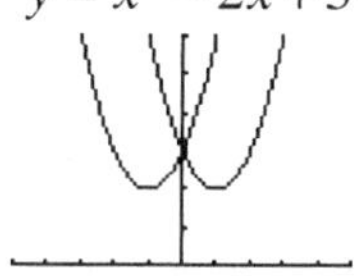

The graphs do not coincide because $\dfrac{x^3 + 3x^2 + 5x + 3}{x+1} = x^2 + 2x + 3$.

Graph $y = \dfrac{x^3 + 3x^2 + 5x + 3}{x+1}$ and $y = x^2 + 2x + 3$ on the same set of axes. The graphs coincide.

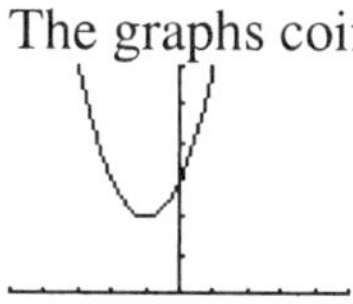

62. $2x - y \geq 4$

$x + y \leq -1$

Graph $2x - y \geq 4$:
Graph $2x - y = 4$ as a solid line with x-intercept 2 and y-intercept −4. Since $2(0) - 0 \geq 4$ is false, shade the half-plane *not* containing (0,0).
Graph $x + y \leq -1$;
Graph $x + y = -1$ as a solid line with x-intercept 1, and y-intercept 1. Since $0 + 0 \leq -1$ is false, shade the half-plane not containing (0,0).
The solution set of the system is the intersection (overlap) of the two shaded regions.

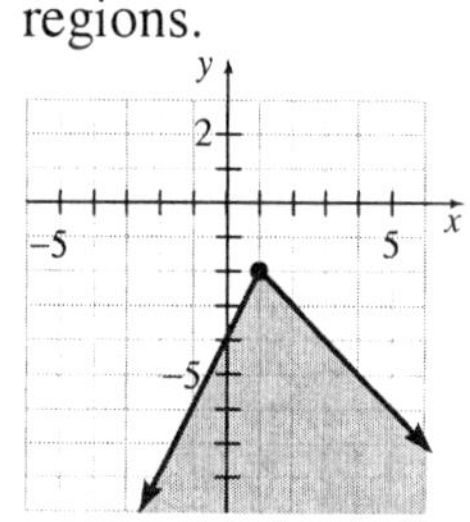

63. $A = PB$; $P = 6\% = 0.06$, $B = 20$

$A = PB$

$A = (0.06)(20)$

1.2

1.1 is 60% of 20.

64. $\frac{x}{3}+\frac{2}{5}=\frac{x}{5}-\frac{2}{5}$

To clear fractions, multiply by the LCD, 15.

$$15\left(\frac{x}{3}+\frac{2}{5}\right)=15\left(\frac{x}{5}-\frac{2}{5}\right)$$
$$15\left(\frac{x}{3}\right)+15\left(\frac{2}{5}\right)=15\left(\frac{x}{5}\right)-15\left(\frac{2}{5}\right)$$
$$5x+6=3x-6$$
$$2x+6=-6$$
$$2x=-12$$
$$x=-6$$

The solution is −6.

6.7 Exercise Set

1. $8^{-2}=\frac{1}{8^2}=\frac{1}{64}$

3. $5^{-3}=\frac{1}{5^3}=\frac{1}{125}$

5. $(-6)^{-2}=\frac{1}{(-6)^2}=\frac{1}{36}$

7. $-6^{-2}=-\frac{1}{6^2}=-\frac{1}{36}$

9. $4^{-1}=\frac{1}{4^1}=\frac{1}{4}$

11. $2^{-1}+3^{-1}=\frac{1}{2^1}+\frac{1}{3^1}=\frac{1}{2}+\frac{1}{3}$
$=\frac{3}{6}+\frac{2}{6}=\frac{5}{6}$

13. $\frac{1}{3^{-2}}=3^2=9$

15. $\frac{1}{(-3)^{-2}}=(-3)^2=9$

17. $\frac{2^{-3}}{8^{-2}}=\frac{8^2}{2^3}=\frac{64}{8}=8$

19. $\left(\frac{1}{4}\right)^{-2}=\frac{1^{-2}}{4^{-2}}=\frac{4^2}{1^2}=\frac{16}{1}=16$

21. $\left(\frac{3}{5}\right)^{-3}=\frac{3^{-3}}{5^{-3}}=\frac{5^3}{3^3}=\frac{125}{27}$

23. $\frac{1}{6x^{-5}}=\frac{1\cdot x^5}{6}=\frac{x^5}{6}$

25. $\frac{x^{-8}}{y^{-1}}=\frac{y^1}{x^8}=\frac{y}{x^8}$

27. $\frac{3}{(-5)^{-3}}=3\cdot(-5)^3=5(-125)=-375$

29. $x^{-8}\cdot x^3=x^{-8+3}=x^{-5}=\frac{1}{x^5}$

31. $(4x^{-5})(2x^2)=8x^{-5+2}=8x^{-3}=\frac{8}{x^3}$

33. $\frac{x^3}{x^9}=x^{3-9}=x^{-6}=\frac{1}{x^6}$

35. $\frac{y}{y^{100}}=\frac{y^1}{y^{100}}=y^{1-100}=y^{-99}=\frac{1}{y^{99}}$

37. $\frac{30z^5}{10z^{10}}=\frac{30}{10}\cdot\frac{z^5}{z^{10}}=3z^{5-10}$
$=-3z^{-5}=\frac{3}{z^5}$

39. $\dfrac{-8x^3}{2x^7} = \dfrac{-8}{2} \cdot \dfrac{x^3}{x^7} = -4x^{-4} = -\dfrac{4}{x^4}$

41. $\dfrac{-9a^5}{27a^8} = \dfrac{-9}{27} \cdot \dfrac{a^5}{a^8} = -\dfrac{1}{3}a^{-3} = -\dfrac{1}{3a^3}$

43. $\dfrac{7w^5}{5w^{13}} = \dfrac{7}{5} \cdot \dfrac{w^5}{w^{13}} = \dfrac{7}{5}w^{-8} = \dfrac{7}{5w^8}$

45. $\dfrac{x^3}{\left(x^4\right)^2} = \dfrac{x^3}{x^{4\cdot 2}} = \dfrac{x^3}{x^8} = x^{-5} = \dfrac{1}{x^5}$

47. $\dfrac{y^{-3}}{\left(y^4\right)^2} = \dfrac{y^{-3}}{y^8} = y^{-3-8} = y^{-11} = \dfrac{1}{y^{11}}$

49. $\dfrac{\left(4x^3\right)^2}{x^8} = \dfrac{4^2x^6}{x^8} = 16x^{-2} = \dfrac{16}{x^2}$

51. $\dfrac{\left(6y^4\right)^3}{y^{-5}} = \dfrac{6^3y^{12}}{y^{-5}} = 216y^{12-(-5)} = 216y^{17}$

53. $\left(\dfrac{x^4}{x^2}\right)^{-3} = \left(x^2\right)^{-3} = x^{-6} = \dfrac{1}{x^6}$

55. $\left(\dfrac{4x^5}{2x^2}\right)^{-4} = \left(2x^3\right)^{-4} = 2^{-4}x^{-12} = \dfrac{1}{2^4x^{12}}$

$= \dfrac{1}{16x^{12}}$

57. $\left(3x^{-1}\right)^{-2} = 3^{-2}\left(x^{-1}\right)^{-2} = 3^{-2}x^2$

$= \dfrac{x^2}{3^2} = \dfrac{x^2}{9}$

59. $\left(-2y^{-1}\right)^{-3} = (-2)^{-3}\left(y^{-1}\right)^{-3} = \dfrac{y^3}{(-2)^3}$

$= \dfrac{y^3}{-8} = -\dfrac{y^3}{8}$

61. $\dfrac{2x^5 \cdot 3x^7}{15x^6} = \dfrac{6x^{12}}{15x^6} = \dfrac{6}{15} \cdot \dfrac{x^{12}}{x^6}$

$= \dfrac{2}{5} \cdot x^6 = \dfrac{2x^6}{5}$

63. $\left(x^3\right)^5 \cdot x^{-7} = x^{15} \cdot x^{-7} = x^{15+(-7)} = x^8$

65. $\left(2y^3\right)^4 y^{-6} = 2^4\left(y^3\right)^4 y^{-6} = 16y^{12}y^{-6}$

$= 16y^6$

67. $\dfrac{\left(y^3\right)^4}{\left(y^2\right)^7} = \dfrac{y^{12}}{y^{14}} = y^{-2} = \dfrac{1}{y^2}$

69. $\left(y^{10}\right)^{-5} = y^{(10)(-5)} = y^{-50} = \dfrac{1}{y^{50}}$

71. $\left(a^4b^5\right)^{-3} = \left(a^4\right)^{-3}\left(b^5\right)^{-3} = a^{-12}b^{-15}$

$= \dfrac{1}{a^{12}b^{15}}$

73. $\left(a^{-2}b^6\right)^{-4} = a^8b^{-24} = \dfrac{a^8}{b^{24}}$

75. $\left(\dfrac{x^2}{2}\right)^{-2} = \dfrac{x^{-4}}{2^{-2}} = \dfrac{2^2}{x^4} = \dfrac{4}{x^4}$

77. $\left(\dfrac{x^2}{y^3}\right)^{-3} = \dfrac{\left(x^2\right)^{-3}}{\left(y^3\right)^{-3}} = \dfrac{x^{-6}}{y^{-9}} = \dfrac{y^9}{x^6}$

79. $8.7\times10^2 = 870$ (Move decimal point 2 places to the right.)

81. $9.23\times10^5 = 923,000$ (Move right 5.)

83. $3.4\times10^0 = 3.4$ (Don't move decimal point.)

85. $7.9\times10^{-1} = 0.79$ (Move left 1.)

87. $2.15\times10^{-2} = 0.0215$ (Move left 2.)

89. $7.86\times10^{-4} = 0.000786$ (Move left 4.)

91. $32,400 = 3.24\times10^4$

93. $220,000,000 = 2.2\times10^8$

95. $713 = 7.13\times10^2$

97. $6751 = 6.751\times10^3$

99. $0.0027 = 2.7\times10^{-3}$

101. $0.000020 = 2.02\times10^{-5}$

103. $0.005 = 5\times10^{-3}$

105. $3.14159 = 3.14159\times10^0$

107. $(2\times10^3)(3\times10^2) = 6\times10^{3+2} = 6\times10^5$

109. $(2\times10^5)(8\times10^3) = 16\times10^{5+3} = 16\times10^8$
$= 1.6\times10^9$

111. $\dfrac{12\times10^6}{4\times10^2} = 3\times10^{6-2} = 3\times10^4$

113. $\dfrac{15\times10^4}{5\times10^{-2}} = 3\times10^{4+2} = 3\times10^6$

115. $\dfrac{15\times10^{-4}}{5\times10^2} = 3\times10^{-4-2} = 3\times10^{-6}$

117. $\dfrac{180\times10^6}{2\times10^3} = 90\times10^{6-3} = 90\times10^3$
$= 9\times10^4$

119. $\dfrac{3\times10^4}{12\times10^{-3}} = 0.25\times10^{4+3} = 0.25\times10^7$
$= 2.5\times10^6$

121. $(5\times10^2)^3 = 5^3\times10^{2(3)} = 125\times10^6$
$= 1.25\times10^8$

123. $(3\times10^{-2})^4 = 3^4\times10^{-2(4)} = 81\times10^{-8}$
$= 8.1\times10^{-7}$

125. $(4\times10^6)^{-1} = 4^{-1}\times10^{6(-1)} = 0.25\times10^{-6}$
$= 2.6\times10^{-7}$

127. $\dfrac{(x^{-2}y)^{-3}}{(x^2y^{-1})^3} = \dfrac{x^6y^{-3}}{x^6y^{-3}}$
$= x^{6-6}y^{-3-(-3)} = x^0y^0 = 1$

128. $\dfrac{(xy^{-2})^{-2}}{(x^{-2}y)^{-3}} = \dfrac{x^{-2}y^4}{x^6y^{-3}}$
$= x^{-2-6}y^{4-(-3)} = x^{-8}y^7 = \dfrac{y^7}{x^8}$

129. $(2x^{-3}yz^{-6})(2x)^{-5} = 2x^{-3}yz^{-6}\cdot2^{-5}x^{\cdot-5}$
$= 2^{-4}x^{-8}yz^{-6} = \dfrac{y}{2^4x^8z^6} = \dfrac{y}{16x^8z^6}$

130. $\left(3x^{-4}yz^{-7}\right)\left(3x\right)^{-3} = 3x^{-4}yz^{-7} \cdot 3^{-3}x^{-3}$

$= 3^{-2}x^{-7}yz^{-7} = \dfrac{y}{3^2x^7z^7} = \dfrac{y}{9x^8z^6}$

131. $\left(\dfrac{x^3y^4z^5}{x^{-3}y^{-4}z^{-5}}\right)^{-2} = \left(x^6y^8z^{10}\right)^{-2}$

$= x^{-12}y^{-16}z^{-20} = \dfrac{1}{x^{12}y^{16}z^{20}}$

132. $\left(\dfrac{x^4y^5z^6}{x^{-4}y^{-5}z^{-6}}\right)^{-4} = \left(x^8y^{10}z^{12}\right)^{-4}$

$= x^{-32}y^{-40}z^{-48} = \dfrac{1}{x^{32}y^{40}z^{48}}$

133. $\dfrac{\left(2^{-1}x^{-2}y^{-1}\right)^{-2}\left(2x^{-4}y^3\right)^{-2}\left(16x^{-3}y^3\right)^0}{\left(2x^{-3}y^{-5}\right)^2}$

$= \dfrac{\left(2^2x^2y^2\right)\left(2^{-2}x^8y^{-6}\right)(1)}{\left(2^2x^{-6}y^{-10}\right)}$

$= \dfrac{x^{18}y^6}{4}$

134. $\dfrac{\left(2^{-1}x^{-3}y^{-1}\right)^{-2}\left(2x^{-6}y^4\right)^{-2}\left(9x^3y^{-3}\right)^0}{\left(2x^{-4}y^{-6}\right)^2}$

$= \dfrac{\left(2^2x^6y^2\right)\left(2^{-2}x^{12}y^{-8}\right)(1)}{\left(2^2x^{-8}y^{-12}\right)}$

$= \dfrac{x^{26}y^6}{4}$

135. $\dfrac{\left(5\times10^3\right)\left(1.2\times10^{-4}\right)}{\left(2.4\times10^2\right)} = 2.5\times10^{-3}$

136. $\dfrac{\left(2\times10^2\right)\left(2.6\times10^{-3}\right)}{\left(4\times10^3\right)} = 1.3\times10^{-4}$

137. $\dfrac{\left(1.6\times10^4\right)\left(7.2\times10^{-3}\right)}{\left(3.6\times10^8\right)\left(4\times10^{-3}\right)} = 0.8\times10^{-4} = 8\times10^{-5}$

138. $\dfrac{\left(1.2\times10^6\right)\left(8.7\times10^{-2}\right)}{\left(2.9\times10^6\right)\left(3\times10^{-3}\right)} = 1.2\times10^1$

139. $9200 = 9.2\times10^3$

141. $0.0000000000000000025 = 2.5\times10^{-16}$

143. $600\times10^6 = 6\times10^2\times10^6 = 6\times10^8$

145. $399\times10^9 = 3.99\times10^2\times10^9 = 3.99\times10^{11}$

147. $20\%\left(2\times10^{12}\right) = 0.2\left(2\times10^{12}\right)$

$= 2\times10^{-1}\left(2\times10^{12}\right) = 4\times10^{11}$

The government spends $\$4\times10^{11}$.

149. $120\left(2.9\times10^8\right) = 348\times10^8$

$= 3.48\times10^2\times10^8 = 3.48\times10^{10}$

The total annual spending in the United States on ice cream is about $\$3.48\times10^{10}$.

151. $\dfrac{2.325\times10^5}{1.86\times10^5} = 1.25$ seconds

153. When moving a base and exponent from numerator to denominator, keep the base and switch the sign of the exponent.

Example: $\dfrac{x^2}{y^{-3}} = \dfrac{y^3}{x^{-2}}$

155. The number will be written as a number between 1 and 10 (not including 10) times a power of 10.

157. If the number is greater than 1 or less than -1, move the decimal point so it is immediately following the first nonzero digit in the number and raise 10 to the number of places the decimal point moved.

If the number is between –1 and 1, move the decimal point so it is immediately following the first nonzero digit in the number and raise 10 to the negative of the number of places the decimal point moved.

Example:
$123.4567 = 1.234567 \times 10^2$
$0.0001234567 = 1.234567 \times 10^{-4}$

159. Statement b is true.

$5^{-2} = \frac{1}{25}$ and $2^{-5} = \frac{1}{32}$

Since $\frac{1}{25} > \frac{1}{32}$, $5^{-2} > 2^{-5}$

161. There is no advantage in using scientific notation to represent a number greater than or equal to 1 and less than 10 because the decimal point will not b moved and it is simpler to write it without the zero exponent.

Example: $7.75 = 7.75 \times 10^0$

163. Students will check their work with a calculator. Results will depend on the exercises chosen.

165. Students will check their work with a calculator. Results will depend on the exercises chosen.

167. Let x = the number of deer in the park.

$$\frac{\text{Original number of tagged deer}}{\text{Total number of deer}} = \frac{\text{Number of tagged deer in sample}}{\text{Number of deer in sample}}$$

$$\frac{25}{x} = \frac{4}{36}$$
$$4x = 900$$
$$x = 225$$

There are approximately 225 deer in the park.

168. $24 \div 8 \cdot 3 + 28 \div (-7) = 3 \cdot 3 + 28 \div (-7)$
$= 9 + (-4) = 5$

169. The whole numbers in the given set are 0 and $\sqrt{16}\,(=4)$.

Chapter 6 Review Exercises

1. $7x^4 + 9x$ is a binomial of degree 4.

2. $3x + 5x^2 - 2$ is a trinomial of degree 2.

3. $16x$ is a monomial of degree 1.

4. $(-6x^3 + 7x^2 - 9x + 3)$
$+(14x^3 + 3x^2 - 11x - 7)$
$= (-6x^3 + 14x^3) + (7x^2 + 3x^2)$
$+(-9x - 11x) + (3 - 7)$
$= 8x^3 + 10x^2 - 20x - 4$

5. $(9y^3-7y^2+5)+(4y^3-y^2+7y-10)$
$=(9y^3+4y^3)+(-7y^2-y^2)+7y$
$+(5-10)$
$=13y^3-8y^2+7y-5$

6. $(5y^2-y-8)-(-6y^2+3y-4)$
$=(5y^2-y-8)+(6y^2-3y+4)$
$=(5y^2+6y^2)+(-y-3y)+(-8+4)$
$=11y^2-4y-4$

7. $(13x^4-8x^3+2x^2)-(5x^4-3x^3+2x^2-6)$
$=(13x^4-8x^3+2x^2)$
$+(-5x^4+3x^3-2x^2+6)$
$=(13x^4-5x^4)+(-8x^3+3x^3)$
$+(2x^2-2x^2)+6$
$=8x^4-5x^3+6$

8. $(-13x^4-6x^2+5x)-(x^4+7x^2-11x)$
$=(-13x^4-6x^2+5x)$
$+(-x^4-7x^2+11x)$
$=(-13x^4-x^4)+(-6x^2-7x^2)$
$+(5x+11x)$
$=-14x^4-13x^2+16x$

9. Add:

$$\begin{array}{r} 7y^4-6y^3+4y^2-4y \\ \underline{y^3-\ \ y^2+3y-4} \\ 7y^4-5y^3+3y^2-\ \ y-4 \end{array}$$

10. Subtract:

$$\begin{array}{r} 7x^2-9x+2 \\ \underline{-(4x^2-2x-7)} \end{array}$$

Add:

$$\begin{array}{r} 7x^2-9x+2 \\ \underline{-4x^2+2x+7} \\ 3x^2-7x+9 \end{array}$$

11.

$$\begin{array}{r} 5x^3-6x^2-\ \ 9x+14 \\ \underline{-(-5x^3+3x^2-11x+\ \ 3)} \end{array}$$

Add:

$$\begin{array}{r} 5x^3-6x^2-\ \ 9x+14 \\ \underline{5x^3-3x^2+11x-\ \ 3} \\ 10x^3-9x^2+\ \ 2x+11 \end{array}$$

12. $104.5x^2-1501.5x+6016;\ x=10$

$104.5x^2-1501.5x+6016$
$=104.5(10)^2-1501.5(10)+6016$
$=10,450-15,015+6016$
$=1451$

The death rate for men averaging 10 hours of sleep per night is 1451 men per 10,000 men.

13. $x^{20}\cdot x^3=x^{20+3}=x^{23}$

14. $y\cdot y^5\cdot y^8=y^1\cdot y^5\cdot y^8=y^{1+5+8}=y^{14}$

15. $(x^{20})^5=x^{20\cdot 5}=x^{100}$

16. $(10y)^2=10^2y^2=100y^2$

17. $\left(-4x^{10}\right)^3 = (-4)^3\left(x^{10}\right)^3 = -64x^{30}$

18. $(5x)\left(10x^3\right) = (5\cdot 10)\left(x^1\cdot x^3\right) = 50x^4$

19. $\left(-12y^7\right)\left(3y^4\right) = -36y^{11}$

20. $\left(-2x^5\right)\left(-3x^4\right)\left(5x^3\right) = 30x^{12}$

21. $7x\left(3x^2+9\right) = 7x\left(3x^2\right)+(7x)(9)$
$= 21x^3+63x$

22. $5x^3\left(4x^2-11x\right) = 5x^3\left(4x^2\right)-5x^3(11x)$
$= 20x^5-55x^4$

23. $3y^2\left(-7y^2+3y-6\right)$
$= 3y^2\left(-7y^2\right)+3y^2(3y)+3y^2(-6)$
$= -21y^4+9y^3-18y^2$

24. $2y^5\left(8y^3-10y^2+1\right)$
$= 2y^5\left(8y^3\right)+2y^5\left(-10y^2\right)+2y^5(1)$
$= 16y^8-20y^7+2y^5$

25. $(x+3)\left(x^2-5x+2\right)$
$= x\left(x^2-5x+2\right)+3\left(x^2-5x+2\right)$
$= x^3-5x^2+2x+3x^2-15x+6$
$= x^3-2x^2-13x+6$

26. $(3y-2)\left(4y^2+3y-5\right)$
$= 3y\left(4y^2+3y-5\right)-2\left(4y^2+3y-5\right)$
$= 12y^3+9y^2-15y-8y^2-6y+10$
$= 12y^3+y^2-21y+10$

27.
$$\begin{array}{r} y^2-4y+7 \\ 3y-5 \\ \hline -5y^2+20y-35 \\ 3y^3-12y^2+21y \quad\quad \\ \hline 3y^3-17y^2+41y-35 \end{array}$$

28.
$$\begin{array}{r} 4x^3-2x^2-6x-1 \\ 2x+3 \\ \hline 12x^3-6x^2-18x-3 \\ 8x^4-4x^3-12x^2-2x \quad\quad \\ \hline 8x^4+8x^3-18x^2-20x-3 \end{array}$$

29. $(x+6)(x+2)$
$= x\cdot x+x\cdot 2+6\cdot x+6\cdot 2$
$= x^2+2x+6x+12$
$= x^2+8x+12$

30. $(3y-5)(2y+1) = 6y^2+3y-10y-5$
$= 6y^2-7y-5$

31. $\left(4x^2-2\right)\left(x^2-3\right)$
$= 4x^2\cdot x^2+4x^2(-3)-2\cdot x^2-2(-3)$
$= 4x^4-12x^2-2x^2+6$
$= 4x^4-14x^2+6$

32. $(5x+4)(5x-4) = (5x)^2-4^2$
$= 25x^2-16$

33. $(7-2y)(7+2y) = 7^2-(2y)^2 = 49-4y^2$

34. $\left(y^2+1\right)\left(y^2-1\right) = \left(y^2\right)^2-1^2 = y^4-1$

35. $(x+3)^2 = x^2+2(x)(3)+3^2$
$= x^2+6x+9$

36. $(3y+4)^2 = (3y)^2 + 2(3y)(4) + 16$
$= 9y^2 + 24y + 16$

37. $(y-1)^2 = y^2 - 2y + 1$

38. $(5y-2)^2 = (5y)^2 - 2(5y)(2) + 2^2$
$= 25y^2 - 20y + 4$

39. $(x^2+4)^2 = (x^2)^2 + 2(x^2)(4) + 4^2$
$= x^4 + 8x^2 + 16$

40. $(x^2+4)(x^2-4) = (x^2)^2 - 4^2 = x^4 - 16$

41. $(x^2+4)(x^2-5) = (x^2)^2 - 5x^2 + 4x^2 - 20$
$= x^4 - x^2 - 20$

42. $A = (x+3)(x+4)$
$= x^2 + 4x + 3x + 12$
$= x^2 + 7x + 12$

43. $A = (x+30)(x+20)$
$= x^2 + 20x + 30x + 600$
$= x^2 + 50x + 600$
The area of the expanded garage is $(x^2 + 50x + 500)$ yards^2.

44. $2x^3y - 4xy^2 + 5y + 6;\ x = -1,\ y = 2$
$2x^3y - 4xy^2 + 5y + 6$
$= 2(-1)^3(2) - 4(-1)(2)^2 + 5(2) + 6$
$= 2(-1)(2) + 4(1)(4) + 5(2) + 6$
$= -4 + 16 + 10 + 6 = 28$

45.

Term	Coefficient	Degree
$4x^2y$	4	2+1=3
$9x^3y^2$	9	3+2=5
$-17x^4$	−17	4
−12	−12	0

Degree of the polynomial = 5

46. $(7x^2 - 8xy + y^2) + (-8x^2 - 9xy + 4y^2)$
$= (7x^2 - 8x^2) + (-8xy - 9xy)$
$+ (y^2 + 4y^2)$
$= -x^2 - 17xy + 5y^2$

47. $(13x^3y^2 - 5x^2y - 9x^2)$
$-(11x^3y^2 - 6x^2y - 3x^2 + 4)$
$= (13x^3y^2 - 5x^2y - 9x^2)$
$+(-11x^3y^2 + 6x^2y + 3x^2 - 4)$
$= (13x^3y^2 - 11x^3y^2) + (-5x^2y + 6x^2y)$
$+(-9x^2 + 3x^2) - 4$
$= 2x^3y^3 + x^2y - 6x^2 - 4$

48. $(-7x^2y^3)(5x^4y^6)$
$= (-7)(-5)x^{2+4}y^{3+6}$
$= -35x^6y^9$

49. $5ab^2(3a^2b^3 - 4ab)$
$= 5ab^2(3a^2b^3) + 5ab^2(-4ab)$
$= 15a^3b^5 - 20a^2b^3$

50. $(x+7y)(3x-5y)$
$= x(3x) + x(-5y) + 7y(3x) + 7y(-5y)$
$= 3x^2 - 5xy + 21xy - 35y^2$
$= 3x^2 + 16xy - 35y^2$

51. $$\begin{aligned}(4xy-3)(9xy-1) &= 4xy(9xy)+4xy(-1)-3(9xy)-3(-1)\\ &= 36x^2y^2-4xy-27xy+3\\ &= 36x^2y^2-31xy+3\end{aligned}$$

52. $$\begin{aligned}(3x+5y)^2 &= (3x)^2+2(3x)(5y)+(5y)^2\\ &= 9x^2+30xy+25y^2\end{aligned}$$

53. $$\begin{aligned}(xy-7)^2 &= (xy)^2-2(xy)(7)+7^2\\ &= x^2y^2-14xy+49\end{aligned}$$

54. $$\begin{aligned}(7x+4y)(7x-4y) &= (7x)^2-(4y)^2\\ &= 49x^2-16y^2\end{aligned}$$

55. $$\begin{aligned}&(a-b)(a^2+ab+b^2)\\ &= a(a^2+ab+b^2)-b(a^2+ab+b^2)\\ &= a^3+a^2b+ab^2-a^2b-ab^2-b^3\\ &= a^3+(a^2b-a^2b)+(ab^2-ab^2)-b^3\\ &= a^3-b^3\end{aligned}$$

56. $$\frac{6^{40}}{6^{10}} = 6^{40-10} = 6^{30}$$

57. $$\frac{x^{18}}{x^3} = x^{18-x} = x^{15}$$

58. $$(-10)^0 = 1$$

59. $$-10^0 = -(1) = -1$$

60. $$400x^0 = 400\cdot 1 = 400$$

61. $$\left(\frac{x^4}{2}\right)^3 = \frac{(x^4)^3}{2^3} = \frac{x^{4\cdot 3}}{8} = \frac{x^{12}}{8}$$

62. $$\left(\frac{-3}{2y^6}\right)^4 = \frac{(-3)^4}{(2y^6)^4} = \frac{81}{(2^4y^6)^4} = \frac{81}{16y^{24}}$$

63. $$\frac{-15y^8}{3y^2} = \frac{-15}{3}\cdot\frac{y^8}{y^2} = -5y^6$$

64. $$\frac{40x^8y^6}{5xy^3} = \frac{40}{5}\cdot\frac{x^8}{x^1}\cdot\frac{y^6}{y^3} = 5x^7y^3$$

65. $$\begin{aligned}\frac{18x^4-12x^2+36x}{6x} &= \frac{18x^4}{6x}-\frac{12x^2}{6x}+\frac{36x}{6x}\\ &= 3x^2-2x+6\end{aligned}$$

66. $$\begin{aligned}&\frac{30x^8-25x^7-40x^5}{-5x^3}\\ &= \frac{30x^8}{-5x^3}-\frac{25x^7}{-5x^3}-\frac{40x^5}{-5x^3}\\ &= -6x^5+5x^4+8x^2\end{aligned}$$

67. $$\begin{aligned}&\frac{27x^3y^2-9x^2y-18xy^2}{3xy}\\ &= \frac{27x^3y^2}{3xy}-\frac{9x^2y}{3xy}-\frac{18xy^2}{3xy}\\ &= 9x^2-3x-6y\end{aligned}$$

68. $$\begin{array}{r} 2x+7 \\ x-2\overline{)2x^2+3x-14} \\ \underline{2x^2-4x} \\ 7x-14 \\ \underline{7x-14} \\ 0 \end{array}$$

$$\frac{2x^2+3x-14}{x-2} = 2x+7$$

69.

$$\begin{array}{r}
x^2-3x+5 \\
2x+1\overline{)2x^3-5x^2+7x+5} \\
\underline{2x^3+\ \ x^2} \qquad\qquad \\
-6x^2+7x \qquad \\
\underline{-6x^2-3x} \qquad \\
10x+5 \\
\underline{10x+5} \\
0
\end{array}$$

$$\frac{2x^3-5x^2+7x+5}{2x+1}=x^2-3x+5$$

70.

$$\begin{array}{r}
x^2+5x+2 \\
x-7\overline{)x^3-2x^2-33x-7} \\
\underline{x^3-7x^2} \qquad\qquad \\
5x^2-33x \qquad \\
\underline{5x^2-35x} \qquad \\
2x-\ \ 7 \\
\underline{2x-14} \\
7
\end{array}$$

$$\frac{x^3-2x^2-33x-7}{x-7}=x^2+5x+2+\frac{7}{x-7}$$

71.

$$\begin{array}{r}
y^2+3y+9 \\
y-3\overline{)y^3+0y^2+0y-27} \\
\underline{y^3-3y^2} \qquad\qquad \\
3y^2+0y \qquad \\
\underline{3y^2-9y} \qquad \\
9y-27 \\
\underline{9y-27} \\
0
\end{array}$$

$$\frac{y^2-27}{y-3}=y^2+3y+9$$

72. $7^{-2}=\frac{1}{7^2}=\frac{1}{49}$

73. $(-4)^{-3}=\frac{1}{(-4)^3}=\frac{1}{-64}=-\frac{1}{64}$

74. $2^{-1}+4^{-1}=\frac{1}{2}+\frac{1}{4}=\frac{3}{4}$

75. $\frac{1}{5^{-2}}=5^2=25$

76. $\left(\frac{2}{5}\right)^{-3}=\frac{2^{-3}}{5^{-3}}=\frac{5^3}{2^3}=\frac{125}{8}$

77. $\frac{x^3}{x^9}=x^{3-9}=x^{-6}=\frac{1}{x^6}$

78. $\frac{30y^6}{5y^8}=\frac{30}{5}\cdot\frac{y^6}{y^8}=6y^{-2}=\frac{6}{y^2}$

79. $(5x^{-7})(6x^2)=(5\cdot 6)(x^{-7+2})$
$=30x^{-5}=\frac{30}{x^5}$

80. $\frac{x^4\cdot x^{-2}}{x^{-6}}=\frac{x^{4+(-2)}}{x^{-6}}=\frac{x^2}{x^{-6}}$
$=x^{2-(-6)}=x^8$

81. $\frac{(3y^3)^4}{y^{10}}=\frac{3^4y^{3(4)}}{y^{10}}=\frac{81y^{12}}{y^{10}}$
$=81y^{12-10}=81y^2$

82. $\frac{y^{-7}}{(y^4)^3}=\frac{y^{-7}}{y^{12}}=y^{-7-12}=y^{-19}=\frac{1}{y^{19}}$

83. $(2x^{-1})^{-3} = 2^{-3}(x^{-1})^{-3} = 2^{-3}x^3$
$= \frac{x^3}{2^{-3}} = \frac{x^3}{8}$

84. $\left(\frac{x^7}{x^4}\right)^{-2} = (x^3)^{-2} = x^{-6} = \frac{1}{x^6}$

85. $\frac{(y^3)^4}{(y^{-2})^4} = \frac{y^{12}}{y^{-8}} = y^{12-(-8)} = y^{20}$

86. $2.3\times10^4 = 23,000$
(Move decimal point to right 4 places.)

87. $1.76\times10^{-3} = 0.00176$ (Move left 3 places.)

88. $9\times10^{-1} = 0.9$

89. $73,900,000 = 7.39\times10^7$

90. $0.00062 = 6.2\times10^{-4}$

91. $0.38 = 3.8\times10^{-1}$

92. $3.8 = 3.8\times10^0$

93. $(6\times10^{-3})(1.5\times10^6) = 6(1.5)\times10^{-3+6}$
$= 9\times10^3$

94. $\frac{2\times10^2}{4\times10^{-3}} = 0.5\cdot10^{2+3} = 0.5\times10^5$
$= 5\times10^{-1}\times10^5$
$= 5.0\times10^4$

95. $(4\times10^{-2}) = 4^2\times10^{-2(2)} = 16\times10^{-4}$
$= 1.6\times10^1\times10^{-4} = 1.6\times10^{1-4}$
$= 1.6\times10^{-3}$

96. $\frac{10^{-6}}{10^{-9}} = \frac{10^9}{10^6} = 10^{9-6} = 10^3 = 1000$
There are 1000 nanoseconds in a microsecond.

97. $2(6.3\times10^9) = 12.6\times10^9 = 1.26\times10^{10}$

In 40 years, there will be approximately 1.26×10^{10} people in the world.

Chapter 6 Test

1. $9x + 6x^2 - 4$ is a trinomial of degree 2.

2. $(7x^3 + 3x^2 - 5x - 11)$
$+(6x^3 - 2x^2 + 4x - 13)$
$= (7x^3 + 6x^3) + (3x^2 - 2x^2)$
$+(-5x + 4x) + (-11 - 13)$
$= 13x^3 + x^2 - x - 24$

3. $(9x^3 - 6x^2 - 11x - 4)$
$-(4x^3 - 8x^2 - 13x + 5)$
$= (9x^3 - 6x^2 - 11x - 4)$
$+(-4x^3 + 8x^2 + 13x - 5)$
$= (9x^3 - 4x^3) + (-6x^2 + 8x^2)$
$+(-11x + 13x) + (-4 - 5)$
$= 5x^3 + 2x^2 + 2x - 9$

4. $(-7x^3)(5x^8) = (-7\cdot5)(x^{3+8}) = -35x^{11}$

5. $6x^2(8x^3 - 5x - 2)$
$= 6x^2(8x^3) + 6x^2(-5x) + 6x^2(-2)$
$= 48x^5 - 30x^3 - 12x^2$

6. $(3x+2)(x^2-4x-3)$
$= 3x(x^2-4x-3)+2(x^2-4x-3)$
$= 3x^3-12x^2-9x+2x^2-8x-6$
$= 3x^3-10x^2-17x-6$

7. $(3y+7)(2y-9)=6y^2+14y-27y-63$
$=6y^2-13y-63$

8. $(7x+5)(7x-5)=(7x)^2-5^2=49x^2-25$

9. $(x^2+3)^2=(x^2)^2+2(x^2)(3)+3^2$
$=x^4+6x^2+9$

10. $(5x-3)^2=(5x)^2-2(5x)(3)+3^2$
$=25x^2-30x+9$

11. $4x^2y+5xy-6x;\ x=-2,\ y=3$
$4x^2y+5xy-6x$
$=4(-2)^2(3)+5(-2)(3)-6(-2)$
$=4(4)(3)+5(-2)(3)-6(-2)$
$=48-30+12=30$

12. $(8x^2y^3-xy+2y^2)-(6x^2y^3-4xy-10y^2)$
$=(8x^2y^3-xy+2y^2)$
$\quad+(-6x^2y^3+4xy+10y^2)$
$=(8x^2y^3-6x^2y^3)+(-xy+4xy)$
$\quad+(2y^2+10y^2)$
$=2x^2y^3+3xy+12y^2$

13. $(3a-7b)(4a+5b)$
$=(3a)(4a)+(3a)(5b)-(7b)(4a)$
$\quad-(7b)(5b)$
$=12a^2+15ab-28ab-35b^2$
$=12a^2-13ab-35b^2$

14. $(2x+3y)^2=(2x)^2+2(2x)(3y)+(3y)^2$
$=4x^2+12xy+9y^2$

15. $\dfrac{-25x^{16}}{5x^4}=\dfrac{-25}{5}\cdot\dfrac{x^{16}}{x^4}=-5x^{16-4}$
$=-5x^{12}$

Check by multiplication:
$5x^4(-5x^{12})=-25x^{4+12}=-25x^{16}$

16. $\dfrac{15x^4-10x^3+25x^2}{5x}$
$=\dfrac{15x^4}{5x}-\dfrac{10x^3}{5x}+\dfrac{25x^2}{5x}$
$=3x^3-2x^2+5x$

Check by multiplication:
$5x(3x^3-2x^2+5x)$
$=5x(3x^3)+5x(-2x^2)+5x(5x)$
$=15x^4-10x^3+25x^2$

17.

$$\begin{array}{r} x^2-2x+3 \\ 2x+1\overline{)2x^3-3x^2+4x+4} \\ \underline{2x^3+\ x^2} \\ -4x^2+4x \\ \underline{-4x^2-2x} \\ 6x+4 \\ \underline{6x+3} \\ 1 \end{array}$$

$$\frac{2x^3-3x^2+4x+4}{2x+1}=x^2-2x+3+\frac{1}{2x+1}$$

Check by multiplication:

$$\begin{aligned}&(2x+1)(x^2-2x+3)+1\\ &=\left[2x(x^2-2x+3)+1(x^2-2x+3)\right]+1\\ &=(2x^3-4x^2+6x+x^2-2x+3)+1\\ &=(2x^3-3x^2+4x+3)+1\\ &=2x^3-3x^2+4x+4\end{aligned}$$

18. $10^{-2}=\dfrac{1}{10^2}=\dfrac{1}{100}$

19. $\dfrac{1}{4^{-3}}=1\cdot 4^3=4^3=64$

20. $(-3x^2)^3=(-3)^3(x^2)^3=-27x^6$

21. $\dfrac{20x^3}{5x^8}=\dfrac{4}{x^5}$

22. $(-7x^{-8})(3x^2)=-21x^{-8+2}=-\dfrac{21}{x^6}$

23. $\dfrac{(2y^3)^4}{y^8}=\dfrac{2^4(y^3)^4}{y^8}=\dfrac{16y^{12}}{y^8}=16y^4$

24.

$$\begin{aligned}(5x^{-4})^{-2}&=5^{-2}(x^{-4})^{-2}=5^{-2}x^8\\ &=\frac{x^8}{5^2}=\frac{x^8}{25}\end{aligned}$$

25.

$$\begin{aligned}\left(\frac{x^{10}}{x^5}\right)^{-3}&=(x^{10-5})^{-3}=(x^5)^{-3}\\ &=x^{-15}=\frac{1}{x^{15}}\end{aligned}$$

26. $3.7\times10^{-4}=0.00037$

27. $7{,}600{,}000=7.6\times10^6$

28.

$$\begin{aligned}&(4.1\times10^2)(3\times10^{-5})\\ &=(4.1\cdot3)(10^2\cdot10^{-5})\\ &=12.3\times10^{-3}\\ &=1.23\times10^{-2}\end{aligned}$$

29.

$$\begin{aligned}\frac{8.4\times10^6}{4\times10^{-2}}&=\frac{8.4}{4}\times\frac{10^6}{10^{-2}}\\ &=2.1\times10^{6-(-2)}\\ &=2.1\times10^8\end{aligned}$$

30.

$$\begin{aligned}A&=(x+8)(x+2)\\ &=x^2+2x+8x+16\\ &=x^2+10x+16\end{aligned}$$

Chapter 6 Cumulative Review Exercises (Chapters 1-6)

1.

$$\begin{aligned}(-7)(-5)\div(12-3)&=(-7)(-5)\div9\\ &=35\div9=\frac{35}{9}\end{aligned}$$

2.

$$\begin{aligned}(3-7)^2(9-11)^3&=(-4)^2(-2)^3\\ &=16(-8)=-128\end{aligned}$$

3. $14,300-(-750)=14,300+750$
$$=15,050$$
The difference in elevation between the plane and the submarine is 15,050 feet.

4.
$$2(x+3)+2x=x+4$$
$$2x+6+2x=x+4$$
$$4x+6=x+4$$
$$3x+6=4$$
$$3x=-2$$
$$x=-\frac{2}{3}$$
The solution is $-\frac{2}{3}$.

5. $\frac{x}{5}-\frac{1}{3}=\frac{x}{10}-\frac{1}{2}$
To clear fractions, multiply by the LCD = 30.
$$30\left(\frac{x}{5}-\frac{1}{3}\right)=30\left(\frac{x}{10}-\frac{1}{2}\right)$$
$$30\left(\frac{x}{5}\right)-30\left(\frac{1}{3}\right)=30\left(\frac{x}{10}\right)-30\left(\frac{1}{2}\right)$$
$$6x-10=3x-15$$
$$3x-10=-15$$
$$3x=-5$$
$$x=-\frac{5}{3}$$
The solution is $-\frac{5}{3}$.

6. Let x = width of sign.
Then $3x$ - 2 = length of sign.
$$2x+2(3x-2)=28$$
$$2x+6x-4=28$$
$$8x-4=28$$
$$8x=32$$
$$x=4$$
$$3x-2=3(4)-2=10$$
The length of the sign is 10 feet and the width is 4 feet, so the dimensions are 10 feet by 4 feet.

7.
$$7-8x\le -6x-5$$
$$7-8x+6x\le -6x-5+6x$$
$$-2x+7\le -5$$
$$-2x+7-7\le -5-7$$
$$-2x\le -12$$
$$\frac{-2x}{-2}\ge\frac{-12}{-2}$$
$$x\ge 6$$
$\{x|x\ge 6\}$

8.

	Rate ·	Time =	Distance
You	13	x	$13x$
Friend	11	x	$11x$

$$13x+11x=72$$
$$24x=72$$
$$x=3$$
It will take 3 hours to meet.

9. Let x = the number of pounds of fertilizer needed to cover 26,000 square feet.

$$\frac{20 \text{ pounds}}{5000 \text{ square feet}} = \frac{x \text{ pounds}}{26{,}000 \text{ square feet}}$$

$$\frac{20}{5000} = \frac{x}{26{,}000}$$

$$5000x = 20(26{,}000)$$

$$500x = 520{,}000$$

$$\frac{5000x}{5000} = \frac{520{,}000}{5000}$$

$$x = 104$$

To cover an area of 26,000 square feet, 104 pounds of fertilizer are needed.

$$\frac{104}{20} = 5.2$$

Since the fertilizer is sold in 20-pound bags and you cannot buy a fraction of a bag, 6 bags of fertilizer are needed.

10. $y = -\frac{2}{5}x + 2$

slope = $-\frac{2}{5} = \frac{-2}{5}$; y-intercept = 2

Plot (0,2). Move 2 units *down* (since −2 is negative) and 5 units to the *right* to reach the point (5,0).

Draw a line through (0,2) and (5,0).

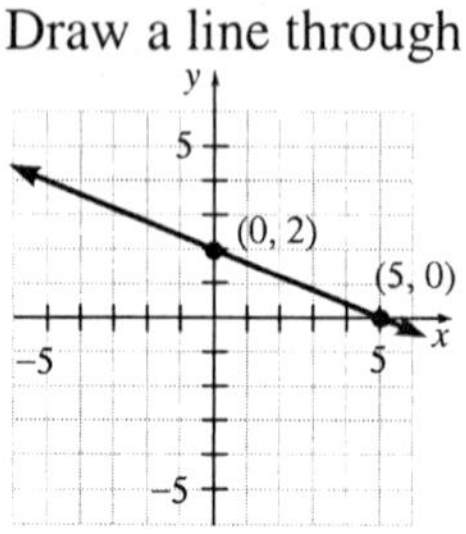

11. $x - 2y = 4$

x-intercept: 4

y-intercept: −2

checkpoint: (−2, −3)

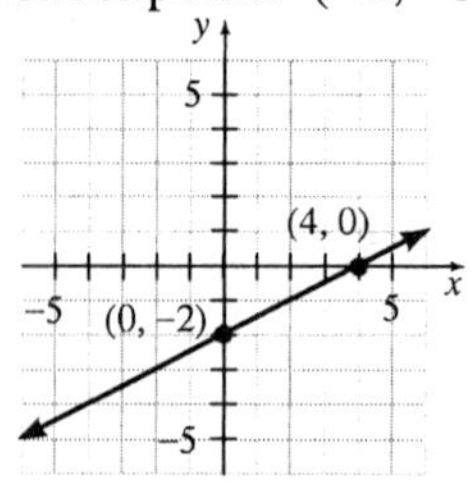

12. (−3,2) and (2, −4)

$$m = \frac{y_2 - y_1}{x_2 - x_1}$$

$$= \frac{-4-2}{2-(-3)} = \frac{-6}{5} = -\frac{6}{5}$$

Because the slope is negative, the line is falling.

13.

$$y-(-1) = -2(x-3)$$

$$y+1 = -2x+6$$

$$y = -2x+5$$

14.

$$3x + 2y = 10$$

$$4x - 3y = -15$$

Multiply the first equation by 3 and the second equation by −2:

$$9x + 6y = 30$$

$$8x - 6y = -30$$

$$17x + 0y = 0$$

$$17x = 0$$

$$x = 0$$

Back-substitute $x = 0$ to find y:

$$3(0) + 2y = 10$$

$$2y = 10$$

$$y = 5$$

The solution is (0, 5).

15. $2x + 3y = -6$

$y = 3x - 13$

Substitute the second equation in for y in the first equation:

$$2x+3y=-6$$
$$2x+3(3x-13)=-6$$
$$2x+9x-39=-6$$
$$11x-39=-6$$
$$11x=33$$
$$x=3$$

Back-substitute $x=3$ to find y:

$y=3x-13=3(3)-13=-4$

The solution is (3, -4).

16. Let y = total charge.
Let x = # of minutes.

Plan A: $y=0.05x+15$

Plan B: $y=0.07x+5$

To find when the plans are the same, substitute the second equation into the first equation:

$$0.07x+5=0.05x+15$$
$$0.02x+5=15$$
$$0.02x=10$$
$$x=500$$

Back-substitute to find y:

$y=0.07x+5=0.07(500)+5=40$

The plans will be the same for 500 minutes at $40 a plan.

17. $2x+5y\le 10$

$x-y\ge 4$

Graph $2x+5y\le 10$:

Graph $2x+5y=10$ as a solid line using its x-intercept, 5 and y-intercept, 2. Since $2(0)+5(0)\le 10$ is true, shade the half-plane containing (0,0).

Graph $x-y\ge 4$:

Graph $x-y=4$ as a solid line using its x-intercept, 4 and y-intercept, -4. Since $0-0\ge 4$ is false, shade the half-plane *not* containing (0,0).

The solution set of the system is the intersection of the two shaded regions.

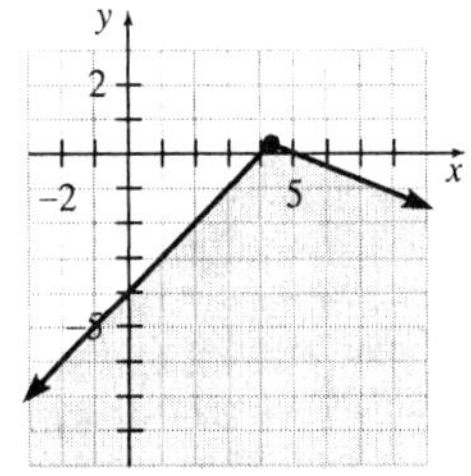

18. $(9x^5-3x^3+2x-7)-(6x^5+3x^3-7x-9)$

$=(9x^5-3x^3+2x-7)$
$\quad+(-6x^5-3x^3+7x+9)$

$=(9x^5-6x^5)+(-3x^3-3x^3)+(2x+7x)$
$\quad+(-7+9)$

$=3x^5-6x^3+9x+2$

19.

$$\begin{array}{r|l} & x^2+2x+3 \\ x+1 & x^3+3x^2+5x+3 \\ & \underline{x^3+x^2} \\ & 2x^2+5x \\ & \underline{2x^2+2x} \\ & 3x+3 \\ & \underline{3x+3} \\ & 0 \end{array}$$

$$\frac{x^3+3x^2+5x+3}{x+1}=x^2+2x+3$$

20. $\dfrac{(3x^2)^4}{x^{10}}=\dfrac{3^4(x^2)^4}{x^{10}}-\dfrac{81x^8}{x^{10}}$

$=81x^{8-10}=81x^{-2}=\dfrac{81}{x^2}$

Chapter 7
Factoring Polynomials

7.1 Exercise Set

1. Possible answers:
$8x^3 = (2x)(4x^2)$
$8x^3 = (4x)(2x^2)$
$8x^3 = (8x)(x^2)$

3. Possible answers:
$-12x^5 = (-4x^3)(3x^2)$
$-12x^5 = (2x^2)(-6x^3)$
$-12x^5 = (-3)(4x^5)$

5. Possible answers:
$36x^4 = (6x^2)(6x^2)$
$36x^4 = (-2x)(-18x^3)$
$36x^4 = (4x^3)(9x)$

7. The GCF (greatest common factor) of 4 and $8x$ is 4.

9. $12x^2 + 8x$
Since 4 is the numerical coefficient of the GCF, and x is the variable factor of the GCF, the GCF of $12x^2$ and $8x$ is $4x$.

11. The GCF of $-2x^4$ and $6x^3$ is $2x^3$.

13. The GCF of $9y^5, 18y^2$, and $-3y$ is $3y$.

15. The GCF of xy, xy^2, and xy^3 is xy.

17. The GCF of $16x^5y^4, 8x^6y^3$, and $20x^4y^5$ is $4x^4y^3$.

19. $8x + 8 = 8 \cdot x + 8 \cdot 1$
$= 8(x+1)$

21. $4y - 4 = 4 \cdot y - 4 \cdot 1$
$= 4(y-1)$

23. $5x + 30 = 5 \cdot x + 5 \cdot 6$
$= 5(x+6)$

25. $30x - 12 = 6 \cdot 5x - 6 \cdot 2$
$= 6(5x-2)$

27. $x^2 + 5x = x \cdot x + x \cdot 5$
$= x(x+5)$

29. $18y^2 + 12 = 6 \cdot 3y^2 + 6 \cdot 2$
$= 6(3y^2+2)$

31. $14x^3 + 21x^2 = 7x^2 \cdot 2x + 7x^2 \cdot 3$
$= 7x^2(2x+3)$

33. $13y^2 - 25y = y \cdot 13y - y \cdot 25$
$= y(13y-25)$

35. $9y^4 + 27y^6 = 9y^4 \cdot 1 + 9y^4 \cdot 3y^2$
$= 9y^4(1+3y^2)$

37. $8x^2 - 4x^4 = 4x^2(2) - 4x^2(x^2)$
$= 4x^2(2-x^2)$

39. $12y^2+16y-8=4(3y^2)+4(4y)-4(2)$
$=4(3y^2+4y-2)$

41. $9x^4+18x^3+6x^2$
$=3x^2(3x^2)+3x^2(6x)+3x^2(2)$
$=3x^2(3x^2+6x+2)$

43. $100y^5-50y^3+100y^2$
$=50y^2(2y^3)-50y^2(y)+50y^2(2)$
$=50y^2(2y^3-y+2)$

45. $10x-20x^2+5x^3$
$=5x(2)-5x(4x)+5x(x^2)$
$=5x(2-4x+x^2)$

47. $11x^2-23$ cannot be factored because the two terms have no common factor other than 1.

49. $6x^3y^2+9xy=3xy(2x^2+y)+3xy(3)$
$=3xy(2x^2y+3)$

51. $30x^2y^2-10xy^2+20xy$
$=10xy(3xy^2)-10xy(y)+10xy(2)$
$=10xy(3xy^2-y+2)$

53. $32x^3y^2-24x^3y-16x^2y$
$=8x^2y(4xy)-8x^2y(3x)-8x^2y(2)$
$=8x^2y(4xy-3x-2)$

55. $x(x+5)+3(x+5)=(x+5)(x+3)$
Here, $(x+5)$ is the greatest common binomial factor.

57. $x(x+2)-4(x+2)=(x+2)(x-4)$

59. $x(y+6)-7(y+6)=(y+6)(x-7)$

61. $3x(x+y)-(x+y)$
$=3x(x+y)-1(x+y)$
$=(x+y)(3x-1)$

63. $4x(3x+1)+3x+1$
$=4x(3x+1)+1(3x+1)$
$=(3x+1)(4x+1)$

65. $7x^2(5x+4)+5x+4$
$=7x^2(5x+4)+1(5x+4)$
$=(5x+4)(7x^2+1)$

67. $x^2+2x+4x+8=(x^2+2x)+(4x+8)$
$=x(x+2)+4(x+2)$
$=(x+2)(x+4)$

69. $x^2+3x-5x-15=(x^2+3x)+(-5x-15)$
$=x(x+3)-5(x+3)$
$=(x+3)(x-5)$

71. $x^3-2x^2+5x-10$
$=(x^3-2x^2)+(5x-10)$
$=x^2(x-2)+5(x-2)$
$=(x-2)(x^2+5)$

73. $x^3-x^2+2x-2=x^2(x-1)+2(x-1)$
$=(x-1)(x^2+2)$

75. $xy+5x+9y+45=x(y+5)+9(y+5)$
$=(y+5)(x+9)$

77. $xy - x + 5y - 5 = x(y-1) + 5(y-1)$
$= (y-1)(x+5)$

79. $3x^2 - 6xy + 5xy - 10y^2$
$= 3x(x-2y) + 5y(x-2y)$
$= (x-2y)(3x+5y)$

81. $3x^3 - 2x^2 - 6x + 4$
$= x^2(3x-2) - 2(3x-2)$
$= (3x-2)(x^2-2)$

83. $x^2 - ax - bx + ab = x(x-a) - b(x-a)$
$= (x-a)(x-b)$

85. $24x^3y^3z^3 + 30x^2y^2z + 18x^2yz^2$
$= 6x^2yz(4xy^2z^2)$
$+ 6x^2yz(5y) + 6x^2yz(3z)$
$= 6x^2yz(4xy^2z^2 + 5y + 3z)$

86. $16x^2y^2z^2 + 32x^2yz^2 + 24x^2yz$
$= 8x^2yz(2yz) + 8x^2yz(4z) + 8x^2yz(3)$
$= 8x^2yz(2yz + 4z + 3)$

87. $x^3 - 4 + 3x^3y - 12y$
$= 1(x^3-4) + 3y(x^3-4)$
$= (x^3-4)(1+3y)$

88. $x^3 - 5 + 2x^3y - 10y$
$= 1(x^3-5) + 2y(x^3-5)$
$= (x^3-5)(1+2y)$

89. $4x^5(x+1) - 6x^3(x+1) - 8x^2(x+1)$
$= 2x^2(x+1)\cdot 2x^3 - 2x^2(x+1)\cdot 3x$
$- 2x^2(x+1)\cdot 4$
$= 2x^2(x+1)(2x^3 - 3x - 4)$

90. $8x^5(x+2) - 10x^3(x+2) - 2x^2(x+2)$
$= 2x^2(x+2)\cdot 4x^3 - 2x^2\cdot 5x$
$- 2x^2(x+2)\cdot 1$
$= 2x^2(x+2)(4x^3 - 5x - 1)$

91. $3x^5 - 3x^4 + x^3 - x^2 + 5x - 5$
$= (3x^5 - 3x^4) + (x^3 - x^2) + (5x-5)$
$= 3x^4(x-1) + x^2(x-1) + 5(x-1)$
$= (x-1)(3x^4 + x^2 + 5)$

92 $7x^5 - 7x^4 + x^3 - x^2 + 3x - 3$
$= (7x^5 - 7x^4) + (x^3 - x^2) + (3x-3)$
$= 7x^4(x-1) + x^2(x-1) + 3(x-1)$
$= (x-1)(7x^4 + x^2 + 3)$

93. The area of the square is $6x \cdot 6x = 36x^2$. The area of the circle is $\pi(2x)^2 = \pi \cdot 4x^2 = 4\pi x^2$. So the shaded area is the area of the square minus the area of the circle, which is $36x^2 - 4\pi x^2 = 4x^2(9-\pi)$.

94. The area of the square is $4x \cdot 4x = 16x^2$. The area of each circle is πx^2. The area of both circles is $2\pi x^2$. So the shaded area is the area of the square minus the area of the two circles, which is $16x^2 - 2\pi x^2 = 2x^2(8-\pi)$.

95. **a.** Use the formula, $64x-16x^2$, for the height of the debris above the ground. Substitute 3 for x.

$64x-16x^2=64(3)-16(3)^2$

$=192-16(9)=192-144=48$

Therefore, the height of the debris after 3 seconds is 48 feet.

b. $64x-16x^2=16x(4-x)$

c. Substitute 3 for x in the factored polynomial.

$16\cdot 3(4-3)=48(1)=48$

You do get the same answer as in part (a) but this does not prove your factorization is correct.

97. Use the formula for the area of a rectangle, $A=l\cdot w$. Substitute $5x^4-10x$ for A and $5x$ for w.

$A=l\cdot w$

$5x^4-10x=l(5x)$

To find a polynomial representing l, factor $5x^4-10x$.

$5x^4-10x=5x(x^3-2)$ or $(x^3-2)\cdot 5x$

which is $l\cdot w$.

Therefore, the l, the length, is (x^3-2) units.

99-103. Answers will vary.

105. Statement d is true.

Either $-4x$ or $4x$ can be used as the GCF.

Multiplying $-4x(x-3)=-4x^2+12x$

and $4x(-x+3)=-4x^2+12x$

107. Answers will vary. One example is $4y^4-8y^3+2y^2-16y$.

109.

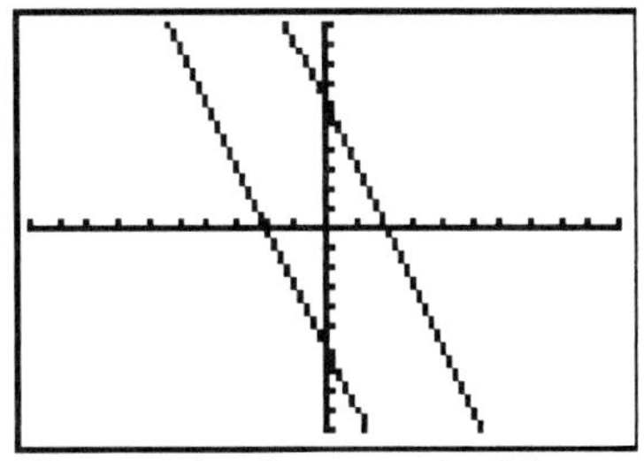

The graphs do not coincide.

Factor out GCF from left side.

$-3x-6=-3(x+2)$. Change the expression on the right side to $-3(x+2)$.

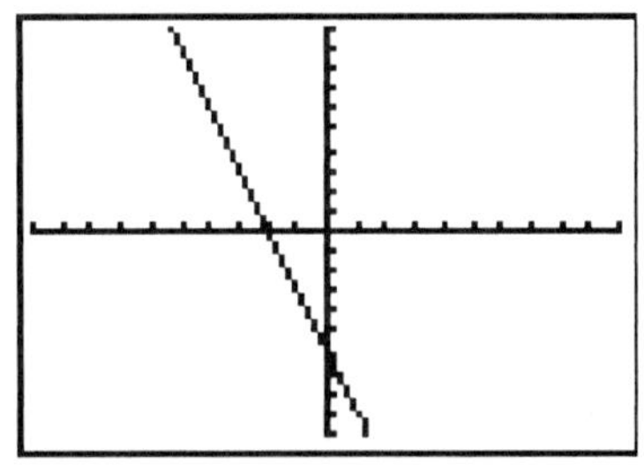

Now the graphs coincide.

111.

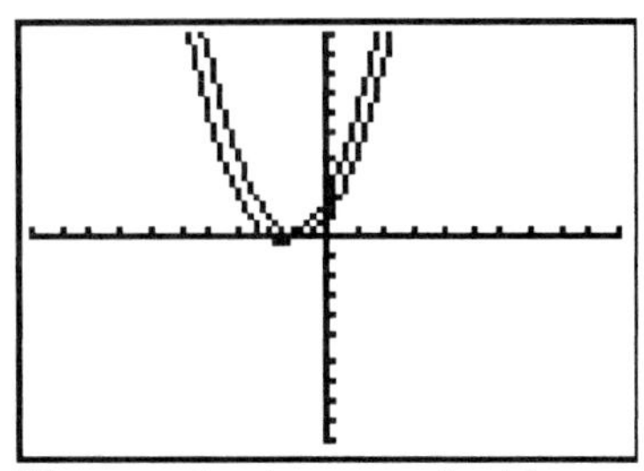

The graphs do not coincide.

Factor by grouping.

$x^2+2x+x+2=x(x+2)+1(x+2)$

$=(x+2)(x+1)$

Change the expression on the right side to $(x+2)(x+1)$.

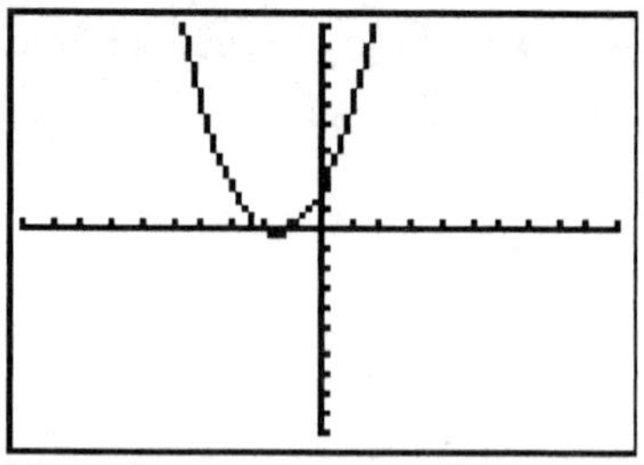

Now the graphs coincide.

112. $(x+7)(x+10) = x^2 + 10x + 7x + 70$
$= x^2 + 17x + 70$

113. $2x - y = -4$
$x - 3y = 3$
Graph both equations on the same axes.
$2x - y = -4$:
x-intercept: -2; y-intercept: 4
$x - 3y = 3$:
x-intercept: 3; y-intercept: -1

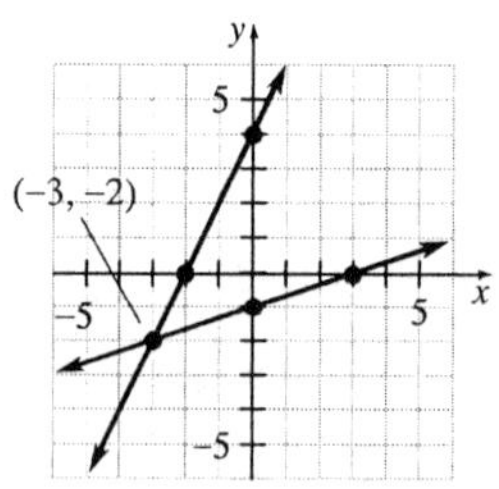

The lines intersect at $(-3,-2)$.
Solution: $(-3,-2)$

114. Line through $(-7,2)$ and $(-4,5)$
First, find the slope

$$m = \frac{5-2}{-4-(-7)} = \frac{3}{3} = 1$$

Write the point-slope equation using $m = 1$ and $(x_1, y_1) = (-7, 2)$ and rewrite this equation in slope-intercept form.

$$y - y_1 = m(x - x_1)$$
$$y - 2 = 1[x - (-7)]$$
$$y - 2 = 1(x + 7)$$
$$y - 2 = x + 7$$
$$y = x + 9$$

Note: If $(-4,5)$ is used as $(x_1 y_1)$, the point-slope equation will be

$$y - 5 = 1[x - (-4)]$$
$$y - 5 = x + 4$$

This also leads to the slope-intercept equation $y = x + 9$.

7.2 Exercise Set

In Exercises 1-41, each factorization should be checked using FOIL multiplication. The check will be only shown here for Exercise 1.

1. $x^2 + 7x + 6$

Factors of 6	6,1	−6, −1
Sum of Factors	7	−7

The factors of 6 whose sum is 7 are 6 and 1.
Thus, $x^2 + 7x + 6 = (x+6)(x+1)$.
Check:
$(x+6)(x+1) = x^2 + 1x + 6x + 6$
$= x^2 + 7x + 6$

3. $x^2 + 7x + 10 = (x+5)(x+2)$
$5(2) = 10;\ 5 + 2 = 7$

5. $x^2 + 11x + 10 = (x+10)(x+1)$
$10(1) = 10;\ 10 + 1 = 11$

7. $x^2 - 7x + 12 = (x-4)(x-3)$
$-4(-3) = 12;\ -4 + -3 = -7$

9. $x^2 - 12x + 36 = (x-6)(x-6)$
$-6(-6) = 36;\ -6 + -6 = -12$

11. $y^2 - 8y + 15 = (y-5)(y-3)$
$-5(-3) = 15;\ -5 + -3 = -8$

13. $x^2 + 3x - 10 = (x+5)(x-2)$
$5(-2) = -10;\ 5 + -2 = 3$

15. $y^2 + 10y - 39 = (y+13)(y-3)$
$(13)(-3) = -39;\ 13 + -3 = 10$

17. $x^2 - 2x - 15 = (x-5)(x+3)$
$(-5)(3) = -15;\ -5 + 3 = -2$

19. $x^2 - 2x - 8 = (x-4)(x+2)$
$(-4)(2) = -8;\ -4 + 2 = -2$

21. $x^2 + 4x + 12$ is prime because there is no pair of integers whose product is 12 and whose sum is 4.

23. $y^2 - 16y + 48 = (y-4)(y-12)$
$(-4)(-12) = 48;\ -4 + -12 = -16$

25. $x^2 - 3x + 6$ is prime because there is no pair of integers whose product is 6 and whose sum is −3.

27. $w^2 - 30w - 64 = (w-32)(w+2)$
$(-32)(2) = -64;\ -32 + 2 = -30$

29. $y^2 - 18y + 65 = (y-5)(y-13)$
$(-5)(-13) = 65;\ -5 + -13 = -18$

31. $r^2 + 12r + 27 = (r+3)(r+9)$
$(3)(9) = 27;\ 3 + 9 = 12$

33. $y^2 - 7y + 5$ is prime because there is no pair of integers whose product is 5 and whose sum is −7.

35. $x^2 + 7xy + 6y^2 = (x+6y)(x+y)$
$(6)(1) = 6;\ 6 + 1 = 7$

37. $x^2 - 8xy + 15y^2 = (x-3y)(x-5y)$
$(-3)(-5) = 15;\ -3 + -5 = -8$

39. $x^2 - 3xy - 18y^2 = (x-6y)(x+3y)$
$(-6)(3) = -18;\ -6 + 3 = -3$

41. $a^2 - 18ab + 45b^2 = (a-15b)(a-3b)$
$(-15)(-3) = 45;\ -15 + -3 = -18$

43. $3x^2 + 15x + 18$
First factor out the GCF, 3. Then factor the resulting binomial.
$$\begin{aligned} 3x^2 + 15x + 18 &= 3(x^2 + 5x + 6) \\ &= 3(x+2)(x+3) \end{aligned}$$

45.
$$\begin{aligned} 4y^2 - 4y - 8 &= 4(y^2 - y - 2) \\ &= 4(y-2)(y+1) \end{aligned}$$

47.
$$\begin{aligned} 10x^2 - 40x - 600 &= 10(x^2 - 4x - 60) \\ &= 10(x-10)(x+6) \end{aligned}$$

49.
$$\begin{aligned} 3x^2 - 33x + 54 &= 3(x^2 - 11x + 18) \\ &3(x-2)(x-9) \end{aligned}$$

51.
$$\begin{aligned} 2r^3 + 6r^2 + 4r &= 2r(r^2 + 3r + 2) \\ &= 2r(r+2)(r+1) \end{aligned}$$

53. $4x^3+12x^2-72x=4x(x^2+3x-18)$
$=4x(x+6)(x-3)$

55. $2r^3+8r^2-64r=2r(r^2+4r-32)$
$=2r(r+8)(r-4)$

57. $y^4+2y^3-80y^2=y^2(y^2+2y-80)$
$=y^2(y+10)(y-8)$

59. $x^4-3x^3-10x^2=x^2(x^2-3x-10)$
$=x^2(x-5)(x+2)$

61. $2w^4-26w^3-96w^2$
$=2w^2(w^2-13w-48)$
$=2w^2(w-16)(w+3)$

63. $15xy^2+45xy-60x=15x(y^2+3y-4)$
$=15x(y+4)(y-1)$

65. $x^5+3x^4y-4x^3y^2=x^3(x^2+3xy-4y^2)$
$=x^3(x+4y)(x-y)$

67. $2x^2y^2-32x^2yz+30x^2z^2$
$=2x^2(y^2-16yz+15z^2)$
$=2x^2(y-15z)(y-z)$

68. $2x^2y^2-30x^2yz+28x^2z^2$
$=2x^2(y^2-15yz+14z^2)$
$=2x^2(y-14z)(y-z)$

69. $(a+b)x^2+(a+b)x-20(a+b)$
$=(a+b)(x^2+x-20)$
$=(a+b)(x+5)(x-4)$

70. $(a+b)x^2-13(a+b)x+36(a+b)$
$=(a+b)(x^2-13x+36)$
$=(a+b)(x-9)(x-4)$

71. $x^2+0.5x+0.06=(x+0.2)(x+0.3)$
$0.2(0.3)=0.06;\ 0.2+0.3=0.5$

72. $x^2-0.5x-0.06=(x-0.6)(x+0.1)$
$-0.6(0.1)=0.06;\ -0.6+0.1=-0.5$

73. $x^2-\frac{2}{5}x+\frac{1}{25}=\left(x-\frac{1}{5}\right)\left(x-\frac{1}{5}\right)$
$\frac{1}{5}\left(\frac{1}{5}\right)=\frac{1}{25};\ -\frac{1}{5}+-\frac{1}{5}=-\frac{2}{5}$

74. $x^2+\frac{2}{3}x+\frac{1}{9}=\left(x+\frac{1}{3}\right)\left(x+\frac{1}{3}\right)$
$\left(\frac{1}{3}\right)\left(\frac{1}{3}\right)=\frac{1}{9};\ \frac{1}{3}+\frac{1}{3}=\frac{2}{3}$

75. $-x^2-3x+40=-(x^2+3x-40)$
$=-(x+8)(x-5)$
$8(-5)=-40;\ 8+-5=3$

76. $-x^2-4x+45=-(x^2+4x-45)$
$=-(x+9)(x-5)$
$9(-5)=-45;\ 9+-5=4$

77. **a.** $-16t^2+16t+32=-16(t^2-t-2)$
$=-16(t-2)(t+1)$

b. Substitute 2 for t in the original polynomial:

$$-16(2)^2+16(2)+32$$
$$=-16(4)+32+32$$
$$=-64+64=0$$

Substitute 2 for t in the factored polynomial:
$-16(2-2)(2+1)=-16(0)(3)=0$
This answer means that after 2 seconds you hit the water.

79-81. Answers will vary.

83. Statement c is true.
$$y^2+5y-24=(y-3)(y+8)$$

85. In order for x^2+4x+b to be factorable, b must be an integer with two positive factors whose sum is 4. The only such pairs are 3 and 1, or 2 and 2.
$$(x+3)(x+1)=x^2+4x+3$$
$$(x+2)(x+2)=x^2+4x+4$$
Therefore, the possible values of b are 3 and 4.

87. $x^3+3x^2+2x=x(x^2+3x+2)$
$=x(x+1)(x+2)$
The trinomial represents the product of three consecutive integers.

89.
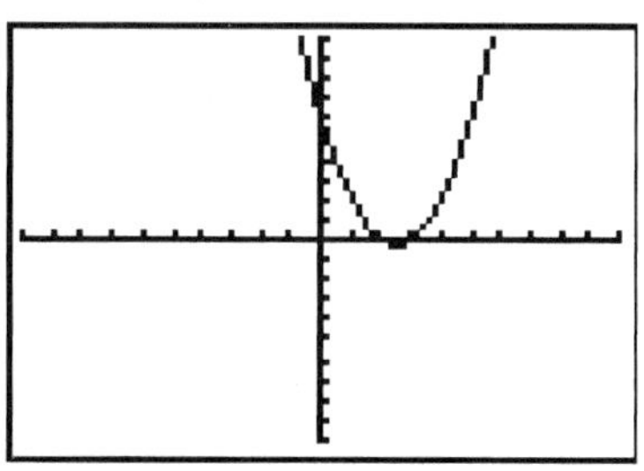

The graphs coincide.
This verifies the factorization $x^2-5x+6=(x-2)(x-3)$.

91.
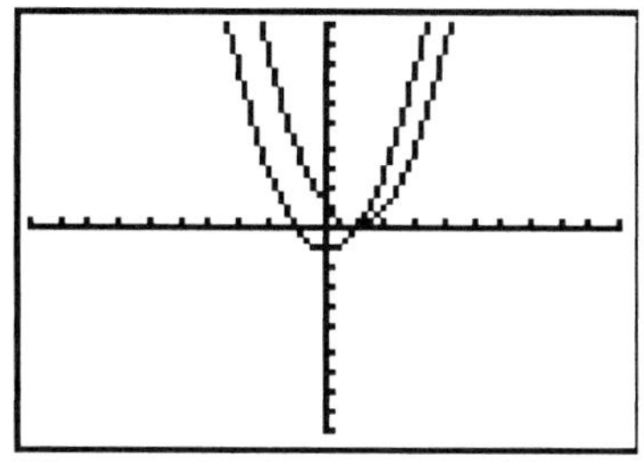

The graphs do not coincide.

$x^2-2x+1=(x-1)(x-1)$

Change the polynomial on the right to $(x-1)(x-1)$.

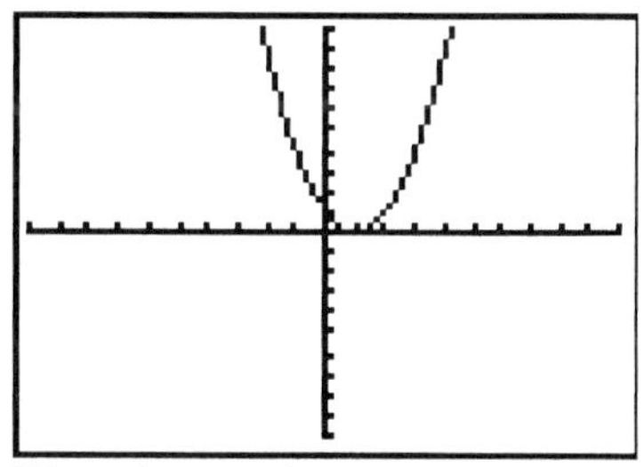

Now the graphs coincide.

93. $(2x+3)(x-2)=2x^2-4x+3x-6$
$=2x^2-x-6$

94. $(3x+4)(3x+1)=9x^2+3x+12x+4$
$=9x^2+15x+4$

95. $4(x-2)=3x+5$
$4x-8=3x+5$
$x-8=5$
$x=13$
The solution is 13.

7.3 Exercise Set

In Exercises 1-57, each trinomial may be factored by either trial and error or by grouping. Both methods will be illustrated here. Each factorization should be checked by FOIL multiplication. The check will be shown here only for Exercise 1. In all answers, the factors may be written in either order.

1. $2x^2+5x+3$

Factor by trial and error.

Step 1 $2x^2+5x+3=(2x\quad)(x\quad)$

Step 2 The number 3 has pairs of factors that are either both positive or both negative. Because the middle term, $5x$, is positive, both factors must be positive. The only positive factorization is $(1)(3)$.

Step 3

Possible Factors of $2x^2+5x+3$	Sum of Outside and Inside Products
$(2x+1)(x+3)$	$6x+x=7x$
$(2x+3)(x+1)$	$2x+3x=5x$

Thus, $2x^2+5x+3=(2x+3)(x+1)$.

Check:

$$\begin{aligned}(2x+3)(x+1)&=2x^2+2x+3x+3\\&=2x^2+5x+3\end{aligned}$$

3. $3x^2+13x+4$

Factor by trial and error.

The only possibility for the first terms is $(3x)(x)=3x^2$.

Because the middle term is positive and the last term is also positive, the possible factorizations of 4 are $(1)(4)$ and $(2)(2)$.

Possible Factors of $3x^2+13x+4$	Sum of Outside and Inside Products
$(3x+1)(x+4)$	$12x+x=13x$
$(3x+4)(x+1)$	$3x+4x=7x$
$(3x+2)(x+2)$	$6x+2x=8x$

Thus, $3x^2+13x+4=(3x+1)(x+4)$.

5. $2x^2+11x+12$

Factor by grouping.

$a=2$ and $c=12$, so $ac=2(12)=24$.

The factors of 24 whose sum is 11 are 8 and 3.

$$\begin{aligned}2x^2+11x+12&=2x^2+8x+3x+12\\&=2x(x+4)+3(x+4)\\&=(x+4)(2x+3)\end{aligned}$$

7. $5y^2-16y+3$

Factor by trial and error. The first terms must be $5y$ and y. Because the middle term is negative, the factors of 3 must be -3 and -1.

$$(5y-1)(y-3)=5y^2-16y+3$$
$$(5y-3)(y-1)=5y^2-8y+3$$

Thus, $y^2-16y+3=(5y-1)(y-3)$.

9. $3y^2+y-4$

Factor by trial and error.

$(3y+1)(y-4)=3y^2-11y-4$

$(3y-1)(y+4)=3y^2+11y-4$

$(3y+4)(y-1)=3y^2+y-4$

$(3y-4)(y+1)=3y^2-y-4$

$(3y+2)(y-2)=3y^2-4y-4$

$(3y-2)(y+2)=3y^2+4y-4$

Thus, $3y^2+y-4=(3y+4)(y-1)$.

11. $3x^2+13x-10$
Factor by grouping.
$a=3$ and $c=-10$, so $ac=-30$.
The factors of -30 whose sum is 13 are 15 and -2.

$$\begin{aligned}3x^2+13x-10&=3x^2+15x-2x-10\\&=3x(x+5)-2(x+5)\\&=(x+5)(3x-2)\end{aligned}$$

13. $3x^2-22x+7$
Factor by trial and error.

$(3x-7)(x-1)=3x^2-10x+7$

$(3x-1)(x-7)=3x^2-22x+7$

Thus, $3x^2-22x+7=(3x-1)(x-7)$.

15. $5y^2-16y+3$
Factor by trial and error.

$(5y-3)(y-1)=5y^2-8y+3$

$(5y-1)(y-3)=5y^2-16y+3$

Thus, $5y^2-16y+3=(5y-1)(y-3)$.

17. $3x^2-17x+10$
Factor by grouping.
$a=3$ and $c=10$, so $ac=30$.
The factors of 30 whose sum is -17 are -15 and -2.

$$\begin{aligned}3x^2-17x+10&=3x^2-15x-2x+10\\&=3x(x-5)-2(x-5)\\&=(x-5)(3x-2)\end{aligned}$$

19. $6w^2-11w+4$
Factor by grouping.
$a=6$ and $c=4$, so $ac=24$.
The factors of 24 whose sum is -11 are -3 and -8.

$$\begin{aligned}6w^2-11w+4&=6w^2-3w-8w+4\\&=3w(2w-1)-4(2w-1)\\&=(2w-1)(3w-4)\end{aligned}$$

21. $8x^2+33x+4$
Factor by grouping.
$a=8$ and $c=4$, so $ac=32$.
The factors of 32 whose sum is 33 are 32 and 1.

$$\begin{aligned}8x^2+33x+4&=8x^2+32x+x+4\\&=8x(x+4)+1(x+4)\\&=(x+4)(8x+1)\end{aligned}$$

23. $5x^2+33x-14$
Factor by trial and error.

$(5x-7)(x+2)=5x^2+3x-14$

$(5x+7)(x-2)=5x^2-3x-14$

$(5x-2)(x+7)=5x^2+33x-14$

Because the correct factorization has been found, there is no need to try additional possibilities.
Thus, $5x^2+33x-14=(5x-2)(x+7)$.

25. $14y^2+15y-9$
Factor by trial and error. The sign in one factor must be positive and the other negative.

$(7y+9)(2y-1)=14y^2+11y-9$

$(7y+1)(2y-9)=14y^2-61y-9$

$(7y+3)(2y-3)=14y^2-15y-9$

$(7y-3)(2y+3)=14y^2+15y-9$

Thus,
$14y^2+15y-9=(7y-3)(2y+3)$.

27. $6x^2 - 7x + 3$
Factor by trial and error. List all the possibilities in which both signs are negative.
$(6x-1)(x-3) = 6x^2 - 19x + 3$
$(6x-3)(x-1) = 6x^2 - 9x + 3$
$(3x-1)(2x-3) = 6x^2 - 11x + 3$
$(3x-3)(2x-1) = 6x^2 - 9x + 3$
None of these possibilities gives the required middle term, $-7x$, and there are no more possibilities to try, so $6x^2 - 7x + 3$ is prime.

29. $25z^2 - 30z + 9$
Factor by trial and error until the correct factorization is obtained. The signs in both factors must be negative.
$(5z-1)(5z-9) = 25z^2 - 50z + 9$
$(5z-3)(5z-3) = 25z^2 - 30z + 9$
Thus, $25z^2 - 30z + 9 = (5z-3)(5z-3)$.

31. $15y^2 - y - 2$
Factor by grouping.
$a = 15$ and $c = -2$, so $ac = -30$.
The factors of -30 whose sum is -1 are -6 and 5.

$$\begin{aligned} 15y^2 - y - 2 &= 15y^2 - 6y + 5y - 2 \\ &= 3y(5y-2) + 1(5y-2) \\ &= (5y-2)(3y+1) \end{aligned}$$

33. $5x^2 + 2x + 9$
Factor by trial and error. The signs in both factors must be positive.
$(5x+3)(x+3) = 5x^2 + 18x + 9$
$(5x+9)(x+1) = 5x^2 + 14x + 9$
$(5x+1)(x+9) = 5x^2 + 46x + 9$
None of these possibilities gives the required middle term, $2x$, and there are no more possibilities to try, so $5x^2 + 2x + 9$ is prime.

35. $10y^2 + 43y - 9$
Factor by grouping.
$a = 10$ and $c = -9$ so $ac = -90$.
The factors of -90 whose sum is 43 are 45 and -2.

$$\begin{aligned} 10y^2 + 43y - 9 &= 10y^2 + 45y - 2y - 9 \\ &= 5y(2y+9) - 1(2y+9) \\ &= (2y+9)(5y-1) \end{aligned}$$

37. $8x^2 - 2x - 1$
Factor by trial and error until the correct factorization is obtained. The sign must be negative in one factor and positive in the other.
$(4x-1)(2x+1) = 8x^2 + 2x - 1$
$(4x+1)(2x-1) = 8x^2 - 2x - 1$
Thus, $8x^2 - 2x - 1 = (4x+1)(2x-1)$.

39. $9y^2 - 9y + 2$
Factor by grouping.
$a = 9$ and $c = 2$, so $ac = 18$.
The factors of 18 whose sum is -9 are -3 and -6.

$$\begin{aligned} 9y^2 - 9y + 2 &= 9y^2 - 3y - 6y + 2 \\ &= 3y(3y-1) - 2(3y-1) \\ &= (3y-1)(3y-2) \end{aligned}$$

41. $20x^2 + 27x - 8$
Factor by grouping.
$a = 20$ and $c = -8$, so $ac = -160$.
The factors of -160 whose sum is 27 are -5 and 32.

$$\begin{aligned} 20x^2 + 27x - 8 &= 20x^2 - 5x + 32x - 8 \\ &= 5x(4x-1) + 8(4x-1) \\ &= (4x-1)(5x+8) \end{aligned}$$

43. $2x^2 + 3xy + y^2 = (2x+y)(x+y)$
(In this case, there are no other combinations to try.)

45. $3x^2+5xy+2y^2$
Factor by trial and error.
$(3x+y)(x+2y)=3x^2+7xy+2y^2$
$(3x+2y)(x+y)=3x^2+5xy+2y^2$
Thus,
$3x^2+5xy+2y^2=(3x+2y)(x+y)$.

47. $2x^2-9xy+9y^2$
Factor by trial and error until the correct factorization is obtained. The signs in both factors must be negative.
$(2x-9y)(x-y)=2x^2-11xy+9y^2$
$(2x+9y)(x+y)=2x^2+11xy+9y^2$
$(2x-3y)(x-3y)=2x^2-9xy+9y^2$
Thus,
$2x^2-9xy+9y^2=(2x-3y)(x-3y)$.

49. $6x^2-5xy-6y^2$
Factor by grouping.
$a=6$ and $c=-6$, so $ac=-36$.
The factors of -36 whose sum is -5 are -9 and 4.
$$\begin{aligned}&6x^2-5xy-6y^2\\&=6x^2-9xy+4xy-6y^2\\&=3x(2x-3y)+2y(2x-3y)\\&=(2x-3y)(3x+2y)\end{aligned}$$

51. $15x^2+11xy-14y^2$
Factor by grouping.
$a=15$ and $c=-14$, so $ac=-210$.
The factors of -210 whose sum is 11 are 21 and -10.
$$\begin{aligned}&15x^2+11xy-14y^2\\&=15x^2+21xy-10xy-14y^2\\&=3x(5x+7y)-2y(5x+7y)\\&=(5x+7y)(3x-2y)\end{aligned}$$

53. $2a^2+7ab+5b^2$
Factor by trial and error.
$(2a+5b)(a+b)=2a^2+7ab+5b^2$
$(2a+b)(a+5b)=2a^2+11ab+5b^2$
Thus,
$2a^2+7ab+5b^2=(2a+5b)(a+b)$.

55. $15a^2-ab-6b^2$
Factor by grouping.
$a=15$ and $c=-6$, so $ac=-90$.
The factors of -90 whose sum is -1 are 9 and -10.
$$\begin{aligned}&15a^2-ab-6b^2\\&=15a^2+9ab-10ab-6b^2\\&=3a(5a+3b)-2b(5a+3b)\\&=(5a+3b)(3a-2b)\end{aligned}$$

57. $12x^2-25xy+12y^2$
Factor by grouping.
$a=12$ and $c=12$, so $ac=144$.
The factors of 144 whose sum is -25 are -9 and -16.
$$\begin{aligned}&12x^2-25xy+12y^2\\&=12x^2-9xy-16xy+12y^2\\&=3x(4x-3y)-4y(4x-3y)\\&=(4x-3y)(3x-4y)\end{aligned}$$

59. $4x^2+26x+30$
First factor out the GCF, 2. Then factor the resulting trinomial by trial and error or grouping.
$$\begin{aligned}4x^2+26x+30&=2(2x^2+13x+15)\\&=2(2x+3)(x+5)\end{aligned}$$

61. $9x^2-6x-24$
The GCF is 3.
$$\begin{aligned}9x^2-6x-24&=3(3x^2-2x-8)\\&=3(3x+4)(x-2)\end{aligned}$$

63. $4y^2+2y-30=2(2y^2+y-15)$
$=2(2y-5)(y+3)$

65. $9y^2+33y-60=3(3y^2+11y-20)$
$=3(3y-4)(y+5)$

67. $3x^3+4x^2+x$
The GCF is x.
$3x^3+4x^2+x=x(3x^2+4x+1)$
$=x(3x+1)(x+1)$

69. $2x^3-3x^2-5x=x(2x^2-3x-5)$
$=x(2x-5)(x+1)$

71. $9y^3-39y^2+12y$
The GCF is $3y$.
$9y^3-39y^2+12y=3y(3y^2-13y+4)$
$=3y(3y-1)(y-4)$

73. $60z^3+40z^2+5z=5z(12z^2+8z+1)$
$=5z(6z+1)(2z+1)$

75. $15x^4-39x^3+18x^2=3x^2(5x^2-13x+6)$
$=3x^2(5x-3)(x-2)$

77. $10x^5-17x^4+3x^3=x^3(10x^2-17x+3)$
$=x^3(2x-3)(5x-1)$

79. $6x^2-3xy-18y^2=3(2x^2-xy-6y^2)$
$=3(2x+3y)(x-2y)$

81. $12x^2+10xy-8y^2=2(6x^2+5xy-4y^2)$
$=2(2x-y)(3x+4y)$

83. $8x^2y+34xy-84y=2y(4x^2+17x-42)$
$=2y(4x-7)(x+6)$

85. $12a^2b-46ab^2+14b^3$
$=2b(6a^2-23ab+7b^2)$
$=2b(2a-7b)(3a-b)$

87. $30(y+1)x^2+10(y+1)x-20(y+1)$
$=10(y+1)(3x^2+x-2)$
$=10(y+1)(3x-2)(x+1)$

88. $6(y+1)x^2+33(y+1)x+15(y+1)$
$=3(y+1)(2x^2+11x+5)$
$=3(y+1)(2x+1)(x+5)$

89. $-32x^2y^4+20xy^4+12y^4$
$=-4y^4(8x^2-5x-3)$
$=-4y^4(8x+3)(x-1)$

90. $-10x^2y^4+14xy^4+12y^4$
$=-2y^4(5x^2-7x-6)$
$=-2y^4(x-2)(5x+3)$

91. **a.** $2x^2-5x-3=(2x+1)(x-3)$

b. $2(y+1)^2-5(y+1)-3$
$=[2(y+1)+1][(y+1)-3]$
$=[2y+2+1][y+1-3]$
$=(2y+3)(y-2)$

92. **a.** $3x^2+5x-2=(3x-1)(x+2)$

b. $3(y+1)^2+5(y+1)-2$
$=[3(y+1)-1][(y+1)+2]$
$=[3y+3-1][y+1+2]$
$=(3y+2)(y+3)$

93.

$$\begin{array}{r|l} x-2 & 3x^3-11x^2+12x-4 \end{array}$$

Quotient: $3x^2-5x+2$

$$\begin{array}{l} 3x^3-6x^2 \\ \hline -5x^2+12x \\ -5x^2+10x \\ \hline 2x-4 \\ 2x-4 \\ \hline \end{array}$$

The quotient $3x^2-5x+2$ into $(3x-2)(x-1)$.

Thus, $3x^3-11x^2+12x-4=(x-2)(3x-2)(x-1)$.

94.

$$\begin{array}{r|l} x-2 & 2x^3+x^2-13x+6 \end{array}$$

Quotient: $2x^2+5x-3$

$$\begin{array}{l} 2x^3-4x^2 \\ \hline 5x^2-13x \\ 5x^2-10x \\ \hline -3x+6 \\ -3x+6 \\ \hline \end{array}$$

The quotient $2x^2+5x-3$ into $(2x-1)(x+3)$.

Thus, $3x^3-11x^2+12x-4=(x-2)(2x-1)(x+3)$.

95. **a.** x^2+3x+2

b. $(x+2)(x+1)$

c. Yes, the pieces are the same in both figures: one large square, three long rectangles, and two small squares. This geometric model illustrates the factorization: $x^2+3x+2=(x+2)(x+1)$.

97. – 99. Answers will vary.

101. Statement *a* is true.
$18y^2-6y+6=9(y^2-3y+3)$, and y^2-3y+3 is prime.

103. $2x^2+bx+3$
The possible factorizations that will give $2x^2$ as the first term and 3 as the last term are:
$(2x+3)(x+1)=2x^2+5x+3$
$(2x+1)(x+3)=2x^2+7x+3$
$(2x-3)(x-1)=2x^2-5x+3$
$(2x-1)(x-3)=2x^2-7x+3$
The possible middle terms are $5x, 7x, -5x$ and $-7x$, so $2x^2+bx+3$ can be factored if *b* is 5, 7, –5, or –7.

105. $2x^{2n}-7x^n-4$
Since $x^n\cdot x^n=x^{n+n}=x^{2n}$, the first terms of the factors will be $2x^n$ and x^n. Use trial and error or grouping to obtain the correct factorization.
$2x^{2n}-7x^n-4=(2x^n+1)(x^n-4)$

106. $(9x+10)(9x-10)=(9x)^2-10^2$
$=81x^2-100$

107. $(4x+5y)^2=(4x)^2+2(4x)(5y)+(5y)^2$
$=16x^2+40xy+25y^2$

108. $(x+2)(x^2-2x+4)$
$= x(x^2-2x+4)+2(x^2-2x+4)$
$= x^3-2x^2+4x+2x^2-4x+8$
$= x^3+8$

Mid-Chapter Check Point – Chapter 7

1. $x^5+x^4=x^4(x+1)$
GCF is x^4.

2. $x^2+7x-18=(x-2)(x+9)$
Factor by trial and error. The only factors of -18 whose sum is 7 are -2 and 9.

3. $x^2y^3-x^2y^2+x^2y=x^2y(y^2-y+1)$
GCF is x^2y. The polynomial in the parentheses is prime because there are no factors of 1 whose sum is -1.

4. x^2-2x+4 is prime because there are no factors of 4 whose sum is -2.

5. $7x^2-22x+3$
Factor by grouping.
$a=7$ and $c=3$, so $ac=21$.
The only factors of 21 whose sum is -22 are -21 and -1.
$7x^2-22x+3=7x^2-21x-x+3$
$=7x(x-3)-1(x-3)$
$=(x-3)(7x-1)$

6. $x^3+5x^2+3x+15$
Factor by grouping.
$x^3+5x^2+3x+15$
$=(x^3+5x^2)+(3x+15)$
$=x^2(x+5)+3(x+5)$
$=(x+5)(x^2+3)$

7. $2x^3-11x^2+5x$
GCF is x.
$2x^3-11x^2+5x=x(2x^2-11x+5)$
$=x(2x-1)(x-5)$

8. $xy-7x-4y+28$
Factor by grouping.
$xy-7x-4y+28$
$=(xy-7x)+(-4y+28)$
$=x(y-7)-4(y-7)$
$=(y-7)(x-4)$

9. $x^2-17xy+30y^2$
Factor by trial and error. The only factors of 30 whose sum is -17 are -15 and -2.
$x^2-17xy+30y^2=(x-15y)(x-2y)$

10. $25x^2-25x-14$
Factor by trial and error.
$(5x-2)(5x+7)=25x^2+25x-14$
$(5x+2)(5x-7)=25x^2-25x-14$
Thus,
$25x^2-25x-14=(5x+2)(5x-7)$.
Because the correct factorization has been found, there is no need to try additional possibilities.

11. $16x^2 - 70x + 24$
GCF is 2.
$16x^2 - 70x + 24 = 2(8x^2 - 35x + 12)$

Factor the polynomial in parentheses by grouping.
$a = 8$ and $c = 12$, so $ac = 96$.
The only factors of 96 whose sum is -35 are -32 and -3.

$$\begin{aligned} &2(8x^2 - 35x + 12) \\ &= 2(8x^2 - 32x - 3x + 12) \\ &= 2[8x(x-4) - 3(x-4)] \\ &= 2(x-4)(8x-3) \end{aligned}$$

12. $3x^2 + 10xy + 7y^2$
Factor by grouping.
$a = 3$ and $c = 7$, so $ac = 21$.
The only factors of 21 whose sum is 10 are 3 and 7.

$$\begin{aligned} 3x^2 + 10xy + 7y^2 &= 3x^2 + 3xy + 7xy + 7y^2 \\ &= 3x(x+y) + 7y(x+y) \\ &= (x+y)(3x+7y) \end{aligned}$$

7.4 Exercise Set

1. $x^2 - 25 = x^2 - 5^2 = (x+5)(x-5)$

3. $y^2 - 1 = y^2 - 1^2 = (y+1)(y-1)$

5. $4x^2 - 9 = (2x)^2 - 3^2 = (2x+3)(2x-3)$

7. $25 - x^2 = 5^2 - x^2 = (5+x)(5-x)$

9. $1 - 49x^2 = 1^2 - (7x)^2 = (1+7x)(1-7x)$

11. $9 - 25y^2 = 3^2 - (5y)^2 = (3+5y)(3-5y)$

13. $x^4 - 9 = (x^2)^2 - 3^2 = (x^2+3)(x^2-3)$

15.
$$\begin{aligned} 49y^4 - 16 &= (7y^2)^2 - 4^2 \\ &= (7y^2+4)(7y^2-4) \end{aligned}$$

17. $x^{10} - 9 = (x^5)^2 - 3^2 = (x^5+3)(x^5-3)$

19.
$$\begin{aligned} 25x^2 - 16y^2 &= (5x)^2 - (4y)^2 \\ &= (5x+4y)(5x-4y) \end{aligned}$$

21.
$$\begin{aligned} x^4 - y^{10} &= (x^2)^2 - (y^5)^2 \\ &= (x^2+y^5)(x^2-y^5) \end{aligned}$$

23. $x^4 - 16 = (x^2)^2 - 4^2 = (x^2+4)(x^2-4)$

Because $x^2 - 4$ is also the difference of two squares, the factorization must be continued. The complete factorization is

$$\begin{aligned} x^4 - 16 &= (x^2+4)(x^2-4) \\ &= (x^2+4)(x^2-2^2) \\ &= (x^2+4)(x+2)(x-2). \end{aligned}$$

25.
$$\begin{aligned} 16x^4 - 81 &= (4x^2)^2 - 9^2 \\ &= (4x^2+9)(4x^2-9) \\ &= (4x^2+9)[(2x)^2 - 3^2] \\ &= (4x^2+9)(2x+3)(2x-3) \end{aligned}$$

27. $2x^2 - 18 = 2(x^2 - 9) = 2(x+3)(x-3)$

29.
$$\begin{aligned} 2x^3 - 72x &= 2x(x^2 - 36) \\ &= 2x(x+6)(x-6) \end{aligned}$$

31. $x^2 + 36$ is prime because it is the sum of two squares with no common factor other than 1.

33. $3x^3 + 27x = 3x(x^2 + 9)$

35. $18 - 2y^2 = 2(9 - y^2) = 2(3 + y)(3 - y)$

37. $3y^3 - 48y = 3y(y^2 - 16)$
$= 3y(y + 4)(y - 4)$

39. $18x^3 - 2x = 2x(9x^2 - 1)$
$= 2x(3x + 1)(3x - 1)$

41. $x^2 + 2x + 1 = x^2 + 2(1x) + 1^2$
$= (x + 1)^2$

43. $x^2 - 14x + 49 = x^2 - 2(7x) + 7^2$
$= (x - 7)^2$

45. $x^2 - 2x + 1 = x^2 - 2(1x) + 1^2$
$= (x - 1)^2$

47. $x^2 + 22x + 121 = x^2 + 2(11x) + 11^2$
$= (x + 11)^2$

49. $4x^2 + 4x + 1 = (2x)^2 + 2(2x) + 1^2$
$= (2x + 1)^2$

51. $25y^2 - 10y + 1 = (5y)^2 - 2(5y) + 1^2$
$= (5y - 1)^2$

53. $x^2 - 10x + 100$ is prime.
To be a perfect square trinomial, the middle term would have to be $2(-10x) = -20x$ rather than $-10x$.

55. $x^2 + 14xy + 49y^2 = x^2 + 2(7xy) + (7y)^2$
$= (x + 7y)^2$

57. $x^2 - 12xy + 36y^2 = x^2 - 2(6xy) + (6y)^2$
$= (x - 6y)^2$

59. $x^2 - 8xy + 64y^2$ is prime.
To be a perfect square trinomial, the middle term would have to be $2(-8xy) = -16xy$ rather than $-8xy$.

61. $16x^2 - 40xy + 25y^2$
$= (4x)^2 - 2(4x \cdot 5y) + (5y)^2$
$= (4x - 5y)^2$

63. $12x^2 - 12x + 3 = 3(4x^2 - 4x + 1)$
$= 3\left[(2x)^2 - 2(2x) + 1^2\right]$
$= 3(2x - 1)^2$

65. $9x^3 + 6x^2 + x$
$= x(9x^2 + 6x + 1)$
$= x\left[(3x)^2 + 2(3x) + 1^2\right]$
$= x(3x + 1)^2$

67. $2y^2 - 4y + 2 = 2(y^2 - 2y + 1)$
$= 2(y - 1)^2$

69. $2y^3 + 28y^2 + 98y = 2y(y^2 + 14y + 49)$
$= 2y(y + 7)^2$

71. x^3+1
$=x^3+1^3$
$=(x+1)(x^2-x\cdot 1+1^2)$
$=(x+1)(x^2-x+1)$

73. x^3-27
$=x^3-3^3$
$=(x-3)(x^2+x\cdot 3+3^2)$
$=(x-3)(x^2+3x+9)$

75. $8y^3-1$
$=(2y)^3-1^3$
$=(2y-1)\left[(2y)^2+2y\cdot 1+1\right]$
$=(2y-1)(4y^2+2y+1)$

77. $27x^3+8$
$=(3x)^3+2^3$
$=(3x+2)\left[(3x)^2-3x\cdot 2+2^2\right]$
$=(3x+2)(9x^2-6x+4)$

79. x^3y^3-64
$=(xy)^3-4^3$
$=(xy-4)\left[(xy)^2+xy\cdot 4+4^2\right]$
$=(xy-4)(x^2y^2+4xy+16)$

81. $27y^4+8y$
$=y(27y^3+8)$
$=y\left[(3y)^3+2^3\right]$
$=y(3y+2)\left[(3y)^2-3y\cdot 2+2^2\right]$
$=y(3y+2)(9y^2-6y+4)$

83. $54-16y^3$
$=2(27-8y^3)$
$=2\left[3^3-(2y)^3\right]$
$=2(3-2y)\left[3^2+3\cdot 2y+(2y)^2\right]$
$=2(3-2y)(9+6y+4y^2)$

85. $64x^3+27y^3$
$=(4x)^3+(3y)^3$
$=(4x+3y)\left[(4x)^2-4x\cdot 3y+(3y)^2\right]$
$=(4x+3y)(16x^2-12xy+9y^2)$

87. $125x^3-64y^3$
$=(5x)^3-(4y)^3$
$=(5x-4y)\left[(5x)^2+5x\cdot 4y+(4y)^2\right]$
$=(5x-4y)(25x^2+20xy+16y^2)$

89. $25x^2-\frac{4}{49}=(5x)^2-\left(\frac{2}{7}\right)^2$
$=\left(5x+\frac{2}{7}\right)\left(5x-\frac{2}{7}\right)$

90. $16x^2-\frac{9}{25}=(4x)^2-\left(\frac{3}{5}\right)^2$
$=\left(4x+\frac{3}{5}\right)\left(4x-\frac{3}{5}\right)$

91.
$$y^4 - \frac{y}{1000} = y\left(y^3 - \frac{1}{1000}\right)$$
$$= y\left[y^3 - \left(\frac{1}{10}\right)^3\right]$$
$$= y\left(y - \frac{1}{10}\right)\left[y^2 + y\cdot\frac{1}{10} + \left(\frac{1}{10}\right)^2\right]$$
$$= y\left(y - \frac{1}{10}\right)\left(y^2 + \frac{y}{10} + \frac{1}{100}\right)$$

92.
$$y^4 - \frac{y}{8} = y\left(y^3 - \frac{1}{8}\right) = y\left[y^3 - \left(\frac{1}{2}\right)^3\right]$$
$$= y\left(y - \frac{1}{2}\right)\left[y^2 + y\cdot\frac{1}{2} + \left(\frac{1}{2}\right)^2\right]$$
$$= y\left(y - \frac{1}{2}\right)\left(y^2 + \frac{y}{2} + \frac{1}{4}\right)$$

93.
$$0.25x - x^3 = x\left(0.25 - x^2\right)$$
$$= x\left[(0.5)^2 - x^2\right] = x(0.5+x)(0.5-x)$$

94.
$$0.64x - x^3 = x\left(0.64 - x^2\right)$$
$$= x\left[(0.8)^2 - x^2\right] = x(0.8+x)(0.8-x)$$

95.
$$(x+1)^2 - 25 = (x+1)^2 - 5^2$$
$$= \left[(x+1)+5\right]\left[(x+1)-5\right]$$
$$= (x+6)(x-4)$$

96.
$$(x+2)^2 - 49 = (x+2)^2 - 7^2$$
$$= \left[(x+2)+7\right]\left[(x+2)-7\right]$$
$$= (x+9)(x-5)$$

97.
$$\begin{array}{r} x^2+2x+1 \\ x-3\overline{\smash{)}x^3-x^2-5x-3} \\ \underline{x^3-3x^2} \\ 2x^2-5x \\ \underline{2x^2-6x} \\ x-3 \\ \underline{x-3} \end{array}$$

The quotient x^2+2x+1 factors further.

$x^2+2x+1=(x+1)^2$.

Thus, $x^3-x^2-5x-3=(x-3)(x+1)^2$.

98.
$$\begin{array}{r} x^2+6x+9 \\ x-2\overline{\smash{)}x^3+4x^2-3x-18} \\ \underline{x^3-2x^2} \\ 6x^2-3x \\ \underline{6x^2-12x} \\ 9x-18 \\ \underline{9x-18} \end{array}$$

The quotient x^2+6x+9 factors further.

$x^2+6x+9=(x+3)^2$.

Thus,

$x^3+4x^2-3x-18=(x-2)(x+3)^2$.

99. Area of outer square = x^2

Area of inner square = $5^2 = 25$

Area of shaded region $= x^2 - 25$

$= (x+5)(x-5)$

101. Area of large square = x^2

Area of each small corner squares

$= 2^2 = 4$

Area of four corner squares $= 4\cdot 4 = 16$

Area of shaded region = $x^2 - 16$

$= (x+4)(x-4)$

103. – 105. Answers will vary.

107. Statement *b* is true.

109. $x^2 - y^2 + 3x + 3y$
$= (x+y)(x-y) + 3(x+y)$
$= (x+y)((x-y)+3)$
$= (x+y)(x-y+3)$

111. $4x^{2n} + 12x^n + 9$
$= (2x^n)^2 + 2(6x^n) + 3^2$
$= (2x^n + 3)^2$

113. $9x^2 + kx + 1$
In order to get $9x^2$ as the first tem of the perfect square trinomial, the possibilities are
$(3x+1)^2 = 9x^2 + 6x + 1$
$(3x-1)^2 = 9x^2 - 6x + 1$
Therefore, for $9x^2 + kx + 1$ to be a perfect square trinomial, *k* must be –6 or 6.

115.

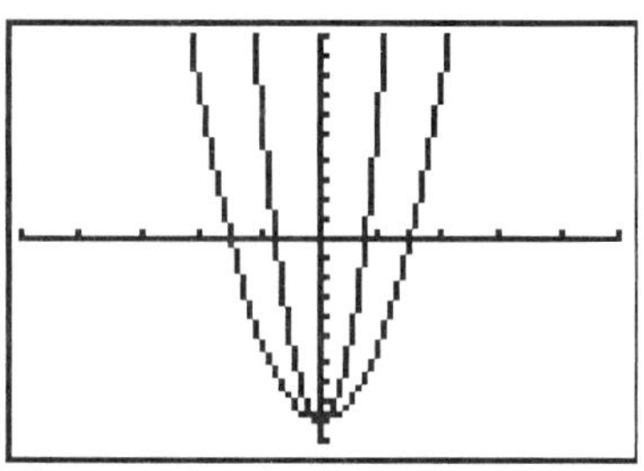

The graphs do not coincide.

$4x^2 - 9 = (2x+3)(2x-3)$
The expression on the right should be changed to $(2x+3)(2x-3)$.

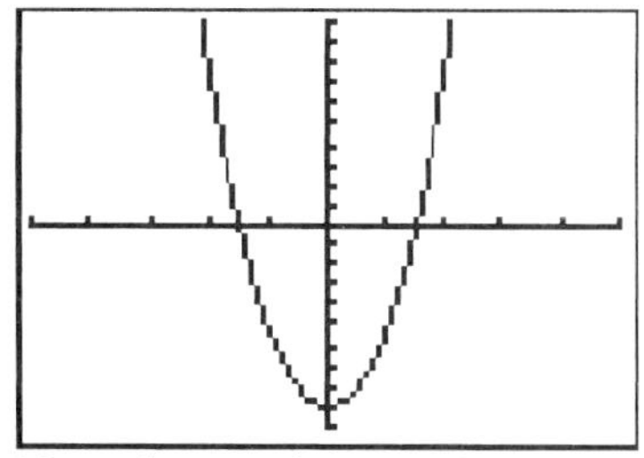

Now the graphs coincide.

117.

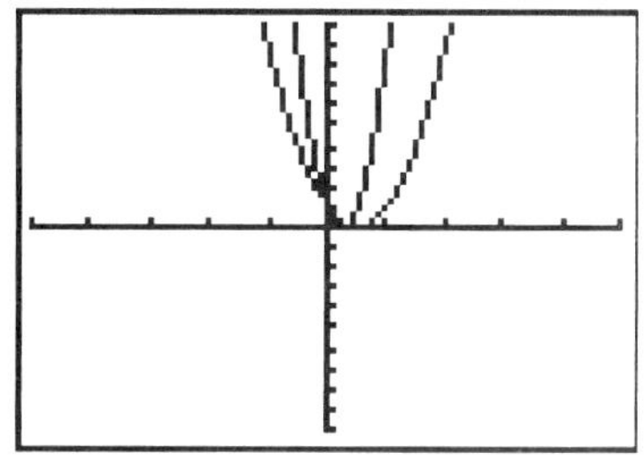

The graphs do not coincide.

$4x^2 - 4x + 1 = (2x)^2 - 2 \cdot 2x \cdot 1 = (2x-1)^2$

The expression on the right should be changed to $(2x-1)^2$.

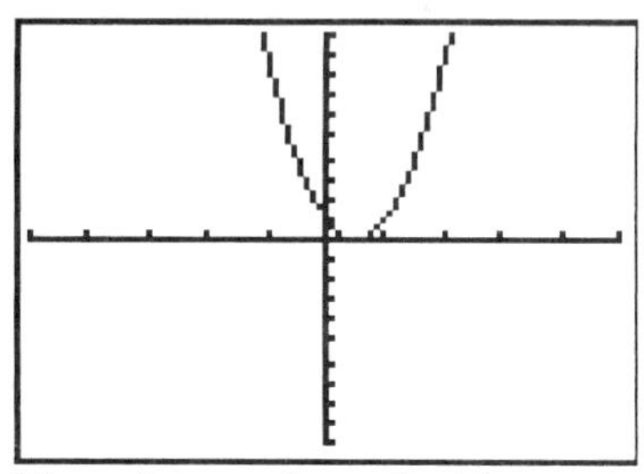

Now the graphs coincide.

119. $(2x^2y^3)^4(5xy^2)$
$= \left[2^4(x^2)^4(y^3)^4\right] \cdot (5xy^2)$
$= (16x^8y^{12})(5xy^2)$
$= (16 \cdot 5)(x^8 \cdot x^1)(y^{12} \cdot y^2)$
$= 80x^9y^{14}$

120. $(10x^2-5x+2)-(14x^2-5x-1)$
$=(10x^2-5x+2)+(-14x^2+5x+1)$
$=(10x^2-14x^2)+(-5x+5x)+(2+1)$
$=-4x^2+3$

121.

$$\begin{array}{r} 2x+5 \\ 3x-2\overline{\smash{)}6x^2+11x-10} \\ \underline{6x^2-\ \ 4x} \\ 15x-10 \\ \underline{15x-10} \\ 0 \end{array}$$

$$\frac{6x^2+11x-10}{3x-2}=2x+5$$

7.5 Exercise Set

In Exercises 1-61, all factorizations should be checked using multiplication or a graphing utility. Checks will not be shown here.

1. $5x^3-20x=5x(x^2-4)$
$=5x(x+2)(x-2)$

3. $7x^3+7x=7x(x^2+1)$

5. $5x^2-5x-30=5(x^2-x-6)$
$=5(x+2)(x-3)$

7. $2x^4-162=2(x^4-81)$
$=2(x^2+9)(x^2-9)$
$=2(x^2+9)(x+3)(x-3)$

9. $x^3+2x^2-9x-18$
$=(x^3+2x^2)+(-9x-18)$
$=x^2(x+2)-9(x+2)$
$=(x+2)(x^2-9)$
$=(x+2)(x+3)(x-3)$

11. $3x^3-24x^2+48x=3x(x^2-8x+16)$
$=3x(x-4)^2$

13. $2x^5+2x^2=2x^2(x^3+1)$
$=2x^2(x+1)(x^2-x+1)$

15. $6x^2+8x=2x(3x+4)$

17. $2y^2-2y-112=2(y^2-y-56)$
$=2(y-8)(y+7)$

19. $7y^4+14y^3+7y^2=7y^2(y^2+2y+1)$
$=7y^2(y+1)^2$

21. $y^2+8y-16$ is prime because there are no two integers whose product is -16 and whose sum is 8.

23. $16y^2-4y-2=2(8y^2-2y-1)$
$=2(4y+1)(2y-1)$

25. $r^2-25r=r(r-25)$

27. $4w^2+8w-5=(2w+5)(2w-1)$

29. $x^3-4x=x(x^2-4)=x(x+2)(x-2)$

31. x^2+64 is prime because it is the sum of two squares with no common factor other than 1.

33. $9y^2+13y+4=(9y+4)(y+1)$

35. y^3+2y^2-4y-8
$=(y^3+2y^2)+(-4y-8)$
$=y^2(y+2)-4(y+2)$
$=(y+2)(y^2-4)$
$=(y+2)(y+2)(y-2)$
or $(y+2)^2(y-2)$

37. $16y^2+24y+9$
$=(4y)^2+2(4y\cdot 3)+3^2$
$=(4y+3)^2$

39. $4y^3-28y^2+40y$
$=4y(y^2-7y+10)$
$=4y(y-5)(y-2)$

41. y^5-81y
$=y(y^4-81)$
$=y(y^2+9)(y^2-9)$
$=y(y^2+9)(y+3)(y-3)$

43. $20a^4-45a^2$
$=5a^2(4a^2-9)$
$=5a^2(2a+3)(2a-3)$

45. $12y^2-11y+2=(4y-1)(3y-2)$

47. $9y^2-64=(3y)^2-8^2$
$=(3y+8)(3y-8)$

49. $9y^2+64$ is prime because it is the sum of two squares with no common factor other than 1.

51. $2y^3+3y^2-50y-75$
$=(2y^3+3y^2)+(-50y-75)$
$=y^2(2y+3)-25(2y+3)$
$=(2y+3)(y^2-25)$
$=(2y+3)(y+5)(y-5)$

53. $2r^3+30r^2-68r$
$=2r(r^2+15r-34)$
$=2r(r+17)(r-2)$

55. $8x^5-2x^3=2x^3(4x^2-1)$
$=2x^3\left[(2x)^2-1^2\right]$
$=2x^3(2x+1)(2x-1)$

57. $3x^2+243=3(x^2+81)$

59. $x^4+8x=x(x^3+8)$
$=x(x^3+2^3)$
$=x(x+2)(x^2-2x+4)$

61. $2y^5-2y^2$
$=2y^2(y^3-1)$
$=2y^2(y-1)(y^2+y+1)$

63. $6x^2+8xy=2x(3x+4y)$

65. $xy-7x+3y-21$
$=(xy-7x)+(3y-21)$
$=x(y-7)+3(y-7)$
$=(y-7)(x+3)$

67. $x^2-3xy-4y^2=(x-4y)(x+y)$

69. $72a^3b^2+12a^2-24a^4b^2$
$=12a^2(6ab^2+1-2a^2b^2)$

71. $3a^2+27ab+54b^2$
$=3(a^2+9ab+18b^2)$
$=3(a+6b)(a+3b)$

73. $48x^4y-3x^2y$
$=3x^2y(16x^2-1)$
$=3x^2y(4x+1)(4x-1)$

75. $6a^2b+ab-2b$
$=b(6a^2+a-2)$
$=b(3a+2)(2a-1)$

77. $7x^5y-7xy^5$
$=7xy(x^4-y^4)$
$=7xy(x^2+y^2)(x^2-y^2)$
$=7xy(x^2+y^2)(x+y)(x-y)$

79. $10x^3y-14x^2y^2+4xy^3$
$=2xy(5x^2-7xy+2y^2)$
$=2xy(5x-2y)(x-y)$

81. $2bx^2+44bx+242b$
$=2b(x^2+22x+121)$
$=2b(x^2+2(11x)+11^2)$
$=2b(x+11)^2$

83. $15a^2+11ab-14b^2=(5a+7b)(3a-2b)$

85. $36x^3y-62x^2y^2+12xy^3$
$=2xy(18x^2-31xy+6y^2)$
$=2xy(9x-2y)(2x-3y)$

87. $a^2y-b^2y-a^2x+b^2x$
$=(a^2y-b^2y)+(-a^2x+b^2x)$
$=y(a^2-b^2)-x(a^2-b^2)$
$=(a^2-b^2)(y-x)$
$=(a+b)(a-b)(y-x)$

89. $9ax^3+15ax^2-14ax$
$=ax(9x^2+15x-14)$
$=ax(3x+7)(3x-2)$

91. $81x^4y-y^5$
$=y(81x^4-y^4)$
$=y(9x^2+y^2)(9x^2-y^2)$
$=y(9x^2+y^2)(3x+y)(3x-y)$

93. $10x^2(x+1)-7x(x+1)-6(x+1)$
$=(x+1)(10x^2-7x-6)$
$=(x+1)(5x-6)(2x+1)$

94. $12x^2(x-1)-4x(x-1)-5(x-1)$
$=(x-1)(12x^2-4x-5)$
$=(x-1)(6x-5)(2x+1)$

95. $6x^4+35x^2-6=(x^2+6)(6x^2-1)$

96. $7x^4+34x^2-5=(7x^2-1)(x^2+5)$

97. $(x-7)^2-4a^2=(x-7)^2-(2a)^2$
$=[(x-7)+2a][(x-7)-2a]$
$=(x-7+2a)(x-7-2a)$

98. $(x-6)^2-9a^2=(x-6)^2-(3a)^2$
$=[(x-6)+3a][(x-6)-3a]$
$=(x-6+3a)(x-6-3a)$

99. $x^2+8x+16-25a^2$
$=(x^2+8x+16)-(5a)^2$
$=(x+4)^2-(5a)^2$
$=[(x+4)+5a][(x+4)-5a]$
$=(x+4+5a)(x+4-5a)$

100. $x^2+14x+49-16a^2$
$=(x^2+14x+49)-(4a)^2$
$=(x+7)^2-(4a)^2$
$=[(x+7)+4a][(x+7)-4a]$
$=(x+7+4a)(x+7-4a)$

101. $y^7+y=y(y^6+1)=y\left[(y^2)^3+1^3\right]$
$=y(y^2+1)(y^4-y^2+1)$

102. $(y+1)^3+1=(y+1)^3+1^3$
$=[(y+1)+1]\left[(y+1)^2-(y+1)+1\right]$
$=(y+2)\left[(y^2+2y+1)-y-1+1\right]$
$=(y+2)(y^2+2y+1-y-1+1)$
$=(y+2)(y^2+y+1)$

103. $256-16t^2=16(16-t^2)$
$=16(4+t)(4-t)$

105. Area of outer circle = πb^2
Area of inner circle = πa^2
Area of shaded ring = $\pi b^2-\pi a^2$

$\pi b^2-\pi a^2=\pi(b^2-a^2)$
$=\pi(b+a)(b-a)$

107. Answers will vary.

109. Statement *d* is true.

$3x^2y^3+9xy^2+21xy$
$=3xy(xy^2+3y+7)$,

and xy^2+3y+7 cannot be factored further.

111. $5y^5-5y^4-20y^3+20y^2$
$=5y^2(y^3-y^2-4y+4)$
$=5y^2\left[y^2(y-1)-4(y-1)\right]$
$=5y^2(y-1)(y^2-4)$
$=5y^2(y-1)(y+2)(y-2)$

113. $(x+5)^2-20(x+5)+100$
This is a perfect square trinomial.

$(x+5)^2-20(x+5)+100$
$=(x+5)^2-2(x+5)(10)+10^2$
$=[(x+5)-10]^2$
$=(x-5)^2$

115.

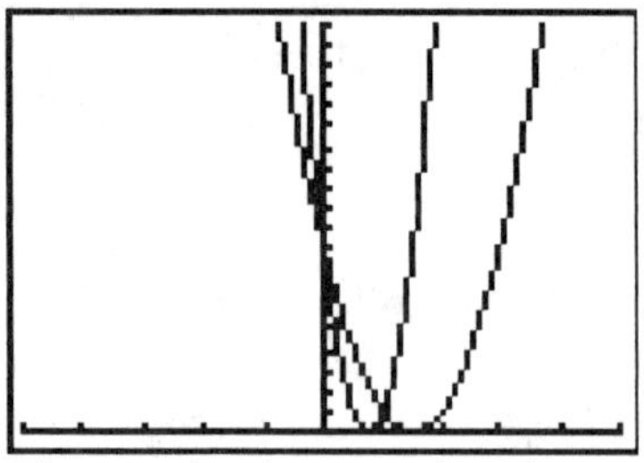

The graphs do not coincide.

$$4x^2 - 12x + 9 = (2x)^2 - 2(2x \cdot 3) + 3^2$$
$$= (2x-3)^2$$

Change the polynomial on the right side to $(2x-3)^2$.

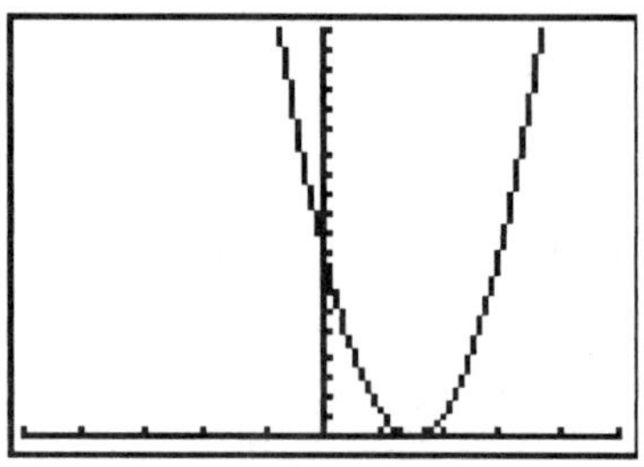

Now the graphs coincide.

117.

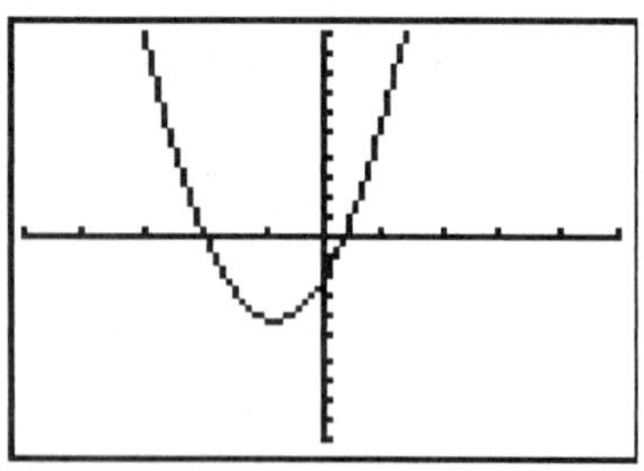

The graphs coincide.

This verifies that the factorization $6x^2 + 10x - 4 = 2(3x-1)(x+2)$ is correct.

119.

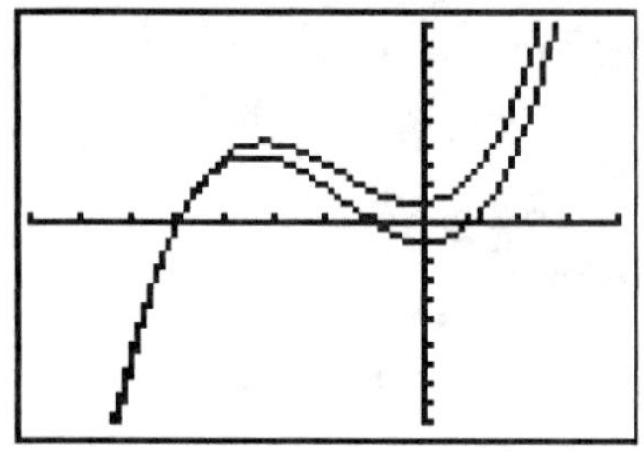

The graphs do not coincide

$$2x^3 + 10x^2 - 2x - 10$$
$$= 2(x^3 + 5x^2 - x - 5)$$
$$= 2\left[(x^3 + 5x^2) + (-x-5)\right]$$
$$= 2\left[x^2(x+5) - 1(x+5)\right]$$
$$= 2(x+5)(x^2-1)$$
$$= 2(x+5)(x+1)(x-1)$$

Change the polynomial on the right side to $2(x+5)(x+1)(x-1)$.

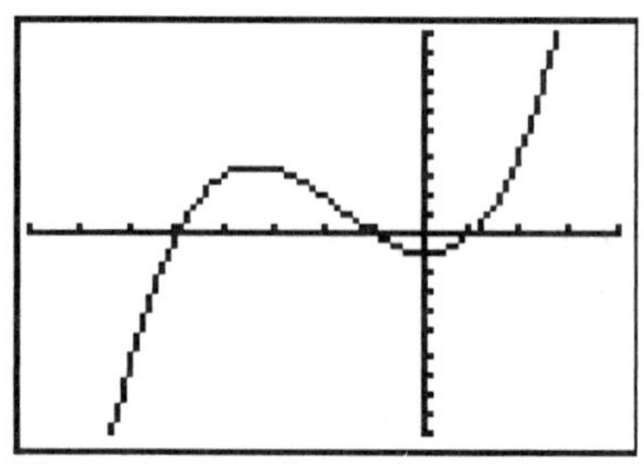

Now the graphs coincide.

120. $9x^2 - 16 = (3x)^2 - 4^2$
$$= (3x+4)(3x-4)$$

121. $5x - 2y = 10$

To find the x-intercept, let $y = 0$.

$$5x - 2(0) = 10$$
$$5x = 10$$
$$x = 2$$

To find the y-intercept, let $x = 0$.

$$5(0)-2y=10$$
$$-2y=10$$
$$y=-5$$

checkpoint: (4,5)

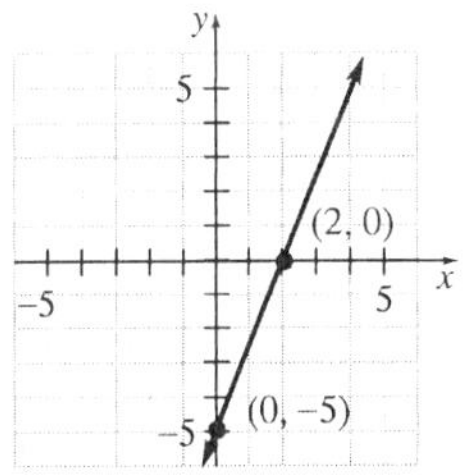

122. Let x = the measure of the first angle.
Then $3x$ = the measure of the second angle;
and $x + 80$ = the measure of the third angle.

$$x+3x+(x+80)=180$$
$$5x+80=180$$
$$5x=100$$
$$x=20$$

Measure of first angle, $x = 20°$
Measure of second angle, $3x = 60°$
Measure of third angle, $x + 80 = 100°$

7.6 Exercise Set

1. $x(x+7)=0$

$x=0$ or $x+7=0$

$x=-7$

The solutions are 0 and −7.

3. $(x-6)(x+4)=0$

$x-6=0$ or $x+4=0$

$x=6$ $\qquad$ $x=-4$

The solutions are 6 and −4.

5. $(x-9)(5x+4)=0$

$x-9=0$ or $5x+4=0$

$x=9$ $\qquad$ $5x=-4$

$x=-\frac{4}{5}$

The solutions are 9 and $-\frac{4}{5}$.

7. $10(x-4)(2x+9)=0$

$x-4=0$ or $2x+9=0$

$x=4$ $\qquad$ $2x=-9$

$x=-\frac{9}{2}$

The solutions are 4 and $-\frac{9}{2}$.

In Exercises 9-55, all solutions should be checked by substitution or by using a graphing utility and identifying x-intercepts. The check by substitution will be shown here for Exercise 9 only.

9. $x^2+8x+15=0$

$(x+5)(x+3)=0$

$x+5=0$ or $x+3=0$

$x=-5$ $\qquad$ $x=-3$

Check −5:

$$x^2+8x+15=0$$
$$(-5)^2+8(-5)+15=0$$
$$25-40+15=0$$
$$0=0 \text{ true}$$

Check −3:

$$x^2+8x+15=0$$
$$(-3)^2+8(-3)+15=0$$
$$9-24+15=0$$
$$0=0 \text{ true}$$

The solutions are −5 and −3.

11.
$$x^2-2x-15=0$$
$$(x+3)(x-5)=0$$
$$x+3=0 \quad \text{or} \quad x-5=0$$
$$x=-3 \qquad\qquad x=5$$
The solutions are –3 and 5.

13.
$$x^2-4x=21$$
$$x^2-4x-21=0$$
$$(x+3)(x-7)=0$$
$$x+3=0 \quad \text{or} \quad x-7=0$$
$$x=-3 \qquad\qquad x=7$$
The solutions are –3 and 7.

15.
$$x^2+9x=-8$$
$$x^2+9x+8=0$$
$$(x+8)(x+1)=0$$
$$x+8=0 \quad \text{or} \quad x+1=0$$
$$x=-8 \qquad\qquad x=-1$$
The solutions are –8 and –1.

17.
$$x^2+4x=0$$
$$x(x+4)=0$$
$$x=0 \quad \text{or} \quad x+4=0$$
$$x=-4$$
The solutions are 0 and –4.

19.
$$x^2-5x=0$$
$$x(x-5)=0$$
$$x=0 \quad \text{or} \quad x-5=0$$
$$x=5$$
The solutions are 0 and 5.

21.
$$x^2=4x$$
$$x^2-4x=0$$
$$x(x-4)=0$$
$$x=0 \quad \text{or} \quad x-4=0$$
$$x=4$$
The solutions are 0 and 4.

23.
$$2x^2=5x$$
$$2x^2-5x=0$$
$$x(2x-5)=0$$
$$x=0 \quad \text{or} \quad 2x-5=0$$
$$2x=5$$
$$x=\frac{5}{2}$$
The solutions are 0 and $\frac{5}{2}$.

25.
$$3x^2=-5x$$
$$3x^2+5x=0$$
$$x(3x+5)=0$$
$$x=0 \quad \text{or} \quad 3x+5=0$$
$$3x=-5$$
$$x=-\frac{5}{3}$$
The only solution is 0 and $-\frac{5}{3}$.

27.
$$x^2+4x+4=0$$
$$(x-2)^2=0$$
$$x+2=0$$
$$x=-2$$
The only solution is –2.

29.
$$x^2=12x-36$$
$$x^2-12x+36=0$$
$$(x-6)^2=0$$
$$x-6=0$$
$$x=6$$
The only solution is 6.

31.
$$4x^2 = 12x - 9$$
$$4x^2 - 12x + 9 = 0$$
$$(2x-3)^2 = 0$$
$$2x - 3 = 0$$
$$2x = 3$$
$$x = \frac{3}{2}$$
The only solution is $\frac{3}{2}$.

33.
$$2x^2 = 7x + 4$$
$$2x^2 - 7x - 4 = 0$$
$$(2x+1)(x-4) = 0$$
$$2x + 1 = 0 \quad \text{or} \quad x - 4 = 0$$
$$2x = -1 \qquad x = 4$$
$$x = -\frac{1}{2}$$
The solutions are $-\frac{1}{2}$ and 4.

35.
$$5x^2 = 18 - x$$
$$5x^2 + x - 18 = 0$$
$$(5x-9)(x+2) = 0$$
$$5x - 9 = 0 \quad \text{or} \quad x + 2 = 0$$
$$5x = 9 \qquad x = -2$$
$$x = \frac{9}{5}$$
The solutions are $\frac{9}{5}$ and -2.

37.
$$x^2 - 49 = 0$$
$$(x+7)(x-7) = 0$$
$$x + 7 = 0 \quad \text{or} \quad x - 7 = 0$$
$$x = -7 \qquad x = 7$$
The solutions are -7 and 7.

39.
$$4x^2 - 25 = 0$$
$$(2x+5)(2x-5) = 0$$
$$2x + 5 = 0 \quad \text{or} \quad 2x - 5 = 0$$
$$2x = -5 \qquad 2x = 5$$
$$x = -\frac{5}{2} \qquad x = \frac{5}{2}$$
The solutions are $-\frac{5}{2}$ and $\frac{5}{2}$.

41.
$$81x^2 = 25$$
$$81x^2 - 25 = 0$$
$$(9x+5)(9x-5) = 0$$
$$9x + 5 = 0 \quad \text{or} \quad 9x - 5 = 0$$
$$9x = -5 \qquad 9x = 5$$
$$x = -\frac{5}{9} \qquad x = \frac{5}{9}$$
The solutions are $-\frac{5}{9}$ and $\frac{5}{9}$.

43.
$$x(x-4) = 21$$
$$x^2 - 4x = 21$$
$$x^2 - 4x - 21 = 0$$
$$(x+3)(x-7) = 0$$
$$x + 3 = 0 \quad \text{or} \quad x - 7 = 0$$
$$x = -3 \qquad x = 7$$
The solutions are -3 and 7.

45.
$$4x(x+1) = 15$$
$$4x^2 + 4x = 15$$
$$4x^2 + 4x - 15 = 0$$
$$(2x+5)(2x-3) = 0$$
$$2x + 5 = 0 \quad \text{or} \quad 2x - 3 = 0$$
$$2x = -5 \qquad 2x = 3$$
$$x = -\frac{5}{2} \qquad x = \frac{3}{2}$$
The solutions are $-\frac{5}{2}$ and $\frac{3}{2}$.

47.
$$(x-1)(x+4)=14$$
$$x^2+3x-4=14$$
$$x^2+3x-18=0$$
$$(x+6)(x-3)=0$$
$$x+6=0 \quad \text{or} \quad x-3=0$$
$$x=-6 \qquad\qquad x=3$$
The solutions are −6 and 3.

49.
$$(x+1)(2x+5)=-1$$
$$2x^2+7x+5=-1$$
$$2x^2+7x+6=0$$
$$(2x+3)(x+2)=0$$
$$2x+3=0 \quad \text{or} \quad x+2=0$$
$$2x=-3 \qquad\qquad x=-2$$
$$x=-\frac{3}{2}$$
The solutions are $-\frac{3}{2}$ and −2.

51.
$$y(y+8)=16(y-1)$$
$$y^2+8y=16y-16$$
$$y^2-8y+16=0$$
$$(y-4)^2=0$$
$$y-4=0$$
$$y=4$$
The only solution is 4.

53.
$$4y^2+20y+25=0$$
$$(2y+5)^2=0$$
$$2y+5=0$$
$$2y=-5$$
$$y=-\frac{5}{2}$$
The only solution is $-\frac{5}{2}$.

55.
$$64w^2=48w-9$$
$$64w^2-48w+9=0$$
$$(8w-3)^2=0$$
$$8w-3=0$$
$$8w=3$$
$$w=\frac{3}{8}$$
The only solution is $\frac{3}{8}$.

57.
$$(x-4)(x^2+5x+6)=0$$
$$(x-4)(x+3)(x+2)=0$$
$$x-4=0 \quad \text{or} \quad x+3=0 \quad \text{or} \quad x+2=0$$
$$x=4 \qquad\qquad x=-3 \qquad\qquad x=-2$$
The solutions are 4, −3, and −2.

58.
$$(x-5)(x^2-3x+2)=0$$
$$(x-5)(x-2)(x-1)=0$$
$$x-5=0 \quad \text{or} \quad x-2=0 \quad \text{or} \quad x-1=0$$
$$x=5 \qquad\qquad x=2 \qquad\qquad x=1$$
The solutions are 5, 2, and 1.

59.
$$x^3-36x=0$$
$$x(x^2-36)=0$$
$$x(x+6)(x-6)=0$$
$$x=0 \quad \text{or} \quad x+6=0 \quad \text{or} \quad x-6=0$$
$$x=-6 \qquad\qquad x=6$$
The solutions are 0, −6, and 6.

60.
$$x^3-4x=0$$
$$x(x^2-4)=0$$
$$x(x+2)(x-2)=0$$
$$x=0 \quad \text{or} \quad x+2=0 \quad \text{or} \quad x-2=0$$
$$x=-2 \qquad\qquad x=2$$
The solutions are 0, −2, and 2.

61. $y^3+3y^2+2y=0$

$y(y^2+3y+2)=0$

$y(y+2)(y+1)=0$

$y=0$ or $y+2=0$ or $y+1=0$

$y=-2 \qquad y=-1$

The solutions are $0, -2$ and -1.

62. $y^3+2y^2-3y=0$

$y(y^2+2y-3)=0$

$y(y+3)(y-1)=0$

$y=0$ or $y+3=0$ or $y-1=0$

$y=-3 \qquad y=1$

The solutions are 0, −3, and 1.

63. $2(x-4)^2+x^2=x(x+50)-46x$

$2(x^2-8x+16)+x^2=x^2+50x-46x$

$2x^2-16x+32+x^2=x^2+4x$

$3x^2-16x+32=x^2+4x$

$2x^2-20x+32=0$

$2(x^2-10x+16)=0$

$2(x-8)(x-2)=0$

$x-8=0$ or $x-2=0$

$x=8 \qquad x=2$

The solutions are 8 and 2.

64. $(x-4)(x-5)+(2x+3)(x-1)$

$=x(2x-25)-13$

$x^2-9x+20+2x^2+x-3$

$=2x^2-25x-13$

$3x^2-8x+17=2x^2-25x-13$

$x^2+17x+30=0$

$(x+15)(x+2)=0$

$x+15=0$ or $x+2=0$

$x=-15 \qquad x=-2$

The solutions are −15 and −2.

65. $(x-2)^2-5(x-2)+6=0$

$[(x-2)-3][(x-2)-2]=0$

$(x-5)(x-4)=0$

$x-5=0$ or $x-4=0$

$x=5 \qquad x=4$

The solutions are 5 and 4.

66. $(x-3)^2+2(x-3)-8=0$

$[(x-3)-2][(x-3)+4]=0$

$(x-5)(x+1)=0$

$x-5=0$ or $x+1=0$

$x=5 \qquad x=-1$

The solutions are 5 and −1.

67. $h=-16t^2+20t+300$

Substitute 0 for h and solve for t.

$0=-16t^2+20t+300$

$-16t^2+20t+300=0$

$-4t(4t^2-5t-75)=0$

$-4t(4t+15)(t-5)=0$

$-4t=0$ or $4t+15=0$ or $t-5=0$

$t=0 \qquad 4t=-15 \qquad t=5$

$t=-\frac{15}{4}=-3.75$

Discard $t=0$ since this represents the time before the ball was thrown. Also discard $t=-3.75$ since time cannot be negative.

The only solution that makes sense is 5. So it will take 5 seconds for the ball to hit the ground.

Each tick mark represents one second.

69. Substitute 276 for h and solve for t.

$$276 = -16t^2 + 20t + 300$$
$$16t^2 - 20t - 24 = 0$$
$$4(4t^2 - 5t - 6) = 0$$
$$4(4t + 3)(t - 2) = 0$$

$4t + 3 = 0$ or $t - 2 = 0$

$4t = -3$ $\quad$ $t = 2$

$t = -\frac{3}{4}$

Discard $t = -\frac{3}{4}$ since time cannot be negative. The ball's height will be 276 feet 2 seconds after it is thrown. This corresponds to the point $(2, 276)$ on the graph.

71. $h = -16t^2 + 72t$

Substitute 32 for h and solve for t.

$$32 = -16t^2 + 72t$$
$$16t^2 - 72t + 32 = 0$$
$$8(2t^2 - 9t + 4) = 0$$
$$8(2t - 1)(t - 4) = 0$$

$2t - 1 = 0$ or $t - 4 = 0$

$t = \frac{1}{2}$ $\quad$ $t = 4$

The debris will be 32 feet above the ground $\frac{1}{2}$ second after the explosion and 4 seconds after the explosion.

73. $N = 2x^2 + 22x + 320$

Substitute 1100 for N and solve for x.

$$1100 = 2x^2 + 22x + 320$$
$$0 = 2x^2 + 22x - 780$$
$$0 = 2(x^2 + 11x - 390)$$
$$0 = 2(x + 26)(x - 15)$$

$x + 26 = 0$ or $x - 15 = 0$

$x = -26$ $\quad$ $x = 15$

Discard $x = -26$ because the model starts at $x = 0$ to represent 1980. Since $x = 15$ represents the year 1995, the model shows that there were 1100 thousand (or 1,100,000) inmates in U.S. state and federal prisons in 1995. This corresponds to the point $(15, 1100)$ on the graph.

75. $P = -10x^2 + 475x + 3500$

Substitute 7250 for P and solve for x.

$$7250 = -10x^2 + 475x + 3500$$
$$10x^2 - 475x + 3750 = 0$$
$$5(2x^2 - 95x + 750) = 0$$
$$5(x - 10)(2x - 75) = 0$$

$x - 10 = 0$ or $2x - 75 = 0$

$x = 10$ $\quad$ $2x = 75$

$x = \frac{75}{2}$ or 37.5

The alligator population will have increased to 7250 after 10 years. (Discard 37.5 because this value is outside of $0 \le x \le 12$.)

77. The solution in Exercise 75 corresponds to the point $(10, 7250)$ on the graph.

79. $N = \frac{t^2 - t}{2}$

Substitute 45 for N and solve for t.

$$45 = \frac{t^2 - t}{2}$$
$$2 \cdot 45 = 2\left(\frac{t^2 - t}{2}\right)$$
$$90 = t^2 - t$$
$$0 = t^2 - t - 90$$
$$0 = (t - 10)(t + 9)$$

$t - 10 = 0$ or $t + 9 = 0$

$t = 10$ $\quad$ $t = -9$

Discard $t=-9$ since the number of teams cannot be negative. If 45 games are scheduled, there are 10 teams in the league.

81. Let x = the width of the parking lot. Then $x+3$ = the length.

$$l\cdot w=A$$
$$(x+3)(x)=180$$
$$x^2+3x=180$$
$$x^2+3x-180=0$$
$$(x+15)(x-12)=0$$
$$x+15=0 \quad \text{or} \quad x-12=0$$
$$x=-15 \qquad\qquad x=12$$

Discard $x=-15$ since the width cannot be negative. Then $x=12$ and $x+3=15$, so the length is 15 yards and the width is 12 yards.

83. Use the formula for the area of a triangle where x is the base and $x+1$ is the height.

$$\frac{1}{2}bh=A$$
$$\frac{1}{2}x(x+1)=15$$
$$2\left[\frac{1}{2}x(x+1)\right]=2\cdot 15$$
$$x(x+1)=30$$
$$x^2+x=30$$
$$x^2+x-30=0$$
$$(x+6)(x-5)=0$$
$$x+6=0 \quad \text{or} \quad x-5=0$$
$$x=-6 \qquad\qquad x=5$$

Discard $x=-6$ since the length of the base cannot be negative.
Then $x=5$ and $x+1=6$, so the base is 5 centimeters and the height is 6 centimeters.

85. **a.** Area of a large rectangle

$$(2x+12)(2x+10)$$
$$=4x^2+20x+24x+120$$
$$=4x^2+44x+120$$

Area of a flower bed = $10\cdot 12=120$

Area of border

$$=(4x^2+44x+120)-120$$
$$=4x^2+44x$$

b. Find the width of the border for which the area of the border would be 168 square feet.

$$4x^2+44x=168$$
$$4x^2+44x-168=0$$
$$4(x^2+11x-42)=0$$
$$4(x+14)(x-3)=0$$
$$x+14=0 \quad \text{or} \quad x-3=0$$
$$x=-14 \qquad\qquad x=3$$

Discard $x=-14$ since the width of the border cannot be negative. You should prepare a strip that is 3 feet wide for the border.

87. Answers will vary.

89. Statement d is true.

$$x(x+\pi)=0$$
$$x=0 \quad \text{or} \quad x+\pi=0$$
$$x=-\pi$$

The solutions are 0 and π.

91. $x^3 - x^2 - 16x + 16 = 0$

$\left(x^3 - x^2\right) + \left(-16x + 16\right) = 0$

$x^2(x-1) - 16(x-1) = 0$

$(x-1)\left(x^2 - 16\right) = 0$

$(x-1)(x+4)(x-4) = 0$

$x - 1 = 0$ or $x + 4 = 0$ or $x - 4 = 0$

$x = 1$ $\quad x = -4$ $\quad x = 4$

The solutions are 1, –4, and 4.

93. $\left(x^2 - 5x + 5\right)^3 = 1$

The only number that can be cubed (raised to the third power) to give 1 is 1. Therefore, the given equation is equivalent to the quadratic equation

$x^2 - 5x + 5 = 1.$

Solve this equation

$x^2 - 5x + 4 = 0$

$(x-1)(x-4) = 0$

$x - 1 = 0$ or $x - 4 = 0$

$x = 1$ $\quad x = 4$

The solutions are 1 and 4.

95. $y = x^2 + x - 2$

To match this equation with its graph, find the intercepts.

To find the $y-$intercepts, let $x = 0$ and solve for y.

$y = 0^2 + 0 - 2$

$y = -2$

The y-intercept is –2.

To find the $x-$intercepts, let $y = 0$ and solve for x.

$0 = x^2 + x - 2$

$0 = (x+2)(x-1)$

$x + 2 = 0$ or $x - 1 = 0$

$x = -2$ $\quad x = 1$

The x intercepts are –2 and 1.

The only graph with y-intercept –2 and x-intercepts –2 and 1 is graph a.

97. $y = x^2 - 4x$

To match this equation with its graph, find the intercepts.

To find the $y-$intercept, let $x = 0$ and solve for y.

$y = 0^2 - 4(0) = 0$

The y-intercept is 0, which means that the graph passes through the origin.

To find the $x-$intercepts, let $y = 0$ and solve for x.

$0 = x^2 - 4x$

$0 = x(x-4)$

$x = 0$ or $x - 4 = 0$

$x = 4$

The x-intercepts are 0 and 4.

The only graph with y-intercept 0 and x-intercepts 0 and 4 is graph b.

99. $y = x^2 + x - 6$

$x^2 + x - 6 = 0$

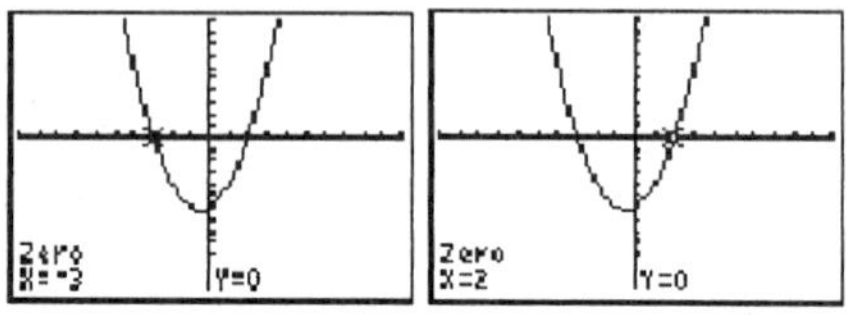

The calculator shows that the x-intercepts for the graph are –3 and 2. This means that the solutions of the equation $x^2 + x - 6 = 0$ are –3 and 2.

Check –3:

$x^2 + x - 6 = 0$

$(-3)^2 + (-3) - 6 = 0$

$9 - 3 - 6 = 0$

$6 - 6 = 0$

$0 = 0$ true

Check 2:

$x^2 + x - 6 = 0$

$2^2 + 2 - 6 = 0$

$4 + 2 - 6 = 0$

$6 - 6 = 0$

$0 = 0$ true

The check verifies that the solutions of $x^2 + x - 6 = 0$ are −3 and 2.

101. $y = x^2 - 2x + 1$

$x^2 - 2x + 1 = 0$

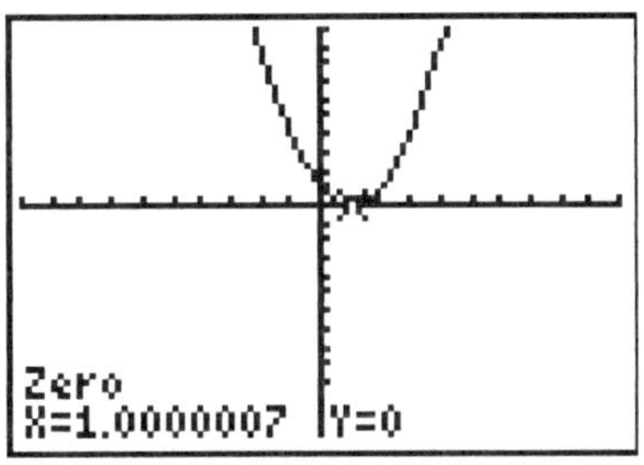

The calculator shows that the graph has one *x*-intercept, 1. This means that the only solution of the equation $x^2 - 2x + 1 = 0$ is 1.

Check 1:

$x^2 - 2x + 1 = 0$

$1^2 - 2(1) + 1 = 0$

$1 - 2 + 1 = 0$

$-1 + 1 = 0$

$0 = 0$ true

The check verifies that the solution of $x^2 - 2x + 1$ is 1.

103. Answers will vary depending on the exercises chosen.

104. $y > -\frac{2}{3}x + 1$

Graph $y = -\frac{2}{3}x + 1$ as a dashed line using the slope $-\frac{2}{3} = \frac{-2}{3}$ and *y*-intercept 1. (Plot (0,1) and move 2 units *down* and 3 units to the *right* to reach the point (3, −1). Draw a line through (0,1) and (3, −1).)

Use (0,0) as a test point. Since $0 > -\frac{2}{3}(0) + 1$ is false, shade the half-plane *not* containing (0,0).

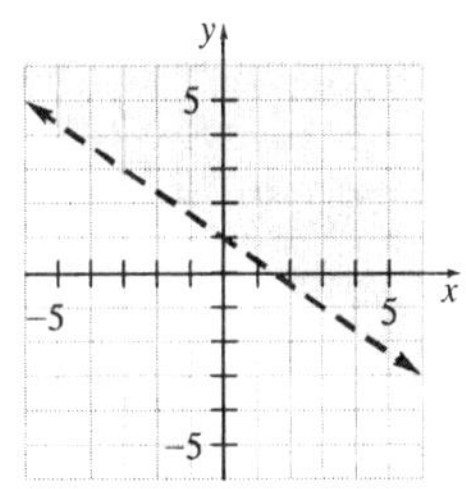

105. $\left(\frac{8x^4}{4x^7}\right)^2 = \left(\frac{8}{4} \cdot x^{4-7}\right) = \left(2x^{-3}\right)^2$

$= 2^2 \cdot \left(x^{-3}\right)^2 = 4x^{-6} = \frac{4}{x^6}$

106.

$5x + 28 = 6 - 6x$

$5x + 6x + 28 = 6 - 6x + 6x$

$11x + 28 = 6$

$11x + 28 - 28 = 6 - 28$

$11x = -22$

$\frac{11x}{11} = \frac{-22}{11}$

$x = -2$

Chapter 7 Review Exercises

1. $30x-45=15(2x-3)$

2. $12x^3+16x^2-400x=4x(3x^2+4x-100)$

3. $30x^4y+15x^3y+5x^2y$
$=5x^2y(6x^2+3x+1)$

4. $7(x+3)-2(x+3)$
$=(x+3)(7-2)$
$=(x+3)\cdot 5$ or $5(x+3)$

5. $7x^2(x+y)-(x+y)$
$=7x^2(x+y)-1(x+y)$
$=(x+y)(7x^2-1)$

6. $x^3+3x^2+2x+6=(x^3+3x^2)+(2x+6)$
$=x^2(x+3)+2(x+3)$
$=(x+3)(x^2+2)$

7. $xy+y+4x+4=(xy+y)+(4x+4)$
$=y(x+1)+4(x+1)$
$=(x+1)(y+4)$

8. $x^3+5x+x^2+5=(x^3+5x)+(x^2+5)$
$=x(x^2+5)+1(x^2+5)$
$=(x^2+5)(x+1)$

9. $xy+4x-2y-8=(xy+4x)+(-2y-8)$
$=x(y+4)-2(y+4)$
$=(y+4)(x-2)$

10. $x^2-3x+2=(x-2)(x-1)$

11. $x^2-x-20=(x-5)(x+4)$

12. $x^2+19x+48=(x+3)(x+16)$

13. $x^2-6xy+8y^2=(x-4y)(x-2y)$

14. x^2+5x-9 is prime because there is no pair of integers whose product is −9 and whose sum is 5.

15. $x^2+16xy-17y^2=(x+17y)(x-y)$

16. $3x^2+6x-24=3(x^2+2x-8)$
$=3(x+4)(x-2)$

17. $3x^3-36x^2+33x=3x(x^2-12x+11)$
$=3x(x-11)(x-1)$

18. $3x^2+17x+10$
Factor by trial and error or by grouping. To factor by grouping, find two integers whose product is $ac=3\cdot 10=30$ and whose sum is $b=17$. These integers are 15 and 2.
$3x^2+17x+10=3x^2+15x+2x+10$
$=3x(x+5)+2(x+5)$
$=(x+5)(3x+2)$

19. $5y^2-17y+6$
Factor by trial and error or by grouping. To factor by trial and error, start with the First terms, which must be $5y$ and y. Because the middle term is negative, the factors of 6 must both be negative. Try various combinations until the correct middle term is obtained.

$$(5y-1)(y-6)=5y^2-31y+6$$
$$(5y-6)(y-1)=5y^2-11y+6$$
$$(5y-3)(y-2)=5y^2-13y+6$$
$$(5y-2)(y-3)=5y^2-17y+6$$

Thus, $5y^2-17y+6=(5y-2)(y-3)$.

20. $4x^2+4x-15=(2x+5)(2x-3)$

21. $5y^2+11y+4$

Use trial and error. The first terms must be 5y and y. Because the middle term is positive, the factors of 4 must both be positive. Try all the combinations.

$$(5y+2)(y+2)=5y^2+12y+4$$
$$(5y+4)(y+1)=5y^2+9y+4$$
$$(5y+1)(y+4)=5y^2+21y+4$$

None of these possibilities gives the required middle term, $11x$, and there are no more possibilities to try, so $5y^2+11y+4$ is prime.

22. $8x^2+8x-6$

First factor out the GCF, 2. Then factor the resulting trinomial by trial and error or by grouping.

$$\begin{aligned}8x^2+8x-6&=2(4x^2+4x-3)\\&=2(2x+3)(2x-1)\end{aligned}$$

23. $$\begin{aligned}2x^3+7x^2-72x&=x(2x^2+7x-72)\\&=x(2x-9)(x+8)\end{aligned}$$

24. $$\begin{aligned}12y^3+28y^2+8y&=4y(3y^2+7y+2)\\&=4y(3y+1)(y+2)\end{aligned}$$

25. $2x^2-7xy+3y^2=(2x-y)(x-3y)$

26. $5x^2-6xy-8y^2=(5x+4y)(x-2y)$

27. $4x^2-1=(2x)^2-1^2=(2x+1)(2x-1)$

28. $$\begin{aligned}81-100y^2&=9^2-(10y)^2\\&=(9+10y)(9-10y)\end{aligned}$$

29. $$\begin{aligned}25a^2-49b^2&=(5a)^2-(7b)^2\\&=(5a+7b)(5a-7b)\end{aligned}$$

30. $$\begin{aligned}z^4-16&=(z^2)^2-4^2\\&=(z^2+4)(z^2-4)\\&=(z^2+4)(z+2)(z-2)\end{aligned}$$

31. $2x^2-18=2(x^2-9)=2(x+3)(x-3)$

32. x^2+1 is prime because it is the sum of two squares with no common factor other than 1.

33. $9x^3-x=x(9x^2-1)=x(3x+1)(3x-1)$

34. $$\begin{aligned}18xy^2-8x&=2x(9y^2-4)\\&=2x(3y+2)(3y-2)\end{aligned}$$

35. $$\begin{aligned}x^2+22x+121&=x^2+2(11x)+11^2\\&=(x+11)^2\end{aligned}$$

36. $$\begin{aligned}x^2-16x+64&=x^2-2(8\cdot x)+8^2\\&=(x-8)^2\end{aligned}$$

37. $$\begin{aligned}9y^2+48y+64&=(3y)^2+2(3y\cdot 8)+8^2\\&=(3y+8)^2\end{aligned}$$

38. $16x^2 - 40x + 25 = (4x)^2 - 2(4x \cdot 5) + 5^2$
$= (4x-5)^2$

39. $25x^2 + 15x + 9$ is prime.
(To be a perfect square trinomial, the middle term would have to be $2(5x \cdot 3) = 30x$.)

40. $36x^2 + 60xy + 25y^2$
$= (6x)^2 + 2(6x \cdot 5y) + (5y)^2$
$= (6x + 5y)^2$

41. $25x^2 - 40xy + 16y^2$
$= (5x)^2 - 2(5x \cdot 4y) + (4y)^2$
$= (5x - 4y)^2$

42. $x^3 - 27 = x^3 - 3^2 = (x-3)(x^2 + 3x + 9)$

43. $64x^3 + 1$
$= (4x)^3 + 1^3$
$= (4x+1)\left[(4x)^2 - 4x \cdot 1 + 1^2\right]$
$= (4x+1)(16x^2 - 4x + 1)$

44. $54x^3 - 16y^3$
$= 2(27x^3 - 8y^3)$
$= 2\left[(3x)^3 - (2y)^3\right]$
$= 2(3x - 2y)\left[(3x)^2 + 3x \cdot 2y + (2y)^2\right]$
$= 2(3x - 2y)(9x^2 + 6xy + 4y^2)$

45. $27x^3y + 8y$
$= y(27x^3 + 8)$
$= y\left[(3x)^3 + 2^3\right]$
$= y(3x+2)\left[(3x)^2 - 3x \cdot 2 + 2^2\right]$
$= y(3x+2)(9x^2 - 6x + 4)$

46. Area of outer square = a^2
Area of inner square = $3^2 = 9$
Area of shaded region $= a^2 - 9$
$= (a+3)(a-3)$

47. Area of large square = a^2
Area of each small corner square = b^2
Area of four corner squares = $4b^2$
Area of shaded region
$= a^2 - 4b^2$
$= (a + 2b)(a - 2b)$

48. Area on the left:
Area of large square = A^2
Area of each rectangle: $A \cdot 1 = A$
Area of two rectangles = $2A$
Area of small square = $1^2 = 1$
Area on the right:
Area of square = $(A+1)^2$
This geometric model illustrates the factorization $A^2 + 2A - 1 = (A+1)^2$

49. $x^3 - 8x^2 + 7x = x(x^2 - 8x + 7)$
$= x(x-7)(x-1)$

50. $10y^2 + 9y + 2 = (5y+2)(2y+1)$

51. $128 - 2y^2 = 2(64 - y^2)$
$= 2(8+y)(8-y)$

52. $9x^2+6x+1=(3x)^2+2(3x)+1^2$
$=(3x+1)^2$

53. $20x^7-36x^3=4x^3(5x^4-9)$

54. $x^3-3x^2-9x+27$
$=(x^3-3x^2)+(-9x+27)$
$=x^2(x-3)-9(x-3)$
$=(x-3)(x^2-9)$
$=(x-3)(x+3)(x-3)$
or $(x-3)^2(x+3)$

55. y^2+16 is prime because it is the sum of two squares with no common factor other than 1.

56. $2x^3+19x^2+35x=x(2x^2+19x+35)$
$=x(2x+5)(x+7)$

57. $3x^3-30x^2+75x=3x(x^2-10x+25)$
$=3x(x-5)^2$

58. $3x^5-24x^2=3x^2(x^3-8)$
$=3x^2(x^3-2^3)$
$=3x^2(x-2)(x^2+2x+4)$

59. $4y^4-36y^2=4y^2(y^2-9)$
$=4y^2(y+3)(y-3)$

60. $5x^2+20x-105=5(x^2+4x-21)$
$=5(x+7)(x-3)$

61. $9x^2+8x-3$ is prime because there are no two integers whose product is $ac=-27$ and whose sum is 8.

62. $10x^5-44x^4+16x^3=2x^3(5x^2-22x+8)$
$=2x^3(5x-2)(x-4)$

63. $100y^2-49=(10y)^2-7^2$
$=(10y+7)(10y-7)$

64. $9x^5-18x^4=9x^4(x-2)$

65. $x^4-1=(x^2)^2-1^2$
$=(x^2+1)(x^2-1)$
$=(x^2+1)(x+1)(x-1)$

66. $2y^3-16=2(y^3-8)$
$=2(y^3-2^3)$
$=2(y-2)(y^2+2y+2^2)$
$=2(y-2)(y^2+2y+4)$

67. $x^3+64=x^3+4^3$
$=(x+4)(x^2-4x+4^2)$
$=(x+4)(x^2-4x+16)$

68. $6x^2+11x-10=(3x-2)(2x+5)$

69. $3x^4-12x^2=3x^2(x^2-4)$
$=3x^2(x+2)(x-2)$

70. $x^2-x-90=(x-10)(x+9)$

71. $25x^2+25xy+6y^2$
$=(5x+2y)(5x+3y)$

72. $x^4+125x = x(x^3+125)$
$= x(x^3+5^3)$
$= x(x+5)(x^2-5x+5^2)$
$= x(x+5)(x^2-5x+25)$

73. $32y^3+32y^2+6y = 2y(16y^2+16y+3)$
$= 2y(4y+3)(4y+1)$

74. $2y^2-16y+32 = 2(y^2-8y+16)$
$= 2(y-4)^2$

75. $x^2-2xy-35y^2 = (x+5y)(x-7y)$

76. $x^2+7x+xy+7y = x(x+7)+y(x+7)$
$= (x+7)(x+y)$

77. $9x^2+24xy+16y^2$
$= (3x)^2+2(3x\cdot 4y)+(4y)^2$
$= (3x+4y)^2$

78. $2x^4y-2x^2y = 2x^2y(x^2-1)$
$= 2x^2y(x+1)(x-1)$

79. $100y^2-49z^2 = (10y)^2-(7z)^2$
$= (10y+7z)(10y-7z)$

80. x^2+xy+y^2 is prime.
(To be a perfect square trinomial, the middle term would have to be $2xy$.)

81. $3x^4y^2-12x^2y^4$
$= 3x^2y^2(x^2-4y^2)$
$= 3x^2y^2(x+2y)(x-2y)$

82. $x(x-12)=0$
$x=0$ or $x-12=0$
$x=12$
The solutions are 0 and 12.

83. $3(x-7)(4x+9)=0$
$x-7=0$ or $4x+9=0$
$x=7$ $\quad 4x=-9$
$x=-\frac{9}{4}$
The solutions are 7 and $-\frac{9}{4}$.

84. $x^2+5x-14=0$
$(x+7)(x-2)=0$
$x+7=0$ or $x-2=0$
$x=-7$ $\quad x=2$
The solutions are -7 and 2.

85. $5x^2+20x=0$
$5x(x+4)=0$
$5x=0$ or $x+4=0$
$x=0$ $\quad x=-4$
The solutions are 0 and -4.

86. $2x^2+15x=8$
$2x^2+15x-8=0$
$(2x-1)(x+8)=0$
$2x-1=0$ or $x+8=0$
$2x=1$ $\quad x=-8$
$x=\frac{1}{2}$
The solutions are $\frac{1}{2}$ and -8.

87.
$$x(x-4)=32$$
$$x^2-4x=32$$
$$x^2-4x-32=0$$
$$(x+4)(x-8)=0$$
$$x+4=0 \quad \text{or} \quad x-8=0$$
$$x=-4 \qquad\qquad x=8$$
The solutions are –4 and 8.

88.
$$(x+3)(x-2)=50$$
$$x^2+x-6=50$$
$$x^2+x-56=0$$
$$(x+8)(x-7)=0$$
$$x+8=0 \quad \text{or} \quad x-7=0$$
$$x=-8 \qquad\qquad x=7$$
The solutions are –8 and 7.

89.
$$x^2=14x-49$$
$$x^2-14x+49=0$$
$$(x-7)^2=0$$
$$x-7=0$$
$$x=7$$
The only solution is 7.

90.
$$9x^2=100$$
$$9x^2-100=0$$
$$(3x+10)(3x-10)=0$$
$$3x+10=0 \quad \text{or} \quad 3x-10=0$$
$$3x=-10 \qquad\qquad 3x=10$$
$$x=-\frac{10}{3} \qquad\qquad x=\frac{10}{3}$$
The solutions are $-\frac{10}{3}$ and $\frac{10}{3}$

91.
$$3x^2+21x+30=0$$
$$3(x^2+7x+10)=0$$
$$3(x+5)(x+2)=0$$
$$x+5=0 \quad \text{or} \quad x+2=0$$
$$x=-5 \qquad\qquad x=-2$$
The solutions are –5 and –2.

92.
$$3x^2=22x-7$$
$$3x^2-22x+7=0$$
$$(3x-1)(x-7)=0$$
$$3x-1=0 \quad \text{or} \quad x-7=0$$
$$3x=1 \qquad\qquad x=7$$
$$x=\frac{1}{3}$$
The solutions are $\frac{1}{3}$ and 7.

93. $h=-16t^2+16t+32$
Substitute 0 for h and solve for t.
$$0=-16t^2+16t+32$$
$$16t^2-16t-32=0$$
$$16(t^2-t-2)=0$$
$$16(t+1)(t-2)=0$$
$$t+1=0 \quad \text{or} \quad t-2=0$$
$$t=-1 \qquad\qquad t=2$$
Because time cannot be negative, discard the solution $t=-1$. The solution $t=2$ indicates that you will hit the water after 2 seconds.

94. Let x = the width of the sign.
Then $x + 3$ = the length of the sign.

Use the formula for the area of a rectangle.

$$l \cdot w = A$$
$$(x+3)(x) = 40$$
$$x^2 + 3x = 40$$
$$x^2 + 3x - 40 = 0$$
$$(x+8)(x-5) = 0$$
$$x+8=0 \quad \text{or} \quad x-5=0$$
$$x=-8 \qquad\qquad x=5$$

A rectangle cannot have a negative length. Thus $x = 5$, and $x+3=8$. The length of the sign is 8 feet and the width is 5 feet. This solution checks because

$$A = lw = (8 \text{ feet})(5 \text{ feet})$$
$$= 40 \text{ square feet.}$$

95. Area of garden = $x(x-3)=88$

$$x(x-3)=88$$
$$x^2-3x=88$$
$$x^2-3x-88=0$$
$$(x-11)(x+8)=0$$
$$x-11=0 \quad \text{or} \quad x+8=0$$
$$x=11 \qquad\qquad x=-8$$

Because a length cannot be negative, discard $x = -8$. Each side of the square lot is 11 meters, that is, the dimensions of the square lot are 11 meters by 11 meters.

Chapter 7 Test

1. $x^2-9x+18=(x-3)(x-6)$

2. $x^2-14x+49=x^2-2(x\cdot 7)+7^2$
$=(x-7)^2$

3. $15y^4-35y^3+10y^2=5y^2(3y^2-7y+2)$
$=5y^2(3y-1)(y-2)$

4. $x^3+2x^2+3x+6=(x^3+2x^2)+(3x+6)$
$=x^2(x+2)+3(x+2)$
$=(x+2)(x^2+3)$

5. $x^2-9x=x(x-9)$

6. $x^3+6x^2-7x=x(x^2+6x-7)$
$=x(x+7)(x-1)$

7. $14x^2+64x-30=2(7x^2+32x-15)$
$=2(7x-3)(x+5)$

8. $25x^2-9=(5x)^2-3^2$
$=(5x+3)(5x-3)$

9. $x^3+8=x^3+2^3=(x+2)(x^2-2x+2^2)$
$=(x+2)(x^2-2x+4)$

10. $x^2-4x-21=(x+3)(x-7)$

11. x^2+4 is prime.

12. $6y^3+9y^2+3y=3y(2y^2+3y+1)$
$=3y(2y+1)(y+1)$

13. $4y^2-36=4(y^2-9)=4(y+3)(y-3)$

14. $16x^2+48x+36$
$=4(4x^2+12x+9)$
$=4[(2x)^2+2(2x\cdot 3)+3^2]$
$=4(2x+3)^2$

15. $2x^4-32=2(x^4-16)$
$=2(x^2+4)(x^2-4)$
$=2(x^2+4)(x+2)(x-2)$

16. $36x^2-84x+49=(6x)^2-2(6x\cdot 7)+7^2$
$=(6x-7)^2$

17. $7x^2-50x+7=(7x-1)(x-7)$

18. $x^3+2x^2-5x-10$
$=(x^3+2x^2)+(-5x-10)$
$=x^2(x+2)-5(x+2)$
$=(x+2)(x^2-5)$

19. $12y^3-12y^2-45y=3y(4y^2-4y-15)$
$=3y(2y+3)(2y-5)$

20. $y^3-125=y^3-5^3$
$=(y-5)(y^2+5y+5^2)$
$=(y-5)(y^2+5y+25)$

21. $5x^2-5xy-30y^2=5(x^2-xy-6y^2)$
$=5(x-3y)(x+2y)$

22. $x^2+2x-24=0$
$(x+6)(x-4)=0$
$x+6=0$ or $x-4=0$
$x=-6$ $\quad$ $x=4$
The solutions are −6 and 4.

23. $3x^2-5x=2$
$3x^2-5x-2=0$
$(3x+1)(x-2)=0$
$3x+1=0$ or $x-2=0$
$3x=-1$ $\quad$ $x=2$
$x=-\frac{1}{3}$
The solutions are $-\frac{1}{3}$ and 2.

24. $x(x-6)=16$
$x^2-6x=16$
$x^2-6x-16=0$
$(x+2)(x-8)=0$
$x+2=0$ or $x-8=0$
$x=-2$ $\quad$ $x=8$
The solutions are −2 and 8.

25. $6x^2=21x$
$6x^2-21x=0$
$3x(2x-7)=0$
$3x=0$ or $2x-7=0$
$x=0$ $\quad$ $2x=7$
$x=\frac{7}{2}$
The solutions are 0 and $\frac{7}{2}$.

26.
$$16x^2 = 81$$
$$16x^2 - 81 = 0$$
$$(4x+9)(4x-9) = 0$$
$$4x+9=0 \quad \text{or} \quad 4x-9=0$$
$$4x=-9 \qquad 4x=9$$
$$x=-\frac{9}{4} \qquad x=\frac{9}{4}$$
The solutions are $-\frac{9}{4}$ and $\frac{9}{4}$.

27.
$$(5x+4)(x-1)=2$$
$$5x^2-x-4=2$$
$$5x^2-x-6=0$$
$$(5x-6)(x+1)=0$$
$$5x-6=0 \quad \text{or} \quad x+1=0$$
$$5x=6 \qquad x=-1$$
$$x=\frac{6}{5}$$
The solutions are $\frac{6}{5}$ and -1.

28. Area of large square = x^2
Area of each small (corner) square = $1^2 = 1$
Area of four corner squares = $4 \cdot 1 = 4$
Area of shaded region
$= x^2 - 4$
$= (x+2)(x-2)$

29. $h = -16t^2 + 80t + 96$
Substitute 0 for h and solve for t.
$$0 = -16t^2 + 80t + 96$$
$$16t^2 - 80t - 96 = 0$$
$$16(t^2 - 5t - 6) = 0$$
$$16(t-6)(t+1) = 0$$
$$t-6=0 \quad \text{or} \quad t+1=0$$
$$t=6 \qquad t=-1$$
Since time cannot be negative, disregard $t=-1$. The rocket will reach the ground after 6 seconds.

30. Let x = the width of the garden.
Then $x+6$ = the length of the garden.
$$(x+6)(x)=55$$
$$x^2+6x=55$$
$$x^2+6x-55=0$$
$$(x+11)(x-5)=0$$
$$x+11=0 \quad \text{or} \quad x-5=0$$
$$x=-11 \qquad x=5$$
Since the width cannot be negative, discard $x=-11$. Then $x = 5$ and $x+6=11$, so the width is 5 feet and the length is 11 feet.

Chapter 7 Cumulative Review Exercises (Chapters 1-7)

1.
$$6[5+2(3-8)-3] = 6[5+2(-5)-3]$$
$$= 6[5-10-3]$$
$$= 6(-8) = -48$$

2.
$$4(x-2) = 2(x-4)+3x$$
$$4x-8 = 2x-8+3x$$
$$4x-8 = 5x-8$$
$$-x = 0$$
$$x = 0$$
The solution is 0.

3.
$$\frac{x}{2}-1=\frac{x}{3}+1$$
$$6\left(\frac{x}{2}-1\right)=6\left(\frac{x}{3}+1\right)$$
$$3x-6=2x+6$$
$$x=12$$
The solution is 12.

4.
$$5-5x>2(5-x)+1$$
$$5-5x>10-2x+1$$
$$5-5x>11-2x$$
$$5-5x+2x>11-2x+2x$$
$$5-3x>11$$
$$5-3x-5>11-5$$
$$-3x>6$$
$$\frac{-3x}{-3}<\frac{6}{-3}$$
$$x<-2$$
Solution set: $\{x|x<-2\}$

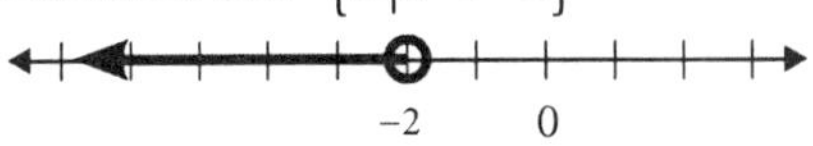

5. Let x = the measure of each of the two base angles.
Then $3x-10$ = the measure of the third angle.
The three angles of any triangle is 180°, so
$$x+x+(3x-10)=180.$$
Solve this equation.
$$5x-10=180$$
$$5x=190$$
$$x=38$$
If $x=38, 3x-10=3(38)-10=104$.
The measures of the three angles of the triangle are 38°, 38°, and 104°.

6. Let x = the cost of the dinner before tax.
$$x+0.06x=159$$
$$1.06x=159$$
$$\frac{1.06x}{1.06}=\frac{159}{1.06}$$
$$x\approx 150$$
The cost of the dinner before tax was \$150.

7.
$$y=-\frac{3}{5}x+3$$
slope = $-\frac{3}{5}=\frac{-3}{5}$; y-intercept = 3
Plot (0,3). From this point, move 3 units *down* (because −3 is negative) and 5 units to the *right* to reach the point (5,0). Draw a line through (0,3) and (5,0).

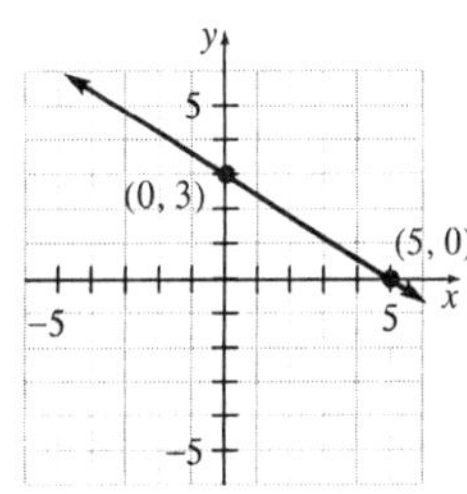

8. Line passing through (2, −4), and (3,1)
$$m=\frac{1-(-4)}{3-2}=\frac{5}{1}=5$$
Use the point (2, −4) in the point-slope equation.
$$y-y_1=m(x-x_1)$$
$$y-(-4)=5(x-2)$$
$$y+4=5(x-2)$$
Rewrite this equation in slope-intercept form.
$$y+4=5x-10$$
$$y=5x-14$$

9. $5x-6y>30$
Graph $5x-6y=30$ as a dashed line through (6,0) and (0, −5). Use (0,0) as a test point. Since $0-0>30$ is false, shade the half-plane *not* containing (0,0).

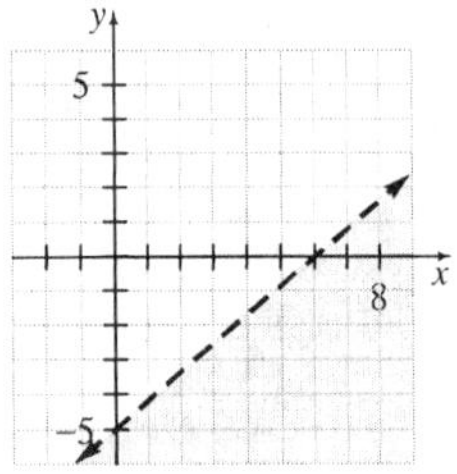

10. $5x+2y=13$
$y=2x-7$
The substitution method is a good choice for solving this system because the second equation is already solved for *y*.
Substitute $2x-7$ for *y* in the first equation.

$$5x+2y=13$$
$$5x+2(2x-7)=13$$
$$5x+4x-14=13$$
$$9x-14=13$$
$$9x=27$$
$$x=3$$

Back-substitute into the second given equation.

$$y=2x-7$$
$$y=2(3)-7=-1$$

Solution: $(3,-1)$

11. $2x+3y=5$
$3x-2y=-4$
The addition method is a good choice for solving this system because both equations are written in the form $Ax+By=C$.

Multiply the first equation by 2 and the second equation by 3; then add the results.

$$4x+6y=10$$
$$9x-6y=-12$$
$$13x=-2$$
$$x=-\frac{2}{13}$$

Instead of back-substituting $-\frac{2}{13}$ and working with fractions, go back to the original system and eliminate *x*. Multiply the first equation by 3 and the second equation by −2; then add the results.

$$6x+9y=15$$
$$-6x+4y=8$$
$$13y=23$$
$$y=\frac{23}{3}$$

Solution: $\left(-\frac{2}{13},\frac{23}{3}\right)$

12. $$\frac{4}{5}-\frac{9}{8}=\frac{4}{5}\cdot\frac{8}{8}-\frac{9}{8}\cdot\frac{5}{5}$$
$$=\frac{32}{40}-\frac{45}{40}=-\frac{13}{40}$$

13. $$\frac{6x^5-3x^4+9x^2+27x}{3x}$$
$$=\frac{6x^5}{3x}-\frac{3x^4}{3x}+\frac{9x^2}{3x}+\frac{27x}{3x}$$
$$=2x^4-x^3+3x+9$$

14. $$(3x-5y)(2x+9y)$$
$$=6x^2+27xy-10xy-45y^2$$
$$=6x^2+17xy-45y^2$$

15.

$$\begin{array}{r} 2x^2+5x-3 \\ 3x-5\overline{\big)6x^3+5x^2-34x+13} \\ \underline{6x^3-10x^2} \qquad\qquad \\ 15x^2-34x \qquad \\ \underline{15x^2-25x} \qquad \\ -9x+13 \\ \underline{-9x+15} \\ -2 \end{array}$$

$$\frac{6x^3+5x^2-34x+13}{3x-5}$$
$$= 2x^2+5x-3+\frac{-2}{3x-5}$$
$$\text{or } \; 2x^2+5x-3-\frac{2}{3x-5}$$

16. To write 0.0071 in scientific notation, move the decimal point 3 places to the right. Because the given number is between 0 and 1, the exponent will be negative.

$$0.0071 = 7.1\times 10^{-3}$$

17. $3x^2+11x+6$

Factor by trial and error or by grouping. To factor by grouping, find two integers whose product is $ac = 3\cdot 6 = 18$ and whose sum is $b = 11$. These integers are 9 and 2.

$$\begin{aligned} 3x^2+11x+6 &= 3x^2+9x+2x+6 \\ &= 3x(x+3)+2(x+3) \\ &= (x+3)(3x+2) \end{aligned}$$

18.

$$\begin{aligned} y^5-16y &= y(y^4-16) \\ &= y(y^2+4)(y^2-4) \\ &= y(y^2+4)(y+2)(y-2) \end{aligned}$$

19.

$$\begin{aligned} 4x^2+12x+9 &= (2x)^2+2(2x\cdot 3)+3x^2 \\ &= (2x+3)^2 \end{aligned}$$

20. Let x = the width of the rectangle.
Then $x + 2$ = the length of the rectangle.
Use the formula for the area of a rectangle.

$$\begin{aligned} l\cdot w &= A \\ (x+2)(x) &= 24 \\ x^2+2x &= 24 \\ x^2+2x-24 &= 0 \\ (x+6)(x-4) &= 0 \end{aligned}$$

$$x+6=0 \quad \text{or} \quad x-4=0$$
$$x=-6 \qquad\qquad x=4$$

Discard -6 because the width cannot be negative. Then $x = 4$ and $x+2=6$, so the width is 4 feet and the length is 6 feet. The dimensions of the rectangle are 6 feet by 4 feet.

Chapter 8
Rational Expressions

8.1 Exercise Set

1. $\frac{5}{2x}$

Set the denominator equal to 0 and solve for x.

$2x = 0$

$x = 0$

The rational expression is undefined for $x = 0$.

3. $\frac{x}{x-8}$

Set the denominator equal to 0 and solve for x.

$x - 8 = 0$

$x = 8$

The rational expression is undefined for $x = 8$.

5. $\frac{13}{5x-20}$

$5x - 20 = 0$

$5x = 20$

$x = 4$

The rational expression is undefined for $x = 4$.

7. $\frac{x+3}{(x+9)(x-2)}$

$(x+9)(x-2) = 0$

$x + 9 = 0$ or $x - 2 = 0$

$x = -9$ $\quad x = 2$

The rational expression is undefined for $x = -9$ and $x = 2$.

9. $\frac{4x}{(3x-17)(x+3)}$

$(3x-17)(x+3) = 0$

$3x - 17 = 0$ or $x + 3 = 0$

$3x = 17$ $\quad x = -3$

$x = \frac{17}{3}$

The rational expression is undefined for $x = -\frac{17}{3}$ and $x = -3$.

11. $\frac{x+5}{x^2+x-12}$

$x^2 + x - 12 = 0$

$(x+4)(x-3) = 0$

$x + 4 = 0$ or $x - 3 = 0$

$x = -4$ $\quad x = 3$

The rational expression is undefined for $x = -4$ and $x = 3$.

13. $\frac{x+5}{5}$

Because the denominator, 5, is not zero for any value of x, the rational expression is defined for all real numbers.

15. $\frac{y+3}{4y^2+y-3}$

$4y^2 + y - 3 = 0$

$(y+1)(4y-3) = 0$

$y + 1 = 0$ or $4y - 3 = 0$

$y = -1$ $\quad 4y = 3$

$y = \frac{3}{4}$

The rational expression is undefined for $y = -1$ and $y = \frac{3}{4}$.

17. $\dfrac{y+5}{y^2-25}$

$y^2-25=0$

$(y+5)(y-5)=0$

$y+5=0 \quad \text{or} \quad y-5=0$

$y=-5 \qquad\qquad y=5$

The rational expression is undefined for $y=-5$ and $y=5$.

19. $\dfrac{5}{x^2+1}$

The smallest possible value of x^2 is 0, so $x^2+1 \ge 1$ for all real numbers of *x*. This means that there is no real number *x* for which $x^2+1=0$. Thus, the rational expression is defined for all real numbers.

21. $\dfrac{14x^2}{7x}=\dfrac{2\cdot 7\cdot x\cdot x}{7\cdot x}=\dfrac{2x}{1}=2x$

23. $\dfrac{5x-15}{25}=\dfrac{5(x-3)}{5\cdot 5}=\dfrac{x-3}{5}$

25. $\dfrac{2x-8}{4x}=\dfrac{2(x-4)}{2\cdot 2x}=\dfrac{x-4}{2x}$

27. $\dfrac{3}{3x-9}=\dfrac{3}{3(x-3)}=\dfrac{1}{x-3}$

29. $\dfrac{-15}{3x-9}=\dfrac{-15}{3(x-3)}=\dfrac{-5}{x-3}$ or $-\dfrac{5}{x-3}$

31. $\dfrac{3x+9}{x+3}=\dfrac{3(x+3)}{x+3}=\dfrac{3}{1}=3$

33. $\dfrac{x+5}{x^2-25}=\dfrac{x+5}{(x+5)(x-5)}=\dfrac{1}{x-5}$

35. $\dfrac{2y-10}{3y-15}=\dfrac{2(y-5)}{3(y-5)}=\dfrac{2}{3}$

37. $\dfrac{x+1}{x^2-2x-3}=\dfrac{x+1}{(x+1)(x-3)}=\dfrac{1}{x-3}$

39. $\dfrac{4x-8}{x^2-4x+4}=\dfrac{4(x-2)}{(x-2)(x-2)}=\dfrac{4}{x-2}$

41. $\dfrac{y^2-3y+2}{y^2+7y-18}=\dfrac{(y-1)(y-2)}{(y+9)(y-2)}=\dfrac{y-1}{y+9}$

43. $\dfrac{2y^2-7y+3}{2y^2-5y+2}=\dfrac{(2y-1)(y-3)}{(2y-1)(y-2)}=\dfrac{y-3}{y-2}$

45. $\dfrac{2x+3}{2x+5}$

The numerator and denominator have no common factor (other than 1), so this rational expression cannot be simplified.

47. $\dfrac{x^2+12x+36}{x^2-36}=\dfrac{(x+6)(x+6)}{(x+6)(x-6)}=\dfrac{x+6}{x-6}$

49.
$$\dfrac{x^3-2x^2+x-2}{x-2}=\dfrac{x^2(x-2)+1(x-2)}{x-2}$$
$$=\dfrac{(x-2)(x^2+1)}{x-2}$$
$$=x^2+1$$

51.
$$\dfrac{x^3-8}{x-2}=\dfrac{(x-2)(x^2+2x+4)}{x-2}$$
$$=x^2+2x+4$$

53. $\dfrac{(x-4)^2}{x^2-16}=\dfrac{(x-4)(x-4)}{(x+4)(x-4)}=\dfrac{x-4}{x+4}$

55. $\dfrac{x}{x+1}$
The numerator and denominator have no common factor (other than 1), so this rational expression cannot be simplified.

57. $\dfrac{x+4}{x^2+16}$
The numerator and denominator are both prime polynomials. They have no common factor (other than 1), so this rational expression cannot be simplified.

59. $\dfrac{x-5}{5-x}=\dfrac{-1(5-x)}{5-x}=-1$
Notice that the numerator and denominator of the given rational expression are additive inverses.

61. $\dfrac{2x-3}{3-2x}$
The numerator and denominator of this rational expression are additive inverses, so $\dfrac{2x-3}{3-2x}=-1.$

63. $\dfrac{x-5}{x+5}$
The numerator and denominator have no common factor and they are not additive inverses, so this rational expression cannot be simplified.

65. $\dfrac{4x-6}{3-2x}=\dfrac{2(2x-3)}{3-2x}=\dfrac{-2(3-2x)}{3-2x}=-2$

67.
$$\begin{aligned}\frac{4-6x}{3x^2-2x}&=\frac{2(2-3x)}{x(3x-2)}\\&=\frac{-2(3x-2)}{x(3x-2)}\\&=-\frac{2}{x}\end{aligned}$$

69.
$$\begin{aligned}\frac{x^2-1}{1-x}&=\frac{(x+1)(x-1)}{1-x}\\&=\frac{(x+1)\cdot-1(1-x)}{1-x}\\&=-1(x+1)=-x-1\end{aligned}$$

71.
$$\begin{aligned}\frac{y^2-y-12}{4-y}&=\frac{(y-4)(y+3)}{4-y}\\&=\frac{-1(4-y)(y+3)}{4-y}\\&=-1(y+3)=-y-3\end{aligned}$$

73.
$$\begin{aligned}\frac{x^2y-x^2}{x^3-x^3y}&=\frac{x^2(y-1)}{x^3(1-y)}\\&=\frac{x^2\cdot-1(1-y)}{x^3(1-y)}\\&=-\frac{1}{x}\end{aligned}$$

75.
$$\begin{aligned}\frac{x^2+2xy-3y^2}{2x^2+5xy-3y^2}&=\frac{(x-y)(x+3y)}{(2x-y)(x+3y)}\\&=\frac{x-y}{2x-y}\end{aligned}$$

77.
$$\frac{x^2-9x+18}{x^3-27}=\frac{(x-3)(x-6)}{(x-3)(x^2+3x+9)}$$
$$=\frac{x-6}{x^2+3x+9}$$

78. $\frac{x^3-8}{x^2+2x-8}=\frac{(x-2)(x^2+2x+4)}{(x-2)(x+4)}$
$=\frac{x^2+2x+4}{x+4}$

79. $\frac{9-y^2}{y^2-3(2y-3)}=\frac{(3+y)(3-y)}{y^2-6y+9}$
$=\frac{(3+y)(3-y)}{(y-3)(y-3)}=\frac{(3+y)\cdot-1(y-3)}{(y-3)(y-3)}$
$=\frac{-1(3+y)}{y-3}$ or $\frac{3+y}{-1(y-3)}=\frac{3+y}{3-y}$

80. $\frac{16-y^2}{y(y-8)+16}=\frac{(4-y)(4+y)}{y^2-8y+16}$
$=\frac{-1\cdot(y-4)(4+y)}{(y-4)(y-4)}=\frac{-1(4+y)}{y-4}$
or $\frac{4+y}{-1(y-4)}=\frac{4+y}{4-y}$

81. $\frac{xy+2y+3x+6}{x^2+5x+6}=\frac{y(x+2)+3(x+2)}{(x+2)(x+3)}$
$=\frac{(x+2)(y+3)}{(x+2)(x+3)}=\frac{y+3}{x+3}$

82. $\frac{xy+4y-7x-28}{x^2+11x+28}=\frac{y(x+4)-7(x+4)}{(x+4)(x+7)}$
$=\frac{(x+4)(y-7)}{(x+4)(x+7)}=\frac{y-7}{x+7}$

83. $\frac{8x^2+4x+2}{1-8x^3}=\frac{2(4x^2+2x+1)}{(1-2x)(1+2x+4x^2)}$
$=\frac{2}{1-2x}$

84. $\frac{x^3-3x^2+9x}{x^3+27}=\frac{x(x^2-3x+9)}{(x+3)(x^2-3x+9)}$
$=\frac{x}{x+3}$

85. $\frac{130x}{100-x}$

a. $x=40$:
$\frac{130x}{100-x}=\frac{130(40)}{100-40}$
$=\frac{5200}{60}$
≈ 86.67

This means it costs about \$86.67 million to inoculate 40% of the population.

$x=80$:
$\frac{130x}{100-x}=\frac{130(80)}{100-80}$
$=\frac{10,400}{20}$
$=520$

This means it costs \$520 million to inoculate 80% of the population.

$x=90$:
$\frac{130x}{100-x}=\frac{130(90)}{100-90}$
$=\frac{11,700}{10}$
$=1170$

This means it costs \$1170 million (\$1,170,000,000) to inoculate 90% of the population.

b. Set the denominator equal to 0 and solve for *x*.

$$100 - x = 0$$
$$100 = x$$

The rational expression is undefined for $x = 100$.

c. The cost keeps rising as *x* approaches 100. No amount of money will be enough to inoculate 100% of the population.

87. $\frac{DA}{A+12}$; $D = 1000, A = 8$

$$\frac{DA}{A+12} = \frac{1000 \cdot 8}{8+12} = \frac{8000}{20} = 400$$

The correct dosage for an 8-year old is 400 milligrams.

89. $$C = \frac{100x + 100,000}{x}$$

a. $x = 500$

$$C = \frac{100(500) + 100,000}{500} = \frac{150,000}{500} = 300$$

The cost per bicycle when manufacturing 500 bicycles is $300.

b. $x = 4000$

$$C = \frac{100(4000) + 100,000}{4000} = \frac{400,000 + 100,000}{4000} = \frac{500,000}{4000} = 125$$

The cost per bicycle when manufacturing 4000 bicycles is $125.

c. The cost per bicycle decreases as more bicycles are manufactured. One possible reason for this is that there could be fixed costs for equipment, so the more the equipment is used, the lower the cost per bicycle.

91. $$y = \frac{5x}{x^2 + 1}; x = 3$$

$$y = \frac{5 \cdot 3}{3^2 + 1} + \frac{15}{10} = 1.5$$

The equation indicates that the drug's concentration after 3 hours is 1.5 milligram per liter. The point $(3, 1.5)$ on the graph conveys this information.

93. Let $w = 145$ and $h = 70$,

$$\text{BMI} = \frac{703(145)}{70^2} = \frac{101,935}{4900} \approx 20.8$$

This person is not considered underweight.

95. **a.** $$\frac{-0.4t + 14.2}{3.7t + 257.4}$$

b. $t = 7$ for the year 2001

$$\frac{-0.4(7) + 14.2}{3.7(7) + 257.4} = \frac{11.4}{283.3} \approx 0.04$$

This indicates there are about 4 crimes per 100 inhabitants or 4000 crimes per 100,000 inhabitants.

c. The rational expression models this fairly well. There is only a difference of about 161 crimes per 100,000 inhabitants.

97. – 101. Answers will vary.

103. Any rational expression in which the numerator and denominator have no common factor other than 1 cannot be simplified. Student examples will vary.

105. $x^2 - x - 6 = (x-3)(x+2)$

Therefore,

$$\frac{x^2 - x - 6}{x+2} = \frac{(x+2)(x-3)}{x+2} = x - 3$$

So $\frac{x^2 - x - 6}{x+2}$ is the desired rational expression.

107.

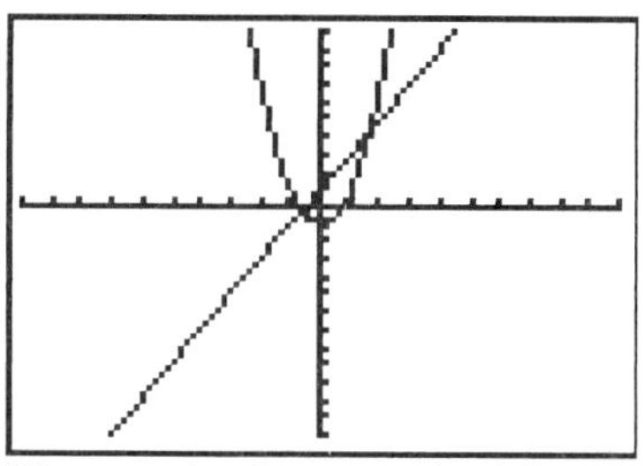

The graphs do not coincide.

$$\frac{2x^2 - x - 1}{x-1} = \frac{(2x+1)(x-1)}{x-1}$$
$$= 2x+1, x \neq 1$$

Change the expression on the right from $2x^2 - 1$ to $2x+1$.

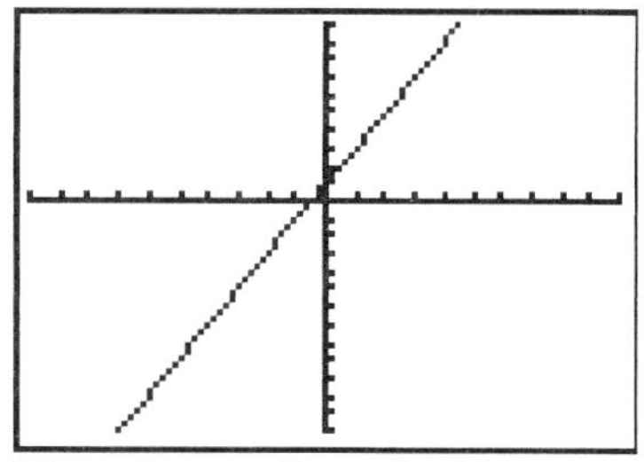

Now the graphs coincide.

109. Answers will vary.

110. $$\frac{5}{6} \cdot \frac{9}{25} = \frac{\cancel{5}^{1}}{\cancel{6}_{2}} \cdot \frac{\cancel{9}^{3}}{\cancel{25}_{5}} = \frac{3}{10}$$

111. $$\frac{2}{3} \div 4 = \frac{2}{3} \cdot \frac{1}{4} = \frac{2}{12} = \frac{2 \cdot 1}{2 \cdot 6} = \frac{1}{6}$$

112. $2x - 5y = -2$

$3x + 4y = 20$

Multiply the first equation by 3 and the second equation by -2; then add the results.

$$6x - 15y = -6$$
$$\underline{-6x - 8y = -40}$$
$$-23y = -46$$
$$y = 2$$

Back-substitute into the first equation of the original system.

$$2x - 5y = -2$$
$$2x - 5(2) = -2$$
$$2x - 10 = -2$$
$$2x = 8$$
$$x = 4$$

Solution: (4,2)

8.2 Exercise Set

1. $$\frac{4}{x+3}\cdot\frac{x-5}{9}=\frac{4(x-5)}{(x+3)9}=\frac{4x-20}{9x+27}$$

3. $$\frac{x}{3}\cdot\frac{12}{x+5}=\frac{3\cdot 4x}{3(x+5)}=\frac{4x}{x+5}$$

5. $$\frac{3}{x}\cdot\frac{4x}{15}=\frac{3\cdot 4x}{3\cdot 5x}=\frac{4}{5}$$

7. $$\frac{x-3}{x+5}\cdot\frac{4x+20}{9x-27}=\frac{x-3}{x+5}\cdot\frac{4(x+5)}{9(x-3)}=\frac{4}{9}$$

9. $$\frac{x^2+9x+14}{x+7}\cdot\frac{1}{x+2}=\frac{(x+7)(x+2)\cdot 1}{(x+7)(x+2)}=1$$

11. $$\frac{x^2-25}{x^2-3x-10}\cdot\frac{x+2}{x}$$
$$=\frac{(x+5)(x-5)}{(x+2)(x-5)}\cdot\frac{(x+2)}{x}$$
$$=\frac{x+5}{x}$$

13. $$\frac{4y+30}{y^2-3y}\cdot\frac{y-3}{2y+15}$$
$$=\frac{2(2y+15)}{y(y-3)}\cdot\frac{(y-3)}{(2y+15)}$$
$$=\frac{2}{y}$$

15. $$\frac{y^2-7y-30}{y^2-6y-40}\cdot\frac{2y^2+5y+2}{2y^2+7y+3}$$
$$=\frac{(y+3)(y-10)}{(y+4)(y-10)}\cdot\frac{(2y+1)(y+2)}{(2y+1)(y+3)}$$
$$=\frac{y+2}{y+4}$$

17. $$\left(y^2-9\right)\cdot\frac{4}{y-3}=\frac{y^2-9}{1}\cdot\frac{4}{y-3}$$
$$=\frac{(y+3)(y-3)}{1}\cdot\frac{4}{y-3}$$
$$=4(y+3)\text{ or }4y+12$$

19. $$\frac{x^2-5x+6}{x^2-2x-3}\cdot\frac{x^2-1}{x^2-4}$$
$$=\frac{(x-2)(x-3)}{(x+1)(x-3)}\cdot\frac{(x+1)(x-1)}{(x+2)(x-2)}$$
$$=\frac{x-1}{x+2}$$

21. $$\frac{x^3-8}{x^2-4}\cdot\frac{x+2}{3x}$$
$$=\frac{(x-2)(x^2+2x+4)}{(x+2)(x-2)}\cdot\frac{(x+2)}{3x}$$
$$=\frac{x^2+2x+4}{3x}$$

23. $$\frac{(x-2)^3}{(x-1)^3}\cdot\frac{x^2-2x+1}{x^2-4x+4}$$
$$=\frac{(x-2)^3}{(x-1)^3}\cdot\frac{(x-1)^2}{(x-2)^2}$$
$$=\frac{x-2}{x-1}$$

25. $$\frac{6x+2}{x^2-1}\cdot\frac{1-x}{3x^2+x}$$
$$=\frac{2(3x+1)}{(x+1)(x-1)}\cdot\frac{(1-x)}{x(3x+1)}$$
$$=\frac{2(3x+1)}{(x+1)(x-1)}\cdot\frac{-1(x-1)}{x(3x+1)}$$
$$=\frac{-2}{x(x+1)}\text{ or }-\frac{2}{x(x+1)}$$

27. $$\frac{25-y^2}{y^2-2y-35}\cdot\frac{y^2-8y-20}{y^2-3y-10} = \frac{(5+y)(5-y)}{(y+5)(y-7)}\cdot\frac{(y-10)(y+2)}{(y-5)(y+2)} = \frac{-(y-10)}{y-7} \text{ or } -\frac{y-10}{y-7}$$

29. $$\frac{x^2-y^2}{x}\cdot\frac{x^2+xy}{x+y} = \frac{(x+y)(x-y)}{x}\cdot\frac{x(x+y)}{(x+y)} = (x-y)(x+y) \text{ or } x^2-y^2$$

31. $$\frac{x^2+2xy+y^2}{x^2-2xy+y^2}\cdot\frac{4x-4y}{3x+3y} = \frac{(x+y)(x+y)}{(x-y)(x-y)}\cdot\frac{4(x-y)}{3(x+y)} = \frac{4(x+y)}{3(x-y)}$$

33. $$\frac{x}{7}\div\frac{5}{3} = \frac{x}{7}\cdot\frac{3}{5} = \frac{3x}{35}$$

35. $$\frac{3}{x}\div\frac{12}{x} = \frac{3}{x}\cdot\frac{x}{12} = \frac{1}{4}$$

37. $$\frac{15}{x}\div\frac{3}{2x} = \frac{15}{x}\cdot\frac{2x}{3} = 10$$

39. $$\frac{x+1}{3}\div\frac{3x+3}{7} = \frac{x+1}{3}\cdot\frac{7}{3x+3} = \frac{x+1}{3}\cdot\frac{7}{3(x+1)} = \frac{7}{9}$$

41. $$\frac{7}{x-5}\div\frac{28}{3x-15} = \frac{7}{x-5}\cdot\frac{3x-15}{28} = \frac{7}{(x-5)}\cdot\frac{3(x-5)}{7\cdot 4} = \frac{3}{4}$$

43. $$\frac{x^2-4}{x}\div\frac{x+2}{x-2} = \frac{x^2-4}{x}\cdot\frac{x-2}{x+2} = \frac{(x+2)(x-2)}{x}\cdot\frac{x-2}{x+2} = \frac{(x-2)^2}{x}$$

45. $$(y^2-16)\div\frac{y^2+3y-4}{y^2+4} = \frac{y^2-16}{1}\cdot\frac{y^2+4}{y^2+3y-4} = \frac{(y+4)(y-4)}{1}\cdot\frac{y^2+4}{(y+4)(y-1)} = \frac{(y-4)(y^2+4)}{y-1}$$

47. $$\frac{y^2-y}{15}\div\frac{y-1}{5} = \frac{y^2-y}{15}\cdot\frac{5}{y-1} = \frac{y(y-1)}{15}\cdot\frac{5}{(y-1)} = \frac{y}{3}$$

49. $\frac{4x^2+10}{x-3} \div \frac{6x^2+15}{x^2-9}$

$= \frac{4x^2+10}{x-3} \cdot \frac{x^2-9}{6x^2+15}$

$= \frac{2(2x^2+5)}{(x-3)} \cdot \frac{(x+3)(x-3)}{3(2x^2+5)}$

$= \frac{2(x+3)}{3}$ or $\frac{2x+6}{3}$

51. $\frac{x^2-25}{2x-2} \div \frac{x^2+10x+25}{x^2+4x-5}$

$= \frac{x^2-25}{2x-2} \cdot \frac{x^2+4x-5}{x^2+10x+25}$

$= \frac{(x+5)(x-5)}{2(x-1)} \cdot \frac{(x+5)(x-1)}{(x+5)(x+5)}$

$= \frac{x-5}{2}$

53. $\frac{y^3+y}{y^2-y} \div \frac{y^3-y^2}{y^2-2y+1}$

$= \frac{y^3+y}{y^2-y} \cdot \frac{y^2-2y+1}{y^3-y^2}$

$= \frac{y(y^2+1)}{y(y-1)} \cdot \frac{(y-1)(y-1)}{y^2(y-1)}$

$= \frac{y^2+1}{y^2}$

55. $\frac{y^2+5y+4}{y^2+12y+32} \div \frac{y^2-12y+35}{y^2+3y-40}$

$= \frac{y^2+5y+4}{y^2+12y+32} \cdot \frac{y^2+3y-40}{y^2-12y+35}$

$= \frac{(y+4)(y+1)}{(y+4)(y+8)} \cdot \frac{(y+8)(y-5)}{(y-7)(y-5)}$

$= \frac{y+1}{y-7}$

57. $\frac{2y^2-128}{y^2+16y+64} \div \frac{y^2-6y-16}{3y^2+30y+48}$

$= \frac{2y^2-128}{y^2+16y+64} \cdot \frac{3y^2+30y+48}{y^2-6y-16}$

$= \frac{2(y^2-64)}{(y+8)(y+8)} \cdot \frac{3(y^2+10y+16)}{(y+2)(y-8)}$

$= \frac{2(y+8)(y-8)}{(y+8)(y+8)} \cdot \frac{3(y+2)(y+8)}{(y+2)(y-8)} = 6$

59. $\frac{2x+2y}{3} \div \frac{x^2-y^2}{x-y}$

$= \frac{2x+2y}{3} \cdot \frac{x-y}{x^2-y^2}$

$= \frac{2(x+y)}{3} \cdot \frac{x-y}{(x+y)(x-y)} = \frac{2}{3}$

61. $\frac{x^2-y^2}{8x^2-16xy+8y^2} \div \frac{4x-4y}{x+y}$

$= \frac{x^2-y^2}{8x^2-16xy+8y^2} \cdot \frac{x+y}{4x-4y}$

$= \frac{(x+y)(x-y)}{8(x^2-2xy+y^2)} \cdot \frac{x+y}{4(x-y)}$

$= \frac{(x+y)(x-y)}{8(x-y)(x-y)} \cdot \frac{x+y}{4(x-y)}$

$= \frac{(x+y)^2}{32(x-y)^2}$

63. $\frac{xy-y^2}{x^2+2x+1} \div \frac{2x^2+xy-3y^2}{2x^2+5xy+3y^2}$

$= \frac{xy-y^2}{x^2+2x+1} \cdot \frac{2x^2+5xy+3y^2}{2x^2+xy-3y^2}$

$= \frac{y(x-y)}{(x+1)(x+1)} \cdot \frac{(2x+3y)(x+y)}{(2x+3y)(x-y)}$

$= \frac{y(x+y)}{(x+1)^2}$

65. $\left(\frac{y-2}{y^2-9y+18}\cdot\frac{y^2-4y-12}{y+2}\right)\div\frac{y^2-4}{y^2+5y+6}=\left(\frac{y-2}{y^2-9y+18}\cdot\frac{y^2-4y-12}{y+2}\right)\cdot\frac{y^2+5y+6}{y^2-4}$

$=\left(\frac{y-2}{(y-6)(y-3)}\cdot\frac{(y-6)(y+2)}{y+2}\right)\cdot\frac{(y+2)(y+3)}{(y+2)(y-2)}=\left(\frac{y-2}{y-3}\right)\cdot\frac{y+3}{y-2}=\frac{y+3}{y-3}$

66. $\left(\frac{6y^2+31y+18}{3y^2-20y+12}\cdot\frac{2y^2-15y+18}{6y^2+35y+36}\right)\div\frac{2y^2-13y+15}{9y^2+15y+4}$

$=\left(\frac{6y^2+31y+18}{3y^2-20y+12}\cdot\frac{2y^2-15y+18}{6y^2+35y+36}\right)\cdot\frac{9y^2+15y+4}{2y^2-13y+15}$

$=\left(\frac{(3y+2)(2y+9)}{(3y-2)(y-6)}\cdot\frac{(2y-3)(y-6)}{(3y+4)(2y+9)}\right)\cdot\frac{(3y+4)(3y+1)}{(2y-3)(y-5)}$

$=\left(\frac{(3y+2)(2y-3)}{(3y-2)(3y+4)}\right)\cdot\frac{(3y+4)(3y+1)}{(2y-3)(y-5)}=\frac{(3y+2)(3y+1)}{(3y-2)(y-5)}$

67. $\frac{3x^2+3x-60}{2x-8}\div\left(\frac{30x^2}{x^2-7x+10}\cdot\frac{x^3+3x^2-10x}{25x^3}\right)$

$=\frac{3x^2+3x-60}{2x-8}\div\left(\frac{30x^2}{(x-2)(x-5)}\cdot\frac{x(x^2+3x-10)}{25x^3}\right)$

$=\frac{3(x^2+x-20)}{2x-8}\div\left(\frac{30x^2}{(x-2)(x-5)}\cdot\frac{x(x+5)(x-2)}{25x^3}\right)$

$=\frac{3(x+5)(x-4)}{2(x-4)}\div\frac{6(x+5)}{5(x-5)}=\frac{3(x+5)(x-4)}{2(x-4)}\cdot\frac{5(x-5)}{6(x+5)}=\frac{5(x-5)}{4}$

68. $\frac{5x^2-x}{3x+2}\div\left(\frac{6x^2+x-2}{10x^2+3x-1}\cdot\frac{2x^2-x-1}{2x^2-x}\right)=\frac{x(5x-1)}{3x+2}\div\left(\frac{(2x-1)(3x+2)}{(5x-1)(2x+1)}\cdot\frac{(2x+1)(x-1)}{x(2x-1)}\right)$

$=\frac{x(5x-1)}{3x+2}\div\left(\frac{(3x+2)(x-1)}{x(5x-1)}\right)=\frac{x(5x-1)}{3x+2}\cdot\frac{x(5x-1)}{(3x+2)(x-1)}=\frac{x^2(5x-1)^2}{(3x+2)^2(x-1)}$

69. $\frac{x^2+xz+xy+yz}{x-y}\div\frac{x+z}{x+y}=\frac{x(x+z)+y(x+z)}{x-y}\cdot\frac{x+y}{x+z}=\frac{(x+z)(x+y)}{x-y}\cdot\frac{x+y}{x+z}=\frac{(x+y)^2}{x-y}$

70. $$\frac{x^2-xz+xy-yz}{x-y}\div\frac{x-z}{y-x}=\frac{x(x-z)+y(x-z)}{x-y}\cdot\frac{y-x}{x-z}=\frac{(x-z)(x+y)}{x-y}\cdot\frac{-1(x-y)}{x-z}$$
$$=-1(x+y)=-x-y$$

71. $$\frac{3xy+ay+3xb+ab}{9x^2-a^2}\div\frac{y^3+b^3}{6x-2a}=\frac{3xy+ay+3xb+ab}{9x^2-a^2}\cdot\frac{6x-2a}{y^3+b^3}$$
$$=\frac{y(3x+a)+b(3x+a)}{(3x+a)(3x-a)}\cdot\frac{2(3x-a)}{(y+b)(y^2-by+b^2)}$$
$$=\frac{(3x+a)(y+b)}{(3x+a)(3x-a)}\cdot\frac{2(3x-a)}{(y+b)(y^2-by+b^2)}=\frac{2}{y^2-by+b^2}$$

72. $$\frac{5xy-ay-5xb+ab}{25x^2-a^2}\div\frac{y^3-b^3}{15x+3a}=\frac{5xy-ay-5xb+ab}{25x^2-a^2}\cdot\frac{15x+3a}{y^3-b^3}$$
$$=\frac{y(5x-a)-b(5x-a)}{(5x+a)(5x-a)}\cdot\frac{3(5x+a)}{(y-b)(y^2+by+b^2)}=\frac{(5x-a)(y-b)}{(5x+a)(5x-a)}\cdot\frac{3(5x+a)}{(y-b)(y^2+by+b^2)}$$
$$=\frac{3}{y^2+by+b^2}$$

73. $$\frac{1}{2}\cdot\frac{250x}{100-x}=\frac{125x}{100-x}$$
The rational expression $\frac{125x}{100-x}$ represents the reduced cost.

75. – 77. Answers will vary.

79. $$\frac{?}{?}\cdot\frac{3x-12}{2x}=\frac{3}{2}$$
$$\frac{?}{?}\cdot\frac{3(x-4)}{2x}=\frac{3}{2}$$
The numerator of the unknown rational expression must contain a factor of x. The denominator of the unknown rational expression must contain a factor of $(x-4)$. Therefore, the simplest pair of polynomials that will work are x in the numerator and $x-4$ in the denominator, to give the rational expression $\frac{x}{x-4}$.

Check:
$$\frac{x}{x-4}\cdot\frac{3x-12}{2x}=\frac{x}{x-4}\cdot\frac{3(x-4)}{2x}=\frac{3}{2}$$

80. $\dfrac{9x^2-y^2+15x-5y}{3x^2+xy+5x} \div \dfrac{3x+y}{9x^3+6x^2y+xy^2} = \dfrac{9x^2-y^2+15x-5y}{3x^2+xy+5x} \cdot \dfrac{9x^3+6x^2y+xy^2}{3x+y}$

$= \dfrac{(3x+y)(3x-y)+5(3x-y)}{x(3x+y+5)} \cdot \dfrac{x(9x^2+6xy+y^2)}{3x+y} = \dfrac{(3x-y)(3x+y+5)}{x(3x+y+5)} \cdot \dfrac{x(3x+y)(3x+y)}{3x+y}$

$= (3x-y)(3x+y)$

83. 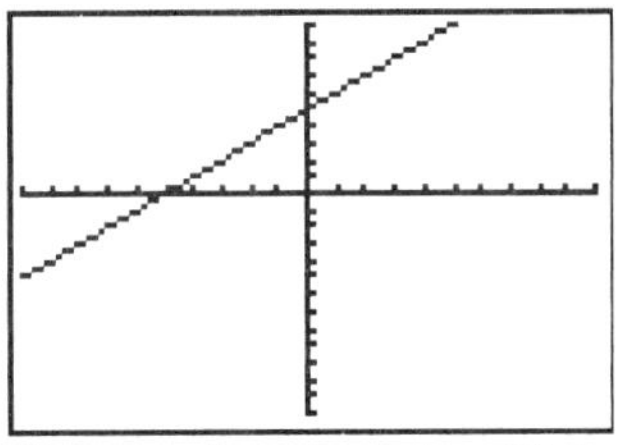

The graph coincides. This verifies that $\dfrac{x^3-25x}{x^2-3x-10} \cdot \dfrac{x+2}{x} = x+5.$

85. 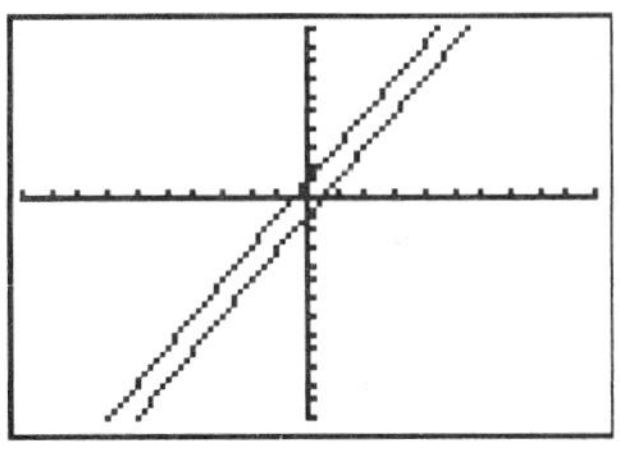

The graphs do not coincide

$(x-5) \div \dfrac{2x^2-11x+5}{4x^2-1}$

$= \dfrac{x-5}{1} \cdot \dfrac{4x^2-1}{2x^2-11x+5}$

$= \dfrac{x-5}{1} \cdot \dfrac{(2x+1)(2x-1)}{(2x-1)(x-5)}$

$= 2x+1$

Change the expression on the right from $(2x-1)$ to $(2x+1)$.

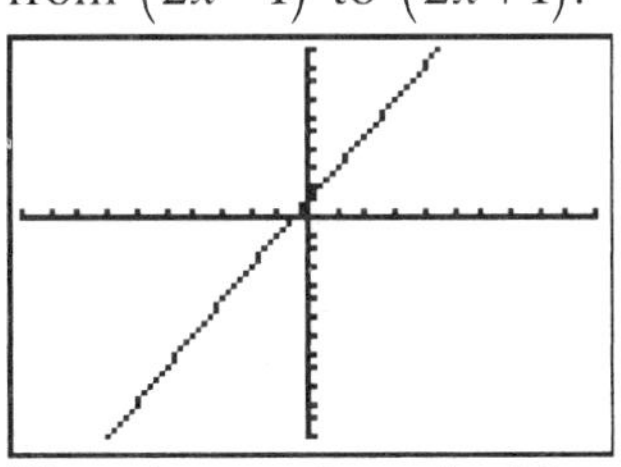

Now the graphs coincide.

86.

$$\begin{aligned} 2x+3 &< 3(x-5) \\ 2x+3 &< 3x-15 \\ -x+3 &< -15 \\ -x &< -18 \\ x &> 18 \end{aligned}$$

$\{x \mid x > 18\}$

87. $3x^2-15x-42 = 3(x^2-5x-14)$
$= 3(x-7)(x+2)$

88.

$$\begin{aligned} x(2x+9) &= 5 \\ 2x^2+9x &= 5 \\ 2x^2+9x-5 &= 0 \\ (2x-1)(x+5) &= 0 \end{aligned}$$

$2x-1=0$ or $x+5=0$

$2x=1$ $\qquad x=-5$

$x=\dfrac{1}{2}$

The solutions are $\dfrac{1}{2}$ and -5.

8.3 Exercise Set

1. $\dfrac{7x}{13}+\dfrac{2x}{13}=\dfrac{9x}{13}$

3. $\dfrac{8x}{15}+\dfrac{x}{15}=\dfrac{9x}{15}=\dfrac{3x}{5}$

5. $\frac{x-3}{12}+\frac{5x+21}{12}=\frac{6x+18}{12}$
$=\frac{6(x+3)}{12}$
$=\frac{x+3}{2}$

7. $\frac{4}{x}+\frac{2}{x}=\frac{6}{x}$

9. $\frac{8}{9x}+\frac{13}{9x}=\frac{21}{9x}=\frac{7}{3x}$

11. $\frac{5}{x+3}+\frac{4}{x+3}=\frac{9}{x+3}$

13. $\frac{x}{x-3}+\frac{4x+5}{x-3}=\frac{5x+5}{x-3}$

15. $\frac{4x+1}{6x+5}+\frac{8x+9}{6x+5}=\frac{12x+10}{6x+5}$
$=\frac{2(6x+5)}{6x+5}=2$

17. $\frac{y^2+7y}{y^2-5y}+\frac{y^2-4y}{y^2-5y}=\frac{y^2+7y+y^2-4y}{y^2-5y}$
$=\frac{2y^2+3y}{y^2-5y}$
$=\frac{y(2y+3)}{y(y-5)}$
$=\frac{2y+3}{y-5}$

19. $\frac{4y-1}{5y^2}+\frac{3y+1}{5y^2}=\frac{4y-1+3y+1}{5y^2}$
$=\frac{7y}{5y^2}=\frac{7}{5y}$

21. $\frac{x^2-2}{x^2+x-2}+\frac{2x-x^2}{x^2+x-2}$
$=\frac{x^2-2+2x-x^2}{x^2+x-2}$
$=\frac{2x-2}{x^2+x-2}=\frac{2(x-1)}{(x+2)(x-1)}=\frac{2}{x+2}$

23. $\frac{x^2-4x}{x^2-x-6}+\frac{4x-4}{x^2-x-6}$
$=\frac{x^2-4x+4x-4}{x^2-x-6}$
$=\frac{x^2-4}{x^2-x-6}=\frac{(x+2)(x-2)}{(x-3)(x+2)}=\frac{x-2}{x-3}$

25. $\frac{3x}{5x-4}-\frac{4}{5x-4}=\frac{3x-4}{5x-4}$

27. $\frac{4x}{4x-3}-\frac{3}{4x-3}=\frac{4x-3}{4x-3}=1$

29. $\frac{14y}{7y+2}-\frac{7y-2}{7y+2}=\frac{14y-(7y-2)}{7y+2}$
$=\frac{14y-7y+2}{7y+2}$
$=\frac{7y+2}{7y+2}=1$

31. $\frac{3x+1}{4x-2}-\frac{x+1}{4x-2}=\frac{(3x+1)-(x+1)}{4x-2}$
$=\frac{3x+1-x-1}{4x-2}$
$=\frac{2x}{4x-2}$
$=\frac{2x}{2(2x-1)}$
$=\frac{x}{2x-1}$

33. $\frac{3y^2-1}{3y^3}-\frac{6y^2-1}{3y^3}$
$=\frac{(3y^2-1)-(6y^2-1)}{3y^3}$
$=\frac{3y^2-1-6y^2+1}{3y^3}=\frac{-3y^2}{3y^3}=-\frac{1}{y}$

35. $\frac{4y^2+5}{9y^2-64}-\frac{y^2-y+29}{9y^2-64}$
$=\frac{(4y^2+5)-(y^2-y+29)}{9y^2-64}$
$=\frac{4y^2+5-y^2+y-29}{9y^2-64}$
$=\frac{3y^2+y-24}{9y^2-64}$
$=\frac{(3y-8)(y+3)}{(3y+8)(3y-8)}=\frac{y+3}{3y+8}$

37. $\frac{6y^2+y}{2y^2-9y+9}-\frac{2y+9}{2y^2-9y+9}$
$-\frac{4y-3}{2y^2-9y+9}$
$=\frac{(6y^2+y)-(2y+9)-(4y-3)}{2y^2-9y+9}$
$=\frac{6y^2+y-2y-9-4y+3}{2y^2-9y+9}$
$=\frac{6y^2-5y-6}{2y^2-9y+9}$
$=\frac{(2y-3)(3y+2)}{(2y-3)(y-3)}$
$=\frac{3y+2}{y-3}$

39. $\frac{4}{x-3}+\frac{2}{3-x}=\frac{4}{x-3}+\frac{(-1)}{(-1)}\cdot\frac{2}{3-x}$
$=\frac{4}{x-3}+\frac{-2}{x-3}$
$=\frac{2}{x-3}$

41. $\frac{6x+7}{x-6}+\frac{3x}{6-x}=\frac{6x+7}{x-6}+\frac{(-1)}{(-1)}\cdot\frac{3x}{6-x}$
$=\frac{6x+7}{x-6}+\frac{-3x}{x-6}$
$=\frac{3x+7}{x-6}$

43. $\frac{5x-2}{3x-4}+\frac{2x-3}{4-3x}=\frac{5x-2}{3x-4}+\frac{(-1)}{(-1)}\cdot\frac{2x-3}{4-3x}$
$=\frac{5x-2}{3x-4}+\frac{-2x+3}{3x-4}$
$=\frac{5x-2-2x+3}{3x-4}$
$=\frac{3x+1}{3x-4}$

45. $\frac{x^2}{x-2}+\frac{4}{2-x}=\frac{x^2}{x-2}+\frac{(-1)}{(-1)}\cdot\frac{4}{2-x}$
$=\frac{x^2}{x-2}+\frac{-4}{x-2}$
$=\frac{x^2-4}{x-2}$
$=\frac{(x+2)(x-2)}{x-2}$
$=x+2$

47. $\frac{y-3}{y^2-25}+\frac{y-3}{25-y^2}$

$=\frac{y-3}{y^2-25}+\frac{(-1)}{(-1)}\cdot\frac{y-3}{25-y^2}$

$=\frac{y-3}{y^2-25}+\frac{-y+3}{y^2-25}$

$=\frac{y-3-y+3}{y^2-25}=\frac{0}{y^2-25}=0$

49. $\frac{6}{x-1}-\frac{5}{1-x}=\frac{6}{x-1}-\frac{(-1)}{(-1)}\cdot\frac{5}{1-x}$

$=\frac{6}{x-1}-\frac{-5}{x-1}$

$=\frac{6+5}{x-1}=\frac{11}{x-1}$

51. $\frac{10}{x+3}-\frac{2}{-x-3}=\frac{10}{x+3}-\frac{(-1)}{(-1)}\cdot\frac{2}{-x-3}$

$=\frac{10}{x+3}-\frac{-2}{x+3}$

$=\frac{10+2}{x+3}=\frac{12}{x+3}$

53. $\frac{y}{y-1}-\frac{1}{1-y}=\frac{y}{y-1}-\frac{(-1)}{(-1)}\cdot\frac{1}{1-y}$

$=\frac{y}{y-1}-\frac{-1}{y-1}$

$=\frac{y+1}{y-1}$

55. $\frac{3-x}{x-7}-\frac{2x-5}{7-x}=\frac{3-x}{x-7}-\frac{(-1)}{(-1)}\cdot\frac{2x-5}{7-x}$

$=\frac{3-x}{x-7}-\frac{-2x+5}{x-7}$

$=\frac{(3-x)-(-2x+5)}{x-7}$

$=\frac{3-x+2x-5}{x-7}$

$=\frac{x-2}{x-7}$

57. $\frac{x-2}{x^2-25}-\frac{x-2}{25-x^2}$

$=\frac{x-2}{x^2-25}-\frac{(-1)}{(-1)}\cdot\frac{x-2}{25-x^2}$

$=\frac{x-2}{x^2-25}-\frac{-x+2}{x^2-25}$

$=\frac{(x-2)-(-x+2)}{x^2-25}$

$=\frac{x-2+x-2}{x^2-25}=\frac{2x-4}{x^2-25}$

59. $\frac{x}{x-y}+\frac{y}{y-x}=\frac{x}{x-y}+\frac{(-1)}{(-1)}\cdot\frac{y}{y-x}$

$=\frac{x}{x-y}+\frac{-y}{x-y}$

$=\frac{x-y}{x-y}=1$

61. $\frac{2x}{x^2-y^2}+\frac{2y}{y^2-x^2}$

$=\frac{2x}{x^2-y^2}+\frac{(-1)}{(-1)}\cdot\frac{2y}{y^2-x^2}$

$=\frac{2x}{x^2-y^2}+\frac{-2y}{x^2-y^2}$

$=\frac{2x-2y}{x^2-y^2}=\frac{2(x-y)}{(x+y)(x-y)}=\frac{2}{x+y}$

63. $\dfrac{x^2-2}{x^2+6x-7}+\dfrac{19-4x}{7-6x-x^2}$

$=\dfrac{x^2-2}{x^2+6x-7}+\dfrac{(-1)}{(-1)}\cdot\dfrac{19-4x}{7-6x-x^2}$

$=\dfrac{x^2-2}{x^2+6x-7}+\dfrac{-19+4x}{-7+6x+x^2}$

$=\dfrac{x^2-2}{x^2+6x-7}+\dfrac{-19+4x}{x^2+6x-7}$

$=\dfrac{x^2-2-19+4x}{x^2+6x-7}$

$=\dfrac{x^2+4x-21}{x^2+6x-7}$

$=\dfrac{(x+7)(x-3)}{(x+7)(x-1)}=\dfrac{x-3}{x-1}$

65. $\dfrac{6b^2-10b}{16b^2-48b+27}+\dfrac{7b^2-20b}{16b^2-48b+27}-\dfrac{6b-3b^2}{16b^2-48b+27}$

$=\dfrac{6b^2-10b+7b^2-20b-6b+3b^2}{16b^2-48b+27}$

$=\dfrac{16b^2-36b}{16b^2-48b+27}=\dfrac{4b(4b-9)}{(4b-9)(4b-3)}$

$=\dfrac{4b}{4b-3}$

66. $\dfrac{22b+15}{12b^2+52b-9}+\dfrac{30b-20}{12b^2+52b-9}-\dfrac{4-2b}{12b^2+52b-9}$

$=\dfrac{22b+15+30b-20-4+2b}{12b^2+52b-9}$

$=\dfrac{54b-9}{12b^2+52b-9}=\dfrac{9(6b-1)}{(6b-1)(2b+9)}$

$=\dfrac{9}{2b+9}$

67. $\dfrac{2y}{y-5}-\left(\dfrac{2}{y-5}+\dfrac{y-2}{y-5}\right)$

$=\dfrac{2y}{y-5}-\left(\dfrac{2+y-2}{y-5}\right)$

$=\dfrac{2y}{y-5}-\dfrac{y}{y-5}=\dfrac{y}{y-5}$

68. $\dfrac{3x}{(x+1)^2}-\left[\dfrac{5x+1}{(x+1)^2}-\dfrac{3x+2}{(x+1)^2}\right]$

$=\dfrac{3x}{(x+1)^2}-\left[\dfrac{5x+1-3x-2}{(x+1)^2}\right]$

$=\dfrac{3x}{(x+1)^2}-\dfrac{2x-1}{(x+1)^2}$

$=\dfrac{3x-2x+1}{(x+1)^2}=\dfrac{x+1}{(x+1)^2}=\dfrac{1}{x+1}$

69. $\dfrac{b}{ac+ad-bc-bd}-\dfrac{a}{ac+ad-bc-bd}$

$=\dfrac{b-a}{ac+ad-bc-bd}$

$=\dfrac{b-a}{a(c+d)-b(c+c)}$

$=\dfrac{b-a}{(c+d)(a-b)}=\dfrac{(-1)}{(-1)}\cdot\dfrac{b-a}{(c+d)(a-b)}$

$=\dfrac{a-b}{-(c+d)(a-b)}=\dfrac{-1}{c+d}$

70. $\dfrac{y}{ax+bx-ay-by}-\dfrac{x}{ax+bx-ay-by}$

$=\dfrac{y-x}{ax+bx-ay-by}=\dfrac{y-x}{x(a+b)-y(a+b)}$

$=\dfrac{y-x}{(a+b)(x-y)}=\dfrac{(-1)}{(-1)}\cdot\dfrac{y-x}{(a+b)(x-y)}$

$=\dfrac{x-y}{-(a+b)(x-y)}=\dfrac{-1}{a+b}$

71. $\frac{(y-3)(y+2)}{(y+1)(y-4)}-\frac{(y+2)(y+3)}{(y+1)(4-y)}-\frac{(y+5)(y-1)}{(y+1)(4-y)}$

$=\frac{y^2-y-6}{(y+1)(y-4)}-\frac{y^2+5y+6}{(y+1)(4-y)}-\frac{y^2+4y-5}{(y+1)(4-y)}$

$=\frac{y^2-y-6}{(y+1)(y-4)}-\frac{(-1)}{(-1)}\cdot\frac{y^2+5y+6}{(y+1)(4-y)}-\frac{(-1)}{(-1)}\cdot\frac{y^2+4y-5}{(y+1)(4-y)}$

$=\frac{y^2-y-6}{(y+1)(y-4)}+\frac{y^2+5y+6}{(y+1)(y-4)}+\frac{y^2+4y-5}{(y+1)(y-4)}$

$=\frac{y^2-y-6+y^2+5y+6+y^2+4y-5}{(y+1)(y-4)}=\frac{3y^2+8y-5}{(y+1)(y-4)}$

72. $\frac{(y+1)(2y-1)}{(y-2)(y-3)}+\frac{(y+2)(y-1)}{(y-2)(y-3)}-\frac{(y+5)(2y+1)}{(3-y)(2-y)}$

$=\frac{2y^2+y-1}{(y-2)(y-3)}+\frac{y^2+y-2}{(y-2)(y-3)}-\frac{2y^2+11y+5}{-1(y-3)\cdot-1(y-2)}$

$=\frac{2y^2+y-1}{(y-2)(y-3)}+\frac{y^2+y-2}{(y-2)(y-3)}-\frac{2y^2+11y+5}{(y-3)(y-2)}$

$=\frac{2y^2+y-1+y^2+y-2-2y^2-11y-5}{(y-2)(y-3)}=\frac{y^2-9y-8}{(y-2)(y-3)}$

73. **a.** $\frac{L+60W}{L}-\frac{L-40W}{L}$

$=\frac{(L+60W)-(L-40W)}{L}$

$=\frac{L+60W-L+40W}{L}$

$=\frac{100W}{L}$

b. $\frac{100W}{L}$; $W=5, L=6$

$\frac{100W}{L}=\frac{100\cdot 5}{6}\approx 83.3$

Since this value is over 80, the skull is round.

75. $P=2L+2W$

$=2\left(\frac{5x+10}{x+3}\right)+2\left(\frac{5}{x+3}\right)$

$=\frac{10x+20}{x+3}+\frac{10}{x+3}$

$=\frac{10x+30}{x+3}=\frac{10(x+3)}{x+3}=10$

The perimeter is 10 meters.

77. – 79. Answers will vary.

81. Statement *d* is true.

$\frac{2x+1}{x-7}+\frac{3x+1}{x-7}-\frac{5x+2}{x-7}$

$=\frac{5x+2}{x-7}-\frac{5x+2}{x-7}=0$

83. $\left(\frac{3x^2-4x+4}{3x^2+7x+2}-\frac{10x+9}{3x^2+7x+2}\right)\div\frac{x-5}{x^2-4}$

$=\left(\frac{(3x^2-4x+4)-(10x+9)}{3x^2+7x+2}\right)\div\frac{x-5}{x^2-4}$

$=\frac{3x^2-4x+4-10x-9}{3x^2+7x+2}\div\frac{x-5}{x^2-4}$

$=\frac{3x^2-14x-5}{3x^2+7x+2}\div\frac{x-5}{x^2-4}$

$=\frac{3x^2-14x-5}{3x^2+7x+2}\cdot\frac{x^2-4}{x-5}$

$=\frac{(3x+1)(x-5)}{(3x+1)(x+2)}\cdot\frac{(x+2)(x-2)}{(x-5)}$

$=x-2$

85. $\frac{3x}{x+2}-\frac{?}{x+2}=\frac{6-17x}{x+2}$

The difference of the numerators on the left side must be $6-17x$, so the missing expression is $20x-6$.

Check:

$\frac{3x}{x+2}-\frac{20x-6}{x+2}=\frac{3x-(20x-6)}{x+2}$

$=\frac{3x-20x+6}{x+2}$

$=\frac{-17x+6}{x+2}$

$=\frac{6-17x}{x+2}$

87. $\frac{a^2}{a-4}-\frac{?}{a-4}=a+3$

In order to reduce $a+3$, the difference on the left must be

$\frac{(a-4)(a+3)}{a-4}=\frac{a^2-a-12}{a-4}$

Since $a^2-(a+12)=a^2-a-12$, the missing expression is $a+12$.

Check:

$\frac{a^2}{a-4}-\frac{a+12}{a-4}=\frac{a^2-(a+12)}{a-4}$

$=\frac{a^2-a-12}{a-4}=\frac{(a-4)(a-3)}{a-4}=a+3$

89.

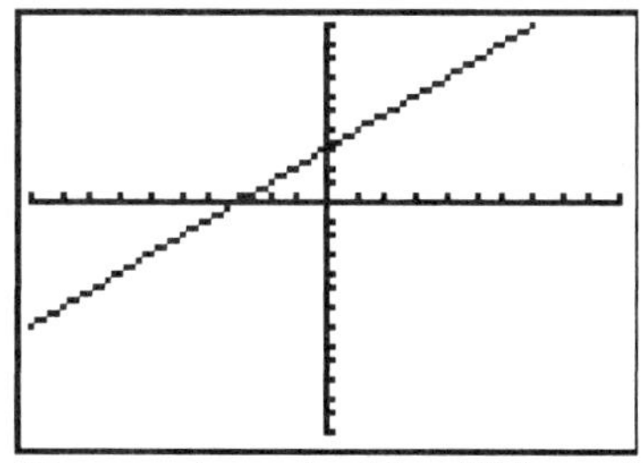

The graphs coincide. This verifies that $\frac{3x+6}{2}-\frac{x}{2}=x+3$.

91.

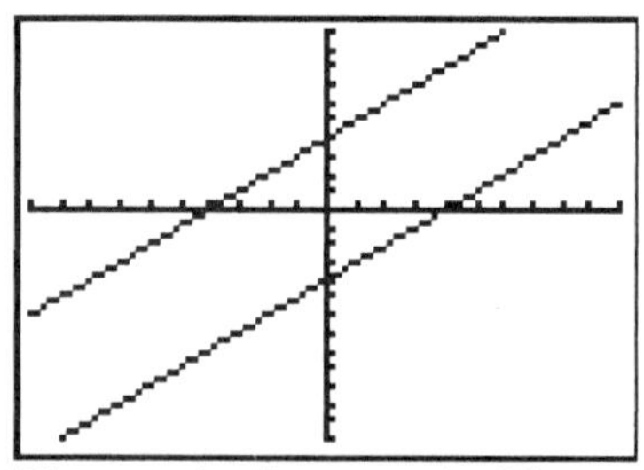

The graphs do not coincide.

$\frac{x^2-13}{x+4}-\frac{3}{x+4}=\frac{x^2-16}{x+4}$

$=\frac{(x+4)(x-4)}{x+4}$

$=x-4$

Change $x+4$ to $x-4$.

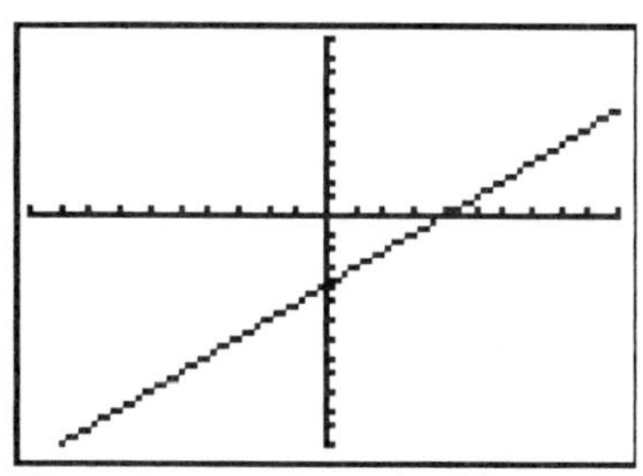

Now the graphs coincide.

92. $\frac{13}{15}-\frac{8}{45}=\frac{13}{15}\cdot\frac{3}{3}-\frac{8}{45}$
$=\frac{39}{45}-\frac{8}{45}=\frac{31}{45}$

93. $81x^4-1=(9x^2+1)(9x^2-1)$
$=(9x^2+1)(3x+1)(3x-1)$

94.
$$\begin{array}{r} 3x^2-7x-5 \\ x+3\overline{)3x^3+2x^2-26x-15} \\ \underline{3x^3+9x^2} \\ -7x^2-26x \\ \underline{-7x^2-21x} \\ -5x-15 \\ \underline{-5x-15} \\ 0 \end{array}$$

$\frac{3x^3+2x^2-26x-15}{x+3}=3x^2-7x-5$

8.4 Exercise Set

1. $\frac{7}{15x^2}$ and $\frac{13}{24x}$
$15x^2=3\cdot 5x^2$
$24=2^3\cdot 3x$
LCD = $2^3\cdot 3\cdot 5x^2=120x^2$

3. $\frac{8}{15x^2}$ and $\frac{5}{6x^5}$
$15x^2=3\cdot 5x^2$
$6x^5=2\cdot 3x^5$
LCD = $2\cdot 3\cdot 5\cdot x^5=30x^5$

5. $\frac{4}{x-3}$ and $\frac{7}{x+1}$
LCD = $(x-3)(x+1)$

7. $\frac{5}{7(y+2)}$ and $\frac{10}{y}$
LCD = $7y(y+2)$

9. $\frac{17}{x+4}$ and $\frac{18}{x^2-16}$
$x+4=1(x+4)$
$x^2-16=(x+4)(x-4)$
LCD = $(x+4)(x-4)$

11. $\frac{8}{y^2-9}$ and $\frac{14}{y(y+3)}$
$y^2-9=(y+3)(y-3)$
$y(y+3)=y(y+3)$
LCD = $y(y+3)(y-3)$

13. $\frac{7}{y^2-1}$ and $\frac{y}{y^2-2y+1}$
$y^2-1=(y+1)(y-1)$
$y^2-2y+1=(y-1)(y-1)$
LCD = $(y+1)(y-1)(y-1)$

15. $\frac{3}{x^2-x-20}$ and $\frac{x}{2x^2+7x-4}$
$x^2-x-20=(x-5)(x+4)$
$2x^2+7x-4=(2x-1)(x+4)$
LCD = $(x-5)(x+4)(2x-1)$

17. $\frac{3}{x}+\frac{5}{x^2}$
LCD = x^2
$\frac{3}{x}+\frac{5}{x^2}=\frac{3}{x}\cdot\frac{x}{x}+\frac{5}{x^2}=\frac{3x+5}{x^2}$

19. $\frac{2}{9x}+\frac{11}{6x}$

LCD = $18x$

$$\frac{2}{9x}+\frac{11}{6x}=\frac{2}{9x}\cdot\frac{2}{2}+\frac{11}{6x}\cdot\frac{3}{3}$$
$$=\frac{4}{18x}+\frac{33}{18x}=\frac{37}{18x}$$

21. $\frac{4}{x}+\frac{7}{2x^2}$

LCD = $2x^2$

$$\frac{4}{x}+\frac{7}{2x^2}=\frac{4}{x}\cdot\frac{2x}{2x}+\frac{7}{2x^2}=\frac{8x}{2x^2}+\frac{7}{2x^2}$$
$$=\frac{8x+7}{2x^2}$$

23. $6+\frac{1}{x}$

LCD = x

$$6+\frac{1}{x}=\frac{6}{1}\cdot\frac{x}{x}+\frac{1}{x}=\frac{6x}{x}+\frac{1}{x}=\frac{6x+1}{x}$$

25. $\frac{2}{x}+9$

LCD = x

$$\frac{2}{x}+9=\frac{2}{x}+\frac{9}{1}\cdot\frac{x}{x}=\frac{2}{x}+\frac{9x}{x}=\frac{2+9x}{x}$$

27. $\frac{x-1}{6}+\frac{x+2}{3}$

LCD = 6

$$\frac{x-1}{6}+\frac{x+2}{3}=\frac{x-1}{6}+\frac{(x+2)}{3}\cdot\frac{2}{2}$$
$$=\frac{x-1}{6}+\frac{2x+4}{6}=\frac{3x+3}{6}=\frac{3(x+1)}{6}$$
$$=\frac{x+1}{2}$$

29. $\frac{4}{x}+\frac{3}{x-5}$

LCD = $x(x-5)$

$$\frac{4}{x}+\frac{3}{x-5}=\frac{4(x-5)}{x(x-5)}+\frac{3}{x-5}\cdot\frac{x}{x}$$
$$=\frac{4(x-5)}{x(x-5)}+\frac{3x}{x(x-5)}$$
$$=\frac{4x-20+3x}{x(x-5)}$$
$$=\frac{7x-20}{x(x-5)}$$

31. $\frac{2}{x-1}+\frac{3}{x+2}$

LCD = $(x-1)(x+2)$

$$\frac{2}{x-1}+\frac{3}{x+2}$$
$$=\frac{2(x+2)}{(x-1)(x+2)}+\frac{3(x-1)}{(x-1)(x+2)}$$
$$=\frac{2x+4+3x-3}{(x-1)(x+2)}$$
$$=\frac{5x+1}{(x-1)(x+2)}$$

33. $\frac{2}{y+5}+\frac{3}{4y}$

LCD = $4y(y+5)$

$$\frac{2}{y+5}+\frac{3}{4y}=\frac{2(4y)}{(4y)(y+5)}+\frac{3(y+5)}{4y(y+5)}$$
$$=\frac{2(4y)+3(y+5)}{4y(y+5)}$$
$$=\frac{8y+3y+15}{4y(y+5)}$$
$$=\frac{11y+15}{4y(y+5)}$$

35. $\dfrac{x}{x+7}-1$

LCD = $x+7$

$$\frac{x}{x+7}-1=\frac{x}{x+7}-\frac{x+7}{x+7}$$
$$=\frac{x-(x+7)}{x+7}$$
$$=\frac{x-x-7}{x+7}$$
$$=\frac{-7}{x+7} \text{ or } -\frac{7}{x+7}$$

37. $\dfrac{7}{x+5}-\dfrac{4}{x-5}$

LCD = $(x+5)(x-5)$

$$\frac{7}{x+5}-\frac{4}{x-5}$$
$$=\frac{7(x-5)}{(x+5)(x-5)}-\frac{4(x+5)}{(x+5)(x-5)}$$
$$=\frac{7(x-5)-4(x+5)}{(x+5)(x-5)}$$
$$=\frac{7x-35-4x-20}{(x+5)(x-5)}$$
$$=\frac{3x-55}{(x+5)(x-5)}$$

39. $\dfrac{2x}{x^2-16}+\dfrac{x}{x-4}$

$x^2-16=(x+4)(x-4)$

$x-4=1(x-4)$

LCD = $(x+4)(x-4)$

$$\frac{2x}{x^2-16}+\frac{x}{x-4}$$
$$=\frac{2x}{(x+4)(x-4)}+\frac{x}{x-4}$$
$$=\frac{2x}{(x+4)(x-4)}+\frac{x(x+4)}{(x+4)(x-4)}$$
$$=\frac{2x+x(x+4)}{(x+4)(x-4)}$$
$$=\frac{2x+x^2+4x}{(x+4)(x-4)}$$
$$=\frac{x^2+6x}{(x+4)(x-4)}$$

41. $\dfrac{5y}{y^2-9}-\dfrac{4}{y+3}$

LCD = $(y+3)(y-3)$

$$\frac{5y}{y^2-9}-\frac{4}{y+3}$$
$$=\frac{5y}{(y+3)(y-3)}-\frac{4}{y+3}$$
$$=\frac{5y}{(y+3)(y-3)}-\frac{4(y-3)}{(y+3)(y-3)}$$
$$=\frac{5y-4(y-3)}{(y+3)(y-3)}$$
$$=\frac{5y-4y+12}{(y+3)(y-3)}$$
$$=\frac{y+12}{(y+3)(y-3)}$$

43. $\dfrac{7}{x-1}-\dfrac{3}{(x-1)(x-1)}$

LCD = $(x-1)(x-1)$

$$\frac{7}{x-1}-\frac{3}{(x-1)(x-1)}$$
$$=\frac{7(x-1)}{(x-1)(x-1)}-\frac{3}{(x-1)(x-1)}$$
$$=\frac{7x-7-3}{(x-1)(x-1)}$$
$$=\frac{7x-10}{(x-1)(x-1)} \text{ or } \frac{7x-10}{(x-1)^2}$$

45. $\frac{3y}{4y-20}+\frac{9y}{6y-30}$

$4y-20=4(y-5)$

$6y-30=6(y-5)$

LCD = $12(y-5)$

$$\frac{3y}{4y-20}+\frac{9y}{6y-30}$$
$$=\frac{4y}{4(y-5)}+\frac{9y}{6(y-5)}$$
$$=\frac{4y}{4(y-5)}\cdot\frac{3}{3}+\frac{9y}{6(y-5)}\cdot\frac{2}{2}$$
$$=\frac{12y}{12(y-5)}+\frac{18y}{12(y-5)}$$
$$=\frac{9y+18y}{12(y-5)}=\frac{27y}{12(y-5)}$$
$$=\frac{9y}{4(y-5)}$$

47. $\frac{y+4}{y}-\frac{y}{y+4}$

LCD = $y(y+4)$

$$\frac{y+4}{y}-\frac{y}{y+4}$$
$$=\frac{(y+4)(y+4)}{y(y+4)}-\frac{y\cdot y}{y(y+4)}$$
$$=\frac{y^2+8y+16-y^2}{y(y+4)}$$
$$=\frac{8y+16}{y(y+4)}$$

49. $\frac{2x+9}{x^2-7x+12}=\frac{2}{x-3}$

$x^2-7x+12=(x-3)(x-4)$

$x-3=1(x-3)$

LCD = $(x-3)(x-4)$

$$\frac{2x+9}{x^2-7x+12}-\frac{2}{x-3}$$
$$=\frac{2x+9}{(x-3)(x-4)}-\frac{2}{x-3}$$
$$=\frac{2x+9}{(x-3)(x-4)}-\frac{2(x-4)}{(x-3)(x-4)}$$
$$=\frac{2x+9-2(x-4)}{(x-3)(x-4)}$$
$$=\frac{2x+9-2x+8}{(x-3)(x-4)}$$
$$=\frac{17}{(x-3)(x-4)}$$

51. $\frac{3}{x^2-1}+\frac{4}{(x+1)^2}$

$x^2-1=(x+1)(x-1)$

$(x+1)^2=(x+1)(x+1)$

LCD = $(x+1)(x+1)(x-1)$

$$\frac{3}{x^2-1}+\frac{4}{(x+1)^2}$$
$$=\frac{3}{(x+1)(x-1)}+\frac{4}{(x+1)(x+1)}$$
$$=\frac{3(x+1)}{(x+1)(x+1)(x-1)}$$
$$+\frac{4(x-1)}{(x+1)(x+1)(x-1)}$$
$$=\frac{3(x+1)+4(x-1)}{(x+1)(x+1)(x-1)}$$
$$=\frac{3x+3+4x-4}{(x+1)(x+1)(x-1)}$$
$$=\frac{7x-1}{(x+1)(x+1)(x-1)}$$

53. $\frac{3x}{x^2+3x-10}-\frac{2x}{x^2+x-6}$

$x^2+3x-10=(x-2)(x+5)$

$x^2+x-6=(x+3)(x-2)$

LCD = $(x+3)(x-2)(x+5)$

$\frac{3x}{x^2+3x-10}-\frac{2x}{x^2+x-6}$

$=\frac{3x}{(x-2)(x+5)}-\frac{2x}{(x+3)(x-2)}$

$=\frac{3x(x+3)}{(x+3)(x-2)(x+5)}$

$-\frac{2x(x+5)}{(x+3)(x-2)(x+5)}$

$=\frac{3x(x+3)-2x(x+5)}{(x+3)(x-2)(x+5)}$

$=\frac{3x^2+9x-2x^2-10x}{(x+3)(x-2)(x+5)}$

$=\frac{x^2-x}{(x+3)(x-2)(x+5)}$

55. $\frac{y}{y^2+2y+1}+\frac{4}{y^2+5y+4}$

$y^2+2y+1=(y+1)(y+1)$

$y^2+5y+4=(y+4)(y+1)$

LCD = $(y+4)(y+1)(y+1)$

$\frac{y}{y^2+2y+1}+\frac{4}{y^2+5y+4}$

$=\frac{y}{(y+1)(y+1)}+\frac{4}{(y+4)(y+1)}$

$=\frac{y(y+4)}{(y+4)(y+1)(y+1)}$

$+\frac{4(y+1)}{(y+4)(y+1)(y+1)}$

$=\frac{y(y+4)+4(y+1)}{(y+4)(y+1)(y+1)}$

$=\frac{y^2+4y+4y+4}{(y+4)(y+1)(y+1)}$

$=\frac{y^2+8y+4}{(y+4)(y+1)(y+1)}$

57. $\frac{x-5}{x+3}+\frac{x+3}{x-5}$

LCD = $(x+3)(x-5)$

$\frac{x-5}{x+3}+\frac{x+3}{x-5}$

$=\frac{(x-5)(x-5)}{(x+3)(x-5)}+\frac{(x+3)(x+3)}{(x-5)(x+3)}$

$=\frac{(x-5)(x-5)+(x+3)(x+3)}{(x+3)(x-5)}$

$=\frac{(x^2-10x+25)+(x^2+6x+9)}{(x+3)(x-5)}$

$=\frac{2x^2-4x+34}{(x+3)(x-5)}$

59. $\frac{5}{2y^2-2y}-\frac{3}{2y-2}$

$2y^2-2y=2y(y-1)$

$2y-2=2(y-1)$

LCD = $2y(y-1)$

$\frac{5}{2y^2-2y}-\frac{3}{2y-2}$

$=\frac{5}{2y(y-1)}-\frac{3}{2(y-1)}$

$=\frac{5}{2y(y-1)}-\frac{3\cdot y}{2y(y-1)}$

$=\frac{5-3y}{2y(y-1)}$

61. $\dfrac{4x+3}{x^2-9}-\dfrac{x+1}{x-3}$

LCD $=(x+3)(x-3)$

$$\dfrac{4x+3}{x^2-9}-\dfrac{x+1}{x-3}$$
$$=\dfrac{4x+3}{(x+3)(x-3)}-\dfrac{(x+1)(x+3)}{(x+3)(x-3)}$$
$$=\dfrac{(4x+3)-(x+1)(x+3)}{(x+3)(x-3)}$$
$$=\dfrac{(4x+3)-(x^2+4x+3)}{(x+3)(x-3)}$$
$$=\dfrac{4x+3-x^2-4x-3}{(x+3)(x-3)}$$
$$=\dfrac{-x^2}{(x+3)(x-3)}=-\dfrac{x^2}{(x+3)(x-3)}$$

63. $\dfrac{y^2-39}{y^2+3y-10}-\dfrac{y-7}{y-2}$

$y^2+3y-10=(y-2)(y+5)$

$y-2=1(y-2)$

LCD $=(y-2)(y+5)$

$$\dfrac{y^2-39}{y^2+3y-10}-\dfrac{y-7}{y-2}$$
$$=\dfrac{y^2-39}{(y-2)(y+5)}-\dfrac{y-7}{y-2}$$
$$=\dfrac{y^2-39}{(y-2)(y+5)}-\dfrac{(y-7)(y+5)}{(y-2)(y+5)}$$
$$=\dfrac{(y^2-39)-(y-7)(y+5)}{(y-2)(y+5)}$$
$$=\dfrac{(y^2-39)-(y^2-2y-35)}{(y-2)(y+5)}$$
$$=\dfrac{y^2-39-y^2+2y+35}{(y-2)(y+5)}$$
$$=\dfrac{2y-4}{(y-2)(y+5)}=\dfrac{2(y-2)}{(y-2)(y+5)}$$
$$=\dfrac{2}{y+5}$$

65. $4+\dfrac{1}{x-3}$

LCD $=x-3$

$$4+\dfrac{1}{x-3}=\dfrac{4(x-3)}{x-3}+\dfrac{1}{x-3}$$
$$=\dfrac{4(x-3)+1}{x-3}$$
$$=\dfrac{4x-12+1}{x-3}$$
$$=\dfrac{4x-11}{x-3}$$

67. $3-\dfrac{3y}{y+1}$

LCD $=y+1$

$$3-\dfrac{3y}{y+1}=\dfrac{3(y+1)}{y+1}-\dfrac{3y}{y+1}$$
$$=\dfrac{3(y+1)-3y}{y+1}$$
$$=\dfrac{3y+3-3y}{y+1}$$
$$=\dfrac{3}{y+1}$$

69. $\dfrac{9x+3}{x^2-x-6}+\dfrac{x}{3-x}$

$x^2-x-6=(x-3)(x+2)$

$3-x=-1(x-3)$

LCD $=(x-3)(x+2)$

$$\frac{9x+3}{x^2-x-6}+\frac{x}{3-x}$$
$$=\frac{9x+3}{(x-3)(x+2)}+\frac{(-1)}{(-1)}\cdot\frac{x}{3-x}$$
$$=\frac{9x+3}{(x-3)(x+2)}+\frac{-x}{x-3}$$
$$=\frac{9x+3}{(x-3)(x+2)}+\frac{-x(x+2)}{(x-3)(x+2)}$$
$$=\frac{9x+3-x(x+2)}{(x-3)(x+2)}$$
$$=\frac{9x+3-x^2-2x}{(x-3)(x+2)}$$
$$=\frac{-x^2+7x+3}{(x-3)(x+2)}$$

71. $$\frac{x+3}{x^2+x-2}-\frac{2}{x^2-1}$$

$x^2+x-2=(x-1)(x+2)$

$x^2-1=(x+1)(x-1)$

LCD = $(x+1)(x-1)(x+2)$

$$\frac{x+3}{x^2+x-2}-\frac{2}{x^2-1}$$
$$=\frac{x+3}{(x-1)(x+2)}-\frac{2}{(x+1)(x-1)}$$
$$=\frac{(x+3)(x+1)}{(x+1)(x-1)(x+2)}-\frac{2(x+2)}{(x+1)(x-1)(x+2)}$$
$$=\frac{(x+3)(x+1)-2(x+2)}{(x+1)(x-1)(x+2)}$$
$$=\frac{x^2+4x+3-2x-4}{(x+1)(x-1)(x+2)}$$
$$=\frac{x^2+2x-1}{(x+1)(x-1)(x+2)}$$

73. $$\frac{y+3}{5y^2}-\frac{y-5}{15y}$$

LCD = $15y^2$

$$\frac{y+3}{5y^2}-\frac{y-5}{15y}$$
$$=\frac{(y+3)(3)}{5y^2(3)}-\frac{(y-5)(y)}{15y(y)}$$
$$=\frac{(3y+9)-(y^2-5y)}{15y^2}$$
$$=\frac{3y+9-y^2+5y}{15y^2}$$
$$=\frac{-y^2+8y+9}{15y^2}$$

75. $$\frac{x+3}{3x+6}+\frac{x}{4-x^2}$$

$3x+6=3(x+2)$

$4-x^2=(2+x)(2-x)$

Note that $-1(2-x)=x-2$

LCD = $3(x+2)(x-2)$

$$\frac{x+3}{3x+6}+\frac{x}{4-x^2}$$
$$=\frac{x+3}{3(x+2)}+\frac{x}{(2+x)(2-x)}$$
$$=\frac{x+3}{3(x+2)}+\frac{(-1)}{(-1)}\cdot\frac{x}{(2+x)(2-x)}$$
$$=\frac{x+3}{3(x+2)}+\frac{-x}{(x+2)(x-2)}$$
$$=\frac{(x+3)(x-2)}{3(x+2)(x-2)}+\frac{-x(3)}{3(x+2)(x-2)}$$
$$=\frac{x^2+x-6-3x}{3(x+2)(x-2)}$$
$$=\frac{x^2-2x-6}{3(x+2)(x-2)}$$

77. $\frac{y}{y^2-1}+\frac{2y}{y-y^2}$

$y^2-1=(y+1)(y-1)$

$y-y^2=y(1-y)$

Note that $-1(1-y)=y-1$

LCD = $y(y+1)(y-1)$

$$\frac{y}{y^2-1}+\frac{2y}{y-y^2}$$
$$=\frac{y}{(y+1)(y-1)}+\frac{2y}{y(1-y)}$$
$$=\frac{y}{(y+1)(y-1)}+\frac{(-1)}{(-1)}\cdot\frac{2y}{y(1-y)}$$
$$=\frac{y}{(y+1)(y-1)}+\frac{-2y}{y(y-1)}$$
$$=\frac{y\cdot y}{y(y+1)(y-1)}+\frac{-2y(y+1)}{y(y+1)(y-1)}$$
$$=\frac{y^2-2y(y+1)}{y(y+1)(y-1)}=\frac{y^2-2y^2-2y}{y(y+1)(y-1)}$$
$$=\frac{-y^2-2y}{y(y+1)(y-1)}=\frac{-y(y+2)}{y(y+1)(y-1)}$$
$$=\frac{-1(y+2)}{(y+1)(y-1)}=\frac{-y-2}{(y+1)(y-1)}$$

79. $\frac{x-1}{x}+\frac{y+1}{y}$

LCD = xy

$$\frac{x-1}{x}+\frac{y+1}{y}$$
$$=\frac{(x-1)(y)}{xy}+\frac{(y+1)(x)}{xy}$$
$$=\frac{xy-y+xy+x}{xy}$$
$$=\frac{x+2xy-y}{xy}$$

81. $\frac{3x}{x^2-y^2}-\frac{2}{y-x}$

$x^2-y^2=(x+y)(x-y)$

Note that $y-x=-1(x-y)$

LCD = $(x+y)(x-y)$

$$\frac{3x}{x^2-y^2}-\frac{2}{y-x}$$
$$=\frac{3x}{(x+y)(x-y)}-\frac{(-1)}{(-1)}\cdot\frac{2}{y-x}$$
$$=\frac{3x}{(x+y)(x-y)}-\frac{-2}{x-y}$$
$$=\frac{3x}{(x+y)(x-y)}-\frac{-2(x+y)}{(x+y)(x-y)}$$
$$=\frac{3x+2(x+y)}{(x+y)(x-y)}=\frac{3x+2x+2y}{(x+y)(x-y)}$$
$$=\frac{5x+2y}{(x+y)(x-y)}$$

83. $\frac{x+6}{x^2-4}-\frac{x+3}{x+2}+\frac{x-3}{x-2}$

LCD = $(x+2)(x-2)$

$$\frac{x+6}{x^2-4}-\frac{x+3}{x+2}+\frac{x-3}{x-2}$$
$$=\frac{x+6}{(x+2)(x-2)}-\frac{x+3}{x+2}+\frac{x-3}{x-2}$$
$$=\frac{x+6}{(x+2)(x-2)}-\frac{(x+3)(x-2)}{(x+2)(x-2)}+\frac{(x-3)(x+2)}{(x-2)(x+2)}$$
$$=\frac{x+6-(x+3)(x-2)+(x-3)(x+2)}{(x+2)(x-2)}$$
$$=\frac{x+6-(x^2+x-6)+(x^2-x-6)}{(x+2)(x-2)}$$

$$= \frac{x+6-x^2-x+6+x^2-x-6}{(x+2)(x-2)}$$

$$= \frac{-x+6}{(x+2)(x-2)}$$

84. $\frac{x+8}{x^2-9} - \frac{x+2}{x+3} + \frac{x-2}{x-3}$

LCD = $(x+3)(x-3)$

$$\frac{x+8}{x^2-9} - \frac{x+2}{x+3} + \frac{x-2}{x-3}$$

$$= \frac{x+8}{(x+3)(x-3)} - \frac{x+2}{x+3} + \frac{x-2}{x-3}$$

$$= \frac{x+8}{(x+3)(x-3)} - \frac{(x+2)(x-3)}{(x+3)(x-3)} + \frac{(x-2)(x+3)}{(x-3)(x+3)}$$

$$= \frac{x+8-(x+2)(x-3)+(x-2)(x+3)}{(x+3)(x-3)}$$

$$= \frac{x+8-(x^2-x-6)+(x^2+x-6)}{(x+3)(x-3)}$$

$$= \frac{x+8-x^2+x+6+x^2+x-6}{(x+3)(x-3)}$$

$$= \frac{3x+8}{(x+3)(x-3)}$$

85. $\frac{5}{x^2-25} + \frac{4}{x^2-11x+30} - \frac{3}{x^2-x-30}$

$x^2-25 = (x+5)(x-5)$

$x^2-11x+30 = (x-6)(x-5)$

$x^2-x-30 = (x-6)(x+5)$

LCD = $(x+5)(x-5)(x-6)$

$$\frac{5}{x^2-25} + \frac{4}{x^2-11x+30} - \frac{3}{x^2-x-30}$$

$$= \frac{5}{(x+5)(x-5)} + \frac{4}{(x-6)(x-5)} - \frac{3}{(x-6)(x+5)}$$

$$= \frac{5(x-6)}{(x+5)(x-5)(x-6)} + \frac{4(x+5)}{(x-6)(x-5)(x+5)} - \frac{3(x-5)}{(x-6)(x+5)(x-5)}$$

$$= \frac{5(x-6)+4(x+5)-3(x-5)}{(x+5)(x-5)(x-6)}$$

$$= \frac{5x-30+4x+20-3x+15}{(x+5)(x-5)(x-6)}$$

$$= \frac{6x+5}{(x+5)(x-5)(x-6)}$$

86. $\frac{3}{x^2-49} + \frac{2}{x^2-15x+56} - \frac{5}{x^2-x-56}$

$x^2-49 = (x+7)(x-7)$

$x^2-15x+56 = (x-7)(x-8)$

$x^2-x-56 = (x-8)(x+7)$

LCD = $(x+7)(x+7)(x-8)$

$$\frac{3}{x^2-49} + \frac{2}{x^2-15x+56} - \frac{5}{x^2-x-56}$$

$$= \frac{3}{(x+7)(x-7)} + \frac{2}{(x-7)(x-8)} - \frac{5}{(x-8)(x+7)}$$

$$= \frac{3(x-8)}{(x+7)(x-7)(x-8)} + \frac{2(x+7)}{(x-7)(x-8)(x+7)} - \frac{5(x-7)}{(x-8)(x+7)(x-7)}$$

$$= \frac{3(x-8)+2(x+7)-5(x-7)}{(x+7)(x-7)(x-8)}$$

$$= \frac{3x-24+2x+14-5x+35}{(x+7)(x-7)(x-8)}$$

$$= \frac{25}{(x+7)(x-7)(x-8)}$$

87. $\frac{x+6}{x^3-27} - \frac{x}{x^3+3x^2+9x}$

$x^3-27 = (x-3)(x^2+3x+9)$

$x^3+3x^2+9x = x(x^2+3x+9)$

LCD = $x(x-3)(x^2+3x+9)$

$$\frac{x+6}{x^3-27} - \frac{x}{x^3+3x^2+9x}$$

$$= \frac{(x+6)x}{(x-3)(x^2+3x+9)x} - \frac{x(x-3)}{x(x^2+3x+9)(x-3)}$$

$$= \frac{x+6}{(x-3)(x^2+3x+9)} - \frac{x}{x(x^2+3x+9)}$$

$$= \frac{x(x+6)-x(x-3)}{x(x-3)(x^2+3x+9)}$$

$$= \frac{x^2+6x-x^2+3x}{x(x-3)(x^2+3x+9)}$$

$$= \frac{9x}{x(x-3)(x^2+3x+9)}$$

$$= \frac{9}{(x-3)(x^2+3x+9)}$$

88. $\frac{x+8}{x^3-8} - \frac{x}{x^3+2x^2+4x}$

$x^3-8 = (x-2)(x^2+2x+4)$

$x^3+2x^2+4x = x(x^2+2x+4)$

LCD = $x(x-2)(x^2+2x+4)$

$$\frac{x+8}{x^3-8} - \frac{x}{x^3+2x^2+4x}$$

$$= \frac{x+8}{(x-2)(x^2+2x+4)} - \frac{x}{x(x^2+2x+4)}$$

$$= \frac{(x+8)x}{(x-2)(x^2+2x+4)x} - \frac{x(x-2)}{x(x^2+2x+4)(x-2)}$$

$$= \frac{x(x+8)-x(x-2)}{x(x-2)(x^2+2x+4)}$$

$$= \frac{x^2+8x-x^2+2x}{x(x-2)(x^2+2x+4)}$$

$$= \frac{10x}{x(x-2)(x^2+2x+4)}$$

$$= \frac{10}{(x-2)(x^2+2x+4)}$$

89. $\frac{9y+3}{y^2-y-6}+\frac{y}{3-y}+\frac{y-1}{y+2}$

$y^2-y-6=(y-3)(y+2)$

$3-y=-1(y-3)$

$y+2=1(y+2)$

LCD = $(y-3)(y+2)$

$\frac{9y+3}{y^2-y-6}+\frac{y}{3-y}+\frac{y-1}{y+2}$

$=\frac{9y+3}{(y-3)(y+2)}+\frac{y}{-1(y-3)}+\frac{y-1}{y+2}$

$=\frac{9y+3}{(y-3)(y+2)}+\frac{-y(y+2)}{(y-3)(y+2)}+\frac{(y-1)(y-3)}{(y+2)(y-3)}$

$=\frac{9y+3+-y(y+2)+(y-1)(y-3)}{(y-3)(y+2)}$

$=\frac{9y+3-y^2-2y+y^2-4y+3}{(y-3)(y+2)}$

$=\frac{3y+6}{(y-3)(y+2)}=\frac{3(y+2)}{(y-3)(y+2)}$

$=\frac{3}{y-3}$

90. $\frac{7y-2}{y^2-y-12}+\frac{2y}{4-y}+\frac{y+1}{y+3}$

$y^2-y-12=(y-4)(y+3)$

$4-y=-1(y-4)$

$y+3=1(y+3)$

LCD = $(y-4)(y+3)$

$\frac{7y-2}{y^2-y-12}+\frac{2y}{4-y}+\frac{y+1}{y+3}$

$=\frac{7y-2}{(y-4)(y+3)}+\frac{2y}{-1(y-4)}+\frac{y+1}{y+3}$

$=\frac{7y-2}{(y-4)(y+3)}+\frac{-2y(y+3)}{(y-4)(y+3)}+\frac{(y+1)(y-4)}{(y+3)(y-4)}$

$=\frac{7y-2+-2y(y+3)+(y+1)(y-4)}{(y-4)(y+3)}$

$=\frac{7y-2-2y^2-6y+y^2-3y-4}{(y-4)(y+3)}$

$=\frac{-y^2-2y-6}{(y-4)(y+3)}$ or $-\frac{y^2+2y+6}{(y-4)(y+3)}$

91. $\frac{3}{x^2+4xy+3y^2}-\frac{5}{x^2-2xy-3y^2}+\frac{2}{x^2-9y^2}$

$x^2+4xy+3y^2=(x+y)(x+3y)$

$x^2-2xy-3y^2=(x-3y)(x+y)$

$x^2-9y^2=(x+3y)(x-3y)$

LCD = $(x+y)(x+3y)(x-3y)$

$\frac{3}{x^2+4xy+3y^2}-\frac{5}{x^2-2xy-3y^2}+\frac{2}{x^2-9y^2}$

$=\frac{3}{(x+y)(x+3y)}-\frac{5}{(x-3y)(x+y)}+\frac{2}{(x+3y)(x-3y)}$

$$= \frac{3(x-3y)}{(x+y)(x+3y)(x-3y)} - \frac{5(x+3y)}{(x-3y)(x+y)(x+3y)} + \frac{2(x+y)}{(x+3y)(x-3y)(x+y)}$$

$$= \frac{3(x-3y)-5(x+3y)+2(x+y)}{(x+y)(x+3y)(x-3y)}$$

$$= \frac{3x-9y-5x-15y+2x+2y}{(x+y)(x+3y)(x-3y)}$$

$$= \frac{-22y}{(x+y)(x+3y)(x-3y)}$$

92. $$\frac{5}{x^2+3xy+2y^2} - \frac{7}{x^2-xy-2y^2} + \frac{4}{x^2-4y^2}$$

$x^2+3xy+2y^2 = (x+y)(x+2y)$

$x^2-xy-2y^2 = (x+y)(x-2y)$

$x^2-4y^2 = (x+2y)(x-2y)$

LCD = $(x+y)(x+2y)(x-2y)$

$$\frac{5}{x^2+3xy+2y^2} - \frac{7}{x^2-xy-2y^2} + \frac{4}{x^2-4y^2}$$

$$= \frac{5}{(x+y)(x+2y)} - \frac{7}{(x+y)(x-2y)} + \frac{4}{(x+2y)(x-2y)}$$

$$= \frac{5(x-2y)}{(x+y)(x+2y)(x-2y)} - \frac{7(x+2y)}{(x+y)(x-2y)(x+2y)} + \frac{4(x+y)}{(x+2y)(x-2y)(x+y)}$$

$$= \frac{5(x-2y)-7(x+2y)+4(x+y)}{(x+y)(x+2y)(x-2y)}$$

$$= \frac{5x-10y-7x-14y+4x+4y}{(x+y)(x+2y)(x-2y)}$$

$$= \frac{2x-20y}{(x+y)(x+2y)(x-2y)}$$

93. Young's Rule $C = \frac{DA}{A+12}$

$A = 8;$

$$C = \frac{D \cdot 8}{8+12} = \frac{8D}{20} = \frac{2D}{5}$$

$A = 3;$

$$C = \frac{D \cdot 3}{3+12} = \frac{3D}{15} = \frac{D}{5}$$

Difference:

$$\frac{2D}{5} - \frac{D}{5} = \frac{D}{5}$$

The difference in dosages for an 8-year-old child and a 3-year-old child is $\frac{D}{5}$. This means that an 8-year-old should be given $\frac{1}{5}$ of the adult dosage more than a 3-year-old.

95. Young's Rule:

$$C = \frac{DA}{A+12}$$

Cowling's Rule:

$$C = \frac{D(A+1)}{24}$$

For $A = 12$, Young's Rule gives

$$C = \frac{D \cdot 12}{12+12} = \frac{12D}{24} = \frac{D}{2}$$

and Cowling's Rule gives

$$C = \frac{D(12+1)}{24} = \frac{13D}{24}$$

The difference between the dosages given by Cowling's Rule and Young's Rule is

$$\frac{13D}{24} - \frac{12D}{24} = \frac{D}{24}.$$

This means that Cowling's Rule says to give a 12-year-old $\frac{1}{24}$ of the adult dose more than Young's Rule says the dosage should be.

97. No, because the graphs cross, neither formula gives a consistently smaller dosage.

99. The difference in dosage is greatest at 5 years. This is where the graphs are farthest apart.

101. $P = 2L + 2W$

$$= 2\left(\frac{x}{x+3}\right) + 2\left(\frac{x}{x-4}\right)$$

$$= \frac{2x}{x+3} + \frac{2x}{x+4}$$

$$= \frac{2x(x+4)}{(x+3)(x+4)} + \frac{2x(x+3)}{(x+3)(x+4)}$$

$$= \frac{2x^2 + 8x + 2x^2 + 6x}{(x+3)(x+4)}$$

$$= \frac{4x^2 + 14x}{(x+3)(x+4)}$$

103. Answers will vary.

105. Explanations will vary. The right side of the equation should be charged from $\frac{3}{x+5}$ to $\frac{5+2x}{5x}$.

107. Answers will vary.

109.
$$\frac{y^2+5y+4}{y^2+2y-3} \cdot \frac{y^2+y-6}{y^2+2y-3} - \frac{2}{y-1}$$

$$= \frac{(y+4)(y+1)}{(y+3)(y-1)} \cdot \frac{(y+3)(y-2)}{(y+3)(y-1)} - \frac{2}{y-1}$$

$$= \frac{(y+4)(y+1)(y-2)}{(y+3)(y-1)(y-1)} - \frac{2}{y-1}$$

$$= \frac{(y+4)(y+1)(y-2)}{(y+3)(y-1)(y-1)} - \frac{2(y-1)(y+3)}{(y-1)(y-1)(y+3)}$$

$$= \frac{(y+4)(y^2-y-2)}{(y+3)(y-1)(y-1)} - \frac{2(y^2+2y-3)}{(y+3)(y-1)(y-1)}$$

$$= \frac{y^3-y^2-2y+4y^2-4y-8}{(y+3)(y-1)(y-1)} - \frac{2y^2+4y-6}{(y+3)(y-1)(y-1)}$$

$$= \frac{y^3+3y^2-6y-8}{(y+3)(y-1)(y-1)} - \frac{2y^2+4y-6}{(y+3)(y-1)(y-1)}$$

$$= \frac{y^3+3y^2-6y-8-2y^2-4y+6}{(y+3)(y-1)(y-1)}$$

$$= \frac{y^3+y^2-10y-2}{(y+3)(y-1)(y-1)}$$

111. $\dfrac{2}{x-1} - \dfrac{?}{?} = \dfrac{2x^2+3x-1}{x^2(x-1)}$

If the first rational expression is multiplied by $\dfrac{x^2}{x^2}$, the result will be

$\dfrac{2}{x-2} \cdot \dfrac{x^2}{x^2} = \dfrac{2x^2}{x^2(x-1)}$.

Then,

$\dfrac{2x^2}{x^2(x-1)} + \dfrac{3x-1}{x^2(x-1)} = \dfrac{2x^2+3x-1}{x^2(x-1)}$.

Therefore, the missing rational expression is

$\dfrac{3x-1}{x^2(x-1)}$.

113. $(3x+5)(2x-7) = 6x^2 - 21x + 10x - 35$
$= 6x^2 - 11x - 35$

114. $3x - y < 3$

Graph $3x - y = 3$ as a dashed line using the x-intercept, 1, and the y-intercept -3. Use (9,0) as a test point. Since $3 \cdot 0 - 9 < 3$ is a true statement, shade the half-plane including (0,0).

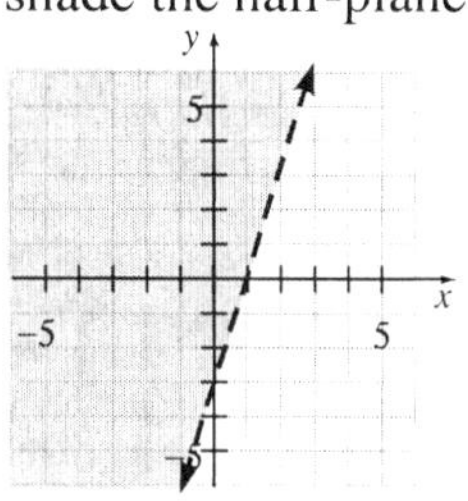

115. Line passing through (−3, −4) and (1,0)

First find the slope.

$$m = \frac{0-(-4)}{1-(-3)} = \frac{4}{4} = 1$$

Use $m = (1,0)$ and $(x_1, y_1) = (1,0)$ in the point-slope form and simplify to find the slope-intercept form.

$$y - y_1 = m(x - x_1)$$
$$y - 0 = 1(x-1)$$
$$y = x - 1$$

Mid-Chapter Check Point – Chapter 8

1. $\dfrac{x^2-4}{x^2-2x-8}$

$$x^2 - 2x - 8 = 0$$
$$(x-4)(x+2) = 0$$
$$x - 4 = 0 \quad \text{or} \quad x + 2 = 0$$
$$x = 4 \qquad\qquad x = -2$$

The rational expression is undefined for $x = 4$ and $x = -2$.

2. $\dfrac{3x^2-7x+2}{6x^2+x-1} = \dfrac{(3x-1)(x-2)}{(3x-1)(2x+1)} = \dfrac{x-2}{2x+1}$

3. $\dfrac{9-3y}{y^2-5y+6} = \dfrac{3(3-y)}{(y-3)(y-2)}$

$= \dfrac{-3(y-3)}{(y-3)(y-2)} = \dfrac{-3}{y-2}$

4. $\dfrac{16w^3-24w^2}{8w^4-12w^3} = \dfrac{8w^2(2w-3)}{4w^3(2w-3)} = \dfrac{2}{w}$

5. $\dfrac{7x-3}{x^2+3x-4} - \dfrac{3x+1}{x^2+3x-4}$

$= \dfrac{7x-3-3x-1}{(x-1)(x+4)}$

$= \dfrac{4x-4}{(x-1)(x+4)}$

$= \dfrac{4(x-1)}{(x-1)(x+4)} = \dfrac{4}{x+4}$

6. $$\frac{x+2}{2x-4}\cdot\frac{8}{x^2-4}$$
$$=\frac{x+2}{2(x-2)}\cdot\frac{8}{(x+2)(x-2)}$$
$$=\frac{4}{(x-2)(x-2)} \text{ or } \frac{4}{(x-2)^2}$$

7. $$1+\frac{7}{x-2}=\frac{x-2}{x-2}+\frac{7}{x-2}=\frac{x+5}{x-2}$$

8. $$\frac{2x^2+x-1}{2x^2-7x+3}\div\frac{x^2-3x-4}{x^2-x-6}$$
$$=\frac{2x^2+x-1}{2x^2-7x+3}\cdot\frac{x^2-x-6}{x^2-3x-4}$$
$$=\frac{(2x-1)(x+1)}{(2x-1)(x-3)}\cdot\frac{(x-3)(x+2)}{(x-4)(x+1)}$$
$$=\frac{x+2}{x-4}$$

9. $$\frac{1}{x^2+2x-3}+\frac{1}{x^2+5x+6}$$
$$x^2+2x-3=(x+3)(x-1)$$
$$x^2+5x+6=(x+2)(x+3)$$
LCD = $(x+3)(x-1)(x+2)$
$$\frac{1}{x^2+2x-3}+\frac{1}{x^2+5x+6}$$
$$=\frac{1}{(x+3)(x-1)}+\frac{1}{(x+2)(x+3)}$$
$$=\frac{1(x+2)}{(x+3)(x-1)(x+2)}+\frac{1(x-1)}{(x+2)(x+3)(x-1)}$$
$$=\frac{x+2+x-1}{(x+3)(x-1)(x+2)}$$
$$=\frac{2x+1}{(x+3)(x-1)(x+2)}$$

10. $$\frac{17}{x-5}+\frac{x+8}{5-x}$$
Note: $5-x=-1(x-5)$
LCD = $x-5$
$$\frac{17}{x-5}+\frac{-1(x+8)}{-1(5-x)}=\frac{17}{x-5}+\frac{-x-8}{x-5}$$
$$=\frac{17-x-8}{x-5}=\frac{9-x}{x-5}$$

11. $$\frac{4y^2-1}{9y-3y^2}\cdot\frac{y^2-7y+12}{2y^2-7y-4}$$
$$=\frac{(2y+1)(2y-1)}{3y(3-y)}\cdot\frac{(y-4)(y-3)}{(2y+1)(y-4)}$$
$$=\frac{-1(2y+1)(2y-1)}{-1\cdot 3y(3-y)}\cdot\frac{(y-4)(y-3)}{(2y+1)(y-4)}$$
$$=\frac{-1(2y+1)(2y+1)}{3y(y-3)}\cdot\frac{(y-4)(y-3)}{(2y+1)(y-4)}$$
$$=\frac{-(2y+1)}{3y}=\frac{-2y-1}{3y}$$

12. $$\frac{y}{y+1}-\frac{2y}{y+2}$$
LCD = $(y+1)(y+2)$
$$\frac{y(y+2)}{(y+1)(y+2)}-\frac{2y(y+1)}{(y+2)(y+1)}$$
$$=\frac{y^2+2y-2y^2-2y}{(y+1)(y+2)}=\frac{-y^2}{(y+1)(y+2)}$$

13. $\frac{w^2+6w+5}{7w^2-63} \div \frac{w^2+10w+25}{7w+21}$

$= \frac{w^2+6w+5}{7w^2-63} \cdot \frac{7w+21}{w^2+10w+25}$

$= \frac{(w+5)(w+1)}{7(w^2-9)} \cdot \frac{7(w+3)}{(w+5)(w+5)}$

$= \frac{(w+5)(w+1)}{7(w+3)(w-3)} \cdot \frac{7(w+3)}{(w+5)(w+5)}$

$= \frac{w+1}{(w-3)(w+5)}$

14. $\frac{2z}{z^2-9} - \frac{5}{z^2+4z+3}$

$z^2-9=(z+3)(z-3)$

$z^2+4z+3=(z+3)(z+1)$

LCD $=(z+3)(z-3)(z+1)$

$\frac{2z}{z^2-9} - \frac{5}{z^2+4z+3}$

$= \frac{2z}{(z+3)(z-3)} - \frac{5}{(z+3)(z+1)}$

$\frac{2z(z+1)}{(z+3)(z-3)(z+1)}$

$- \frac{5(z-3)}{(z+3)(z+1)(z-3)}$

$= \frac{2z^2+2z-5z+15}{(z+3)(z-3)(z+1)}$

$= \frac{2z^2-3z+15}{(z+3)(z-3)(z+1)}$

15. $\frac{z+2}{3z-1} + \frac{5}{(3z-1)^2}$

LCD = $(3z-1)(3z-1)$

$\frac{(z+2)(3z-1)}{(3z-1)(3z-1)} + \frac{5}{(3z-1)^2}$

$= \frac{3z^2+5z-2+5}{(3z-1)^2} = \frac{3z^2+5z+3}{(3z-1)^2}$

16. $\frac{8}{x^2+4x-21} + \frac{3}{x+7}$

$x^2+4x-21=(x+7)(x-3)$

$x+7=1(x+7)$

LCD $=(x+7)(x-3)$

$\frac{8}{x^2+4x-21} + \frac{3}{x+7}$

$= \frac{8}{(x+7)(x-3)} + \frac{3}{x+7}$

$= \frac{8}{(x+7)(x-3)} + \frac{3(x-3)}{(x+7)(x-3)}$

$= \frac{8+3x-9}{(x+7)(x-3)} = \frac{3x-1}{(x+7)(x-3)}$

17. $\frac{x^4-27x}{x^2-9} \cdot \frac{x+3}{x^2+3x+9}$

$= \frac{x(x^3-27)}{(x+3)(x-3)} \cdot \frac{x+3}{x^2+3x+9}$

$= \frac{x(x-3)(x^2+3x+9)}{(x+3)(x-3)} \cdot \frac{x+3}{x^2+3x+9}$

$= \frac{x}{1} = x$

18. $\dfrac{x-1}{x^2-x-2}-\dfrac{x+2}{x^2+4x+3}$

$x^2-x-2=(x-2)(x+1)$

$x^2+4x+3=(x+3)(x+1)$

LCD = $(x-2)(x+1)(x+3)$

$\dfrac{x-1}{x^2-x-2}-\dfrac{x+2}{x^2+4x+3}$

$=\dfrac{x-1}{(x-2)(x+1)}-\dfrac{x+2}{(x+1)(x+3)}$

$=\dfrac{(x-1)(x+3)}{(x-2)(x+1)(x+3)}$

$-\dfrac{(x+2)(x-2)}{(x+1)(x+3)(x-2)}$

$=\dfrac{x^2+2x-3-(x^2-4)}{(x-2)(x+1)(x+3)}$

$=\dfrac{x^2+2x-3-x^2+4}{(x-2)(x+1)(x+3)}$

$=\dfrac{2x+1}{(x-2)(x+1)(x+3)}$

19. $\dfrac{x^2-2xy+y^2}{x+y}\div\dfrac{x^2-xy}{5x+5y}$

$=\dfrac{x^2-2xy+y^2}{x+y}\cdot\dfrac{5x+5y}{x^2-xy}$

$=\dfrac{(x-y)(x-y)}{x+y}\cdot\dfrac{5(x+y)}{x(x-y)}$

$=\dfrac{5(x-y)}{x}=\dfrac{5x-5y}{x}$

20. $\dfrac{5}{x+5}+\dfrac{x}{x-4}-\dfrac{11x-8}{x^2+x-20}$

$x^2+x-20=(x+5)(x-4)$

LCD $=(x+5)(x-4)$

$\dfrac{5}{x+5}+\dfrac{x}{x-4}-\dfrac{11x-8}{x^2+x-20}$

$=\dfrac{5}{x+5}+\dfrac{x}{x-4}-\dfrac{11x-8}{(x+5)(x-4)}$

$=\dfrac{5(x-4)}{(x+5)(x-4)}+\dfrac{x(x+5)}{(x-4)(x+5)}$

$-\dfrac{11x-8}{(x+5)(x-4)}$

$=\dfrac{5x-20+x^2+5x-11x+8}{(x+5)(x-4)}$

$=\dfrac{x^2-x-12}{(x+5)(x-4)}=\dfrac{(x+3)(x-4)}{(x+5)(x-4)}$

$=\dfrac{x+3}{x+5}$

8.5 Exercise Set

In Exercises 1-39, each complex rational expression can be simplified by either of the two methods introduced in this section of the textbook. Both methods will be illustrated here.

1. $\dfrac{\frac{1}{2}+\frac{1}{4}}{\frac{1}{2}+\frac{1}{3}}$

Add to get a single rational expression in the numerator.

$\frac{1}{2}+\frac{1}{4}=\frac{2}{4}+\frac{1}{4}=\frac{3}{4}$

Add to get a single rational expression in the denominator.

$\frac{1}{2}+\frac{1}{3}=\frac{3}{6}+\frac{2}{6}=\frac{5}{6}$

Perform the division indicated by the fraction bar. Invert and multiply.

$$\frac{\frac{1}{2}+\frac{1}{4}}{\frac{1}{2}+\frac{1}{3}}=\frac{\frac{3}{4}}{\frac{5}{6}}=\frac{3}{4}\cdot\frac{6}{5}=\frac{9}{10}$$

3. $$\frac{5+\frac{2}{5}}{7-\frac{1}{10}}=\frac{\frac{25}{5}+\frac{2}{5}}{\frac{70}{10}-\frac{1}{10}}$$
$$=\frac{\frac{27}{5}}{\frac{69}{10}}=\frac{27}{5}\cdot\frac{10}{69}=\frac{9\cdot 3\cdot 2\cdot 5}{5\cdot 3\cdot 23}=\frac{18}{23}$$

5. $$\frac{\frac{2}{5}-\frac{1}{3}}{\frac{2}{3}-\frac{3}{4}}$$
LCD = 60
$$\frac{\frac{2}{5}-\frac{1}{3}}{\frac{2}{3}-\frac{3}{4}}=\frac{60\cdot\left(\frac{2}{5}-\frac{1}{3}\right)}{60\cdot\left(\frac{2}{3}-\frac{3}{4}\right)}$$
$$=\frac{60\cdot\frac{2}{5}-60\cdot\frac{1}{3}}{60\cdot\frac{2}{3}-60\cdot\frac{3}{4}}$$
$$=\frac{24-20}{40-45}=\frac{4}{-5}=-\frac{4}{5}$$

7. $$\frac{\frac{3}{4}-x}{\frac{3}{4}+x}=\frac{\frac{3}{4}-\frac{4x}{4}}{\frac{3}{4}+\frac{4x}{4}}$$
$$=\frac{\frac{3-4x}{4}}{\frac{3+4x}{4}}$$
$$=\frac{3-4x}{4}\cdot\frac{4}{3+4x}=\frac{3-4x}{3+4x}$$

9. $$\frac{7-\frac{2}{x}}{5+\frac{1}{x}}=\frac{\frac{7x-2}{x}}{\frac{5x+1}{x}}=\frac{7x-2}{x}\cdot\frac{x}{5x+1}=\frac{7x-2}{5x+1}$$

11. $$\frac{2+\frac{3}{y}}{1-\frac{7}{y}}=\frac{\frac{2y+3}{y}}{\frac{y-7}{y}}$$
$$=\frac{2y+3}{y}\cdot\frac{y}{y-7}=\frac{2y+3}{y-7}$$

13. $$\frac{\frac{1}{y}-\frac{3}{2}}{\frac{1}{y}+\frac{3}{4}}=\frac{\frac{2-3y}{2y}}{\frac{4+3y}{4y}}$$
$$=\frac{2-3y}{2y}\cdot\frac{4y}{4+3y}$$
$$=\frac{2(2-3y)}{4+3y}=\frac{4-6y}{4+3y}$$

15. $$\frac{\frac{x}{5}-\frac{5}{x}}{\frac{1}{5}+\frac{1}{x}}$$
LCD = 5x
$$\frac{\frac{x}{5}-\frac{5}{x}}{\frac{1}{5}+\frac{1}{x}}=\frac{5x\cdot\left(\frac{x}{5}-\frac{5}{x}\right)}{5x\cdot\left(\frac{1}{5}+\frac{1}{x}\right)}$$
$$=\frac{5x\cdot\frac{x}{5}-5x\cdot\frac{5}{x}}{5x\cdot\frac{1}{5}+5x\cdot\frac{1}{x}}$$
$$=\frac{x^2-25}{x+5}$$
$$=\frac{(x+5)(x-5)}{x+5}=x-5$$

17. $$\frac{1+\frac{1}{x}}{1-\frac{1}{x^2}}=\frac{\frac{x+1}{x}}{\frac{x^2-1}{x^2}}$$
$$=\frac{x+1}{x}\cdot\frac{x^2}{x^2-1}$$
$$=\frac{x+1}{x}\cdot\frac{x^2}{(x+1)(x-1)}$$
$$=\frac{x}{x-1}$$

19. $$\frac{\frac{1}{7}-\frac{1}{y}}{\frac{7-y}{7}}$$
LCD = $7y$
$$\frac{\frac{1}{7}-\frac{1}{y}}{\frac{7-y}{7}}=\frac{7y\left(\frac{1}{7}-\frac{1}{y}\right)}{7y\left(\frac{7-y}{7}\right)}$$
$$=\frac{7y\left(\frac{1}{7}\right)-7y\left(\frac{1}{y}\right)}{7y\left(\frac{7-y}{7}\right)}$$
$$=\frac{y-7}{y(7-y)}$$
$$=\frac{-1(7-y)}{y(7-y)}=-\frac{1}{y}$$

21. $$\frac{x+\frac{2}{y}}{\frac{x}{y}}=\frac{\frac{xy+2}{y}}{\frac{x}{y}}=\frac{xy+2}{y}\cdot\frac{y}{x}=\frac{xy+2}{x}$$

23. $$\frac{\frac{1}{x}+\frac{1}{y}}{xy}$$
LCD = xy
$$\frac{\frac{1}{x}+\frac{1}{y}}{xy}=\frac{xy\left(\frac{1}{x}+\frac{1}{y}\right)}{xy(xy)}=\frac{y+x}{x^2y^2}$$

25. $$\frac{\frac{x}{y}+\frac{1}{x}}{\frac{y}{x}+\frac{1}{x}}=\frac{\frac{x^2+y}{xy}}{\frac{y+1}{x}}=\frac{x^2+y}{xy}\cdot\frac{x}{y+1}$$
$$=\frac{x^2+y}{y(y+1)}$$

27. $$\frac{\frac{1}{y}+\frac{2}{y^2}}{\frac{2}{y}+1}$$
LCD = y^2
$$\frac{\frac{1}{y}+\frac{2}{y^2}}{\frac{2}{y}+1}=\frac{y^2\left(\frac{1}{y}+\frac{2}{y^2}\right)}{y^2\left(\frac{2}{y}+1\right)}$$
$$=\frac{y^2\left(\frac{1}{y}\right)+y^2\left(\frac{2}{y^2}\right)}{y^2\left(\frac{2}{y}\right)+y^2(1)}$$
$$=\frac{y+2}{2y+y^2}$$
$$=\frac{(y+2)}{y(2+y)}=\frac{1}{y}$$

29. $$\frac{\frac{12}{x^2}-\frac{3}{x}}{\frac{15}{x}-\frac{9}{x^2}}=\frac{\frac{12}{x^2}-\frac{3x}{x^2}}{\frac{15x}{x^2}-\frac{9}{x^2}}=\frac{\frac{12-3x}{x^2}}{\frac{15x-9}{x^2}}$$
$$=\frac{12-3x}{x^2}\cdot\frac{x^2}{15x-9}=\frac{12-3x}{15x-9}$$
$$=\frac{3(4-x)}{3(5x-3)}=\frac{4-x}{5x-3}$$

31. $\dfrac{2+\frac{6}{y}}{1-\frac{9}{y^2}}$

LCD = y^2

$$\frac{2+\frac{6}{y}}{1-\frac{9}{y^2}} = \frac{y^2\left(2+\frac{6}{y}\right)}{y^2\left(1-\frac{9}{y^2}\right)}$$

$$= \frac{2y^2+6y}{y^2-9}$$

$$= \frac{2y(y+3)}{(y+3)(y-3)} = \frac{2y}{y-3}$$

33. $\dfrac{\frac{1}{x+2}}{1+\frac{1}{x+2}}$

LCD = $x+2$

$$\frac{\frac{1}{x+2}}{1+\frac{1}{x+2}} = \frac{(x+2)\left(\frac{1}{x+2}\right)}{(x+2)\left(1+\frac{1}{x+2}\right)}$$

$$= \frac{1}{x+2+1} = \frac{1}{x+3}$$

35. $\dfrac{x-5+\frac{3}{x}}{x-7+\frac{2}{x}}$

LCD = x

$$\frac{x-5+\frac{3}{x}}{x-7+\frac{2}{x}} = \frac{x\left(x-5+\frac{3}{x}\right)}{x\left(x-7+\frac{2}{x}\right)}$$

$$= \frac{x^2-5x+3}{x^2-7x+2}$$

37.

$$\frac{\frac{3}{xy^2}+\frac{2}{x^2y}}{\frac{1}{x^2y}+\frac{2}{xy^3}} = \frac{\frac{3x}{x^2y^2}+\frac{2y}{x^2y^2}}{\frac{y^2}{x^2y^3}+\frac{2x}{x^2y^3}}$$

$$= \frac{\frac{3x+2y}{x^2y^2}}{\frac{y^2+2x}{x^2y^3}}$$

$$= \frac{3x+2y}{x^2y^2}\cdot\frac{x^2y^3}{y^2+2x}$$

$$= \frac{(3x+2y)(y)}{y^2+2x}$$

$$= \frac{3xy+2y^2}{y^2+2x}$$

39.

$$\frac{\frac{3}{x+1}-\frac{3}{x-1}}{\frac{5}{x^2-1}}$$

$$= \frac{\frac{3(x-1)-3(x+1)}{(x+1)(x-1)}}{\frac{5}{x^2-1}}$$

$$= \frac{\frac{3x-3-3x-3}{(x+1)(x-1)}}{\frac{5}{x^2-1}}$$

$$= \frac{\frac{-6}{(x+1)(x-1)}}{\frac{5}{x^2-1}}$$

$$= \frac{-6}{(x+1)(x-1)}\cdot\frac{x^2-1}{5}$$

$$= \frac{-6}{(x+1)(x-1)}\cdot\frac{(x+1)(x-1)}{5}$$

$$= -\frac{6}{5}$$

41.

$$\frac{\frac{6}{x^2+2x-15}-\frac{1}{x-3}}{\frac{1}{x+5}+1}=\frac{\frac{6}{(x+5)(x-3)}-\frac{1}{x-3}}{\frac{1}{x+5}+1}$$

LCD = $(x+5)(x-3)$

$$\frac{\frac{6}{(x+5)(x-3)}-\frac{1}{x-3}}{\frac{1}{x+5}+1}$$

$$=\frac{(x+5)(x-3)\left[\frac{6}{(x+5)(x-3)}-\frac{1}{x-3}\right]}{(x+5)(x-3)\left[\frac{1}{x+5}+1\right]}$$

$$=\frac{6-(x+5)}{x-3+(x+5)(x-3)}$$

$$=\frac{6-x-5}{x-3+x^2+2x-15}$$

$$=\frac{-x+1}{x^2+3x-18}=\frac{1-x}{(x-3)(x+6)}$$

42.

$$\frac{\frac{1}{x-2}-\frac{6}{x^2+3x-10}}{1+\frac{1}{x-2}}=\frac{\frac{1}{x-2}-\frac{6}{(x-2)(x+5)}}{1+\frac{1}{x-2}}$$

LCD $=(x-2)(x+5)$

$$\frac{\frac{1}{x-2}-\frac{6}{(x-2)(x+5)}}{1+\frac{1}{x-2}}$$

$$=\frac{(x-2)(x+5)\left[\frac{1}{x-2}-\frac{6}{(x-2)(x+5)}\right]}{(x-2)(x+5)\left[1+\frac{1}{x-2}\right]}$$

$$=\frac{x+5-6}{(x-2)(x+5)+x+5}$$

$$=\frac{x-1}{x^2+3x-10+x+5}$$

$$=\frac{x-1}{x^2+4x-5}=\frac{x-1}{(x-1)(x+5)}=\frac{1}{x+5}$$

43.

$$\frac{y^{-1}-(y+5)^{-1}}{5}=\frac{\frac{1}{y}-\frac{1}{y+5}}{5}$$

LCD= $y(y+5)$

$$\frac{\frac{1}{y}-\frac{1}{y+5}}{5}=\frac{y(y+5)\left(\frac{1}{y}-\frac{1}{y+5}\right)}{y(y+5)(5)}$$

$$=\frac{y+5-y}{5y(y+5)}=\frac{5}{5y(y+5)}=\frac{1}{y(y+5)}$$

44.

$$\frac{y^{-1}-(y+2)^{-1}}{2}=\frac{\frac{1}{y}-\frac{1}{y+2}}{2}$$

LCD $=y(y+2)$

$$\frac{\frac{1}{y}-\frac{1}{y+2}}{2}=\frac{y(y+2)\left(\frac{1}{y}-\frac{1}{y+2}\right)}{y(y+2)(2)}$$

$$=\frac{y+2-y}{2y(y+2)}=\frac{2}{2y(y+2)}=\frac{1}{y(y+2)}$$

45. $\dfrac{1}{1-\frac{1}{x}}-1=\dfrac{x(1)}{x\left(1-\frac{1}{x}\right)}-1=\dfrac{x}{x-1}-1$

$=\dfrac{x}{x-1}-\dfrac{x-1}{x-1}=\dfrac{x-x+1}{x-1}=\dfrac{1}{x-1}$

46. $\dfrac{1}{1-\frac{1}{x+1}}-1=\dfrac{(x+1)(1)}{(x+1)\left(1-\frac{1}{x+1}\right)}-1$

$=\dfrac{x+1}{x+1-1}-1=\dfrac{x+1}{x}-1=\dfrac{x+1}{x}-\dfrac{x}{x}$

$=\dfrac{x+1-x}{x}=\dfrac{1}{x}$

47. $\dfrac{1}{1+\frac{1}{1+\frac{1}{x}}}=\dfrac{1}{1+\frac{x(1)}{x\left(1+\frac{1}{x}\right)}}=\dfrac{1}{1+\frac{x}{x+1}}$

$=\dfrac{(x+1)(1)}{(x+1)\left(1+\frac{x}{x+1}\right)}=\dfrac{x+1}{x+1+x}=\dfrac{x+1}{2x+1}$

48. $\dfrac{1}{1+\frac{1}{1+\frac{1}{2}}}=\dfrac{1}{1+\frac{(2)1}{(2)\left(1+\frac{1}{2}\right)}}=\dfrac{1}{1+\frac{2}{2+1}}$

$=\dfrac{1}{1+\frac{2}{3}}=\dfrac{1}{\frac{3}{3}+\frac{2}{3}}=\dfrac{1}{\frac{5}{3}}=1\cdot\dfrac{3}{5}=\dfrac{3}{5}$

49. $\dfrac{2d}{\frac{d}{r_1}+\frac{d}{r_2}}$

LCD = r_1r_2

$\dfrac{2d}{\frac{d}{r_1}+\frac{d}{r_2}}=\dfrac{r_1r_2(2d)}{r_1r_2\left(\frac{d}{r_1}+\frac{d}{r_2}\right)}$

$=\dfrac{2r_1r_2d}{r_2d+r_1d}$

$=\dfrac{2r_1r_2d}{d(r_2+r_1)}=\dfrac{2r_1r_2}{r_2+r_1}$

If $r_1=40$ and $r_2=30$, the value of this expression will be

$\dfrac{2\cdot 40\cdot 30}{30+40}=\dfrac{2400}{70}$

$=34\dfrac{2}{7}.$

Your average speed will be $34\frac{2}{7}$ miles per hour.

51. – 53. Answers will vary.

55. Simplify the given complex fraction

LCD = x^5

$\dfrac{x^6}{x^6}\cdot\dfrac{\left(\frac{1}{x}+\frac{1}{x^2}+\frac{1}{x^4}\right)}{\left(\frac{1}{x^4}+\frac{1}{x^5}+\frac{1}{x^6}\right)}$

$=\dfrac{\frac{x^6}{x}+\frac{x^6}{x^2}+\frac{x^6}{x^3}}{\frac{x^6}{x^4}+\frac{x^6}{x^5}+\frac{x^6}{x^6}}$

$=\dfrac{x^5+x^4+x^3}{x^2+x+1}$

$=\dfrac{x^3(x^2+x+1)}{x^2+x+1}$

$=x^3$

Because the rational expression can be simplified to x^3, this is what it does to each number *x*; it cubes *x*.

57. $$\frac{1+\frac{1}{y}-\frac{6}{y^2}}{1-\frac{5}{y}+\frac{6}{y^2}}-\frac{1-\frac{1}{y}}{1-\frac{2}{y}-\frac{3}{y^2}}$$

Simplify the first complex rational expression using the LCD method.

$$\frac{y^2}{y^2}\cdot\frac{\left(1+\frac{1}{y}-\frac{6}{y^2}\right)}{\left(1-\frac{5}{y}+\frac{6}{y^2}\right)}=\frac{y^2+y-6}{y^2-5y+6}$$

Simplify the second complex algebraic expression by the LCD method.

$$\frac{y^2}{y^2}\cdot\frac{\left(1-\frac{1}{y}\right)}{\left(1-\frac{2}{y}-\frac{3}{y^2}\right)}=\frac{y^2-y}{y^2-2y-3}$$

Now subtract.

$$\frac{y^2+y-6}{y^2-5y+6}-\frac{y^2-y}{y^2-2y-3}$$
$$=\frac{y^2+y-6}{(y-2)(y-3)}-\frac{y^2-y}{(y-3)(y+1)}$$
$$=\frac{(y-2)(y+3)}{(y-2)(y-3)}-\frac{y^2-y}{(y-3)(y+1)}$$
$$=\frac{y+3}{y-3}-\frac{y^2-y}{(y-3)(y+1)}$$
$$=\frac{(y+3)(y+1)}{(y-3)(y+1)}-\frac{y^2-y}{(y-3)(y+1)}$$
$$=\frac{(y+3)(y+1)-(y^2-y)}{(y-3)(y+1)}$$
$$=\frac{(y^2+4y+3)-(y^2-y)}{(y-3)(y+1)}$$
$$=\frac{y^2+4y+3-y^2+y}{(y-3)(y+1)}$$
$$=\frac{5y+3}{(y-3)(y+1)}$$

59.

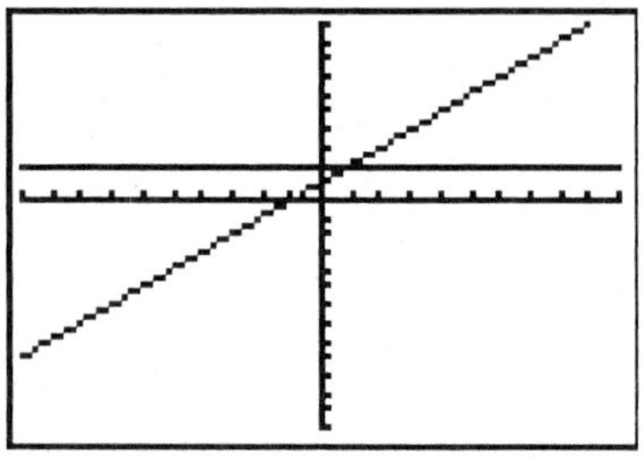

The graphs do not coincide.

$$\frac{\frac{1}{x}+1}{\frac{1}{x}}=\frac{\frac{1}{x}+\frac{x}{x}}{\frac{1}{x}}=\frac{\frac{1+x}{x}}{\frac{1}{x}}$$
$$=\frac{1+x}{x}\cdot\frac{x}{1}=1+x$$

Change the expression on the right to $1+x$.

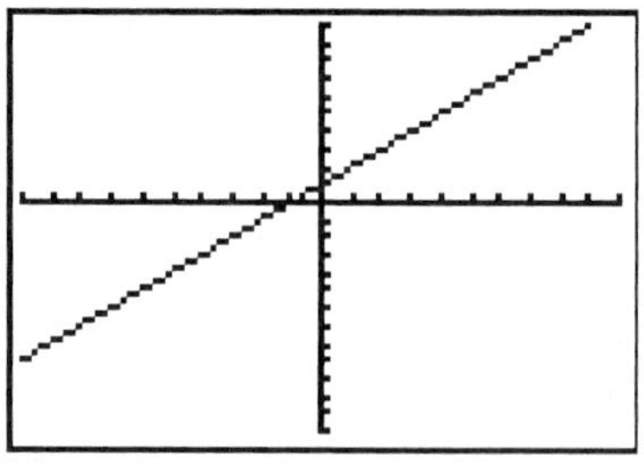

Now the graphs coincide.

61. $$2x^3-20x^2+50x=2x(x^2-10x+25)$$
$$=2x(x-5)^2$$

62. $$2-3(x-2)=5(x+5)-1$$
$$2-3x+6=5x+25-1$$
$$8-3x=5x+24$$
$$8-3x-5x=5x+24-5x$$
$$8-8x=24$$
$$8-8x-8=24-8$$
$$-8x=16$$
$$\frac{-8x}{-8}=\frac{16}{-8}$$
$$x=-2$$

The solution is -2.

63. $(x+y)(x^2-xy+y^2)$
$$= x(x^2-xy+y^2)+y(x^2-xy+y^2)$$
$$= x^3-x^2y+xy^2+x^2y-xy^2+y^3$$
$$= x^3+y^3$$

8.6 Exercise Set

In Exercises 1-43, all proposed solutions that are on the list of restrictions on the variable should be rejected and all other proposed solutions should be checked in the original equation. Checks will not be shown here.

1. $\frac{x}{3}=\frac{x}{2}-2$

There are no restrictions on the variable because the variable does not appear in any denominator.
The LCD is 6.

$$\frac{x}{3}=\frac{x}{2}-2$$
$$6\left(\frac{x}{3}\right)=6\left(\frac{x}{2}-2\right)$$
$$6\cdot\frac{x}{3}=6\cdot\frac{x}{2}-6\cdot 2$$
$$2x=3x-12$$
$$0=x-12$$
$$12=x$$

The solution is 12.

3. $\frac{4x}{3}=\frac{x}{18}-\frac{x}{6}$

There are no restrictions.
The LCD is 18.

$$\frac{4x}{3}=\frac{x}{18}-\frac{x}{6}$$
$$18\left(\frac{4x}{3}\right)=18\left(\frac{x}{18}-\frac{x}{6}\right)$$
$$18\cdot\frac{4x}{3}=18\cdot\frac{x}{18}-18\cdot\frac{x}{6}$$
$$24x=x-3x$$
$$24x=-2x$$
$$26x=0$$
$$x=0$$

The solution is 0.

5. $2-\frac{8}{x}=6$

The restriction is $x \neq 0$.
The LCD is x.

$$2-\frac{8}{x}=6$$
$$x\left(2-\frac{8}{x}\right)=x\cdot 6$$
$$x\cdot 2-x\cdot\frac{8}{x}=x\cdot 6$$
$$2x-8=6x$$
$$-8=4x$$
$$-2=x$$

The solution is −2.

7. $\frac{2}{x}+\frac{1}{3}=\frac{4}{x}$

The restriction is $x \neq 0$.
The LCD is $3x$.

$$\frac{2}{x}+\frac{1}{3}=\frac{4}{x}$$
$$3x\left(\frac{2}{x}+\frac{1}{3}\right)=3x\left(\frac{4}{x}\right)$$
$$3x\cdot\frac{2}{x}+3x\cdot\frac{1}{3}=3x\cdot\frac{4}{x}$$
$$6+x=12$$
$$x=6$$

The solution is 6.

9. $\frac{2}{x}+3=\frac{5}{2x}+\frac{13}{4}$

The restriction is $x\neq 0$

The LCD is $4x$.

$$\frac{2}{x}+3=\frac{5}{2x}+\frac{13}{4}$$
$$4x\left(\frac{2}{x}+3\right)=4x\left(\frac{5}{2x}+\frac{13}{4}\right)$$
$$8+12x=10+13x$$
$$8=10+x$$
$$-2=x$$

The solution is –2.

11. $\frac{2}{3x}+\frac{1}{4}=\frac{11}{6x}-\frac{1}{3}$

The restriction is $x\neq 0$.

The LCD is $12x$.

$$\frac{2}{3x}+\frac{1}{4}=\frac{11}{6x}-\frac{1}{3}$$
$$12x\left(\frac{2}{3x}+\frac{1}{4}\right)=12x\left(\frac{11}{6x}-\frac{1}{3}\right)$$
$$8+3x=22-4x$$
$$8+7x=22$$
$$7x=14$$
$$x=2$$

The solution is 2.

13. $\frac{6}{x+3}=\frac{4}{x-3}$

Restrictions: $x\neq -3, x\neq 3$

LCD = $(x+3)(x-3)$

$$\frac{6}{x+3}=\frac{4}{x-3}$$
$$(x+3)(x-3)\cdot\frac{6}{x+3}=(x+3)(x-3)\cdot\frac{4}{x-3}$$
$$(x-3)\cdot 6=(x+3)\cdot 4$$
$$6x-18=4x+12$$
$$2x-18=12$$
$$2x=30$$
$$x=15$$

The solution is 15.

15. $\frac{x-2}{2x}+1=\frac{x+1}{x}$

Restriction: $x\neq 0$

LCD = $2x$.

$$\frac{x-2}{2x}+1=\frac{x+1}{x}$$
$$2x\left(\frac{x-2}{2x}+1\right)=2x\left(\frac{x+1}{x}\right)$$
$$x-2+2x=2(x+1)$$
$$3x-2=2x+2$$
$$x-2=2$$
$$x=4$$

The solution is 4.

17. $x+\frac{6}{x}=-7$

Restriction: $x\neq 0$

LCD = x

$$x+\frac{6}{x}=-7$$
$$x\left(x+\frac{6}{x}\right)=x(-7)$$
$$x^2+6=-7x$$
$$x^2+7x+6=0$$
$$(x+6)(x+1)=0$$
$$x+6=0 \quad\text{or}\quad x+1=0$$
$$x=-6 \qquad\qquad x=-1$$

The solutions are –6 and –1.

19. $\frac{x}{5}-\frac{5}{x}=0$

Restriction: $x \neq 0$

LCD = $5x$

$$\frac{x}{5}-\frac{5}{x}=0$$
$$5x\left(\frac{x}{5}-\frac{5}{x}\right)=5x\cdot 0$$
$$5x\cdot\frac{x}{5}-5x\cdot\frac{5}{x}=0$$
$$x^2-25=0$$
$$(x+5)(x-5)=0$$
$$x+5=0 \quad \text{or} \quad x-5=0$$
$$x=-5 \qquad\qquad x=5$$

The solutions are −5 and 5.

21. $x+\frac{3}{x}=\frac{12}{x}$

Restriction: $x \neq 0$

LCD = x

$$x+\frac{3}{x}=\frac{12}{x}$$
$$x\left(x+\frac{3}{x}\right)=x\left(\frac{12}{x}\right)$$
$$x^2+3=12$$
$$x^2-9=0$$
$$(x+3)(x-3)=0$$
$$x+3=0 \quad \text{or} \quad x-3=0$$
$$x=-3 \qquad\qquad x=3$$

The solutions are −3 and 3.

23. $\frac{4}{y}-\frac{y}{2}=\frac{7}{2}$

Restrictions: $y \neq 0$

LCD = $2y$

$$2y\left(\frac{4}{y}-\frac{y}{2}\right)=2y\left(\frac{7}{2}\right)$$
$$8-y^2=7y$$

$$\frac{4}{y}-\frac{y}{2}=\frac{7}{2}$$
$$0=y^2+7y-8$$
$$0=(y+8)(y-1)$$
$$y+8=0 \quad \text{or} \quad y-1=0$$
$$y=-8 \qquad\qquad y=1$$

The solutions are −8 and 1.

25. $\frac{x-4}{x}=\frac{15}{x+4}$

Restrictions: $x \neq 0, x \neq -4$

LCD = $x(x+4)$

$$\frac{x-4}{x}=\frac{15}{x+4}$$
$$x(x+4)\left(\frac{x-4}{x}\right)=x(x+4)\left(\frac{15}{x+4}\right)$$
$$(x+4)(x-4)=x\cdot 15$$
$$x^2-16=15x$$
$$x^2-15x-16=0$$
$$(x+1)(x-16)=0$$
$$x+1=0 \quad \text{or} \quad x-16=0$$
$$x=-1 \qquad\qquad x=16$$

The solutions are −1 and 16.

27. $\frac{1}{x-1}+5=\frac{11}{x-1}$

Restriction: $x \neq 1$

LCD = $x-1$

$$\frac{1}{x-1}+5=\frac{11}{x-1}$$
$$(x-1)\left(\frac{1}{x-1}+5\right)=(x-1)\left(\frac{11}{x-1}\right)$$
$$1+(x-1)\cdot 5=11$$
$$1+5x-5=11$$
$$5x-4=11$$
$$5x=15$$
$$x=3$$

The solution is 3.

29. $\frac{8y}{y+1} = 4 - \frac{8}{y+1}$

Restriction: $y \neq -1$

LCD = $y+1$

$$\frac{8y}{y+1} = 4 - \frac{8}{y+1}$$
$$(y+1)\left(\frac{8y}{y+1}\right) = (y+1)\left(4 - \frac{8}{y+1}\right)$$
$$8y = (y+1)\cdot 4 - 8$$
$$8y = 4y + 4 - 8$$
$$8y = 4y - 4$$
$$4y = -4$$
$$y = -1$$

The proposed solution, -1, is *not* a solution because of the restriction $x \neq -1$. Notice that -1 makes two of the denominators zero in the original equation. Therefore, the equation has no solution.

31. $\frac{3}{x-1} + \frac{8}{x} = 3$

Restrictions: $x \neq 1, x \neq 0$

LCD = $x(x-1)$

$$\frac{3}{x-1} + \frac{8}{x} = 3$$
$$x(x-1)\left(\frac{3}{x-1} + \frac{8}{x}\right) = x(x-1)\cdot 3$$
$$x(x-1)\left(\frac{3}{x-1} + \frac{8}{x}\right) = 3x(x-1)$$
$$3x + 8(x-1) = 3x^2 - 3x$$
$$3x + 8x - 8 = 3x^2 - 3x$$
$$11x - 8 = 3x^2 - 3x$$
$$0 = 3x^2 - 14x + 8$$
$$0 = (3x-2)(x-4)$$

$$3x - 2 = 0 \quad \text{or } x - 4 = 0$$
$$3x = 2 \qquad x = 4$$
$$x = \frac{2}{3}$$

The solutions are $\frac{2}{3}$ and 4.

33. $\frac{3y}{y-4} - 5 = \frac{12}{y-4}$

Restriction: $y \neq 4$

LCD = $y-4$

$$\frac{3y}{y-4} - 5 = \frac{12}{y-4}$$
$$(y-4)\left(\frac{3y}{y-4} - 5\right) = (y-4)\left(\frac{12}{y-4}\right)$$
$$3y - 5(y-4) = 12$$
$$3y - 5y + 20 = 12$$
$$-2y + 20 = 12$$
$$-2y = -8$$
$$y = 4$$

The proposed solution, 4, is *not* a solution because of the restriction $y \neq 4$.Therefore, this equation has no solution.

35. $\frac{1}{x} + \frac{1}{x-3} = \frac{x-2}{x-3}$

Restrictions: $x \neq 0, x \neq 3$

LCD = $x(x-3)$

$$\frac{1}{x} + \frac{1}{x-3} = \frac{x-2}{x-3}$$
$$x(x-3)\left(\frac{1}{x} + \frac{1}{x-3}\right) = x(x-3)\cdot\frac{x-2}{x-3}$$
$$x - 3 + x = x(x-2)$$
$$2x - 3 = x^2 - 2x$$
$$0 = x^2 - 4x + 3$$
$$0 = (x-3)(x-1)$$

$x-3=0$ or $x-1=0$

$x=3 \qquad x=1$

The proposed solution 3 is *not* a solution because of the restriction $x \neq 3$.

The proposed solution 1 checks in the original equation.

The solution is 1.

37. $\dfrac{x+1}{3x+9}+\dfrac{x}{2x+6}=\dfrac{2}{4x+12}$

To find any restrictions and the LCD, factor the denominators.

$$\frac{x+1}{3(x+3)}+\frac{x}{2(x+3)}=\frac{2}{4(x+3)}$$

Restriction: $x \neq -3$

LCD = $12(x+3)$

$$12(x+3)\left[\frac{x+1}{3(x+3)}+\frac{x}{2(x+3)}\right]=12(x+3)\left[\frac{2}{4(x+3)}\right]$$

$$4(x+1)+6x=6$$
$$4x+4+6x=6$$
$$10x+4=6$$
$$10x=2$$
$$x=\frac{2}{10}=\frac{1}{5}$$

The solution is $\frac{1}{5}$.

39. $\dfrac{4y}{y^2-25}+\dfrac{2}{y-5}=\dfrac{1}{y+5}$

To find any restrictions and the LCD, factor the first denominator.

$$\frac{4y}{(y+5)(y-5)}+\frac{2}{y-5}=\frac{1}{y+5}$$

Restrictions: $y \neq -5, y \neq 5$

LCD = $(y+5)(y-5)$

$$(y+5)(y-5)\left[\frac{4y}{(y+5)(y-5)}+\frac{2}{y-5}\right]=(y+5)(y-5)\cdot\frac{1}{y+5}$$

$$4y+2(y+5)=y-5$$
$$4y+2y+10=y-5$$
$$6y+10=y-5$$
$$5y+10=-5$$
$$5y=-15$$
$$y=-3$$

The solution is −3.

41. $\dfrac{1}{x-4}-\dfrac{5}{x+2}=\dfrac{6}{x^2-2x-8}$

Factor the last denominator.

$$\frac{1}{x-4}-\frac{5}{x+2}=\frac{6}{(x-4)(x+2)}$$

Restrictions: $x \neq 4, x \neq -2$

LCD = $(x-4)(x+2)$

$$(x-4)(x+2)\left[\frac{1}{x-4}-\frac{5}{x+2}\right]=(x-4)(x+2)\left[\frac{6}{(x-4)(x+2)}\right]$$

$$(x+2)\cdot 1-(x-4)\cdot 5=6$$
$$x+2-5x+20=6$$
$$-4x+22=6$$
$$-4x=-16$$
$$x=4$$

The proposed solution 4 is *not* a solution because of the restriction $x \neq 4$. Therefore, the given equation has no solution.

43. $\frac{2}{x+3}-\frac{2x+3}{x-1}=\frac{6x-5}{x^2+2x-3}$

Factor the last denominator.

$\frac{2}{x+3}-\frac{2x+3}{x-1}=\frac{6x-5}{(x+3)(x-1)}$

Restrictions: $x\neq -3, x\neq 1$

LCD = $(x+3)(x-1)$

$$(x+3)(x-1)\left[\frac{2}{x+3}-\frac{2x+3}{x-1}\right]$$
$$=(x+3)(x-1)\left[\frac{6x-5}{(x+3)(x-1)}\right]$$
$$(x-1)\cdot 2-(x+3)(2x+3)=6x-5$$
$$2x-2-(2x^2+9x+9)=6x-5$$
$$2x-2-2x^2-9x-9=6x-5$$
$$-2x^2-7x-11=6x-5$$
$$0=2x^2+13x+6$$
$$0=(x+6)(2x+1)$$

$x+6=0$ or $2x+1=0$

$x=-6 \qquad 2x=-1$

$x=-\frac{1}{2}$

The solutions are -6 and $-\frac{1}{2}$.

45. $\frac{x^2-10}{x^2-x-20}=1+\frac{7}{x-5}$

Factor the first denominator.

$\frac{x^2-10}{(x-5)(x+4)}=1+\frac{7}{x-5}$

Restrictions: $x\neq 5, x\neq -4$

LCD = $(x-5)(x+4)$

$$(x-5)(x+4)\left(\frac{x^2-10}{(x-5)(x+4)}\right)$$
$$=(x-5)(x+4)\cdot 1+(x-5)(x+4)\left(\frac{7}{x-5}\right)$$
$$x^2-10=(x-5)(x+4)+(x+4)\cdot 7$$
$$x^2-10=x^2-x-20+7x+28$$
$$x^2-10=x^2+6x+8$$
$$-10=6x+8$$
$$-18=6x$$
$$-3=x$$

The solution is -3.

46. $\frac{x^2+4x-2}{x^2-2x-8}=1+\frac{4}{x-4}$

Factor the first denominator.

$\frac{x^2+4x-2}{(x-4)(x+2)}=1+\frac{4}{x-4}$

Restrictions: $x\neq 4, x\neq -2$

LCD = $(x-4)(x+2)$

$$(x-4)(x+2)\left(\frac{x^2+4x-2}{x^2-2x-8}\right)$$
$$=(x-4)(x+2)\cdot 1$$
$$+(x-4)(x+2)\left(\frac{4}{x-4}\right)$$
$$x^2+4x-2=x^2-2x-8+(x+2)\cdot 4$$
$$x^2+4x-2=x^2-2x-8+4x+8$$
$$x^2+4x-2=x^2+2x$$
$$4x-2=2x$$
$$2x=2$$
$$x=1$$

The solution is 1.

47. $\frac{x^2-10}{x^2-x-20}-1-\frac{7}{x-5}$

Factor the first denominator.

$\frac{x^2-10}{(x-5)(x+4)}-1-\frac{7}{x-5}$

LCD = $(x-5)(x+4)$

$$\frac{x^2-10}{(x-5)(x+4)}-\frac{(x-5)(x+4)}{(x-5)(x+4)}-\frac{7(x+4)}{(x-5)(x+4)}$$

$$\frac{x^2-10-(x-5)(x+4)-7(x+4)}{(x-5)(x+4)}$$

$$=\frac{x^2-10-(x^2-x-20)-7x-28}{(x-5)(x+4)}$$

$$=\frac{x^2-10-x^2+x+20-7x-28}{(x-5)(x+4)}$$

$$=\frac{-6x-8}{(x-5)(x+4)}$$

48. $\frac{x^2+4x-2}{x^2-2x-8}-1-\frac{4}{x-4}$

Factor the first denominator.

$$\frac{x^2+4x-2}{(x-4)(x+2)}-1-\frac{4}{x-4}$$

LCD = $(x-4)(x+2)$

$$\frac{x^2+4x-2}{(x-4)(x+2)}-\frac{(x-4)(x+2)}{(x-4)(x+2)}-\frac{4(x+2)}{(x-4)(x+2)}$$

$$\frac{x^2+4x-2-(x-4)(x+2)-4(x+2)}{(x-4)(x+2)}$$

$$=\frac{x^2+4x-2-(x^2-2x-8)-4x-8}{(x-4)(x+2)}$$

$$=\frac{x^2+4x-2-x^2+2x+8-4x-8}{(x-4)(x+2)}$$

$$=\frac{2x-2}{(x-4)(x+2)}$$

49. $5y^{-2}+1=6y^{-1}$

$$\frac{5}{y^2}+1=\frac{6}{y}$$

Restrictions: $y \neq 0$

LCD = y^2

$$y^2\left(\frac{5}{y^2}+1\right)=y^2\left(\frac{6}{y}\right)$$

$$y^2\cdot\frac{5}{y^2}+y^2\cdot 1=6y$$

$$5+y^2=6y$$

$$y^2-6y+5=0$$

$$(y-5)(y-1)=0$$

$y-5=0$ or $y-1=0$

$y=5$ $\quad$ $y=1$

The solutions are 5 and 1.

50. $3y^{-2}+1=4y^{-1}$

$$\frac{3}{y^2}+1=\frac{4}{y}$$

Restrictions: $y \neq 0$

LCD = y^2

$$y^2\left(\frac{3}{y^2}+1\right)=y^2\left(\frac{4}{y}\right)$$

$$y^2\cdot\frac{3}{y^2}+y^2\cdot 1=4y$$

$$3+y^2=4y$$

$$y^2-4y+3=0$$

$$(y-3)(y-1)=0$$

$y-3=0$ or $y-1=0$

$y=3$ $\quad$ $y=1$

The solutions are 3 and 1.

51. $\dfrac{3}{y+1}-\dfrac{1}{1-y}=\dfrac{10}{y^2-1}$

Factor the denominators.

$$\frac{3}{y+1}-\frac{(-1)\cdot 1}{(-1)(1-y)}=\frac{10}{(y+1)(y-1)}$$

$$\frac{3}{y+1}-\frac{-1}{y-1}=\frac{10}{(y+1)(y-1)}$$

$$\frac{3}{y+1}+\frac{1}{y-1}=\frac{10}{(y+1)(y-1)}$$

Restrictions: $y\neq -1, y\neq 1$

LCD = $(y+1)(y-1)$

$$(y+1)(y-1)\left(\frac{3}{y+1}+\frac{1}{y-1}\right)=(y+1)(y-1)\left(\frac{10}{(y+1)(y-1)}\right)$$

$$(y-1)\cdot 3+(y+1)\cdot 1=10$$
$$3y-3+y+1=10$$
$$4y-2=10$$
$$4y=12$$
$$y=3$$

The solution is 3.

52. $\dfrac{4}{y-2}-\dfrac{1}{2-y}=\dfrac{25}{y+6}$

$$\frac{4}{y-2}+\frac{1}{y-2}=\frac{25}{y+6}$$

Restrictions: $y\neq 2, y\neq -6$

LCD = $(y-2)(y+6)$

$$(y-2)(y+6)\left(\frac{4}{y-2}+\frac{1}{y-2}\right)=(y-2)(y+6)\left(\frac{25}{y+6}\right)$$

$$(y+6)\cdot 4+(y+6)\cdot 1=(y-2)\cdot 25$$
$$4y+24+y+6=25y-50$$
$$5y+30=25y-50$$
$$80=20y$$
$$4=y$$

The solution is 4.

53. $C=\dfrac{400x+500{,}000}{x}; C=450$

$$450=\frac{400x+500{,}000}{x}$$

LCD = x

$$x\cdot 450=x\left(\frac{400x+500{,}000}{x}\right)$$
$$450x=400x+500{,}000$$
$$50x=500{,}000$$
$$x=10{,}000$$

At an average cost of \$450 per wheelchair, 10,000 wheelchairs can be produced.

55. $C=\dfrac{2x}{100-x}; C=2$

$$2=\frac{2x}{100-x}$$

LCD = $100-x$

$$(100-x)\cdot 2=(100-x)\cdot\frac{2x}{100-x}$$
$$200-2x=2x$$
$$200=4x$$
$$50=x$$

For \$2 million, 50% of the contaminants can be removed.

57. $C = \frac{DA}{A+12}; C = 300, D = 1000$

$$300 = \frac{1000A}{A+12}$$

LCD = $A+12$

$$(A+12)\cdot 300 = (A+12)\left(\frac{1000A}{A+12}\right)$$

$$300A + 3600 = 1000A$$

$$3600 = 700A$$

$$\frac{3600}{700} = A$$

$$A = \frac{36}{7} \approx 5.14$$

To the nearest year, the child is 5 years old.

59. $C = \frac{10,000}{x} + 3x; C = 350$

$$350 = \frac{10,000}{x} + 3x$$

LCD = x

$$x \cdot 350 = x\left(\frac{10,000}{x} + 3x\right)$$

$$350x = 10,000 + 3x^2$$

$$0 = 3x^2 - 350x + 10,000$$

$$0 = (3x - 200)(x - 50)$$

$3x - 200 = 0$ or $x - 50 = 0$

$3x = 200$ $\quad x = 50$

$$x = \frac{200}{3}$$

$$= 66\frac{2}{3} \approx 67$$

For yearly inventory costs to be \$350, the owner should order either 50 or approximately 67 cases. These solutions correspond to the points $(50, 350)$ and $\left(66\frac{2}{3}, 350\right)$ on the graph.

61. Let x = the number of additional hits needed.

After x additional consecutive hits, the player's batting average will be

$$\frac{12+x}{40+x}$$

so solve the equation

$$\frac{12+x}{40+x} = 0.440.$$

Multiply both sides by the LCD, $40+x$.

$$(40+x)\left(\frac{12+x}{40+x}\right) = (40+x)(0.440)$$

$$12 + x = 17.6 + 0.44x$$

$$12 + x - 12 = 17.6 + 0.44x - 12$$

$$x = 5.6 + 0.44x$$

$$x - 0.44x = 5.6 + 0.44x - 0.44x$$

$$0.56x = 5.6$$

$$\frac{0.56x}{0.56} = \frac{5.6}{0.56}$$

$$x = 10$$

The player must get 10 additional consecutive hits to achieve a batting average of 0.440.

63. – 67. Answers will vary.

69. Statement b is true.

$$\frac{a}{x} + 1 = \frac{a}{x}$$

$$x\left(\frac{a}{x} + 1\right) = x\left(\frac{a}{x}\right)$$

$$a + x = a$$

$$x = 0$$

The proposed solution is a restricted value for x, so the given equation has no solution.

71. $f = \dfrac{f_1 f_2}{f_1 + f_2}$ for f_2

$$f = \frac{f_1 f_2}{f_1 + f_2}$$

Multiply both sides by the LCD, $f_1 + f_2$.

$$(f_1 + f_2) \cdot f = (f_1 + f_2)\left(\frac{f_1 f_2}{f_1 + f_2}\right)$$

$$ff_1 + ff_2 = f_1 f_2$$

Get all terms containing f_2 on one side and all terms not containing f_2 on the other side.

$$ff_2 - f_1 f_2 = -f_1 f$$

Factor out the common factor f_2 on the left side.

$$f_2(f - f_1) = -f_1 f$$

Divide both sides by $f - f_1$.

$$\frac{f_2(f - f_1)}{f - f_1} = \frac{-f_1 f}{f - f_1}$$

$$f_2 = \frac{-f_1 f}{f - f_1} \text{ or } \frac{ff_1}{f_1 - f}$$

73. $\left(\dfrac{x+1}{x+7}\right)^2 \div \left(\dfrac{x+1}{x+7}\right)^4 = 0$

$$\left(\frac{x+1}{x+7}\right)^2 \cdot \left(\frac{x+7}{x+1}\right)^4 = 0$$

$$\frac{(x+1)^2}{(x+7)^2} \cdot \frac{(x+7)^4}{(x+1)^4} = 0$$

Restrictions: $x \neq -7, x \neq -1$

$$\frac{(x+7)^2}{(x+1)^2} = 0$$

Multiply both sides by $(x+1)^2$.

$$(x+1)^2\left[\frac{(x+7)^2}{(x+1)^2}\right] = (x+1)^2 \cdot 0$$

$$(x+7)^2 = 0$$

$$x + 7 = 0$$

$$x = -7$$

The proposed solution, −7, is *not* a solution of the original equation because it is on the list of restrictions. Therefore, the given equation has no solution.

75. $\dfrac{x}{2} + \dfrac{x}{4} = 6$

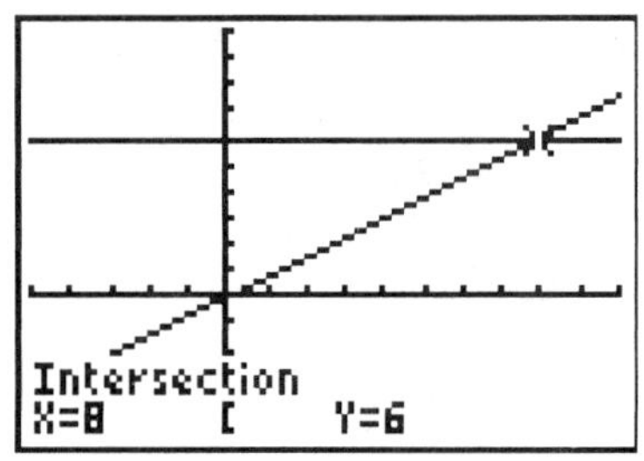

The solution is 8.

Check $x = 8$:

$$\frac{8}{2} + \frac{8}{4} = 6$$

$$4 + 2 = 6$$

$$6 = 6 \text{ true}$$

77. $x + \dfrac{6}{x} = -5$

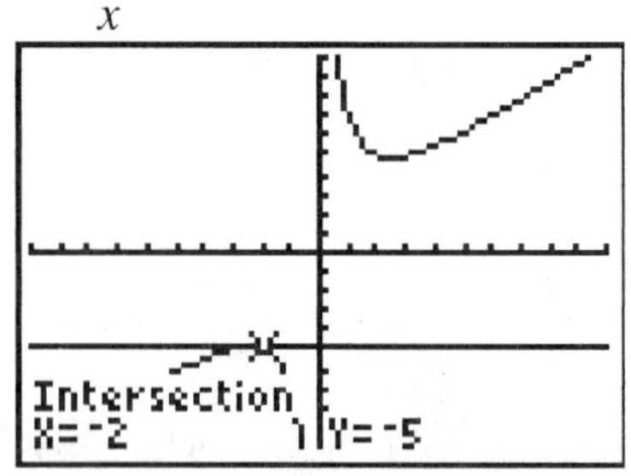

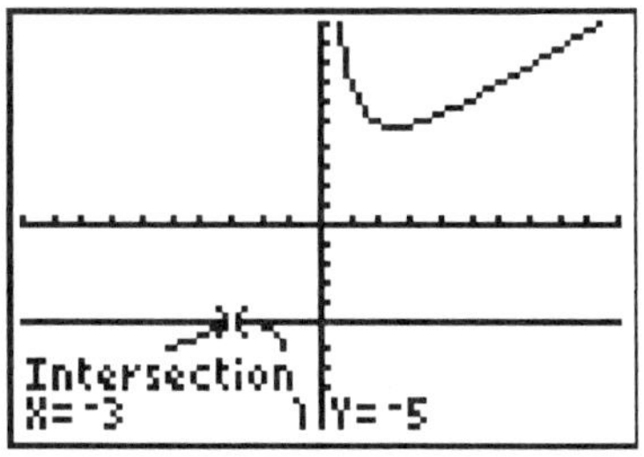

The solutions are −3 and −2.

Check −3:

$$x+\frac{6}{x}=-5$$
$$-3+\frac{6}{-3}=-5$$
$$-3+(-2)=-5$$
$$-5=-5 \text{ true}$$

Check −2:

$$x+\frac{6}{x}=-5$$
$$-2+\frac{6}{-2}=-5$$
$$-2+(-3)=-5$$
$$-5=-5 \text{ true}$$

78. x^4+2x^3-3x-6

Factor by grouping.

$$\begin{aligned} x^4+2x^3-3x-6 &= (x^4+2x^3)+(-3x-6) \\ &= x^3(x+2)-3(x+2) \\ &= (x+2)(x^3-3) \end{aligned}$$

79. $$\begin{aligned} (3x^2)(-4x^{-10}) &= (3\cdot -4)(x^2\cdot x^{-10}) \\ &= -12x^{2+(-10)} = -12x^{-8} \\ &= -\frac{12}{x^8} \end{aligned}$$

80. $$\begin{aligned} -5[4(x-2)-3] &= -5[4x-8-3] \\ &= -5[4x-11] \\ &= -20x+55 \end{aligned}$$

8.7 Exercise Set

1. The times are equal, so

$$\frac{10}{x}=\frac{15}{x+3}$$

To solve this equation, multiply both sides by the LCD, $x(x+3)$.

$$\begin{aligned} x(x+3)\cdot\frac{10}{x} &= x(x+3)\cdot\frac{15}{x+3} \\ 10(x+3) &= 15x \\ 10x+30 &= 15x \\ 30 &= 5x \\ 6 &= x \end{aligned}$$

If $x=6, x+3=9$.

Note: The equation

$$\frac{10}{x}=\frac{15}{x+3}$$

is a proportion, so it can also be solved by using the cross-products principle.

$$10(x+3)=15x$$

This allows you to skip the first step of the solution process shown above. The walking rate is 6 miles per hour and the car's rate is 9 miles per hour.

3. Let x = the jogger's rate running uphill

Then $x+4$ = the jogger's rate running downhill

	Dist	**Rate**	**Time**
Down	5	$x+4$	$\frac{5}{x+4}$
Up	3	x	$\frac{3}{x}$

The times are equal, so

$$\frac{5}{x+4}=\frac{3}{x}.$$

Use the cross-products principle to solve this equation.

$5x = 3(x+4)$

$5x = 3x + 12$

$2x = 12$

$x = 6$

If $x = 6$, $x + 4 = 10$.

The jogger runs 10 miles per hour downhill and 6 miles per hour uphill.

5. Let x = the rate of the current.
Then $15 + x$ = the boat's rate with the current.
and $15 - x$ = the boat's rate against the current

	Dist	Rate	Time
With the current	20	$15+x$	$\frac{20}{15+x}$
Against the current	10	$15-x$	$\frac{10}{15-x}$

$$\frac{20}{15+x} = \frac{10}{15-x}$$

Use the cross-products principle to solve this equation.

$20(15-x) = 10(15+x)$

$300 - 20x = 150 + 10x$

$300 = 150 + 30x$

$150 = 30x$

$5 = x$

The rate of the current is 5 miles per hour.

7. Let x = walking rate.
Then $2x$ = jogging rate.

	Dist	Rate	Time
Walking	2	x	$\frac{2}{x}$
Jogging	2	$2x$	$\frac{2}{2x}$

The total time is 1 hour, so

$\frac{2}{x} + \frac{2}{2x} = 1$

$\frac{2}{x} + \frac{1}{x} = 1.$

To solve this equation, multiply both sides by the LCD, x.

$x\left(\frac{2}{x} + \frac{1}{x}\right) = x \cdot 1$

$2 + 1 = x$

$3 = x$

If $x = 3$, $2x = 6$.

The walking rate is 3 miles per hour and the jogging rate is 6 miles per hour.

9. Let x = the boat's average rate in still water.
Then $x + 2$ = the boat's rate with the current (downstream).
and $x - 2$ = the boat's rate against the current (upstream).

	Dist	Rate	Time
Down	6	$x+2$	$\frac{6}{x+2}$
Up	4	$x-2$	$\frac{4}{x-2}$

The times are equal so solve the following equation.

$\frac{6}{x+2} = \frac{4}{x-2}$

$6(x-2) = 4(x+2)$

$6x - 12 = 4x + 8$

$2x - 12 = 8$

$2x = 20$

$x = 10$

The boat's average rate in still water is 10 miles per hour.

11. Let x = the time in minutes, for both people to shovel the driveway together.

	Fractional part of job completed in 1 minute	Time working together	Fractional part of job completed in x minutes
You	$\frac{1}{20}$	x	$\frac{x}{20}$
Your brother	$\frac{1}{15}$	x	$\frac{x}{15}$

Working together, you and your brother complete the whole job, so

$\frac{x}{20}+\frac{x}{15}=1.$

Multiply both sides by the LCD, 60.

$$60\left(\frac{x}{20}+\frac{x}{15}\right)=60\cdot 1$$
$$3x+4x=60$$
$$7x=60$$
$$x=\frac{60}{7}\approx 8.6$$

It will take about 8.6 minutes, which is enough time.

13. Let x = the time, in hours, for both teams to clean the streets working together.

	Fractional part of job completed in 1 hour	Time working together	Fractional part of job completed in x hours
First team	$\frac{1}{400}$	x	$\frac{x}{400}$
Second team	$\frac{1}{300}$	x	$\frac{x}{300}$

Working together, the two teams complete one whole job, so

$\frac{x}{400}+\frac{x}{300}=1.$

Multiply both sides by the LCD, 1200.

$$1200\left(\frac{x}{400}+\frac{x}{300}\right)=1200\cdot 1$$
$$3x+4x=1200$$
$$7x=1200$$
$$x=\frac{1200}{7}\approx 171.4$$

It will take about 171.4 hours for both teams to clean the streets working together. One week is $7\cdot 24=168$ hours, so even if both crews work 24 hours a day, there is not enough time.

15. Let x = the time, in hours, for both pipes to fill in the pool.

$$\frac{x}{4}+\frac{x}{6}=1$$
$$12\left(\frac{x}{4}+\frac{x}{6}\right)=12\cdot 1$$
$$3x+2x=12$$
$$5x=12$$
$$x=\frac{12}{5}=2.4$$

Using both pipes, it will take 2.4 hours or 2 hours 24 minutes to fill the pool.

17. $$\frac{18}{9}=\frac{10}{x}$$
$$18x=9\cdot 10$$
$$18x=90$$
$$x=5$$

The length of the side marked x is 5 inches.

19. $$\frac{10}{30}=\frac{x}{18}$$
$$30x=10\cdot 18$$
$$30x=180$$
$$x=6$$

The length of the side marked x is 6 meters.

21. $$\frac{20}{15}=\frac{x}{12}$$
$$15x=12\cdot 20$$
$$15x=240$$
$$x=16$$

The length of the side marked x is 16 inches.

23. $$\frac{8}{6}=\frac{x}{12}$$
$$6x=8\cdot 12$$
$$6x=96$$
$$x=16$$

The tree is 16 feet tall.

25. $g=kh$

27. $w=\frac{k}{v}$

29. $y=kx$

To find k, substitute 80 for y and 4 for x.

$$80=k\cdot 4$$
$$20=k$$

The constant of variation is 20.

31. $W=\frac{k}{r}$

To find k, substitute 600 for W and 10 for r.

$$600=\frac{k}{10}$$
$$600\cdot 10=\frac{k}{10}\cdot 10$$
$$6000=k$$

The constant of variation is 6000.

33. *Step 1* Write an equation.

$y=kx$

Step 2 Use the given values to find k. Substitute 35 for y and 5 for x.

$$35=k\cdot 5$$
$$7=k$$

Step 3 Substitute the value of k into the equation

$y = 7k$

Step 4 Answer the question.
Substitute 12 for x and solve for y.

$y = 7 \cdot 12 = 84$

35. *Step 1* $y = \frac{k}{x}$

Step 2 Substitute 10 for y and 5 for x.

$$10 = \frac{k}{5}$$
$$50 = k$$

Step 3 $y = \frac{50}{x}$

Step 4 Substitute 2 for x and solve for y.

$$y = \frac{50}{2}$$
$$y = 25$$

37. **a.** $G = kW$

b. $G = 0.02W$

c. $G = 0.02(52) = 1.04$
Your fingernails would grow 1.04 inches in one year.

39. *Step 1* Write an equation.

$C = kM$

Step 2 Use the given values to find k.

$$400 = k \cdot 3000$$
$$\frac{400}{3000} = k$$
$$\frac{2}{15} = k$$

Step 3 Substitute the value of k into the equation.

$$C = \frac{2}{15}M$$

Step 4 Answer the problem's question. Substitute 450 for M and solve for C.

$$C = \frac{2}{15}(450) = 60$$

The cost of a 450-mile trip is \$60.

41. Let s = speed.
Then M = Mach number.

Step 1 $s = kM$

Step 2 To find k, substitute 1502.2 for s and 2.03 for M.

$$1502.2 = k \cdot 2.03$$
$$\frac{150.2}{2.03} = k$$
$$740 = k$$

Step 3 Substitute 740 for k.

$s = 740M$

Step 4 Substitute 3.3 for M and solve for s.

$s = 740(3.3) = 2442$

The speed of the Blackbird is 2442 miles per hour.

43. Let t = driving time
r = driving rate

Step 1 $t = \frac{k}{r}$

Step 2
$$1.5 = \frac{k}{20}$$
$$1.5 \cdot 20 = \frac{k}{20} \cdot 20$$
$$30 = k$$

Step 3 $t = \frac{30}{r}$

Step 4 $t = \frac{30}{60} = 0.5$

The trip would take 0.5 hour (or 30 minutes) at an average rate of 60 miles per hour.

45. Let V = volume and P = pressure

Step 1 $V = \frac{k}{P}$

Step 2
$$32 = \frac{k}{8}$$
$$256 = k$$

Step 3 $V = \frac{256}{P}$

Step 4
$$40 = \frac{256}{P}$$
$$40P = 256$$
$$P = 6.4$$

When the volume is 40 cubic centimeters, the pressure is 6.4 pounds per square centimeter.

47. Let n = the number of pens. Then p = the price per pen.

Step 1 $n = \frac{k}{p}$

Step 2 To find k, substitute 4000 for n and 1.50 for p.
$$4000 = \frac{k}{1.50}$$
$$4000 \cdot 1.50 = \frac{k}{1.50} \cdot 150$$
$$6000 = k$$

Step 3 $n = \frac{6000}{p}$

Step 4 Substitute 1.20 for p and solve for n.
$$n = \frac{6000}{1.20} = 5000$$

There will be 5000 pens sold at $1.20 each.

49. – 61. Answers will vary.

63. Let x = the usual average rate, in miles per hour, of the bus.
Then $x+15$ = the average rate, in miles per hour, of the bus in the snowstorm.

	Distance	Rate	Time
Usual conditions	60	x	$\frac{60}{x}$
Snowstorm conditions	60	$x-15$	$\frac{60}{x-15}$

Since the time during the snowstorm is 2 hours longer than the usual time solve the following equation.

$$\frac{60}{x}+2=\frac{60}{x-15}$$

Multiply both sides of the equation by the LCD, $x(x-15)$

$$x(x-15)\left(\frac{60}{x}+2\right)=x(x-15)\left(\frac{60}{x-15}\right)$$

$$(x-15)\cdot 60+x(x-15)\cdot 2=60x$$

$$60x-900+2x^2-30x=60x$$

$$2x^2+30x-900=60x$$

$$2x^2-30x-900=0$$

$$x^2-15x-450=0$$

$$(x-30)(x+15)=0$$

$$x-30=0 \quad \text{or} \quad x+15=0$$

$$x=30 \qquad\qquad x=-15$$

Since the rate cannot be negative, the solution is 30. Therefore, the usual average rate of the bus is 30 miles per hour.

65. Let x = the time, in hours, it takes to prepare a report working together.

	Fractional part of job completed in 1 hour	Time working together	Fractional part of job completed in x hours
Ben	$\frac{1}{3}$	x	$\frac{x}{3}$
Shane	$\frac{1}{4.2}=\frac{5}{21}$	x	$\frac{5x}{21}$

Working together, Ben and Shane prepare one report, so

$$\frac{x}{3}+\frac{5x}{21}=1$$

To solve this equation, multiply both sides by the LCD, 21.

$$21\cdot\left(\frac{x}{3}+\frac{5x}{21}\right)=21\cdot 1$$
$$7x+5x=21$$
$$12x=21$$
$$x=\frac{21}{12}=1.75$$

Ben and Shane can prepare one report in 1.75 hours. Multiply this by four to determine how many hours it takes to prepare four reports. $4(1.75)=7$.

Therefore, working together Ben and Shane can prepare four reports in 7 hours.

67. Let $x=$ time, in hours, to fill empty swimming pool

$$\frac{x}{2}-\frac{x}{10}=1$$

Multiply both sides of the equation by the LCD, 20.

$$20\cdot\left(\frac{x}{2}-\frac{x}{10}\right)=20\cdot 1$$
$$10x-2x=20$$
$$8x=20$$
$$x=2.5$$

It will take 2.5 hours to fill the empty swimming pool.

69. Let $x=$ lower interest rate and $x+1=$ higher interest rate.

	Principal	**Interest rate**	**Interest earned**
Investment at higher interest rate	$\frac{200}{x+1}$	$x+1$	200
Investment at lower interest rate	$\frac{175}{x}$	x	175

Since the principal is the same at each rate, solve the following equation.

$$\frac{200}{x+1}=\frac{175}{x}$$
$$200x=175(x+1)$$
$$200x=175x+175$$
$$25x=175$$
$$x=7$$

Therefore, the lower interest rate is 7% and the higher interest rate is 8%.

70. $25x^2 - 81 = (5x)^2 - 9^2$
$= (5x+9)(5x-9)$

71. $x^2 - 12x + 36 = 0$
$(x-6)^2 = 0$
$x - 6 = 0$
$x = 6$
The only solution is 6.

72. $y = -\frac{2}{3}x + 4$
slope = $-\frac{2}{3} = \frac{-2}{3}$
y-intercept = 4
Plot (0,4). From this point, move 2 units *down* and 3 units to the *right* to reach the point (3,2). Draw a line through (0,4) and (3,2).

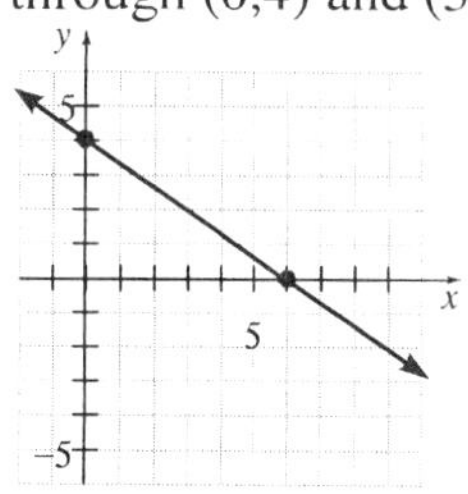

Chapter 8 Review Exercises

1. $\frac{5x}{6x-24}$
Set the denominator equal to 0 and solve for x.
$6x - 24 = 0$
$6x = 24$
$x = 4$
The rational expression is undefined for $x = 4$.

2. $\frac{x+3}{(x-2)(x+5)}$
Set the denominator equal to 0 and solve for x.
$(x-2)(x+5) = 0$
$x - 2 = 0$ or $x + 5 = 0$
$x = 2$ $\quad x = -5$
The rational expression is undefined for $x = 2$ and $x = -5$.

3. $\frac{x^2+3}{x^2-3x+2}$
$x^2 - 3x + 2 = 0$
$(x-1)(x-2) = 0$
$x - 1 = 0$ or $x - 2 = 0$
$x = 1$ $\quad x = 2$
The rational expression is undefined for $x = 1$ and $x = 2$.

4. $\frac{7}{x^2+81}$
The smallest possible value of x^2 is 0, so $x^2 + 81 \geq 81$ for all real numbers x. This means that there is no real number for x for which $x^2 + 81 = 0$. Thus, the rational expression is defined for all real numbers.

5. $\frac{16x^2}{12x} = \frac{4 \cdot 4 \cdot x \cdot x}{4 \cdot 3 \cdot x} = \frac{4x}{3}$

6. $\frac{x^2-4}{x-2} = \frac{(x+2)(x-2)}{(x-2)} = x + 2$

7. $\frac{x^3+2x^2}{x+2} = \frac{x^2(x+2)}{(x+2)} = x^2$

8. $\dfrac{x^2+3x-18}{x^2-36}=\dfrac{(x+6)(x-3)}{(x+6)(x-6)}$
$=\dfrac{x-3}{x-6}$

9. $\dfrac{x^2-4x-5}{x^2+8x+7}=\dfrac{(x+1)(x-5)}{(x+1)(x+7)}$
$=\dfrac{x-5}{x+7}$

10. $\dfrac{y^2+2y}{y^2+4y+4}=\dfrac{y(y+2)}{(y+2)(y+2)}$
$=\dfrac{y}{y+2}$

11. $\dfrac{x^2}{x^2+4}$
The numerator and denominator have no common factor, so this rational expression cannot be simplified.

12. $\dfrac{2x^2-18y^2}{3y-x}=\dfrac{2(x^2-9y^2)}{3y-x}$
$=\dfrac{2(x+3y)(x-3y)}{(3y-x)}$
$=\dfrac{2(x+3y)(-1)(3y-x)}{(3y-x)}$
$=-2(x+3y)$ or $-2x-6y$

13. $\dfrac{x^2-4}{12x}\cdot\dfrac{3x}{x+2}=\dfrac{(x+2)(x-2)}{12x}\cdot\dfrac{3x}{(x+2)}$
$=\dfrac{x-2}{4}$

14. $\dfrac{5x+5}{6}\cdot\dfrac{3x}{x^2+x}=\dfrac{5(x+1)}{6}\cdot\dfrac{3x}{x(x+1)}$
$=\dfrac{5}{2}$

15. $\dfrac{x^2+6x+9}{x^2-4}\cdot\dfrac{x-2}{x+3}$
$=\dfrac{(x+3)(x+3)}{(x+2)(x-2)}\cdot\dfrac{x-2}{x+3}$
$=\dfrac{x+3}{x+2}$

16. $\dfrac{y^2-2y+1}{y^2-1}\cdot\dfrac{2y^2+y-1}{5y-5}$
$=\dfrac{(y-1)(y-1)}{(y+1)(y-1)}\cdot\dfrac{(2y-1)(y+1)}{5(y-1)}$
$=\dfrac{2y-1}{5}$

17. $\dfrac{2y^2+y-3}{4y^2-9}\cdot\dfrac{3y+3}{5y-5y^2}$
$=\dfrac{(2y+3)(y-1)}{(2y+3)(2y-3)}\cdot\dfrac{3(y+1)}{5y(1-y)}$
$=$
$=\dfrac{-3(y+1)}{5y(2y-3)}$ or $-\dfrac{3(y+1)}{5y(2y-3)}$

18. $\dfrac{x^2+x-2}{10}\div\dfrac{2x+4}{5}$
$=\dfrac{x^2+x-2}{10}\cdot\dfrac{5}{2x+4}$
$=\dfrac{(x-1)(x+2)}{10}\cdot\dfrac{5}{2(x+2)}$
$=\dfrac{x-1}{4}$

19. $\dfrac{6x+2}{x^2-1} \div \dfrac{3x^2+x}{x-1}$

$= \dfrac{6x+2}{x^2-1} \cdot \dfrac{x-1}{3x^2+x}$

$= \dfrac{2(3x+1)}{(x+1)(x-1)} \cdot \dfrac{(x-1)}{x(3x+1)}$

$= \dfrac{2}{x(x+1)}$

20. $\dfrac{1}{y^2+8y+15} \div \dfrac{7}{y+5}$

$= \dfrac{1}{y^2+8y+15} \cdot \dfrac{y+5}{7}$

$= \dfrac{1}{(y+3)(y+5)} \cdot \dfrac{(y+5)}{7}$

$= \dfrac{1}{7(y+3)}$

21. $\dfrac{y^2+y-42}{y-3} \div \dfrac{y+7}{(y-3)^2}$

$= \dfrac{y^2+y-42}{y-3} \cdot \dfrac{(y-3)^2}{y+7}$

$= \dfrac{(y+7)(y-6)}{(y-3)} \cdot \dfrac{(y-3)(y-3)}{y+7}$

$= (y-6)(y-3)$ or $y^2-9y+18$

22. $\dfrac{8x+8y}{x^2} \div \dfrac{x^2-y^2}{x^2}$

$= \dfrac{8x+8y}{x^2} \cdot \dfrac{x^2}{x^2-y^2}$

$= \dfrac{8(x+y)}{x^2} \cdot \dfrac{x^2}{(x+y)(x-y)}$

$= \dfrac{8}{x-y}$

23. $\dfrac{4x}{x+5} + \dfrac{20}{x+5} = \dfrac{4x+20}{x+5} = \dfrac{4(x+5)}{x+5} = 4$

24. $\dfrac{8x-5}{3x-1} + \dfrac{4x+1}{3x-1} = \dfrac{8x-5+4x+1}{3x-1}$

$= \dfrac{12x-4}{3x-1}$

$= \dfrac{4(3x-1)}{3x-1} = 4$

25. $\dfrac{3x^2+2x}{x-1} - \dfrac{10x-5}{x-1}$

$= \dfrac{(3x^2+2x)-(10x-5)}{x-1}$

$= \dfrac{3x^2+2x-10x+5}{x-1}$

$= \dfrac{3x^2-8x+5}{x-1}$

$= \dfrac{(3x-5)(x-1)}{x-1}$

$= 3x-5$

26. $\dfrac{6y^2-4y}{2y-3} - \dfrac{12-3y}{2y-3}$

$= \dfrac{(6y^2-4y)-(12-3y)}{2y-3}$

$= \dfrac{6y^2-4y-12+3y}{2y-3}$

$= \dfrac{6y^2-y-12}{2y-3}$

$= \dfrac{(2y-3)(3y+4)}{2y-3}$

$= 3y+4$

27. $$\frac{x}{x-2}+\frac{x-4}{2-x}=\frac{x}{x-2}+\frac{(-1)}{(-1)}\cdot\frac{x-4}{x-2}$$
$$=\frac{x}{x-2}+\frac{-x+4}{x-2}$$
$$=\frac{x-x+4}{x-2}=\frac{4}{x-2}$$

28. $$\frac{x+5}{x-3}-\frac{x}{3-x}=\frac{x+5}{x-3}-\frac{(-1)}{(-1)}\cdot\frac{x}{3-x}$$
$$=\frac{x+5}{x-3}+\frac{x}{x-3}$$
$$=\frac{x+5+x}{x-3}=\frac{2x+5}{x-5}$$

29. $\frac{7}{9x^3}$ and $\frac{5}{12x}$
$$9x^3=3^2x^3$$
$$12x=2^2\cdot 3x$$
$$\text{LCD} = 2^2\cdot 3^2\cdot x^3=36x^3$$

30. $\frac{3}{x^2(x-1)}$ and $\frac{11}{x(x-1)^2}$
$$\text{LCD} = x^2(x-1)^2$$

31. $\frac{x}{x^2+4x+3}$ and $\frac{17}{x^2+10x+21}$
$$x^2+4x+3=(x+3)(x+1)$$
$$x^2+10x+21=(x+3)(x+7)$$
$$\text{LCD} = (x+3)(x+1)(x+7)$$

32. $$\frac{7}{3x}+\frac{5}{2x^2}$$
$$\text{LCD} = 6x^2$$
$$\frac{7}{3x}+\frac{6}{2x^2}=\frac{7}{3x}\cdot\frac{2x}{2x}+\frac{5}{2x^2}\cdot\frac{3}{3}$$
$$=\frac{14x+15}{6x^2}$$

33. $$\frac{5}{x+1}+\frac{2}{x}$$
$$\text{LCD} = x(x+1)$$
$$\frac{5}{x+1}+\frac{2}{x}=\frac{5x}{x(x+1)}+\frac{2(x+1)}{x(x+1)}$$
$$=\frac{5x+2(x+1)}{x(x+1)}=\frac{5x+2x+2}{x(x+1)}$$
$$=\frac{7x+2}{x(x+1)}$$

34. $$\frac{7}{x+3}+\frac{4}{(x+3)^2}$$
$$\text{LCD} = (x+3)^2 \text{ or } (x+3)(x+3)$$
$$\frac{7}{x+3}+\frac{4}{(x+3)^2}$$
$$=\frac{7}{x+3}+\frac{4}{(x+3)(x+3)}$$
$$=\frac{7(x+3)}{(x+3)(x+3)}+\frac{4}{(x+3)(x+3)}$$
$$=\frac{7(x+3)+4}{(x+3)(x+3)}=\frac{7x+21+4}{(x+3)(x+3)}$$
$$=\frac{7x+25}{(x+3)(x+3)} \text{ or } \frac{7x+25}{(x+3)^2}$$

35. $$\frac{6y}{y^2-4}-\frac{3}{y+2}$$
$$y^2-4=(y+2)(y-2)$$
$$y+2=1(y+2)$$
$$\text{LCD} = (y+2)(y-2)$$
$$\frac{6y}{y^2-4}-\frac{3}{y+2}$$
$$=\frac{6y}{(y+2)(y-2)}-\frac{3}{y+2}$$
$$=\frac{6y}{(y+2)(y-2)}-\frac{3(y-2)}{(y+2)(y-2)}$$

$$= \frac{6y-3(y-2)}{(y+2)(y-2)} = \frac{6y-3y+6}{(y+2)(y-2)}$$
$$= \frac{3y+6}{(y+2)(y-2)} = \frac{3(y+2)}{(y+2)(y-2)}$$
$$= \frac{3}{y-2}$$

36. $$\frac{y-1}{y^2-2y+1} - \frac{y+1}{y-1}$$
$$= \frac{y-1}{(y-1)(y-1)} - \frac{y+1}{y-1}$$
$$= \frac{1}{y-1} - \frac{y+1}{y-1}$$
$$= \frac{1-(y+1)}{y-1} = \frac{1-y-1}{y-1}$$
$$= \frac{-y}{y-1} \text{ or } -\frac{y}{y-1}$$

37. $$\frac{x+y}{y} - \frac{y-x}{x}$$
LCD = xy
$$\frac{x+y}{y} - \frac{y-x}{x}$$
$$= \frac{(x+y)}{y}\cdot\frac{x}{x} - \frac{(x-y)}{x}\cdot\frac{y}{y}$$
$$= \frac{x^2+xy}{xy} - \frac{xy-y^2}{xy}$$
$$= \frac{(x^2+xy)-(xy-y^2)}{xy}$$
$$= \frac{x^2+xy-xy+y^2}{xy} = \frac{x^2+y^2}{xy}$$

38. $$\frac{2x}{x^2+2x+1} + \frac{x}{x^2-1}$$
$$x^2+2x+1 = (x+1)(x+1)$$
$$x^2-1 = (x+1)(x-1)$$
LCD = $(x+1)(x+1)(x-1)$
$$\frac{2x}{x^2+2x+1} + \frac{x}{x^2-1}$$
$$= \frac{2x}{(x+1)(x+1)} + \frac{x}{(x+1)(x-1)}$$
$$= \frac{2x(x-1)}{(x+1)(x+1)(x-1)} + \frac{x(x+1)}{(x+1)(x-1)(x+1)}$$
$$= \frac{2x(x-1)+x(x+1)}{(x+1)(x+1)(x-1)}$$
$$= \frac{2x^2-2x+x^2+x}{(x+1)(x+1)(x-1)}$$
$$= \frac{3x^2-x}{(x+1)(x+1)(x-1)}$$

39. $$\frac{5x}{x+1} - \frac{2x}{1-x^2}$$
$$x+1 = 1(x+1)$$
$$1-x^2 = -1(x^2-1) = -(x+1)(x-1)$$
LCD = $(x+1)(x-1)$
$$\frac{5x}{x+1} - \frac{2x}{1-x^2}$$
$$= \frac{5x}{x+1} - \frac{(-1)}{(-1)}\cdot\frac{2x}{1-x^2}$$
$$= \frac{5x}{x+1} - \frac{-2x}{x^2-1}$$
$$= \frac{5x(x-1)}{(x+1)(x-1)} - \frac{-2x}{(x+1)(x-1)}$$
$$= \frac{5x(x-1)+2x}{(x+1)(x-1)}$$
$$= \frac{5x^2-5x+2x}{(x+1)(x-1)}$$
$$= \frac{5x^2-3x}{(x+1)(x-1)}$$

40. $\dfrac{4}{x^2-x-6}-\dfrac{4}{x^2-4}$

$x^2-x-6=(x+2)(x-3)$

$x^2-4=(x+2)(x-2)$

$\text{LCD} = (x+2)(x-3)(x-2)$

$$\frac{4}{x^2-x-6}-\frac{4}{x^2-4}$$
$$=\frac{4}{(x+2)(x-3)}-\frac{4}{(x+2)(x-2)}$$
$$=\frac{4(x-2)}{(x+2)(x-3)(x-2)}-\frac{4(x-3)}{(x+2)(x-3)(x-2)}$$
$$=\frac{4(x-2)-4(x-3)}{(x+2)(x-3)(x-2)}$$
$$=\frac{4x-8-4x+12}{(x+2)(x-3)(x-2)}$$
$$=\frac{4}{(x+2)(x-3)(x-2)}$$

41. $\dfrac{7}{x+3}+2$

$\text{LCD} = x+3$

$$\frac{7}{x+3}+2=\frac{7}{x+3}+\frac{2(x+3)}{x+3}$$
$$=\frac{7+2(x+3)}{x+3}$$
$$=\frac{7+2x+6}{x+3}$$
$$=\frac{2x+13}{x+3}$$

42. $\dfrac{2y-5}{6y+9}-\dfrac{4}{2y^2+3y}$

$6y+9=3(2y+3)$

$2y^2+3y=y(2y+3)$

$\text{LCD} = 3y(2y+3)$

$$\frac{2y-5}{6y+9}-\frac{4}{2y^2+3y}$$
$$=\frac{2y-5}{3(2y+3)}-\frac{4}{y(2y+3)}$$
$$=\frac{(2y-5)(y)}{3(2y+3)(y)}-\frac{4(3)}{y(2y+3)(3)}$$
$$=\frac{2y^2-5y-12}{3y(2y+3)}=\frac{(2y+3)(y-4)}{3y(2y+3)}$$
$$=\frac{y-4}{3y}$$

In Exercises 43-47, each complex rational expression can be simplified by either of the two methods introduced in Section 8.5 of the textbook. Both methods will be illustrated here.

43. $$\frac{\frac{1}{2}+\frac{3}{8}}{\frac{3}{4}-\frac{1}{2}}=\frac{\frac{4}{8}+\frac{3}{8}}{\frac{3}{4}-\frac{2}{4}}=\frac{\frac{7}{8}}{\frac{1}{4}}=\frac{7}{8}\cdot\frac{4}{1}=\frac{7}{2}$$

44. $\dfrac{\frac{1}{x}}{1-\frac{1}{x}}$

$\text{LCD} = x$

$$\frac{\frac{1}{x}}{1-\frac{1}{x}}=\frac{x}{x}\cdot\frac{\left(\frac{1}{x}\right)}{\left(1-\frac{1}{x}\right)}$$
$$=\frac{x\cdot\frac{1}{x}}{x\cdot 1-x\cdot\frac{1}{x}}$$
$$=\frac{1}{x-1}$$

45. $\dfrac{\frac{1}{x}+\frac{1}{y}}{\frac{1}{xy}}$

LCD = xy

$$\frac{\frac{1}{x}+\frac{1}{y}}{\frac{1}{xy}} = \frac{xy}{xy}\cdot\frac{\left(\frac{1}{x}+\frac{1}{y}\right)}{\left(\frac{1}{xy}\right)}$$

$$= \frac{xy\cdot\frac{1}{x}+xy\cdot\frac{1}{y}}{xy\cdot\frac{1}{xy}}$$

$$= \frac{y+x}{1} = y+x \text{ or } x+y$$

46. $\dfrac{\frac{1}{x}-\frac{1}{2}}{\frac{1}{3}-\frac{x}{6}} = \dfrac{\frac{2}{2x}-\frac{x}{2x}}{\frac{2}{6}-\frac{x}{6}}$

$$= \frac{\frac{2-x}{2x}}{\frac{2-x}{6}} = \frac{2-x}{2x}\cdot\frac{6}{2-x} = \frac{3}{x}$$

47. $\dfrac{3+\frac{12}{x}}{1-\frac{16}{x^2}}$

LCD = x^2

$$\frac{3+\frac{12}{x}}{1-\frac{16}{x^2}} = \frac{x^2}{x^2}\cdot\frac{\left(3+\frac{12}{x}\right)}{\left(1-\frac{16}{x^2}\right)}$$

$$= \frac{3x^2+12x}{x^2-16}$$

$$= \frac{3x(x+4)}{(x+4)(x-4)} = \frac{3x}{x-4}$$

48. $\frac{3}{x}-\frac{1}{6}=\frac{1}{x}$

The restriction is $x \neq 0$.

The LCD is $6x$.

$$\frac{3}{x}-\frac{1}{6}=\frac{1}{x}$$

$$6x\left(\frac{3}{x}-\frac{1}{6}\right)=6x\left(\frac{1}{x}\right)$$

$$18-x=6$$

$$-x=-12$$

$$x=12$$

The solution is 12.

49. $\frac{3}{4x}=\frac{1}{x}+\frac{1}{4}$

The restriction is $x \neq 0$.

The LCD is $4x$.

$$\frac{3}{4x}=\frac{1}{x}+\frac{1}{4}$$

$$4x\left(\frac{3}{4x}\right)=4x\left(\frac{1}{x}+\frac{1}{4}\right)$$

$$3=4+x$$

$$-1=x$$

The solution is -1.

50. $x+5=\frac{6}{x}$

The restriction is $x \neq 0$.

The LCD is x.

$$x+5=\frac{6}{x}$$

$$x(x+5)=x\left(\frac{6}{x}\right)$$

$$x^2+5x=6$$

$$x^2+5x-6=0$$

$$(x+6)(x-1)=0$$

$$x+6=0 \quad \text{or} \quad x-1=0$$

$$x=-6 \qquad\qquad x=1$$

The equation has two solutions, -6 and 1.

51. $4-\frac{x}{x+5}=\frac{5}{x+5}$

The restriction is $x \neq -5$.

The LCD is $x+5$.

$$(x+5)\left(4-\frac{x}{x+5}\right)=(x+5)\left(\frac{5}{x+5}\right)$$

$$(x+5)\cdot 4-(x+5)\left(\frac{x}{x+5}\right)=(x+5)\left(\frac{5}{x+5}\right)$$

$$4x+20-x=5$$
$$3x+20=5$$
$$3x=-15$$
$$x=-5$$

The only proposed solution, −5, is *not* a solution because of the restriction $x \neq -5$. Notice that −5 makes two of the denominators zero in the original equation. Therefore, the given equation has no solution.

52. $\frac{2}{x-3}=\frac{4}{x+3}+\frac{8}{x^2-9}$

To find any restrictions and the LCD, all denominators should be written in factored form.

$$\frac{2}{x-3}=\frac{4}{x+3}+\frac{8}{(x+3)(x-3)}$$

Restrictions: $x \neq 3, x \neq -3$

LCD = $(x+3)(x-3)$

$$(x+3)(x-3)\cdot\frac{2}{x-3}=(x+3)(x-3)\left(\frac{4}{x+3}+\frac{8}{(x+3)(x-3)}\right)$$

$$2(x+3)=4(x-3)+8$$
$$2x+6=4x-12+8$$
$$2x+6=4x-4$$
$$10=2x$$
$$5=x$$

The solution is 5.

53. $\frac{2}{x}=\frac{2}{3}+\frac{x}{6}$

Restriction: $x \neq 0$

LCD = $6x$

$$6x\left(\frac{2}{x}\right)=6x\left(\frac{2}{3}+\frac{x}{6}\right)$$

$$12=4x+x^2$$
$$0=x^2+4x-12$$
$$0=(x+6)(x-2)$$
$$x+6=0 \quad \text{or} \quad x-2=0$$
$$x=-6 \qquad x=2$$

The solutions −6 and 2.

54. $\frac{13}{y-1}-3=\frac{1}{y-1}$

Restrictions: $y \neq 1$

LCD = $y-1$

$$(y-1)\left(\frac{13}{y-1}-3\right)=(y-1)\left(\frac{1}{y-1}\right)$$

$$13-3(y-1)=1$$
$$13-3y+3=1$$
$$16-3y=1$$
$$-3y=-15$$
$$y=5$$

The solution is 5.

55. $\frac{1}{x+3}-\frac{1}{x-1}=\frac{x+1}{x^2+2x-3}$

$$\frac{1}{x+3}-\frac{1}{x-1}=\frac{x+1}{(x+3)(x-1)}$$

Restrictions: $x \neq -3, x \neq 1$

LCD = $(x+3)(x-1)$

$$(x+3)(x-1)\left[\frac{1}{x+3}-\frac{1}{x-1}\right]=(x+3)(x-1)\cdot\left[\frac{x+1}{(x+3)(x-1)}\right]$$

$$(x-1)-(x+3)=x+1$$
$$x-1-x-3=x+1$$
$$-4=x+1$$
$$-5=x$$

The solution is −5.

56. $P=\dfrac{250(3t+5)}{t+25}; P=125$

$$125=\frac{250(3t+5)}{t+25}$$
$$125(t+25)=\frac{250(3t+5)}{t+25}\cdot(t+25)$$
$$125t+3125=250(3t+5)$$
$$125t+3125=750t+1250$$
$$3125=625t+1250$$
$$1875=625t$$
$$3=t$$

It will take 3 years for the population to reach 125 elk.

57. $S=\dfrac{C}{1-r};\ S=200,\ C=140$

$$200=\frac{140}{1-r}$$
$$200(1-r)=\frac{140}{1-r}\cdot 1-r$$
$$200-200r=140$$
$$-200r=-60$$
$$r=\frac{-60}{-200}=\frac{3}{10}=30\%$$

The markup is 30%.

58. Let $x=$ the rate of the current.
Then $20+x=$ the rate of the boat with the current
and $20-x=$ the rate of the boat against the current.

	Distance	Rate	Time
With Current	72	$20+x$	$\dfrac{72}{20+x}$
Against Current	48	$20-x$	$\dfrac{48}{20-x}$

The times are equal, so

$$\frac{72}{20+x}=\frac{48}{20-x}$$

This equation is a proportion, so it can be solved using the cross-products principle.

$$72(20-x)=48(20+x)$$
$$1440-72x=960+48x$$
$$1440=960+120x$$
$$480=120x$$
$$4=x$$

The rate of the current is 4 miles per hour

59. Let $x=$ the rate of the slower car.
Then $x+10=$ the rate of the faster car.

	Distance	Rate	Time
Slower car	60	x	$\dfrac{60}{x}$
Faster car	90	$x+10$	$\dfrac{90}{x+10}$

$$\frac{60}{x}=\frac{90}{x+10}$$
$$60(x+10)=90x$$
$$60x+600=90x$$
$$600=30x$$
$$20=x$$

If $x=20,\ x+10=30$.
The rate of the slower car is 20 miles per hour and the rate of the faster car is 30 miles per hour.

60. Let x = the time, in hours, for both people to paint the fence together.

	Fractional part of job completed in 1 hour	Time working together	Fractional part of job completed in x hour
Painter	$\frac{1}{6}$	x	$\frac{x}{6}$
Apprentice	$\frac{1}{12}$	x	$\frac{x}{12}$

Working together, the two people complete one whole job, so

$$\frac{x}{6}+\frac{x}{12}=1.$$

$$12\left(\frac{x}{6}+\frac{x}{12}\right)=12\cdot 1$$

$$2x+x=12$$

$$3x=12$$

$$x=4$$

It would take them 4 hours to paint the fence working together.

61. $\frac{8}{4}=\frac{10}{x}$

$$8x=40$$

$$x=5$$

The length of the side marked with an x is 5 feet.

62. Write a proportion relating the corresponding sides of the large and small triangle. Notice that the length of the base of the larger triangle is 9 ft + 6 ft = 15 ft.

$$\frac{x}{5}=\frac{15}{6}$$

$$6x=5\cdot 15$$

$$6x=75$$

$$x=\frac{75}{6}=12.5$$

The height of the lamppost is 12.5 feet.

63. Let b = electric bill (in dollars). Then e = number of kilowatts of electricity used.

Step 1 $b=ke$

Step 2 To find k, substitute 98 for b and 1400 for e.

$$98=k\cdot 1400$$

$$\frac{98}{1400}=k$$

$$0.07=k$$

Step 3 $b=0.07e$

Step 4 Substitute 2200 for e and solve for b.

$$b=0.07(2200)=154$$

The bill is \$154 for 2200 kilowatts of electricity.

64. *Step 1* $t=\frac{k}{r}$

Step 2 To find *k*, substitute *k*, substitute 4 for *t* and 50 for *r*.

$$4=\frac{k}{50}$$
$$200=k$$

Step 3 $t=\frac{200}{r}$

Step 4 Substitute 40 for *r* and solve for *t*.

$$t=\frac{200}{40}=5$$

At 40 miles per hour, the trip will take 5 hours.

Chapter 8 Test

1. $\frac{x+7}{x^2+5x-36}$

Set the denominator equal to 0 and solve for *x*.

$$x^2+5x-36=0$$
$$(x+9)(x-4)=0$$
$$x+9=0 \quad \text{or} \quad x-4=0$$
$$x=-9 \qquad x=4$$

The rational expression is undefined for $x=-9$ and $x=4$.

2. $\frac{x^2+2x-3}{x^2-3x+2}=\frac{(x-1)(x+3)}{(x-1)(x-2)}=\frac{x+3}{x-2}$

3. $\frac{4x^2-20x}{x^2-4x-5}=\frac{4x(x-5)}{(x+1)(x-5)}=\frac{4x}{x+1}$

4. $\frac{x^2-16}{10}\cdot\frac{5}{x+4}=\frac{(x+4)(x-4)}{10}\cdot\frac{5}{(x+4)}$

$$=\frac{x-4}{2}$$

5. $\frac{x^2-7x+12}{x^2-4x}\cdot\frac{x^2}{x^2-9}$

$$=\frac{(x-3)(x-4)}{x(x-4)}\cdot\frac{x^2}{(x+3)(x-3)}$$
$$=\frac{x}{x+3}$$

6. $\frac{2x+8}{x-3}\div\frac{x^2+5x+4}{x^2-9}$

$$=\frac{2x+8}{x-3}\cdot\frac{x^2-9}{x^2+5x+4}$$
$$=\frac{2(x+4)}{(x-3)}\cdot\frac{(x+3)(x-3)}{(x+4)(x+1)}$$
$$=\frac{2(x+3)}{x+1}=\frac{2x+6}{x+1}$$

7. $\frac{5y+5}{(y-3)^2}\div\frac{y^2-1}{y-3}$

$$=\frac{5y+5}{(y-3)^2}\cdot\frac{y-3}{y^2-1}$$
$$=\frac{5(y+1)}{(y-3)(y-3)}\cdot\frac{(y-3)}{(y+1)(y-1)}$$
$$=\frac{5}{(y-3)(y-1)}$$

8. $\dfrac{2y^2+5}{y+3}+\dfrac{6y-5}{y+3}$

$$=\frac{(2y^2+5)+(6y-5)}{y+3}$$

$$=\frac{2y^2+5+6y-5}{y+3}$$

$$=\frac{2y^2+6y}{y+3}=\frac{2y(y+3)}{y+3}=2y$$

9. $\dfrac{y^2-2y+3}{y^2+7y+12}-\dfrac{y^2-4y-5}{y^2+7y+12}$

$$=\frac{(y^2-2y+3)-(y^2-4y-5)}{y^2+7y+12}$$

$$=\frac{y^2-2y+3-y^2+4y+5}{y^2+7y+12}$$

$$=\frac{2y+8}{y^2+7y+12}$$

$$=\frac{2(y+4)}{(y+3)(y+4)}=\frac{2}{y+3}$$

10. $\dfrac{x}{x+3}+\dfrac{5}{x-3}$

LCD = $(x+3)(x-3)$

$\dfrac{x}{x+3}+\dfrac{5}{x-3}$

$$=\frac{x(x-3)}{(x+3)(x-3)}+\frac{5(x+3)}{(x+3)(x-3)}$$

$$=\frac{x(x-3)+5(x+3)}{(x+3)(x-3)}$$

$$=\frac{x^2-3x+5x+15}{(x+3)(x-3)}$$

$$=\frac{x^2+2x+15}{(x+3)(x-3)}$$

11. $\dfrac{2}{x^2-4x+3}+\dfrac{6}{x^2+x-2}$

$x^2-4x+3=(x-1)(x-3)$

$x^2+x-2=(x-1)(x+2)$

LCD = $(x-1)(x-3)(x+2)$

$\dfrac{2}{x^2-4x+3}+\dfrac{6}{x^2+x-2}$

$$=\frac{2}{(x-1)(x-3)}+\frac{6}{(x-1)(x+2)}$$

$$=\frac{2(x+2)}{(x-1)(x-3)(x+2)}+\frac{6(x-3)}{(x-1)(x-3)(x+2)}$$

$$=\frac{2(x+2)+6(x-3)}{(x-1)(x-3)(x+2)}$$

$$=\frac{2x+4+6x-18}{(x-1)(x-3)(x+2)}$$

$$=\frac{8x-14}{(x-1)(x-3)(x+2)}$$

12. $\dfrac{4}{x-3}+\dfrac{x+5}{3-x}$

$3-x=-1(x-3)$

LCD = $x-3$

$\dfrac{4}{x-3}+\dfrac{x+5}{3-x}$

$$=\frac{4}{x-3}+\frac{(-1)}{(-1)}\cdot\frac{(x+5)}{(3-x)}$$

$$=\frac{4}{x-3}+\frac{-x-5}{x-3}$$

$$=\frac{4-x-5}{x-3}=\frac{-x-1}{x-3}$$

13. $1+\frac{3}{x-1}$

LCD = $x-1$

$$1+\frac{3}{x-1}=\frac{1(x-1)}{x-1}+\frac{3}{x-1}$$
$$=\frac{x-1+3}{x-1}=\frac{x+2}{x-1}$$

14. $\frac{2x+3}{x^2-7x+12}-\frac{2}{x-3}$

$x^2-7x+12=(x-3)(x-4)$

$x-3=1(x-3)$

LCD = $(x-3)(x-4)$

$$\frac{2x+3}{x^2-7x+12}-\frac{2}{x-3}$$
$$=\frac{2x+3}{(x-3)(x-4)}-\frac{2(x-4)}{(x-3)(x-4)}$$
$$=\frac{2x+3-2(x-4)}{(x-3)(x-4)}$$
$$=\frac{2x+3-2x+8}{(x-3)(x-4)}$$
$$=\frac{11}{(x-3)(x-4)}$$

15. $\frac{8y}{y^2-16}-\frac{4}{y-4}$

$y^2-16=(y+4)(y-4)$

$y-4=1(y-4)$

LCD = $(y+4)(y-4)$

$$\frac{8y}{y^2-16}-\frac{4}{y-4}$$
$$=\frac{8y}{(y+4)(y-4)}-\frac{4}{y-4}$$
$$=\frac{8y}{(y+4)(y-4)}-\frac{4(y+4)}{(y+4)(y-4)}$$
$$=\frac{8y-4(y+4)}{(y+4)(y-4)}$$
$$=\frac{8y-4y-16}{(y+4)(y-4)}$$
$$=\frac{4y-16}{(y+4)(y-4)}$$
$$=\frac{4(y-4)}{(y+4)(y-4)}=\frac{4}{y+4}$$

16. $\frac{(x-y)^2}{x+y}\div\frac{x^2-xy}{3x+3y}$

$$=\frac{(x-y)^2}{x+y}\cdot\frac{3x+3y}{x^2-xy}$$
$$=\frac{(x-y)(x-y)}{(x+y)}\cdot\frac{3(x+y)}{x(x-y)}$$
$$=\frac{3(x-y)}{x}=\frac{3x-3y}{x}$$

17.
$$\frac{5+\frac{5}{x}}{2+\frac{1}{x}}=\frac{\frac{5x}{x}+\frac{5}{x}}{\frac{2x}{x}+\frac{1}{x}}=\frac{\frac{5x+5}{x}}{\frac{2x+1}{x}}$$
$$=\frac{5x+5}{x}\cdot\frac{x}{2x+1}$$
$$=\frac{5x+5}{2x+1}$$

18. $\frac{\frac{1}{x}-\frac{1}{y}}{\frac{1}{x}}$

LCD = xy

$$\frac{xy}{xy}\cdot\frac{\left(\frac{1}{x}-\frac{1}{y}\right)}{\left(\frac{1}{x}\right)}=\frac{xy\cdot\frac{1}{x}-xy\cdot\frac{1}{y}}{xy\cdot\frac{1}{x}}=\frac{y-x}{y}$$

19. $\frac{5}{x}+\frac{2}{3}=2-\frac{2}{x}-\frac{1}{6}$

Restriction: $x \neq 0$

LCD = $6x$

$$6x\left(\frac{5}{x}+\frac{2}{3}\right)=6x\left(2-\frac{2}{x}-\frac{1}{6}\right)$$
$$6x\cdot\frac{5}{x}+6x\cdot\frac{2}{3}=6x\cdot 2-6x\cdot\frac{2}{x}-6x\cdot\frac{1}{6}$$
$$30+4x=12x-12-x$$
$$30+4x=11x-12$$
$$30=7x-12$$
$$42=7x$$
$$6=x$$

The solution is 6.

20. $\frac{3}{y+5}-1=\frac{4-y}{2y+10}$

$\frac{3}{y+5}-1=\frac{4-y}{2(y+5)}$

Restriction: $y \neq -5$

LCD = $2(y+5)$

$$2(y+5)\left(\frac{3}{y+5}-1\right)=2(y+5)\left[\frac{4-y}{2(y+5)}\right]$$
$$6-2(y+5)=4-y$$
$$6-2y-10=4-y$$
$$-4-2y=4-y$$
$$-4=4+y$$
$$-8=y$$

The solution is −8.

21. $\frac{2}{x-1}=\frac{3}{x^2-1}+1$

$\frac{2}{x-1}=\frac{3}{(x+1)(x-1)}+1$

Restrictions: $x \neq 1, x \neq -1$

LCD = $(x+1)(x-1)$

$$(x+1)(x-1)\left(\frac{2}{x-1}\right)=(x+1)(x-1)\left[\frac{3}{(x+1)(x-1)}+1\right]$$
$$2(x+1)=3+(x+1)(x-1)$$
$$2x+2=3+x^2-1$$
$$2x+2=2+x^2$$
$$0=x^2-2x$$
$$0=x(x-2)$$
$$x=0 \text{ or } x-2=0$$
$$x=2$$

The equation has two solutions, 0 and 2.

22. Let x = the rate of the current

Then $30+x$ = the rate of the boat with the current

and $30-x$ = the rate of the boat against the current

	Dist	Rate	Time
With the Current	16	$30+x$	$\frac{16}{30+x}$
Against the Current	14	$30-x$	$\frac{14}{30-x}$

$$\frac{16}{30+x}=\frac{14}{30-x}$$
$$16(30-x)=14(30+x)$$
$$480-16x=420+14x$$
$$480=420+30x$$
$$60=30x$$
$$2=x$$

The rate of the current is 2 miles per hour.

23. Let x = the time (in minutes) for both pipes to fill the hot tub.

$$\frac{x}{20}+\frac{x}{30}=1$$

LCD = 60

$$60\left(\frac{x}{20}+\frac{x}{30}\right)=60\cdot 1$$
$$3x+2x=60$$
$$5x=60$$
$$x=12$$

It will take 12 minutes for both pipes to fill the hot tub.

24. $$\frac{10}{4}=\frac{8}{x}$$
$$10x=8\cdot 4$$
$$10x=32$$
$$x=3.2$$

The length of the side marked with an x is 3.2 inches.

25. Let C = the current (in amperes). Then R = the resistance (in ohms).

Step 1 $C=\frac{k}{R}$

Step 2 To find k, substitute 42 for C and 5 for R.

$$42=\frac{k}{5}$$
$$42\cdot 5=\frac{k}{5}\cdot 5$$
$$210=k$$

Step 3 $C=\frac{210}{R}$

Step 4 Substitute 4 for R and solve for C.

$$C=\frac{210}{4}=52.5$$

When the resistance is 4 ohms, the current is 52.5 amperes.

Chapter 8 Cumulative Review Exercises (Chapters 1-8)

1. $$2(x-3)+5x=8(x-1)$$
$$2x-6+5x=8x-8$$
$$7x-6=8x-8$$
$$-6=x-8$$
$$2=x$$

The solution is 2.

2. $$-3(2x-4)>2(6x-12)$$
$$-6x+12>12x-24$$
$$-18x+12>-24$$
$$-18x>-36$$
$$\frac{-18x}{-18}<\frac{-36}{-18}$$
$$x<2$$

Solution set: $\{x|x<2\}$

3. $$x^2+3x=18$$
$$x^2+3x-18=0$$
$$(x+6)(x-3)=0$$
$$x+6=0 \quad\text{or}\quad x-3=0$$
$$x=-6 \qquad x=3$$

The solutions are −6 and 3.

4. $$\frac{2x}{x^2-4}+\frac{1}{x-2}=\frac{2}{x+2}$$
$$x^2-4=(x+2)(x-2)$$

Restrictions: $x\neq 2, x\neq -2$

LCD = $(x+2)(x-2)$

$$(x+2)(x-2)\left[\frac{2x}{(x+2)(x-2)}+\frac{1}{x-2}\right]$$
$$=(x+2)(x-2)\cdot\frac{2}{x+2}$$
$$2x+(x+2)=2(x-2)$$
$$3x+2=2x-4$$
$$x=-6$$

The solution is −6.

5. $y = 2x - 3$

$x + 2y = 9$

To solve this system by the substitution method, substitute $2x - 3$ for y in the second equation.

$$x + 2y = 9$$
$$x + 2(2x - 3) = 9$$
$$x + 4x - 6 = 9$$
$$5x - 6 = 9$$
$$5x = 15$$
$$x = 3$$

Back-substitute 3 for x into the first equation.

$$y = 2x - 3$$
$$y = 2 \cdot 3 - 3 = 3$$

Solution: $(3,3)$

6. $3x + 2y = -2$

$-4x + 5y = 18$

To solve this system by the addition method, multiply the first equation by 4 and the second equation by 3.
Then add the equations.

$$\begin{array}{r} 12x + \ \ 8y = -8 \\ -12x + 15y = 54 \\ \hline 23y = 46 \end{array}$$
$$y = 2$$

Back-substitute 2 for y in the first equation of the original system.

$$3x + 2y = -2$$
$$3x + 2(2) = -2$$
$$3x + 4 = -2$$
$$3x = -6$$
$$x = -2$$

Solution: $(-2,2)$

7. $3x - 2y = 6$

x-intercept: 2
y-intercept: -3
checkpoint: (4,3)
Draw a line through (2,0), (0, -3) and (4,3).

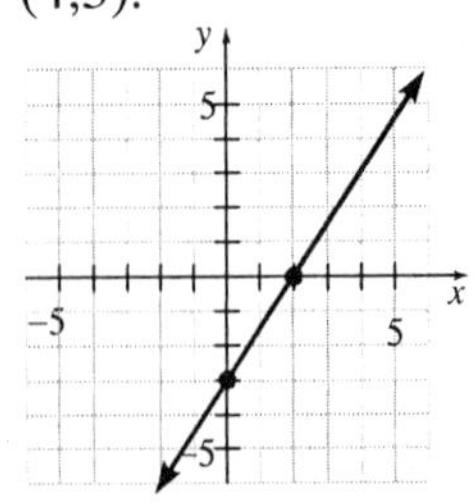

8. $y > -2x + 3$

Graph $y = -2x + 3$ as a dashed line using its slope, $-2 = \frac{-2}{1}$, and its y-intercept, 3.

Use (0,0) as a test point. Because $0 > 2 \cdot 0 + 3$ is false, shade the half-plane *not* containing (0,0).

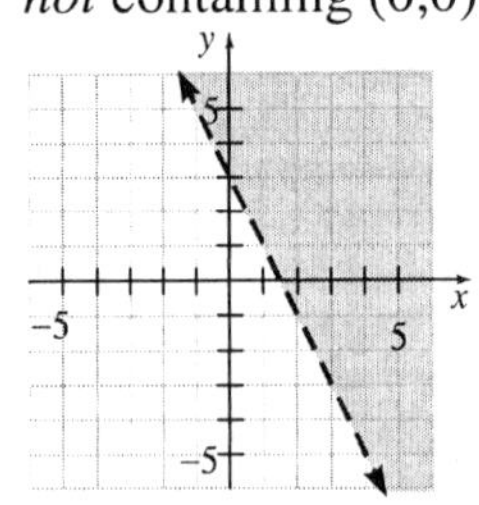

9. $y = -3$

The graph is a horizontal line with y-intercept -3.

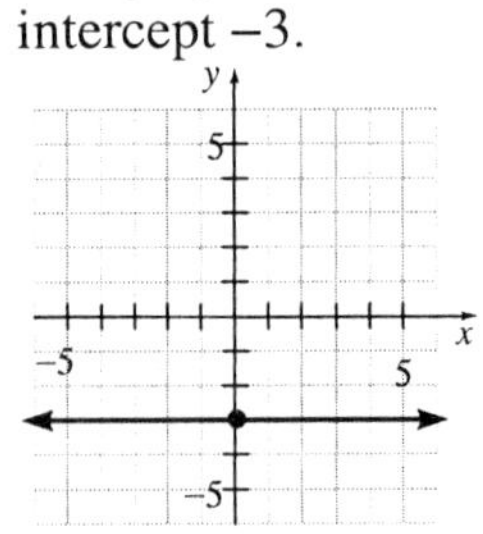

10.
$$-21 - 16 - 3(2 - 8) = -21 - 16 - 3(-6)$$
$$= -21 - 16 + 18$$
$$= -37 + 18 = -19$$

11. $\left(\frac{4x^5}{2x^2}\right)^3 = \left(2x^3\right)^3 = 2^3 \cdot \left(x^3\right)^3 = 8x^9$

12. $\frac{\frac{1}{x}-2}{4-\frac{1}{x}}$

LCD = x

$$\frac{\frac{1}{x}-2}{4-\frac{1}{x}} = \frac{x\left(\frac{1}{x}-2\right)}{x\left(4-\frac{1}{x}\right)}$$

$$= \frac{x\cdot\frac{1}{x}-x\cdot 2}{x\cdot 4-x\cdot\frac{1}{x}} = \frac{1-2x}{4x-1}$$

13. $4x^2-13x+3$

Factor by trial and error. Try various combinations until the correct one is found

$4x^2-13x+3=(4x-1)(x-3)$

14. $4x^2-20x+25=(2x)^2-2(2x\cdot 5)+5^2$

$=(2x-5)^2$

15. $3x^2-75=3\left(x^2-25\right)$

$=3(x+5)(x-5)$

16. $\left(4x^2-3x+2\right)-\left(5x^2-7x-6\right)$

$=\left(4x^2-3x+2\right)+\left(-5x^2+7x+6\right)$

$=-x^2+4x+8$

17. $\frac{-8x^6+12x^4-4x^2}{4x^2} = \frac{-8x^6}{4x^2}+\frac{12x^4}{4x^2}-\frac{4x^2}{4x^2}$

$=-2x^4+3x^2-1$

18. $\frac{x+6}{x-2}+\frac{2x+1}{x+3}$

LCD = $(x-2)(x+3)$

$\frac{x+6}{x-2}+\frac{2x+1}{x+3}$

$=\frac{(x+6)(x+3)}{(x-2)(x+3)}+\frac{(2x+1)(x-2)}{(x-2)(x+3)}$

$=\frac{(x+6)(x+3)+(2x+1)(x-2)}{(x-2)(x+3)}$

$=\frac{x^2+9x+18+2x^2-3x-2}{(x-2)(x+3)}$

$=\frac{3x^2+6x+16}{(x-2)(x+3)}$

19. Let x = the amount invested at 5%
Then $4000-x$ = the amount invested at 9%

$0.05x+0.09(4000-x)=311$

$0.05x+360-0.09x=311$

$-0.04x+360=311$

$-0.04x=-49$

$x=\frac{-49}{-0.04}$

$x=1225$

If x = 1225, then $4000-x=2775$.
\$1225 was invested at 5% and \$2775 at 9%.

20. Let x = the length of the shorter piece.
Then $3x$ = the length of the larger piece.

$x+3x=68$

$4x=68$

$x=17$

If x = 17, then $3x$ = 51.
The lengths of the pieces are 17 inches and 51 inches.

Chapter 9
Roots and Radicals

9.1 Exercise Set

1. $\sqrt{36}=6$
The principal square root of 36 is 6.

3. $-\sqrt{36}=-6$
The negative square root of 36 is −6.

5. $\sqrt{-36}$ is not a real number.
There is no real number whose square is −36.

7. $\sqrt{\frac{1}{9}}=\frac{1}{3}$ because $\left(\frac{1}{3}\right)^2=\frac{1}{9}$.

9. $\sqrt{\frac{1}{100}}=\frac{1}{10}$ because $\left(\frac{1}{10}\right)^2=\frac{1}{100}$.

11. $-\sqrt{\frac{1}{36}}=-\frac{1}{6}$ because $\sqrt{\frac{1}{36}}=\frac{1}{6}$.

13. $\sqrt{-\frac{1}{36}}$ is not a real number.

15. $\sqrt{0.04}=0.2$ because $(0.2)^2=0.04$ and 0.2 is positive.

17. $\sqrt{33-8}=\sqrt{25}=5$

19. $\sqrt{2\cdot 32}=\sqrt{64}=8$

21. $\sqrt{144+25}=\sqrt{169}=13$

23. $\sqrt{144}+\sqrt{25}=12+5=17$

25. $\sqrt{25-144}=\sqrt{-119}$ which is not a real number.

27. $y=\sqrt{x-1}$

x	$y=\sqrt{x-1}$	(x,y)
1	$y=\sqrt{1-1}=0$	$(1,0)$
2	$y=\sqrt{2-1}=1$	$(2,1)$
5	$y=\sqrt{5-1}=2$	$(5,2)$
10	$y=\sqrt{10-1}=3$	$(10,3)$
17	$y=\sqrt{17-1}=4$	$(17,4)$

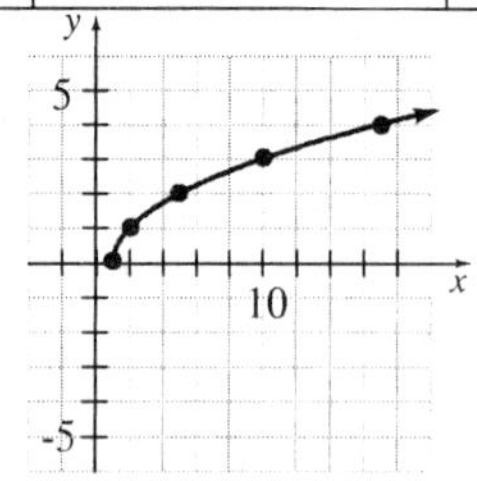

29. Answers will vary. Both curves are increasing and open down. They both have a range of $y\geq 0$.

31. $\sqrt{7}\approx 2.646$

33. $\sqrt{23}\approx 4.796$

35. $-\sqrt{65}\approx -8.062$

37. $12+\sqrt{11}\approx 15.317$

39. $\frac{12+\sqrt{11}}{2}\approx 7.658$

41. $\frac{-5+\sqrt{321}}{6} \approx 2.15$

43. $\sqrt{13-5} = \sqrt{8} \approx 2.82$

45. $\sqrt{5-13} = \sqrt{-8}$, which is not a real number

47. $\sqrt[3]{64} = 4$ because $4^3 = 64$.

49. $\sqrt[3]{-27} = -3$ because $(-3)^3 = -27$

51. $-\sqrt[3]{8} = -2$ because $(2)^3 = 8$

53. $\sqrt[3]{\frac{1}{125}} = \frac{1}{5}$ because $\left(\frac{1}{5}\right)^3 = \frac{1}{125}$.

55. $\sqrt[3]{-1000} = -10$ because $(-10)^3 = -1000$

57. $\sqrt[4]{1} = 1$ because $1^4 = 1$.

59. $\sqrt[4]{16} = 2$ because $2^4 = 16$.

61. $-\sqrt[4]{16} = -2$ because $(2)^4 = 16$

63. $\sqrt[4]{-16}$ is not a real number because the index, 4, is even and the radicand, −16 is negative.

65. $\sqrt[5]{-1} = -1$ because $(-1)^5 = -1$

67. $\sqrt[6]{-1}$ is not a real number because the index, 6, is even and the radicand, −1 is negative.

69. $-\sqrt[4]{256} = -4$ because $\sqrt[4]{256} = 4$.

71. $\sqrt[6]{64} = 2$ because $2^6 = 64$.

73. $-\sqrt[5]{32} = -2$ because $\sqrt[5]{32} = 2$.

75. $\sqrt{2x}$ yields a real number if
$2x \geq 0$
$x \geq 0$

76. $\sqrt{3x}$ yields a real number if
$3x \geq 0$
$x \geq 0$

77. $\sqrt{x-2}$ yields a real number if
$x-2 \geq 0$
$x \geq 2$

78. $\sqrt{x-3}$ yields a real number if
$x-3 \geq 0$
$x \geq 3$

79. $\sqrt{2-x}$ yields a real number if
$2-x \geq 0$
$-x \geq -2$
$x \leq 2$

80. $\sqrt{3-x}$ yields a real number if
$3-x \geq 0$
$-x \geq -3$
$x \leq 3$

81. $\sqrt{x^2+2}$ yields a real number for all real numbers x since x^2+2 is always positive.

82. $\sqrt{x^2+3}$ yields a real number for all real numbers x since x^2+3 is always positive.

83. $\sqrt{12-2x}$ yields a real number if

$$12-2x \geq 0$$
$$-2x \geq -12$$
$$x \leq 6$$

84. $\sqrt{8-2x}$ yields a real number if

$$8-2x \geq 0$$
$$-2x \geq -8$$
$$x \leq 4$$

85. $v = 4\sqrt{r};\ r = 9$

$$v = 4\sqrt{9} = 4 \cdot 3 = 12$$

The maximum velocity is 12 miles per hour.

87. $v = \sqrt{20L}; L = 245$

$$v = \sqrt{20 \cdot 245} = \sqrt{4900} = 70$$

The motorist was traveling 70 miles per hour, so she was speeding.

89. **a.** At birth we have $x = 0$.

$$y = 2.9\sqrt{x} + 36$$
$$= 2.9\sqrt{0} + 36$$
$$= 2.9(0) + 36$$
$$= 36$$

According to the model, the head circumference at birth is 36 cm.

b. At 9 months we have $x = 9$.

$$y = 2.9\sqrt{x} + 36$$
$$= 2.9\sqrt{9} + 36$$
$$= 2.9(3) + 36$$
$$= 44.7$$

According to the model, the head circumference at 9 months is 44.7 cm.

c. At 14 months we have $x = 14$.

$$y = 2.9\sqrt{x} + 36$$
$$= 2.9\sqrt{14} + 36$$
$$\approx 46.9$$

According to the model, the head circumference at 14 months is roughly 46.9 cm.

d. The model describes healthy children.

91. **a.**

$$y = a\sqrt{x} + b$$
$$261 = a\sqrt{0} + b$$
$$261 = b$$

Therefore, $y = a\sqrt{x} + 261$.

b.

$$y = a\sqrt{x} + 261$$
$$791 = a\sqrt{9} + 261$$
$$791 = 3a + 261$$
$$530 = 3a$$
$$177 \approx a$$

Therefore, $y = 177\sqrt{x} + 261$.

c. In 2001, we have $x = 10$.

$$y = 177\sqrt{10} + 261 \approx 821$$

According to the model, there were roughly 821,000 cumulative AIDS cases in 2001.
The estimate is a little high, but fairly close to the actual value.

d. In 2007, we have $x = 16$.

$$y = 177\sqrt{16} + 261 = 969$$

According to the model, the cumulative AIDS cases is predicted to be about 969,000 in 2007.

93. The symbol $\sqrt{\ }$ denotes the principal square root. From 92, the answer 6 is given by this symbol. To obtain the other answer in 92, we need the symbol $-\sqrt{\ }$.

95. $\sqrt[3]{8}$ is 2 because $2^3 = 8$. $\sqrt[n]{a}$ means that nth root of a. That is, the number raised to the nth power that will yield the value a.

97. The number of cumulative cases is increasing each year, but at a slower rate.

99. Answers will vary.

101. $\sqrt{\sqrt[3]{64}} = \sqrt{4} = 2$

103. $\sqrt{\sqrt{16}} - \sqrt[3]{\sqrt{64}} = \sqrt{4} - \sqrt[3]{8}$
$= 2 - 2$
$= 0$

105. $y_1 = \sqrt{x}$
$y_2 = \sqrt{x+4}$
$y_3 = \sqrt{x-3}$

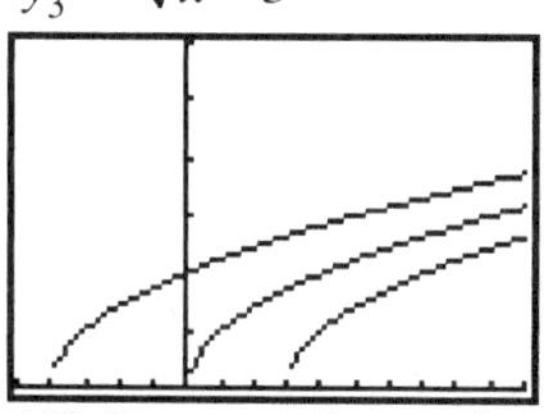

All three graphs are increasing and have a range of $y \geq 0$. The graphs of y_2 and y_3 look like the graph of y_1 but are shifted left 4 units and shifted right 3 units, respectively.

107. $4x - 5y = 20$
$-5y = -4x + 20$
$y = \frac{4}{5}x - 4$
x-intercept: 5
y-intercept: −4
checkpoint: (−5, −8)

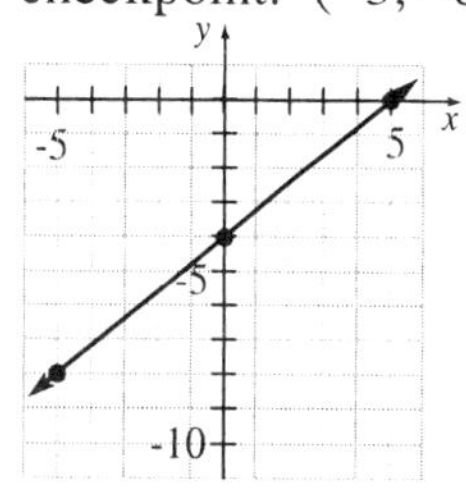

108. $2(x-3) > 4x + 10$
$2x - 6 > 4x + 10$
$-2x - 6 > 10$
$-2x > 16$
$x < -8$
$\{x | x < -8\}$

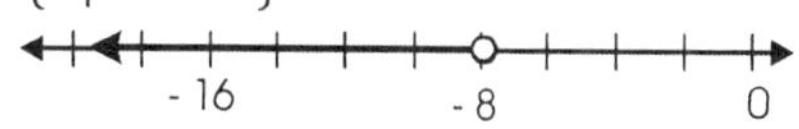

109. $\frac{1}{x^2 - 17x + 30} \div \frac{1}{x^2 + 7x - 18}$
$= \frac{1}{x^2 - 17x + 30} \cdot \frac{x^2 + 7x - 18}{1}$
$= \frac{1}{(x-15)(x-2)} \cdot \frac{(x+9)(x-2)}{1}$
$= \frac{x+9}{x-15}$

9.2 Exercise Set

1. $\sqrt{2}\cdot\sqrt{7}=\sqrt{2\cdot 7}=\sqrt{14}$

3. $\sqrt{3x}\cdot\sqrt{5y}=\sqrt{3x\cdot 5y}=\sqrt{15xy}$

5. $\sqrt{5}\cdot\sqrt{5}=\sqrt{25}=5$

7. $\sqrt{\frac{2}{3}}\cdot\sqrt{\frac{5}{7}}=\sqrt{\frac{2}{3}\cdot\frac{5}{7}}=\sqrt{\frac{10}{21}}$

9. $\sqrt{0.1x}\cdot\sqrt{5y}=\sqrt{0.5xy}$

11. $\sqrt{\frac{1}{5}a}\cdot\sqrt{\frac{1}{5}b}=\sqrt{\frac{1}{25}ab}=\sqrt{\frac{1}{25}}\cdot\sqrt{ab}$
$=\frac{1}{5}\sqrt{ab}$

13. $\sqrt{\frac{2x}{9}}\cdot\sqrt{\frac{9}{2}}=\sqrt{\frac{2x\cdot 9}{9\cdot 2}}=\sqrt{\frac{18x}{18}}=\sqrt{x}$

15. $\sqrt{50}=\sqrt{25\cdot 2}=\sqrt{25}\sqrt{2}=5\sqrt{2}$

17. $\sqrt{45}=\sqrt{9\cdot 5}=\sqrt{9}\sqrt{5}=3\sqrt{5}$

19. $\sqrt{200}=\sqrt{100\cdot 2}=\sqrt{100}\sqrt{2}=10\sqrt{2}$

21. $\sqrt{75x}=\sqrt{25\cdot 3x}=\sqrt{25}\sqrt{3x}=5\sqrt{3x}$

23. $\sqrt{9x}=\sqrt{9}\sqrt{x}=3\sqrt{x}$

25. $\sqrt{35}$ cannot be simplified because 35 has no perfect square factors other than 1.

27. $\sqrt{y^2}=y$

29. $\sqrt{64x^2}=8x$

31. $\sqrt{11x^2}=\sqrt{x^2}\sqrt{11}=x\sqrt{11}$

33. $\sqrt{8x^2}=\sqrt{4x^2}\sqrt{2}=2x\sqrt{2}$

35. $\sqrt{x^{20}}=x^{10}$ because $\left(x^{10}\right)^2=x^{20}.$

37. $\sqrt{25y^{10}}=5y^5$

39. $\sqrt{20x^6}-\sqrt{4x^6}\sqrt{5}=2x^3\sqrt{5}$

41. $\sqrt{72y^{100}}=\sqrt{36y^{100}}\sqrt{2}=6y^{50}\sqrt{2}$

43. $\sqrt{x^3}=\sqrt{x^2}\sqrt{x}=x\sqrt{x}$

45. $\sqrt{x^7}=\sqrt{x^6}\sqrt{x}=x^3\sqrt{x}$

47. $\sqrt{y^{17}}=\sqrt{y^{16}}\sqrt{y}=y^8\sqrt{y}$

49. $\sqrt{25x^5}=\sqrt{25x^4}\sqrt{x}=5x^2\sqrt{x}$

51. $\sqrt{8x^{17}}=\sqrt{4x^{16}}\sqrt{2x}=2x^8\sqrt{2x}$

53. $\sqrt{90y^{19}}=\sqrt{9y^{18}}\sqrt{10y}=3y^9\sqrt{10y}$

55. $\sqrt{3}\cdot\sqrt{15}=\sqrt{45}=\sqrt{9}\sqrt{5}=3\sqrt{5}$

57. $\sqrt{5x}\cdot\sqrt{10y}=\sqrt{50xy}=\sqrt{25}\sqrt{2xy}$
$=5\sqrt{2xy}$

59. $\sqrt{12x}\cdot\sqrt{3x}=\sqrt{36x^2}=6x$

61. $\sqrt{15x^2}\cdot\sqrt{3x}=\sqrt{45x^3}=\sqrt{9x^2}\sqrt{5x}$
$=3x\sqrt{5x}$

63. $\sqrt{15x^4}\cdot\sqrt{5x^9}=\sqrt{75x^{13}}$
$=\sqrt{25x^{12}}\sqrt{3x}$
$=5x^6\sqrt{3x}$

65. $\sqrt{7x}\cdot\sqrt{3y}=\sqrt{21xy}$

67. $\sqrt{50xy}\cdot\sqrt{4xy^2}=\sqrt{200x^2y^3}$
$=\sqrt{100x^2y^2}\sqrt{2y}$
$=10xy\sqrt{2y}$

69. $\sqrt{\frac{49}{16}}=\frac{\sqrt{49}}{\sqrt{16}}=\frac{7}{4}$

71. $\sqrt{\frac{3}{4}}=\frac{\sqrt{3}}{\sqrt{4}}=\frac{\sqrt{3}}{2}$

73. $\sqrt{\frac{x^2}{36}}=\frac{\sqrt{x^2}}{6}=\frac{x}{6}$

75. $\sqrt{\frac{7}{x^4}}=\frac{\sqrt{7}}{\sqrt{x^4}}=\frac{\sqrt{7}}{x^2}$

77. $\sqrt{\frac{72}{y^{20}}}=\frac{\sqrt{72}}{\sqrt{y^{20}}}=\frac{\sqrt{36}\sqrt{2}}{y^{10}}=\frac{6\sqrt{2}}{y^{10}}$

79. $\frac{\sqrt{54}}{\sqrt{6}}=\sqrt{\frac{54}{6}}=\sqrt{9}=3$

81. $\frac{\sqrt{24}}{\sqrt{3}}=\sqrt{\frac{24}{3}}=\sqrt{8}=\sqrt{4}\sqrt{2}=2\sqrt{2}$

83. $\frac{\sqrt{75}}{\sqrt{15}}=\sqrt{\frac{75}{15}}=\sqrt{5}$

85. $\frac{\sqrt{48x}}{\sqrt{3x}}=\sqrt{\frac{48x}{3x}}=\sqrt{16}=4$

87. $\frac{\sqrt{32x^3}}{\sqrt{8x}}=\sqrt{\frac{32x^3}{8x}}=\sqrt{4x^2}=2x$

89. $\frac{\sqrt{150x^4}}{\sqrt{3x}}=\sqrt{\frac{150x^4}{3x}}=\sqrt{50x^3}$
$=\sqrt{25x^2}\sqrt{2x}=5x\sqrt{2x}$

91. $\frac{\sqrt{400x^{10}}}{\sqrt{10x^3}}=\sqrt{\frac{400x^{10}}{10x^3}}=\sqrt{40x^7}$
$=\sqrt{4x^6}\sqrt{10x}=2x^3\sqrt{10x}$

93. $\sqrt[3]{16}=\sqrt[3]{8\cdot 2}=\sqrt[3]{8}\cdot\sqrt[3]{2}=2\sqrt[3]{2}$

95. $\sqrt[3]{54}=\sqrt[3]{27\cdot 2}=\sqrt[3]{27}\cdot\sqrt[3]{2}=3\sqrt[3]{2}$

97. $\sqrt[4]{32}=\sqrt[4]{16\cdot 2}=\sqrt[4]{16}\cdot\sqrt[4]{2}=2\sqrt[4]{2}$

99. $\sqrt[3]{4}\cdot\sqrt[3]{2}=\sqrt[3]{8}=2$

101. $\sqrt[3]{9}\cdot\sqrt[3]{6}=\sqrt[3]{54}=\sqrt[3]{27}\sqrt[3]{2}=3\sqrt[3]{2}$

103. $\sqrt[4]{4}\cdot\sqrt[4]{8}=\sqrt[4]{32}=\sqrt[4]{16}\cdot\sqrt[4]{2}=2\sqrt[4]{2}$

105. $\sqrt[3]{\frac{27}{8}}=\frac{\sqrt[3]{27}}{\sqrt[3]{8}}=\frac{3}{2}$

107. $\sqrt[3]{\frac{3}{8}}=\frac{\sqrt[3]{3}}{\sqrt[3]{8}}=\frac{\sqrt[3]{3}}{2}$

109. $\sqrt{90(x+4)^3}=\sqrt{9(x+4)^2}\cdot\sqrt{10(x+4)}$
$=3(x+4)\sqrt{10(x+4)}$

110. $\sqrt{150(x+8)^3} = \sqrt{25(x+8)^2} \cdot \sqrt{6(x+8)}$
$= 5(x+8)\sqrt{6(x+8)}$

111. $\sqrt{x^2 - 6x + 9} = \sqrt{(x-3)^2} = x - 3$

112. $\sqrt{x^2 - 10x + 25} = \sqrt{(x-5)^2} = x - 5$

113. $\sqrt{2^{43}x^{104}y^{13}} = \sqrt{2^{42}x^{104}y^{12}} \cdot \sqrt{2y}$
$= 2^{21}x^{52}y^{6}\sqrt{2y}$

114. $\sqrt{3^{41}x^{102}y^{17}} = \sqrt{3^{40}x^{102}y^{16}} \cdot \sqrt{3y}$
$= 3^{20}x^{51}y^{8}\sqrt{3y}$

115. $\sqrt[3]{24x^5} = \sqrt[3]{8x^3} \cdot \sqrt[3]{3x^2}$
$= 2x\sqrt[3]{3x^2}$

117. $2\sqrt{5L}; L = 40$
$2\sqrt{5 \cdot 40} = 2\sqrt{200} = 2\sqrt{100}\sqrt{2}$
$= 2 \cdot 10\sqrt{2} = 20\sqrt{2}$

The speed of the car was $20\sqrt{2}$ miles per hour.

119. $A = l \cdot w$
$= \sqrt{15} \cdot \sqrt{5} = \sqrt{75}$
$= \sqrt{25}\sqrt{3} = 5\sqrt{3}$

The area is $5\sqrt{3}$ square feet.

For Exercises 121-127, answers may vary.

129. $\sqrt{\square x^{\square}} = 5x^7$

Since $(5x^7)^2 = 5^2(x^7)^2 = 25x^{14}$, the radicand is $25x^{14}$. The missing coefficient is 25 and the missing exponent is 14.

131. Results will vary depending on the exercises chosen.

133.

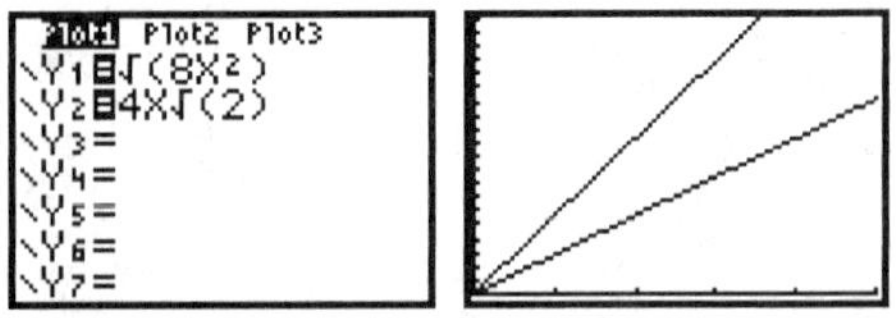

The graphs do not coincide.

$\sqrt{8x^2} = \sqrt{4x^2 \cdot 2} = \sqrt{4x^2}\sqrt{2} = 2x\sqrt{2}$

Change y_2 to $2x\sqrt{2}$.

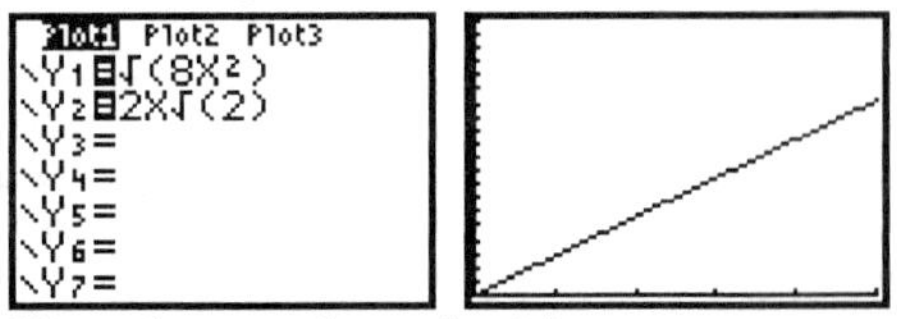

Now the graphs coincide.

135. $4x + 3y = 18$
$5x - 9y = 48$

To solve this system by the addition method, multiply the first equation by 3 and add the result to the second equation.

$$\begin{aligned} 12x + 9y &= 54 \\ 5x - 9y &= 48 \\ \hline 17x \qquad &= 102 \\ x &= 6 \end{aligned}$$

Back-substitute into the first equation of the original system.

$$\begin{aligned} 4x + 3y &= 18 \\ 4(6) + 3y &= 18 \\ 24 + 3y &= 18 \\ 3y &= -6 \\ y &= -2 \end{aligned}$$

Solution: (6,–2).

136. $\frac{6x}{x^2-4}-\frac{3}{x+2}$

Factor the first denominator.

$x^2-4=(x+2)(x-2)$

The LCD = $(x+2)(x-2)$.

$$\frac{6x}{x^2-4}-\frac{3}{x+2}$$
$$=\frac{6}{(x+2)(x-2)}-\frac{3(x-2)}{(x+2)(x-2)}$$
$$=\frac{6x-3(x-2)}{(x+2)(x-2)}$$
$$=\frac{6x-3x+6}{(x+2)(x-2)}$$
$$=\frac{3x+6}{(x+2)(x-2)}$$
$$=\frac{3(x+2)}{(x+2)(x-2)}$$
$$=\frac{3}{x-2}$$

137. $2x^3-16x^2+30x=2x\left(x^2-8x+15\right)$
$=2x(x-3)(x-5)$

9.3 Exercise Set

1. $8\sqrt{3}+5\sqrt{3}=(8+5)\sqrt{3}=13\sqrt{3}$

3. $17\sqrt{6}-2\sqrt{6}=(17-2)\sqrt{6}=15\sqrt{6}$

5. $3\sqrt{13}-8\sqrt{13}=(3-8)\sqrt{13}=-5\sqrt{13}$

7. $12\sqrt{x}+3\sqrt{x}=(12+3)\sqrt{x}=15\sqrt{x}$

9. $70\sqrt{y}-76\sqrt{y}=(70-76)\sqrt{y}$
$=-6\sqrt{y}$

11. $7\sqrt{10x}+2\sqrt{10x}=(7+2)\sqrt{10x}$
$=9\sqrt{10x}$

13. $7\sqrt{5y}-\sqrt{5y}=7\sqrt{5y}-1\sqrt{5y}$
$=(7-1)\sqrt{5y}=6\sqrt{5y}$

15. $\sqrt{5}+\sqrt{5}=1\sqrt{5}+1\sqrt{5}=(1+1)\sqrt{5}$
$=2\sqrt{5}$

17. $4\sqrt{2}+3\sqrt{2}+5\sqrt{2}=(4+3+5)\sqrt{2}$
$=12\sqrt{2}$

19. $4\sqrt{7}-5\sqrt{7}+8\sqrt{7}=(4-5+8)\sqrt{7}$
$=7\sqrt{7}$

21. $4\sqrt{11}-6\sqrt{11}+2\sqrt{11}=(4-6+2)\sqrt{11}$
$=0\sqrt{11}=0$

23. $\sqrt{5}+\sqrt{20}=\sqrt{5}+\sqrt{4\cdot 5}=\sqrt{5}+2\sqrt{5}$
$=1\sqrt{5}+2\sqrt{5}=3\sqrt{5}$

25. $\sqrt{8}-\sqrt{2}=\sqrt{4\cdot 2}-\sqrt{2}=\sqrt{4}\sqrt{2}-\sqrt{2}$
$=2\sqrt{2}-1\sqrt{2}=(2-1)\sqrt{2}$
$=\sqrt{2}$

27. $\sqrt{50}+\sqrt{18}=\sqrt{25}\sqrt{2}+\sqrt{9}\sqrt{2}$
$=5\sqrt{2}+3\sqrt{2}=8\sqrt{2}$

29. $7\sqrt{12}+\sqrt{75}=7\sqrt{4}\sqrt{3}+\sqrt{25}\sqrt{3}$
$=7\cdot 2\sqrt{3}+5\sqrt{3}$
$=14\sqrt{3}+5\sqrt{3}=19\sqrt{3}$

31. $3\sqrt{27}-2\sqrt{18}=3\sqrt{9\cdot 3}-2\sqrt{9\cdot 2}$
$$=3\cdot 3\sqrt{3}-2\cdot 3\sqrt{2}$$
$$=9\sqrt{3}-6\sqrt{2}$$

Because $\sqrt{3}$ and $\sqrt{2}$ are unlike radicals, it is not possible to combine terms and simplify further.

33. $2\sqrt{45x}-2\sqrt{20x}$
$$=2\sqrt{9}\sqrt{5x}-2\sqrt{4}\sqrt{5x}$$
$$=2\cdot 3\sqrt{5x}-2\cdot 2\sqrt{5x}$$
$$=6\sqrt{5x}-4\sqrt{5x}$$
$$=(6-4)\sqrt{5x}=2\sqrt{5x}$$

35. $\sqrt{8}+\sqrt{16}+\sqrt{18}+\sqrt{25}$
$$=\sqrt{4}\sqrt{2}+4+\sqrt{9}\sqrt{2}+5$$
$$=2\sqrt{2}+4+3\sqrt{2}+5$$
$$=(4+5)+\left(2\sqrt{2}+3\sqrt{2}\right)$$
$$=9+5\sqrt{2}$$

37. $\sqrt{2}+\sqrt{11}$

These are unlike radicals, so the terms cannot be combined.

39. $2\sqrt{80}+3\sqrt{75}=2\sqrt{16}\sqrt{5}+3\sqrt{25}\sqrt{3}$
$$=2\cdot 4\sqrt{5}+3\cdot 5\sqrt{3}$$
$$=8\sqrt{5}+15\sqrt{3}$$

Because $\sqrt{5}$ and $\sqrt{3}$ are unlike radicals, it is not possible to combine terms.

41. $3\sqrt{54}-2\sqrt{20}+4\sqrt{45}-\sqrt{24}$
$$=3\sqrt{9}\sqrt{6}-2\sqrt{4}\sqrt{5}+4\sqrt{9}\sqrt{5}-\sqrt{4}\sqrt{6}$$
$$=3\cdot 3\sqrt{6}-2\cdot 2\sqrt{5}+4\cdot 3\sqrt{5}-2\sqrt{6}$$
$$=9\sqrt{6}-4\sqrt{5}+12\sqrt{5}-2\sqrt{6}$$
$$=(9-2)\sqrt{6}+(-4+12)\sqrt{5}$$
$$=7\sqrt{6}+8\sqrt{5}$$

43. $\sqrt{2}\left(\sqrt{3}+\sqrt{5}\right)$

Use the distributive property.
$$\sqrt{2}\left(\sqrt{3}+\sqrt{5}\right)=\sqrt{2}\cdot\sqrt{3}+\sqrt{2}\cdot\sqrt{5}$$
$$=\sqrt{6}+\sqrt{10}$$

45. $\sqrt{7}\left(\sqrt{6}-\sqrt{10}\right)=\sqrt{7}\cdot\sqrt{6}-\sqrt{7}\cdot\sqrt{10}$
$$=\sqrt{42}-\sqrt{70}$$

47. $\sqrt{3}\left(5+\sqrt{3}\right)=\sqrt{3}\cdot 5+\sqrt{3}\cdot\sqrt{3}$
$$=5\sqrt{3}+3$$

49. $\sqrt{3}\left(\sqrt{6}-\sqrt{3}\right)=\sqrt{3}\cdot\sqrt{6}-\sqrt{3}\cdot\sqrt{3}$
$$=\sqrt{18}-3=\sqrt{9}\sqrt{2}-3$$
$$=3\sqrt{2}-3$$

51. $\left(5+\sqrt{2}\right)\left(6+\sqrt{2}\right)$

Use the FOIL method.
$$\left(5+\sqrt{2}\right)\left(6+\sqrt{2}\right)$$
$$=5\cdot 6+5\sqrt{2}+6\sqrt{2}+\sqrt{2}\cdot\sqrt{2}$$
$$=30+5\sqrt{2}+6\sqrt{2}+2$$
$$=(30+2)+(5+6)\sqrt{2}$$
$$=30+11\sqrt{2}$$

53. $\left(4+\sqrt{5}\right)\left(10-3\sqrt{5}\right)$

$=4\cdot 10+4\left(-3\sqrt{5}\right)+\sqrt{5}\cdot 10$

$+\sqrt{5}\left(-3\sqrt{5}\right)$

$=40+12\sqrt{5}+10\sqrt{5}-3\cdot 5$

$=40-12\sqrt{5}+10\sqrt{5}-15$

$=(40-15)+(-12+10)\sqrt{5}$

$=25-2\sqrt{5}$

55. $\left(6-3\sqrt{7}\right)\left(2-5\sqrt{7}\right)$

$=6\cdot 2+6\left(-5\sqrt{7}\right)-3\sqrt{7}(2)$

$-3\sqrt{7}\left(-5\sqrt{7}\right)$

$=12-30\sqrt{7}-6\sqrt{7}+15\cdot 7$

$=12-30\sqrt{7}-6\sqrt{7}+105$

$=(12+105)+(-30-6)\sqrt{7}$

$=117-36\sqrt{7}$

57. $\left(\sqrt{10}-3\right)\left(\sqrt{10}-5\right)$

$=\sqrt{10}\cdot\sqrt{10}+\sqrt{10}(-5)-3\sqrt{10}-3(-5)$

$=10-5\sqrt{10}-3\sqrt{10}+15$

$=25-8\sqrt{10}$

59. $\left(\sqrt{3}+\sqrt{6}\right)\left(\sqrt{3}+2\sqrt{6}\right)$

$=\sqrt{3}\cdot\sqrt{3}+\sqrt{3}\cdot 2\sqrt{6}+\sqrt{6}\cdot 3$

$+\sqrt{6}\cdot 2\sqrt{6}$

$=3+2\sqrt{18}+\sqrt{18}+2\cdot 6$

$=3+2\sqrt{18}+\sqrt{18}+12$

$=15+3\sqrt{18}=15+3\sqrt{9}\sqrt{2}$

$=15+3\cdot 3\sqrt{2}$

$=15+9\sqrt{2}$

61. $\left(\sqrt{2}+1\right)\left(\sqrt{3}-6\right)$

$=\sqrt{2}\cdot\sqrt{3}+\sqrt{2}(-6)+1\cdot\sqrt{3}+1(-6)$

$=\sqrt{6}-6\sqrt{2}+\sqrt{3}-6$

63. $\left(3+\sqrt{5}\right)\left(3-\sqrt{5}\right)$

These two radical expressions are conjugates. Use the special-product formula

$(A+B)(A-B)=A^2-B^2$

$\left(3+\sqrt{5}\right)\left(3-\sqrt{5}\right)=3^2-\left(\sqrt{5}\right)^2$

$=9-5$

$=4$

65. $\left(1-\sqrt{6}\right)\left(1+\sqrt{6}\right)=1^2-\left(\sqrt{6}\right)^2$

$=1-6$

$=-5$

67. $\left(\sqrt{11}+5\right)\left(\sqrt{11}-5\right)=\left(\sqrt{11}\right)^2-5^2$

$=11-25=-14$

69. $\left(\sqrt{7}-\sqrt{5}\right)\left(\sqrt{7}+\sqrt{5}\right)=\left(\sqrt{7}\right)^2-\left(\sqrt{5}\right)^2$

$=7-5=2$

71. $\left(2\sqrt{3}+7\right)\left(2\sqrt{3}-7\right)=\left(2\sqrt{3}\right)^2-7^2$

$=12-49$

$=-37$

73. $\left(2\sqrt{3}+\sqrt{5}\right)\left(2\sqrt{3}-\sqrt{5}\right)$

$=\left(2\sqrt{3}\right)^2-\left(\sqrt{5}\right)^2$

$=12-5$

$=7$

75. $\left(\sqrt{2}+\sqrt{3}\right)^2$

Use the special-product formula.

$(A+B)^2 = A^2+2AB+B^2$

$\left(\sqrt{2}+\sqrt{3}\right)$

$=\left(\sqrt{2}\right)^2+2\cdot\sqrt{2}\cdot\sqrt{3}+\left(\sqrt{3}\right)^2$

$=2+2\sqrt{6}+3=5+2\sqrt{6}$

77. $\left(\sqrt{x}-\sqrt{10}\right)^2$

Use the special-product formula

$(A+B)^2 = A^2-2AB+B^2$

$\left(\sqrt{x}-\sqrt{10}\right)^2$

$=\left(\sqrt{x}\right)^2-2\cdot\sqrt{x}\cdot\sqrt{10}+\left(\sqrt{10}\right)^2$

$=x-2\sqrt{10x}+10$

79. $5\sqrt{27x^3}-3x\sqrt{12x}$

$=5\sqrt{9x^2}\cdot\sqrt{3x}-3x\sqrt{4}\cdot\sqrt{3x}$

$=5(3x)\sqrt{3x}-3x(2)\sqrt{3x}$

$=15x\sqrt{3x}-6x\sqrt{3x}$

$=9x\sqrt{3x}$

80. $7\sqrt{32x^3}-3x\sqrt{50x}$

$=7\sqrt{16x^2}\cdot\sqrt{2x}-3x\sqrt{25}\cdot\sqrt{2x}$

$=7(4x)\sqrt{2x}-3x(5)\sqrt{2x}$

$=28x\sqrt{2x}-15x\sqrt{2x}$

$=13x\sqrt{2x}$

81. $6y^2\sqrt{x^5y}+2x^2\sqrt{xy^5}$

$=6y^2\sqrt{x^4}\cdot\sqrt{xy}+2x^2\sqrt{y^4}\cdot\sqrt{xy}$

$=6y^2\left(x^2\right)\sqrt{xy}+2x^2\left(y^2\right)\sqrt{xy}$

$=6x^2y^2\sqrt{xy}+2x^2y^2\sqrt{xy}$

$=8x^2y^2\sqrt{xy}$

82. $9y^2\sqrt{x^5y}+x^2\sqrt{xy^5}$

$=9y^2\sqrt{x^4}\cdot\sqrt{xy}+x^2\sqrt{y^4}\cdot\sqrt{xy}$

$=9y^2\left(x^2\right)\sqrt{xy}+x^2\left(y^2\right)\sqrt{xy}$

$=9x^2y^2\sqrt{xy}+x^2y^2\sqrt{xy}$

$=10x^2y^2\sqrt{xy}$

83. $3\sqrt[3]{54}-4\sqrt[3]{16}$

$=3\sqrt[3]{27}\cdot\sqrt[3]{2}-4\sqrt[3]{8}\cdot\sqrt[3]{2}$

$=3(3)\sqrt[3]{2}-4(2)\sqrt[3]{2}$

$=9\sqrt[3]{2}-8\sqrt[3]{2}$

$=\sqrt[3]{2}$

84. $7\sqrt[3]{24}-5\sqrt[3]{81}$

$=7\sqrt[3]{8}\cdot\sqrt[3]{3}-5\sqrt[3]{27}\cdot\sqrt[3]{3}$

$=7(2)\sqrt[3]{3}-5(3)\sqrt[3]{3}$

$=14\sqrt[3]{3}-15\sqrt[3]{3}$

$=-\sqrt[3]{3}$

85. $x\sqrt[3]{32x}+9\sqrt[3]{4x^4}$

$=x\sqrt[3]{8}\sqrt[3]{4x}+9\sqrt[3]{x^3}\cdot\sqrt[3]{4x}$

$=x(2)\sqrt[3]{4x}+9(x)\sqrt[3]{4x}$

$=2x\sqrt[3]{4x}+9x\sqrt[3]{4x}$

$=11x\sqrt[3]{4x}$

86. $x\sqrt[3]{48x}+11\sqrt[3]{6x^4}$

$=x\sqrt[3]{8}\cdot\sqrt[3]{6x}+11\sqrt[3]{x^3}\cdot\sqrt[3]{6x}$

$=x(2)\sqrt[3]{6x}+11(x)\sqrt[3]{6x}$

$=2x\sqrt[3]{6x}+11x\sqrt[3]{6x}$

$=13x\sqrt[3]{6x}$

87. Use the formulas for perimeter and area of a square with $s=\sqrt{3}+\sqrt{5}$.

$P=4x=4\left(\sqrt{3}+\sqrt{5}\right)$

$=4\sqrt{3}+4\sqrt{5}$

The perimeter is $\left(4\sqrt{3}+4\sqrt{5}\right)$ inches.

$A=s^2$

$=\left(\sqrt{3}+\sqrt{5}\right)^2$

$=\left(\sqrt{3}\right)^2+2\sqrt{3}\sqrt{5}+\left(\sqrt{5}\right)^2$

$=3+2\sqrt{15}+5$

$=8+2\sqrt{15}$

The area is $\left(8+2\sqrt{15}\right)$ square inches.

89. Use the formulas for the perimeter and area of a rectangle with $l=\sqrt{6}+1$ and $w=\sqrt{6}-1$.

$P=2l+2w=2\left(\sqrt{6}+1\right)+2\left(\sqrt{6}-1\right)$

$=2\sqrt{6}+2+2\sqrt{6}-2$

$=4\sqrt{6}$

The perimeter is $4\sqrt{6}$ inches.

$A=lw=\left(\sqrt{6}+1\right)\left(\sqrt{6}-1\right)$

$=\left(\sqrt{6}\right)^2-1^2$

$=6-1=5$

The area is 5 square inches.

91. To find the perimeter of a triangle, add the lengths of the three sides.

$P=\sqrt{2}+\sqrt{2}+2=2+2\sqrt{2}$

The perimeter is $\left(2+2\sqrt{2}\right)$ inches.

Use the formula for the area of a triangle with $b=\sqrt{2}$ and $h=\sqrt{2}$.

$A=\frac{1}{2}bh=\frac{1}{2}\left(\sqrt{2}\right)\left(\sqrt{2}\right)$

$=\frac{1}{2}\cdot 2=1$

The area is 1 square inch.

93. $\sqrt{2}+\sqrt{8}; a=2, b=8$

$\sqrt{a}+\sqrt{b}=\sqrt{(a+b)+2\sqrt{ab}}$

$\sqrt{2}+\sqrt{8}=\sqrt{(2+8)+2\sqrt{2\cdot 8}}$

$=\sqrt{10+2\sqrt{16}}$

$=\sqrt{10+2\cdot 4}$

$=\sqrt{18}=\sqrt{9}\sqrt{2}=3\sqrt{2}$

$\sqrt{2}+\sqrt{8}=\sqrt{2}+\sqrt{4\cdot 2}$

$=\sqrt{2}+\sqrt{4}\sqrt{2}$

$=\sqrt{2}+2\sqrt{2}$

$=(1+2)\sqrt{2}=3\sqrt{2}$

Explanations of preferences will vary.

For Exercises 95-101, answers may vary.

95. Like radicals are radicals with the same index and the same radicand (in simplified form).

97. $\sqrt{8}$ can be written as $2\sqrt{2}$.

99. Use the FOIL method as you would with two binomials, then simplify by collecting like terms.

101. Use the special product
$(a-b)(a+b)=a^2-b^2$

103. $\sqrt{5}\cdot\sqrt{15}+6\sqrt{3}=\sqrt{75}+6\sqrt{3}$
$=\sqrt{25}\sqrt{3}+6\sqrt{3}$
$=5\sqrt{3}+6\sqrt{3}$
$=11\sqrt{3}$

104. $\left(\sqrt[3]{4}+1\right)\left(\sqrt[3]{2}-3\right)$
$=\sqrt[3]{4}\cdot\sqrt[3]{2}-3\sqrt[3]{4}+1\sqrt[3]{2}+1(-3)$
$=\sqrt[3]{8}-3\sqrt[3]{4}+\sqrt[3]{2}-3$
$=2-3\sqrt[3]{4}+\sqrt[3]{2}-3$
$=-1-3\sqrt[3]{4}+\sqrt[3]{2}$

105. $\left(5+\sqrt{\square}\right)\left(5-\sqrt{\square}\right)$
$\left(5+\sqrt{a}\right)\left(5-\sqrt{a}\right)=5^2-\left(\sqrt{a}\right)^2$
$=25-a=22$
Therefore, the missing radicand is $a=3$.
$\left(5+\sqrt{3}\right)\left(5-\sqrt{3}\right)=22$

107. $y_1=\sqrt{4x}+\sqrt{9x}$
$y_2=5\sqrt{x}$

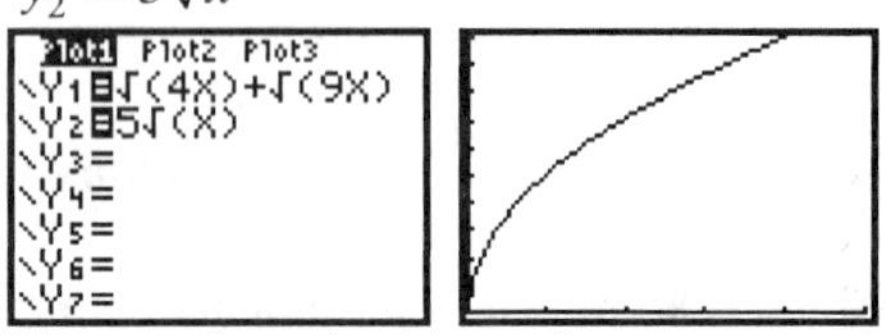

The graphs coincide so the simplification is correct.

109. $y_1=\left(\sqrt{x}-1\right)\left(\sqrt{x}-1\right)$
$y_2=x+1$

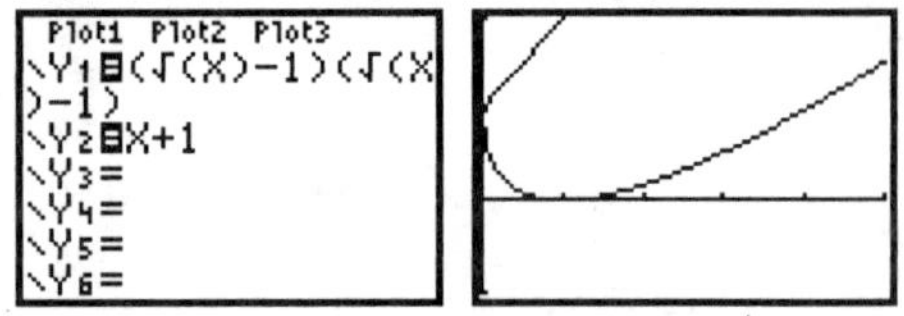

The graphs do not coincide so the simplification is not correct. The right side should be $x-2\sqrt{x}+1$.

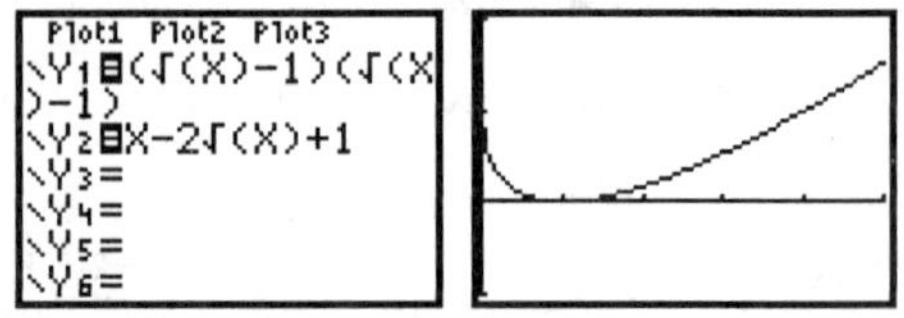

Now the graphs coincide.

111. $(5x+3)(5x-3)=(5x)^2-3^2$
$=25x^2-9$

112. $64x^3-x=x\left(64x^2-1\right)$
$=x\left[(8x)^2-1^2\right]$
$=x(8x+1)(8x-1)$

113. $y=-\frac{1}{4}x+3$

slope = $-\frac{1}{4}=\frac{-1}{4}$; *y*-intercept = 3

Plot (0,3). From this point, move 1 unit *down* and 4 units to the *right* to reach the point (4,2). Draw a line through (0,3) and (4,2).

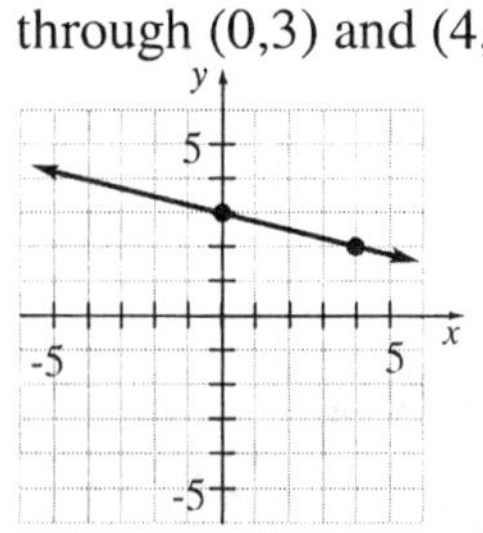

Chapter 9 Mid-Chapter Check Points

1. $\sqrt{50} \cdot \sqrt{6} = \sqrt{50 \cdot 6} = \sqrt{300}$
$= \sqrt{100} \cdot \sqrt{3} = 10\sqrt{3}$

2. $\sqrt{6} + 9\sqrt{6} = (1+9)\sqrt{6} = 10\sqrt{6}$

3. $\sqrt{96x^3} = \sqrt{16x^2} \cdot \sqrt{6x} = 4x\sqrt{6x}$

4. $\sqrt[5]{\frac{4}{32}} = \frac{\sqrt[5]{4}}{\sqrt[5]{32}} = \frac{\sqrt[5]{4}}{2}$

5. $\sqrt{27} + 3\sqrt{12} = \sqrt{9} \cdot \sqrt{3} + 3\sqrt{4} \cdot \sqrt{3}$
$= 3\sqrt{3} + 3(2)\sqrt{3}$
$= 3\sqrt{3} + 6\sqrt{3}$
$= 9\sqrt{3}$

6. $\left(\sqrt{10} + \sqrt{3}\right)\left(\sqrt{10} - \sqrt{3}\right)$
$= \left(\sqrt{10}\right)^2 - \left(\sqrt{3}\right)^2 = 10 - 3 = 7$

7. $\frac{\sqrt{5}}{2}\left(4\sqrt{3} - 6\sqrt{20}\right)$
$= \frac{4}{2}\sqrt{5 \cdot 3} - \frac{6}{2}\sqrt{5 \cdot 20}$
$= 2\sqrt{15} - 3\sqrt{100}$
$= 2\sqrt{15} - 3(10)$
$= 2\sqrt{15} - 30$

8. $-\sqrt{32x^{21}} = -\sqrt{16x^{20}} \cdot \sqrt{2x}$
$= -4x^{10}\sqrt{2x}$

9. $\sqrt{6x^3} \cdot \sqrt{2x^4} = \sqrt{6x^3 \cdot 2x^4}$
$= \sqrt{12x^7}$
$= \sqrt{4x^6} \cdot \sqrt{3x}$
$= 2x^3\sqrt{3x}$

10. $\frac{\sqrt[3]{32}}{\sqrt[3]{2}} = \sqrt[3]{\frac{32}{2}} = \sqrt[3]{16} = \sqrt[3]{8} \cdot \sqrt[3]{2} = 2\sqrt[3]{2}$

11. $-3\sqrt{90} - 5\sqrt{40}$
$= -3\sqrt{9} \cdot \sqrt{10} - 5\sqrt{4} \cdot \sqrt{10}$
$= -3(3)\sqrt{10} - 5(2)\sqrt{10}$
$= -9\sqrt{10} - 10\sqrt{10}$
$= -19\sqrt{10}$

12. $\left(2 - \sqrt{3}\right)\left(5 + 2\sqrt{3}\right)$
$= 10 + 4\sqrt{3} - 5\sqrt{3} - 2\left(\sqrt{3}\right)^2$
$= 10 - \sqrt{3} - 6$
$= 4 - \sqrt{3}$

13. $\frac{\sqrt{56x^5}}{\sqrt{7x^3}} = \sqrt{\frac{56x^5}{7x^3}} = \sqrt{8x^2}$
$= \sqrt{4x^2} \cdot \sqrt{2} = 2x\sqrt{2}$

14. $-\sqrt[4]{32} = -\sqrt[4]{16} \cdot \sqrt[4]{2} = -2\sqrt[4]{2}$

15. $\left(\sqrt{2} + \sqrt{7}\right)^2$
$= \left(\sqrt{2}\right)^2 + 2\left(\sqrt{2}\right)\left(\sqrt{7}\right) + \left(\sqrt{7}\right)^2$
$= 2 + 2\sqrt{2 \cdot 7} + 7$
$= 9 + 2\sqrt{14}$

16. $\sqrt[3]{\frac{1}{2}}\cdot\sqrt[3]{32}=\sqrt[3]{\frac{1}{2}\cdot 32}=\sqrt[3]{16}$
$=\sqrt[3]{8}\cdot\sqrt[3]{2}=2\sqrt[3]{2}$

17. $\sqrt{5}+\sqrt{20}+\sqrt{45}$
$=\sqrt{5}+\sqrt{4}\cdot\sqrt{5}+\sqrt{9}\cdot\sqrt{5}$
$=1\sqrt{5}+2\sqrt{5}+3\sqrt{5}$
$=6\sqrt{5}$

18. $\frac{1}{3}\sqrt{\frac{90}{16}}=\frac{1}{3}\frac{\sqrt{90}}{\sqrt{16}}=\frac{\sqrt{9}\cdot\sqrt{10}}{3\cdot 4}$
$=\frac{3\sqrt{10}}{12}=\frac{\sqrt{10}}{4}$

19. $3\sqrt{2}\left(\sqrt{2}+\sqrt{5}\right)$
$=3\sqrt{2}\cdot\sqrt{2}+3\sqrt{2}\cdot\sqrt{5}$
$=3\sqrt{2\cdot 2}+3\sqrt{2\cdot 5}$
$=3\sqrt{4}+3\sqrt{10}$
$=3(2)+3\sqrt{10}$
$=6+3\sqrt{10}$

20. $\left(5-\sqrt{2}\right)\left(5+\sqrt{2}\right)=5^2-\left(\sqrt{2}\right)^2$
$=25-2$
$=23$

9.4 Exercise Set

1. $\frac{1}{\sqrt{10}}=\frac{1}{\sqrt{10}}\cdot\frac{\sqrt{10}}{\sqrt{10}}=\frac{\sqrt{10}}{10}$

3. $\frac{5}{\sqrt{5}}=\frac{5}{\sqrt{5}}\cdot\frac{\sqrt{5}}{\sqrt{5}}=\frac{5\sqrt{5}}{5}=\sqrt{5}$

5. $\frac{2}{\sqrt{6}}=\frac{2}{\sqrt{6}}\cdot\frac{\sqrt{6}}{\sqrt{6}}=\frac{2\sqrt{6}}{6}=\frac{\sqrt{6}}{3}$

7. $\frac{28}{\sqrt{7}}=\frac{28}{\sqrt{7}}\cdot\frac{\sqrt{7}}{\sqrt{7}}=\frac{28\sqrt{7}}{7}=4\sqrt{7}$

9. $\sqrt{\frac{3}{5}}=\frac{\sqrt{3}}{\sqrt{5}}=\frac{\sqrt{3}}{\sqrt{5}}\cdot\frac{\sqrt{5}}{\sqrt{5}}=\frac{\sqrt{15}}{5}$

11. $\sqrt{\frac{7}{3}}=\frac{\sqrt{7}}{\sqrt{3}}=\frac{\sqrt{7}}{\sqrt{3}}\cdot\frac{\sqrt{3}}{\sqrt{3}}=\frac{\sqrt{21}}{3}$

13. $\sqrt{\frac{x^2}{3}}=\frac{\sqrt{x^2}}{\sqrt{3}}=\frac{x}{\sqrt{3}}\cdot\frac{\sqrt{3}}{\sqrt{3}}=\frac{x\sqrt{3}}{3}$

15. $\sqrt{\frac{11}{x}}=\frac{\sqrt{11}}{\sqrt{x}}=\frac{\sqrt{11}}{\sqrt{x}}\cdot\frac{\sqrt{x}}{\sqrt{x}}=\frac{\sqrt{11x}}{x}$

17. $\sqrt{\frac{x}{y}}=\frac{\sqrt{x}}{\sqrt{y}}=\frac{\sqrt{x}}{\sqrt{y}}\cdot\frac{\sqrt{y}}{\sqrt{y}}=\frac{\sqrt{xy}}{y}$

19. $\sqrt{\frac{x^4}{2}}=\frac{\sqrt{x^4}}{\sqrt{2}}=\frac{x^2}{\sqrt{2}}$
$=\frac{x^2}{\sqrt{2}}\cdot\frac{\sqrt{2}}{\sqrt{2}}=\frac{x^2\sqrt{2}}{2}$

21. $\frac{\sqrt{7}}{\sqrt{5}}=\frac{\sqrt{7}}{\sqrt{5}}\cdot\frac{\sqrt{5}}{\sqrt{5}}=\frac{\sqrt{35}}{5}$

23. $\frac{\sqrt{3x}}{\sqrt{14}}=\frac{\sqrt{3x}}{\sqrt{14}}\cdot\frac{\sqrt{14}}{\sqrt{14}}=\frac{\sqrt{42x}}{14}$

25. $\frac{1}{\sqrt{20}}=\frac{1}{\sqrt{4}\sqrt{5}}=\frac{1}{2\sqrt{5}}=\frac{1}{2\sqrt{5}}\cdot\frac{\sqrt{5}}{\sqrt{5}}$
$=\frac{\sqrt{5}}{2\cdot 5}=\frac{\sqrt{5}}{10}$

27. $\dfrac{12}{\sqrt{32}}=\dfrac{12}{\sqrt{6}\sqrt{2}}=\dfrac{12}{4\sqrt{2}}=\dfrac{3}{\sqrt{2}}$
$=\dfrac{3}{\sqrt{2}}\cdot\dfrac{\sqrt{2}}{\sqrt{2}}=\dfrac{3\sqrt{2}}{2}$

29. $\dfrac{15}{\sqrt{12}}=\dfrac{15}{\sqrt{4}\sqrt{3}}=\dfrac{15}{2\sqrt{3}}=\dfrac{15}{2\sqrt{3}}\cdot\dfrac{\sqrt{3}}{\sqrt{3}}$
$=\dfrac{15\sqrt{3}}{2\cdot 3}=\dfrac{15\sqrt{3}}{6}=\dfrac{5\sqrt{3}}{2}$

31. $\sqrt{\dfrac{5}{18}}=\dfrac{\sqrt{5}}{\sqrt{18}}=\dfrac{\sqrt{5}}{\sqrt{9}\sqrt{2}}=\dfrac{\sqrt{5}}{3\sqrt{2}}$
$=\dfrac{\sqrt{5}}{3\sqrt{2}}\cdot\dfrac{\sqrt{2}}{\sqrt{2}}=\dfrac{\sqrt{10}}{3\cdot 2}=\dfrac{\sqrt{10}}{6}$

33. $\sqrt{\dfrac{x}{32}}=\dfrac{\sqrt{x}}{\sqrt{32}}=\dfrac{\sqrt{x}}{\sqrt{16}\sqrt{2}}=\dfrac{\sqrt{x}}{4\sqrt{2}}$
$=\dfrac{\sqrt{x}}{4\sqrt{2}}\cdot\dfrac{\sqrt{2}}{\sqrt{2}}=\dfrac{\sqrt{2x}}{4\cdot 2}=\dfrac{\sqrt{2x}}{8}$

35. $\sqrt{\dfrac{1}{45}}=\dfrac{\sqrt{1}}{\sqrt{45}}=\dfrac{1}{\sqrt{45}}=\dfrac{1}{\sqrt{9}\sqrt{5}}=\dfrac{1}{3\sqrt{5}}$
$=\dfrac{1}{3\sqrt{5}}\cdot\dfrac{\sqrt{5}}{\sqrt{5}}=\dfrac{\sqrt{5}}{3\cdot 5}=\dfrac{\sqrt{5}}{15}$

37. $\dfrac{\sqrt{7}}{\sqrt{12}}=\dfrac{\sqrt{7}}{\sqrt{4}\sqrt{3}}=\dfrac{\sqrt{7}}{2\sqrt{3}}\cdot\dfrac{\sqrt{3}}{\sqrt{3}}$
$=\dfrac{\sqrt{21}}{2\cdot 3}=\dfrac{\sqrt{21}}{6}$

39. $\dfrac{8x}{\sqrt{8}}=\dfrac{8x}{\sqrt{4}\sqrt{2}}=\dfrac{8x}{2\sqrt{2}}=\dfrac{4x}{\sqrt{2}}$
$=\dfrac{4x}{\sqrt{2}}\cdot\dfrac{\sqrt{2}}{\sqrt{2}}=\dfrac{4x\sqrt{2}}{2}$
$=2x\sqrt{2}$

41. $\dfrac{\sqrt{7y}}{\sqrt{8}}=\dfrac{\sqrt{7y}}{\sqrt{4}\sqrt{2}}=\dfrac{\sqrt{7y}}{2\sqrt{2}}\cdot\dfrac{\sqrt{2}}{\sqrt{2}}$
$=\dfrac{\sqrt{14y}}{2\cdot 2}=\dfrac{\sqrt{14y}}{4}$

43. $\sqrt{\dfrac{7x}{12}}=\dfrac{\sqrt{7x}}{\sqrt{12}}=\dfrac{\sqrt{7x}}{\sqrt{4}\sqrt{3}}=\dfrac{\sqrt{7x}}{2\sqrt{3}}$
$=\dfrac{\sqrt{7x}}{2\sqrt{3}}\cdot\dfrac{\sqrt{3}}{\sqrt{3}}=\dfrac{\sqrt{21x}}{2\cdot 3}$
$=\dfrac{\sqrt{21x}}{6}$

45. $\sqrt{\dfrac{45}{x}}=\dfrac{\sqrt{45}}{\sqrt{x}}=\dfrac{\sqrt{9}\sqrt{5}}{\sqrt{x}}=\dfrac{3\sqrt{5}}{\sqrt{x}}$
$=\dfrac{3\sqrt{5}}{\sqrt{x}}\cdot\dfrac{\sqrt{x}}{\sqrt{x}}=\dfrac{3\sqrt{5x}}{x}$

47. $\dfrac{5}{\sqrt{x^3}}=\dfrac{5}{\sqrt{x^2}\sqrt{x}}=\dfrac{5}{x\sqrt{x}}=\dfrac{5}{x\sqrt{x}}\cdot\dfrac{\sqrt{x}}{\sqrt{x}}$
$=\dfrac{5\sqrt{x}}{x\cdot x}=\dfrac{5\sqrt{x}}{x^2}$

49. $\sqrt{\dfrac{27}{y^3}}=\dfrac{\sqrt{27}}{\sqrt{y^3}}=\dfrac{\sqrt{9}\sqrt{3}}{\sqrt{y^2}\sqrt{y}}$
$=\dfrac{3\sqrt{3}}{y\sqrt{y}}=\dfrac{3\sqrt{3}}{y\sqrt{y}}\cdot\dfrac{\sqrt{y}}{\sqrt{y}}$
$=\dfrac{3\sqrt{3y}}{y\cdot y}=\dfrac{3\sqrt{3y}}{y^2}$

51. $\dfrac{\sqrt{50x^2}}{\sqrt{12y^3}}=\dfrac{\sqrt{25x^2}\sqrt{2}}{\sqrt{4y^2}\sqrt{3y}}=\dfrac{5x\sqrt{2}}{2y\sqrt{3y}}$

$=\dfrac{5x\sqrt{2}}{2\sqrt{3y}}\cdot\dfrac{\sqrt{3y}}{\sqrt{3y}}=\dfrac{5x\sqrt{6y}}{2y\cdot 3y}$

$=\dfrac{5x\sqrt{6y}}{6y^2}$

53. $\dfrac{1}{4+\sqrt{3}}$

Multiply the numerator and denominator by the conjugate of the denominator, $4-\sqrt{3}$.

$\dfrac{1}{4+\sqrt{3}}\cdot\dfrac{4-\sqrt{3}}{4-\sqrt{3}}=\dfrac{1\left(4-\sqrt{3}\right)}{4^2-\left(\sqrt{3}\right)^2}$

$=\dfrac{4-\sqrt{3}}{16-3}$

$=\dfrac{4-\sqrt{3}}{13}$

55. $\dfrac{9}{2-\sqrt{7}}=\dfrac{9}{2-\sqrt{7}}\cdot\dfrac{2+\sqrt{7}}{2+\sqrt{7}}$

$=\dfrac{9\left(2+\sqrt{7}\right)}{2^2-\left(\sqrt{7}\right)^2}=\dfrac{9\left(2+\sqrt{7}\right)}{4-7}$

$=\dfrac{9\left(2+\sqrt{7}\right)}{-3}$

$=-3\left(2+\sqrt{7}\right)$

$-6-3\sqrt{7}$

57. $\dfrac{16}{\sqrt{11}+3}=\dfrac{16}{\sqrt{11}+3}\cdot\dfrac{\sqrt{11}-3}{\sqrt{11}-3}$

$=\dfrac{16\left(\sqrt{11}-3\right)}{\left(\sqrt{11}\right)^2-3^2}=\dfrac{16\left(\sqrt{11}-3\right)}{11-9}$

$=\dfrac{16\left(\sqrt{11}-3\right)}{2}$

$=8\left(\sqrt{11}-3\right)$

$-8\sqrt{11}-24$

59. $\dfrac{18}{3-\sqrt{3}}=\dfrac{18}{3-\sqrt{3}}\cdot\dfrac{3+\sqrt{3}}{3+\sqrt{3}}$

$=\dfrac{18\left(3+\sqrt{3}\right)}{3^2-\left(\sqrt{3}\right)^2}=\dfrac{18\left(3+\sqrt{3}\right)}{9-3}$

$=\dfrac{18\left(3+\sqrt{3}\right)}{6}$

$=3\left(3+\sqrt{3}\right)$

$=9+3\sqrt{3}$

61. $\dfrac{\sqrt{2}}{\sqrt{2}+1}=\dfrac{\sqrt{2}}{\sqrt{2}+1}\cdot\dfrac{\sqrt{2}-1}{\sqrt{2}-1}$

$=\dfrac{\sqrt{2}\left(\sqrt{2}-1\right)}{\left(\sqrt{2}\right)^2-1^2}=\dfrac{\sqrt{2}\left(\sqrt{2}-1\right)}{2-1}$

$=\dfrac{\sqrt{2}\left(\sqrt{2}-1\right)}{1}$

$=2-\sqrt{2}$

63.
$$\frac{\sqrt{10}}{\sqrt{10}-\sqrt{7}}=\frac{\sqrt{10}}{\sqrt{10}-\sqrt{7}}\cdot\frac{\sqrt{10}+\sqrt{7}}{\sqrt{10}+\sqrt{7}}$$
$$=\frac{\sqrt{10}\left(\sqrt{10}+\sqrt{7}\right)}{\left(\sqrt{10}\right)^2-\left(\sqrt{7}\right)^2}$$
$$=\frac{\sqrt{10}\left(\sqrt{10}+\sqrt{7}\right)}{10-7}$$
$$=\frac{\sqrt{10}\left(\sqrt{10}+\sqrt{7}\right)}{3}$$
$$=\frac{10+\sqrt{70}}{3}$$

65.
$$\frac{6}{\sqrt{6}+\sqrt{3}}=\frac{6}{\sqrt{6}+\sqrt{3}}\cdot\frac{\sqrt{6}-\sqrt{3}}{\sqrt{6}-\sqrt{3}}$$
$$=\frac{6\left(\sqrt{6}-\sqrt{3}\right)}{\left(\sqrt{6}\right)^2-\left(\sqrt{3}\right)^2}$$
$$=\frac{6\left(\sqrt{6}-\sqrt{3}\right)}{6-3}$$
$$=\frac{6\left(\sqrt{6}-\sqrt{3}\right)}{3}$$
$$=2\left(\sqrt{6}-\sqrt{3}\right)$$
$$=2\sqrt{6}-2\sqrt{3}$$

67.
$$\frac{2}{\sqrt{5}-\sqrt{3}}=\frac{2}{\sqrt{5}-\sqrt{3}}\cdot\frac{\sqrt{5}+\sqrt{3}}{\sqrt{5}+\sqrt{3}}$$
$$=\frac{2\left(\sqrt{5}+\sqrt{3}\right)}{\left(\sqrt{5}\right)^2-\left(\sqrt{3}\right)^2}$$
$$=\frac{2\left(\sqrt{5}+\sqrt{3}\right)}{5-3}$$
$$=\frac{2\left(\sqrt{5}+\sqrt{3}\right)}{2}$$
$$=\sqrt{5}+\sqrt{3}$$

69.
$$\frac{2}{4+\sqrt{x}}=\frac{2}{4+\sqrt{x}}\cdot\frac{4-\sqrt{x}}{4-\sqrt{x}}$$
$$=\frac{2\left(4-\sqrt{x}\right)}{4^2-\left(\sqrt{x}\right)^2}=\frac{2\left(4-\sqrt{x}\right)}{16-x}$$
$$=\frac{8-2\sqrt{x}}{16-x}$$

71.
$$\frac{2\sqrt{3}}{\sqrt{15}+2}=\frac{2\sqrt{3}}{\sqrt{15}+2}\cdot\frac{\sqrt{15}-2}{\sqrt{15}-2}$$
$$=\frac{2\sqrt{3}\left(\sqrt{15}-2\right)}{\left(\sqrt{15}\right)^2-2^2}$$
$$=\frac{2\sqrt{3}\left(\sqrt{15}-2\right)}{15-4}$$
$$=\frac{2\sqrt{3}\left(\sqrt{15}-2\right)}{11}$$
$$=\frac{2\sqrt{45}-4\sqrt{3}}{11}$$
$$=\frac{2\sqrt{9}\sqrt{5}-4\sqrt{3}}{11}$$
$$=\frac{2\cdot 3\sqrt{5}-4\sqrt{3}}{11}$$
$$=\frac{6\sqrt{5}-4\sqrt{3}}{11}$$

73. $$\frac{\sqrt{5}+\sqrt{2}}{\sqrt{5}-\sqrt{2}}=\frac{\sqrt{5}+\sqrt{2}}{\sqrt{5}-\sqrt{2}}\cdot\frac{\sqrt{5}+\sqrt{2}}{\sqrt{5}+\sqrt{2}}$$
$$=\frac{\left(\sqrt{5}+\sqrt{2}\right)^2}{\left(\sqrt{5}\right)^2-\left(\sqrt{2}\right)^2}$$
$$=\frac{\left(\sqrt{5}\right)^2+2\sqrt{5}\sqrt{2}+\left(\sqrt{2}\right)^2}{\left(\sqrt{5}\right)^2-\left(\sqrt{2}\right)^2}$$
$$=\frac{5+2\sqrt{10}+2}{5-2}$$
$$=\frac{7+2\sqrt{10}}{3}$$

75. $$\frac{\sqrt{36x^2y^5}}{\sqrt{2x^3y}}=\sqrt{\frac{36x^2y^5}{2x^3y}}=\sqrt{\frac{18y^4}{x}}$$
$$=\frac{\sqrt{9y^4}\sqrt{2}}{\sqrt{x}}=\frac{3y^2\sqrt{2}}{\sqrt{x}}$$
$$=\frac{3y^2\sqrt{2}}{\sqrt{x}}\cdot\frac{\sqrt{x}}{\sqrt{x}}=\frac{3y^2\sqrt{2x}}{x}$$

76. $$\frac{\sqrt{100x^5y^2}}{\sqrt{2xy^3}}=\sqrt{\frac{100x^5y^2}{2xy^3}}=\sqrt{\frac{50x^4}{y}}$$
$$=\frac{\sqrt{25x^4}\sqrt{2}}{\sqrt{y}}=\frac{5x^2\sqrt{2}}{\sqrt{y}}$$
$$=\frac{5x^2\sqrt{2}}{\sqrt{y}}\cdot\frac{\sqrt{y}}{\sqrt{y}}=\frac{5x^2\sqrt{2y}}{y}$$

77. $$\frac{2}{\sqrt{x+2}-\sqrt{x}}$$
$$=\frac{2}{\sqrt{x+2}-\sqrt{x}}\cdot\frac{\sqrt{x+2}+\sqrt{x}}{\sqrt{x+2}+\sqrt{x}}$$
$$=\frac{2\left(\sqrt{x+2}+\sqrt{x}\right)}{\left(\sqrt{x+2}\right)^2-\left(\sqrt{x}\right)^2}$$
$$=\frac{2\left(\sqrt{x+2}+\sqrt{x}\right)}{x+2-x}$$
$$=\frac{2\left(\sqrt{x+2}+\sqrt{x}\right)}{2}$$
$$=\sqrt{x+2}+\sqrt{x}$$

78. $$\frac{3}{\sqrt{x+3}-\sqrt{x}}$$
$$=\frac{3}{\sqrt{x+3}-\sqrt{x}}\cdot\frac{\sqrt{x+3}+\sqrt{x}}{\sqrt{x+3}+\sqrt{x}}$$
$$=\frac{3\left(\sqrt{x+3}+\sqrt{x}\right)}{\left(\sqrt{x+3}\right)^2-\left(\sqrt{x}\right)^2}$$
$$=\frac{3\left(\sqrt{x+3}+\sqrt{x}\right)}{x+3-x}$$
$$=\frac{3\left(\sqrt{x+3}+\sqrt{x}\right)}{3}$$
$$=\sqrt{x+3}+\sqrt{x}$$

79. $$\frac{\sqrt{2}}{\sqrt{3}}+\frac{\sqrt{3}}{\sqrt{2}}=\frac{\sqrt{2}}{\sqrt{3}}\cdot\frac{\sqrt{3}}{\sqrt{3}}+\frac{\sqrt{3}}{\sqrt{2}}\cdot\frac{\sqrt{2}}{\sqrt{2}}$$
$$=\frac{\sqrt{6}}{3}+\frac{\sqrt{6}}{2}=\frac{2\sqrt{6}}{6}+\frac{3\sqrt{6}}{6}$$
$$=\frac{5\sqrt{6}}{6}$$

80. $\frac{\sqrt{2}}{\sqrt{7}}+\frac{\sqrt{7}}{\sqrt{2}}=\frac{\sqrt{2}}{\sqrt{7}}\cdot\frac{\sqrt{7}}{\sqrt{7}}+\frac{\sqrt{7}}{\sqrt{2}}\cdot\frac{\sqrt{2}}{\sqrt{2}}$

$$=\frac{\sqrt{14}}{7}+\frac{\sqrt{14}}{2}$$
$$=\frac{2\sqrt{14}}{14}+\frac{7\sqrt{14}}{14}$$
$$=\frac{9\sqrt{14}}{14}$$

81. $\frac{2x+4-2h}{\sqrt{x+2-h}}$

$$=\frac{2(x+2-h)}{\sqrt{x+2-h}}\cdot\frac{\sqrt{x+2-h}}{\sqrt{x+2-h}}$$
$$=\frac{2(x+2-h)\sqrt{x+2-h}}{x+2-h}$$
$$=2\sqrt{x+2-h}$$

82. $\frac{4x+12-4h}{\sqrt{x+3-h}}$

$$=\frac{4(x+3-h)}{\sqrt{x+3-h}}\cdot\frac{\sqrt{x+3-h}}{\sqrt{x+3-h}}$$
$$=\frac{4(x+3-h)\sqrt{x+3-h}}{x+3-h}$$
$$=4\sqrt{x+3-h}$$

83. **a.** $P=\frac{x(13+\sqrt{x})}{5\sqrt{x}};x=25$

$$P=\frac{25(13+\sqrt{25})}{5\sqrt{25}}$$
$$=\frac{25+(13+5)}{5\cdot 5}$$
$$=\frac{25\cdot 18}{25}=18$$

According to the formula, 18% of 25-year-olds must pay more taxes.

b. $\frac{x(13+\sqrt{x})}{5\sqrt{x}}\cdot\frac{\sqrt{x}}{\sqrt{x}}$

$$=\frac{x\sqrt{x}(13+\sqrt{x})}{5\sqrt{x}\sqrt{x}}$$
$$=\frac{x\sqrt{x}\cdot 13+x\sqrt{x}\sqrt{x}}{5\sqrt{x}\sqrt{x}}$$
$$=\frac{13x\sqrt{x}+x\cdot x}{5x}$$
$$=\frac{x(13\sqrt{x}+x)}{5x}$$
$$=\frac{13\sqrt{x}+x}{5}$$

c. $\frac{13\sqrt{25}+25}{5}=\frac{13(5)+25}{5}=18$

According to the formula, 18% of 25-year-olds must pay more taxes. This is the same result as in part (a).

85. $\frac{w}{h}=\frac{2}{\sqrt{5}-1}$

$$=\frac{2}{\sqrt{5}-1}\cdot\frac{\sqrt{5}+1}{\sqrt{5}+1}$$
$$=\frac{2(\sqrt{5}+1)}{5-1}$$
$$=\frac{\sqrt{5}+1}{2}\approx 1.62$$

87. The value stays the same because we simply multiply by 1. To rationalize the denominator, we multiply the original expression by something like $\frac{\sqrt{2}}{\sqrt{2}}$ or $\frac{\sqrt{5}+1}{\sqrt{5}+1}$ which is equivalent to 1 (but in a different form).

89. $P = \dfrac{x\left(13+\sqrt{x}\right)}{5\sqrt{x}}$

$x = 30:$

$$P = \frac{30\left(13+\sqrt{30}\right)}{5\sqrt{30}} \approx 20$$

$x = 40:$

$$P = \frac{40\left(13+\sqrt{40}\right)}{5\sqrt{40}} \approx 24$$

$x = 50:$

$$P = \frac{50\left(13+\sqrt{50}\right)}{5\sqrt{50}} \approx 28$$

These results show that about 20% of 30-year-old taxpayers, 24% of 40-year-old taxpayers, and 28% of 50-year old taxpayers must pay more taxes. The trend is for an increasing percentage of taxpayers to pay more taxes as the taxpayers get older. Explanations may vary.

91. $\dfrac{1}{\sqrt[3]{2}}$

Because the denominator is a cube root rather than a square root, multiply numerator and denominator by a radical that will make the radicand a perfect cube rather than a perfect square. Since 8 is a perfect cube, multiply numerator and denominator by $\sqrt[3]{4}$.

$$\frac{1}{\sqrt[3]{2}} \cdot \frac{\sqrt[3]{4}}{\sqrt[3]{4}} = \frac{\sqrt[3]{4}}{\sqrt[3]{8}} = \frac{\sqrt[3]{4}}{2}$$

93. $\sqrt{13+\sqrt{2}+\dfrac{7}{3+\sqrt{2}}}$

$$= \sqrt{13+\sqrt{2}+\frac{7}{3+\sqrt{2}} \cdot \frac{3-\sqrt{2}}{3-\sqrt{2}}}$$

$$= \sqrt{13+\sqrt{2}+\frac{7\left(3-\sqrt{2}\right)}{3^2-\left(\sqrt{2}\right)^2}}$$

$$= \sqrt{13+\sqrt{2}+\frac{7\left(3-\sqrt{2}\right)}{9-2}}$$

$$= \sqrt{13+\sqrt{2}+\frac{7\left(3-\sqrt{2}\right)}{7}}$$

$$= \sqrt{13+\sqrt{2}+3-\sqrt{2}}$$

$$= \sqrt{16} = 4$$

95. $2x-1 = x^2-4x+4$

$$0 = x^2-6x+5$$

$$0 = (x-5)(x-1)$$

$x-5=0$ or $x-1=0$

$x=5$ $\quad$ $x=1$

The solutions are 5 and 1.

96. $\left(2x^2\right)^{-3} = \dfrac{1}{\left(2x^2\right)^3} = \dfrac{1}{2^3\left(x^2\right)^3} = \dfrac{1}{8x^6}$

97. $\dfrac{x^2-6x+9}{12} \cdot \dfrac{3}{x^2-9}$

$$= \frac{(x-3)(x-3)}{12} \cdot \frac{3}{(x+3)(x-3)}$$

$$= \frac{x-3}{4(x+3)}$$

9.5 Exercise Set

In Exercises 1-43, it is *essential* to check all proposed solutions in the original equation in order to eliminate extraneous solutions.

1.
$$\sqrt{x} = 5$$
$$\left(\sqrt{x}\right)^2 = 5^2$$
$$x = 25$$
Check:
$$\sqrt{x} = 5$$
$$\sqrt{25} = 5$$
$$5 = 5 \text{ true}$$
The solution is 5.

3.
$$\sqrt{x} - 4 = 0$$
$$\sqrt{x} = 4$$
$$\left(\sqrt{x}\right)^2 = 4^2$$
$$x = 16$$
Check:
$$\sqrt{x} - 4 = 0$$
$$\sqrt{16} - 4 = 0$$
$$4 - 4 = 0$$
$$0 = 0 \text{ true}$$
The solution is 16.

5.
$$\sqrt{x+2} = 3$$
$$\left(\sqrt{x+2}\right)^2 = 3^2$$
$$x + 2 = 9$$
$$x = 7$$

Substitute 7 for x in the original equation to verify that the solution is 7.

7.
$$\sqrt{x-3} - 11 = 0$$
$$\sqrt{x-3} = 11$$
$$\left(\sqrt{x-3}\right)^2 = 11^2$$
$$x - 3 = 121$$
$$x = 124$$
Substitute 124 for x in the original equation to verify that the solution is 124.

9.
$$\sqrt{3x-5} = 4$$
$$\left(\sqrt{3x-5}\right)^2 = 4^2$$
$$3x - 5 = 16$$
$$3x = 21$$
$$x = 7$$
Substitute 7 for x in the original equation to verify that 7 is the solution.

11.
$$\sqrt{x+5} + 2 = 5$$
$$\sqrt{x+5} = 3$$
$$\left(\sqrt{x+5}\right)^2 = 3^2$$
$$x + 5 = 9$$
$$x = 4$$
Substitute 4 for x in the original equation to verify that the solution is 4.

13.
$$\sqrt{x+3} = \sqrt{4x-3}$$
$$\left(\sqrt{x+3}\right)^2 = \left(\sqrt{4x-3}\right)^2$$
$$x + 3 = 4x - 3$$
$$-3x + 3 = -3$$
$$-3x = -6$$
$$x = 2$$
Substitute 2 for x in the original equation to verify that the solution is 2.

15. $\sqrt{6x-2} = \sqrt{4x+4}$

$\left(\sqrt{6x-2}\right)^2 = \left(\sqrt{4x+4}\right)$

$6x-2 = 4x+4$

$2x-2 = 4$

$2x = 6$

$x = 3$

Substitute 3 for x in the original equation to verify that the solution is 3.

17. $11 = 6+\sqrt{x+1}$

$5 = \sqrt{x+1}$

$5^2 = \left(\sqrt{x+1}\right)^2$

$25 = x+1$

$24 = x$

Substitute 24 for x in the original equation to verify that the solution is 24.

19. $\sqrt{x}+10 = 0$

$\sqrt{x} = -10$

$\left(\sqrt{x}\right)^2 = (-10)^2$

$x = 100$

Check 100:

$\sqrt{x}+10 = 0$

$\sqrt{100}+10 = 0$

$10+10 = 0$

$20 = 0$ false

This false statement indicates that 100 is not a solution. Since the only proposed solution is extraneous, the given equation has no solution.

21. $\sqrt{x-1} = -3$

$\left(\sqrt{x-1}\right)^2 = (-3)^2$

$x-1 = 9$

$x = 10$

Check 10:

$\sqrt{x-1} = -3$

$\sqrt{10-1} = -3$

$\sqrt{9} = -3$

$3 = -3$ false

The false statement shows that 10 is an extraneous solution. Since it is the only proposed solution, the given equation has no solution.

23. $3\sqrt{x} = \sqrt{8x+16}$

$\left(3\sqrt{x}\right)^2 = \left(\sqrt{8x+16}\right)^2$

$9x = 8x+16$

$x = 16$

Check 16:

$3\sqrt{x} = \sqrt{8x+16}$

$3\sqrt{16} = \sqrt{8\cdot16+16}$

$3\cdot4 = \sqrt{128+16}$

$12 = \sqrt{144}$

$12 = 12$ true

The solution is 16.

25. $\sqrt{2x-3}+5 = 0$

$\sqrt{2x-3} = -5$

$\left(\sqrt{2x-3}\right)^2 = (-5)^2$

$2x-3 = 25$

$2x = 28$

$x = 14$

Check 14:

$$\sqrt{2x-3}+5=0$$
$$\sqrt{2\cdot 14-3}+5=0$$
$$\sqrt{28-3}+5=0$$
$$\sqrt{25}+5=0$$
$$5+5=0$$
$$10=0 \text{ false}$$

The false statement shows that 14 is an extraneous solution, so the given equation has no solution.

27. $$\sqrt{3x+4}-2=3$$
$$\sqrt{3x+4}=5$$
$$\left(\sqrt{3x+4}\right)^2=5^2$$
$$3x+4=25$$
$$3x=21$$
$$x=7$$

Substitute 7 for x in the original equation to verify that the solution is 7.

29. $$3\sqrt{x-1}=\sqrt{3x+3}$$
$$\left(3\sqrt{x-1}\right)^2=\left(\sqrt{3x+3}\right)^2$$
$$9(x-1)=3x+3$$
$$9x-9=3x+3$$
$$6x=12$$
$$x=2$$

Substitute 2 for x in the original equation to verify that the solution is 2.

31. $$\sqrt{x+7}=x+5$$

Square both sides,

$$\left(\sqrt{x+7}\right)^2=(x+5)^2$$

Square the binomial on the right.

$$x+7=x^2+10x+25$$

Simplify and solve this quadratic equation.

$$0=x^2+9x+18$$
$$0=(x+3)(x+6)$$
$$x+3=0 \quad \text{or} \quad x+6=0$$
$$x=-3 \qquad\qquad x=-6$$

There are two proposed solutions. Each must checked separately in the original equation.

Check –3:

$$\sqrt{x+7}=x+5$$
$$\sqrt{-3+7}=-3+5$$
$$\sqrt{4}=2$$
$$2=2 \text{ true}$$

Check –6:

$$\sqrt{x+7}=x+5$$
$$\sqrt{-6+7}=-6+5$$
$$\sqrt{1}=-1$$
$$1=-1 \text{ false}$$

Thus –6 is an extraneous solution, while –3 satisfies the equation. The only solution is –3.

33. $$\sqrt{2x+13}=x+7$$
$$\left(\sqrt{2x+13}\right)^2=(x+7)^2$$
$$2x+13=x^2+14x+49$$
$$0=x^2+12x+36$$
$$0=(x+6)^2$$
$$0=x+6$$
$$-6=x$$

Check –6:

$$\sqrt{2x+13}=x+7$$
$$\sqrt{2(-6)+13}=-6+7$$
$$\sqrt{-12+13}=1$$
$$\sqrt{1}=1$$
$$1=1 \text{ true}$$

The solution is –6.

35.
$$\sqrt{9x^2+2x-4}=3x$$
$$\left(\sqrt{9x^2+2x-4}\right)=(3x)^2$$
$$9x^2+2x-4=9x^2$$
$$2x-4=0$$
$$2x=4$$
$$x=2$$
Substitute 2 for x in the original equation to verify that the solution is 2.

37.
$$x=\sqrt{2x-2}+1$$
$$x-1=\sqrt{2x-2}$$
$$(x-1)^2=\left(\sqrt{2x-2}\right)^2$$
$$x^2+2x+1=2x-2$$
$$x^2-4x+3=0$$
$$(x-1)(x-3)=0$$
$$x-1=0 \text{ or } x-3=0$$
$$x=1 \qquad x=3$$

Check 1:
$$x=\sqrt{2x-2}+1$$
$$1=\sqrt{2\cdot 1-2}+1$$
$$1=\sqrt{2-2}+1$$
$$1=0+1$$
$$1=1 \text{ true}$$

Check 3:
$$x=\sqrt{2x-2}+1$$
$$3=\sqrt{2\cdot 3-2}+1$$
$$3=\sqrt{6-2}+1$$
$$3=\sqrt{4}+1$$
$$3=2+1$$
$$3=3 \text{ true}$$

Both proposed solutions, 1 and 3, satisfy the original equation, so the equation has two solutions, 1 and 3.

39.
$$x=\sqrt{8-7x}+2$$
$$x-2=\sqrt{8-7x}$$
$$(x-2)^2=\left(\sqrt{8-7x}\right)^2$$
$$x^2-4x+4=8-7x$$
$$x^2+3x-4=0$$
$$(x+4)(x-1)=0$$
$$x+4=0 \text{ or } x-1=0$$
$$x=-4 \qquad x=1$$
Check –4:
$$x=\sqrt{8-7x}+2$$
$$-4=\sqrt{8-7\cdot 1}+2$$
$$-4=\sqrt{8-7}+2$$
$$-4=\sqrt{1}+2$$
$$-4=1+2$$
$$-4=3 \text{ false}$$
Both of the proposed solutions, –4 and 1, are extraneous so the given equation has no solution.

41.
$$\sqrt{3x}+10=x+4$$
$$\sqrt{3x}=x-6$$
$$\left(\sqrt{3x}\right)^2=(x-6)^2$$
$$3x=x^2-12x+36$$
$$0=x^2-15x+36$$
$$0=(x-3)(x-12)$$
$$x-3=0 \text{ or } x-12=0$$
$$x=3 \qquad x=12$$
Check 3:
$$\sqrt{3x}+10=x+4$$
$$\sqrt{3\cdot 3}+10=3+4$$
$$\sqrt{9}+10=7$$
$$3-10=7$$
$$13=7 \text{ false}$$

Check 12:

$$\sqrt{3x}+10=x+4$$
$$\sqrt{3\cdot12}+10=12+4$$
$$\sqrt{36}+10=16$$
$$6+10=16$$
$$16=16 \text{ true}$$

The proposed solution 3 is extraneous, while 12 satisfies the equation. Therefore, the solution is 12.

43. $$3\sqrt{x}+5=2$$
$$3\sqrt{x}=-3$$
$$\left(3\sqrt{x}\right)^2=(-3)^2$$
$$9x=9$$
$$x=1$$

Check 1:

$$3\sqrt{x}+5=2$$
$$3\sqrt{1}+5=2$$
$$3\cdot1+5=2$$
$$3+5=2$$
$$8=2 \text{ false}$$

The proposed solution 1 is extraneous, so the equation has no solution.

45. Let x = the number.

$$2+\sqrt{4x}=10$$
$$\sqrt{4x}=8$$
$$\left(\sqrt{4x}\right)^2=8^2$$
$$4x=64$$
$$x=16$$

Check 16:

$$2+\sqrt{4(16)}=10$$
$$2+\sqrt{64}=10$$
$$2+8=10$$
$$10=10 \text{ true}$$

The number is 16.

46. Let x = the number.

$$5+\sqrt{6x}=8$$
$$\sqrt{6x}=3$$
$$\left(\sqrt{6x}\right)^2=3^2$$
$$6x=9$$
$$x=\frac{3}{2}$$

Check $\frac{3}{2}$: $5+\sqrt{6\left(\frac{3}{2}\right)}=8$

$$5+\sqrt{9}=8$$
$$5+3=8$$
$$8=8 \text{ true}$$

The number is $\frac{3}{2}$.

47. Let x = the number.

$$x=4+\sqrt{2x}$$
$$x-4=\sqrt{2x}$$
$$(x-4)^2=\left(\sqrt{2x}\right)^2$$
$$x^2-8x+16=2x$$
$$x^2-10x+16=0$$
$$(x-8)(x-2)=0$$
$$x-8=0 \quad\text{or}\quad x-2=0$$
$$x=8 \qquad\qquad x=2$$

Check 8: $8=4+\sqrt{2(8)}$

$$8=4+\sqrt{16}$$
$$8=4+4$$
$$8=8 \text{ true}$$

Check 2: $2=4+\sqrt{2(2)}$

$$2=4+\sqrt{4}$$
$$2=4+2$$
$$2=6 \text{ false}$$

Discard 2. The solution is 8.

48. Let x = the number.

$$x = 6 + \sqrt{3x}$$
$$x - 6 = \sqrt{3x}$$
$$(x-6)^2 = \left(\sqrt{3x}\right)^2$$
$$x^2 - 12x + 36 = 3x$$
$$x^2 - 15x + 36 = 0$$
$$(x-12)(x-3) = 0$$
$$x - 12 = 0 \quad \text{or} \quad x - 3 = 0$$
$$x = 12 \qquad\qquad x = 3$$

Check 12: $12 = 6 + \sqrt{3(12)}$
$$12 = 6 + \sqrt{36}$$
$$12 = 6 + 6$$
$$12 = 12 \text{ true}$$

Check 3: $3 = 6 + \sqrt{3(3)}$
$$3 = 6 + \sqrt{9}$$
$$3 = 6 + 3$$
$$3 = 9 \text{ false}$$

Discard 3. The solution is 12.

49.
$$v = \sqrt{2gh}$$
$$v^2 = \left(\sqrt{2gh}\right)^2$$
$$v^2 = 2gh$$
$$\frac{v^2}{2g} = \frac{2gh}{2g}$$
$$\frac{v^2}{2g} = h$$

50.
$$t = \frac{\pi}{2}\sqrt{\frac{l}{2}}$$
$$\frac{2t}{\pi} = \sqrt{\frac{l}{2}}$$
$$\left(\frac{2t}{\pi}\right)^2 = \frac{l}{2}$$
$$2 \cdot \frac{4t^2}{\pi^2} = l$$
$$\frac{8t^2}{\pi^2} = l$$

51.
$$\sqrt{x} + 2 = \sqrt{x+8}$$
$$\left(\sqrt{x}+2\right)^2 = \left(\sqrt{x+8}\right)^2$$
$$\left(\sqrt{x}\right)^2 + 2(2)\left(\sqrt{x}\right) + 2^2 = x + 8$$
$$x + 4\sqrt{x} + 4 = x + 8$$
$$4\sqrt{x} = 4$$
$$\sqrt{x} = 1$$
$$\left(\sqrt{x}\right)^2 = 1^2$$
$$x = 1$$

Check: $\sqrt{1} + 2 = \sqrt{1+8}$
$$1 + 2 = \sqrt{9}$$
$$3 = 3 \text{ true}$$

The solution is 1.

52.
$$\sqrt{x}+6=\sqrt{x+72}$$
$$\left(\sqrt{x}+6\right)^2=\left(\sqrt{x+72}\right)^2$$
$$\left(\sqrt{x}\right)^2+2\left(\sqrt{x}\right)(6)+6^2=x+72$$
$$x+12\sqrt{x}+36=x+72$$
$$12\sqrt{x}=36$$
$$\sqrt{x}=3$$
$$\left(\sqrt{x}\right)^2=3^2$$
$$x=9$$

Check: $\sqrt{9}+6=\sqrt{9+72}$
$$3+6=\sqrt{81}$$
$$9=9 \text{ true}$$

The solution is 9.

53.
$$\sqrt{x-8}=\sqrt{x}-2$$
$$\left(\sqrt{x-8}\right)^2=\left(\sqrt{x}-2\right)^2$$
$$x-8=\left(\sqrt{x}\right)^2-2\left(\sqrt{x}\right)(2)+2^2$$
$$x-8=x-4\sqrt{x}+4$$
$$4\sqrt{x}=12$$
$$\sqrt{x}=3$$
$$\left(\sqrt{x}\right)^2=3^2$$
$$x=9$$

Check: $\sqrt{9-8}=\sqrt{9}-2$
$$\sqrt{1}=3-2$$
$$1=1 \text{ true}$$

The solution is 9.

54.
$$\sqrt{x-4}=\sqrt{x}-2$$
$$\left(\sqrt{x-4}\right)^2=\left(\sqrt{x}-2\right)^2$$
$$x-4=\left(\sqrt{x}\right)^2-2\left(\sqrt{x}\right)(2)+2^2$$
$$x-4=x-4\sqrt{x}+4$$
$$4\sqrt{x}=8$$
$$\sqrt{x}=2$$
$$\left(\sqrt{x}\right)^2=2^2$$
$$x=4$$

Check: $\sqrt{4-4}=\sqrt{4}-2$
$$\sqrt{0}=2-2$$
$$0=0 \text{ true}$$

The solution is 4.

55. **a.** For 1995 we have $x=4$.
$$y=3.2\sqrt{x}+11$$
$$=3.2\sqrt{4}+11$$
$$=3.2(2)+11$$
$$=17.4$$
According to the model, 17.4% of U.S. adults were obese in 1995. Explanations will vary.

b. Here we let $y=25$ and solve for x.
$$25=3.2\sqrt{x}+11$$
$$14=3.2\sqrt{x}$$
$$4.375=\sqrt{x}$$
$$(4.375)^2=\left(\sqrt{x}\right)^2$$
$$x\approx 19$$
According to the model, 25% of U.S. adults will be obese in $1991+19=2010$.

57. $N = 5000\sqrt{100-x}; N = 25,000$

$$25,000 = 5000\sqrt{100-x}$$
$$5 = \sqrt{100-x}$$
$$5^2 = \left(\sqrt{100-x}\right)^2$$
$$25 = 100 - x$$
$$-75 = -x$$
$$75 = x$$

According to the formula, 25,000 people in the group will survive to 75 years old.

59. $d = 3.5\sqrt{h}; d = 200$

$$200 = 3.5\sqrt{h}$$
$$\frac{200}{3.5} = \sqrt{h}$$
$$\left(\frac{200}{3.5}\right)^2 = h$$
$$h \approx 3265$$

After losing altitude, the plane's altitude is about 3265 meters or 3.265 kilometers. Because the plane was flying at an altitude of 8 kilometers and dropped to an altitude of about 3 kilometers, it lost about 5 kilometers in altitude.

61. $R = \sqrt{A^2 + B^2}; R = 500, A = 300$

$$500 = \sqrt{300^2 + B^2}$$
$$500 = \sqrt{90,000 + B^2}$$
$$500^2 = \left(\sqrt{90,000 + B^2}\right)^2$$
$$250,000 = 90,000 + B^2$$
$$160,000 = B^2$$
$$0 = B^2 - 160,000$$
$$0 = (B + 400)(B - 400)$$

$B + 400 = 0$ or $B - 400 = 0$

$B = -400$ $\quad$ $B = 400$

Although both proposed solutions satisfy the given equation, reject −400 because the size of a force cannot be negative. Tractor B is exerting a force of 400 pounds.

63. Answers will vary. Isolating the radical is a good idea so that we can square both sides to eliminate the radical. If we square both sides without isolating the radical, we will still have a radical in the equation.

65. $\sqrt{x} = -1$ has no real solution because the principal square root is never negative in the real number system.

67. Statement b is true.
This can be seen simply by looking at the equation because the square root of a real number can never be negative.

69. $y = \sqrt{x-2} + 2$

$z = \sqrt{y-2} + 2$

$w = \sqrt{z-2} + 2$

$w = 2$

Substitute 2 for w in the third equation and solve for z.

$2 = \sqrt{z-2} + 2$

$0 = \sqrt{z-2}$

$0^2 = \left(\sqrt{z-2}\right)^2$

$0 = z - 2$

$z = 2$

Now substitute 2 for z in the second equation.

$2 = \sqrt{y-2} + 2$

This is the same as the equation $2 = \sqrt{z-2} + 2$ with just the variable changes, so from the previous work we know that $y = 2$. Similarly, substituting 2 for y in the first equation gives

$2 = \sqrt{x-2} + 2$

which leads to $x = 2$.

Thus, $x = 2$, $y = 2$, and $z = 2$.

71. $\sqrt{x} + 3 = 5$

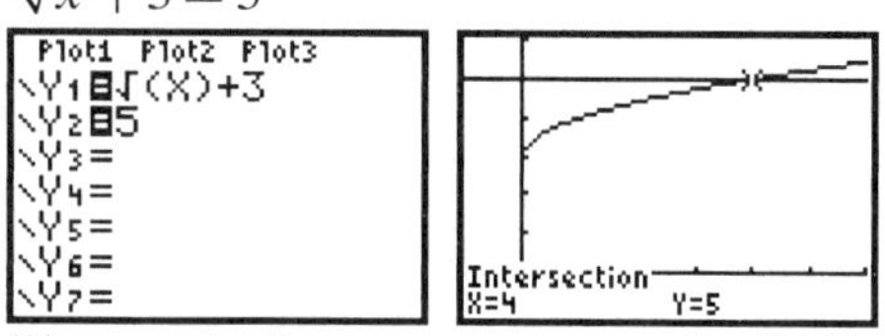

The graphs intersect at one point (4,5), so the x-intercept of the intersection point is 4. Therefore, the solution of the given equation is 4.

Check 4:

$\sqrt{x} + 3 = 5$

$\sqrt{4} + 3 = 5$

$2 + 3 = 5$

$5 = 5$ true

73. $4\sqrt{x} = x + 3$

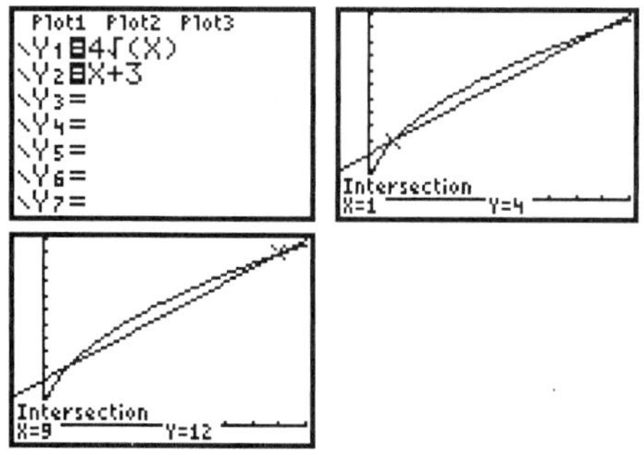

The graphs intersect at (1,4) and (9,12). Therefore, the x-intercepts of the intersection points (and the solutions of the equation) are 1 and 9.

Check 1:	Check 9:
$4\sqrt{1} = 1 + 3$	$4\sqrt{9} = 9 + 3$
$4 \cdot 1 = 1 + 3$	$4 \cdot 3 = 12$
$4 = 4$ true	$12 = 12$ true

75. Answers will vary depending on selected exercises. For example, #29:

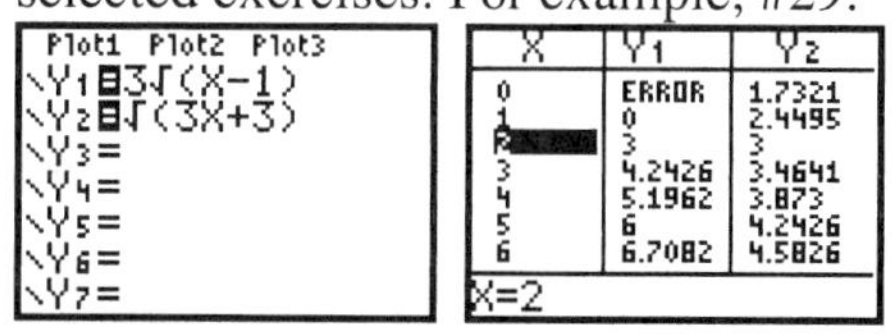

76. Let x = the amount invested at 6%. Then $9000 - x =$ the amount invested at 4%.

The investments earned a total of \$500 in interest, so

$0.06x + 0.04(9000 - x) = 500.$

Solve this equation.

$$0.06x + 360 - 0.04x = 500$$

$$0.02x + 360 = 500$$

$$0.02x = 140$$

$$\frac{0.02x}{0.02} = \frac{140}{0.02}$$

$$x = 7000$$

$$9000 - x = 2000$$

\$7000 was invested at 6% and \$2000 was invested at 4%.

77. Let x = the price of an orchestra seat. Then y = the price of a mezzanine seat.
The given information leads to the system
$$4x+2y=22$$
$$2x+3y=16$$
Because both equations are written in the form $Ax+By=C$, the addition method is a good choice for solving this system. Because the problem only asks for the price of an orchestra seat, it is only necessary to solve the system for x. To do this, it is necessary to eliminate y.
Multiply the first equation by 3 and the second equation by −2. Then add the results.
$$\begin{aligned} 12x+6y &= 66 \\ -4x-6y &= -32 \\ \hline 8x \quad &= 34 \end{aligned}$$
$$x=\frac{34}{8}=4.25$$
The price of an orchestra seat is \$4.25.

78. $2x+y=-4$
$x+y=-3$
Graph $2x+y=-4$ using its x-intercept -2 and its y-intercept −4.
Graph $x+y=-3$ using its x-intercept −3 and y-intercept −3.

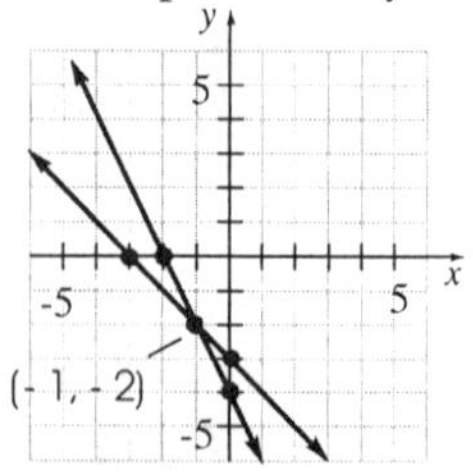

The two lines intersect at the point $(-1,-2)$ so the solution of the system is $(-1,-2)$

9.6 Exercise Set

1. $49^{\frac{1}{2}}=\sqrt{49}=7$

3. $121^{\frac{1}{2}}=\sqrt{121}=11$

5. $27^{\frac{1}{3}}=\sqrt[3]{27}=3$

7. $-125^{\frac{1}{3}}=-\left(\sqrt[3]{125}\right)=-5$

9. $16^{\frac{1}{4}}=\sqrt[4]{16}=2$

11. $-32^{\frac{1}{5}}=-\left(\sqrt[5]{32}\right)=-2$

13. $\left(\frac{1}{9}\right)^{\frac{1}{2}}=\sqrt{\frac{1}{9}}=\frac{1}{3}$

15. $\left(\frac{27}{64}\right)^{\frac{1}{3}}=\sqrt[3]{\frac{27}{64}}=\frac{\sqrt[3]{27}}{\sqrt[3]{64}}=\frac{3}{4}$

17. $81^{\frac{3}{2}}=\left(\sqrt{81}\right)^3=9^3=729$

19. $125^{\frac{2}{3}}=\left(\sqrt[3]{125}\right)^2=5^2=25$

21. $9^{\frac{3}{2}}=\left(\sqrt{9}\right)^3=3^3=27$

23. $(-32)^{\frac{3}{5}}=\left(\sqrt[5]{-32}\right)^3=(-2)^3=-8$

25. $9^{-\frac{1}{2}}=\frac{1}{9^{\frac{1}{2}}}=\frac{1}{\sqrt{9}}=\frac{1}{3}$

27. $125^{-\frac{1}{3}} = \dfrac{1}{125^{\frac{1}{3}}} = \dfrac{1}{\sqrt[3]{125}} = \dfrac{1}{5}$

29. $32^{-\frac{1}{5}} = \dfrac{1}{32^{\frac{1}{5}}} = \dfrac{1}{\sqrt[5]{32}} = \dfrac{1}{2}$

31. $\left(\dfrac{1}{4}\right)^{-\frac{1}{2}} = \dfrac{1}{\left(\frac{1}{4}\right)^{\frac{1}{2}}} = \dfrac{1}{\sqrt{\frac{1}{4}}} = \dfrac{1}{\frac{1}{2}} = 2$

33. $16^{-\frac{3}{4}} = \dfrac{1}{16^{\frac{3}{4}}} = \dfrac{1}{\left(\sqrt[4]{16}\right)^3} = \dfrac{1}{2^3} = \dfrac{1}{8}$

35. $81^{-\frac{5}{4}} = \dfrac{1}{81^{\frac{5}{4}}} = \dfrac{1}{\left(\sqrt[4]{81}\right)^5} = \dfrac{1}{3^5} = \dfrac{1}{243}$

37. $8^{-\frac{2}{3}} = \dfrac{1}{8^{\frac{2}{3}}} = \dfrac{1}{\left(\sqrt[3]{8}\right)^2} = \dfrac{1}{2^2} = \dfrac{1}{4}$

39. $\left(\dfrac{4}{25}\right)^{-\frac{1}{2}} = \dfrac{1}{\left(\frac{4}{25}\right)^{\frac{1}{2}}} = \dfrac{1}{\sqrt{\frac{4}{25}}} = \dfrac{1}{\frac{2}{5}} = \dfrac{5}{2}$

41. $\left(\dfrac{8}{125}\right)^{-\frac{1}{3}} = \dfrac{1}{\left(\frac{8}{125}\right)^{\frac{1}{3}}} = \dfrac{1}{\sqrt[3]{\frac{8}{125}}} = \dfrac{1}{\frac{2}{5}} = \dfrac{5}{2}$

43. $(-8)^{-\frac{2}{3}} = \dfrac{1}{(-8)^{\frac{2}{3}}} = \dfrac{1}{\left(\sqrt[3]{-8}\right)^2}$

$= \dfrac{1}{(-2)^2} = \dfrac{1}{4}$

45. $27^{\frac{2}{3}} + 16^{\frac{3}{4}} = \left(\sqrt[3]{27}\right)^2 + \left(\sqrt[4]{16}\right)^3$

$= 3^2 + 2^3 = 9 + 8 = 17$

47. $25^{\frac{3}{2}} \cdot 81^{\frac{1}{4}} = \left(\sqrt{25}\right)^3 \cdot \left(\sqrt[4]{81}\right)$

$= 5^3 \cdot 3 = 125 \cdot 3$

$= 375$

49. $x^{\frac{1}{3}} \cdot x^{\frac{1}{4}} = x^{\frac{1}{3}+\frac{1}{4}} = x^{\frac{4}{12}+\frac{3}{12}} = x^{\frac{7}{12}}$

50. $x^{\frac{1}{4}} \cdot x^{\frac{1}{5}} = x^{\frac{1}{4}+\frac{1}{5}} = x^{\frac{5}{20}+\frac{4}{20}} = x^{\frac{9}{20}}$

51. $\dfrac{x^{\frac{1}{6}}}{x^{\frac{5}{6}}} = x^{\frac{1}{6}-\frac{5}{6}} = x^{-\frac{4}{6}} = x^{-\frac{2}{3}} = \dfrac{1}{x^{\frac{2}{3}}}$

52. $\dfrac{x^{\frac{1}{4}}}{x^{\frac{3}{4}}} = x^{\frac{1}{4}-\frac{3}{4}} = x^{-\frac{2}{4}} = x^{-\frac{1}{2}} = \dfrac{1}{x^{\frac{1}{2}}}$

53. $\left(x^{1/4}y^3\right)^{2/3} = \left(x^{1/4}\right)^{2/3} \cdot \left(y^3\right)^{2/3}$

$= x^{\frac{1}{4}\cdot\frac{2}{3}} \cdot y^{3\cdot\frac{2}{3}}$

$= x^{\frac{1}{6}}y^2$

54. $\left(x^{1/6}y^{15}\right)^{3/5} = \left(x^{1/6}\right)^{3/5}\left(y^{15}\right)^{3/5}$

$= x^{\frac{1}{6}\cdot\frac{3}{5}}y^{15\cdot\frac{3}{5}}$

$= x^{\frac{1}{10}}y^9$

55.
$$\left(\frac{x^{2/5}}{x^{6/5}\cdot x^{3/5}}\right)^5=\frac{\left(x^{2/5}\right)^5}{\left(x^{6/5}\right)^5\cdot\left(x^{3/5}\right)^5}$$
$$=\frac{x^2}{x^6\cdot x^3}=\frac{x^2}{x^9}$$
$$=x^{2-9}=x^{-7}=\frac{1}{x^7}$$

56.
$$\left(\frac{x^{4/7}}{x^{3/7}\cdot x^{2/7}}\right)^{49}=\frac{\left(x^{4/7}\right)^{49}}{\left(x^{3/7}\right)^{49}\cdot\left(x^{2/7}\right)^{49}}$$
$$=\frac{x^{28}}{x^{21}\cdot x^{14}}=\frac{x^{28}}{x^{35}}$$
$$=x^{28-35}=x^{-7}=\frac{1}{x^7}$$

57.
$$v=\left(\frac{5r}{2}\right)^{\frac{1}{2}};r=250$$
$$v=\left(\frac{5\cdot 250}{2}\right)^{\frac{1}{2}}$$
$$=\left(\frac{1250}{2}\right)^{\frac{1}{2}}$$
$$=625^{\frac{1}{2}}$$
$$=\sqrt{625}=25$$
If the curve has a radius of 250 feet, the maximum velocity a car can travel without skidding is 25 miles per hour.

59.
$$P=\frac{73t^{\frac{1}{3}}-28t^{\frac{2}{3}}}{t};t=8\ (\text{for }1993)$$
$$P=\frac{73\cdot 8^{\frac{1}{3}}-28\cdot 8^{\frac{2}{3}}}{8}$$
$$=\frac{73\cdot 2-28\cdot 4}{8}$$
$$=\frac{34}{8}=4.25$$
According to the formula, about 4.25% of people applying for jobs in 2001 tested positive for illegal drugs.

61.
$$V=194.5t^{\frac{1}{6}}\qquad E=339.6t^{\frac{2}{3}}$$
$$V=194.5\sqrt[6]{t}\qquad E=339.6\left(\sqrt[3]{t}\right)^2$$

For Exercises 63–67, answers may vary.

63.
$a^{\frac{1}{n}}$ means the nth root of a. For example, $8^{\frac{1}{3}}=\sqrt[3]{8}=2$.

65.
$a^{-\frac{m}{n}}$ means to take the reciprocal of the nth root of a raised to the mth power. For example,
$$16^{-\frac{3}{4}}=\frac{1}{16^{\frac{3}{4}}}=\frac{1}{\left(\sqrt[4]{16}\right)^3}=\frac{1}{2^3}=\frac{1}{8}$$

67.
It would be better to use $a^{\frac{m}{n}}=\left(\sqrt[n]{a}\right)^m$ since it is easier to take the square root of 36.

69. Statement **a** is correct.

$$2^{\frac{1}{2}} \cdot 2^{\frac{2}{3}} = 2^{\frac{1}{2}+\frac{2}{3}} = 2^{\frac{4}{2}} = 2^2 = 4$$

$$\left(\frac{1}{4}\right)^{-1} = \frac{1}{\left(\frac{1}{4}\right)^1} = \frac{1}{\frac{1}{4}} = 1$$

Statement **b** is false.

$$8^{-1/2} = \frac{1}{8^{1/2}} = \frac{1}{\sqrt{8}} = \frac{1}{2\sqrt{2}} = \frac{\sqrt{2}}{4}$$

Statement **c** is false.

$$25^{-1/2} = \frac{1}{25^{1/2}} = \frac{1}{\sqrt{25}} = \frac{1}{5}$$

Statement **d** is false.

$$-3^{-2} = -\frac{1}{3^2} = -\frac{1}{9}$$

71.

$$25^{\frac{1}{4}} \cdot 25^{-\frac{3}{4}} = 25^{\frac{1}{4}+\left(-\frac{3}{4}\right)} = 25^{-\frac{2}{4}}$$

$$= 25^{-\frac{1}{2}} = \frac{1}{25^{\frac{1}{2}}}$$

$$= \frac{1}{\sqrt{25}} = \frac{1}{5}$$

73. **a.**

X	Y1
0	0
25	93.561
50	248.63
150	1170.3
200	1755.7
250	2404.9
300	3109.9

Y1=X^1.41

b.

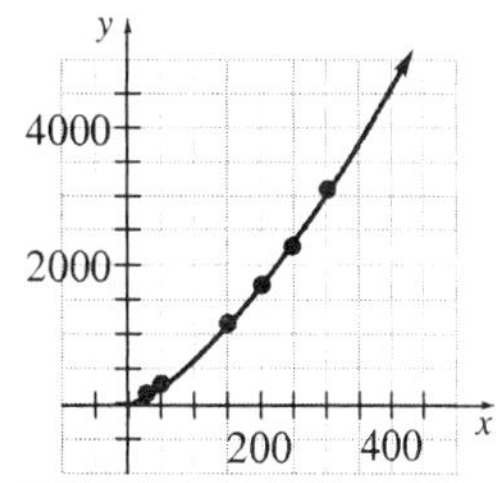

The graph indicates that as body weight increases, territorial area increases.

c. The following graph is drawn in the viewing rectangle $[0, 400, 50]$ by $[0, 4500, 500]$.

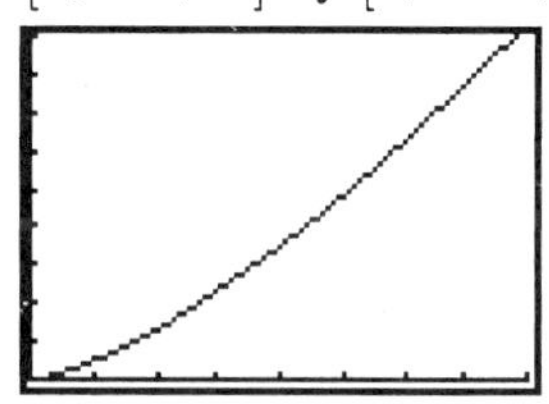

75.

$$7x - 3y = -14$$
$$y = 3x + 6$$

To solve this system by the substitution method, substitute $3x + 6$ for y in the first equation and solve for x.

$$7x - 3(3x + 6) = -14$$
$$7x - 9x - 18 = -14$$
$$-2x - 18 = -14$$
$$-2x = 4$$
$$x = -2$$

Back-substitute -2 for x into the second equation.

$$y = 3x + 6$$
$$y = 3(-2) + 6 = -6 + 6 = 0$$

Solution: $(-2, 0)$

76. $-3x+4y\le 12$

$x\ge 2$

To graph the solutions of this system if inequalities, first graph $-3x+4y=12$ as a solid line using its x-intercept, –4, and its y-intercept 3. Use (0,0) as a test point. Since $-3(0)+4(0)\le 12$ is true, shade the half-plane containing (0,0). Now graph x = 2 as a solid vertical line. Since $0\ge 2$ is false, shade the half-plane *not* containing (0,0), which is the half-plane to the right of the vertical line. The solution set of the system is the intersection (overlap) of the two shaded regions.

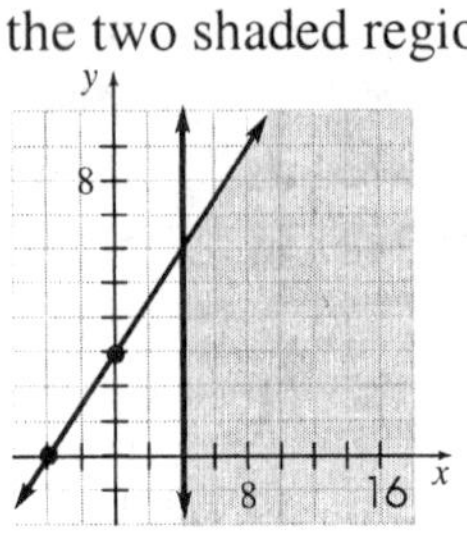

77. $\frac{(2x)^5}{x^3}=\frac{2^5x^5}{x^3}=\frac{32x^5}{x^3}=32x^2$

Chapter 9 Review Exercises

1. $\sqrt{121}=11$
The principal square root of 121 is 11.

2. $-\sqrt{121}=-11$
The negative square root of 121 is –11.

3. $\sqrt{-121}$ is not a real number because the square of a real number is never negative.

4. $\sqrt[3]{\frac{8}{125}}=\frac{2}{5}$ because $\left(\frac{2}{5}\right)^3=\frac{8}{125}$.

5. $\sqrt[5]{-32}=-2$ because $(-2)^5=-32$.

6. $-\sqrt[4]{81}=-3$ because $3^4=81$.

7. $\sqrt{75}\approx 8.660$

8. $\sqrt{398-5}=\sqrt{393}\approx 19.824$

9. $P=26.5\sqrt{t};\ t=9$ (for 1999)

$P=26.5\sqrt{9}$
$=26.5\cdot 3=79.5$

According to the formula, there were 79.5 thousand or 79,500 people over age 85 in Arizona in 1999.

10. As t increases $\sqrt{t}$ increases, so $26.5\sqrt{t}$ increases. This indicates that Arizona's over-85 population is increasing over time.

11. $d=\sqrt{\frac{3h}{2}};h=1575$

$d=\sqrt{\frac{3\cdot 1575}{2}}=\sqrt{\frac{4725}{2}}$
$=\sqrt{2362.5}\approx 49$

Visitor's will be able to see about 49 miles from the top of the building.

12. $\sqrt{54}=\sqrt{9\cdot 6}=\sqrt{9}\sqrt{6}=3\sqrt{6}$

13. $6\sqrt{20}=6\sqrt{4\cdot 5}=6\sqrt{4}\sqrt{5}$
$=6\cdot 2\sqrt{5}=12\sqrt{5}$

14. $\sqrt{63x^2}=\sqrt{9x^2}\sqrt{7}=3x\sqrt{7}$

15. $\sqrt{48x^3}=\sqrt{16x^2}\sqrt{3x}=4x\sqrt{3x}$

16. $\sqrt{x^8} = x^4$ because $\left(x^4\right)^2 = x^8$.

17. $\sqrt{75x^9} = \sqrt{25x^8}\sqrt{3x} = 5x^4\sqrt{3x}$

18. $\sqrt{45x^{23}} = \sqrt{9x^{22}}\sqrt{5x} = 3x^{11}\sqrt{5x}$

19. $\sqrt[3]{24} = \sqrt[3]{8\cdot 3} = \sqrt[3]{8}\sqrt[3]{3} = 2\sqrt[3]{3}$

20. $\sqrt{7}\cdot\sqrt{11} = \sqrt{7\cdot 11} = \sqrt{77}$

21. $\sqrt{3}\cdot\sqrt{12} = \sqrt{36} = \sqrt{6}$

22. $\sqrt{5x}\cdot\sqrt{10x} = \sqrt{50x^2} = \sqrt{25x^2}\sqrt{2}$
$= 5x\sqrt{2}$

23. $\sqrt{3x^2}\cdot\sqrt{4x^3} = \sqrt{12x^5} = \sqrt{4x^4}\sqrt{3x}$
$= 2x^2\sqrt{3x}$

24. $\sqrt[3]{6}\cdot\sqrt[3]{9} = \sqrt[3]{6\cdot 9} = \sqrt[3]{54} = \sqrt[3]{27}\cdot\sqrt[3]{2}$
$= 3\sqrt[3]{2}$

25. $\sqrt{\frac{5}{2}}\cdot\sqrt{\frac{3}{8}} = \sqrt{\frac{5\cdot 3}{2\cdot 8}} = \sqrt{\frac{15}{16}}$
$= \frac{\sqrt{15}}{\sqrt{16}} = \frac{\sqrt{15}}{4}$

26. $\sqrt{\frac{121}{4}} = \frac{\sqrt{121}}{\sqrt{4}} = \frac{11}{2}$

27. $\sqrt{\frac{7x}{25}} = \frac{\sqrt{7x}}{\sqrt{25}} = \frac{\sqrt{7x}}{5}$

28. $\sqrt{\frac{18}{x^2}} - \frac{\sqrt{18}}{\sqrt{x^2}} = \frac{\sqrt{9}\sqrt{2}}{x} = \frac{3\sqrt{2}}{x}$

29. $\frac{\sqrt{200}}{\sqrt{2}} = \sqrt{\frac{200}{2}} = \sqrt{100} = 10$

30. $\frac{\sqrt{96}}{\sqrt{3}} = \sqrt{32} = \sqrt{16}\sqrt{2} = 4\sqrt{2}$

31. $\frac{\sqrt{72x^8}}{\sqrt{x^3}} = \sqrt{\frac{72x^8}{x^3}} = \sqrt{72x^5}$
$= \sqrt{36x^4}\sqrt{2x} = 6x^2\sqrt{2x}$

32. $\sqrt[3]{\frac{5}{64}} = \frac{\sqrt[3]{5}}{\sqrt[3]{64}} = \frac{\sqrt[3]{5}}{4}$

33. $\sqrt[3]{\frac{40}{27}} = \frac{\sqrt[3]{40}}{\sqrt[3]{27}} = \frac{\sqrt[3]{8}\sqrt[3]{5}}{3} = \frac{2\sqrt[3]{5}}{3}$

34. $7\sqrt{5} + 13\sqrt{5} = (7+13)\sqrt{5} = 20\sqrt{5}$

35. $\sqrt{8} + \sqrt{50} = \sqrt{4}\sqrt{2} + \sqrt{25}\sqrt{2}$
$= 2\sqrt{2} + 5\sqrt{2}$
$= (2+5)\sqrt{2} = 7\sqrt{2}$

36. $\sqrt{75} - \sqrt{48} = \sqrt{25}\sqrt{3} - \sqrt{16}\sqrt{3}$
$= 5\sqrt{3} - 4\sqrt{3}$
$= (5-4)\sqrt{3} = \sqrt{3}$

37. $2\sqrt{80} + 3\sqrt{45} = 2\sqrt{16}\sqrt{5} + 3\sqrt{9}\sqrt{5}$
$= 2\cdot 4\sqrt{5} + 3\cdot 3\sqrt{5}$
$= 8\sqrt{5} + 9\sqrt{5} = 17\sqrt{5}$

38. $4\sqrt{72} - 2\sqrt{48} = 4\sqrt{36}\sqrt{2} - 2\sqrt{16}\sqrt{3}$
$= 4\cdot 6\sqrt{2} - 2\cdot 4\sqrt{3}$
$= 24\sqrt{2} - 8\sqrt{3}$

39. $2\sqrt{18}+3\sqrt{27}-\sqrt{12}$
$=2\sqrt{9}\sqrt{2}+3\sqrt{9}\sqrt{3}-\sqrt{4}\sqrt{3}$
$=2\cdot 3\sqrt{2}+3\cdot 3\sqrt{3}-2\sqrt{3}$
$=6\sqrt{2}+9\sqrt{3}-2\sqrt{3}$
$=6\sqrt{2}+7\sqrt{3}$

40. $\sqrt{10}\left(\sqrt{5}+\sqrt{6}\right)=\sqrt{10}\cdot\sqrt{5}+\sqrt{10}\cdot\sqrt{6}$
$=\sqrt{50}+\sqrt{60}$
$=\sqrt{25}\sqrt{2}+\sqrt{4}\sqrt{15}$
$=5\sqrt{2}+2\sqrt{15}$

41. $\sqrt{3}\left(\sqrt{6}-\sqrt{12}\right)=\sqrt{3}\cdot\sqrt{6}-\sqrt{3}\cdot\sqrt{12}$
$=\sqrt{18}-\sqrt{36}$
$=\sqrt{9}\sqrt{2}-6=3\sqrt{2}-6$

42. $\left(9+\sqrt{2}\right)\left(10+\sqrt{2}\right)$
$=9\cdot 10+9\sqrt{2}+10\sqrt{2}+\sqrt{2}\cdot\sqrt{2}$
$=90+19\sqrt{2}+2=92+19\sqrt{2}$

43. $\left(1+3\sqrt{7}\right)\left(4-\sqrt{7}\right)$
$=1\cdot 4-1\sqrt{7}+3\sqrt{7}\cdot 4-3\cdot\sqrt{7}\sqrt{7}$
$=4-\sqrt{7}+12\sqrt{7}-3\cdot 7$
$=4+11\sqrt{7}-21$
$=-17+11\sqrt{7}$

44. $\left(\sqrt{3}+2\right)\left(\sqrt{6}-4\right)$
$=\sqrt{3}\cdot\sqrt{6}+4\sqrt{3}+2\sqrt{6}-2\cdot 4$
$=\sqrt{18}-4\sqrt{3}+2\sqrt{6}-8$
$=\sqrt{9}\sqrt{2}-4\sqrt{3}+2\sqrt{6}-8$
$=3\sqrt{2}-4\sqrt{3}+2\sqrt{6}-8$

45. $\left(2+\sqrt{7}\right)\left(2-\sqrt{7}\right)=2^2-\left(\sqrt{7}\right)^2$
$=4-7=-3$

46. $\left(\sqrt{11}-\sqrt{5}\right)\left(\sqrt{11}+\sqrt{5}\right)$
$=\left(\sqrt{11}\right)^2-\left(\sqrt{5}\right)^2$
$=11-5=6$

47. $\left(1+\sqrt{2}\right)^2=1^2+2\cdot 1\cdot\sqrt{2}+\left(\sqrt{2}\right)^2$
$=1+2\sqrt{2}+2$
$=3+2\sqrt{2}$

48. $\frac{30}{\sqrt{5}}=\frac{30}{\sqrt{5}}\cdot\frac{\sqrt{5}}{\sqrt{5}}=\frac{30\sqrt{5}}{5}=6\sqrt{5}$

49. $\frac{13}{\sqrt{50}}=\frac{13}{\sqrt{25}\sqrt{2}}=\frac{13}{5\sqrt{2}}\cdot\frac{\sqrt{2}}{\sqrt{2}}$
$=\frac{13\sqrt{2}}{5\cdot 2}=\frac{13\sqrt{2}}{10}$

50. $\sqrt{\frac{2}{3}}=\frac{\sqrt{2}}{\sqrt{3}}=\frac{\sqrt{2}}{\sqrt{3}}\cdot\frac{\sqrt{3}}{\sqrt{3}}=\frac{\sqrt{6}}{3}$

51. $\sqrt{\frac{3}{8}}=\frac{\sqrt{3}}{\sqrt{8}}=\frac{\sqrt{3}}{\sqrt{4}\sqrt{2}}=\frac{\sqrt{3}}{2\sqrt{2}}$
$=\frac{\sqrt{3}}{2\sqrt{2}}\cdot\frac{\sqrt{2}}{\sqrt{2}}=\frac{\sqrt{6}}{2\cdot 2}=\frac{\sqrt{6}}{4}$

52. $\sqrt{\frac{17}{x}}=\frac{\sqrt{17}}{\sqrt{x}}=\frac{\sqrt{17}}{\sqrt{x}}\cdot\frac{\sqrt{x}}{\sqrt{x}}=\frac{\sqrt{17x}}{x}$

53.
$$\frac{11}{\sqrt{5}+2}=\frac{11}{\sqrt{5}+2}\cdot\frac{\sqrt{5}-2}{\sqrt{5}-2}$$
$$=\frac{11\left(\sqrt{5}-2\right)}{\left(\sqrt{5}\right)^2-2^2}$$
$$=\frac{11\left(\sqrt{5}-2\right)}{5-4}$$
$$=\frac{11\left(\sqrt{5}-2\right)}{1}$$
$$=11\sqrt{5}-22$$

54.
$$\frac{21}{4-\sqrt{3}}=\frac{21}{4-\sqrt{3}}\cdot\frac{4+\sqrt{3}}{4+\sqrt{3}}$$
$$=\frac{21\left(4+\sqrt{3}\right)}{4^2-\left(\sqrt{3}\right)^2}$$
$$=\frac{21\left(4+\sqrt{3}\right)}{16-3}$$
$$=\frac{21\left(4+\sqrt{3}\right)}{13}$$
$$=\frac{84+21\sqrt{3}}{13}$$

55.
$$\frac{12}{\sqrt{5}+\sqrt{3}}=\frac{12}{\sqrt{5}+\sqrt{3}}\cdot\frac{\sqrt{5}-\sqrt{3}}{\sqrt{5}-\sqrt{3}}$$
$$=\frac{12\left(\sqrt{5}-\sqrt{3}\right)}{\left(\sqrt{5}\right)^2-\left(\sqrt{3}\right)^2}$$
$$=\frac{12\left(\sqrt{5}-\sqrt{3}\right)}{5-3}$$
$$=\frac{12\left(\sqrt{5}-\sqrt{3}\right)}{2}$$
$$=6\left(\sqrt{5}-\sqrt{3}\right)$$
$$=6\sqrt{5}-6\sqrt{3}$$

56.
$$\frac{7\sqrt{2}}{\sqrt{2}-4}=\frac{7\sqrt{2}}{\sqrt{2}-4}\cdot\frac{\sqrt{2}+4}{\sqrt{2}+4}$$
$$=\frac{7\sqrt{2}\left(\sqrt{2}+4\right)}{\left(\sqrt{2}\right)^2-4^2}$$
$$=\frac{7\sqrt{2}\left(\sqrt{2}+4\right)}{2-16}$$
$$=\frac{7\sqrt{2}\left(\sqrt{2}+4\right)}{-14}$$
$$=\frac{7\cdot\sqrt{2}\sqrt{2}+7\cdot\sqrt{2}\cdot 4}{-14}$$
$$=\frac{7\cdot 2+28\sqrt{2}}{-14}$$
$$=\frac{14+28\sqrt{2}}{-14}$$
$$=\frac{14\left(1+2\sqrt{2}\right)}{14(-1)}$$
$$=-1\left(1+2\sqrt{2}\right)$$
$$=-1-2\sqrt{2}$$

57.
$$\sqrt{x+3}=4$$
$$\left(\sqrt{x+3}\right)=4^2$$
$$x+3=16$$
$$x=13$$

Check 13:
$$\sqrt{x+3}=4$$
$$\sqrt{13+3}=4$$
$$\sqrt{16}=4$$
$$4=4 \text{ true}$$
The solution is 13.

58. $\sqrt{2x+3}=5$

$\left(\sqrt{2x+3}\right)^2=5^2$

$2x+3=25$

$2x+22$

$x=11$

Check 11:

$\sqrt{2x+3}=5$

$\sqrt{2(11)+3}=5$

$\sqrt{22+3}=5$

$\sqrt{25}=5$

$5=5$ true

The solution is 11.

59. $3\sqrt{x}=\sqrt{6x+15}$

$\left(3\sqrt{x}\right)^2=\left(\sqrt{6x+15}\right)^2$

$9x=6x+15$

$3x=15$

$x=5$

Substitute 5 for x in the original equation to verify that the solution is 5.

60. $\sqrt{5x+1}=x+1$

$\left(\sqrt{5x+1}\right)^2=(x+1)^2$

$5x+1=x^2+2x+1$

$0=x^2-3x$

$0=x(x-3)$

$x=0$ or $x-3=0$

$x=3$

Each of the proposed solutions must be checked separately in the original equation.

Check 0:

$\sqrt{5x+1}=x+1$

$\sqrt{5\cdot 0+1}=0+1$

$\sqrt{1}=0+1$

$1=1$ true

Check 3:

$\sqrt{5x+1}=x+1$

$\sqrt{5\cdot 3+1}=3+1$

$\sqrt{15+1}=4$

$\sqrt{16}=4$

$4=4$ true

The solutions are 0 and 3.

61. $\sqrt{x+1}+5=x$

$\sqrt{x+1}=x-5$

$\left(\sqrt{x+1}\right)^2=(x-5)^2$

$x+1=x^2-10x+25$

$0=x^2-11x+24$

$0=(x-3)(x-8)$

$x-3=0$ or $x-8=0$

$x=3$ $\quad$ $x=8$

Check 3:

$\sqrt{x+1}+5=x$

$\sqrt{3+1}+5=3$

$\sqrt{4}+5=3$

$2+5=3$

$7=3$ false

Check 8:

$$\sqrt{x+1}+5=x$$
$$\sqrt{8+1}+5=8$$
$$\sqrt{9}+5=8$$
$$3+5=8$$
$$8=8 \text{ true}$$

The false statement indicates that 3 does *not* satisfy the original equation; it is an extraneous solution. The true statement indicates that 8 satisfies the equation. Therefore, the only solution is 8.

62.

$$\sqrt{x-2}+5=1$$
$$\sqrt{x-2}=-4$$
$$\left(\sqrt{x-2}\right)^2=(-4)^2$$
$$x-2=16$$
$$x=18$$

Check 18:

$$\sqrt{x-2}+5=1$$
$$\sqrt{18-2}+5=1$$
$$\sqrt{16}+5=1$$
$$4+5=1$$
$$9=1 \text{ false}$$

The only proposed solution, 18, is extraneous, so the equation has no solution.

63.

$$x=\sqrt{x^2+4x+4}$$
$$x^2=\left(\sqrt{x^2+4x+4}\right)^2$$
$$x^2=x^2+4x+4$$
$$0=4x+4$$
$$-4=4x$$
$$-1=x$$

Check:

$$x=\sqrt{x^2+4x+4}$$
$$-1=\sqrt{(-1)^2+4(-1)+4}$$
$$-1=\sqrt{1-4+4}$$
$$-1=\sqrt{1}$$
$$-1=1 \text{ false}$$

The only proposed solution, −1, is extraneous, so the equation has no solution.

64.

$$t=\sqrt{\frac{d}{16}};t=3$$
$$3=\sqrt{\frac{d}{16}}$$
$$3^2=\left(\sqrt{\frac{d}{16}}\right)^2$$
$$9=\frac{d}{16}$$
$$9\cdot 16=d$$
$$144=d$$

The bridge is 144 feet above the water.

65.

$$D=\sqrt{2H};D=50$$
$$50=\sqrt{2H}$$
$$50^2=\left(\sqrt{2H}\right)^2$$
$$2500=2H$$
$$1250=H$$

The mountain is 1250 feet high.

66. $16^{\frac{1}{2}}=\sqrt{16}=4$

67. $125^{\frac{1}{3}}=\sqrt[3]{125}=5$

68. $64^{\frac{2}{3}} = \left(\sqrt[3]{64}\right)^2 = 4^2 = 16$

69. $25^{-\frac{1}{2}} = \dfrac{1}{25^{\frac{1}{2}}} = \dfrac{1}{\sqrt{25}} = \dfrac{1}{5}$

70. $27^{-\frac{1}{3}} = \dfrac{1}{27^{\frac{1}{3}}} = \dfrac{1}{\sqrt[3]{27}} = \dfrac{1}{3}$

71. $(-8)^{-\frac{4}{3}} = \dfrac{1}{(-8)^{\frac{4}{3}}} = \dfrac{1}{\left(\sqrt[3]{-8}\right)^4}$

$= \dfrac{1}{(-2)^4} = \dfrac{1}{16}$

72. $S = 28.6A^{\frac{1}{3}};\ A = 8$

$S = 28.6 \cdot 8^{\frac{1}{3}} = 28.6\sqrt[3]{8}$

$= 28.6 \cdot 2 = 57.2 \approx 57$

There are approximately 57 species on a Galapagos island whose area is 8 square miles.

Chapter 9 Test

1. $-\sqrt{64} = -8$

The negative square root of 64 is –8.

2. $\sqrt[3]{64} = 4$ because $4^3 = 64$.

3. $\sqrt{48} = \sqrt{16 \cdot 3} = \sqrt{16}\sqrt{3} = 4\sqrt{3}$

4. $\sqrt{72x^3} = \sqrt{36x^2}\sqrt{2x} = 6x\sqrt{2x}$

5. $\sqrt{x^{29}} = \sqrt{x^{28} \cdot x} = \sqrt{x^{28}}\sqrt{x} = x^{14}\sqrt{x}$

6. $\sqrt{\dfrac{25}{x^2}} = \dfrac{\sqrt{25}}{\sqrt{x^2}} = \dfrac{5}{x}$

7. $\sqrt{\dfrac{75}{27}} = \dfrac{\sqrt{75}}{\sqrt{27}} = \dfrac{\sqrt{25}\sqrt{3}}{\sqrt{9}\sqrt{3}}$

$= \dfrac{5\sqrt{3}}{3\sqrt{3}} = \dfrac{5}{3}$

8. $\sqrt[3]{\dfrac{5}{8}} = \dfrac{\sqrt[3]{5}}{\sqrt[3]{8}} = \dfrac{\sqrt[3]{5}}{2}$

9. $\dfrac{\sqrt{80x^4}}{\sqrt{2x^2}} = \sqrt{\dfrac{80x^4}{2x^2}} = \sqrt{40x^2}$

$= \sqrt{4x^2}\sqrt{10} = 2x\sqrt{10}$

10. $\sqrt{10} \cdot \sqrt{5} = \sqrt{50} = \sqrt{25 \cdot 2}$

$= \sqrt{25}\sqrt{2} = 5\sqrt{2}$

11. $\sqrt{6x} \cdot \sqrt{6y} = \sqrt{6x \cdot 6y}$

$= \sqrt{36xy}$

$= \sqrt{36} \cdot \sqrt{xy}$

$= 6\sqrt{xy}$

12. $\sqrt{10x^2} \cdot \sqrt{2x^3} = \sqrt{20x^5} = \sqrt{4x^4}\sqrt{5x}$

$= 2x^2\sqrt{5x}$

13. $\sqrt{24} + 3\sqrt{54} = \sqrt{4}\sqrt{6} + 3\sqrt{9}\sqrt{6}$

$= 2\sqrt{6} + 3 \cdot 3\sqrt{6}$

$= 2\sqrt{6} + 9\sqrt{6}$

$= 11\sqrt{6}$

14. $7\sqrt{8} - 2\sqrt{32} = 7\sqrt{4}\sqrt{2} - 2\sqrt{16}\sqrt{2}$

$= 7 \cdot 2\sqrt{2} - 2 \cdot 4\sqrt{2}$

$= 14\sqrt{2} - 8\sqrt{2} = 6\sqrt{2}$

15. $\sqrt{3}\left(\sqrt{10}+\sqrt{3}\right)=\sqrt{3}\cdot\sqrt{10}+\sqrt{3}\cdot\sqrt{3}$
$=\sqrt{30}+3$

16. $\left(7-\sqrt{5}\right)\left(10+3\sqrt{5}\right)$
$=7\cdot 10+7\cdot 3\sqrt{5}-10\sqrt{5}-3\sqrt{5}\cdot\sqrt{5}$
$=70+21\sqrt{5}-10\sqrt{5}-3\cdot 5$
$=70+11\sqrt{5}-15=55+11\sqrt{5}$

17. $\left(\sqrt{6}+2\right)\left(\sqrt{6}-2\right)=\left(\sqrt{6}\right)^2-2^2$
$=6-4=2$

18. $\left(3+\sqrt{7}\right)^2=3^2+2\cdot 3\cdot\sqrt{7}+\left(\sqrt{7}\right)^2$
$=9+6\sqrt{7}+7=16+6\sqrt{7}$

19. $\frac{4}{\sqrt{5}}=\frac{4}{\sqrt{5}}\cdot\frac{\sqrt{5}}{\sqrt{5}}=\frac{4\sqrt{5}}{5}$

20. $\frac{5}{4+\sqrt{3}}=\frac{5}{4+\sqrt{3}}\cdot\frac{4-\sqrt{3}}{4-\sqrt{3}}$
$=\frac{5\left(4-\sqrt{3}\right)}{4^2-\left(\sqrt{3}\right)^2}$
$=\frac{5\left(4-\sqrt{3}\right)}{16-3}$
$=\frac{5\left(4-\sqrt{3}\right)}{13}$
$=\frac{20-5\sqrt{5}}{13}$

21. $\sqrt{3x}+5=11$
$\sqrt{3x}=6$
$\left(\sqrt{3x}\right)^2=6^2$
$3x=36$
$x=12$

Check the proposed solution in the original equation.
$\sqrt{3x}+5=11$
$\sqrt{3\cdot 12}+5=11$
$\sqrt{36}+5=11$
$6+5=11$
$11=11$
The solution is 12.

22. $\sqrt{2x-1}=x-2$
$\left(\sqrt{2x-1}\right)^2=(x-2)^2$
$2x-1=x^2-4x+4$
$0=x^2-6x+5$
$0=(x-1)(x-5)$
$x-1=0$ or $x-5=0$
$x=1$ $\quad$ $x=5$
Check each proposed solution in the original equation.

Check 1:
$\sqrt{2x-1}=x-2$
$\sqrt{2\cdot 1-1}=1-2$
$\sqrt{2-1}=1-2$
$\sqrt{1}=-1$
$1=-1$ false
Check 5:
$\sqrt{2x-1}=x-2$
$\sqrt{2\cdot 5-1}=5-2$
$\sqrt{10-1}=3$
$\sqrt{9}=3$
$3=3$ true
The check shows that 1 is an extraneous solution, while 5 satisfies the equation.
Therefore, the solution is 5.

23. $t=\sqrt{\dfrac{d}{16}};t=10$

$$10=\sqrt{\frac{d}{16}}$$

$$10^2=\left(\sqrt{\frac{d}{16}}\right)^2$$

$$100=\frac{d}{16}$$

$$1600=d$$

The skydiver will fall 1600 feet in 10 seconds.

24. $8^{\frac{2}{3}}=\left(\sqrt[3]{8}\right)^2=2^2=4$

25. $9^{-\frac{1}{2}}=\dfrac{1}{9^{\frac{1}{2}}}=\dfrac{1}{\sqrt{9}}=\dfrac{1}{3}$

Cumulative Review Exercises (Chapters 1-9)

1. $2x+3x-5+7=10x+3-6x-4$

$$5x+2=4x-1$$

$$x+2=-1$$

$$x=-3$$

The solution is -3.

2.

$$2x^2+5x=12$$

$$2x^2+5x-12=0$$

$$(2x-3)(x+4)=0$$

$$2x-3=0 \quad \text{or} \quad x+4=0$$

$$2x=3 \qquad\qquad x=-4$$

$$x=\frac{3}{2}$$

The solutions are -4 and $\dfrac{3}{2}$.

3. $8x-5y=-4$

$2x+15y=-66$

Multiply the first equation by 3 and add the two equation.

$$24x-15y=-12$$

$$\underline{2x+15y=-66}$$

$$26x \qquad =-78$$

$$x \qquad =-3$$

Back-substitute $x=-3$ into the first equation and solve for y.

$$8(-3)-5y=-4$$

$$-24-5y=-4$$

$$-5y=20$$

$$y=-4$$

The solution is $(-3,-4)$.

4. $\dfrac{15}{x}-4=\dfrac{6}{x}+3$

Restriction: $x\neq 0$

LCD = x

Multiply both sides by the LCD, which is x.

$$x\left(\frac{15}{x}-4\right)=x\left(\frac{6}{x}+3\right)$$

$$x\cdot\frac{15}{x}-x\cdot 4=x\cdot\frac{6}{x}+x\cdot 3$$

$$15-4x=6+3x$$

$$15-7x=6$$

$$-7x=-9$$

$$x=\frac{9}{7}$$

The solution is $\dfrac{9}{7}$.

5. $-3x-7=8$

$$-3x=15$$

$$x=-5$$

The solution is -5.

6.
$$\sqrt{2x-1}-x=-2$$
$$\sqrt{2x-1}=x-2$$
$$\left(\sqrt{2x-1}\right)^2=(x-2)^2$$
$$2x-1=x^2-4x+4$$
$$0=x^2-6x+5$$
$$0=(x-1)(x-5)$$
$$x-1=0 \quad \text{or} \quad x-5=0$$
$$x=1 \qquad\qquad x=5$$
Check each proposed solution in the original equation.

Check 1: $\sqrt{2x-1}-x=-2$
$$\sqrt{2\cdot 1-1}-1=-2$$
$$\sqrt{2-1}-1=-2$$
$$\sqrt{1}-1=-2$$
$$1-1=-2$$
$$0=-2 \text{ false}$$
Check 5: $\sqrt{2x-1}-x=-2$
$$\sqrt{2\cdot 5-1}-5=-2$$
$$\sqrt{10-1}-5=-2$$
$$\sqrt{9}-5=-2$$
$$3-5=-2$$
$$-2=-2 \text{ true}$$
The check shows that 1 is an extraneous solution, while 5 satisfies the equation, so the only solution is 5.

7.
$$\frac{8x^3}{-4x^7}=\frac{8}{-4}\cdot x^{3-7}=-2x^{-4}$$
$$=\frac{-2}{x^4}=-\frac{2}{x^4}$$

8.
$$6\sqrt{75}-4\sqrt{12}=6\sqrt{25}\sqrt{3}-4\sqrt{4}\sqrt{3}$$
$$=6\cdot 5\sqrt{3}-4\cdot 2\sqrt{3}$$
$$=30\sqrt{3}-8\sqrt{3}$$
$$=22\sqrt{3}$$

9.
$$\frac{\frac{1}{x}-\frac{1}{2}}{\frac{1}{3}-\frac{x}{6}}$$
LCD = $6x$
$$\frac{\frac{1}{x}-\frac{1}{2}}{\frac{1}{3}-\frac{x}{6}}=\frac{6x}{6x}\cdot\frac{\left(\frac{1}{x}-\frac{1}{2}\right)}{\left(\frac{1}{3}-\frac{x}{6}\right)}$$
$$=\frac{6x\cdot\frac{1}{x}-6x\cdot\frac{1}{2}}{6x\cdot\frac{1}{3}-6x\cdot\frac{x}{6}}$$
$$=\frac{6-3x}{2x-x^2}$$
$$=\frac{3(2-x)}{x(2-x)}=\frac{3}{x}$$

10.
$$\frac{4-x^2}{3x^2-5x-2}=\frac{(2+x)(2-x)}{(3x+1)(x-2)}$$
$$=\frac{(2+x)(-1)(x-2)}{(3x+1)(x-2)}$$
$$=\frac{-1(2+x)}{3x+1}$$
$$=\frac{2+x}{3x+1}$$

11.
$$-5-(-8)-(4-6)$$
$$=-5-(-8)-(-2)$$
$$=-5+8+2$$
$$=3+2$$
$$=5$$

12. $x^2 - 18x + 77$

To factor this trinomial, find two integers whose product is 77 and whose sum is −18. These integers are −7 and −11.

$x^2 - 18x + 77 = (x-7)(x-11)$

13.
$$\begin{aligned} x^3 - 25x &= x\left(x^2 - 25\right) \\ &= x(x-5)(x-5) \end{aligned}$$

14.
$$\begin{array}{r} 6x^2 - 7x + 2 \\ x-2\overline{)6x^3 - 19x^2 + 16x - 4} \\ \underline{6x^3 - 12x^2} \qquad\qquad \\ -7x^2 + 16x \quad \\ \underline{-7x^2 + 14x} \quad \\ 2x - 4 \\ \underline{2x - 4} \\ 0 \end{array}$$

$$\frac{6x^3 - 19x^2 + 16x - 4}{x-2} = 6x^2 - 7x + 2$$

15.
$$\begin{aligned} &(2x-3)\left(4x^2 + 6x + 9\right) \\ &= 2x\left(4x^2 + 6x + 9\right) - 3\left(4x^2 + 6x + 9\right) \\ &= 8x^3 + 12x^2 + 18x - 12x^2 - 18x - 27 \\ &= 8x^3 - 27 \end{aligned}$$

16.
$$\begin{aligned} &\frac{3x}{x^2 + x - 2} - \frac{2}{x+2} \\ &= \frac{3x}{(x+2)(x-1)} - \frac{2}{x+2} \\ &= \frac{3x}{(x+2)(x-1)} - \frac{2(x-1)}{(x+2)(x-1)} \\ &= \frac{3x - 2(x-1)}{(x+2)(x-1)} \\ &= \frac{3x - 2x + 2}{(x+2)(x-1)} \\ &= \frac{x+2}{(x+2)(x-1)} \\ &= \frac{1}{x-1} \end{aligned}$$

17.
$$\begin{aligned} &\frac{5x^2 - 6x + 1}{x^2 - 1} \div \frac{16x^2 - 9}{4x^2 + 7x + 3} \\ &= \frac{5x^2 - 6x + 1}{x^2 - 1} \cdot \frac{4x^2 + 7x + 3}{16x^2 - 9} \\ &= \frac{(5x-1)(x-1)}{(x+1)(x-1)} \cdot \frac{(4x+3)(x+1)}{(4x+3)(4x-3)} \\ &= \frac{5x-1}{4x-3} \end{aligned}$$

18.
$$\begin{aligned} \sqrt{12} - 4\sqrt{75} &= \sqrt{4} \cdot \sqrt{3} - 4\sqrt{25} \cdot \sqrt{3} \\ &= 2\sqrt{3} - 4(5)\sqrt{3} \\ &= 2\sqrt{3} - 20\sqrt{3} \\ &= -18\sqrt{3} \end{aligned}$$

19. $2x - y = 4$

The graph is a line with x-intercept 2 and y-intercept −4. The point (1, −2) can be used as a checkpoint. Draw a line through (2,0), (0, −4), and (1, −2).

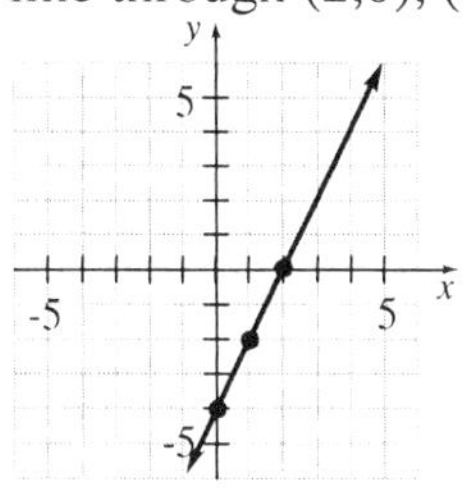

20. $y = -\frac{2}{3}x$

The graph is a line with slope $-\frac{2}{3} = \frac{-2}{3}$ and y-intercept 0. Plot (0,0). From the origin, move 2 units *down* and 3 units to the *right* to reach the point (3, −2). Draw a line through (0,0) and (3, −2).

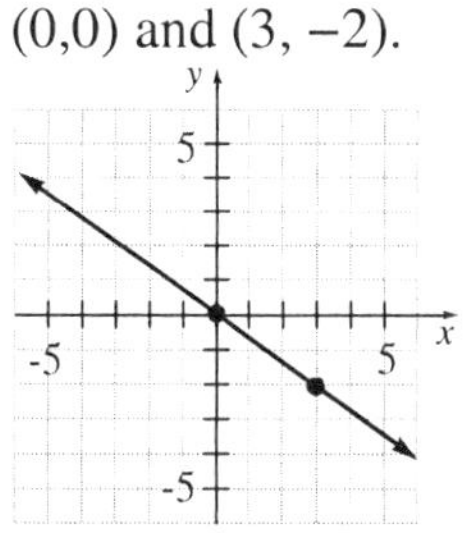

21. $x \geq -1$

Graph $x = 1$ as a solid vertical line. Use (0,0) as a test point. Since $0 \geq -1$ is true, shade the half-plane that contains (0,0). This is the region to the right of the vertical line.

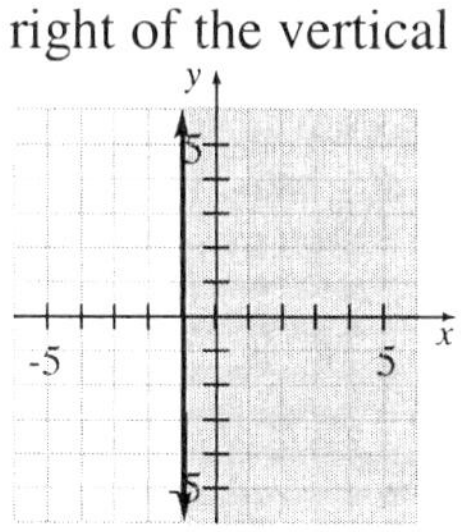

22. $(-1,5)$ and $(2,-3)$

$$m = \frac{y_2 - y_1}{x_2 - x_1} = \frac{-3-5}{2-(-1)}$$
$$= \frac{-8}{3} = -\frac{8}{3}$$

23. Slope 5, passing through (−2, −3). First, substitute 5 for m, −2 for x_1, and −3 for y_1 in the point-slope form.

$$y - y_1 = m(x - x_1)$$
$$y - (-3) = 5[x - (-2)]$$
$$y + 3 = 5(x + 2)$$

Now rewrite the equation in slope-intercept form.

$$y + 3 = 5x + 10$$
$$y = 5x + 7$$

24. Let x = the number.

$$5x - 7 = 208$$
$$5x = 215$$
$$x = 43$$

The number is 43.

25. Let x = the number of deer in the park.

$$\frac{\text{Original number of tagged deer}}{\text{Total number of deer}} = \frac{\text{Number of tagged deer in sample}}{\text{Number of deer in sample}}$$

$$\frac{318}{x} = \frac{56}{168}$$
$$(318)(168) = 56x$$
$$53,424 = 56x$$
$$954 = x$$

There are approximately 954 deer in the park.

Chapter 10
Quadratic Equations and Functions

10.1 Exercise Set

1. $x^2 = 16$

$x = \sqrt{16}$ or $x = -\sqrt{16}$

$x = 4 \qquad x = -4$

The solutions are 4 and −4.

3. $y^2 = 81$

$y = \sqrt{81}$ or $y = -\sqrt{81}$

$y = 9 \qquad y = -9$

The solutions are 9 and −9.

5. $x^2 = 7$

$x = \sqrt{7}$ or $x = -\sqrt{7}$

The solutions are $\sqrt{7}$ and $-\sqrt{7}$.

7. $x^2 = 50$

$x = \sqrt{50}$ or $x = -\sqrt{50}$

Simplify $\sqrt{50}$:

$\sqrt{50} = \sqrt{25}\sqrt{2} = 5\sqrt{2}$.

$x = 5\sqrt{2}$ or $x = -5\sqrt{2}$

The solutions are $5\sqrt{2}$ and $-5\sqrt{2}$.

9. $5x^2 = 20$

$x^2 = 4$

$x = \sqrt{4}$ or $x = -\sqrt{4}$

$x = 2$ or $x = -2$

The solutions are 2 and −2.

11. $4y^2 = 49$

$y^2 = \frac{49}{4}$

$y = \sqrt{\frac{49}{4}}$ or $y = -\sqrt{\frac{49}{4}}$

$y = \frac{7}{2}$ or $y = -\frac{7}{2}$

The solutions are $\frac{7}{2}$ and $-\frac{7}{2}$.

13. $2x^2 + 1 = 51$

$2x^2 = 50$

$x^2 = 25$

$x = \sqrt{25}$ or $x = -\sqrt{25}$

$x = 5$ or $x = -5$

The solutions are 5 and −5.

15. $3x^2 - 2 = 0$

$3x = 2$

$x^2 = \frac{2}{3}$

$x = \sqrt{\frac{2}{3}}$ or $x = -\sqrt{\frac{2}{3}}$

Rationalize the denominators

$\sqrt{\frac{2}{3}} = \frac{\sqrt{2}}{\sqrt{3}} = \frac{\sqrt{2}}{\sqrt{3}} \cdot \frac{\sqrt{3}}{\sqrt{3}} = \frac{\sqrt{6}}{3}$

$x = \frac{\sqrt{6}}{3}$ or $x = -\frac{\sqrt{6}}{3}$

The solutions are $\frac{\sqrt{6}}{3}$ and $-\frac{\sqrt{6}}{3}$.

17. $5z^2 - 7 = 0$

$5z^2 = 7$

$z^2 = \frac{7}{5}$

$z = \sqrt{\frac{7}{5}}$ or $z = -\sqrt{\frac{7}{5}}$

Rationalize the denominators.

$\sqrt{\frac{7}{5}} = \frac{\sqrt{7}}{\sqrt{5}} = \frac{\sqrt{7}}{\sqrt{5}} \cdot \frac{\sqrt{5}}{\sqrt{5}} = \frac{\sqrt{35}}{5}$

$z = \frac{\sqrt{35}}{5}$ or $z = -\frac{\sqrt{35}}{5}$

The solutions are $\frac{\sqrt{35}}{5}$ and $-\frac{\sqrt{35}}{5}$.

19. $(x-3)^2 = 16$

$x - 3 = \sqrt{16}$ or $x - 3 = -\sqrt{16}$

$x - 3 = 4$ or $x - 3 = -4$

$x = 7$ $\quad$ $x = -1$

The solutions are 7 and -1.

21. $(x+5)^2 = 121$

$x + 5 = \sqrt{121}$ or $x + 5 = -\sqrt{121}$

$x + 5 = 11$ or $x + 5 = -11$

$x = 6$ $\quad$ $x = -16$

The solutions are 6 and -16.

23. $(3x+2)^2 = 9$

$3x + 2 = \sqrt{9}$ or $3x + 2 = -\sqrt{9}$

$3x + 2 = 3$ or $3x + 2 = -3$

$3x = 1$ or $3x = -5$

$x = \frac{1}{3}$ $\quad$ $x = -\frac{5}{3}$

The solutions are $\frac{1}{3}$ and $-\frac{5}{3}$

25. $(x-5)^2 = 3$

$x - 5 = \sqrt{3}$ or $x - 5 = -\sqrt{3}$

$x = 5 + \sqrt{3}$ $\quad$ $x = 5 - \sqrt{3}$

The solutions are $5 + \sqrt{3}$ and $5 - \sqrt{3}$.

27. $(y+8)^2 = 11$

$y + 8 = \sqrt{11}$ or $y + 8 = -\sqrt{11}$

$y = -8 + \sqrt{11}$ $\quad$ $y = -8 - \sqrt{11}$

The solutions are $-8 + \sqrt{11}$ and $-8 - \sqrt{11}$.

29. $(z-4)^2 = 18$

$z - 4 = \sqrt{18}$ or $z - 4 = -\sqrt{18}$

$z - 4 = 3\sqrt{2}$ $\quad$ $z - 4 = -3\sqrt{2}$

$z = 4 + 3\sqrt{2}$ $\quad$ $z = 4 - 3\sqrt{2}$

The solutions are $4 + 3\sqrt{2}$ and $4 - 3\sqrt{2}$.

31. $x^2 + 4x + 4 = 16$

$(x+2)^2 = 16$

$x + 2 = \sqrt{16}$ or $x + 2 = -\sqrt{16}$

$x + 2 = 4$ or $x + 2 = -4$

$x = 2$ $\quad$ $x = -6$

The solutions are 2 and -6.

33. $x^2 - 6x + 9 = 36$

$(x-3)^2 = 36$

$x - 3 = \sqrt{36}$ or $x - 3 = -\sqrt{36}$

$x - 3 = 6$ or $x - 3 = -6$

$x = 9$ $\quad$ $x = -3$

35. $x^2 - 10x + 25 = 2$

$(x-5)^2 = 2$

$x - 5 = \sqrt{2}$ or $x - 5 = -\sqrt{2}$

$x = 5 + \sqrt{2}$ $\quad$ $x = 5 - \sqrt{2}$

The solutions are $5 + \sqrt{2}$ and $-1 - \sqrt{5}$

37. $x^2+2x+1=5$

$(x+1)^2=5$

$x+1=\sqrt{5}$ or $x+1=-\sqrt{5}$

$x=-1+\sqrt{5}$ $\quad x=-1-\sqrt{5}$

The solutions are $-1+\sqrt{5}$ and $-1-\sqrt{5}$

39. $y^2-14y+49=12$

$(y-7)^2=12$

$y-7=\sqrt{12}$ or $y-7=-\sqrt{12}$

$y-7=2\sqrt{3}$ or $y-7=-2\sqrt{3}$

$y=7+2\sqrt{3}$ $\quad y=7-2\sqrt{3}$

The solutions are $7+2\sqrt{3}$ and $7-2\sqrt{3}$

In Exercises 41-63, all of the unknown quantities must be positive. Therefore, only the positive square roots are used as solutions.

41. $8^2+15^2=c^2$

$64+225=c^2$

$289=c^2$

$c=\sqrt{289}=17$

The missing length is 17 meters.

43. $15^2+36^2=c^2$

$225+1296=c^2$

$1521=c^2$

$c=\sqrt{1521}$

$=39$

The missing length is 39 meters.

45. $a^2+16^2=20^2$

$a^2+256=440$

$a^2=144$

$a=\sqrt{144}$

$=12$

The missing length is 12 centimeters.

47. $9^2+b^2=16^2$

$81+b^2=256$

$b^2=175$

$b=\sqrt{175}$

$=\sqrt{25}\sqrt{7}$

$=5\sqrt{7}$

The missing length is $5\sqrt{7}$ meters.

49. $d=\sqrt{(x_2-x_1)^2+(y_2-y_1)^2}$

$=\sqrt{(4-3)^2+(1-5)^2}$

$=\sqrt{1^2+(-4)^2}$

$=\sqrt{1+16}=\sqrt{17}\approx 4.12$

51. $d=\sqrt{(x_2-x_1)^2+(y_2-y_1)^2}$

$=\sqrt{(4-(-4))^2+(17-2)^2}$

$=\sqrt{8^2+15^2}=\sqrt{64+225}$

$=\sqrt{289}=17$

53. $d=\sqrt{(x_2-x_1)^2+(y_2-y_1)^2}$

$=\sqrt{(9-6)^2+(5-(-1))^2}$

$=\sqrt{3^2+6^2}=\sqrt{9+36}$

$=\sqrt{45}=3\sqrt{5}\approx 6.71$

55. $d = \sqrt{(x_2 - x_1)^2 + (y_2 - y_1)^2}$

$= \sqrt{(-2-(-7))^2 + (-1-(-5))^2}$

$= \sqrt{5^2 + 4^2} = \sqrt{25+16}$

$= \sqrt{41} \approx 6.40$

57. $d = \sqrt{(x_2 - x_1)^2 + (y_2 - y_1)^2}$

$= \sqrt{\left(4\sqrt{7} - \left(-2\sqrt{7}\right)\right)^2 + (8-10)^2}$

$= \sqrt{\left(6\sqrt{7}\right)^2 + (-2)^2} = \sqrt{252+4}$

$= \sqrt{256} = 16$

59. Let x = the number.

$(x-3)^2 = 25$

$x-3 = \sqrt{25}$ or $x-3 = -\sqrt{25}$

$x = 3+5$ $\quad$ $x = 3-5$

$x = 8$ $\quad$ $x = -2$

The number is -2 or 8.

60. Let x = the number.

$(x-7)^2 = 16$

$x-7 = \sqrt{16}$ or $x-7 = -\sqrt{16}$

$x = 7+4$ $\quad$ $x = 7-4$

$x = 11$ $\quad$ $x = 3$

The number is 3 or 11.

61. Let x = the number.

$(3x+2)^2 = 49$

$3x+2 = \sqrt{49}$ or $3x+2 = -\sqrt{49}$

$3x+2 = 7$ $\quad$ $3x+2 = -7$

$3x = 5$ $\quad$ $3x = -9$

$x = \frac{5}{3}$ $\quad$ $x = -3$

The number is -3 or $\frac{5}{3}$.

62. Let x = the number.

$(4x-3)^2 = 9$

$4x-3 = \sqrt{9}$ or $4x-3 = -\sqrt{9}$

$4x-3 = 3$ $\quad$ $4x-3 = -3$

$4x = 6$ $\quad$ $4x = 0$

$x = \frac{3}{2}$ $\quad$ $x = 0$

The number is 0 or $\frac{3}{2}$.

63. $A = \pi r^2$

$\frac{A}{\pi} = r^2$

$r = \sqrt{\frac{A}{\pi}}$

$= \frac{\sqrt{A}}{\sqrt{\pi}} \cdot \frac{\sqrt{\pi}}{\sqrt{\pi}}$

$= \frac{\sqrt{A\pi}}{\pi}$

64. $ax^2 - b = 0$

$ax^2 = b$

$x^2 = \frac{b}{a}$

$x = \sqrt{\frac{b}{a}} = \frac{\sqrt{b}}{\sqrt{a}}$

$= \frac{\sqrt{b}}{\sqrt{a}} \cdot \frac{\sqrt{a}}{\sqrt{a}}$

$= \frac{\sqrt{ab}}{a}$

65.

$$I = \frac{k}{d^2}$$
$$d^2 I = k$$
$$d^2 = \frac{k}{I}$$
$$d = \sqrt{\frac{k}{I}} = \frac{\sqrt{k}}{\sqrt{I}}$$
$$= \frac{\sqrt{k}}{\sqrt{I}} \cdot \frac{\sqrt{I}}{\sqrt{I}}$$
$$= \frac{\sqrt{kI}}{I}$$

66.

$$A = p(1+r)^2$$
$$\frac{A}{p} = (1+r)^2$$
$$1 + r = \sqrt{\frac{A}{p}}$$
$$r = -1 + \frac{\sqrt{A}}{\sqrt{p}} = -1 + \frac{\sqrt{A}}{\sqrt{p}} \cdot \frac{\sqrt{p}}{\sqrt{p}}$$
$$= -1 + \frac{\sqrt{Ap}}{p} = \frac{-p + \sqrt{Ap}}{p}$$
$$= \frac{\sqrt{Ap} - p}{p}$$

67. Let x = the length of the ladder.

$$8^2 + 10^2 = x^2$$
$$64 + 100 = x^2$$
$$164 = x^2$$
$$x = \sqrt{164} = \sqrt{4}\sqrt{41} = 2\sqrt{41}$$

The length of the ladder is $2\sqrt{41}$ feet.

69.

$$90^2 + 90^2 = x^2$$
$$8100 + 8100 = x^2$$
$$16,200 = x^2$$
$$\sqrt{16,2000} = \sqrt{8100}\sqrt{2} = 90\sqrt{2}$$

The distance from home plate to second base is $90\sqrt{2}$ feet.

71. Let x = the length of a side of the screen.

$$x^2 + x^2 = 25^2$$
$$2x^2 = 625$$
$$x^2 = \frac{625}{2}$$
$$x = \sqrt{\frac{625}{2}}$$

Simplify the radical.
The measure of the side of the screen is $\frac{25\sqrt{2}}{2}$ inches.

73.

$$A = \pi r^2; A = 36\pi$$
$$36\pi = \pi r^2$$
$$36 = r^2$$
$$r = \sqrt{36} = 6$$

The radius is 6 inches.

75.

$$W = 3t^2; W = 108$$
$$108 = 3t^2$$
$$36 = t^2$$
$$t = \sqrt{36} = 6$$

The fetus weighs 108 grams after 6 weeks

77.

$$d = 16t^2; d = 400$$

The rock must fall 400 feet to hit the water.

$$400 = 16t^2$$
$$25 = t^2$$
$$t = \sqrt{25} = 5$$

It will take 5 seconds for the rock to hit the water.

79. The length of each side of the original garden is x meters. Therefore, the length of each larger side is $x + 4$ meters since 2 meters were added to each side.

Larger square: $A = (x+4)^2 ; A = 144$

$$144 = (x+4)^2$$
$$x+4 = \sqrt{144} \quad \text{or} \quad x+4 = -\sqrt{144}$$
$$x+4 = 12 \quad \text{or} \quad x+4 = -12$$
$$x = 8 \qquad x = -16$$

Reject -16 because a length cannot be negative. The length of each side of the original square is 8 meters.

81. The volume of a rectangular solid is given by $V = lwh$. From the problem statement, we have

$V = 200, l = x, w = x, h = 2$

$$200 = x \cdot x \cdot 2$$
$$200 = 2x^2$$
$$100 = x^2$$
$$x = \sqrt{100} = 10$$

The length and width of the open box are both 10 inches.

For problems 83-85, answers will vary.

87. Statement c is true.
There is no real number whose square is negative.

89. 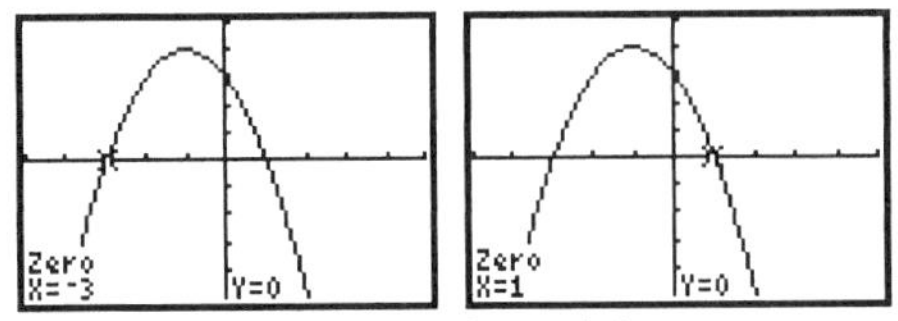

The solutions are -3 and 1.
Check:

$$4-(-3+1)^2 = 0$$
$$4-(-2)^2 = 0$$
$$4-4 = 0$$
$$0 = 0 \text{ true}$$

$$4-(1+1)^2 = 0$$
$$4-(2)^2 = 0$$
$$4-4 = 0$$
$$0 = 0 \text{ true}$$

91. $$12x^2 + 14x - 6 = 2(6x^2 + 7x - 3)$$
$$= 2(2x+3)(3x-1)$$

92. $$\frac{x^2 - x - 6}{3x-3} \div \frac{x^2-4}{x-1}$$
$$= \frac{x^2 - x - 6}{3x-3} \cdot \frac{x-1}{x^2-4}$$
$$= \frac{(x+2)(x-3)}{3(x-1)} \cdot \frac{(x-1)}{(x+2)(x-2)}$$
$$= \frac{x-3}{3(x-2)}$$

93. $4(x-5)=22+2(6x+3)$

$4x-20=22+12x+6$

$4x-20=28+12x$

$-8x-20=28$

$-8x=48$

$x=-6$

The solution is −6.

10.2 Exercise Set

1. x^2+10x

The coefficient of the x-term is 10.

Half of 10 is 5, and $5^2=25$. Add 25.

$x^2+10x+25=(x+5)^2$

3. x^2-2x

The coefficient of the x-term is −2.

Half of −2 is −1, and $(-1)^2=1$. Add 1.

$x^2-2x+1=(x-1)^2$

5. x^2+5x

The coefficient of the x-term is 5. Half of 5 is $\frac{5}{2}$, and $\left(\frac{5}{2}\right)^2=\frac{25}{4}$. Add $\frac{25}{4}$.

$x^2+5x+\frac{25}{4}=\left(x+\frac{5}{2}\right)^2$

7. x^2-7x

$\frac{1}{2}(-7)=-\frac{7}{2};\left(-\frac{7}{2}\right)^2=\frac{9}{4}$

$x^2-7x+\frac{49}{4}=\left(x-\frac{7}{2}\right)^2$

9. $x^2+\frac{1}{2}x$

$\frac{1}{2}\left(\frac{1}{2}\right)=\frac{1}{4};\left(\frac{1}{4}\right)^2=\frac{1}{16}$

$x^2+\frac{1}{2}x+\frac{1}{16}=\left(x+\frac{1}{4}\right)^2$

11. $x^2-\frac{4}{3}x$

$\frac{1}{2}\left(-\frac{4}{3}\right)=-\frac{2}{3};\left(-\frac{2}{3}\right)^2=\frac{4}{9}$

$x^2-\frac{4}{3}x+\frac{4}{9}=\left(x-\frac{2}{3}\right)^2$

13. $x^2+4x=5$

To complete the square on the binomial x^2+4x, take half of 4, which is 2, and square 2, giving 4. Add 4 to both sides of the equation to make the left side a perfect square binomial.

$x^2+4x=5$

$x^2+4x+4=5+4$

$(x+2)^2=9$

$x+2=\sqrt{9}$ or $x+2=-\sqrt{9}$

$x+2=3$ $\quad$ $x+2=-3$

$x=1$ $\quad$ $x=-5$

The solutions are 1 and −5.

15. $x^2-10x=-24$

To complete the square on the binomial x^2-10x, take half of −10, which is−5, and square −5, giving 25. Add 25 to both sides of the equation to make the left side a perfect square binomial.

$x^2-10x+25=-24+25$

$(x-5)^2=1$

The solutions are 6 and 4.

17. $x^2 - 2x = 5$

$\frac{1}{2}(-2) = -1; (-1)^2 = 1$

$x^2 - 2x + 1 = 5 + 1$

$(x-1)^2 = 6$

$x - 1 = \sqrt{6}$ or $x - 1 = -\sqrt{6}$

$x = 1 + \sqrt{6}$ or $x = 1 - \sqrt{6}$

The solutions are $1+\sqrt{6}$ and $1-\sqrt{6}$.

19. $x^2 + 4x + 1 = 0$

First subtract 1 from both sides to isolate the binomial $x^2 + 4x$.

$x^2 + 4x = -1$

$\frac{1}{2}(4) = 2; 2^2 = 4$

$x^2 + 4x + 4 = -1 + 4$

$(x+2)^2 = 3$

$x + 2 = \sqrt{3}$ or $x + 2 = -\sqrt{3}$

$x = -2 + \sqrt{3}$ or $x = -2 - \sqrt{3}$

The solutions are
$-2+\sqrt{3}$ and $-2-\sqrt{3}$.

21. $x^2 - 3x = 28$

$\frac{1}{2}(-3) = -\frac{3}{2}; \left(-\frac{3}{2}\right)^2 = \frac{9}{4}$

$x^2 - 3x + \frac{9}{4} = 28 + \frac{9}{4}$

$\left(x - \frac{3}{2}\right)^2 = \frac{121}{4}$

$x - \frac{3}{2} = \sqrt{\frac{121}{4}}$ or $x - \frac{3}{2} = -\sqrt{\frac{121}{4}}$

$x - \frac{3}{2} = \frac{11}{2}$ or $x - \frac{3}{2} = -\frac{11}{2}$

$x = \frac{14}{2} = 7$ $\quad x = -\frac{8}{2} = -4$

The solutions are 7 and −4.

23. $x^2 + 3x - 1 = 0$

$x^2 + 3x = 1$

$\frac{1}{2}(3) = \frac{3}{2}; \left(\frac{3}{2}\right)^2 = \frac{9}{4}$

$x^2 + 3x + \frac{9}{4} = 1 + \frac{9}{4}$

$\left(x + \frac{3}{2}\right) = \frac{13}{4}$

$x + \frac{3}{2} = \sqrt{\frac{13}{4}}$ or $x + \frac{3}{2} = -\sqrt{\frac{13}{4}}$

$x + \frac{3}{2} = \frac{\sqrt{13}}{2}$ or $x + \frac{3}{2} = -\sqrt{\frac{13}{2}}$

$x = -\frac{3}{2} + \frac{\sqrt{13}}{2}$ or $x = -\frac{3}{2} - \frac{\sqrt{13}}{2}$

$x = \frac{-3+\sqrt{13}}{2}$ or $x = \frac{-3-\sqrt{13}}{2}$

The solutions are $\frac{-3+\sqrt{13}}{2}$ and $\frac{-3-\sqrt{13}}{2}$, which can be written in abbreviated form as $\frac{-3\pm\sqrt{13}}{2}$.

25.
$$x^2 = 7x - 3$$
$$x^2 - 7x = -3$$

$$\frac{1}{2}(-7) = -\frac{7}{2}; \left(-\frac{7}{2}\right)^2 = \frac{49}{4}$$

$$x^2 - 7x + \frac{49}{4} = -3 + \frac{49}{4}$$
$$\left(x - \frac{7}{2}\right)^2 = \frac{-12}{4} + \frac{49}{4}$$
$$\left(x - \frac{7}{2}\right)^2 = \frac{37}{4}$$
$$x - \frac{7}{2} = \sqrt{\frac{37}{4}} \quad \text{or} \quad x - \frac{7}{2} = -\sqrt{\frac{37}{4}}$$
$$x - \frac{7}{2} = \frac{\sqrt{37}}{2} \quad \text{or} \quad x - \frac{7}{2} = -\frac{\sqrt{37}}{2}$$
$$x = \frac{7}{2} + \frac{\sqrt{37}}{2} \quad \text{or} \quad x = \frac{7}{2} - \frac{\sqrt{37}}{2}$$
$$x = \frac{7 + \sqrt{37}}{2} \quad \text{or} \quad x = \frac{7 - \sqrt{37}}{2}$$

The solutions are $x = \frac{7 \pm \sqrt{37}}{2}$.

27. $2x^2 - 2x - 6 = 0$

First, divide both sides of the equation by 2 so that the coefficient of the x^2 term will be 1.

$x^2 - x - 3 = 0$

Next, add 3 to both sides to isolate the binomial.

$x^2 - x = 3$

Complete the square: The coefficient of the x-term is -1, and $\frac{1}{2}(-1) = -\frac{1}{2}$, so add $\left(-\frac{1}{2}\right)^2 = \frac{1}{4}$ to both sides.

$$x^2 - x + \frac{1}{4} = 3 + \frac{1}{4}$$
$$\left(x - \frac{1}{2}\right)^2 = \frac{13}{4}$$
$$x - \frac{1}{2} = \sqrt{\frac{13}{4}} \quad \text{or} \quad x - \frac{1}{2} = -\sqrt{\frac{13}{4}}$$
$$x - \frac{1}{2} = \frac{\sqrt{13}}{2} \quad \text{or} \quad x - \frac{1}{2} = -\frac{\sqrt{13}}{2}$$
$$x = \frac{1 + \sqrt{13}}{2} \quad \text{or} \quad x = \frac{1 - \sqrt{13}}{2}$$

The solutions are $x = \frac{1 \pm \sqrt{13}}{2}$.

29.
$$2x^2 - 3x + 1 = 0$$
$$x^2 - \frac{3}{2}x + \frac{1}{2} = 0$$
$$x^2 - \frac{3}{2}x = -\frac{1}{2}$$

$$\frac{1}{2}\left(-\frac{3}{2}\right) = -\frac{3}{4}; \left(-\frac{3}{4}\right)^2 = \frac{9}{16}$$

$$x^2 - \frac{3}{2}x + \frac{9}{16} = -\frac{1}{2} + \frac{9}{16}$$
$$\left(x - \frac{3}{4}\right)^2 = -\frac{8}{16} + \frac{9}{16}$$
$$\left(x - \frac{3}{4}\right)^2 = \frac{1}{16}$$
$$x - \frac{3}{4} = \sqrt{\frac{1}{16}} \quad \text{or} \quad x - \frac{3}{4} = -\sqrt{\frac{1}{16}}$$
$$x - \frac{3}{4} = \frac{1}{4} \quad \text{or} \quad x - \frac{3}{4} = -\frac{1}{4}$$
$$x = 1 \qquad x = \frac{2}{4} = \frac{1}{2}$$

The solutions are 1 and $\frac{1}{2}$.

31. $2x^2+10x+11=0$

$$x^2+5x+\frac{11}{2}=0$$

$$x^2+5x=-\frac{11}{2}$$

$$\frac{1}{2}(5)=\frac{5}{2};\left(\frac{5}{2}\right)^2=\frac{25}{4}$$

$$x^2+5x+\frac{25}{4}=-\frac{11}{2}+\frac{25}{4}$$

$$\left(x+\frac{5}{2}\right)^2=-\frac{22}{4}+\frac{25}{4}$$

$$\left(x+\frac{5}{2}\right)^2=\frac{3}{4}$$

$$x+\frac{5}{2}=\sqrt{\frac{3}{4}} \quad \text{or} \quad x+\frac{5}{2}=-\sqrt{\frac{3}{4}}$$

$$x+\frac{5}{2}=\frac{\sqrt{3}}{2} \quad \text{or} \quad x+\frac{5}{2}=-\frac{\sqrt{3}}{2}$$

$$x=-\frac{5}{2}+\frac{\sqrt{3}}{2} \quad \text{or} \quad x=-\frac{5}{2}-\frac{\sqrt{3}}{2}$$

$$x=\frac{-5+\sqrt{3}}{2} \quad \text{or} \quad x=\frac{-5-\sqrt{3}}{2}$$

The solutions are $x=\frac{-5\pm\sqrt{3}}{2}$.

33. $4x^2-2x-3=0$

$$x^2-\frac{1}{2}x-\frac{3}{4}=0$$

$$x^2-\frac{1}{2}x=\frac{3}{4}$$

$$\frac{1}{2}\left(-\frac{1}{2}\right)=-\frac{1}{4};\left(-\frac{1}{4}\right)^2=\frac{1}{16}$$

$$x^2-\frac{1}{2}x+\frac{1}{16}=\frac{3}{4}+\frac{1}{16}$$

$$\left(x-\frac{1}{4}\right)^2=\frac{12}{16}+\frac{1}{16}$$

$$\left(x-\frac{1}{4}\right)^2=\frac{13}{16}$$

$$x-\frac{1}{4}=\sqrt{\frac{13}{16}} \quad \text{or} \quad x-\frac{1}{4}=-\sqrt{\frac{13}{16}}$$

$$x-\frac{1}{4}=\frac{\sqrt{13}}{4} \quad \text{or} \quad x-\frac{1}{4}=-\frac{\sqrt{13}}{4}$$

$$x=\frac{1}{4}+\frac{\sqrt{13}}{4} \quad \text{or} \quad x=\frac{1}{4}-\frac{\sqrt{13}}{4}$$

$$x=\frac{1+\sqrt{13}}{4} \quad \text{or} \quad x=\frac{1-\sqrt{13}}{4}$$

The solutions are $x=\frac{1\pm\sqrt{13}}{4}$

35. $\frac{x^2}{6}-\frac{x}{3}-1=0$

Multiply both sides of the equation by 6 to obtain

$$x^2-2x-6=0$$

$$x^2-2x=6$$

The coefficient on x is -2. Divide this by 2 and square the result.

$$\left(\frac{-2}{2}\right)^2=(-1)^2=1$$

Add 1 to both sides of the equation:

$$x^2-2x+1=6+1$$

$$(x-1)^2=7$$

$$x-1=\pm\sqrt{7}$$

$$x=1\pm\sqrt{7}$$

The solutions are $1\pm\sqrt{7}$.

36. $\frac{x^2}{6}+x-\frac{3}{2}=0$

Multiply both sides of the equation by 6 to obtin

$x^2+6x-9=0$

$x^2+6x=9$

The coefficient on x is 6. Divide this by 2 and square the result.

$\left(\frac{6}{2}\right)^2=3^2=9$

Add 9 to both sides of the equation:

$x^2+6x+9=9+9$

$(x+3)^2=18$

$x+3=\pm\sqrt{18}$

$x=-3\pm3\sqrt{2}$

The solutions are $-3\pm3\sqrt{2}$.

37. $(x+2)(x-3)=1$

$x^2-x-6=1$

$x^2-x=7$

The coefficient of x is -1. Divide this by 2 and square the result.

$\left(\frac{-1}{2}\right)^2=\frac{1}{4}$

Add $\frac{1}{4}$ to both sides of the equation.

$x^2-x+\frac{1}{4}=7+\frac{1}{4}$

$\left(x-\frac{1}{2}\right)^2=\frac{29}{4}$

$x-\frac{1}{2}=\pm\sqrt{\frac{29}{4}}$

$x=\frac{1}{2}\pm\frac{\sqrt{29}}{2}=\frac{1\pm\sqrt{29}}{2}$

The solutions are $\frac{1\pm\sqrt{29}}{2}$.

38. $(x-5)(x-3)=-1$

$x^2-8x+15=-1$

$x^2-8x=-16$

The coefficient on x is -8. Divide this by 2 and square the result.

$\left(\frac{-8}{2}\right)^2=(-4)^2=16$

Add 16 to both sides of the equation.

$x^2-8x+16=-16+16$

$(x-4)^2=0$

$x-4=0$

$x=4$

The only solution is 4.

39. $x^2+4bx=5b^2$

The coefficient on x is $4b$. Divide this by 2 and square the result.

$\left(\frac{4b}{2}\right)^2=(2b)^2=4b^2$

Add $4b^2$ to both sides of the equation:

$x^2+4bx+4b^2=5b^2+4b^2$

$(x+2b)^2=9b^2$

$x+2b=\pm\sqrt{9b^2}$

$x=-2b\pm3b$

$x=-2b-3b$ or $x=-2b+3b$

$=-5b$ $\qquad$ $=b$

The solutions are $-5b$ and b.

40. $x^2+6bx=7b^2$

The coefficient on x is $6b$. Divide this by 2 and square the result.

$\left(\frac{6b}{2}\right)^2=(3b)^2=9b^2$

Add $9b^2$ to both sides of the equation:

$$x^2 + 6bx + 9b^2 = 7b^2 + 9b^2$$
$$(x+3b)^2 = 16b^2$$
$$x + 3b = \pm\sqrt{16b^2}$$
$$x = -3b \pm 4b$$
$$x = -3b - 4b \quad \text{or} \quad x = -3b + 4b$$
$$= -7b \qquad\qquad = b$$
The solutions are $-7b$ and b.

41. Answers will vary.

43. Statement d is true.
$$\frac{1}{2}(-7) = -\frac{7}{2}, \text{ and } \left(-\frac{7}{2}\right)^2 = \frac{49}{4}.$$

45. $x^2 + x + c = 0$
Subtract c from both sides:
$x^2 + x = -c$
The coefficient of the x-term is 1. and
$\left(\frac{1}{2}\right)^2 = \frac{1}{4}$, so add $\frac{1}{4}$ to both sides.
$$x^2 + x + \frac{1}{4} = \frac{1}{4} - c$$
$$\left(x + \frac{1}{2}\right)^2 = \frac{1}{4} - \frac{4c}{4}$$
$$\left(x + \frac{1}{2}\right)^2 = \frac{1-4c}{4}$$
$$x + \frac{1}{2} = \pm\sqrt{\frac{1-4c}{4}}$$
$$x = -\frac{1}{2} \pm \frac{\sqrt{1-4c}}{2}$$
$$x = \frac{-1 \pm \sqrt{1-4c}}{2}$$
The solutions are $x = \dfrac{-1 \pm \sqrt{1-4c}}{2}$

47. Answers will vary depending on the equations chosen. As an example, the solution for equation in Exercise 17 is shown here. In Exercise 17, the solutions to the equation $x^2 - 2x = 5$ were found to be $1 + \sqrt{6}$ and $1 - \sqrt{6}$. Use a calculator to obtain decimal approximation for these solutions.
$1 + \sqrt{6} \approx 3.45$
$1 - \sqrt{6} \approx -1.45$
Graph $Y_1 = x^2 - 2x - 5$.

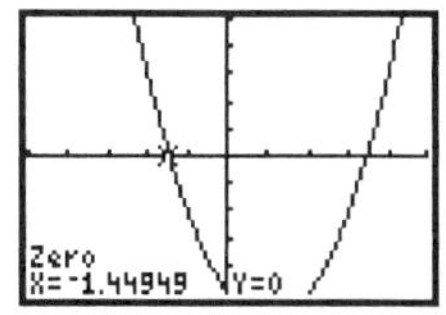

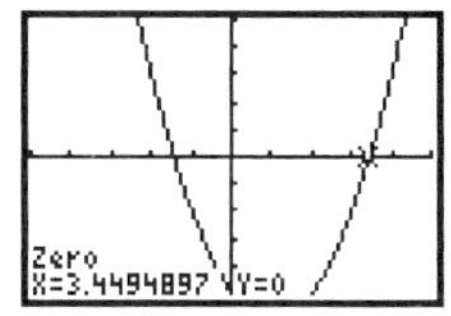

The x-intercepts of $y = x^2 - 2x - 5$ verify the solution.

48.
$$\frac{2x+3}{x^2-7x+12} - \frac{2}{x-3}$$
$$= \frac{2x+3}{(x-3)(x-4)} - \frac{2}{x-3}$$
$$= \frac{2x+3}{(x-3)(x-4)} - \frac{2(x-4)}{(x-3)(x-4)}$$
$$= \frac{(2x-3)-2(x-4)}{(x-3)(x-4)}$$
$$= \frac{2x+3-2x+8}{(x-3)(x-4)}$$
$$= \frac{11}{(x-3)(x-4)}$$

49. $$\frac{x-\frac{1}{3}}{3-\frac{1}{x}}$$
LCD = $3x$

$$\frac{x-\frac{1}{3}}{3-\frac{1}{x}}=\frac{3x}{3x}\cdot\frac{\left(x-\frac{1}{3}\right)}{\left(3-\frac{1}{x}\right)}$$
$$=\frac{3x\cdot x-3x\cdot\frac{1}{3}}{3x\cdot 3-3x\cdot\frac{1}{x}}$$
$$=\frac{3x^2-x}{9x-3}$$
$$=\frac{x(3x-1)}{3(3x-1)}=\frac{x}{3}$$

50. $\sqrt{2x+3}=2x-3$
Square both sides and solve for x:
$$\left(\sqrt{2x+3}\right)^2=(2x-3)^2$$
$$2x+3=(2x)^2-2\cdot 2x\cdot 3+3^2$$
$$2x+3=4x^2-12x+9$$
$$0=4x^2-14x+6$$
$$0=2\left(2x^2-7x+3\right)$$
$$0=2(2x-1)(x-3)$$
$$2x-1=0 \quad\text{or}\quad x-3=0$$
$$x=\frac{1}{2} \qquad\qquad x=3$$
Each of the proposed solutions must be checked in the original equation.

Check $\frac{1}{2}$: $\sqrt{2x+3}=2x-3$
$$\sqrt{2\left(\frac{1}{2}\right)+3}=2\left(\frac{1}{2}\right)-3$$
$$\sqrt{1+3}=1-3$$
$$=\sqrt{4}=1-3$$
$$2=-2 \text{ false}$$

Check 3: $\sqrt{2x+3}=2x-3$
$$\sqrt{2\cdot 3+3}=2\cdot 3-3$$
$$\sqrt{6+3}=6-3$$
$$\sqrt{9}=3$$
$$3=3 \text{ true}$$

Thus, $\frac{1}{2}$ is an extraneous solution, while 3 satisfies the equation. Therefore, the only solution is 3.

10.3 Exercise Set

1. $x^2+5x+6=0$
Identify the values of $a, b,$ and c:
$a=1, b=5,$ and $c=6.$
Substitute these values into the quadratic formula and simplify to get the equation's solutions.
$$x=\frac{-b\pm\sqrt{b^2-4ac}}{2a}$$
$$x=\frac{5\pm\sqrt{5^2-4(1)(6)}}{2(1)}$$
$$=\frac{5\pm\sqrt{25-24}}{2}=\frac{5\pm\sqrt{1}}{2}=\frac{-5\pm 1}{2}$$
$$x=\frac{-5+1}{2} \quad\text{or}\quad x=\frac{-5-1}{2}$$
$$=\frac{-4}{2}=-2 \qquad =\frac{-6}{2}=-3$$
The solutions are −2 and −3.

3. $x^2+5x+3=0$

$a=1, b=5, c=3$

$$x=\frac{-b\pm\sqrt{b^2-4ac}}{2a}$$

$$x=\frac{-5\pm\sqrt{5^2-4(1)(3)}}{2\cdot 1}$$

$$x=\frac{-5\pm\sqrt{25-12}}{2}$$

$$=\frac{-5\pm\sqrt{13}}{2}$$

The solutions are $\frac{-5\pm\sqrt{13}}{2}$.

5. $x^2+4x-6=0$

$a=1, b=4, c=-6$

$$x=\frac{-b\pm\sqrt{b^2-4ac}}{2a}$$

$$x=\frac{-4\pm\sqrt{4^2-4(1)(-6)}}{2\cdot 1}$$

$$=\frac{-4\pm\sqrt{16+24}}{2}$$

$$=\frac{-4\pm\sqrt{40}}{2}$$

$$=\frac{-4\pm 2\sqrt{10}}{2}$$

$$=\frac{2\left(-2\pm\sqrt{10}\right)}{2}$$

$$=-2\pm\sqrt{10}$$

The solutions are $-2\pm\sqrt{10}$.

7. $x^2+4x-7=0$

$a=1, b=4, c=-7$

$$x=\frac{-b\pm\sqrt{b^2-4ac}}{2a}$$

$$=\frac{-4\pm\sqrt{4^2-4(1)(-7)}}{2\cdot 1}$$

$$=\frac{-4\pm\sqrt{16+28}}{2}$$

$$=\frac{-4\pm\sqrt{44}}{2}$$

$$=\frac{-4\pm 2\sqrt{11}}{2}$$

$$=\frac{2\left(-2\pm\sqrt{11}\right)}{2}$$

$$=-2\pm\sqrt{11}$$

The solutions are $-2\pm\sqrt{11}$.

9. $x^2-3x-18=0$

$a=1, b=-3, c=-18$

$$x=\frac{-b\pm\sqrt{b^2-4ac}}{2a}$$

$$=\frac{-(-3)\pm\sqrt{(-3)^2-4(1)(-18)}}{2\cdot 1}$$

$$=\frac{3\pm\sqrt{9+72}}{2}$$

$$=\frac{3\pm\sqrt{81}}{2}$$

$$=\frac{3\pm 9}{2}$$

$$x=\frac{3+9}{2} \quad \text{or} \quad x=\frac{3-9}{2}$$

$$x=\frac{12}{2}=6 \quad \text{or} \quad x=\frac{-6}{2}=-3$$

11. $6x^2-5x-6=0$

$a=6, b=-5, c=-6$

$$x=\frac{-b\pm\sqrt{b^2-4ac}}{2a}$$

$$=\frac{-(-5)\pm\sqrt{(-5)^2-4(6)(-6)}}{2\cdot 6}$$

$$=\frac{5\pm\sqrt{25+144}}{12}$$

$$=\frac{5\pm\sqrt{169}}{12}=\frac{5\pm 13}{12}$$

$$x=\frac{5+13}{12} \text{ or } x=\frac{5-13}{12}$$

$$x=\frac{18}{12}=\frac{3}{2} \text{ or } x=\frac{-8}{12}=-\frac{2}{3}$$

The solutions are $\frac{3}{2}$ and $-\frac{2}{3}$.

13. $x^2-2x-10=0$

$a=1, b=-2, c=-10$

$$x=\frac{-b\pm\sqrt{b^2-4ac}}{2a}$$

$$=\frac{-(-2)\pm\sqrt{(-2)^2-4(1)(-10)}}{2\cdot 1}$$

$$=\frac{2\pm\sqrt{4+40}}{2}=\frac{2\pm\sqrt{44}}{2}$$

$$=\frac{2\pm 2\sqrt{11}}{2}$$

$$=\frac{2(1\pm\sqrt{11})}{2}$$

$$=1\pm\sqrt{11}$$

The solutions are $1\pm\sqrt{11}$.

15. $x^2-x=14$

Rewrite the equation in standard form.

$x^2-x-14=0$

Identify $a, b,$ and c.

$a=1, b=-1, c=-14$

Substitute these values into the quadratic formula.

$$x=\frac{-b\pm\sqrt{b^2-4ac}}{2a}$$

$$=\frac{-(-1)\pm\sqrt{(-1)^2-4(1)(-14)}}{2\cdot 1}$$

$$=\frac{1\pm\sqrt{1+56}}{2}=\frac{1\pm\sqrt{57}}{2}$$

The radical cannot be simplified.

The solutions are $\frac{1\pm\sqrt{57}}{2}$.

17. $6x^2+6x+1=0$

$a=6, b=6, c=1$

$$x=\frac{-b\pm\sqrt{b^2-4ac}}{2a}$$

$$=\frac{-6\pm\sqrt{6^2-4(6)(1)}}{2\cdot 6}$$

$$=\frac{-6\pm\sqrt{36-24}}{12}=\frac{-6\pm\sqrt{12}}{12}$$

$$=\frac{-6\pm 2\sqrt{3}}{12}=\frac{2(-3\pm\sqrt{3})}{12}$$

$$=\frac{-3\pm\sqrt{3}}{6}$$

The solutions are $\frac{-3\pm\sqrt{3}}{6}$.

19. $9x^2 - 12x + 4 = 0$

$a = 9, b = -12, c = 4$

$$x = \frac{-b \pm \sqrt{b^2 - 4ac}}{2a}$$
$$= \frac{-(-12) \pm \sqrt{(-12)^2 - 4(9)(4)}}{2 \cdot 9}$$
$$= \frac{12 \pm \sqrt{144 - 144}}{18} = \frac{12 \pm \sqrt{0}}{18}$$
$$= \frac{12 \pm 0}{18} = \frac{12}{18}$$
$$= \frac{2}{3}$$

The only solution is $\frac{2}{3}$.

21. $4x^2 = 2x + 7$

Rewrite the equation in standard form.

$4x^2 - 2x - 7 = 0$

$a = 4, b = -2, c = -7$

$$x = \frac{-b \pm \sqrt{b^2 - 4ac}}{2a}$$
$$= \frac{-(-2) \pm \sqrt{(-2)^2 - 4(4)(-7)}}{2 \cdot 4}$$
$$= \frac{2 \pm \sqrt{4 + 112}}{8} = \frac{2 \pm \sqrt{116}}{8}$$
$$= \frac{2 \pm 2\sqrt{29}}{8} = \frac{2 \pm \left(1 \pm \sqrt{29}\right)}{8}$$
$$= \frac{1 \pm \sqrt{29}}{4}$$

The solutions are $\frac{1 \pm \sqrt{29}}{4}$.

23. $2x^2 - x = 1$

Write the equation in standard form.

$2x^2 - x - 1 = 0$

Factor the trinomial.

$(2x + 1)(x - 1) = 0$

Use the zero-product property.

$2x + 1 = 0$ or $x - 1 = 0$

$2x = -1$ $\quad x = 1$

$x = -\frac{1}{2}$

The solutions are 1 and $-\frac{1}{2}$.

25. $5x^2 + 2 = 11x$

Write the equation in standard form.

$5x^2 - 11x + 2 = 0$

Factor the trinomial.

$(5x - 1)(x - 2) = 0$

Use the zero-product property.

$5x - 1 = 0$ or $x - 2 = 0$

$5x = 1$ $\quad x = 2$

$x = \frac{1}{5}$

The solutions are $\frac{1}{5}$ and 2.

27. $3x^2 = 60$

$x^2 = 20$

Use the square root property.

$x = \sqrt{20}$ or $x = -\sqrt{20}$

$x = 2\sqrt{5}$ $\quad x = -2\sqrt{5}$

The solutions are $2\sqrt{5}$ and $-2\sqrt{5}$.

29. $x^2 - 2x = 1$

Write the equation in standard form.

$x^2 - 2x - 1 = 0$

The trinomial is prime, so we cannot factor and use the zero-product property. Instead, use the quadratic formula with

$a = 1, b = -2, c = -1$

$$x = \frac{-b \pm \sqrt{b^2 - 4ac}}{2a}$$
$$= \frac{-(-2) \pm \sqrt{(-2)^2 - 4(1)(-1)}}{2 \cdot 1}$$
$$= \frac{2 \pm \sqrt{4+4}}{2} = \frac{2 \pm \sqrt{8}}{2}$$
$$= \frac{2 \pm 2\sqrt{2}}{2} = \frac{2(1 \pm \sqrt{2})}{2}$$
$$= 1 \pm \sqrt{2}$$

The solutions are $1 \pm \sqrt{2}$.

31. $(2x+3)(x+4) = 1$

Write the equation in standard form.

$2x^2 + 11x + 12 = 1$

$2x^2 + 11x + 11 = 0$

The trinomial cannot be factored, so use the quadratic formula with $a = 2, b = 11, c = 11$.

$$x = \frac{-b \pm \sqrt{b^2 - 4ac}}{2a}$$
$$= \frac{-11 \pm \sqrt{11^2 - 4(2)(11)}}{2 \cdot 2}$$
$$= \frac{-11 \pm \sqrt{121 - 88}}{4}$$
$$= \frac{-11 \pm \sqrt{33}}{4}$$

The solutions are $\frac{-11 \pm \sqrt{33}}{4}$.

33. $(3x-4)^2 = 16$

Use the square root property.

$3x - 4 = \sqrt{16}$ or $3x - 4 = -\sqrt{16}$

$3x - 4 = 4$ or $3x - 4 = -4$

$3x = 8$ or $3x = 0$

$x = \frac{8}{3}$ or $x = 0$

The solutions are $\frac{8}{3}$ and 0.

35. $3x^2 - 12x + 12 = 0$

$3(x^2 - 4x + 4) = 0$

$3(x-2)^2 = 0$

$(x-2)^2 = 0$

$x - 2 = 0$

$x = 2$

The only solution is 2.

37. $4x^2 - 16 = 0$

$4(x^2 - 4) = 0$

$4(x+2)(x-2) = 0$

$x + 2 = 0$ or $x - 2 = 0$

$x = -2$ or $x = 2$

The solutions are -2 and 2.

39. $x^2 + 9x = 0$

$x(x+9) = 0$

$x = 0$ or $x + 9 = 0$

$x = -9$

The solutions are 0 and -9.

41. $\frac{3}{4}x^2 - \frac{5}{2}x - 2 = 0$

To clear fractions, multiply both sides by the LCD, 4.

$$4\left(\frac{3}{4}x^2 - \frac{5}{2}x - 2\right) = 4 \cdot 0$$
$$3x^2 - 10x - 8 = 0$$
$$(3x+2)(x-4) = 0$$
$$3x + 2 = 0 \quad \text{or} \quad x - 4 = 0$$
$$3x = -2 \qquad x = 4$$
$$x = -\frac{2}{3}$$

The solutions are $-\frac{2}{3}$ and 4.

43. $(3x-2)^2 = 10$

Use the square root property.

$$(3x-2)^2 = 10$$
$$3x - 2 = \sqrt{10} \qquad 3x - 2 = -\sqrt{10}$$
$$3x = 2 + \sqrt{10} \quad \text{or} \quad 3x = 2 - \sqrt{10}$$
$$x = \frac{2+\sqrt{10}}{3} \qquad x = \frac{2-\sqrt{10}}{3}$$

The solutions are $\frac{2 \pm \sqrt{10}}{3}$.

45. $\frac{x^2}{x+7} - \frac{3}{x+7} = 0$

Multiply both sides by the LCD, $x+7$.

$$x^2 - 3 = 0$$
$$x^2 = 3$$
$$x = \pm\sqrt{3}$$

The solutions are $\pm\sqrt{3}$.

46. $\frac{x^2}{x+9} - \frac{11}{x+9} = 0$

Multiply both sides by the LCD, $x+9$.

$$x^2 - 11 = 0$$
$$x^2 = 11$$
$$x = \pm\sqrt{11}$$

The solutions are $\pm\sqrt{11}$.

47.
$$(x+2)^2 + x(x+1) = 4$$
$$x^2 + 4x + 4 + x^2 + x = 4$$
$$2x^2 + 5x = 0$$
$$x(2x+5) = 0$$
$$x = 0 \quad \text{or} \quad 2x + 5 = 0$$
$$2x = -5$$
$$x = -\frac{5}{2}$$

The solutions are $-\frac{5}{2}$ and 0.

48.
$$(x-1)(3x+2) = -7(x-1)$$
$$3x^2 - 3x + 2x - 2 = -7x + 7$$
$$3x^2 + 6x - 9 = 0$$
$$x^2 + 2x - 3 = 0$$
$$(x+3)(x-1) = 0$$
$$x + 3 = 0 \quad \text{or} \quad x - 1 = 0$$
$$x = -3 \qquad x = 1$$

The solutions are -3 and 1.

49.
$$2x^2 - 9x - 3 = 9 - 9x$$
$$2x^2 - 12 = 0$$
$$x^2 - 6 = 0$$
$$x^2 = 6$$
$$x = \pm\sqrt{6}$$

The solutions are $\pm\sqrt{6}$.

50. $3x^2-6x-3=12-6x$

$$3x^2-15=0$$
$$3x^2=15$$
$$x^2=5$$
$$x=\pm\sqrt{5}$$

The solutions are $\pm\sqrt{5}$.

51. $\frac{1}{x}+\frac{1}{x+3}=\frac{1}{4}$

Multiply both sides by the LCD, $4x(x+3)$.

$$4x(x+3)\left(\frac{1}{x}+\frac{1}{x+3}\right)=4x(x+3)\frac{1}{4}$$
$$4(x+3)+4x=x(x+3)$$
$$4x+12+4x=x^2+3x$$
$$0=x^2-5x-12$$

Here we will use the quadratic formula with $a=1$, $b=-5$, and $c=-12$.

$$x=\frac{-(-5)\pm\sqrt{(-5)^2-4(1)(-12)}}{2(1)}$$
$$=\frac{5\pm\sqrt{25+48}}{2}$$
$$=\frac{5\pm\sqrt{73}}{2}$$

The solutions are $\frac{5\pm\sqrt{73}}{2}$.

52. $\frac{1}{x}+\frac{2}{x+3}=\frac{1}{4}$

Multiply both sides by the LCD, $4x(x+3)$

$$4x(x+3)\left(\frac{1}{x}+\frac{2}{x+3}\right)=4x(x+3)\frac{1}{4}$$
$$4(x+3)+4x(2)=x(x+3)$$
$$4x+12+8x=x^2+3x$$
$$0=x^2-9x-12$$

Here we will use the quadratic formula with $a=1$, $b=-9$, and $c=-12$.

$$x=\frac{-(-9)\pm\sqrt{(-9)^2-4(1)(-12)}}{2(1)}$$
$$=\frac{9\pm\sqrt{81+48}}{2}$$
$$=\frac{9\pm\sqrt{129}}{2}$$

The solutions are $\frac{9\pm\sqrt{129}}{2}$.

53. $h=-16t^2+60t+4; h=0$

$$0=-16t^2+60t+4$$
$$16t^2-60t-4=0$$
$$4\left(4t^2-15t-1\right)=0$$
$$4t^2--15t-1=0$$

Note: Dividing both sides by 4 is not necessary, but it results in smaller numbers to be substituted in the quadratic formula.
$a=4, b=-15, c=-1$

$$t=\frac{-b\pm\sqrt{b^2-4ac}}{2a}$$
$$=\frac{-(-15)\pm\sqrt{(-15)^2-4(4)(-1)}}{2(4)}$$
$$=\frac{15\pm\sqrt{225+16}}{8}=\frac{15\pm\sqrt{241}}{8}$$
$$t=\frac{15+\sqrt{241}}{8} \quad \text{or} \quad t=\frac{15-\sqrt{241}}{8}$$
$$t\approx 3.8 \quad \text{or} \quad t\approx -0.1$$

Reject the negative solution to the quadratic equation because the time cannot be negative. It will take about 3.8 seconds for the football to hit the ground.

55. $h = -0.05x^2 + 27$

$$22 = -0.05x^2 + 27$$
$$-5 = -0.05x^2$$
$$\frac{-5}{-0.05} = \frac{-0.05x^2}{-0.05}$$
$$100 = x^2$$
$$\sqrt{100} = x$$
$$10 = x$$

The arch is 22 feet high at a point that is 10 feet to the right of the center.

57. $N = -0.02x^2 + 0.5x + 10.2$

$$7.2 = -0.02x^2 + 0.5x + 10.2$$
$$0 = -0.02x^2 + 0.5x + 3.0$$

Multiply both sides by -50 to clear the decimals.

$$x^2 - 25x - 150 = 0$$
$$(x-30)(x+5) = 0$$
$$x - 30 = 0 \quad \text{or} \quad x + 5 = 0$$
$$x = 30 \qquad\qquad x = -5$$

Discard the negative. According to the model, there will be 7.2 million property crimes in 1975+30=2005.

59. Let x = the width of the rectangle. Then $x+3$ = the length.

$$A = l2$$
$$36 = (x+3)\cdot x$$
$$36 = x^2 + 3x$$
$$0 = x^2 + 3x - 36$$
$$a = 1, b = 3, c = -36$$
$$x = \frac{-b \pm \sqrt{b^2 - 4ac}}{2a}$$
$$= \frac{-3 \pm \sqrt{(-3)^2 - 4(1)(-36)}}{2\cdot 1}$$
$$= \frac{-3 \pm \sqrt{9+144}}{2} = \frac{-3 \pm \sqrt{153}}{2}$$
$$x = \frac{-3+\sqrt{153}}{2} \quad \text{or} \quad x = \frac{-3-\sqrt{153}}{2}$$
$$x \approx 4.7 \qquad\qquad x \approx -7.7$$

Reject the negative solution of the quadratic equation because the width cannot be negative. If $x = 4.7$, then $x+3 = 7.7$. Thus, to the nearest tenth of a meter, the width is 4.7 meters and the length is7.7 meters.

61. Let x = the length of the shorter leg. Then $x+1$ = the length of the longer leg.

Use the Pythagorean Theorem.

$$x^2 + (x+1) = 4^2$$
$$x^2 + x^2 + 2x + 1 = 16$$
$$2x^2 + 2x - 15 = 0$$

Solve using the quadratic formula.

$$a = 2, b = 2, c = -15$$
$$x = \frac{-2 \pm \sqrt{2^2 - 4(2)(-15)}}{2\cdot 2}$$
$$= \frac{2 \pm \sqrt{4+120}}{4}$$
$$= \frac{2 \pm \sqrt{124}}{4}$$
$$x = \frac{-2+\sqrt{124}}{4} \quad \text{or} \quad x = \frac{-2-\sqrt{124}}{4}$$
$$x \approx 2.3 \qquad\qquad x \approx -3.3$$

The length of a leg cannot be negative, so reject -3.3. If $x = 2.3$, then $x+1$ = 3.3. Thus, to the nearest tenth of a foot, the lengths of the legs are 2.3 feet and 3.3 feet.

63. Set the two formulas equal to each other and solve for A.

$$\frac{DA}{A+12}=\frac{D(A+1)}{24}$$
$$24DA=D(A+1)(A+12)$$
$$24A=(A+1)(A+12)$$
$$24A=A^2+13A+12$$
$$0=A^2-11A+12$$

Solve using the quadratic formula.

$$A=\frac{-(-11)\pm\sqrt{(-11)^2-4(1)(12)}}{2(1)}$$
$$=\frac{11\pm\sqrt{121-48}}{2}=\frac{11\pm\sqrt{73}}{2}$$

$A\approx 9.8$ or $A\approx 1.2$

Discard 1.2 since this age is too young for the formulas to apply. The two formulas give the same child's dosage for a child that is about 9.8 years old.

For Exercises 65-67, answers may vary.

69. If $b^2-4ac>0$, there are two real number solutions. If b^2-4ac is a perfect square, the solutions are rational; if it is not a perfect square, they are irrational.

If $b^2-4ac=0$, there is only one solution, which is rational.

If $b^2-4ac<0$, the solutions are not real numbers.

Therefore, by evaluating b^2-4ac, you can determine the kinds of solutions for any quadratic equation without actually solving it.

71. Let x = the width of the border.

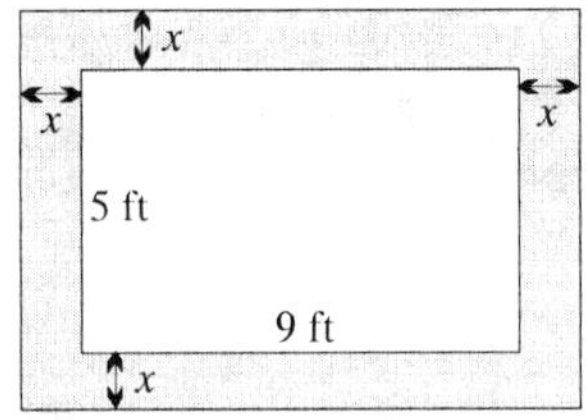

Area of large rectangle (garden plus border) $=(9+2x)(5+2x)$

Area of small rectangle (garden) $=9\cdot 5=45$

Area of border = Area of large rectangle - Area of small rectangle $=(9+2x)(5+2x)-45$

The area of the border is 40 square feet, so

$(9+2x)(5+2x)-45=40.$

Solve this equation.

$$45+28x+4x^2-45=40$$
$$4x^2+28x-40=0$$
$$4(x^2+7x-10)=0$$
$$x^2+7x-10=0$$

$a=1, b=7, c=-10$

$$x=\frac{-b\pm\sqrt{b^2-4ac}}{2a}$$
$$=\frac{-7\pm\sqrt{7^2-4(1)(-10)}}{2(1)}$$
$$=\frac{-7\pm\sqrt{49+40}}{2}$$
$$=\frac{-7\pm\sqrt{89}}{2}$$

$x=\frac{-7+\sqrt{89}}{2}$ or $x=\frac{-7-\sqrt{89}}{2}$

$x\approx 1.2$ $\quad x\approx -8.2$

Reject −8.2 because the width of the border must be positive. The width of the border is about 1.2 feet.

73. $y = -0.02x^2 + 0.5x + 10.2$

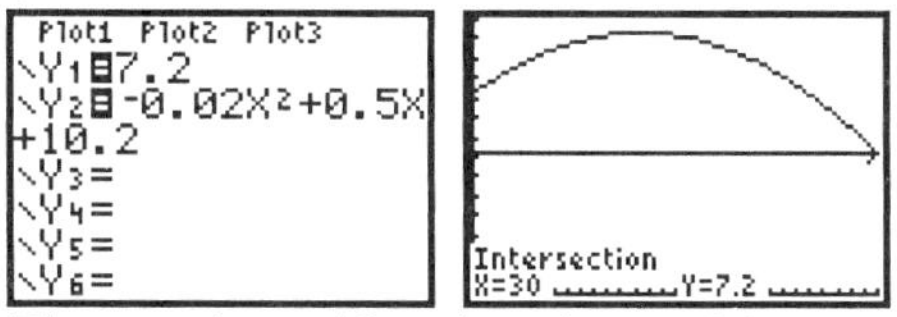

The graph verifies that the positive solution of the quadratic equation is 30.

74. $125^{-\frac{2}{3}} = \frac{1}{125^{\frac{2}{3}}} = \frac{1}{\left(\sqrt[3]{125}\right)^2}$

$= \frac{1}{5^2} = \frac{1}{25}$

75. $\frac{12}{3+\sqrt{5}}$

To rationalize the denominator, multiply numerator and denominator by the conjugate of the denominator.

$\frac{12}{3+\sqrt{5}} = \frac{12}{3+\sqrt{5}} \cdot \frac{3-\sqrt{5}}{3-\sqrt{5}}$

$= \frac{12\left(3-\sqrt{5}\right)}{3^2 - \left(\sqrt{5}\right)^2}$

$= \frac{12\left(3-\sqrt{5}\right)}{9-5}$

$= \frac{12\left(3-\sqrt{5}\right)}{4}$

$= 3\left(3-\sqrt{5}\right) = 9 - 3\sqrt{5}$

76. $(x-y)\left(x^2+xy+y^2\right)$

$= x\left(x^2+xy+y^2\right) - y\left(x^2+xy+y^2\right)$

$= x^3 + x^2y + xy^2 - x^2y - xy^2 - y^3$

$= x^3 - y^3$

Mid-Chapter 10 Check Points

1. $(3x-2)^2 = 100$

$3x - 2 = \pm\sqrt{100}$

$3x - 2 = \pm 10$

$3x = 2 \pm 10$

$x = \frac{2 \pm 10}{3}$

$x = \frac{2+10}{3} = 4$ or $x = \frac{2-10}{3} = -\frac{8}{3}$

The solutions are $-\frac{8}{3}$ and 4.

2. $15x^2 = 5x$

$15x^2 - 5x = 0$

$5x(3x-1) = 0$

$5x = 0$ or $3x - 1 = 0$

$x = 0$ $\quad 3x = 1$

$x = \frac{1}{3}$

The solutions are 0 and $\frac{1}{3}$.

3. $x^2 - 2x - 10 = 0$

$a = 1, b = -2, c = -10$

$x = \frac{-(-2) \pm \sqrt{(-2)^2 - 4(1)(-10)}}{2(1)}$

$= \frac{2 \pm \sqrt{4+40}}{2} = \frac{2 \pm \sqrt{44}}{2}$

$= \frac{2 \pm 2\sqrt{11}}{2} = 1 \pm \sqrt{11}$

The solutions are $1 \pm \sqrt{11}$.

4. $x^2-8x+16=7$

$x^2-8x+9=0$

$a=1, b=-8, c=9$

$$x=\frac{-(-8)\pm\sqrt{(-8)^2-4(1)(9)}}{2(1)}$$

$$=\frac{8\pm\sqrt{64-36}}{2}=\frac{8\pm\sqrt{28}}{2}$$

$$=\frac{8\pm2\sqrt{7}}{2}=4\pm\sqrt{7}$$

The solutions are $4\pm\sqrt{7}$.

5. $3x^2-x-2=0$

$(3x+2)(x-1)=0$

$3x+2=0$ or $x-1=0$

$3x=-2$ $\quad x=1$

$x=-\frac{2}{3}$

The solutions are $-\frac{2}{3}$ and 1.

6. $6x^2=10x-3$

$6x^2-10x+3=0$

$a=6, b=-10, c=3$

$$x=\frac{-(-10)\pm\sqrt{(-10)^2-4(6)(3)}}{2(6)}$$

$$=\frac{10\pm\sqrt{100-72}}{12}=\frac{10\pm\sqrt{28}}{12}$$

$$=\frac{10\pm2\sqrt{7}}{12}=\frac{5\pm\sqrt{7}}{6}$$

The solutions are $\frac{5\pm\sqrt{7}}{6}$.

7. $x^2+(x+1)^2=25$

$x^2+x^2+2x+1=25$

$2x^2+2x-24=0$

$x^2+x-12=0$

$(x+4)(x-3)=0$

$x+4=0$ or $x-3=0$

$x=-4$ $\quad x=3$

The solutions are -4 and 3.

8. $(x+5)^2=40$

$x+5=\pm\sqrt{40}$

$x+5=\pm2\sqrt{10}$

$x=-5\pm2\sqrt{10}$

The solutions are $-5\pm2\sqrt{10}$.

9. $2(x^2-8)=11-x^2$

$2x^2-16=11-x^2$

$3x^2=27$

$x^2=9$

$x=\pm\sqrt{9}$

$x=\pm3$

The solutions are ±3.

10. $2x^2+5x+1=0$

$a=2,\ b=5,\ c=1$

$$x=\frac{-5\pm\sqrt{5^2-4(2)(1)}}{2(2)}$$

$$=\frac{-5\pm\sqrt{25-8}}{4}=\frac{-5\pm\sqrt{17}}{4}$$

The solutions are $\frac{-5\pm\sqrt{17}}{4}$.

11. $(x-8)(2x-3)=34$

$2x^2-16x-3x+24=34$

$2x^2-19x-10=0$

$(2x+1)(x-10)=0$

$2x+1=0$ or $x-10=0$

$2x=-1$ $\quad x=10$

$x=-\frac{1}{2}$

The solutions are $-\frac{1}{2}$ and 10.

12. $x+\frac{16}{x}=8$

Multiply both sides of the equation by x.

$x\left(x+\frac{16}{x}\right)=x(8)$

$x^2+16=8x$

$x^2-8x+16=0$

$(x-4)^2=0$

$x=4$

The only solution is 4.

13. $x^2+14x-32=0$

$x^2+14x=32$

The coefficient on x is 14. Divide this by 2 and square the result.

$\left(\frac{14}{2}\right)^2=7^2=49$

Add 49 to both sides.

$x^2+14x+49=32+49$

$(x+7)^2=81$

$x+7=\pm\sqrt{81}$

$x+7=\pm 9$

$x=-7\pm 9$

$x=-7+9=2$ or $x=-7-9=-16$

The solutions are -16 and 2.

14. Let a = the length of the missing side.

$a^2+6^2=8^2$

$a^2+36=64$

$a^2=28$

$a=\sqrt{28}=2\sqrt{7}$

The missing length is $2\sqrt{7}$.

15. $d=\sqrt{(x_2-x_1)^2+(y_2-y_1)^2}$

$=\sqrt{(9-(-3))^2+(-3-2)^2}$

$=\sqrt{(12)^2+(-5)^2}=\sqrt{144+25}$

$=\sqrt{169}=13$

The distance is 13 units.

16. $(4x)^2+(3x)^2=20^2$

$16x^2+9x^2=400$

$25x^2=400$

$x^2=16$

$x=\sqrt{16}=4$

$3x=3(4)=12$

$4x=4(4)=16$

The lengths of the legs are 12 inches and 16 inches.

10.4 Exercise Set

1. $\sqrt{-36}=\sqrt{36(-1)}=\sqrt{36}\sqrt{-1}=6i$

3. $\sqrt{-13}=\sqrt{13(-1)}=\sqrt{13}\sqrt{-1}=\sqrt{13}\,i$

5. $\sqrt{-50}=\sqrt{50(-1)}=\sqrt{25\cdot 2}\sqrt{-1}=5\sqrt{2}\,i$

7. $\sqrt{-20}=\sqrt{20(-1)}=\sqrt{4\cdot 5}\sqrt{-1}=2\sqrt{5}\,i$

9. $-\sqrt{-28} = -\sqrt{28(-1)}$
$= -\sqrt{4\cdot 7}\sqrt{-1}$
$= -2\sqrt{7}\,i$

11. $7+\sqrt{-16} = 7+\sqrt{16}\sqrt{-1} = 7+4i$

13. $10+\sqrt{-3} = 10+\sqrt{3}\sqrt{-1} = 10+\sqrt{3}i$

15. $6-\sqrt{-98} = 6-\sqrt{98}\sqrt{-1}$
$= 6-\sqrt{49\cdot 2}\sqrt{-1}$
$= 6-7\sqrt{2}i$

17. $(x-3)^2 = -9$
$x-3=\sqrt{-9}$ or $x-3=-\sqrt{-9}$
$x-3=3i$ or $x-3=-3i$
$x=3+3i$ or $x=3-3i$
The solutions are $3+3i$ and $3-3i$ which can be written in abbreviated form as $3\pm 3i$.

19. $(x+7)^2 = -64$
$x+7=\sqrt{-64}$ or $x+7=-\sqrt{-64}$
$x+7=8i$ or $x+7=-\sqrt{8}i$
$x=-7+8i$ or $x=-7-\sqrt{8}i$
The solutions are $-7\pm\sqrt{8}\,i$

21. $(x-2)^2 = -7$
$x-2=\sqrt{-7}$ or $x-2=-\sqrt{-7}$
$x-2=\sqrt{7}i$ or $x-2=-\sqrt{7}i$
$x=2+\sqrt{7}i$ or $x=2-\sqrt{7}i$
The solutions are $2\pm\sqrt{7}i$

23. $(y+3)^2 = -18$
$y+3=\sqrt{-18}$ or $y+3=-\sqrt{-18}$
$y+3=3\sqrt{2}i$ or $y+3=-3\sqrt{2}i$
$y=-3+3\sqrt{2}i$ or $y=-3-3\sqrt{2}i$
The solutions are $-3\pm 3\sqrt{2}i.$

25. $x^2+4x+5=0$
$a=1, b=4, c=5$
$$x=\frac{-b\pm\sqrt{b^2-4ac}}{2a}$$
$$=\frac{-4\pm\sqrt{4^2-4(1)(5)}}{2\cdot 1}$$
$$=\frac{-4\pm\sqrt{16-20}}{2}=\frac{-4\pm\sqrt{-4}}{2}$$
$$=\frac{-4\pm 2i}{2}=\frac{2(-2\pm i)}{2}$$
$$=-2\pm i$$
The solutions are $-2\pm i$.

27. $x^2-6x+13=0$
$a=1, b=-6, c=13$
$$x=\frac{-b\pm\sqrt{b^2-4ac}}{2a}$$
$$=\frac{-(-6)\pm\sqrt{(-6)^2-4(1)(13)}}{2\cdot 1}$$
$$=\frac{6\pm\sqrt{36-52}}{2}=\frac{6\pm\sqrt{-16}}{2}$$
$$=\frac{6\pm 4i}{2}=\frac{2(3\pm 2i)}{2}$$
$$=3\pm 2i$$
The solutions are $3\pm 2i$.

29. $x^2 - 12x + 40 = 0$

$a = 1, b = -12, c = 40$

$$x = \frac{-b \pm \sqrt{b^2 - 4ac}}{2a}$$

$$= \frac{-(-12) \pm \sqrt{(-12)^2 - 4(1)(40)}}{2 \cdot 1}$$

$$= \frac{12 \pm \sqrt{144 - 160}}{2} = \frac{12 \pm \sqrt{-16}}{2}$$

$$= \frac{12 \pm 4i}{2} = \frac{2(6 \pm 2i)}{2}$$

$$= 6 \pm 2i$$

The solutions are $6 \pm 2i$.

31. $x^2 = 10x - 27$

Write the equation in standard form; then identify *a,b,* and *c*.

$x^2 - 10x + 27 = 0$

$a = 1, b = -10, c = 27$

$$x = \frac{-b \pm \sqrt{b^2 - 4ac}}{2a}$$

$$= \frac{-(-10) \pm \sqrt{(-10)^2 - 4(1)(27)}}{2 \cdot 1}$$

$$= \frac{10 \pm \sqrt{100 - 68}}{2} = \frac{10 \pm \sqrt{-32}}{2}$$

$$= \frac{10 \pm 4\sqrt{2}i}{2} = \frac{2(5 \pm 2\sqrt{2}i)}{2}$$

$$= 5 \pm 2\sqrt{2}i$$

The solutions are $5 \pm 2\sqrt{2}i$.

33. $5x^2 = 2x - 3$

Write the equation in standard form.

$5x^2 - 2x + 3 = 0$

$a = 5, b = -2, c = 3$

$$x = \frac{-b \pm \sqrt{b^2 - 4ac}}{2a}$$

$$= \frac{-(-2) \pm \sqrt{(-2)^2 - 4(5)(3)}}{2 \cdot 5}$$

$$= \frac{2 \pm \sqrt{4 - 60}}{10} = \frac{2 \pm \sqrt{-56}}{10}$$

$$= \frac{2 \pm 2\sqrt{14}i}{10} = \frac{2(1 \pm \sqrt{14}i)}{10}$$

$$= \frac{1 \pm \sqrt{14}i}{5}$$

The solutions are $\frac{1 \pm \sqrt{14}i}{5}$.

35. $2y^2 = 4y - 5$

Write the equation in standard form.

$2y^2 - 4y + 5 = 0$

$a = 2, b = -4, c = 5$

$$y = \frac{-b \pm \sqrt{b^2 - 4ac}}{2a}$$

$$= \frac{-(-4) \pm \sqrt{(-4)^2 - 4(2)(5)}}{2 \cdot 2}$$

$$= \frac{4 \pm \sqrt{16 - 40}}{4} = \frac{4 \pm \sqrt{-24}}{4}$$

$$= \frac{4 \pm 2\sqrt{6}i}{4} = \frac{2(2 \pm \sqrt{6}i)}{2 \cdot 2}$$

$$= \frac{2 \pm \sqrt{6}i}{2}$$

The solutions are $\frac{2 \pm \sqrt{6}i}{2}$.

37.
$$12x^2+35=8x^2+15$$
$$4x^2+35=15$$
$$4x^2=-20$$
$$x^2=-5$$
$$x=\pm\sqrt{-5}=\pm\sqrt{5}\,i$$
The solutions are $\pm\sqrt{5}\,i$

38.
$$8x^2-9=5x^2-30$$
$$3x^2-9=-30$$
$$3x^2=-21$$
$$x^2=-7$$
$$x=\pm\sqrt{-7}=\pm\sqrt{7}\,i$$
The solutions are $\pm\sqrt{7}\,i$.

39.
$$\frac{x+3}{5}=\frac{x-2}{x}$$
$$5x\left(\frac{x+3}{5}\right)=5x\left(\frac{x-2}{x}\right)$$
$$x(x+3)=5(x-2)$$
$$x^2+3x=5x-10$$
$$x^2-2x+10=0$$
$$a=1, b=-2, c=10$$
$$x=\frac{-(-2)\pm\sqrt{(-2)^2-4(1)(10)}}{2(1)}$$
$$=\frac{2\pm\sqrt{4-40}}{2}=\frac{2\pm\sqrt{-36}}{2}$$
$$=\frac{2\pm 6i}{2}=1\pm 3i$$
The solutions are $1\pm 3i$.

40.
$$\frac{x+4}{4}=\frac{x-5}{x-2}$$
$$(x+4)(x-2)=4(x-5)$$
$$x^2-2x+4x-8=4x-20$$
$$x^2-2x+12=0$$
$$a=1, b=-2, c=12$$
$$x=\frac{-(-2)\pm\sqrt{(-2)^2-4(1)(12)}}{2(1)}$$
$$=\frac{2\pm\sqrt{4-48}}{2}=\frac{2\pm\sqrt{-44}}{2}$$
$$=\frac{2\pm 2\sqrt{11}\,i}{2}=1\pm\sqrt{11}\,i$$
The solutions are $1\pm\sqrt{11}\,i$.

41.
$$\frac{1}{x+1}-\frac{1}{2}=\frac{1}{x}$$
Multiply both sides by the LCD, $2x(x+1)$.
$$2x(x+1)\left(\frac{1}{x+1}-\frac{1}{2}\right)=2x(x+1)\left(\frac{1}{x}\right)$$
$$2x-x(x+1)=2(x+1)$$
$$2x-x^2-x=2x+2$$
$$-x^2-x-2=0$$
$$x^2+x+2=0$$
$$a=1, b=1, c=2$$
$$x=\frac{-1\pm\sqrt{(1)^2-4(1)(2)}}{2(1)}$$
$$=\frac{-1\pm\sqrt{1-8}}{2}=\frac{-1\pm\sqrt{-7}}{2}$$
$$=\frac{-1\pm\sqrt{7}\,i}{2}$$
The solutions are $\frac{-1\pm\sqrt{7}\,i}{2}$.

42. $\frac{4}{x}=\frac{8}{x^2}+1$

Multiply both sides by the LCD, x^2.

$$x^2\left(\frac{4}{x}\right)=x^2\left(\frac{8}{x^2}+1\right)$$
$$4x=8+x^2$$

$x^2-4x+8=0$
$a=1, b=-4, c=8$

$$x=\frac{-(-4)\pm\sqrt{(-4)^2-4(1)(8)}}{2(1)}$$
$$=\frac{4\pm\sqrt{16-32}}{2}=\frac{4\pm\sqrt{-16}}{2}$$
$$=\frac{4\pm 4i}{2}=2\pm 2i$$

The solutions are $2\pm 2i$.

43. $R=-2x^2+36x; R=200$

$$200=-2x^2+36x$$
$$2x^2+36x+200=0$$
$$x^2+18x+100=0$$

$a=1, b=18, c=100$

$$x=\frac{-b\pm\sqrt{b^2-4ac}}{2a}$$
$$=\frac{-18\pm\sqrt{18^2-4(1)(100)}}{2\cdot 1}$$
$$=\frac{-18\pm\sqrt{324-400}}{2}$$
$$=\frac{-18\pm\sqrt{-76}}{2}$$
$$=\frac{-18\pm 2\sqrt{19}i}{2}$$
$$=\frac{2\left(-9\pm\sqrt{19}i\right)}{2}$$
$$=9\pm\sqrt{19}i$$

The solutions of the equation are $9\pm\sqrt{19}i$, which are not real numbers. Because the equation has no real number solution, it is not possible to generate $200,000 in weekly revenue. The job applicant, has guaranteed to do something that is impossible, so this person will not be hired.

45. i represents $\sqrt{-1}$.

47. A complex number is any pure real number, any pure imaginary number, or any number in the form $a+bi$ where a and b are nonzero real numbers.

49. Answers may vary. The set of real numbers is a subset of the complex numbers. Therefore, every real number must also be a complex number.

51. Statement b is true.

53. Let x represent a number that satisfies the equation $x^2-2x=-5$.
Write this equation in standard form and solve by the quadratic formula.

$x^2-2x+5=0$
$a=1, b=-2, c=5$

$$x=\frac{-b\pm\sqrt{b^2-4ac}}{2a}$$
$$=\frac{-(-2)\pm\sqrt{(-2)^2-4(1)(5)}}{2\cdot 1}$$
$$=\frac{2\pm\sqrt{4-20}}{2}=\frac{2\pm\sqrt{-16}}{2}$$
$$=\frac{2\pm 4i}{2}=\frac{2(1\pm 2i)}{2}$$
$$=1\pm 2i$$

The solutions are $1\pm 2i$. Because these are not real numbers, there is no real number that satisfies the condition given in the exercise.

55.

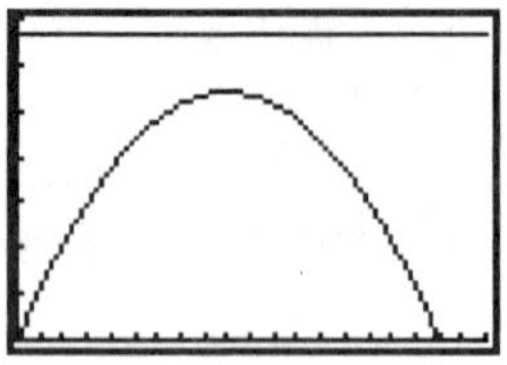

The graph shows that the parabola and the horizontal line do not intersect. The vertex, which is the maximum point on the graph, has a y-coordinate that is less than 200. Therefore, the weekly revenue will never reach $200,000.

56. $y = \frac{1}{3}x - 2$

slope = $\frac{1}{3}$; y-intercept = -2

Plot $(0, -2)$. From this point, go 1 unit *up* and 3 units to the *right* to reach the point $(3, -1)$

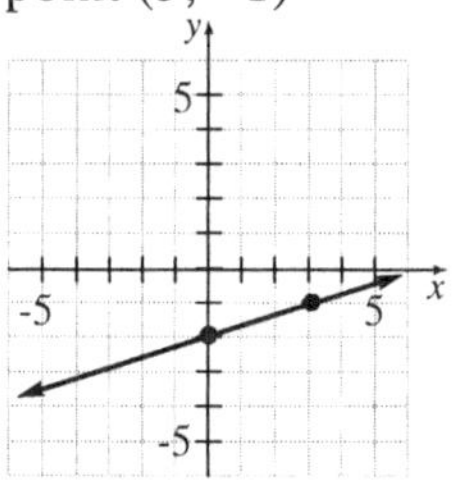

57. $2x - 3y = 6$

x-intercept: 3
y-intercept: -2
checkpoint: $(-3, -4)$
Draw a line through $(3,0)$, $(0, -2)$, and $(-3, -4)$.

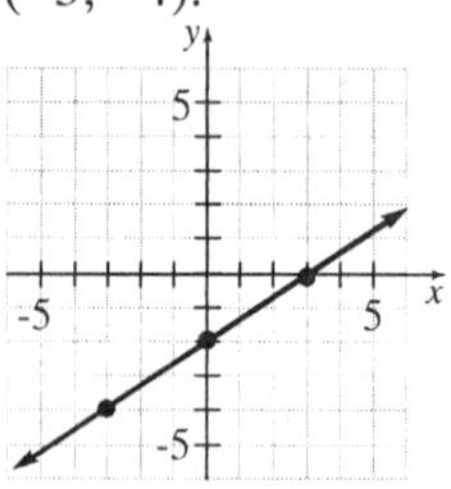

58. $x = -2$

Draw a vertical line with x-intercept -2.

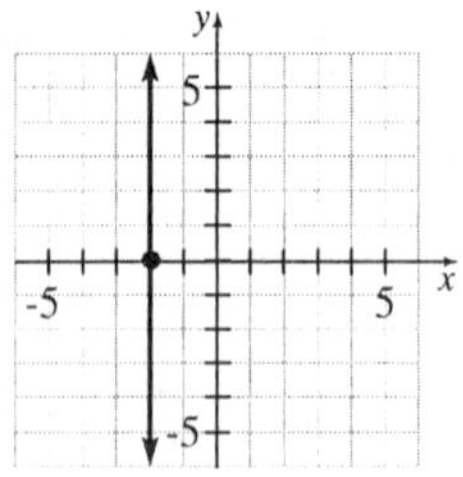

10.5 Exercise Set

1. $y = x^2 - 4x + 3$

Because a, the coefficient of x^2, is 1, which is greater than 0, the parabola opens upward.

3. $y = -2x^2 + x + 6$

Because $a = -2$, which is less than 0, the parabola opens downward.

5. $y = x^2 - 4x + 3$

To find the x-intercepts, replace y with 0 and solve the resulting equation.

$$x^2 - 4x + 3 = 0$$
$$(x-1)(x-3) = 0$$
$$x - 1 = 0 \quad \text{or} \quad x - 3 = 0$$
$$x = 1 \qquad\qquad x = 3$$

The x-intercepts are 1 and 3.

7. $y = -x^2 + 8x - 12$

$$0 = -x^2 + 8x - 12$$
$$x^2 - 8x + 12 = 0$$
$$(x-2)(x-6) = 0$$
$$x - 2 = 0 \quad \text{or} \quad x - 6 = 0$$
$$x = 2 \qquad\qquad x = 6$$

The x-intercepts are 2 and 6.

9. $y = x^2 + 2x - 4$

$x^2 + 2x - 4 = 0$

This equation cannot be solved by factoring, so use the quadratic formula with $a = 1, b = 2,$ and $c = -4$.

$$x = \frac{-b \pm \sqrt{b^2 - 4ac}}{2a}$$

$$= \frac{-2 \pm \sqrt{2^2 - 4(1)(-4)}}{2(1)}$$

$$= \frac{-2 \pm \sqrt{4+16}}{2} = \frac{-2 \pm \sqrt{20}}{2}$$

$$= \frac{-2 \pm 2\sqrt{5}}{2} = -1 \pm \sqrt{5}$$

$x = -1\sqrt{5} \approx -3.2$ or $x = -1 - \sqrt{5} \approx 1.2$

The x-intercepts are approximately -3.2 and 1.2.

11. $y = x^2 - 4x + 3$

To find the y-intercept, replace x with 0.

$y = 0^2 - 4 \cdot 0 + 3 = 0 - 0 + 3 = 3$

The y-intercept is 3.

13. $y = -x^2 + 8x - 12$

$y = -0^2 + 8 \cdot 0 - 12 = 0 + 0 - 12 = -12$

The y-intercept is -12.

15. $y = x^2 + 2x - 4$

$$y = 0^2 + 2 \cdot 0 - 4 = -4$$

The y-intercept is -4.

17. $y = x^2 + 6x$

$$y = 0^2 + 6 \cdot 0 = 0$$

The y-intercept is 0.

19. $y = x^2 - 4x + 3$

$a = 1, b = -4, c = 3$

x-coordinate of vertex

$$= \frac{-b}{2a} = \frac{-(-4)}{2(1)} = \frac{4}{2} = 2$$

y-coordinate of vertex

$= 2^2 - 4(2) + 3 = 4 - 8 + 3 = -1$

The vertex is $(2, -1)$.

21. $y = 2x^2 + 4x - 6$

$a = 2, b = 4, c = -6$

x-coordinate of vertex

$$= \frac{-b}{2a} = \frac{-4}{2(2)} = \frac{-4}{4} = -1$$

y-coordinate of vertex

$= 2(-1)^2 + 4(-1) - 6 = 2 - 4 - 6 = -8$

The vertex is $(-1, -8)$.

23. $y = x^2 + 6x$

$a = 1, b = 6, c = 0$

x-coordinate of vertex

$$= \frac{-b}{2a} = \frac{-6}{2(1)} = \frac{-6}{2} = -3$$

y-coordinate of vertex

$= (-3)^2 + 6(-3) = 9 - 18 = -9$

The vertex is $(-3, -9)$.

25. $y = x^2 + 8x + 7$

Step1 Determine how the parabola opens.

Here a, the coefficient of x^2, is 1. Because $a > 0$, the parabola opens upward.

Step 2 Find the vertex.

For this equation, $a = 1, b = 8,$ and $c = 7$.

x-coordinate of vertex.

$= \frac{-b}{2a} = \frac{-8}{2(1)} = \frac{-8}{2} = -4$

y-coordinate of vertex

$= (-4)^2 + 8(-4) + 7 = 16 - 32 + 7 = -9$

The vertex is $(-4, -9)$.

Step 3 Find the x-intercepts.
Replace y with 0 in $y = x^2 + 8x + 7$ and solve for x.

$x^2 + 8x + 7 = 0$

$(x+7)(x+1) = 0$

$x + 7 = 0$ or $x + 1 = 0$

$x = -7$ $\quad$ $x = -1$

The x-intercepts are -7 and -1.

Step 4 Find the y-intercept.
Replace x with 0 and solve for y.

$y = 0^2 + 8(0) + 7 = 0 + 0 + 7 = 7$

The y-intercept is 7.

Steps 5 and 6 Plot the intercepts and the vertex. Connect these points with a smooth curve.
Plot
$(-4, -9), (-7, 0), (-1, 0)$, and $(0, 7)$, and connect them with a smooth curve.

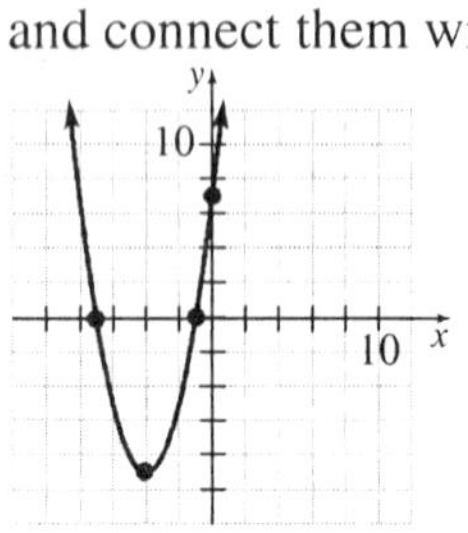

27. $y = x^2 - 2x - 8$

Step 1 $a = 1 > 0$, so the parabola opens upward.

Step 2 $a = 1, b = -2, c = -8$
x-coordinate of vertex

$= \frac{-b}{2a} = \frac{-2(-2)}{2(1)} = \frac{2}{2} = 1$

y-coordinate of vertex

$= 1^2 - 2(1) - 8 = 1 - 2 - 8 = -9$

The vertex is $(1, -9)$

Step 3

$x^2 - 2x - 8 = 0$

$(x+2)(x-4) = 0$

$x + 2 = 0$ or $x - 4 = 0$

$x = -2$ $\quad$ $x = 4$

The x-intercepts are -2 and 4.

Step 4 $y = 0^2 - 2(0) - 8 = 8$

The y-intercept is -8.

Steps 5 and 6 Plot
$(1, -9), (-2, 0), (4, 0)$, and $(0, -8)$, and connect them with a smooth curve.

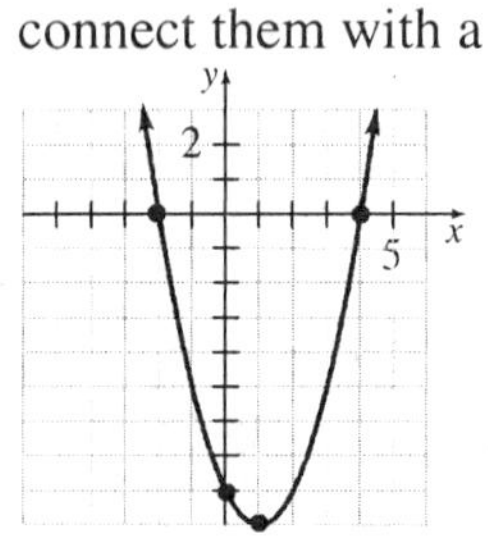

29. $y = -x^2 + 4x - 3$

Step1 $a = -1 < 0$, so the parabola opens downward.

Step 2 $a = -1, b = 4, c = -3$
x-coordinate of vertex
$= \frac{-b}{2a} = \frac{-4}{2(-1)} = \frac{-4}{-2} = 2$
y-coordinate of vertex
$= -2^2 + 4 \cdot 2 - -4 + 8 - 3 = 1$
The vertex is (2,1).

Step 3
$-x^2 + 4x - 3 = 0$
$0 = x^2 - 4x + 3$
$0 = (x-1)(x-3)$
$x - 1 = 0$ or $x - 3 = 0$
$x = 1$ $x = 3$
The x-intercepts are 1 and 3.

Step 4 $y = -0^2 + 4(0) - 3 = -3$
The y-intercept is -3.

Steps 5 and 6 Plot $(2,1), (1,0), (3,0)$, and $(0,-3)$, and connect them with a smooth curve

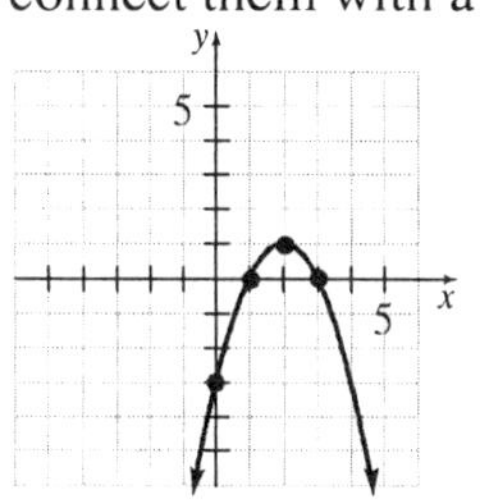

31. $y = x^2 - 1$
Step 1 $a = 1 > 0$, so the parabola opens upward.

Step 2 $a = 1, b = 0, c = -1$
x-coordinate of vertex
$= \frac{-b}{2a} = \frac{-0}{2(1)} = \frac{0}{2} = 0$
y-coordinate of vertex
$= 0^2 - 1 = -1$
The vertex is $(0,1)$.

Step 3
$x^2 - 1 = 0$
$(x+1)(x-1) = 0$
$x + 1 = 0$ or $x - 1 = 0$
$x = -1$ $x = 1$
The x-intercepts are -1 and 1.
Step 4 $y = 0^2 - 1 = -1$
The y-intercept is -1. Notice that this gives the same point as the vertex, $(0,-1)$..

Steps 5 and 6 Plot $(0,-1), (-1,0)$, and $(1,0)$, and connect them with a smooth curve.

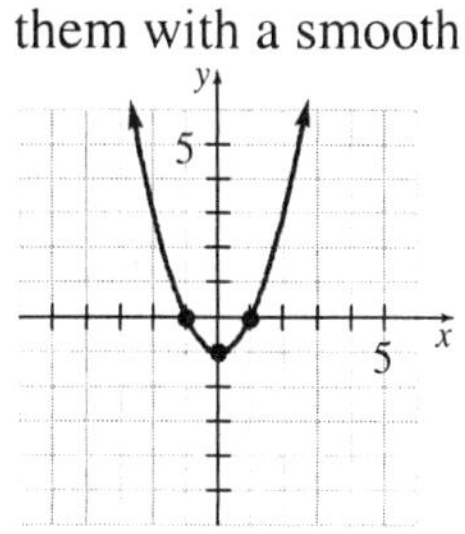

33. $y = x^2 + 2x + 1$

Step 1 $a - 1 > 0$, so the parabola opens upward.

Step 2 $a = 1, b = 2, c = 1$
x-coordinate of vertex
$$= \frac{-b}{2a} = \frac{-2}{2(1)} = \frac{-2}{2} = -1$$
y-coordinate of vertex
$$= (-1)^2 + 2(-1) + 1 = 1 - 2 + 1 = 0$$
The vertex is $(-1, 0)$.

Step 3
$$x^2 + 2x + 1 = 0$$
$$(x+1)^2 = 0$$
$$x + 1 = 0$$
$$x = -1$$
There is only one x-intercept, -1. Notice that this gives the same point as the vertex, $(-1, 0)$.

Step 4 $y = 0^2 + 2 \cdot 0 + 1 = 1$
The y-intercept is 1.

The work in Steps 1-4 has produced only two points, $(-1, 0)$ and $(0, 1)$. At least one additional point is needed. In order to have at least one point on each side of the vertex, choose an x-value less than -1 and find the corresponding y-value.
If $x = -2$,
$$y = (-2)^2 + 2(-2) + 1 = 4 - 4 + 1 = 1.$$

Steps 5 and 6 Plot $(-2, 1), (-1, 0)$, and $(0, 1)$, and connect them with a smooth curve.

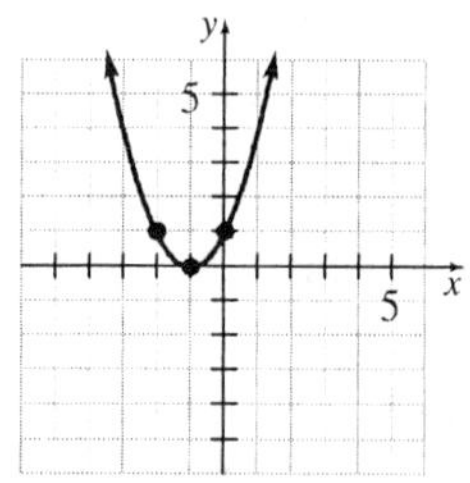

35. $y = -2x^2 + 4x + 5$

Step 1 $a = -2 < 0$, so the parabola opens downward.

Step 2 $a = -2, b = 4, c = 5$
x-coordinate of vertex
$$= \frac{-b}{2a} = \frac{-4}{2(-2)} = \frac{-4}{-4} = 1$$
y-coordinate of vertex
$$= -2(1)^2 + 4(1) + 5 = -2 + 4 + 5 = 7$$
The vertex is $(1, 7)$

Step 3
$$-2x^2 + 4x + 5 = 0$$
$$0 = 2x^2 - 4x - 5$$
The trinomial cannot be factored, so use the quadratic formula with $a = 2, b = -4,$ and $c = -5$.
$$x = \frac{-b \pm \sqrt{b^2 - 4ac}}{2a}$$
$$= \frac{-(-4) \pm \sqrt{(-4)^2 - 4(2)(-5)}}{2 \cdot 2}$$
$$= \frac{4 \pm \sqrt{16 + 40}}{4} = \frac{4 \pm \sqrt{56}}{4}$$
$$x = \frac{4 + \sqrt{56}}{4} \approx 2.9 \quad \text{or} \quad x = \frac{4 - \sqrt{56}}{4} \approx -($$
The x-intercepts are approximately 2.9 and -0.9.

Step 4 $y = -2 \cdot 0^2 + 4.0 + 5 = 5$
The y-intercept is 5.

Steps 5 and 6 Plot $(1,7), (2.9,0), (-0.9,0)$, and $(0,5)$, and connect them with a smooth curve.

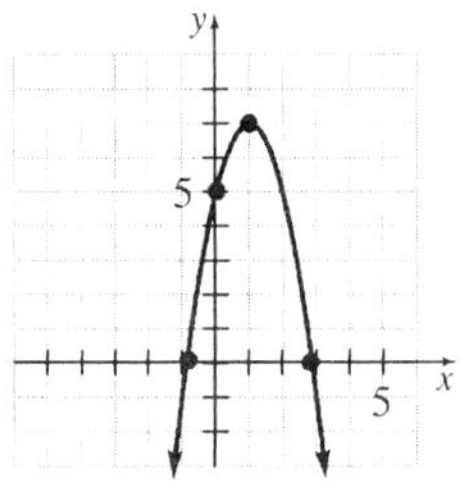

37.
$$y = (x-3)^2 + 2$$
$$y = (x^2 - 6x + 9) + 2$$
$$y = x^2 - 6x + 11$$
$$a = 1, b = -6, c = 11$$
$$x = -\frac{b}{2a} = -\frac{(-6)}{2(1)} = \frac{6}{2} = 3$$
$$y = (3)^2 - 6(3) + 11 = 9 - 18 + 11 = 2$$
The vertex is $(3,2)$.

38.
$$y = (x-4)^2 + 3$$
$$y = (x^2 - 8x + 16) + 3$$
$$y = x^2 - 8x + 19$$
$$a = 1, b = -8, c = 19$$
$$x = -\frac{b}{2a} = -\frac{(-8)}{2(1)} = \frac{8}{2} = 4$$
$$y = (4)^2 - 8(4) + 19 = 16 - 32 + 19 = 3$$
The vertex is $(4,3)$.

39.
$$y = (x+5)^2 - 4$$
$$y = (x^2 + 10x + 25) - 4$$
$$y = x^2 + 10x + 21$$
$$a = 1, b = 10, c = 21$$
$$x = -\frac{b}{2a} = -\frac{10}{2(1)} = -5$$
$$y = (-5)^2 + 10(-5) + 21$$
$$= 25 - 50 + 21 = -4$$
The vertex is $(-5,-4)$.

40.
$$y = (x+6)^2 - 5$$
$$y = (x^2 + 12x + 36) - 5$$
$$y = x^2 + 12x + 31$$
$$a = 1, b = 12, c = 31$$
$$x = -\frac{b}{2a} = -\frac{12}{2(1)} = -6$$
$$y = (-6)^2 + 12(-6) + 31$$
$$= 36 - 72 + 31 = -5$$
The vertex is $(-6,-5)$.

41.
$$y = 2(x-1)^2 - 3$$
$$y = 2(x^2 - 2x + 1) - 3$$
$$y = 2x^2 - 4x + 2 - 3$$
$$y = 2x^2 - 4x - 1$$
$$a = 2, b = -4, c = -1$$
$$x = -\frac{b}{2a} = -\frac{(-4)}{2(2)} = \frac{4}{4} = 1$$
$$y = 2(1)^2 - 4(1) - 1 = 2 - 4 - 1 = -3$$
The vertex is $(1,-3)$.

42. $y = 2(x-1)^2 - 4$

$y = 2(x^2 - 2x + 1) - 4$

$y = 2x^2 - 4x + 2 - 4$

$y = 2x^2 - 4x - 2$

$a = 2, b = -4, c = -2$

$x = -\frac{b}{2a} = -\frac{(-4)}{2(2)} = \frac{4}{4} = 1$

$y = 2(1)^2 - 4(1) - 2$

$= 2 - 4 - 2 = -4$

The vertex is $(1, -4)$.

43. $y = -3(x+2)^2 + 5$

$y = -3(x^2 + 4x + 4) + 5$

$y = -3x^2 - 12x - 12 + 5$

$y = -3x^2 - 12x - 7$

$a = -3, b = -12, c = -7$

$x = -\frac{b}{2a} = -\frac{(-12)}{2(-3)} = -\frac{12}{6} = -2$

$y = -3(-2)^2 - 12(-2) - 7$

$= -12 + 24 - 7 = 5$

The vertex is $(-2, 5)$.

44. $y = -3(x+4)^2 + 6$

$y = -3(x^2 + 8x + 16) + 6$

$y = -3x^2 - 24x - 48 + 6$

$y = -3x^2 - 24x - 42$

$a = -3, b = -24, c = -42$

$x = -\frac{b}{2a} = -\frac{(-24)}{2(-3)} = -\frac{24}{6} = -4$

$y = -3(-4)^2 - 24(-4) - 42$

$= -48 + 96 - 42 = 6$

The vertex is $(-4, 6)$.

45. For a parabola whose equation is $y = a(x-h)^2 + k$, the vertex is the point (h, k).

47. $y = -0.02x^2 + x + 1$

$a = -0.02, b = 1, c = 1$

x-coordinate of vertex

$= \frac{-b}{2a} = \frac{-1}{2(-0.2)} = \frac{-1}{-0.04} = 25$

y-coordinate of vertex

$= -0.02(25)^2 + 25 + 1$

$= -12.5 + 25 + 1 = 13.5$

The vertex is $(25, 13.5)$

This means that the maximum growth of 13.5 inches per year occurs when there is 25 inches of annual rainfall.

49. $y = -16x^2 + 200x + 4$

$a = -16, b = 200, c = 4$

x-coordinate of vertex

$= \frac{-b}{2a} = \frac{-200}{2(-16)} = \frac{-200}{-32} = 6.25$

y-coordinate of vertex

$= -16(6.25)^2 + 200(6.25) + 4$

$= -625 + 1250 + 4 = 629$

The vertex is $(6.25, 629)$.

The fireworks should explode 6.25 seconds after they are launched to reach a maximum height of 629 feet.

51. The area of the plot is $x(120 - 2x)$. To find the maximum possible area, find the vertex of the parabola whose equation is

$y = x(120 - 2x)$

Write this equation in the form

$y = ax^2 + bx + c$

$y = 120x - 2x^2$
$y = -2x^2 + 120x$
$a = -2, b = 120, c = 0$
x-coordinate of vertex
$= \frac{-b}{2a} = \frac{-120}{2(-2)} = \frac{-120}{-4} = 30$
y-coordinate of vertex
$= -2(30)^2 + 120(30)$
$= -1800 + 3600 = 1800$
The vertex is $(30, 1800)$.

If $x = 30$, then
$120 - 2x = 120 - 2(30) = 60$. The area will be maximized (have the maximum value) when the length is 60 feet and the width is 30 feet. The largest area that can be enclosed is 1800 square feet.

53. Answers may vary.

55. Set $y = 0$ and solve for *x*. The solutions are the x-intercepts.

57. Write the equation in the form $y = ax^2 + bx + c$. The x-coordinate of the vertex is then given by $x = -\frac{b}{2a}$. The y-coordinate is found by letting $x = -\frac{b}{2a}$ in the equation and solving for *y*.

59. **b.** is true (to a point). If there is only one x-intercept, then the x-intercept is also the x-coordinate of the vertex.

61.

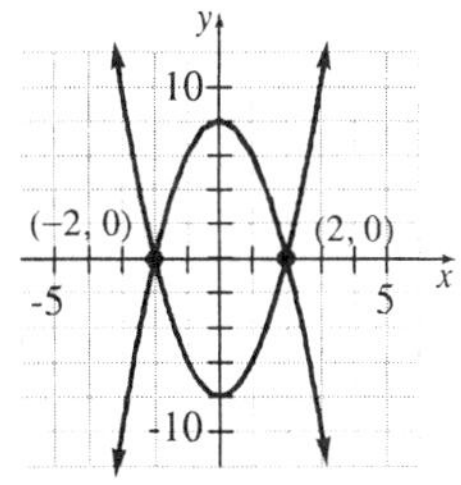

Intersection points: $(-2, 0)$ and $(2, 0)$.

63. Answers will vary.

65. $y = -0.25x^2 + 40x$
$a = -0.25$, $b = 40$, $c = 0$
$x = -\frac{b}{2a} = -\frac{40}{2(-0.25)} = \frac{40}{0.5} = 80$
$y = -0.25(80)^2 + 40(80) = 1600$
The vertex is $(80, 1600)$.
The y-intercept is 0 and the graph opens down.
Window settings will vary. One example would be:

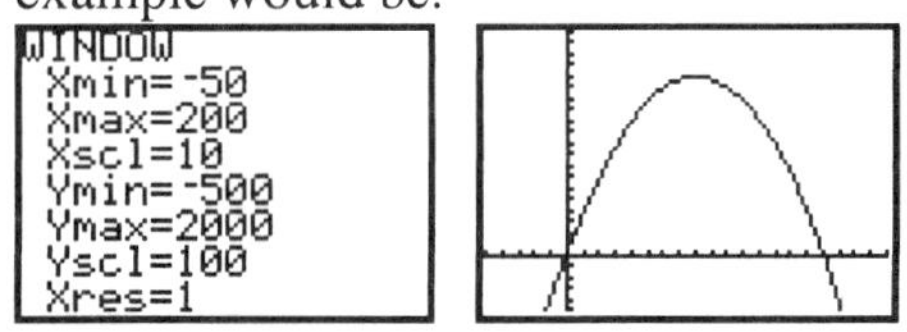

67. $y = 5x^2 + 40x + 600$
$a = 5$, $b = 40$, $c = 600$
$x = -\frac{b}{2a} = -\frac{40}{2(5)} = -\frac{40}{10} = -4$
$y = 5(-4)^2 + 40(-4) + 600 = 520$
The vertex is $(-4, 520)$.
The y-intercept is 600 and the graph opens up.
Window settings will vary. One example would be:

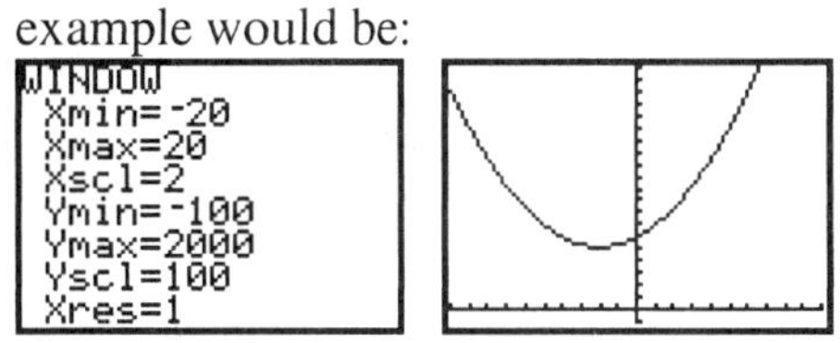

69. $7(x-2)=10-2(x+3)$

$7x-14=10-2x-6$

$7x-14=4-2x$

$9x-14=4$

$9x=18$

$x=2$

The solution is 2.

70. $\frac{7}{x+2}+\frac{2}{x+3}=\frac{1}{x^2+5x+6}$

$\frac{7}{x+2}+\frac{2}{x+3}=\frac{1}{(x+2)(x+3)}$

Restrictions: $x \neq -2, x \neq -3$

LCD = $(x+2)(x+3)$

$(x+2)(x+3)\left[\frac{7}{x+2}+\frac{2}{x+3}\right]$

$=(x+2)(x+3)\left[\frac{1}{(x+2)(x+3)}\right]$

$7(x+3)+2(x+2)=1$

$7x+21+2x+4=1$

$9x+25=1$

$9x=-24$

$x=\frac{-24}{9}=-\frac{8}{3}$

The solution is $-\frac{8}{3}$.

71. $5x-3y=-13$

$x=2-4y$

To solve this system by the substitution method, substitute $2-4y$ for x in the first equation.

$5x-3y=-13$

$5(2-4y)-3y=-13$

$10-20y-3y=-13$

$10-23y=-13$

$-23y=-23$

$y=1$

Back-substitute 1 for y in the second equation of the given system.

$x=2-4y=2-4(1)=-2$

The solution is $(-2,1)$.

10.6 Exercise Set

1. $\{(1,2),(3,4),(5,5)\}$

This relation is a function because no two ordered pairs have the same first component and different second components.

The domain is the set of all first components: $\{1,3,5\}$.

The range is the set of second components: $\{2,4,5\}$.

3. $\{(3,4),(3,5),(4,4),(4,5)\}$

This relation is not a function because the first two ordered pairs have the same first component but different second components. (The same applies to the third and fourth ordered pairs.)

Domain: $\{3,4\}$

Range: $\{4,5\}$

5. $\{(-3,-3),(-2,-2),(-1,-1),(0,0)\}$

This relation is a function.

Domain: $\{-3, -2, -1,0\}$

Range: $\{-3, -2, -1,0\}$

7. $\{(1,4),(1,5),(1,6)\}$
This relation is not a function because all three ordered pairs have the same first component.
Domain: $\{1\}$
Range: $\{4,5,6\}$

9. $f(x)=x+5$

a. $f(7)=7+5=12$

b. $f(-6)=-6+5=-1$

c. $f(0)=0+5=5$

11. $f(x)=7x$

a $f(10)=7\cdot 10=70$

b $f(-4)=7(-4)=-28$

c. $f(0)=7\cdot 0=0$

13. $f(x)=8x-3$

a. $f(12)=8(12)-3=96-3=93$

b. $f\left(-\frac{1}{2}\right)=8\left(-\frac{1}{2}\right)-3=-4-3=-7$

c. $f(0)=8(0)-3=0-3=-3$

15. $g(x)=x^2+3x$

a. $g(2)=2^2+3(2)=4+6=10$

b. $g(-2)=(-2)^2+3(-2)=4-6=-2$

c. $g(0)=0^2+3(0)=0+0=0$

17. $h(x)=x^2-2x+3$

a. $h(4)=4^2-2\cdot 4+3=16-8+3=11$

b. $h(-4)=(-4)^2-2(-4)+3$
$=16+8+3=27$

c. $h(0)=0^2-2\cdot 0+3=3$

19. $f(x)=5$
The value of this function is 5 for every value of x.

a. $f(9)=5$

b. $f(-9)=5$

c. $f(0)=5$

21. $f(r)=\sqrt{r+6}+3$

a. $f(-6)=\sqrt{-6+6}+3=\sqrt{0}+3$
$=0+3=3$

b. $f(10)=\sqrt{10+6}+3=\sqrt{16}+3$
$=4+3=7$

23. $f(x)=\frac{x}{|x|}$

a. $f(6)=\frac{6}{|6|}=\frac{6}{6}=1$

b. $f(-6)=\frac{-6}{|-6|}=\frac{-6}{6}=-1$

25. No vertical line will intersect this graph in more than one point so y is a function of x.

27. No vertical line will intersect this graph in more than one point, so y is a function of x.

29. Many vertical lines will intersect this graph in two points. One such line is the y-axis. Therefore, y is not a function of x.

31. No vertical line will intersect this graph in more than one point, so y is a function of x.

33.
$$f(x)=2x+3;\ \{-1,0,1\}$$
$$f(-1)=2(-1)+3=-2+3=1$$
$$f(0)=2(0)+3=0+3=3$$
$$f(1)=2(1)+3=2+3=5$$
$$\{(-1,1),(0,3),(1,5)\}$$

34.
$$f(x)=3x+5;\ \{-1,0,1\}$$
$$f(-1)=3(-1)+5=-3+5=2$$
$$f(0)=3(0)+5=0+5=5$$
$$f(1)=3(1)+5=3+5=8$$
$$\{(-1,2),(0,5),(1,8)\}$$

35.
$$g(x)=x-x^2;\ \{-2,-1,0,1,2\}$$
$$g(-2)=(-2)-(-2)^2$$
$$=-2-4=-6$$
$$g(-1)=(-1)-(-1)^2$$
$$=-1-1=-2$$
$$g(0)=0-0^2=0$$
$$g(1)=1-1^2=1-1=0$$
$$g(2)=2-2^2=2-4=-2$$
$$\{(-2,-6),(-1,-2),(0,0),(1,0),(2,-2)\}$$

36.
$$g(x)=x-|x|;\ \{-2,-1,0,1,2\}$$
$$g(-2)=(-2)-|-2|=-2-2=-4$$
$$g(-1)=(-1)-|-1|=-1-1=-2$$
$$g(0)=0-|0|=0-0=0$$
$$g(1)=1-|1|=1-1=0$$
$$g(2)=2-|2|=2-2=0$$
$$\{(-2,-4),(-1,-2),(0,0),(1,0),(2,0)\}$$

37.
$$\frac{f(x)-f(h)}{x-h}=\frac{[6x+7]-[6h+7]}{x-h}$$
$$=\frac{6x+7-6h-7}{x-h}$$
$$=\frac{6x-6h}{x-h}=\frac{6(x-h)}{(x-h)}$$
$$=6$$
where $x\neq h$.

38.
$$\frac{f(x)-f(h)}{x-h}=\frac{[8x+9]-[8h+9]}{x-h}$$
$$=\frac{8x+9-8h-9}{x=h}$$
$$=\frac{8x-8h}{x-h}=\frac{8(x-h)}{x-h}$$
$$=8$$
where $x\neq h$.

39.
$$\frac{f(x)-f(h)}{x-h}=\frac{\left[x^2-1\right]-\left[h^2-1\right]}{x-h}$$
$$=\frac{x^2-1-h^2+1}{x-h}$$
$$=\frac{x^2-h^2}{x-h}$$
$$=\frac{(x-h)(x+h)}{x-h}$$
$$=x+h$$
where $x\neq h$.

40. $\dfrac{f(x)-f(h)}{x-h}=\dfrac{\left[x^3-1\right]-\left[h^3-1\right]}{x-h}$

$=\dfrac{x^3-1-h^3+1}{x-h}$

$=\dfrac{x^3-h^3}{x-h}$

$=\dfrac{(x-h)\left(x^2+xh+h^2\right)}{x-h}$

$=x^2+xh+h^2$

where $x \neq h$.

41. **a.** $\{$(U.S., 80%), (Japan, 64%), (France, 64%), (Germany, 61%), (England, 59%), (China, 47%)$\}$

b. Yes, the relation is a function. Each element in the domain corresponds to only one element in the range.

43. $f(x)=0.76x+171.4$

$f(20)=0.76(20)+171.4=186.6$

This means that at age 20, the average cholesterol level for an American man is 186.6, or approximately 187.

45. $W(h)=2.95h-57.32$

$W(64)=2.95(64)-57.32=131.48$

≈ 131

The ideal weight of a woman with a medium frame whose height is 64 inches is 131 pounds.

47. $W(h)=0.077h^2-7.61h+310.11$

$W(70)=0.077(70)^2-7.61(70)+310.11$

$=154.71\approx 155$

The ideal weight of a man with a medium frame whose height is 70 inches is 155 pounds.

49. $V(a)=-0.02a^2+186a+9.90$

$V(20)=-0.02(20)^2+1.86(20)+9.90$

$=39.1$

39.1% of 20-year old Americans say they do volunteer work.

51. To determine if a set of ordered pairs is a function, first examine the x-coordinates. If none are repeated, the relation is a function. If an x-coordinate is repeated, then the relation is a function only if the corresponding y-coordinates are the same.

53. No. $f(x)$ DOES NOT mean *f* times *x*. Rather, $f(x)$ represents the value of the function *f* for a given value of *x*. For example, $f(3)$ means 'the value of the function when $x=3$'. If $f(x)=3x+2$ then $f(3)=3(3)+2=9+2=11$.

55. Answers will vary.

57. Since $f(0)=7$, we know the y-intercept is $b=7$ and that the point $(0,7)$ is on the graph. Since $f(1)=10$, we know the point $(1,10)$ is also on the graph. Using the two points, we can obtain the slope of the line:

$m=\dfrac{10-7}{1-0}=\dfrac{3}{1}=3$

Since we have the y-intercept and the slope, we can write the equation of the line as

$y=3x+7$.

59. Since the car decreases in value by \$3200 each year, we have a linear function with slope $m = -3200$. The initial value of the car is \$22,500 which is the y-intercept (i.e. the value of the car after $x = 0$ years). Therefore, we can write

$V(x) = -3200x + 22{,}500$ for $0 \le x \le 7$

$$V(3) = -3200(3) + 22{,}500$$
$$= -9600 + 22{,}500$$
$$= 12{,}900$$

This indicates that the value of the car will be \$12,900 after 3 years.

60. 0.00397

To write this number in scientific notation, move the decimal point 3 places to the right. Because the number is between 0 and 1, the exponent will be positive.

$0.00397 = 3.97 \times 10^{-3}$

61.

$$x-2\,\overline{)\,x^3 - 7x^2 - 20x + 3} \quad \text{quotient: } x^2 + 9x + 16$$
$$\underline{x^3 - 2x^2}$$
$$9x^2 - 2x$$
$$\underline{9x^2 - 18x}$$
$$16x + 3$$
$$\underline{16x - 32}$$
$$35$$

$$\frac{x^3 + 7x^2 - 20x + 3}{x-2} = x^2 + 9x + 16 + \frac{35}{x-2}$$

62. $3x + 2y = 6$

$8x - 3y = 1$

To solve this system by the addition method, multiply the first equation by 3 and then second equation by 2; then add the equations.

$$9x + 6y = 18$$
$$\underline{16x - 6y = 2}$$
$$25x \quad = 20$$
$$x = \frac{20}{25} = \frac{4}{5}$$

Instead of substituting $\frac{4}{5}$ for x for working with fractions, go back to the original system and eliminate x.

To do this, multiply the first equation by 8 and the second equation by −3; then add.

$$24x + 16y = 48$$
$$\underline{-24x + 9y = -3}$$
$$25y = 45$$
$$y = \frac{45}{25} = \frac{9}{5}$$

The solution is $\left(\frac{4}{5}, \frac{9}{5}\right)$.

Chapter 10 Review Exercises

1. $x^2 = 64$

$x = \sqrt{64}$ or $x = -\sqrt{64}$

$x = 8 \qquad x = -8$

The solutions are 8 and −8.

2. $x^2 = 17$

$x = \sqrt{17}$ or $x = -\sqrt{17}$

The solutions are $\sqrt{17}$ and $-\sqrt{17}$.

3. $2x^2 = 150$

$x^2 = 75$

$x = \sqrt{75}$ or $x = -\sqrt{75}$

Simplify $\sqrt{75}$:

$\sqrt{75} = \sqrt{25}\sqrt{3} = 5\sqrt{3}$

$x = 5\sqrt{3}$ or $x = -5\sqrt{3}$

The solutions are $5\sqrt{3}$ and $-5\sqrt{3}$

4. $(x-3)^2=9$

$x-3=\sqrt{9}$ or $x-3=-\sqrt{9}$

$x-3=3 \qquad x-3=-3$

$x=6 \qquad x=0$

The solutions are 6 and 0.

5. $(y+4)^2=5$

$y+4=\sqrt{5}$ or $y+4=-\sqrt{5}$

$y=-4+\sqrt{5} \qquad y=-4-\sqrt{5}$

The solutions are $-4+\sqrt{5}$ and $-4-\sqrt{5}$.

6. $3y^2-5=0$

$3y^2=5$

$y^2=\frac{5}{3}$

$y=\sqrt{\frac{5}{3}}$ or $y=-\sqrt{\frac{5}{3}}$

Rationalize the denominators.

$\sqrt{\frac{5}{3}}=\frac{\sqrt{5}}{\sqrt{3}}\cdot\frac{\sqrt{3}}{\sqrt{3}}=\frac{\sqrt{15}}{3}$

$y=\frac{\sqrt{15}}{3}$ or $y=-\frac{\sqrt{15}}{3}$

The solutions are $\frac{\sqrt{15}}{3}$ and $-\frac{\sqrt{15}}{3}$

7. $(2x-7)^2=25$

$2x-7=\sqrt{25}$ or $2x-7=-\sqrt{25}$

$2x-7=5$ or $2x-7=-5$

$2x=12 \qquad 2x=2$

$x=6 \qquad x=1$

The solutions are 6 and 1.

8. $(x+5)^2=12$

$x+5=\sqrt{12}$ or $x+5=-\sqrt{12}$

$x+5=2\sqrt{3}$ or $x+5=-2\sqrt{3}$

$x=-5+2\sqrt{3} \qquad x=-5-2\sqrt{3}$

The solutions are $-5+2\sqrt{3}$ and $-5-2\sqrt{3}$.

In Exercises 9-15, all of the unknown quantities must be positive. Therefore, only the positive square roots are used as solutions.

9. Let c = the length of the hypotenuse.

$6^2+8^2=c^2$

$36+64=c^2$

$100=c^2$

$c=\sqrt{100}=10$

The missing length is 10 feet.

10. Let c = the length of the hypotenuse.

$4^2+6^2=c^2$

$16+36=c^2$

$c=\sqrt{52}=\sqrt{4}\sqrt{13}=2\sqrt{13}$

The missing length is $2\sqrt{13}$ inches.

11. Let b = the missing length (length of one of the legs).

$11^2+b^2=15^2$

$121+b^2=225$

$b^2=104$

$b=\sqrt{104}=\sqrt{4}\sqrt{26}=2\sqrt{26}$

The missing length is $2\sqrt{26}$ centimeters.

12. Let x = the distance between the base of the building and the bottom of the ladder.

$x^2 + 20^2 = 25^2$

$x^2 + 400 = 625$

$x = 225$

$x = \sqrt{225} = 15$

The bottom of the ladder is 15 feet away from the building.

13. Let h = the distance up the pole that the wires should be attached.
In the figure below, the pole and one of the wires are shown.

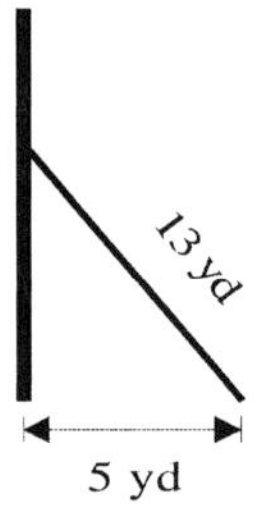

$5^2 + h^2 = 13^2$

$25 + h^2 = 169$

$h^2 = 144$

$h = \sqrt{144} = 12$

The wires will be attached 12 yards up the pole.

14. $W = 3t^2; W = 1200$

$1200 = 3t^2$

$400 = t^2$

$t = \sqrt{400} = 20$

The fetus weighs 1200 grams after 20 weeks.

15. $d = 16t^2; d = 100$

$100 = 16t^2$

$6.25 = t^2$

$t = \sqrt{6.25} = 2.5$

It will take the object 2.5 seconds to hit the water.

16. $d = \sqrt{(x_2 - x_1)^2 + (y_2 - y_1)^2}$

$= \sqrt{[1-(-3)]^2 + [-5-(-2)]^2}$

$= \sqrt{4^2 + (-3)^2}$

$= \sqrt{16+9}$

$= \sqrt{25}$

$= 5$

17. $d = \sqrt{(x_2 - x_1)^2 + (y_2 - y_1)^2}$

$= \sqrt{(5-3)^2 + (4-8)^2}$

$= \sqrt{2^2 + (-4)^2}$

$= \sqrt{4+16}$

$= \sqrt{20} = \sqrt{4 \cdot 5} = 2\sqrt{5} \approx 4.47$

18. $x^2 + 16x$
The coefficient of the x-term is 15. Half of 16 is 8, and $8^2 = 64$. Add 4.

$x^2 + 16x + 64 = (x+8)^2$

19. $x^2 - 6x$

$\frac{1}{2}(-6) = -3; (-3)^2 = 9$

$x^2 - 6x + 9 = (x-3)^2$

20. $x^2 + 3x$

$\frac{1}{2}(3) = \frac{3}{2}; \left(\frac{3}{2}\right)^2 = \frac{9}{4}$

$$x^2 + 3x + \frac{9}{4} = \left(x + \frac{3}{2}\right)^2$$

21. $x^2 - 5x$

$\frac{1}{2}(-5) = -\frac{5}{2}; \left(-\frac{5}{2}\right)^2 = \frac{25}{4}$

$$x^2 - 5x + \frac{25}{4} = \left(x - \frac{5}{2}\right)^2$$

22. $x^2 - 12x + 27 = 0$

First, subtract 27 from both sides to isolate the binomial $x^2 - 12x$.

$x^2 - 12x = -27$

$\frac{1}{2}(-12) = -6; (-6)^2 = 36$

$x^2 - 12x + 36 = -27$

$(x-6)^2 = 9$

$x - 6 = \sqrt{9}$ or $x - 6 = -\sqrt{9}$

$x - 6 = 3$ or $x - 6 = -3$

$x = 9$ $\quad$ $x = 3$

The solutions are 9 and 3.

23. $x^2 - 6x + 4 = 0$

$x^2 - 6x = -4$

$\frac{1}{2}(-6) = -3; (-3)^2 = 9$

$x^2 - 6x + 9 = -4 + 9$

$(x-3)^2 = 5$

$x - 3 = \sqrt{5}$ or $x - 3 = -\sqrt{5}$

$x = 3 + \sqrt{5}$ $\quad$ $x = 3 - \sqrt{5}$

The solutions are $3 + \sqrt{5}$ and $3 - \sqrt{5}$

24. $3x^2 - 12x + 11 = 0$

First, divide both sides of the equation by 3 so that the coefficient of the x^2-term will be 1.

$x^2 - 4x + \frac{11}{3} = 0$

$x^2 - 4x = -\frac{11}{3}$

$x^2 - 4x + 4 = -\frac{11}{3} + 4$

$(x-2)^2 = -\frac{11}{3} + \frac{12}{3}$

$(x-2)^2 = \frac{1}{3}$

$x - 2 = \sqrt{\frac{1}{3}}$ or $x - 2 = -\sqrt{\frac{1}{3}}$

Simplify the radicals.

$\sqrt{\frac{1}{3}} = \frac{\sqrt{1}}{\sqrt{3}} = \frac{1}{\sqrt{3}} \cdot \frac{\sqrt{3}}{\sqrt{3}} = \frac{\sqrt{3}}{3}$

$x - 2 = \frac{\sqrt{3}}{3}$ or $x - 2 = -\frac{\sqrt{3}}{3}$

$x = 2 + \frac{\sqrt{3}}{3}$ or $x = 2 - \frac{\sqrt{3}}{3}$

$x = \frac{6}{3} + \frac{\sqrt{3}}{3}$ or $x = \frac{6}{3} - \frac{\sqrt{3}}{3}$

$x = \frac{6 + \sqrt{3}}{3}$ or $x = \frac{6 - \sqrt{3}}{3}$

The solutions are $\frac{6 \pm \sqrt{3}}{3}$.

25. $2x^2+5x-3=0$

$a=2, b=5, c=-3$

Substitute these values into the quadratic formula.

$$x=\frac{-b\pm\sqrt{b^2-4ac}}{2a}$$

$$x=\frac{-5\pm\sqrt{5^2-4(2)(-3)}}{2(2)}$$

$$=\frac{-5\pm\sqrt{25+24}}{4}$$

$$=\frac{-5\pm\sqrt{49}}{4}=\frac{-5\pm7}{4}$$

$$x=\frac{-5+7}{4} \text{ or } x=\frac{-5-7}{4}$$

$$=\frac{2}{4}=\frac{1}{2} \qquad =\frac{-12}{4}=-3$$

The solutions are $\frac{1}{2}$ and -3.

26. $x^2=2x+4$

Rewrite the equation in standard form.

$x^2-2x-4=0$

Identify $a, b,$ and c.

$a=1, b=-2, c=-4$

Substitute these values into the quadratic formula.

$$x=\frac{-b\pm\sqrt{b^2-4ac}}{2a}$$

$$=\frac{-(-2)\pm\sqrt{(-2)^2-4(1)(-4)}}{2(1)}$$

$$=\frac{2\pm\sqrt{4+16}}{2}=\frac{2\pm\sqrt{20}}{2}$$

$$=\frac{2\pm2\sqrt{5}}{2}=\frac{2\pm\sqrt{20}}{2}$$

$$=1\pm\sqrt{5}$$

The solutions are $1\pm\sqrt{5}$.

27. $3x^2+5=9x$

Rewrite the equation in standard form.

$3x^2-9x+5=0$

$a=3, b=-9, c=5$

$$x=\frac{-b\pm\sqrt{b^2-4ac}}{2a}$$

$$=\frac{-(-9)\pm\sqrt{(-9)^2-4(3)(5)}}{2\cdot3}$$

$$=\frac{9\pm\sqrt{81-60}}{6}=\frac{9\pm\sqrt{21}}{6}$$

The solutions are $\frac{9\pm\sqrt{21}}{6}$.

28. $2x^2-11x+5=0$

This equation can be solved by the factoring method. Factor the trinomial.

$(2x-1)(x-5)=0$

Use the zero-product principle.

$2x-1=0$ or $x-5=0$

$2x=1 \qquad x=5$

$x=\frac{1}{2}$

The solutions are $\frac{1}{2}$ and 5.

29. $(3x+5)(x-3)=5$

Write the equation in standard form.

$3x^2-4x-15=5$

$3x^2-4x-20=0$

This equation can be solved by the factoring method.

$(3x-10)(x+2)=0$

$3x-10=0$ or $x+2=0$

$3x=10 \qquad x=-2$

$x=\frac{10}{3}$

The solutions are $\frac{10}{3}$ and -2.

30. $3x^2 - 7x + 1 = 0$
The trinomial cannot be factored, so use the quadratic formula with $a = 3, b = -7,$ and $c = 1.$

$$x = \frac{-b \pm \sqrt{b^2 - 4ac}}{2a}$$
$$= \frac{-(-7) \pm \sqrt{(-7)^2 - 4(3)(1)}}{2(3)}$$
$$= \frac{7 \pm \sqrt{49 - 12}}{6}$$
$$= \frac{7 \pm \sqrt{37}}{6}$$

The solutions are $\frac{7 \pm \sqrt{37}}{6}.$

31. $x^2 - 9 = 0$
Solve by the factoring method.
$(x + 3)(x - 3) = 0$
$x + 3 = 0$ or $x - 3 = 0$
$x = -3$ $\quad x = 3$
The solutions are −3 and 3.

32. $(2x - 3)^2 = 5$
Use the square root property.
$2x - 3 = \sqrt{5}$ or $2x - 3 = -\sqrt{5}$
$2x = 3 + \sqrt{5}$ $\quad 2x = 3 - \sqrt{5}$
$x = \frac{3 + \sqrt{5}}{2}$ $\quad x = \frac{3 - \sqrt{5}}{2}$
The solutions are $\frac{3 \pm \sqrt{5}}{2}$

33. $N = 0.2x^2 - 1.2x + 2; N = 29$
$29 = 0.2x^2 - 1.2x + 2$
$0 = 0.2x^2 - 1.2x - 27$
$a = 0.2, b = -1.2, c = -27$

$$x = \frac{-b \pm \sqrt{b^2 - 4ac}}{2a}$$
$$= \frac{-(-1.2) \pm \sqrt{(-1.2)^2 - 4(0.2)(-27)}}{2(0.2)}$$
$$= \frac{1.2 \pm \sqrt{1.44 + 21.6}}{0.4} = \frac{1.2 \pm \sqrt{23.04}}{0.4}$$
$$= \frac{1.2 \pm 4.8}{0.4}$$

$x = \frac{1.2 + 4.8}{0.4}$ or $x = \frac{1.2 - 4.8}{0.4}$
$x = 15$ $\quad x = -9$
Reject −9 because the model begins at $x = 0.$ According to the model, there will be 29 infections a month for every 1000 PCs 15 years after 1990, in the year 2005.

34. $h = -16t^2 + 140t + 3; h = 0$
$0 = -16t^2 + 140t + 3$
$16t^2 - 140t - 3 = 0$
$a = 16, b = -140, c = -3$

$$x = \frac{-b \pm \sqrt{b^2 - 4ac}}{2a}$$
$$= \frac{-(-140) \pm \sqrt{(-140)^2 - 4(16)(-3)}}{2 \cdot 16}$$
$$= \frac{140 \pm \sqrt{19{,}600 + 192}}{32}$$
$$= \frac{140 \pm \sqrt{19{,}792}}{32}$$

$x = \frac{140 + \sqrt{19{,}792}}{32}$ or $x = \frac{140 - \sqrt{19{,}792}}{32}$
$x \approx 8.8$ $\quad x \approx -0.02$
Reject −0.02 because the time it takes the ball to hit the ground cannot be negative. It will take about 8.8 seconds for the ball to hit the ground.

35. $\sqrt{-81}=\sqrt{81(-1)}=\sqrt{81}\sqrt{-1}=9i$

36. $\sqrt{-23}=\sqrt{-23(-1)}=\sqrt{23}\sqrt{-1}=\sqrt{23}\,i$

37. $\sqrt{-48}=\sqrt{48}\sqrt{-1}=\sqrt{16\cdot 3}\sqrt{-1}=4\sqrt{3}\,i$

38. $3+\sqrt{-49}=3+\sqrt{49}\sqrt{-1}=3+7i$

39. $x^2=-100$

Use the square root property.

$x=\sqrt{-100}$ or $x=-\sqrt{-100}$

$x=10i \qquad x=-10i$

The solutions are $\pm 10i$.

40. $5x^2=-125$

$x^2=-25$

$x=\sqrt{-25}$ or $x=-\sqrt{-25}$

$x=5i \qquad x=-5i$

The solutions are $\pm 5i$.

41. $(2x+1)^2=-8$

$2x+1=\pm\sqrt{-8}$

$2x+1=\pm 2\sqrt{2}i$

$2x=-1\pm 2\sqrt{2}i$

$x=\dfrac{-1\pm 2\sqrt{2}i}{2}$

The solutions are $\dfrac{-1\pm 2\sqrt{2}i}{2}$.

42. $x^2-4x+13=0$

Use the quadratic formula with $a=1, b=-4$, and $c=13$.

$$x=\frac{-b\pm\sqrt{b^2-4ac}}{2a}$$
$$=\frac{-(-4)\pm\sqrt{(-4)^2-4(1)(13)}}{2\cdot 1}$$
$$=\frac{4\pm\sqrt{16-52}}{2}=\frac{4\pm\sqrt{-36}}{2}$$
$$=\frac{4\pm 6i}{2}=\frac{2(2\pm 3i)}{2}$$
$$=2\pm 3i$$

The solutions are $2\pm 3i$.

43. $3x^2-x+2=0$

$a=3, b=-1, c=2$

$$x=\frac{-b\pm\sqrt{b^2-4ac}}{2a}$$
$$=\frac{-(-1)\pm\sqrt{(-1)^2-4(3)(2)}}{2\cdot 3}$$
$$=\frac{1\pm\sqrt{1-24}}{6}=\frac{1\pm\sqrt{-23}}{6}$$
$$=\frac{1\pm\sqrt{23}i}{6}$$

The solutions are $\dfrac{1\pm\sqrt{23}i}{6}$.

44. $y=x^2-6x-7$

a. Because a, the coefficient of x^2, is 1, which is greater than 0, the parabola opens upward.

b. $x^2-6x-7=0$

$(x+1)(x-7)=0$

$x+1=0$ or $x-7=0$

$x=-1 \qquad x=7$

The x-intercepts are -1 and 7.

c. $y = 0^2 - 6 \cdot 0 - 7 = -7$
The y-intercept is -7.

d. $a = 1, b = -6$
x-coordinate of vertex
$= \frac{-b}{2a} = \frac{-(-6)}{2(1)} = \frac{6}{2} = 3$
y-coordinate of vertex
$= 3^2 - 6 \cdot 3 - 7$
$= 9 - 18 - 7$
$= -16$
The vertex is $(3, -16)$

e. Plot the points
$(-1, 0), (7, 0), (0, -7),$
and $(3, -16)$, and connect these points with a smooth curve.

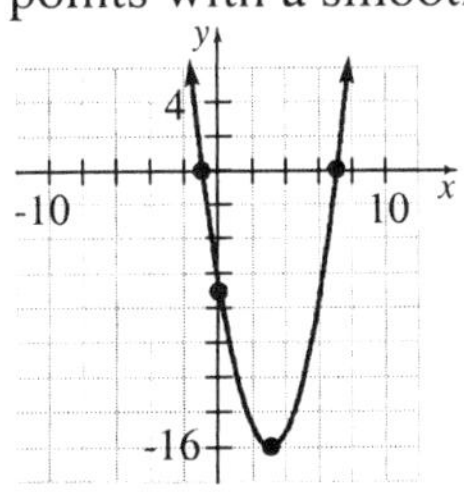

c. $y = -0^2 - 2 \cdot 0 + 3 = 3$
The y-intercept is 3.

d. $a = -1, b = -2$
x-intercept of vertex
$= \frac{-b}{2a} = \frac{-(-2)}{2(-1)} = \frac{2}{-2} = -1$
y-coordinate of vertex
$= -(-1)^2 - 2(-1) + 3$
$= -1 + 2 + 3$
$= 4$
The vertex is $(-1, 4)$.

e. Plot the points $(-3, 0), (1, 0), (0, 3)$, and $(-1, 4)$, and connect them with a smooth curve.

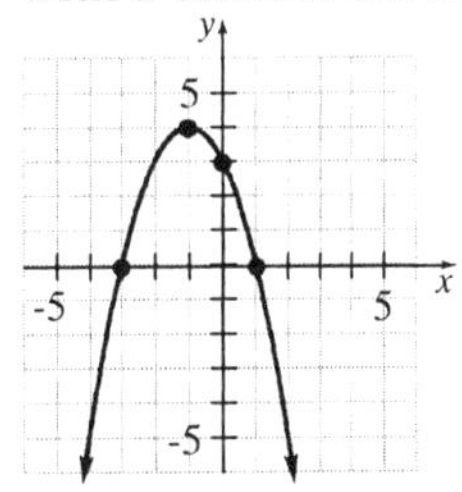

45. $y = -x^2 - 2x + 3$

a. $a = -1 < 0$, so the parabola opens downward.

b. $-x^2 - 2x + 3 = 0$
$0 = x^2 + 2x - 3$
$0 = (x + 3)(x - 1)$
$x + 3 = 0$ or $x - 1 = 0$
$x = -3$ $\quad x = 1$
The x-intercepts are -3 and 1.

46. $y = -3x^2 + 6x + 1$

a. $a = -3 < 0$, so the parabola opens downward.

b. $-3x^2 + 6x + 1 = 0$
$0 = 3x^2 - 6x - 1$
The trinomial cannot be factored, so use the quadratic formula with $a = 3, b = -6,$
and $c = -1$.

$$x = \frac{-b \pm \sqrt{b^2 - 4ac}}{2a}$$
$$= \frac{-(-6) \pm \sqrt{(-6)^2 - 4(3)(-1)}}{2 \cdot 3}$$
$$= \frac{6 \pm \sqrt{36+12}}{6} = \frac{6 \pm \sqrt{48}}{6}$$
$$= \frac{6 \pm 4\sqrt{3}}{6} = \frac{2(3 \pm 2\sqrt{3})}{6}$$
$$= \frac{3 \pm 2\sqrt{3}}{3}$$
$$x = \frac{3+2\sqrt{3}}{3} \quad \text{or} \quad x = \frac{3-2\sqrt{3}}{3}$$
$$x \approx 2.2 \qquad x \approx -0.2$$

The x-intercepts are approximately 2.2 and −0.2.

c. $y = -3 \cdot 0^2 + 6 \cdot 0 + 1 = 1$

The y-intercept is 1.

d. $a = -3, b = 6$

$$x = \frac{-b}{2a} = \frac{-6}{2(-3)} = \frac{-6}{-6} = 1$$
$$y = -3(1)^2 + 6(1) + 1 = -3 + 6 + 1 = 4$$

The vertex is $(1, 4)$.

e. Plot the points $(2.2, 0), (-0.2, 0), (0, 1)$, and $(1, 4)$, and connect them with a smooth curve.

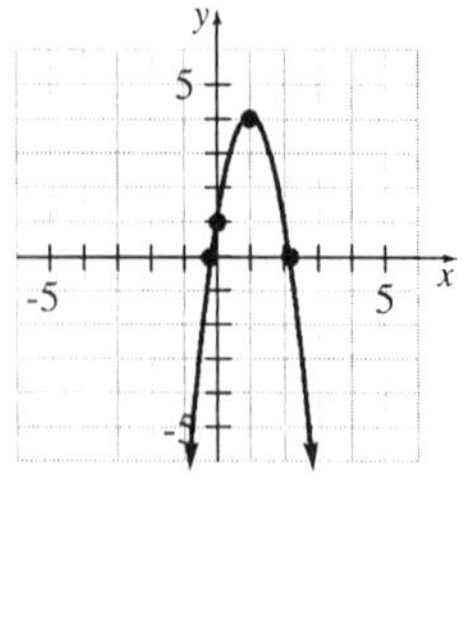

47. $y = x^2 - 4x$

a. $a = 1 > 0$, so the parabola opens upward.

b.
$$x^2 - 4x = 0$$
$$x(x-4) = 0$$
$$x = 0 \quad \text{or} \quad x - 4 = 0$$
$$x = 4$$

The x-intercepts are 0 and 4.

c. $y = 0^2 - 4 \cdot 0 = 0$

The y-intercept is 0. This does not provide an additional point because part (b) already showed that the parabola passes through the origin.

d. $a = 1, b = -4$

$$x = \frac{-b}{2a} = \frac{-(-4)}{2(1)} = \frac{4}{2} = 2$$
$$y = 2^2 - 4 \cdot 2 = 4 - 8 = -4$$

The vertex is $(2, -4)$.

e. Plot the points $(0,0), (4,0)$, and $(2,-4)$, and draw a smooth curve through them.

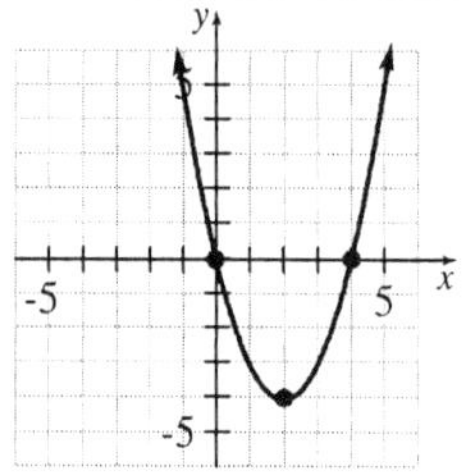

48. $y = -16x^2 + 96x + 3$

Find the vertex of the parabola.

$a = -16, b = 96$

$$x = \frac{-b}{2a} = \frac{-96}{2(-16)} = \frac{-96}{2(-16)} = \frac{-96}{-32} = 3$$

$$y = -16 \cdot 3^2 + 96 \cdot 3 + 3$$
$$= -144 + 288 + 3 = 147$$

The baseball will reach its maximum height 3 seconds after it is hit. The maximum height is 147 feet.

49. $\{(2,7),(3,7),(5,7)\}$

This relation is a function because no two ordered pairs have the same first component and different second components.

The domain is the set of first components:

$\{2, 3, 5\}$.

The range is the set of second components: $\{7\}$

50. $\{(1,10),(2,500),(3,\pi)\}$

This relation is a function.

Domain: $\{1,2,3\}$

Range: $\{10,500,\pi\}$

51. $\{(12,13),(14,15),(12,19)\}$

This relation is not a function because two of the ordered pairs have the same first component, 12, but different second components.

Domain: $\{12,14\}$

Range: $\{13,15,19\}$

52. $f(x) = 3x - 4$

a. $f(-5) = 3(-5) - 4 = -15 - 4 = -19$

b. $f(6) = 3 \cdot 6 - 4 = 18 - 4 = 14$

c. $f(0) = 3 \cdot 0 - 4 = 0 - 4 = -4$

53. $g(x) = x^2 - 5x + 2$

a. $g(-4) = (-4)^2 - 5(-4) + 2$
$= 16 + 20 + 2 = 38$

b. $g(3) = 3^2 - 5 \cdot 3 + 2$
$= 9 - 15 + 2 = -4$

c. $g(0) = 0^2 - 5 \cdot 0 + 2 = -0 + 2 = 2$

54. Many vertical lines will intersect the graph in two points, so *y* is not a function of *x*.

55. No vertical line will intersect this graph in more than one point, so *y* is a function of *x*.

56. No vertical line will intersect this graph in more than one point, so *y* is a function of *x*.

57. Many vertical lines will intersect the graph in two points, so *y* is not a function of *x*.

58. $f(t) = -14t^2 + 42t + 1980$

$$f(10) = -14(10)^2 + 42(10) + 1980$$
$$= -1400 + 420 + 1980$$
$$= 1000$$

The average price of a computer 10 years after 1993 (that is, in 2003) was $1000.

Chapter 10 Test

1. $3x^2 = 48$

$x^2 = 16$

$x = \sqrt{16}$ or $x = -\sqrt{16}$

$x = 4$ or $x = -4$

The solutions are 4 and –4.

2. $(x-3)^2 = 5$

$x - 3 = \sqrt{5}$ or $x - 3 = -\sqrt{5}$

$x = 3 + \sqrt{5}$ $\quad$ $x = 3 - \sqrt{5}$

The solutions are $3 \pm \sqrt{5}$.

3. Let b = distance PQ across the lake.
Use the Pythagorean Theorem.

$8^2 + b^2 = 12^2$

$64 + b^2 = 144$

$b^2 = 80$

$b = \sqrt{80} = \sqrt{16}\sqrt{5} = 4\sqrt{5}$

The distance across the lake is $4\sqrt{5}$ yards.

4.
$$d = \sqrt{(x_2 - x_1)^2 + (y_2 - y_1)^2}$$
$$= \sqrt{(-4-3)^2 + [1-(-2)]^2}$$
$$= \sqrt{(-7)^2 + 3^2}$$
$$= \sqrt{49+9} = \sqrt{58} \approx 7.62$$

5. $x^2 + 4x - 3 = 0$

$x^2 + 4x = 3$

$\frac{1}{2}(4) = 2; 2^2 = 4$

$x^2 + 4x + 4 = 3 + 4$

$(x+2)^2 = 7$

$x + 2 = \sqrt{7}$ or $x + 2 = -\sqrt{7}$

$x = -2 + \sqrt{7}$ $\quad$ $x = -2 - \sqrt{7}$

The solutions are $-2 \pm \sqrt{7}$.

6. $3x^2 + 5x + 1 = 0$

The trinomial cannot be factored, so use the quadratic formula with $a = 3, b = 5,$ and $c = 1$.

$$x = \frac{-b \pm \sqrt{b^2 - 4ac}}{2a}$$
$$= \frac{-5 \pm \sqrt{5^2 - 4(3)(1)}}{2\cdot 3}$$
$$= \frac{-5 \pm \sqrt{25-12}}{6}$$
$$= \frac{-5 \pm \sqrt{13}}{6}$$

The solutions are $\frac{-5 \pm \sqrt{13}}{6}$.

7. $(3x-5)(x+2) = -6$

Write the equation in standard form.

$3x^2 + x - 10 = -6$

$3x^2 + x - 4 = 0$

Factor the trinomial and use the zero-product principle.

$(3x+4)(x-1) = 0$

$3x + 4 = 0$ or $x - 1 = 0$

$3x = -4$ $\quad$ $x = 1$

$x = -\frac{4}{3}$

The solutions are $-\frac{4}{3}$ and 1.

8. $(2x+1)^2 = 36$

$2x + 1 = \sqrt{36}$ or $2x + 1 = -\sqrt{36}$

$2x + 1 = 6$ $\quad$ $2x + 1 = -6$

$2x = 5$ $\quad$ $2x = -7$

$x = \frac{5}{2}$ $\quad$ $x = -\frac{7}{2}$

The solutions are $\frac{5}{2}$ and $-\frac{7}{2}$.

9. $2x^2 = 6x - 1$
Write the equation in standard form.
$2x^2 - 6x + 1 = 0$
The trinomial cannot be factored so use the quadratic formula with $a = 2, b = -6,$
and $c = 1$.

$$x = \frac{-b \pm \sqrt{b^2 - 4ac}}{2a}$$
$$= \frac{-(-6) \pm \sqrt{(-6)^2 - 4(2)(1)}}{2 \cdot 2}$$
$$= \frac{6 \pm \sqrt{36 - 8}}{4} = \frac{6 \pm \sqrt{28}}{4}$$
$$= \frac{6 \pm 2\sqrt{7}}{4} = \frac{2(3 \pm \sqrt{7})}{4}$$
$$= \frac{3 \pm \sqrt{7}}{2}$$

The solutions are $\frac{3 \pm \sqrt{7}}{2}$.

10. $2x^2 + 9x = 5$
Write the equation in standard form.
$2x^2 + 9x - 5 = 0$
Solve by the factoring method.
$(2x - 1)(x + 5) = 0$
$2x - 1 = 0$ or $x + 5 = 0$
$2x = 2$ $\qquad x = -5\text{m}$
$x = \frac{1}{2}$

The solutions are $\frac{1}{2}$ and -5.

11. $\sqrt{-121} = \sqrt{121(-1)} = \sqrt{121}\sqrt{-1} = 11i$

12. $\sqrt{-75} = \sqrt{75(-1)} = \sqrt{25 \cdot 3}\sqrt{-1}$
$= 5\sqrt{3}\,i$

13. $x^2 + 36 = 0$
$x^2 = -36$
$x = \sqrt{-36}$ or $x = -\sqrt{-36}$
$x = 6i$ $\qquad x = -6i$
The solutions are $\pm 6i$.

14. $(x - 5)^2 = 25$
$x - 5 = \sqrt{-25}$ or $x - 5 = -\sqrt{-25}$
$x - 5 = 5i$ or $x - 5 = -5i$
$x = 5 + 5i$ $\qquad x = 5 - 5i$
The solutions are $5 \pm 5i$.

15. $x^2 - 2x + 5 = 0$
The trinomial cannot be factored, so use the quadratic formula with $a = 1, b = -2,$
and $c = 5$.

$$x = \frac{-b \pm \sqrt{b^2 - 4ac}}{2a}$$
$$= \frac{-(-2) \pm \sqrt{(-2)^2 - 4(1)(5)}}{2 \cdot 1}$$
$$= \frac{2 \pm \sqrt{4 - 20}}{2} = \frac{2 \pm \sqrt{-16}}{2}$$
$$= \frac{2 \pm 4i}{2} = \frac{2(1 \pm 2i)}{2}$$
$$= 1 \pm 2i$$

The solutions are $1 \pm 2i$.

16. $y = x^2 + 2x - 8$
Step 1 $a = 1 > 0$, so the parabola opens upward.

Step 2 $a = 1, b = 2, c = -8$
x-coordinate of vertex
$$= \frac{-b}{2a} = \frac{-2}{2(1)} = \frac{-2}{2} = -1$$
y-coordinate of vertex
$$= (-1)^2 + 2(-1) - 8 = 1 - 2 - 8 = -9$$

The vertex is $(-1,-9)$.

Step 3
$$x^2+2x-8=0$$
$$(x+4)(x-2)=0$$
$$x+4=0 \quad \text{or} \quad x-2=0$$
$$x=-4 \qquad x=2$$

The x-intercepts are −4 and 2.

Step 4 $y=0^2+2\cdot0-8=-8$
The y-intercept is −8.

Steps 5 and 6 Plot $(-1,-9),(-4,0),(2,0)$, and $(0,-8)$, and connect them with a smooth curve.

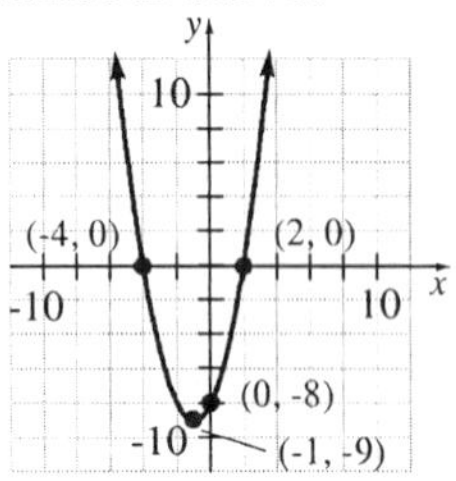

17. $y=-2x^2+16x-24$

Step 1 $a=-2<0,$ so the parabola opens downward.

Step 2 $a=-2, b=16, c=-24$
$$x=\frac{-b}{2a}=\frac{-16}{2(-2)}=\frac{-16}{-4}=4$$
$$y=-2\cdot4^2+16\cdot4-24$$
$$=-32+64-24=8$$

The vertex is $(4,8)$.

Step 3
$$-2x^2+16x-24=0$$
$$0=2x^2-16x+24$$
$$0=2(x^2-8x+12)$$
$$0=2(x-2)(x-6)$$
$$x-2=0 \quad \text{or} \quad x-6=0$$
$$x=2 \qquad x=6$$

The x-intercepts are 2 and 6.

Step 4
$y=-2\cdot0^2+16\cdot0-24=-24$
The y-intercept is -24.

Steps 5 and 6 Plot $(4,8),(2,0),(6,0)$, and $(0,-24)$, and connect them with a smooth curve.

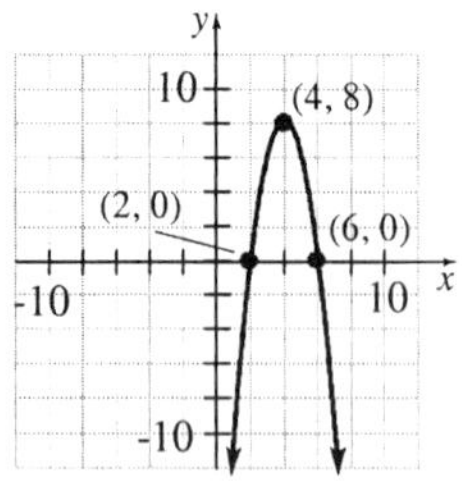

18. $y=-16x^2+64x+5$
The graph of this equation is a parabola opening downward, so its vertex is a maximum point. Find the coordinates of the vertex.
$a=-16, b=64$
$$x=\frac{-b}{2a}=\frac{-64}{2(-16)}=\frac{-64}{-32}=2$$
$$y=-16\cdot2^2+64\cdot2+5$$
$$=-64+128+5=69$$

The baseball reaches its maximum height 2 seconds after it is hit. The maximum height is 69 feet.

19. The baseball will hit the ground when $y = 0$, so solve the quadratic equation
$0 = -16x^2 + 64x + 5$
or
$16x^2 - 64x - 5 = 0$
The trinomial cannot be factored, so use the quadratic formula with $a = 16$, $b = -64$, and $c = -5$.

$$x = \frac{-b \pm \sqrt{b^2 - 4ac}}{2a}$$
$$= \frac{-(-64) \pm \sqrt{(-64)^2 - 4(16)(-5)}}{2 \cdot 16}$$
$$= \frac{64 \pm \sqrt{4096 + 320}}{32} = \frac{64 \pm \sqrt{4416}}{32}$$
$$x = \frac{64 + \sqrt{4416}}{32} \text{ or } x = \frac{64 - \sqrt{4416}}{32}$$
$$x \approx 4.1 \qquad x \approx -0.08$$

Reject −0.08 because it represents a time before the baseball was hit. The baseball hit the ground 4.1 seconds after it was hit.

20. $\{(1,2),(3,4),(5,6),(6,6)\}$
This relation is a function because no two ordered pairs have the same first component and different second components.
Domain: $\{1,3,5,6\}$
Range: $\{2,4,6\}$

21. $\{(2,1),(4,3),(6,5),(6,6)\}$
This relation is not a function because two ordered pairs have the same first component, 6, but different second components.
Domain: $\{2,4,6\}$
Range: $\{1,3,5,6\}$

22. $f(x) = 7x - 3$
$f(10) = 7 \cdot 10 - 3 = 70 - 3 = 67$

23. $g(x) = x^2 - 3x + 7$
$g(-2) = (-2)^2 - 3(-2) + 7$
$= 4 + 6 + 7 = 17$

24. No vertical line will intersect this graph in more than one point, so *y* is a function of *x*.

25. Many vertical lines will intersect this graph in more than one point. One such line is the *y*-axis. Therefore, *y* is not a function of *x*.

26. $f(x) = -0.5x^2 + 4x + 19$
$f(10) = -0.5(10)^2 + 4(10) + 19$
$= -50 + 40 + 19 = 9$
This means that in 2000 (10 years after 1990), 9 million people received food stamps.

Chapter 10 Cumulative Review Exercises (Chapters 1-10)

1. $2-4(x+2)=5-3(2x+1)$

$2-4x-8=5-6x-3$

$-4x-6=2-6x$

$2x-6=2$

$2x=8$

$x=4$

The solution is 4.

2. $\frac{x}{2}-3=\frac{x}{5}$

Multiply both sides by the LCD, 10.

$10\left(\frac{x}{2}-3\right)=10\left(\frac{x}{5}\right)$

$5x-30=2x$

$3x-30=0$

$3x=30$

$x=10$

The solution is 10.

3. $3x+9\geq 5(x-1)$

$3x+9\geq 5x-5$

$-2x+9\geq -5$

$-2x\geq -14$

$\frac{-2x}{-2}\leq\frac{-14}{-2}$

$x\leq 7$

The solution set is $\{x|x\leq 7\}$.

4. $2x+3y=6$

$x+2y=5$

To solve this system by the addition method, multiply the second equation by −2; then add the equations.

$2x+3y=6$

$\underline{-2x-4y=-10}$

$-y=-4$

$y=4$

Back-substitute 4 for y into the second original equation and solve for x.

$x+2y=5$

$x+2\cdot 4=5$

$x+8=5$

$x=-3$

The solution is $(-3,4)$.

5. $3x-2y=1$

$y=10-2x$

To solve this system by the substitution method, substitute $10-2x$ for y into the first equation.

$3x-2y=1$

$3x-2(10-2x)=1$

$3x-20+4x=1$

$7x-20=1$

$7x=21$

$x=3$

Back-substitute 3 for x into the second equation of the given system to find in value of y.

6. $\frac{3}{x+5}-1=\frac{4-x}{2x+10}$

$\frac{3}{x+5}-1=\frac{4-x}{2(x+5)}$

Restriction: $x \neq -5$

LCD = $2(x+5)$

$$2(x+5)\left[\frac{3}{x+5}-1\right]=2(x+5)\left[\frac{4-x}{2(x+5)}\right]$$
$$6-2(x+5)=4-x$$
$$6-2x-10=4-x$$
$$-4-2x=4-x$$
$$-4-x=4$$
$$-x=8$$
$$x=-8$$

The solution is −8.

7. $x+\frac{6}{x}=-5$

Restriction: $x \neq 0$

LCD = x

$$x\left(x+\frac{6}{x}\right)=x(-5)$$
$$x^2+6=-5x$$
$$x^2+5x+6=0$$
$$(x+3)(x+2)=0$$
$$x+3=0 \quad \text{or} \quad x+2=0$$
$$x=-3 \qquad x=-2$$

The solutions are −3 and −2.

8.
$$x-5=\sqrt{x+7}$$
$$(x-5)^2=\left(\sqrt{x+7}\right)^2$$
$$x^2-10x+25=x+7$$
$$x^2-11x+18=0$$
$$(x-9)(x-2)=0$$
$$x-9=0 \quad \text{or} \quad x-2=0$$
$$x=9 \qquad x=2$$

Check each proposed solution in the original equation.

Check 9:	Check 2:
$x-5=\sqrt{x+7}$	$x-5=\sqrt{x+7}$
$9-5=\sqrt{9+7}$	$2-5=\sqrt{2+7}$
$4=\sqrt{16}$	$-3=\sqrt{9}$
$4=4$ true	$-3=3$ false

The checks show that 9 satisfies the equation, while 2 is an extraneous solution. Therefore, the only solution is 9.

9. $(x-2)^2=20$

To solve this quadratic equation, use the square root property.

$$x-2=\sqrt{20} \quad \text{or} \quad x-2=-\sqrt{20}$$
$$x-2=2\sqrt{5} \quad \text{or} \quad x-2=-2\sqrt{5}$$
$$x=2+2\sqrt{5} \qquad x=2-2\sqrt{5}$$

The solutions are $2\pm2\sqrt{5}$.

10. $3x^2-6x+2=0$

Use the quadratic formula with $a=3$, $b=-6$, and $c=2$.

$$x=\frac{-b\pm\sqrt{b^2-4ac}}{2a}$$
$$=\frac{-(-6)\pm\sqrt{(-6)^2-4(3)(2)}}{2\cdot3}$$
$$=\frac{6\pm\sqrt{36-24}}{6}=\frac{6\pm\sqrt{12}}{6}$$
$$=\frac{6\pm2\sqrt{3}}{6}=\frac{2\left(3\pm\sqrt{3}\right)}{6}$$
$$=\frac{3\pm\sqrt{3}}{3}$$

The solutions are $\frac{3\pm\sqrt{3}}{3}$.

11. $A=\frac{5r+2}{t}$ for t

$$tA=t\left(\frac{5r+2}{t}\right)$$
$$tA=5r+2$$
$$\frac{tA}{A}=\frac{5r+2}{A}$$
$$t=\frac{5r+2}{A}$$

12. $$\frac{12x^3}{3x^{12}}=\frac{12}{3}\cdot\frac{x^3}{x^{12}}$$
$$=4x^{3-12}$$
$$=4x^{-9}$$
$$=\frac{4}{x^9}$$

13. $$4\cdot6\div2\cdot3+(-5)$$
$$=24\div2\cdot3+(-5)$$
$$=12\cdot3+(-5)$$
$$=36+(-5)=31$$

14. $$(6x^2-8x+3)-(-4x^2+x-1)$$
$$=(6x^2-8x+3)+(4x^2-x+1)$$
$$=(6x^2+4x^2)+(-8x-x)+(3+1)$$
$$=10x^2-9x+4$$

15. $$(7x+4)(3x-5)$$
$$=7x(3x)+7x(-5)+4(3x)+4(-5)$$
$$=21x^2-35x+12x-20$$
$$=21x^2-23x-20$$

16. $$(5x-2)^2=(5x)^2-2\cdot5x\cdot2+2^2$$
$$=25x^2-20x+4$$

17. $$(x+y)(x^2-xy+y^2)$$
$$=x(x^2-xy+y^2)+y(x^2-xy+y^2)$$
$$=x^3-x^2y+xy^2+x^2y-xy^2+y^3$$
$$=x^3+y^3$$

18. $$\frac{x^2+6x+8}{x^2}\div(3x^2+6x)$$
$$=\frac{x^2+6x+8}{x^2}\cdot\frac{1}{3x^2+6x}$$
$$=\frac{(x+2)(x+4)}{x^2}\cdot\frac{1}{3x(x+2)}$$
$$=\frac{x+4}{3x^3}$$

19. $$\frac{x}{x^2+2x-3}-\frac{x}{x^2-5x+4}$$

To find the LCD, factor the denominators.

$$x^2+2x-3=(x+3)(x-1)$$
$$x^2-5x+4=(x-1)(x-4)$$
LCD = $(x+3)(x-1)(x-4)$

$$\frac{x}{(x+3)(x-1)}-\frac{x}{(x-1)(x-4)}$$
$$=\frac{x(x-4)}{(x+3)(x-1)(x-4)}$$
$$-\frac{x(x+3)}{(x+3)(x-1)(x-4)}$$
$$=\frac{x(x-4)-x(x+3)}{(x+3)(x-1)(x-4)}$$
$$=\frac{x^2-4x-x^2-3x}{(x+3)(x-1)(x-4)}$$
$$=\frac{-7x}{(x+3)(x-1)(x-4)}$$

20. $\dfrac{x-\frac{1}{5}}{5-\frac{1}{x}}$

LCD = $5x$

$$\frac{x-\frac{1}{5}}{5-\frac{1}{x}} = \frac{5x}{5x}\cdot\frac{\left(x-\frac{1}{5}\right)}{\left(5-\frac{1}{x}\right)}$$

$$= \frac{5x\cdot x - 5x\cdot\frac{1}{5}}{5x\cdot 5 - 5x\cdot\frac{1}{x}}$$

$$= \frac{5x^2 - x}{25x-5}$$

$$= \frac{x(5x-1)}{5(5x-1)} = \frac{x}{5}$$

21.
$$3\sqrt{20}+2\sqrt{45} = 3\sqrt{4}\sqrt{5}+2\sqrt{9}\sqrt{5}$$
$$= 3\cdot 2\sqrt{5}+2\cdot 3\sqrt{5}$$
$$= 6\sqrt{5}+6\sqrt{5} = 12\sqrt{5}$$

22.
$$\sqrt{3x}\cdot\sqrt{6x} = \sqrt{18x^2} = \sqrt{9x^2}\sqrt{2}$$
$$= 3x\sqrt{2}$$

23.
$$\frac{2}{\sqrt{3}} = \frac{2}{\sqrt{3}}\cdot\frac{\sqrt{3}}{\sqrt{3}} = \frac{2\sqrt{3}}{3}$$

24.
$$\frac{8}{3-\sqrt{5}} = \frac{8}{3-\sqrt{5}}\cdot\frac{3+\sqrt{5}}{3+\sqrt{5}}$$
$$= \frac{8\left(3+\sqrt{5}\right)}{3^2-\left(\sqrt{5}\right)^2}$$
$$= \frac{8\left(3+\sqrt{5}\right)}{9-5}$$
$$= \frac{8\left(3+\sqrt{5}\right)}{4}$$
$$= 2\left(3+\sqrt{5}\right) = 6+2\sqrt{5}$$

25.
$$4x^2-49 = (2x)^2-7^2$$
$$= (2x+7)(2x-7)$$

26. x^3+3x^2-x-3

Factor by grouping.
$$x^3+3x^2-x-3 = \left(x^3+3x^2\right)+(-x-3)$$
$$= x^2(x+3)-1(x+3)$$
$$= (x+3)\left(x^2-1\right)$$
$$= (x+3)(x+1)(x-1)$$

27.
$$2x^2+8x-42 = 2\left(x^2+4x-21\right)$$
$$= 2(x-3)(x+7)$$

28.
$$x^5-16x = x\left(x^4-16\right)$$
$$= \left[\left(x^2\right)^2-4^2\right]$$
$$= x\left(x^2+4\right)\left(x^2-4\right)$$
$$= x\left(x^2+4\right)(x+2)(x-2)$$

29.
$$x^3-10x^2+25x = x\left(x^2-10x+25\right)$$
$$= x(x-5)^2$$

30. $x^3 - 8$

Use the formula for factoring the difference of two cubes.

$$x^3 - 8 = x^3 - 2^3 = (x-2)(x^2 + 2\cdot x + 2^2)$$
$$= (x-2)(x^2 + 2x + 4)$$

31. $8^{-\frac{2}{3}} = \frac{1}{8^{\frac{2}{3}}} = \frac{1}{\left(\sqrt[3]{8}\right)^2} = \frac{1}{2^2} = \frac{1}{4}$

32. $y = \frac{1}{3}x - 1$

slope = $\frac{1}{3}$; y-intercept = -1

Plot $(0,-1)$. From the point, move 1 unit
up and 3 units to the *right* to reach the point $(3,0)$.Draw a line through $(0,-1)$ and $(3,0)$.

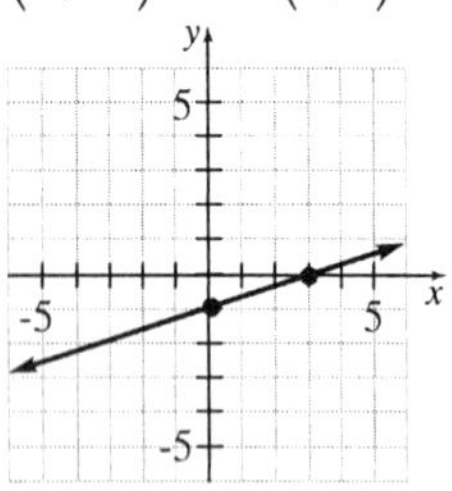

33. $3x + 2y = -6$

x-intercept: -2
y-intercept: -3
checkpoint: $(-4,3)$
Draw a line through $(-2,0), (0,-3)$, and $(-4,3)$.

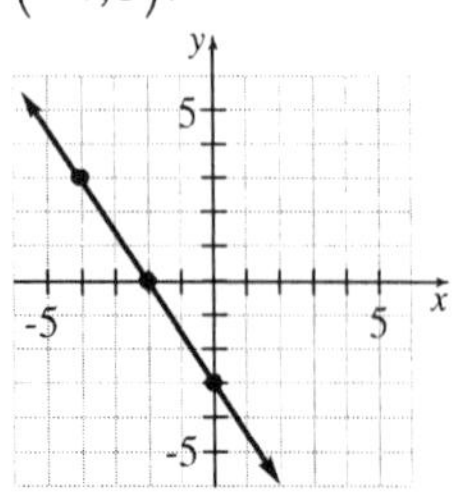

34. $y = -2$

The graph is a horizontal line with y-intercept -2.

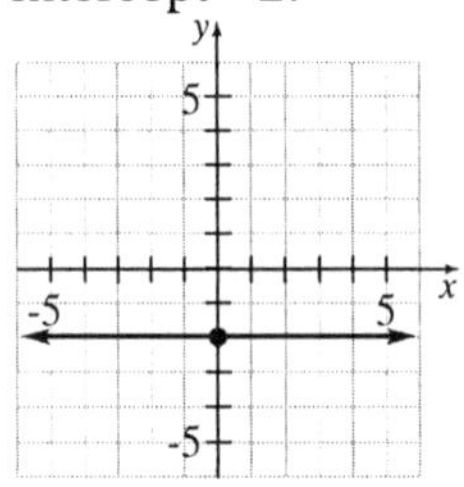

35. $3x - 4y \le 12$

Graph $3x - 4y = 12$ as a solid line using its x-intercept, 4, and its y-intercept -3. Use $(0,0)$ as a test point. Because $3\cdot 0 - 4\cdot 0 \le 12$ is true, shade the half-plane containing $(0,0)$.

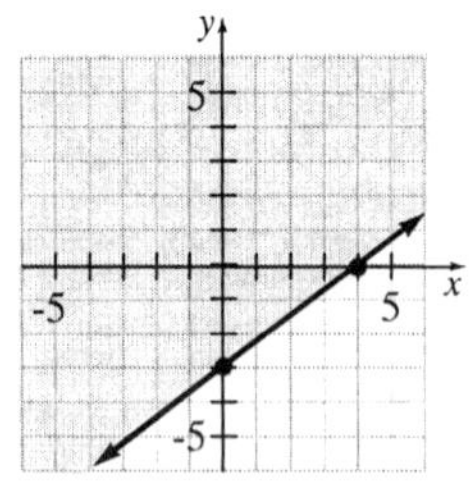

36. $y = x^2 - 2x - 3$

The graph is a parabola opening upward.
Find the vertex:
$a = 1, b = -2$

$$x = \frac{-b}{2a} = \frac{-(-2)}{2(1)} = \frac{2}{2} = 1$$

$$y = 1^2 - 2\cdot 1 - 3 = 1 - 2 - 3 = -4$$

The vertex is $(1,-4)$.

Find the x-intercepts:

$$x^2 - 2x - 3 = 0$$
$$(x+1)(x-3) = 0$$
$$x + 1 = 0 \quad \text{or} \quad x - 3 = 0$$
$$x = -1 \qquad\qquad x = 3$$

The x-intercepts are -1 and 3.

Find the y-intercept:
$y = 0^2 - 2 \cdot 0 - 3 = 3$
The y-intercept is -3.
Plot the points $(1,-4),(-1,0),(3,0)$, and $(0,-3)$, and connect them with a smooth curve.

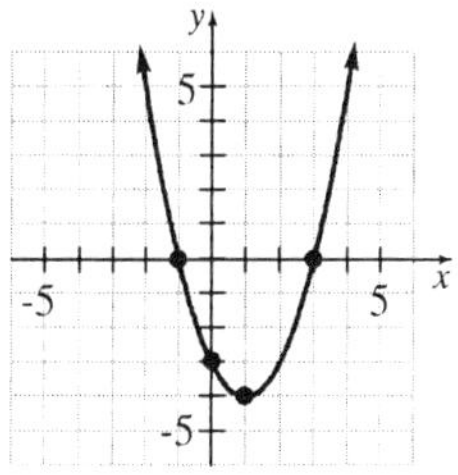

37. $2x + y < 4$
$x > 2$
Graph $2x + y = 4$ as a dashed line using its x-intercept, 2, and y-intercept, 4.
Because $2 \cdot 0 + 0 < 4$ is true, shade the half-plane containing $(0,0)$.
Graph $x = 2$ as a dashed vertical line with x-intercept 2. Because $0 > 2$ is false, shade the half-plane *not* containing $(0,0)$.
This is the region to the right of the vertical line.
The solution set is the intersection of the two shaded regions. The open circle at $(2,0)$ shows that is not included in the graph.

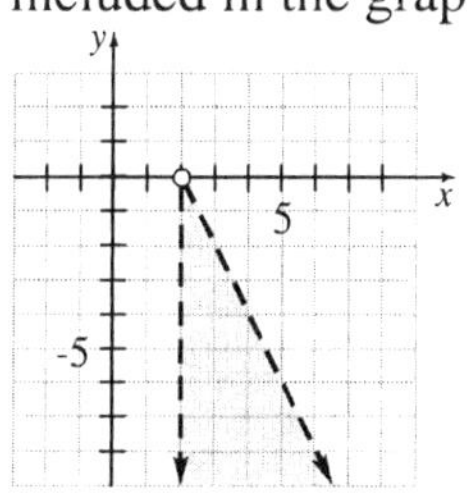

38. $(-1,3)$ and $(2,-3)$
$$m = \frac{y_2 - y_1}{x_2 - x_1} = \frac{-3-3}{2-(-1)} = \frac{-6}{3} = -2$$

39. Line passing through $(1,2)$ and $(3,6)$
First find the slope.
$$m = \frac{6-2}{3-1} = \frac{4}{2} = 2$$
Use the slope and either point in the point-slope form.
$m = 2 \left(x_1 y_1\right) = (1,2)$:
$y - y_1 = m(x - x_1)$
$y - 2 = 2(x - 1)$
$m = 2 \left(x_1 y_1\right) = (3,6)$:
$y - y_1 = m(x - x_1)$
$y - 6 = 2(x - 3)$
Rewrite either of these equations in slope-intercept form.

$y - 2 = 2(x-1)$	$y - 6 = 2(x-3)$
$y - 2 = 2x - 2$	$y - 6 = 2x - 6$
$y = 2x$	$y = 2x$

Notice that the results are the same. The slope-intercept form is $y = 2x$.

40. Let x = the unknown number.
$5x - 7 = 208$
$5x = 215$
$x = 43$
The number is 43.

41. Let x = the price of the camera before the reduction.
$x - 0.20x = 256$
$1x - 0.20x = 256$
$0.80x = 256$
$$\frac{0.80x}{0.80} = \frac{256}{0.80}$$
$x = 320$
The price before the reduction was \$320.

42. Let x = the width of the rectangle.
Then $3x$ = the length.

$$2x+2(3x)=400$$
$$2x+6x=400$$
$$8x=400$$
$$x=50$$
$$3x=150$$

The length is 150 yards and the width is 50 yards.

43. Let x = amount invested at 7%
Then $20,000-x$ = amount invested at 9%.
The total interest earned in one year is 1550, so the equation is
$0.07x+0.09(20,000-x)=1550.$
Solve this equation.

$$0.07x+1800-0.09x=1550$$
$$-0.02x+1800=1550$$
$$-0.02x=-250$$
$$\frac{-0.02x}{-0.02}=\frac{-250}{-0.02}$$
$$x=12,000$$

\$12,500 was invested at 7% and \$20,000 – \$12,500 = \$7500 was invested at 9%.

44. Let x = the number of liters of 40% acid solution.
Then $12-x$ = the number of liters of 70% acid solution.

	Number of liters ×	Percent of Acid =	Amount of Acid
40% Acid solution	x	0.40	$0.4x$
70% Acid solution	$12-x$	0.70	$0.7(12-x)$
50% Acid solution	12	0.50	$0.5(12)$

$$0.40x+0.70(12-x)=0.50(12)$$
$$0.40x+8.4-0.70x=6$$
$$-0.30x+8.4=6$$
$$-0.30x=-2.4$$
$$\frac{-0.30x}{-0.30}=\frac{-2.4}{-0.30}$$
$$x=8$$

8 liters of 40% acid solution and $12-8=4$ liters of 70% acid solution should be used.

45. Let x = the time it will take for the boats to be 232 miles apart.

	Rate ×	Time =	Distance
Boat Going East	13	x =	$13x$
Boat Going West	19	x =	$19x$

$$13x+19x=232$$
$$32x=232$$
$$x=7.25$$

The boats will be 232 miles apart after 7.25 hours or 7 hours, 15 minutes.

46. Let x = the number of students to be enrolled.

$$\frac{x \text{ students}}{176 \text{ faculty members}}=\frac{23}{2}$$
$$\frac{x}{176}=\frac{23}{2}$$
$$2x=176\cdot 23$$
$$2x=4048$$
$$x=2024$$

The university should enroll 2024 students.

47. Let x = the height of the sail.
Use the formula for the area of a triangle.

$$A = \frac{1}{2}bh$$
$$120 = \frac{1}{2}\cdot 15\cdot x$$
$$2\cdot 120 = 2\left(\frac{1}{2}\cdot 15\cdot x\right)$$
$$240 = 15x$$
$$16 = x$$

The height of the sail is 16 feet.

48. Let $x =$ the measure of the second angle.
Then $x+10 =$ the measure of the first angle.
$4x+20 =$ the measure of the third angle.

$$x+(x+10)+(4x+20)=180$$
$$6x+30=180$$
$$6x=150$$
$$x=25$$

Measure of the first angle = $x+10=35°$
Measure of the second angle = $x=25°$
Measure of the third angle = $4x+20=120°$

49. Let x = the price of a TV.
Then $y =$ the price of a stereo.

$$3x+4y=2530$$
$$4x+3y=2510$$

To solve this system by the addition method, multiply the first equation by 4 and the second equation by −3; then add the resulting equations.

$$12x+16y=10{,}120$$
$$-12x-9y=-7530$$
$$7y=2590$$
$$y=370$$

Back-substitute 370 for y in the first equation of the original system.

$$3x+4y=2530$$
$$3x+4(370)=2530$$
$$3x+1480=2530$$
$$3x=1050$$
$$x=350$$

The price of a TV is \$350 and the price of a stereo is \$370.

50. Let x = the width of the rectangle.
Then $x+6 =$ the length of the rectangle.
The area of the rectangle is 55 square meters, so the equation is $(x+6)(x)=55$.
Solve this equation.

$$x^2+6x=55$$
$$x^2+6x-55=0$$
$$(x+11)(x-5)=0$$
$$x+11=0 \quad \text{or} \quad x-5=0$$
$$x=-11 \qquad x=5$$

Reject 11 because the width cannot be negative. The width is 5 meters and the length is 11 meters.